BIBLICAL DOGMATICS

AN EXPOSITION

OF THE

PRINCIPAL DOCTRINES

OF THE

HOLY SCRIPTURES

BY

MILTON S. TERRY, D.D.
Professor of Christian Doctrine in Garrett Biblical Institute

Wipf and Stock Publishers
EUGENE, OREGON

Wipf and Stock Publishers
199 West 8th Avenue, Suite 3
Eugene, Oregon 97401

Biblical Dogmatics
An Exposition of the Principal Doctrines of the Holy Scriptures
By Terry, Milton S.
ISBN: 1-59244-058-4
Publication date: September, 2002
Previously published by Eaton & Mains, 1907.

TO MY STUDENTS
WHO ARE PREACHING THE GOSPEL OF CHRIST
IN MANY LANDS

PREFACE

So long as men continue to think there will be no end of books on a subject so important as the doctrines of the Christian faith. The living truths of God can never be fully expounded. The Scriptures of the Old and New Testaments are a source of religious teaching so inexhaustible that each new generation of biblical scholars discovers therein treasures of knowledge unnoticed by previous research. Other departments of study are also continually furnishing new contributions to the sum of human knowledge and throwing their suggestive side-lights on many portions of the Bible, so that we are not infrequently called upon to revise some of our former opinions and adjust them to the newly discovered facts. No old and permanent truth can ever suffer loss by the incoming of new light, but the weakness and unprofitableness of aged errors become thereby apparent. If the Bible is permitted to speak for itself, and its divers portions are studied in their proper historical connections and in the light of the contemporaneous religious literature of ancient peoples, it will be found to be a remarkably self-interpreting book, and to disclose a real progress in the knowledge of God among the Hebrew prophets and teachers. It is with no assumption of having discovered any remarkably new truths that we put forth this volume, but rather with a conviction that, amid the fresh and increasing light coming from many sources, the old abiding truths may be set forth in a somewhat new and more helpful manner. We are persuaded that the best method of expounding the great truths of the Christian religion is that which most accurately reproduces the teachings of the biblical writers and formulates them in the fullest light of the gospel of Jesus. This volume is such an attempt at a new expression of the things which are most commonly believed among us. No new or strange doctrines are here exploited; no old and well-attested truth is set aside; but certain doctrines of the Christian faith are here presented in a manner somewhat different from that which has long been prevalent. In no such case, however, has any fundamental truth been questioned; the only issue is one of interpretation, and on most questions of interpretation there is room for differences of opinion.

The days of theological controversy are happily well nigh past. There is manifest a growing disposition to subject all questions of doubtful disputation to rational criticism. It is generally conceded that many subjects, which involve biblical exegesis and doctrine, call for revision and restatement. In a volume of this scope and size one cannot reasonably expect all his readers to agree with him throughout. The author indulges no presumption of clearing up the "things hard to be understood" in Paul's epistles, of which the writer of 2 Pet. iii, 16, speaks; much less can he hope to explain all the mysteries of the other apostles, and the evangelists and the prophets. In offering the result of his own study of questions long under investigation and dispute in the Church, he takes pains to tell his readers in advance that some of the expositions of doctrine given in this book are submitted tentatively and with no little hesitation. On sundry questions of eschatology who can at the most do more than "see in a mirror, darkly"? There is a widespread feeling that the real teaching of our Lord and his apostles does not sustain many current popular notions of "times and seasons which the Father has set within his own authority." There are abroad in the world many strange and crass conceptions of the coming of Christ, the resurrection of the dead and the eternal judgment. On such topics as these which transcend the actual experiences of mankind and pertain to the invisible things of God, one should speak with modesty and reserve. Among the mysteries over which great and good men have differed in opinion through many generations there may generally be found a substance of truth of permanent value. It is coming to be recognized that even the biblical writers themselves differ in types of doctrine and in cast of thought, and it is very possible for interpreters of the apostles and prophets to misapprehend the exact import of their various figures of speech. It is possible for the most discreet students of Holy Writ sometimes to teach for revelations of God what are only the mistaken notions of men. There are probably but few men who have not inherited from the past a larger amount of human tradition and dogma than they are aware of.

We have long hesitated over employing the title of *Dogmatics* for a treatise which aims to avoid the dogmatic spirit and style so deservedly unpopular and offensive in the Christian world. It is proper, therefore, to observe that this word has no full or fair equivalent in the English language. In the literature of Christian theology it has long served as the definite scientific term for a systematic exposition of religious truth. Its conformity, moreover, to the scientific titles of the two companion volumes of this series is a special justification of our use of it. Our method is inductive and expository. Our habit is to abstain from *a priori* assumptions and to avoid unprofitable speculation, but always to study to ascertain the demonstrable truth of the biblical teaching. We keep in mind the fact of a progress in divine revelation, and therefore do not forget that the spirit and the ideas of the Old Testament have been largely superseded by the more perfect illumination of the teaching of Christ, who has fulfilled the law and the prophets. It will be seen that the method of this treatise is first to study the nature of man, his sinfulness and the possibilities of his future, as matters of observation and of biblical testimony. We next pass to the great central fact of the religious history of the world, the manifestation of Jesus Christ. This subject, by reason of its vital relation to all Christian thought, naturally occupies the central and largest place in our volume. The doctrine of the God and Father of our Lord Jesus Christ follows as the Holy of holies among religious mysteries. Our method of treating this deepest problem of religion is historical rather than polemical, and aims to show how the everlasting Father has gradually revealed himself in many ways unto all men, but most remarkably through the fathers and prophets of Israel, and finally through his Son Jesus Christ. This method of procedure is quite the opposite of what is commonly followed in systems of theology. It studies visible man first and the invisible God last. It gives no space, except in occasional footnotes, to the old-time polemics. It ignores "plans" and "schemes" and "theories" of atonement. Even the doctrine of the Trinity finds but little more attention in this volume than it finds in the Scriptures. Our method provides no separate section for "eschatology," but simply connects the problems of the future with those facts of the present time to which they are logically and vitally related. This method, of course, will not please the confessional theologian; it may even much offend him. But we believe the great majority of unbiased readers will find it a more simple and excellent way. If it be not the best possible method, it may at least be worth one trial. If any one prefer, he can read our third part first, and our first part last. We assume from the start that our readers are intelligent Christian believers, and can study man's nature and destiny without having first to be informed of the facts of Christ and the existence of God. We advise our readers to make much use of the carefully prepared indexes at the close of this volume, for different phases of the same subject are often treated in different connections, and numerous biblical texts contain doctrines related to several different topics.

In the main text of this volume we have rarely made a citation from any other source than the Scriptures. In occasional footnotes may be found some quotations and references adapted to confirm our views, or to direct the reader to a further study of the same topic. Hundreds of such references, however, at first designed for insertion in footnotes, have been omitted entirely, in order to keep the volume within a moderate size. A select bibliography is given as an appendix, sufficient to direct the special student in his further research. Without the help of the many contributions of the past, the present treatise could not have been written. The author also owes it to his esteemed colleagues, Professor C. M. Stuart, Professor D. A. Hayes, and Professor F. C. Eiselen, to make this public acknowledgment of their invaluable services by way of many helpful suggestions and in the reading of the proofs.

With this publication we complete the trilogy of our contributions to the study of biblical interpretation and doctrine which we began with the issue of Biblical Hermeneutics in 1883. The Biblical Apocalyptics followed in 1898. The numerous gratifying testimonials of welcome which the preceding volumes have received are deeply appreciated, and the hope is indulged that this concluding volume may be found as acceptable as its predecessors.

EVANSTON, FEBRUARY 22, 1907.

CONTENTS

GENERAL OUTLINE

INTRODUCTION
1. Idea and Scope of Biblical Dogmatics.
2. Sources of Biblical Dogmatics.
3. Method of Biblical Dogmatics.

PART FIRST
THE CONSTITUTION AND POSSIBILITIES OF MAN
1. THE NATURE OF MAN.
2. THE SINFULNESS OF MAN.
3. THE REGENERATION AND ETERNAL LIFE OF MAN.

PART SECOND
THE MANIFESTATION OF CHRIST
1. THE PERSON OF CHRIST.
2. THE MEDIATION OF JESUS CHRIST.
3. THE KINGDOM AND COMING OF CHRIST.

PART THIRD
OUR FATHER IN HEAVEN
1. THE UNIVERSAL REVELATION.
2. THE HEBREW REVELATION.
3. THE REVELATION IN JESUS CHRIST.

ANALYTICAL OUTLINE
INTRODUCTION

CHAPTER I.
Idea and Scope of Biblical Dogmatics.
1. Theology and Religion, 1.
2. Universality of Religion and Revelation, 1.
3. Philosophy of Religion, 2.
4. The Christian Religion, 3.
5. Biblical Theology, 3.
6. Systematic Theology, 4.
7. Limits and Aim of Biblical Dogmatics, 4.
8. Theology Old and New, 5.

CHAPTER II.
Sources of Biblical Dogmatics.
1. The Bible a Priceless Treasury, 7.
2. Trammels of Old Tradition, 7.
3. Reaction and Changes of View, 8.
4. Other Sacred Bibles, 9.
5. Limits of the Biblical Canon, 9.
6. Other Traditions Questioned, 11.
7. Variety of Compositions, 12.
8. Three Divisions of the Hebrew Canon, 13.
9. The New Testament Canon, 14.
10. Superiority of the New Testament, 15.
    (1) Shown by Statements of Jesus.
    (2) Shown by other New Testament Teaching.
    (3) Shown by Obvious Facts of the Records.
    (4) The Transition Gradual.
11. The Question of Inspiration, 18.
    (1) Highest Old Testament Claims.
    (2) Witness of the New Testament.
    (3) Such Claims not Applicable to All the Books.
    (4) Our Doctrine should Accord with existing Facts.
    (5) Inerrancy a Dogma of Necessitarian Philosophy.
12. The Dogma of Infallibility, 24.
    (1) Involves a Distorted Notion of the Bible.
    (2) Discredited by Discrepancies and Persistent Controversy.
    (3) The Word itself Irrelevant.
    (4) Sufficiency Rather than Infallibility.
13. Authority as Sources of Doctrine, 28.
    (1) Superiority in Variety of Contents.
    (2) Superiority of Historic Outline and Background.
    (3) Superiority of the Revelation of Christ.
14. The Bible and the Word of God, 32.
15. Necessity of Sound Interpretation, 34.
16. Sufficiency as Sources of Doctrine, 35.

CHAPTER III.
Method of Biblical Dogmatics.
1. Importance of Method, 37.
2. Lack of System in Ancient Writers, 37.
3. Federal and Trinitarian Methods, 38.
4. Methods of some German Writers, 38.
5. Methods of Five American Divines, 39.
6. Outlines of Other Writers, 41.
7. Questions of Scope and Terminology, 42.
8. A Priori and a Posteriori Methods, 43.
9. The Method of this Work, 44.

PART FIRST
THE CONSTITUTION AND POSSIBILITIES OF MAN

SECTION FIRST
THE NATURE OF MAN.

CHAPTER I.
The Natural Constitution of Man.
1. Primary Realities, 45.
2. The Bodily Form, 46.
3. Life, Soul and Blood, 46.
4. The Heart, 47.
5. Reins, Intestines, Breath, 48.
6. The Head, 48.
7. The Mind, 49.
8. The Spirit, 50.
9. The Doctrine of Trichotomy, 51.
    (1) Has no Support in Sound Interpretation.
    (2) The Words Used Indiscriminately.
    (3) Yet with Distinctive Connotation.
10. General Result, 53.

CHAPTER II.
The Moral Element in Man.
1. The Fact of Moral Sense, 55.
2. Conscience, 55.
    (1) Old Testament Illustration.
    (2) New Testament use of συνείδησις.
    (3) Essential Moral Sense.
3. Personality and Freedom of Will, 56.
4. The Moral Element of Social Relations, 58.

CHAPTER III.
The Religious Element in Man.
1. Essential in Normal Human Nature, 60.
2. Biblical Words Expressive of Religious Feeling and Action, 60.
3. Earliest Manifestations of the Religious Sense, 61.
4. Has due Recognition in Scripture, 61.
5. Was Gradually Developed, 62.
6. Universal in Mankind, 63.

CHAPTER IV
Propagation and Dispersion of Mankind.
1. Unity of the Human Race, 64.
2. Propagation of Species, 64.
3. Creationism and its Proof-texts, 65.
4. Dispersion of Races and Tribes, 67.

CHAPTER V.
The Origin of Man.
1. The Definite Modern Question, 69.
2. Two Ways of Answering the Question, 69.
3. Poetical Concepts of Creation, 70.
4. No Definite Answer in Scripture, 71.
5. But Man is the Crowning Work of God, 72.

CHAPTER VI.
Man's Place in the World.
1. Man as the Chief Creation of God, 73.
2. Ancient Concepts of "the Heavens and the Earth," 74.
3. Not Physical Bulk but Rational Nature Man's crowning Excellence, 74.

CHAPTER VII.
Primitive State of Man.
1. Completeness of Natural Constitution, 76.
2. Undeveloped in Knowledge and Civilization, 77.
3. Original Goodness, 77.
4. Made in the Image of God, 78.
    (1) No Explanation in Scripture.
    (2) New Testament Texts in Ephesians iv, 24; Col. iii, 9, 10.
    (3) Interpretation of Wisdom ii, 23.
    (4) Spiritual Personality.

SECTION SECOND
THE SINFULNESS OF MAN.

CHAPTER I.
The Fact and the Nature of Human Sinfulness.
1. The Awful Fact of Sin, 83.
2. Depravity of the Race, 84.
    (1) Depicted in Genesis.
    (2) Paul's dark Picture in Romans i, 18–32.
    (3) Great Antithesis in Romans v, 12–19.
3. Hebrew and Greek Words Indicating Nature of Sin, 86.
4. Sin Conceived as Transgression and Lawlessness, 87.
5. Sin Conceived as Selfishness, 88.
6. Concept of Spiritual Blindness, 88.
7. Concept of Guilt, 89.
    (1) The Fact Explained.
    (2) Significance of αἰτία.
    (3) Significance of ἔνοχος.
    (4) Guilt even in Errors of Ignorance.
8. Degrees of Guilt and Sin, 90.
    (1) Hardening the Heart.
    (2) Blasphemy against the Holy Spirit.
    (3) Doctrine of Hebrews vi, 4–8, and x, 26, 27.
    (4) Other Biblical Testimony.

CHAPTER II.
The Origin and the Persistent Cause of Sin.
1. Adequate Cause Must be Sought, 95.
2. Inadequate Theories, 95.
3. Adequate and Actual Cause in Man's Personality, 97.

4. Illustrated in Genesis iii, 98.
5. Same Efficient Cause Apparent in all Sinning, 99.
6. Nature of Volitional Freedom, 99.
7. Other Resultant Facts of Sin, 100.
8. Biblical Records of Apostasy, 101.
   (1) Israel's Apostasy in the Desert.
   (2) Examples of Saul, David, Solomon.
   (3) New Testament Admonition and Warning.

CHAPTER III.
Divers Aspects of Sin in the Various Biblical Writers.

1. Defective Moral Standards of Old Testament Times, 104.
2. Imprecatory Psalms, 104.
3. Public and National Sins Overshadow the Individual, 105.
4. Divorcing Morality and Public Service, 106.
5. Collective Idea of Sin and Penalty, 107.
6. Deeper Concepts of Psalms and Prophets, 107.
7. Individual Responsibility in Ezekiel and Jeremiah, 109.
8. Sin as Represented in the Wisdom Books, 109.
   (1) In Proverbs.
   (2) In the Book of Job.
   (3) In the Song of Songs.
   (4) In Ecclesiastes.
   (5) In the Later Jewish Literature.
9. Paul's Doctrine of Sin in the Flesh, 114.
10. Pauline Rabbinism, 116.

CHAPTER IV.
The Penal Consequences of Sin.

1. Physical Death as Penalty, 118.
2. Physical Death as Universal Law, 118.
3. Physical Evils not a Penalty for Sin, 119.
4. New Testament Doctrine of Death, 120.
5. Pauline Conception of Sin and Death, 121.
6. Penal Consequences beyond this Life, 122.
7. Biblical Doctrine of Retribution, 122.
   (1) Old Testament Teaching Vague.
   (2) Isaiah lxvi, 24.
   (3) Daniel xii, 2.
   (4) Apocrypha and Pseudepigrapha.
   (5) The New Testament Teaching.
8. Inferences Touching the Nature of Future Punishment, 128.
9. Sheol, Hades, Gehenna, Tartarus, 129.
10. Degrees of Penalty, 130.
11. Duration of Penalty Everlasting, 131.
    (1) Absence of Hope or Promise.
    (2) Question of Matthew xii, 32.
    (3) Question of 1 Peter iii, 18–20.
12. Doctrine of Annihilation of the Wicked, 133.
13. The Question of Theodicy, 134.

SECTION THIRD
THE REGENERATION AND ETERNAL LIFE OF MAN.

CHAPTER I.
Conviction, Repentance, and Conversion.

1. Salvation a Fact of Experience, 136.
2. Blameless Childhood and Youth, 137.
3. Conviction of Sin, 137.
   (1) Expressed in the Penitential Psalms.
   (2) Described in Romans vii.
   (3) Experienced by Millions.
4. Repentance, 140.
5. Conversion, 140.
6. Requires Coöperation of God and Man, 141.

CHAPTER II.
The Doctrine of Faith.

1. Faith Defined, 142.
2. Doctrine of Paul, 142.
3. Theme of the Epistle to the Romans, 143.
4. Example of Abraham in Romans iv, 143.
5. Doctrine of James, 144.
6. Doctrine of the Epistle to the Hebrews, 145.
7. Doctrine of Faith in the Gospels, 145.
8. Personal Confession, 146.

CHAPTER III.
Forgiveness of Sins and Reconciliation.

1. Greek Words for Remission, 147.
2. Peculiarity of Paul's Doctrine of Justification, 148.
3. Reconciliation, 148.

CHAPTER IV.
New Birth and New Life.

1. Comprehensive of the Other Experiences, 150.
2. Idea of a New Heart in the Old Testament, 150.
3. Teaching of Jesus in John iii, 3–8, 151.
4. Significance of Titus iii, 5, and Ephesians v, 26, 152.
5. The New Birth a New Creation, 153.
6. Mystery of Spiritual Life, 155.
7. A Passing out of Death into Life, 156.

CHAPTER V.
Adoption, Sonship, Assurance, and Spiritual Freedom.

1. New Relationship of Adoption, 158.
2. Sons of God, 159.
3. Witness of the Spirit, 160.
4. Boldness, Confidence, and Full Assurance, 161.
5. Christian Freedom, 162.

CHAPTER VI.
Progress in Spiritual Life.
1. New Life Involves Growth, 164.
2. Elements of Spiritual Growth, 165.
3. Argument of Romans vi, 166.
4. Doctrine of 1 John iii, 9, 10, 166.
5. Sanctification and Holiness, 167.
6. Practical Righteousness, 169.
7. Doctrine of Christian Perfection, 171.
8. Specific Christian Virtues, 173.
9. Love the Greatest of All, 174.
10. Continual Cultivation and Growth, 175.
11. The Discipline of Trial, 176.
12. Growth and Discipline a Manifold Experience, 177.
13. The Beautiful in Religion, 177.

CHAPTER VII.
Means of Promoting Spiritual Life.
1. The Fellowship and Ministries of the Church, 179.
2. The Sacraments, 181.
   (1) Christian Baptism.
   (2) The Lord's Supper.
3. The Ministry of the Word, 185.
4. Exercises of Practical Godliness, 187.
5. Prayer, 188.
6. Sevenfold Exhortation of Hebrews x, 19-25, 190.

CHAPTER VIII.
Eternal Life.
1. Meaning of the Phrase, 191.
2. Paul's View of Life, Light, and Liberty, 192.
3. Eternal Life a Present Possession, 193.
4. Endless Permanence in Life, 193.
5. Eternal Life in the Synoptic Gospels, 194.
6. Eternal Life in the Epistles, 194.
7. A Glorious Inheritance, Now and Forever, 195.

CHAPTER IX.
The Doctrine of Immortality.
1. The Fact and the Doctrine, 197.
2. Human Limitation and Doubt, 198.
3. Doctrine of the Old Testament, 198.
   (1) Sundry Intimations.
   (2) Expressed in Many Psalms.
   (3) Job xix, 25-27.
   (4) The Realm of Sheol.
   (5) The Greek Word Hades.
4. Doctrine of the New Testament, 204.
   (1) In the Apocalypse of John.
   (2) In the Epistle to the Hebrews.
   (3) In the Epistles of Paul.
   (4) Teaching of Jesus in the Synoptics.
   (5) Teaching of Jesus in John's Gospel.

CHAPTER X.
The Doctrine of the Resurrection.
1. A Doctrine Variously Apprehended, 212.
2. Vaguely Expressed in Old Testament, 212.
   (1) Psalm xvii, 15.
   (2) Language of Other Poets and Prophets.
   (3) Hosea vi, 1-3.
   (4) Isaiah xxvi, 19.
   (5) Ezekiel xxxvii, 1-14.
   (6) Daniel xii, 2, 3.
   (7) Variety of Later Jewish Opinions.
3. The Fuller Teaching in the New Testament, 219.
4. No Help from Etymology of Greek Words, 220.
5. The Teaching of Jesus Christ, 221.
   (1) Significance of Christ's own Resurrection.
   (2) Significance of the Ascension.
   (3) Rationale of the Forty Days.
   (4) Forty Days in the Flesh.
   (5) Not Glorified During the Forty Days.
   (6) Glorified at the Ascension.
   (7) Jesus's Raising Others from the Dead.
   (8) Jesus's Teaching in the Synoptic Gospels.
   (9) Jesus's Teaching in John's Gospel.
   (10) Jesus Absolutely Assures Immortality, but Offers no Theories.
6. Doctrine of the Apocalypse of John, 230.
7. Paul's Doctrine of the Resurrection,
   (1) Acts xxiv, 15.
   (2) 1 Thessalonians iv, 13-18.
   (3) 1 Corinthians xv. (The Six Paragraphs.)
   (4) 2 Corinthians iv, 16—v, 10.
   (5) In Romans and Philippians.
   (6) In Colossians, Ephesians, and 2 Timothy.
8. Various Types of Biblical Doctrine, 246.
9. No Basis for Many Prevalent Theories, 246.
10. The Main Idea is a New Organism, 247.
11. All the Dead not Raised Simultaneously, 248.
12. The Subject Belongs to the Unseen, 249.
13. Summary of the Biblical Teaching, 250.

CHAPTER XI.
Various Aspects of the Heavenly Glory.
1. The General Conception, 252.
2. Heavenly Recognition, 252.
   (1) Doctrines of Absorption and of Transmigration.
   (2) The Biblical Suggestions.
3. Absence of all Evil, 255.
4. A Sabbath-Rest, 255.
5. Advance in Knowledge and in Heavenly Vision, 256.
6. Increase of Capacity, 257.
7. Reigning with Christ, 257.
8. Glory Through Ages of Ages, 258.

CONTENTS xiii

PART SECOND
THE MANIFESTATION OF THE CHRIST

SECTION FIRST
THE PERSON OF CHRIST.
CHAPTER I.
Facts of His Earthly Life.

1. Born of the House of David, 259.
2. Record of the Virgin Birth, 260.
3. Childhood and Growth, 261.
4. His Baptism and Temptation, 261.
5. His Public Ministry and Death, 262.
6. A Man Among Men, 262.
7. A Man of Transcendent Greatness, 263.
8. Manner and Matter of His Teaching, 264.
9. His Marvelous Self-Expression, 264.
10. His Sinlessness, 265.

CHAPTER II.
The Titles Son of God and Son of Man.

1. The Title Son of God, 266.
   (1) Old Testament Origin and Messianic Significance.
   (2) His Knowledge of the Father.
   (3) The Only Begotten Son.
2. The Title Son of Man, 268.
   (1) Its Usage in the Old Testament.
   (2) "Son of Man" in the Book of Enoch.
   (3) The Lord's own Favorite Title.
   (4) A Person Sublimely Unique.

CHAPTER III.
The Supernatural in the Person of Christ.

1. The Supernatural Birth, 273.
2. The Baptism, Temptation, and Triumph, 274.
3. The Miracles of his Ministry, 275.
4. Miracles Natural with Christ, 276.
5. No Ostentatious Display of Miracles, 277.
6. Miracles Proofs of Divine Wisdom and Power, but not of Omnipotence, 277.
7. The Resurrection and Ascension, 278.

CHAPTER IV.
The Self-Consciousness of Jesus Christ.

1. The Mighty Works and Mighty Words of Jesus Inseparable, 280.
2. His Consciousness of God, 280.
3. His Sense of Subordination, 281.
4. Consciousness of Commitment to a Purpose of the Ages, 282.
5. Consciousness of Pre-existence, 282.
6. Conscious Freedom from Sin, 283.
7. Consciousness of Being Saviour of Men, 284.
8. Consciousness of his Messiahship, 285.
   (1) Assumed in his Fulfilling Law and Prophets.
   (2) Directly Acknowledged.
   (3) Indicated in his Doctrine of the Kingdom.
9. Significance of this Consciousness, 288.

CHAPTER V.
Christology of the First Apostles and of the General Epistles.

1. Sources of Information, 289.
2. The Preaching of Peter, 289.
3. The First Epistle of Peter, 291.
4. Second Peter and Jude, 291.
5. The Epistle of James, 292.

CHAPTER VI.
The Christ of John's Apocalypse.

1. Date and Composition of the Book, 294.
2. The Christophany of i, 12–16, 295.
3. The Lamb in the Midst of the Throne, 295.
4. His Titles, Glory, Triumphs, and Worship, 296.
5. The Grand Total Impression of the Revelation, 296.

CHAPTER VII.
The Pauline Christology.

1. Significance of Paul's Conversion, 297.
2. The Thessalonian Epistles, 297.
3. The Corinthian Epistles, 298.
4. The Epistle to the Galatians, 299.
5. The Epistle to the Romans, 300.
6. The Epistle to Philemon, 300.
7. The Pastoral Epistles, 301.
8. The Ephesian Epistle, 302.
9. The Epistle to the Philippians, 306.
10. The Epistle to the Colossians, 311.
    (1) Fullness of the Deity.
    (2) Significance of i, 13–18.
    (3) Firstborn of all Creation.
    (4) His Pre-eminence.
11. The Pauline Doctrine of Pre-existence, 314.
    (1) The Phrase "sent forth from God."
    (2) Christ the Spiritual Rock.
    (3) 1 Corinthians xv, 45–49.
    (4) 2 Corinthians viii, 9.

12. Pauline Texts which call Christ God, 317.
    (1) 1 Timothy iii, 16.
    (2) Titus ii, 13.
    (3) Romans ix, 5.
    (4) Ephesians v, 5.
    (5) Acts xx, 28.

CHAPTER VIII.
Christology of the Epistle to the Hebrews.

1. Character and Scope of the Epistle, 321.
2. The Facts of the Incarnation, 321.
3. Various Designations of Christ, 321.
4. Doctrine of Pre-existence, 322.
5. Effulgence of Glory and Image of Substance, 323.
6. Question of Divine Titles Applied, 324.

CHAPTER IX.
The Johannine Christology.

1. The Johannine Peculiarities, 326.
2. The Word, or Logos, 326.
3. The Logos in Greek Philosophy and in Philo, 327.
4. Personification of Wisdom in Jewish Writings, 328.
5. Creation by the Word of God, 329.
6. Theophanies and Angelophanies, 329.
7. John's Gospel Gave the Logos New and Deeper Significance, 330.
8. Necessity of Incarnation, 331.
9. Suggestive Words and Phrases, 332.
10. The Word of Life, 332.
11. The Word of Light, 333.
12. Doctrine of Pre-existence, 334.
13. The Idealistic Explanation, 334.
    (1) Does Not Accord with John's Explicit Language.
    (2) Logos Not Synonymous with Abstract Terms.
    (3) More than Memra, Shekina or Angel.
14. John's Doctrine Far above the Current Theosophy, 336.
15. Erroneous Metaphysical Distinctions, 337.
16. Jesus Christ in the Flesh, 337.

CHAPTER X.
Summary of the New Testament Doctrine of the Person of Jesus Christ.

1. The Divers Dogmas of Historical Theology, 339.
2. Divers Types of the Biblical Doctrine, 339.
3. Onesidedness of Polemics, 340.
4. The Simplest Facts of His Life, 341.
5. His Subordinate Relation to God, 341.
6. His Consciousness of Unique Relationship to God, 342.
7. His Heavenly Pre-existence, 342.
8. Self-Coherence of the Supernatural in Christ, 343.
9. A Likeness of Method in Paul and John, 343.
10. The Godhead of Christ Jesus, 344.
11. The Mystery of God, 344.

SECTION SECOND
THE MEDIATION OF JESUS CHRIST.

CHAPTER I.
The Mystery of Mediation and of Incarnation.

1. Nature of Mediation, 346.
2. Doctrine and Ideals of Incarnation, 346.
3. Mystery and Purpose of the Ages, 348.

CHAPTER II.
Old Testament Ideas of Mediation.

1. Value of Old Testament Ideas, 350.
2. Primitive Priesthood and Mediation, 350.
3. Moses and Samuel as Mediators, 351.
4. The Levitical Priesthood, 351.
5. The Sacrificial Offerings, 353.
    (1) Cereal Offerings.
    (2) Blood Offerings.
    (3) The Sin Offering.
6. The Goat for Azazel, 355.
7. Symbolical Significance of Blood, 355.
8. The Consuming of the Flesh, 356.
9. Significance of כפר and its Derivatives, 356.
10. Frequent Biblical Allusion to Sacrifices, 357.
11. Human Sacrifices, 357.
12. Priesthood and Sacrifice Express Deep Religious Convictions, 358.
13. Insufficiency of Animal Sacrifices, 359.
14. Ideas of Mediation in the Prophets, 359.
15. The Suffering Servant of Jehovah in Isa. liii, 361.
    (1) The Preceding Context.
    (2) The Contrasts.
    (3) Mediatorial Soul-Passion.
    (4) Triumph and Exaltation.
    (5) The Christian Interpretation.
16. Idea given in Daniel ix, 24, 362.
17. Doctrine of the Penitential Psalms, 363.
18. Connection with Israel's Messianic Hope, 365.

CHAPTER III.
Sayings of Jesus relative to Redemption.

1. Comparatively Little on this Subject in the Gospels, 366.
2. His Entire Life a Ransom for Many, 366.
3. Words of Jesus at the Last Supper, 369.
4. God's Great Love for the World, 371.

5. Giving his Flesh and Blood for the World, 372.
6. Dying for Others, 373.
7. Intercessory Prayer in Chapter xvii, 373.
8. Words of Jesus on the Cross, 374.

CHAPTER IV.
Doctrine of John and of Peter.

1. Doctrine of the First Epistle of John, 376.
2. Old Testament Imagery of Blood Offerings, 377.
3. The Living Paraclete, 378.
4. The Coming through Water and Blood, 378.
5. Testimony of the Spirit, 379.
6. Doctrine of John's Apocalypse, 380.
7. The Teaching of Peter, 381.
8. Sprinkling of the Blood of Jesus, 381.
9. Bearing our Sins in his Body, 382.
10. Partaking in Christ's Sufferings, 383.

CHAPTER V.
Doctrine of the Pauline Epistles.

1. Christ's Mediation the Substance of Paul's Gospel, 384.
2. The Corinthian Epistles, 384.
3. God in Christ Reconciling the World, 385.
4. Epistle to the Galatians, 388.
5. Becoming a Curse for Us, 389.
6. Epistle to the Romans, 390.
7. Discussion of Romans iii, 21–26, 391.
   (1) Not a New Teaching.
   (2) Originates with God.
   (3) Passing over Former Sins.
   (4) Two Greek Words.
   (5) Realized through Faith.
   (6) Magnifies the Law.
   (7) Mysterious Necessities of the Moral World.
8. Continuous Reconciliation, Romans iv, 25, 400.
9. The Great Antithesis of Romans v, 12–21, 401.
10. The Doctrine in Ephesians and Colossians, 401.
11. In the Pastoral Epistles, 402.

CHAPTER VI.
Doctrine of the Epistle to the Hebrews.

1. Outline of the Epistle, 404.
2. Superior Priesthood of Jesus, 405.
3. Symbolism of the Tabernacle, 406.
4. Mediator of the New Covenant, Hebrews ix, 15–18, 407.
   (1) Reasons for "Testament" in Hebrews ix, 16, 17.
   (2) Reasons for "Covenant."
5. This Not a Covenant between Equals, 411.
6. Alexandrian Cast of the Epistle, 411.
7. Substantial Agreement of All the New Testament Writers, 412.

CHAPTER VII.
Summary of the Biblical Doctrine.

1. A Continuous Process, not a Finished Work, 413.
2. Largely Set Forth by Symbols and Metaphors, 414.
3. Use of Current Forms of Speech, 415.
4. Necessity of Christ's Mediation, 415.
   (1) Necessity in Man.
   (2) Necessity in Nature of God.
5. Such Suffering not Penal, 417.
6. Does Not Remove All Consequences of Sin, 417.
7. Not an Objective Process or Ground of God's Activity, 418.
8. Essentially Spiritual in its Operation, 418.
9. Effectual Through a Living Faith, 418.
10. No Theory of Atonement in the Scriptures, 419.
11. Mystical Body of Christ, 420.
12. The Communion of Saints, 421.

SECTION THIRD
THE KINGDOM AND COMING OF CHRIST.

CHAPTER I.
The Nature of the Kingdom of Christ.

1. Heavenly Enthronement of Jesus Christ, 423.
2. Old Testament Doctrine of the Kingdom of God, 423.
   (1) God Rules in Many and Divers Forms.
   (2) God as the Supreme Judge.
   (3) Apocalyptic Day of Jehovah.
   (4) Messianic Prophecies of the Kingdom.
   (5) The Messiah an Associate with the Most High.
3. Views of the Kingdom Current among the Jews, 429.
4. The Doctrine of Jesus, 430.
   (1) A Kingdom of Heaven.
   (2) Lessons of the Parables.
   (3) A Spiritual Kingdom.
   (4) The Greatest in the Kingdom.
   (5) The Fundamental Law of Love.
   (6) Jesus's Teaching Different from John's Ideal.
   (7) Jesus's Teaching in John's Gospel.
5. Doctrine of Pauline Epistles, 438.
6. Other New Testament Teaching, 439.
7. Contemplates Present and Future Blessedness, 440.
8. Concluding Summary, 440.

CHAPTER II.

The Coming of the Kingdom of Christ.

1. Variety of Biblical Statements, Words and Phrases, 442.
2. Coming in the Near Future, 442.
3. Jesus's Eschatological Discourse, 444.
4. The End of the Age, 444.
5. Supposed Inconsistencies, 446.
    (1) Matthew xxiv, 14.
    (2) The Day and Hour Unknown.
    (3) Apocalyptic Language.
6. The Words $\pi\alpha\rho o\nu\sigma i\alpha$, and $\dot{\epsilon}\rho\chi o\mu\alpha\iota$, 448.
7. Admonition of Luke xvii, 20–37, 449.
8. Synoptic Testimony Quite Decisive, 449.
9. Excludes Literalism, 450.
10. Doctrine of John's Gospel, 451.
    (1) John iii, 3–7; 31–36.
    (2) John xiv, 3.
    (3) John xxi, 22, 23.
11. General Apostolic Allusions, 453.
12. Import of the word $\dot{\epsilon}\pi\iota\phi\acute{a}\nu\epsilon\iota\alpha$, 454.
13. Import of $\dot{a}\pi o\kappa\acute{a}\lambda\nu\psi\iota\varsigma$, and $\phi\alpha\nu\acute{\epsilon}\rho\omega\sigma\iota\varsigma$, 455.
14. The Statement in Acts i, 11, 456.
15. Doctrine of John's Apocalypse, 457.
    (1) The First Part, I–XI.
    (2) The Second Part, XII–XXII.
    (3) New Jerusalem a Symbol of the Kingdom of Heaven.
16. Biblical Doctrine of Antichrist, 460.
    (1) Old Testament Concepts.
    (2) Antichrist in John's Apocalypse.
17. The Pauline Doctrine of Antichrist.
    (1) Relation of Second Thessalonians ii, 1–12, to First Thessalonians iv, 13–18.
    (2) Meaning of Second Thessalonians ii, 2.
    (3) Imagery of Paul's Picture of Antichrist.
    (4) Other Peculiar Words and Phrases.
    (5) Essential Content and Import of the Pauline Doctrine.
18. The Antichrist of the Johannine Epistles.
19. General Conclusion.

CHAPTER III.

Continuous Development of the Kingdom of Christ.

1. Christ to Overcome the World, 473.
2. Old Testament Messianic Ideals, 473.
    (1) Ancient Promises
    (2) Psalms cx and lxxii.
    (3) Isaiah ii, 2–4.
    (4) Isaiah ix, 1–7, and xi, 1–10.
    (5) Daniel ii, 44, and vii, 13.
3. Christ as Ruler and Judge, 477.
4. Days of Judgment, 478.
5. The Judgment in Matthew xxv, 31–46. 478.
6. Times and Modes of Judgment Not Specifically Revealed, 478.
7. Eternal Issues of the Judgment, 479.
8. Judgment of God and of Christ One, 480.
9. A New Power in the World, 480.
10. Its Period One of Untold Ages and Generations, 481.
11. Regeneration and Restitution of All Things, 482.
12. Paul's Statement in First Corinthians xv, 24–28, 483.

CHAPTER IV.

The Mission and Ministry of the Spirit of Christ.

1. Vital Relation of the Kingdom of Christ and the Ministry of His Spirit, 484.
2. The Spirit Operative Before End of Age, 484.
3. Meaning of the Word Spirit, 485.
4. Threefold Elements of Personality, 485.
5. Epithets applied to the Spirit of God, 487.
6. The Spirit Capable of Grief, 487.
7. Advance in the New Testament Doctrine, 488.
8. Christ and the Holy Spirit, 488.
9. The Johannine Teaching, 489.
10. Procession and Personality, 480.
11. The Power of the Spirit After the Glorification of Jesus, 491.
12. The Pentecostal Gifts of Power, 492.
    (1) Foretold by Jesus.
    (2) Expected and Prayed for.
    (3) The Promise Fulfilled.
    (4) Peter's Interpretation.
    (5) Immediate Results.
    (6) Typical Significance.
    (7) Three Fundamental Truths.
13. Ministrations of the Spirit, 495.
    (1) Conviction of Sin, Righteousness, and Judgment.
    (2) Regeneration.
    (3) Sanctification.
    (4) Witness and Communion.
    (5) Revealing the Truth.
    (6) Imparting Gifts of Power.
    (7) The Comforter.
14. The Greater Works of the Spirit, 504.
    (1) Greater than Physical Signs and Wonders.
    (2) Jesus's Estimate of Miracles.
    (3) Lesson from Elijah.
    (4) Paul's Estimate of External Wonders.
15. Shows the Real Nature of the Kingdom of God, 508.
16. Personal Presence of the Living God, 508.

PART THIRD
OUR FATHER IN HEAVEN

SECTION FIRST
THE UNIVERSAL REVELATION.
CHAPTER I.
The Mystery of the Invisible.
1. Witnessed Among All Nations, 509.
2. The Divers Interpretations, 510.
3. Philosophical Theories, 511.
4. Current Theistic Arguments, 512.
5. Words of Zophar and Elihu, 513.

CHAPTER II.
Biblical Recognition of the Gods and Cults of the Nations.
1. Gods of the Nations, 514.
2. Traces of Heathen Myths, 514.
3. Names of the Gods, 515.

CHAPTER III.
Origin of the Concept of God.
1. Involved in the Origin of Religion, 518.
2. Inadequate Theories, 518.
3. A Question of Psychology Rather than of History, 519.
4. The Concept a Revelation, 519.
5. Revelation Gradual and in Parts, 520.
6. Childhood of the World, 521.

SECTION SECOND
THE HEBREW REVELATION.
CHAPTER I.
The Call and Covenant of Abraham.
1. The Migration and the Promise, 523.
2. Meeting with Melchizedek, 523.
3. Defective Ethical Standards, 524.
4. Nomadic Life Favorable to Religious Thought, 524.
5. The Covenant of Promise, 524.
6. Anthropomorphic Conceptions, 525.
7. Other Patriarchal Revelations, 527.
8. The Biblical Narratives Give Truthful Pictures, 527.

CHAPTER II.
The Divine Legation of Moses.
1. The Hebrew Exodus, 529.
2. The New Name Jehovah, 529.
3. The Sinaitic Legislation, 531.
4. Comparative Legislation of the Nations, 532.

CHAPTER III.
Canaanitish Conflicts and Messages of the Prophets.
1. Israel's Apostasy from Jehovah, 534.
2. The Concept of Monolatry, 535.
3. Jehovah a Terrible God, 536.
4. Jehovah of Hosts, 537.
5. Human Sacrifices, 537.
6. Ideas of God Enlarged with National Growth, 537.
7. Significance of the Temple, 538.
8. Concept of a Theocratic Kingdom, 539.
9. Apocalyptic Visions of Jehovah, 540.
10. The Biblical Angelology, 541.
11. The Prophetic Monotheism, 543.
12. Theology of the Psalter, 545.
13. Hebrew Ideal of Creation, 546.
14. The Messianic Hope of Israel, 547.
15. A Purposed Goal in Human History, 548.
16. Concept of God as Father, 549.
17. Summary of Old Testament Doctrine, 550.
    (1) Essential Qualities of Nature.
    (2) Personality of God.
    (3) Divine Attributes in Personality.
        Omnipotence.
        Omniscience.
        Omnisentience.

SECTION THIRD
THE REVELATION IN JESUS CHRIST.
CHAPTER I.
The Threefold Manifestation.
1. Love, Wisdom, and Power in the Person, Mediation, and Kingdom of Christ, 555.
2. Complemental to Old Testament Revelation, 555.
3. Christ the Power of God, 556.
4. Christ the Wisdom of God, 557.
5. Christ the Love of God, 558.

CHAPTER II.
Christ's own Testimony and Teaching.
1. Jesus's Testimony in Matthew xi, 25–27, 560.
    (1) Fuller Revelation of the Father.
    (2) Simplicity of Christ's Gospel of the Father.
    (3) The Father's Delight in His Children.
2. Great Advance on the Old Testament View, 564.
3. The Only One Good, 564.
4. Doctrine of Jesus in the Fourth Gospel, 565.
    (1) God is Spirit.
    (2) God is the Life and the Light.
    (3) God is Love.
    (4) Johannine Concept of the Fatherhood.

CHAPTER III.

Apostolic Concepts of the Father.

1. In the Epistle of John, 569.
2. In the Other Catholic Epistles, 569.
3. In the Pauline Epistles, 570.
   (1) Various Striking Phrases.
   (2) Monotheistic Attributes.
   (3) Sympathy with the Groaning Creation.

CHAPTER IV.

The Everlasting Fatherhood.

1. Monistic, Immanent, Transcendent, 572.
2. God Conceived as Generator and Generatrix, 572.
3. Providential Oversight and Rule, 573.
4. Suffers with the Groaning Creation, 574.
5. The Cry—How Long, O Lord, 575.
6. No Waste of Material or Energy, 576.
7. Defective Concept of Monarchy and Absolutism, 578.
8. The Idea of Divine Maternity, 579.
9. The Everlasting Trinity of Wisdom, Power, and Love, 580.
10. The Everlasting Goal, 581.

Select Bibliography, 583.
Index of Scripture Texts, 595.
General Index, 605.

INTRODUCTION

CHAPTER I

IDEA AND SCOPE OF BIBLICAL DOGMATICS

1. Theology and Religion. Theology is the science of religion, and a scientific treatment of the Christian faith must be a rational conception and statement of its fundamental truths. Religion is found to be an essential element in the spiritual nature of man. There is a necessary relation between man and God, and the consciousness of this fact accounts for the universal prevalence of religion among the various peoples. Religion appears under many different forms, and it has been in all ages an important factor in the progress of civilization. It cannot be accounted for as a product of human reason, or as an invention of priestcraft, or as an effect of ghostly and superstitious fears. Religion, like the moral sense, is a matter of personal consciousness and universal experience, and it compels some form of recognition among all men. The simplest explanation of these facts appears in the biblical teaching that God, the invisible and eternal Spirit, has in various ways revealed himself to all the peoples of the earth. That which may be known of God in his works of creation and in his opposition to all unrighteousness of men is said by Paul to have been revealed from heaven to the conscience and perception of the human soul, and such revelation has been in progress from the beginning until now. Accordingly, men of all nations show the work of a divine law written in their hearts, and their conscience and reason continually bear witness to these unmistakable facts.

2. Universality of Religion and Revelation. That God, the eternal Spirit, has at different times and in many ways revealed himself to mankind is attested by the universality of the religious feeling. If there be any human heart destitute of religious consciousness, it must be either undeveloped or abnormal. Hence we conceive that all true elements of religion are matters of divine revelation. But not all these elements of religion have ever been given at any one time or place as a perfected whole. They have been made known to men in various degrees of clearness, here in part and there in part. According to John i, 9, the all-pervasive, true, eternal Light illumines every man coming into the world. That which has commonly been called "natural religion" proves in its final analysis to be a matter of revelation, for the invisible attributes and powers of the Creator are made manifest through the visible forms of the things which have been made. But this fact that all religion, like the concept of God, is a matter of revelation does not exclude the further fact that various special and remarkable revelations have at different times been made to men. There have been distinctive epochs of religious activity, and there have appeared not a few transcendent teachers of religion, gifted above their fellow men in the knowledge of divine mysteries; and all these are entitled to our most serious and careful consideration.[1] At the same time we should observe that a deep religious feeling may exist without a definite system of religious thought. Religious emotion may also very powerfully impress and actuate one's life, while at the same time his concept of God and the world may be darkened by sundry low and delusive superstitions. One may seriously embrace a falsehood for the truth and propagate it with great zeal. His error may contain elements of truth, and so be the more enthralling. One may also perversely change the truth of God into a lie, or exchange it for a lie, and worship and serve the creature rather than the Creator (comp. Rom. i, 25). The facts of religious aberration, bigotry, and bitterness constitute a mournful exhibit of human frailty. But on the other hand, a study of the efforts of the great and good to formulate their conceptions of God and of the relations between God and man is one of the most interesting and profitable occupations of the seeker after truth.

3. Philosophy of Religion. There are many different forms of religion in the world, and there have been many which, like the peoples who observed them, long ago ceased to exist. The fact that we can speak of "dead religions" and "living religions" is itself an indication that religion is an inseparable factor in the life and growth of nations. Aside from the lower phases of religion which appear among barbarous tribes, there are such conspicuous systems as Buddhism and Mohammedanism which are embraced by millions of enthusiastic devotees. Each of these

---

[1] This fact has been admirably expressed by Professor R. H. Charles: "All true growth in religion, whether in the past or the present, springs from the communion of man with the immediate living God, wherein man learns the will of God, and becomes thereby an organ of God, a personalized conscience, a revealer of divine truth for men less inspired than himself. The truth thus revealed through a man possesses a divine authority for men."—Critical History of the Doctrine of a Future Life, p. 3. London, 1899.

great systems of faith has its own peculiar history and teachings, and they all demand the attention of the thorough student of theology. The "philosophy of religion," so called, has in recent years become a distinct department of study, and is based upon a comparative examination of all the religious cults known among the nations. It studies to reduce the facts of religion to certain fundamental principles, and to explain their origin, their nature, and their relations. Such comparative study is not fairly or profitably pursued without the aid of history, psychology, philosophy, and theology.

4. The Christian Religion. We maintain that the Christian religion is by far the highest and purest among all the great religions now existing. It acknowledges its direct historical connection with the religion of the Jewish people, and makes an important use of their ancient scriptures; but it assumes to supplement and supersede the older Hebrew system. The religious teachings of the Law, the Prophets, and the Psalms of Israel stand aloft and unique; they are without parallel among all the sacred writings that originated in their time; but the teachings of Jesus Christ and his apostles surpass them all in their self-evidencing authority and adaptation to meet the spiritual wants of man. The doctrines of this superior religion are to be learned from the writings of the New Testament. In these simple but remarkable records the precious truths of the older scriptures, even to the jot and tittle, are seen in their higher pleroma (comp. Matt. v, 17). The Christian revelation fulfills and consummates the entire Hebrew cult. It is the purpose of Biblical Dogmatics to gather up and set forth in orderly arrangement the essential doctrines of this superior revelation as they may be clearly proven out of all these sacred writings.

5. Biblical Theology. Biblical Dogmatics, accordingly, differs in its scope from what is known as biblical theology. The latter aims to trace the genesis and growth of religious ideas, and to set forth the various types of doctrine apparent in the different biblical writers. It is, accordingly, a kind of historical discipline, while at the same time it belongs essentially to the department of exegetical theology, for its main task is to furnish a correct grammatico-historical explanation of the teaching of each biblical writer, and also to show as far as possible the origin and development of each distinct religious concept. Biblical Dogmatics, on the other hand, goes beyond the limits of this exegetical and historical discipline, and seeks a logical arrangement of the biblical doctrines into a systematic body of revealed truth. It appropriates the results of exegetical study as presented in biblical theology, and combines them in their inner living connection and their higher unity.[1]

6. Systematic Theology. Systematic Theology claims a still broader field than that of Biblical Dogmatics and of Biblical Theology. It goes beyond the limits of the biblical revelation, although acknowledging the Scriptures as the chief source of religious dogma. It recognizes the creeds and controversies of Christendom, and employs, as occasion offers, both the methods and the facts of science, of philosophy, and of all human research. It deals with doctrines of the Christian faith, sets forth the processes by which the several dogmas have been constructed into scientific statement and confessional formulas, and arranges the whole body of doctrines thus constructed into one complete, logical, self-consistent system. Systematic Theology, or Christian Dogmatics in the broad sense, may well claim the great creeds of Christendom as a magnificent inheritance. Certain specific formulas of doctrine may be discarded; many peculiar opinions of great fathers and teachers of the church may be seen to be no longer tenable; but the ecumenical creeds, the historic confessions, and such names as Athanasius, and Augustine, and Jerome, and Bernard, and Anselm, Luther and Melanchthon, Zwingli and Calvin, Arminius, Bunyan, Edwards, and Wesley are fairly canonized in the thought of the Christian world. We may freely test their statements by all the appliances of later research and we may find not a little in them to be set aside; but we should also appreciate and admire the inestimable substance of truth which they have transmitted to us in their luminous expositions of Christian doctrine.

7. Limits and Aim of Biblical Dogmatics. Biblical Dogmatics may adopt the method of Systematic Theology in the construction of distinctive doctrines of the Scriptures and in arranging them into an orderly and logical system, but it may not go beyond the proper exegesis of the Bible in its construction of doctrine, nor is it to deal with the creeds of the Church and the polemics of theologians. It may, so far as serves its purpose, proceed in the steps of biblical theology, point out the genesis and development of particular doctrines, and give due attention to the distinctive types of doctrine which appear in different biblical writers. So far as the books of the Law and the Prophets and the Psalms of

---

[1] We cannot well overestimate the value of biblical theology to modern Christian thought. It is almost the extreme opposite of the older confessional dogmatics, for its trend has been virtually a revolt from the dialectic and speculative methods of a former time. It seems almost an ironical element, working unconsciously in theologians, when they insist in strong terms that the Scriptures are the "sole and infallible rule of faith," and yet make it their strenuous task to twist luminous statements of the biblical writers from their obvious meaning into a supposable harmony with preconceived extra-biblical schemes of doctrine.

the Old Testament show divergences of thought, or so far as the different books of the New Testament indicate any diversity of doctrinal expression, Biblical Dogmatics is bound to pay careful attention to all the facts. If there be found any contradiction of teaching in the various authors, or if early and imperfect religious ideas are corrected, supplemented or superseded in later times, Biblical Dogmatics should take due account of all such progress and changes of doctrine. At the same time it is the task of Biblical Dogmatics so to combine the truths of Scripture as to exhibit the higher and broader unity under which the varying individual concepts of different writers may be seen to be so many manifestations of the same Spirit.

8. Theology Old and New. The result of a faithful construction of Biblical Dogmatics should be an old and new theology. Not an old theology and a new one, as if they were twain and contradictory, but a theology which is at once both old and new. It is a theology which faithfully maintains and conserves the great religious teachings of the Scriptures, but which may be set forth in new forms of statement and with new life and beauty by the living Spirit of Christ which ever abides and coöperates with the enlargement of human knowledge. "Therefore every scribe who hath been made a disciple to the kingdom of heaven is like unto a man that is a householder, who bringeth forth out of his treasure things new and old" (Matt. xiii, 52). A notable part of the ministry of the Holy Spirit, whom the Father sends as an abiding Comforter, is to teach us and to guide us into all the truth (John xiv, 26; xvi, 13; 1 John ii, 27). By the guidance of this abiding Spirit the disciple of the kingdom of heaven may continually find new confirmations and enlarged conceptions of the truths of Holy Writ. He enjoys numerous advantages over the ancient fathers. There is today a more searching criticism of the biblical records than at any previous period; there prevails a sounder and better exegesis of those records; the comparative study of the great religions of the world and their sacred books has accomplished much for a broader view of the relations between God and man; scientific exploration and commercial and international intercourse have enlarged the knowledge and sympathy of men; the remarkable sociological movements throughout the civilized world and the profound study of the philosophy of human history have lifted whole classes to a higher plane of thought; discoveries in natural science and the inductive methods of investigation so prominent in modern research, the uplifting influence of great reforms and the marvelous achievements of modern Christian missions among the peoples of other faiths, the refining influence of enlarged literary culture and the power of the secular and religious press—these and other like elements of advantage over the former times are of incalculable value for the full equipment of the biblical theologian. The illuminating Spirit of God may be expected to work with increased efficiency by means of the superior knowledge and culture now possible to man. And so the student in any department of theological research ought to profit by the various appliances of learning and science, confident that the Spirit of truth is ever operating through such aids to the discovery of new beauty and treasure in the ancient revelations. Our heavenly Father worketh hitherto, and how shall we be partakers of his Spirit if we neglect any light arising through the advance of human research? Our aim shall be to "combine spiritual things with spiritual words" (1 Cor. ii, 13), and thus conserve and enhance the old eternal truths by a manner of statement somewhat new, but, it is hoped, clearly self-consistent and intelligible.

CHAPTER II

SOURCES OF BIBLICAL DOGMATICS

1. The Bible a Priceless Treasury. The main sources of biblical doctrine are the canonical scriptures of the Old and New Testaments. The writers of these remarkable books were all of them offspring of Abraham, who was of old time called out from his far Eastern country and kindred to become a great nation and a blessing to all the families of the earth (Gen. xii, 1-3). These people and their sacred writings hold a unique place in the history of mankind. In the more ancient times the sons of Abraham were called Hebrews; later they were also called Israelites; and after their restoration from Babylonian captivity they were more commonly called Jews, because most of the survivors of that exile were of the tribe and kingdom of Judah. There came unto them time and again the assurance that they were to be a peculiar possession of God above all other peoples of the earth, "a kingdom of priests, and a holy nation," destined to be a light among the nations to make known the salvation of God to the ends of the earth (Exod. xix, 6; Deut. vii, 6; Isa. xlix, 6). According to Jesus, in John iv, 22, "the salvation is from the Jews," and Paul's conception of the chief advantage of the Jews was in the fact that "they were intrusted with the oracles of God" (Rom. iii. 2). If there be any truth in the common saying that the Romans have been preëminent in teaching the world its highest ideals of government and law, and that the Greeks have excelled in art and philosophy, it may as surely be maintained that the Hebrew nation has been the recipient and custodian of the purest religion and the most profitable scriptures known among men. We accordingly accept the canonical books of the two Testaments as a priceless deposit of religious truth, exceedingly profitable and altogether sufficient for doctrine and for instruction in the revelations of God.

2. Trammels of Old Tradition. But the precious truths of these scriptures have been largely obscured and deprived of their real force and authority by the traditions of men. The early Christian Church inherited from the Jewish synagogue a vast accumulation of conjectures touching the origin of the sacred books, and the nature of their inspiration; and this harmful leaven of erroneous and misleading conceptions has been working through all the Christian centuries. The rabbinical exegesis ran into a cabalistic juggling with the text of Scripture, and was speedily followed by the almost equally fantastic allegorical methods of the Alexandrian school of biblical interpreters, from Philo the Jew to Origen the learned Christian father. In spite of the wholesome reaction of the school of Antioch the mischievous assumptions and the mystic methods of the allegorical treatment of Scripture have persisted until quite modern times, and may be found in some places even to this day. Along with the old rabbinic and allegorical exegesis there was also begotten a theory of biblical inspiration, which in course of time has taken to itself such qualifying terms as *verbal, inerrant,* and *infallible.* It has affirmed that the sacred writers were impassive instruments in the hands of God, and that every word and letter of the Bible were supernaturally dictated by the omniscient Spirit.[1] This strange fiction of mistaken reverence for the letter of Scripture has tended to a materialistic and sentimental bibliolatry, and has fostered the most absurd mental aberrations. The extravagant claims of the old Jewish rabbis, and the mystic vagaries of mediæval cabalists, were paralleled by the declaration of the Helvetic creed of 1675 that "the Hebrew original of the Old Testament is inspired of God not only in its consonants, but in its vowels and the vowel points." The allegorical interpretation itself was in part an effort to get rid of the obvious difficulties of inerrant verbal inspiration, and also to account for the recorded immoralities of the patriarchs which such a strained view of Scripture seemed to sanction.

3. Reaction and Changes of View. The common sense and intelligence of men have for long time been revolting from this distorted handling of the Scriptures. The author of 2 Peter (iii, 16) speaks of Paul's epistles, and also the other scriptures, as having been stretched on the rack and twisted over a windlass (στρεβλοῦσιν) by the ignorant errorists of his time. Such a torturing of a multifarious body of religious literature is sure, sooner or later, to provoke reaction, and such intellectual reactions have too generally been led by men of a rationalistic and iconoclastic spirit. We naturally feel that this ought not so to be; and yet history has often shown that iconoclasts may indirectly serve

---

[1] Thus Quenstedt, in 1685, declared that "all things which were to be written were suggested by the Holy Spirit to the sacred writers in the very act of writing, and were dictated to their intellect as if unto a pen (*quasi in calamum*), so that they could be written in no other circumstances, in this and no other mode or order" (Theologia Didact., iv, 2). Carpzov, in 1728, declared that the divine Power "impelled the will" of the biblical writers, and "directed their hand that they might write infallibly" (Critica Sacra Vet. Test., p. 43). Similar statements might be cited by the hundred from writers both earlier and later than these.

the cause of truth. If they but stimulate men to a remonstrance against aged abuses, to an exposure of unsound and misleading methods, and to the adoption of more tenable beliefs, their very extravagances may help the infirmities of less bold reformers. But changes of opinion on a wide scale and modification of old beliefs are not made suddenly. They usually require several generations to make the necessary discoveries and adjust the results of faithful investigation.

4. Other Sacred Bibles. One of the most important discoveries of the last century is the number of other collections of literature held sacred by the adherents of divers ethnic religions of the world. The Chinese classics, as revised and enlarged by the wisdom of Confucius, have an authority in the civilization and worship of the millions of Eastern Asia that is notably comparable with that of the Hebrew scriptures among the Jewish people. The Kojiki of the old Shinto cult in Japan presents another example that is worthy of comparison. The ancient Vedas of India command a reverence among millions of the Hindus as great as any Jew or Christian ever evinced for the Bible of his faith. The Tripitaka of the Buddhists, the Avesta of the ancient Mazdeans and the modern Parsees, the Koran of the Mohammedans, and sundry other collections of sacred literature hold a similar high place in the estimation of other religionists. For in several of these ethnic books claims of miraculous inspiration are made even more extravagant than those of verbal dictation and literal inerrancy. Among some of the Mohammedans it is held that the Koran is not a human production, but existed from eternity in the essence of God; and some Brahmans put forth similar declarations respecting their ancient Vedas. Acquaintance with these other bibles of the world, and with the remarkable claims put forth in their honor, have admonished us to be more cautious in making assertions about our Holy Bible which are not clearly demonstrable.

5. Limits of the Biblical Canon. Another fact which scientific research has compelled us to acknowledge is the uncertainty of the limits of our canonical scriptures. Faithful historical inquiry nowhere finds that God himself, or Jesus Christ, or any duly accredited person or company of men, has ever settled once for all the exact extent of either the Old Testament or the New. Some of the New Testament writers quote from apocryphal writings with as much respect as they do from Moses and the prophets, and many of the early Christian fathers not only do the same thing but they also call those apocryphal books "holy Scripture." The Greek and Roman Catholic Churches accept the Old Testament Apocrypha as an integral part of the inspired canon. The lists of canonical books found in the writings of Melito, Origen, and other early Christian writers, and those indorsed by the Councils of Laodicea and Hippo, vary in details, and they represent at most only the opinions of men of fallible judgment, no more competent to determine such a question than the painstaking historical students of our day. There is little room to doubt, however, that the thirty-nine books of the Old Testament, as they are now everywhere acknowledged, were accepted as Holy Scriptures by the Jews at the beginning of the Christian era. Josephus specifies them as five books of Moses, thirteen books of the Prophets, and four others containing hymns to God and prescribed rules of life for men.[1] These make in all twenty-two books, according to the number of letters in the Hebrew alphabet; but Josephus nowhere names all the books, or gives us to understand how he condensed our present thirty-nine into twenty-two. It is also a fact not to be overlooked that in the first century of our era the Jewish rabbis were yet discussing the canonicity of Ecclesiastes, Esther, and the Song of Songs.[2] So little weight had these Talmudic discussions of the rabbinic schools of Palestine with the Alexandrian Jews that they freely admitted into their collection of scriptures the books which we now call Apocrypha. The early Christian fathers appear to have accepted the Alexandrian rather than the Palestinian canon, and, as we have said, the Greek and Roman Churches have followed their example in spite of the lists of more limited collections approved by various Church councils. But even could it be shown that the limits of the Old Testament were fixed by Ezra or by Christ and his apostles, where shall we find equal authority for the several books of the New Testament? It is matter of ancient record that the epistles of James, 2 Peter, 2 and 3 John, Jude, the Apocalypse of John, and the epistle to the Hebrews were in the early times regarded by some as spurious, and were long disputed.[3] But while these facts disclose the uncertainty of the limits of the canon, as fixed by any unquestionable authority, it must also be observed that over the

---

[1] Contra Apion, book i, 8.

[2] It is remarkable how a vague tradition, destitute of any trustworthy authority, and notably inconsistent with certain demonstrable facts, may be taken up by a bold writer and affirmed as the end of all controversy on a most important question. Thus J. H. Hottinger, about the middle of the seventeenth century, declared: "Hitherto it has been an unquestioned axiom both among Jews and Christians (who have not a fungus for brains) that the canon of the Old Testament was fixed once for all, with divine authority, by Ezra and the men of the Great Synagogue" (Thesaurus Philologicus, i, 2). This statement is without any proof, but has been repeated by scores of theologians, who seem never to have clearly comprehended the difference between demonstrable facts and bold assertions.

[3] Eusebius, Ecclesiastical History, book iii, chap. xxv; book ii, chap. xxiii.

acceptance of the great majority of the books no serious question has ever arisen; and while some of the apocryphal books are of obviously inferior value, it may be said of all of them, canonical, apocryphal, and pseudepigraphical, that they contain much that is "profitable for doctrine, for reproof, for correction, and for instruction in righteousness"; and it would make no serious difference in results if we should include them all in our sources of biblical dogmatics. In fact, on doctrines not a few we find it necessary to consult these apocryphal sources for information touching the religious opinions of the Jews current at the time these books were written. The book of Tobit, as well as the book of Esther, furnishes us with a noteworthy side-light upon the Jewish life and thought of its time, and the historian of Judaism might well deplore its loss. On the other hand, no important truth of our Christian religion would be invalidated or imperiled if we should omit from our sources of doctrine not only all the apocryphal writings, but also the books of Esther, Ecclesiastes, Song of Songs, Chronicles, James, Hebrews, 2 Peter, 2 and 3 John, Jude, and the Apocalypse, for the canonicity of most of these, as we have observed, was much questioned in the ancient times. There is, moreover, a convenience in the use of the more limited canon, and it seems preferable to confine our sources of doctrine to the scriptures of the Old Testament which are accepted alike by Jews, Greek and Roman Catholics and Protestants, and to the New Testament as commonly received by the Greek, Roman, and Protestant Churches.

6. Other Traditions Questioned. Other traditions of the Jewish synagogue touching the authorship of certain books have also been challenged by modern criticism. A well-known passage in the Talmud assumes to answer the question, "Who wrote the Old Testament books?" That answer, given in the footnote,[1] is a fair specimen of oracular dogma prevalent in the old rabbinic schools. Its value is to be estimated by comparison with scores of similar deliverances found among the teachings of the Gemara. The entire statement is obviously a set of rabbinical conjectures, made at a time when the origin and history of the books named were as uncertain to these Jews as they are to us. The strange idea

---

[1] Moses wrote his own book, and the section about Balaam and Job. Joshua wrote his own book and eight verses of the Law. Samuel wrote his own book and also Judges and Ruth. David wrote the book of Psalms at the direction of (or *in behalf of*) the ten ancients: Adam the first, Melchizedek, Abraham, Moses, Heman, Jeduthun, Asaph, and the three sons of Korah. Jeremiah wrote his own book and the book of Kings and Lamentations. Hezekiah and his company wrote Isaiah, Proverbs, Song, and Ecclesiastes. The men of the Great Synagogue wrote Ezekiel and the Twelve, Daniel, and the roll of Esther. Ezra wrote his own book, and the genealogies of Chronicles down to his own time.—Baba Bathra, 14, b.

that David wrote the Psalms by the aid of Adam, Melchizedek and Abraham, and that the men of the Great Synagogue wrote Ezekiel, is sufficient to disparage the entire tradition and to divest it of all historical value. And yet this old and worthless statement of conjectures, repeated in substance by generations of biblical commentators, has been allowed to go unchallenged so long, that when we now call attention to its obscurity and want of corroborating evidence some people show alarm, and imagine that we are "attacking" the Scriptures themselves. A careful study of the Bible evinces the fact that many of the Old Testament books are anonymous, while the traditional authorship of others is heavily discounted, if not disproved, by the internal witness of the books themselves. The Psalms are not all ascribed to David, and the book of Proverbs contains at least seven different collections, some of them made long after the time of Solomon. Moreover, the titles of many psalms and the superscriptions and subscriptions of some books and portions of books appear to have no more value than the chapter-headings inserted in the "authorized" English version of 1611. Some books long supposed to have come from one writer are found on closer examination to be composite, and this noteworthy feature of books both canonical and apocryphal appears also in most of the religious books of other nations. It ought, therefore, to be no disturbing element in our search for the truth embodied in these ancient books to be apprized of all the facts and features of their origin, so far as such facts can now be ascertained. The books themselves remain precisely what they always have been since they were canonized for religious uses, and the results of continuous searching criticism only serve to present them to us in a clearer light.

7. Variety of Compositions. Another fact brought into prominence by modern research is the remarkable variety of compositions embodied in the scriptures of the two Testaments. There are fragments of very ancient Hebrew song imbedded sometimes in the midst of historic annals; there are sundry collections of odes and proverbs, dramas wrought out in artificial form, alphabetical poems, orations of fervid eloquence, biography of romantic interest, genealogies of tedious length, theocratic history and narratives of many persons and of events of which we possess no other record; there are the oracles of prophecy and the gospel memoirs, unlike any other literature known; the New Testament epistles are unique, and the gospel of John is a monument of Christian thought which persistently confounds the hostile criticism of the centuries. All these writings taken together exhibit also a wealth and variety of rhetorical qualities unsurpassed in other comparable collections of religious literature. There are enigmatical sayings, riddles, fables, parables, allegories, types, symbols, and apocalyptic pictures set in exquisite idealistic form, and often adorned with the most beautiful and forceful figures of speech. It is easily seen now that all portions of this extensive and various body of scripture are not of equal value. Compositions of such great diversity of character and scope, many of them separated from each other by centuries, could not and should not be expected to escape the most searching criticism. The original texts are in many cases corrupt, so that we are at a loss to know precisely what the ancient writer said. Had the biblical writings, like certain well-known inscriptions, been originally graven in the enduring rock with a stylus of iron (comp. Job xix, 24), there might have been less ground for dubious questioning; but they were at first inscribed in perishable manuscripts, and they have been copied by many different hands through successive generations, and a comparison of the various copies and of the several versions shows that they have suffered by way of numerous omissions, interpolations, and verbal changes.

8. Three Divisions of the Hebrew Canon. The three well-known divisions of the Hebrew canon—the Law, the Prophets, and the Writings—appear to have been made some time before the beginning of our era. They are mentioned in Luke xxiv, 44, as "the law of Moses, and the prophets, and the psalms," and in the prologue of Ecclesiasticus as "the law, and the prophets, and the other books of our fathers." All printed copies of the Hebrew Bible show this arrangement of the Palestinian canon. The first five books are called the Law of Moses; the books of the Prophets are separated into two classes, the earlier and the later, the first class embracing Joshua, Judges, Samuel, and Kings, the second the more oracular books of Isaiah, Jeremiah, Ezekiel, and the twelve Minor Prophets. All the other books of the Old Testament belong to the third division called *Kethubim, i. e.,* Writings. By some of the Greek and Latin fathers and by many later writers this third section was called the *Hagiographa, i. e.,* Holy Writings. The book of Psalms is divided into a pentateuch, each section ending with a doxology; and the Jews have a saying that Moses gave five books of law, and David gave five books of psalms; the law is the word of Jehovah to his people, and the psalms are the responsive word of his people to Jehovah. But the critical study of both these pentateuchs has resulted in a prevalent belief that Moses was no more the author of the one than was David of the other. On this question of criticism, however, the last word has not yet been said, and is not likely to be for years to come.

9. The New Testament Canon. The books of the New Testament canon are fewer in number than those of the Old, and would fill less than one third the number of pages, but as sources of Christian doctrine they are very far in advance of the Hebrew scriptures, for they embody the teachings of the Lord Jesus who has fulfilled the law and the prophets, and is the Mediator of a new and better covenant. The three synoptic gospels occupy the first and highest position in this canon, for they contain a remarkably simple and uniform account of the best established traditions of what Jesus said and did, as they were first reported by those "who from the beginning were eyewitnesses and ministers of the word" (Luke i, 2). This oral testimony, which doubtless entered largely into the first preaching of the gospel by the apostles, found its way at an early date into numerous written narratives out of which our first three gospels appear to have been compiled. It is now commonly believed that Mark's gospel is the oldest of the three, and, according to Papias (about A. D. 130), it is in substance what Mark remembered of the things said or done by Christ as they were personally communicated to him by Peter. Papias also says that Matthew wrote out a collection of the sayings of Jesus in the Hebrew language, which others translated and interpreted as they were able.[1] That Hebrew (or Aramaic) original is lost, and we do not know just how much of it has been preserved in translation in our present Greek gospel according to Matthew. The date of Matthew and also that of Luke are quite uncertain, and each of these gospels has recorded words and works of our Lord which are not reported elsewhere. The gospel according to John is so different in its style from the Synoptics that its date and authorship form one of the most persistently disputed problems of New Testament criticism. Those who maintain its genuineness concede that the style and contents are probably due to the mystic temperament of the writer and the advanced age at which he wrote. Long residence in a center of Greek literary activity, and half a century of thinking and speaking repeatedly of personal memories of his beloved Lord, would very naturally color a mystic apostle's manner of reporting his testimony "that Jesus is the Christ, the Son of God" (John xx, 31).

The Acts of the apostles is from the author of the third gospel, and furnishes a most important history of the beginnings of the Christian community, and of the preaching and ministry of the

---

[1] See Eusebius, Ecclesiastical History, book iii, chap. xxxix. Our Greek gospel of Matthew appears to be based upon the Hebrew original referred to by Papias, and to include also a considerable amount of matter derived from other sources. It is also not improbable that our Greek gospel of Mark is a similar enlargement of the original memoranda of Peter's recollections.

first apostles, especially of Peter and Paul. The epistles of Paul to the Romans, Corinthians, and Galatians bear the most indisputable marks of genuineness and are among the earliest writings of the New Testament. The other Pauline epistles have been repeatedly questioned, especially the so-called Pastoral epistles; but they are all so clearly products of earliest Christian teaching, and have so much to commend them as substantially the works of Paul, that we can safely accept them as trustworthy sources of apostolic doctrine. The same, in substance, may be said of the Catholic epistles and the Apocalypse, although Jude and 2 Peter have least value among all the New Testament writings, and the majority of modern critics assign their composition to the first half of the second century.

10. Superiority of the New Testament. When, now, we examine the contents and scope of all these canonical books, and observe that Jesus and his disciples emphasize the transcendent superiority of the new covenant, mediated and ministered by the Christ, the Son of God, we must note that the New Testament revelation consummates and supersedes that of the law and the prophets of the former times. How or why should this be otherwise after "the appearing of our Saviour Christ Jesus, who abolished death, and brought life and immortality to light through the gospel"? There has been such a widespread habit of placing the Old Testament on a full equality with the New, and a consequent failure to observe how Jesus and his apostles inculcate a different doctrine, that we must here call attention to the following facts:

(1) *Shown by Statements of Jesus.* One of the most emphatic statements of Jesus is that he came to fulfill, not to destroy, the law and the prophets (Matt. v, 17). His own most positive teaching in the immediate context and elsewhere, goes to show a complete displacement of the statutes of the old covenant as a norm of ethics and of religious life, and a taking up of all their essential and permanent elements into a new setting in the gospel of the kingdom of heaven. Even the decalogue, the richest kernel of the whole law, becomes, in the teaching of Christ, exalted into a divine fullness and significance unknown to the Jewish fathers. The word, "Thou shalt not kill" is violated by "every one who is angry with his brother." The sin of adultery is committed when one "looketh on a woman to lust after her." The statutes against swearing falsely are all superseded by the new commandment, "Swear not at all." The sabbath law is so enlarged as to become a principle of universal obligation to do good: to be, like the Son of man, not a slave but "lord of the sabbath," and to know that the heavenly Father "worketh even until now." Jesus set aside

the old Mosaic regulations for divorce, and rebuked the disciples who would, like Elijah, have called down fire from heaven upon a Samaritan village that refused to receive him. And if these weightier matters of the law were thus declared defective, how much more the minor regulations about meats, and drinks, and rituals of divine service? We learn from all this that the new covenant of the gospel brings with it new spirit and new life. It does not stop at partial reforms and modifications of old customs, but requires a deep, radical, permanent uplift from the bondage of the letter of laws and prophecy into a Christly freedom of the spirit. All this and more may be shown further by our Lord's own illustration of the impropriety of putting a piece of new, undressed cloth upon an old garment, or of putting new wine into old wine-skins, or of an invited guest fasting at the time of the wedding feast, when the bridegroom and his companions are expected to rejoice together (Matt. ix, 14-17). The old and new cannot thus be pieced together, for the Lord Christ came to "make all things new." Essential elements of the old truth must needs abide; they cannot be destroyed; but they are taken up out of their old limitations and wrought over into a thoroughly new structure. Every jot and tittle of the former revelation, whether it be found in the Law, the Prophets, or the Psalms, must be fulfilled, and pass, as by a process of growth, into a new organism. Thus it was that the law and the prophets reached their finale with the ministry of John, whom Jesus pronounced greater than any one who had up to his time arisen, but, he added significantly, "he that is but little in the kingdom of heaven is greater than he" (Matt. xi, 11; comp. Luke xvi, 16).

(2) *Shown by other New Testament Teaching.* This teaching of Jesus is also affirmed in the New Testament epistles. According to Paul the letter of the old covenant, written in tables of stone, although it came with glory, was relatively a ministration of death and of condemnation, and has been eclipsed by the surpassing glory of the manifestation of the Christ (2 Cor. iii, 6-11). Hence the man who has found life in Christ is "a new creation: the old things are passed away; behold, they are become new" (2 Cor. v, 17; comp. Rev. xxi, 5). Like a woman, who in the event of her husband's death is discharged from the law of subjection to the husband, so "we have been discharged from the law, having died to that wherein we were held; so that we serve in newness of the spirit, and not in the oldness of the letter" (Rom. vii, 6). In like manner the epistle to the Hebrews teaches that by the manifestation and exaltation of Christ there comes "a setting aside (ἀθέτησις) of a foregoing commandment because of its weakness

and unprofitableness, and a bringing in thereupon of a better hope, through which we draw nigh unto God" (vii, 18, 19). For the law made nothing perfect; the first covenant was not faultless, and was at that time becoming old and nigh unto vanishing away (viii, 7, 8, 13). The law and its ceremonial were a shadow of good things to come, and must be taken away in order that the Christ may reveal himself as the Mediator of a better covenant, enacted upon better promises (x, 1; viii, 6). So the old covenant has given place to the new, and we are no longer under the law, but under grace. The old is not destroyed; it remains as a precious and wonderful object lesson to show us how God spoke of old in different ways and portions; but that which in its nature was preparatory must needs be relatively defective and weak and unprofitable as a law for the Christian life. Every jot and tittle, however, that has value for religious discipline is fulfilled in the higher revelation of Christ.

(3) *Shown by Obvious Facts of the Records.* A study of the main contents of the Old Testament will serve, furthermore, to show how defective the law and the prophets of the ancient time are for purposes of direct instruction now. The holy men of old live, act, and speak within the limitations of their time, and we should no more look for perfection in the ethics, or in the definite religious concepts of their writings, than we look for ripe fruit in the young shoot or in the green ear. There is no evidence in their books that those men of God, who wrote the Law and the Prophets and the Psalms, were so overruled by the Spirit as to be independent of their historical environment. The book of Genesis is of the nature of a grand national epic, and, like the poems of Homer and Firdausi, is a composite of the songs and traditions which had been transmitted from parents to children through many generations. The rest of the Pentateuch is mainly given to the record of laws and regulations for the ritual of a Levitical service which long since became old and vanished away. The laws touching slavery, retaliation, cities of refuge, easy-going divorce, matters of inheritance, witchcraft, meats, drinks, ablutions, and such like, are no more binding on the Christian conscience than similar laws of Hammurabi, Lycurgus, or Numa. "For Christ is the end of the law unto righteousness to every one that believeth" (Rom. x, 4). Much the same is the character of the Prophets and the Psalms, so far as their contents may be supposed to supply us with authoritative precepts for Christian faith and practice, for they belong to the pre-Christian ages, and, though abounding in pious sentiment, magnificent oracles, and hymns of divine worship, every jot and tittle of them have found their

consummation in the superior revelation of Jésus Christ. As the Decalogue received at his hand a deeper and fuller setting than it had before, so, too, the prophets and the psalms of Israel have been fulfilled and superseded by "the Apostle and High Priest of our confession," who is the life and the light of the world.

(4) *The Transition Gradual.* But the fulfilling of the old and the establishing of the new were not the accomplishment of a few days. Jewish customs and ritualistic vows and offerings and forms of divine service prevailed for a long time among the Jewish Christians. Jesus himself avoided an open and sudden breach by subjecting himself to the law and the ancient customs. He submitted to baptism by John as a becoming fulfillment of righteousness (Matt. iii, 15). He directed the man whom he healed of his leprosy to go to the priest and offer for his cleansing the things commanded in the law (Mark i, 44). The apostles of the Church in Jerusalem observed with conscientious care the practices of circumcision, fasting, vows, and questions of meats, and drinks, and fast days, and new moons, and sabbath days. Even Paul, after having broken with Jewish rudiments, consented, for the sake of peace, to observe the obligations of a Jewish vow and shave his head (Acts xxi, 24). But these things were only the temporary accommodations to the relaxing bonds of an old system that was then "nigh unto vanishing away."

11. The Question of Inspiration. The divine inspiration of the Scriptures is a fact acknowledged by all who accept them as a treasury of religious truth, but the exact nature and extent of that inspiration have been subjects of persistent controversy. We have no theory of inspiration to propound, but confidently accept the canonical scriptures as containing the highest revelations of divine truth ever imparted to mankind. We are bound, however, to oppose and drive away, so far as we are able, the dogma of the verbal inerrancy of the records, a dogma which we believe to be without any valid support in the Scriptures. The strange notion of a mechanical control of the biblical writers by the power of God's Spirit may be traced back to the ancient Jewish synagogue and the Alexandrian theosophy. Some of the early Christian fathers seem to have imbibed this conception from the assumptions of the allegorical exegesis which was prevalent in those days. Justin Martyr speaks of "the energy of the divine Spirit acting like a plectrum, descending from heaven and using righteous men as an instrument, like a harp or lyre."[1] Such a statement might have had force with the Greeks of Justin's time, who were familiar

---

[1] Address to the Greeks, chap. viii.

with the mantic frenzy of sibyls and soothsayers, but should have no weight with any who soberly inquire after the actual facts. It is, however, conceivable, and it has sometimes occurred, that devout men, under an extraordinary spell of inspiration, have spoken more wisely than they knew. No theist should question the power of the Holy Spirit of God to move the human soul with a supernatural inspiration, or with a heavenly vision. But we find that such extraordinary revelations are the experience of a moment, and, in case the person so inspired essays afterward to write down what he saw, we are not at liberty to affirm, without some specific evidence, that his normal powers were suspended or neutralized in the process of his writing. In such a case what he wrote would not be his own composition, but the supernaturally secured product of another mind. A dogma which involves such a concept of any writings cannot be accepted without the most positive evidence. We must appeal to demonstrable facts, observe what the various scriptures claim for themselves, allow no unwarranted inferences from exceptional statements of prophets or apostles, but seek a sound and trustworthy interpretation of what is written relative to the question before us.

(1) *Highest Old Testament Claims.* If we turn to the scriptures themselves and study the highest claims which any of the sacred writers make for what they have put on record, we find nothing in the Old Testament more impressive than Isaiah's account of his own divine commission (in Isa. vi). However we interpret the vision of Jehovah's throne, and the seraphim, and the live coal that touched the prophet's lips, it is evident that to the seer himself the revelation was profoundly real; and he went forth with that vision of the Holy One in his soul and proclaimed his powerful messages to the people. But there is not a line of evidence that what was afterward written out as Isaiah's oracles was anything other than the prophet's own composition, prepared in the full exercise of all his personal faculties, and within the limitations of his own human thought. Jeremiah tells us that Jehovah destined him before his birth to be a prophet unto the nations, and also that he put forth his hand and touched his mouth, and said unto him, "Behold, I have put my words in thy mouth" (Jer. i, 9). He also commanded him to "write all the words that I have spoken unto thee in a book" (xxx, 2; comp. xxxvi, 4, 32). But in his case, as in that of Isaiah, we have no warrant for supposing that when Jeremiah addressed the people of his time, or sent the messages of Jehovah to the king, or dictated the words which Baruch wrote upon the book-roll, his normal intellectual activity was temporarily arrested or neutralized by

divine power. So, too, when the sweet psalmist of Israel says (as in 2 Sam. xxiii, 2),

> **The Spirit of Jehovah spoke in me,**
> **And his word was upon my tongue,**

he simply utters the impassioned language of sacred poetry, which always breathes human emotion, and shows rhetorical culture, but furnishes no proof that the writer was an impassive machine, controlled by another Person, and miraculously secured against the utterance of any and every kind of error or mistake.

(2) *Witness of the New Testament.* When we turn to the New Testament for its highest claims of inspiration we observe the same lack of any evidence of infallible dictation. Some have appealed to the assurance given the disciples that they should be divinely assisted by the Holy Spirit when arrested and brought before governors and councils (Mark xiii, 11), but that is a promise which Christians of all times may appropriate when beset with like persecution. It was as truly verified by Martin Luther at the Diet of Worms as by Peter before the council at Jerusalem. The assurance of such divine assistance before councils makes no reference whatever to the writing of scriptures. So, too, the promise of the Comforter (in John xiv, 26), who "shall teach you all things, and bring to your remembrance all that I said unto you," contains no word touching a future record of the sayings of Christ, but is applicable to all who believe in Jesus and receive the Holy Spirit. For this "promise of the Father" is no other than the "anointing from the Holy One," of which we read in 1 John ii, 20-27, namely, "the anointing which ye received from him," and which "teacheth you concerning all things." So far as the disciples' recollection of the words of Jesus has furnished any portion of our gospels, we doubtless possess most precious results of that promised help of the Spirit. But no student of the variations and intricacies of the synoptic Gospels should fail to see that the facts which meet him at every step are utterly incompatible with the claim of verbal inerrancy for these divergent records. So far as they report the sayings of Jesus, they are all of them, at the most, Greek translations of what he uttered in another language. The preface of Luke's gospel is especially noteworthy for the statement of the author that he had "traced all things accurately from the first," and had taken pains to secure trustworthy information from those "who were from the beginning eyewitnesses and ministers of the word." He does not give the slightest hint that he received any exceptional assistance of the Holy Spirit. Paul puts forth as lofty claims to special revelation

as any writer of the New Testament. He declares that he received his gospel "not from man, but through revelation of Jesus Christ" (Gal. i, 12). But he obviously refers to the substance of his preaching, and his language cannot be legitimately construed into a claim of inerrancy for his epistles.[1] For his epistles bear some marks of his human infirmity. He confesses his inability to remember whether he baptized any other than Crispus, and Gaius, and the household of Stephanas at Corinth (1 Cor. i, 14, 16). He gave the Corinthians his judgment on a certain question, "as one that hath obtained mercy of the Lord to be trustworthy," and in the expression of such an opinion he said that he "thought that he had the Spirit of God" (1 Cor. vii, 25, 40); but he nowhere puts forth the claim of inerrant inspiration. He shows his high estimate of the Old Testament when he says: "Whatsoever things were written aforetime were written for our learning, that through patience and through comfort of the scriptures we might have hope" (Rom. xv, 4). We read also in 2 Tim. iii, 16, the classic text on inspiration: "Every scripture inspired of God is also profitable for teaching, for reproof, for correction, for instruction which is in righteousness"; but here is not a word that can establish the dogma of verbal inerrancy.

(3) *Such Claims not Applicable to All the Books.* We should further point out the fallacy of applying any high claims made for themselves by certain prophets and apostles to other writers who make no such claim. We may well believe that Isaiah, and Jeremiah, and Paul, and some others, were gifted above all other men by way of an exceptional inspiration for some particular work, but it does not therefore follow that all others, whose writings have been taken up into our canon, were inspired in the same manner and in the same degree. As simple matter of fact, all the books of the Bible are not of equal value, and some portions of a single book are not as valuable as some other portions of the same book. Can any man of sober thought maintain that the laws touching clean and unclean animals in Lev. xi, or the vindictive Psa. cix, or Isaiah's oracle against Moab, are worthy to be placed on an equality with the Sermon on the Mount, or even with the epistle to Philemon? What shall we think of the

---

[1] The fact that such a text as 1 Cor. ii, 13, has been often cited to prove Paul's claim to verbal inspiration shows how unjustifiably men construe irrelevant statements to the support of foregone conclusions. The passage refers, as the whole context shows, to the apostolic preaching of the gospel, not to any records or epistles as such. The apostle's language is also applicable to every minister of the gospel message, and to every child of God who possesses the spiritual mind, "combines spiritual things with spiritual words," or "interprets spiritual things to spiritual men." This endowment was no exclusive prerogative of inspired writers of the first century, but is the blessed gift of all who enjoy the illumination of the Holy Spirit.

statement that the generations of Esau in Gen. xxxvi, the names of the mighty men of David in 2 Samuel, and the genealogies of 1 Chron. i-ix, "*are* the very word of God"? If we maintain that the entire canonical Scripture is the product of a supernatural dictation of verbal statements, we must in all logical consistency apply our theory to the long lists of cities and tribal boundaries in the book of Joshua, the exploits of Ehud, and Jephthah, and Samson in the book of Judges, and the references to apocryphal literature in the epistles of Jude and 2 Peter.[1] Such a theory ought to show some perceptible evidence that the books of Nehemiah and Esther and Ecclesiastes and the Canticles bear marks of divine inspiration not to be found in the Wisdom of Solomon, Ecclesiasticus, and 1 Maccabees. What remarkable advantage by way of demonstrable inspiration has the epistle of Jude over the book of Enoch, who is quoted therein as "the seventh from Adam"?

(4) *Our Doctrine should Accord with existing Facts.* From these various considerations it seems inevitable to conclude that our doctrine of biblical inspiration should accord with all the existing facts of the writings themselves. Sound sense and scientific criticism can accept nothing less. All the biblical writers were men of like passions as we are, and not one of them has put forth the claim, or warranted the inference, that their book-rolls are inerrant and infallible in all which they record. Their manifold peculiarities of thought and style evince the human freedom with which they wrote, and any attempt or presumption at the present time to define the exact nature and extent of each man's inspiration would be an exhibition of human folly. There exists no specific definition of the word *inspiration* as applied to the Scriptures, and there is no statement or theory of the same to be found in any creed, confession, or ecclesiastical formulary of faith, that would be accepted in all Christendom today as having authority for the Christian conscience. How absurd, then, to affirm that any particular theory of inspiration is binding, or has always been the doctrine of the Church! As well might one

---

[1] In his note on Matt. i, 1, John Wesley expresses the opinion that if the biblical genealogies contained some mistakes, it was not the office of inspiration to correct them. If this opinion holds, it must in self-consistency apply alike to all the genealogies, and the chronicles of the kings of Judah and Israel, and the songs and fragments cited from "the book of Jashar," and "the book of the Wars of Jehovah," and from all the other sources of similar kind mentioned in the Old Testament. Seventeen such different sources are acknowledged in the books of Chronicles alone. Critical study is continually discovering evidences of compilation in most of the narratives of the Bible; and if the inspired compilers of these records were not permitted to correct any mistakes found in the documents they employed, what becomes of the inerrant inspiration of so large a portion of the Scriptures? On this principle more than half the narratives recorded in the Old Testament may be shown to be copied from older public records and so to exclude the office of inspiration to correct any errors which they may contain!

claim the consensus of Christendom for the allegorical interpretation of the Scriptures. The one truth conceded by all who revere these sacred writings is that the Holy Spirit of God coöperated with their authors, and the result is a volume immeasurably more profitable, as a whole, for instruction in spiritual things than all the other religious writings of the world. With or without the so-called Apocrypha, these scriptures of the Old and the New Testament are the self-evidencing records of a progressive divine revelation of God in the world of human history. They embody and inculcate all the great religious truths which are anywhere known among men. They vary in the relative value of their different portions, but, when fairly interpreted, they reveal an adorable purpose of God to draw all men unto himself, and they accordingly contain, as in a shrine, all those hallowed and helpful doctrines, reproofs, counsels, consolations, and heavenly promises which answer to the deepest yearnings of the heart of man.

(5) *Inerrancy a Dogma of Necessitarian Philosophy.*—The dogma of verbal inerrancy is inconsistent with existing facts, extravagant in its assumptions, and mischievous in its tendency to provoke continual controversy in the Church. It has so extensively infected popular thought as to become a positive hindrance to the rational study of the Bible. Its habitual bent is either to conceal or to pervert the undeniable human element conspicuous in the sacred writings. It has obvious logical relationship to the necessitarian philosophy of human action, and was, accordingly, adopted by the leading Churches of the Reformation which accepted the Calvinistic creed. These Churches maintained the dogma of divinely secured human volition, and a mechanical theory of biblical inspiration was the natural result. This theory found its logical expression in the Helvetic creed which declared that "the Hebrew original of the Old Testament is inspired of God not only in its consonants, but in its vowels—either the vowel points themselves, or at least the power of the points—not only in its matter but in its words; thus forming together with the original of the New Testament, the sole and complete rule of our faith and life; and to its standard, as to a Lydian stone, all extant versions, Oriental and Occidental, ought to be applied, and whenever they differ, be conformed." With all its extravagance this confession is only a logical conclusion from the postulates of the monergistic theology and the necessitarian philosophy. Once accept the theory of supernaturally secured human volitions, and our thoughts, words, and deeds become as mechanical and necessary as the movements of the planets and the tides. We reject this hypothesis and regard its conclusions as a mischievous leaven

in the realm of Christian thought. The synergistic theology is the opposite of this, and the only tenable alternative. But many who reject the necessitarian theology are so accustomed to the use of words and phrases which had their origin in notions of positively secured human actions that they have unwittingly imbibed the theory of the verbal inerrancy of the entire volume of Holy Scriptures.

12. The Dogma of Infallibility. The necessitarian dogma of inspired verbal inerrancy is usually connected with that of the "infallibility of the Bible." It seems difficult for some to think of a book of divine revelation without associating with it the idea of all the perfections of God, and they allow *a priori* assumptions to divert attention from some of the most simple facts. It is claimed and was formally declared by the Vatican Council of 1870, that the Pope of Rome, whenever he speaks officially on a question of doctrine or of morals, is possessed of inerrant and infallible judgment for determining the very truth of God. But all Protestant Christendom rejects this claim as ludicrously futile, and even the Greek Church resents it as blasphemous. Over against the authority of popes and councils the Protestant reformers placed the clear teaching of the Scriptures as interpreted by valid and convincing reasoning. To these latter Luther made his appeal when called upon to revoke his opinions before the Diet of Worms. These Scriptures contain the treasured revelations of ages and generations of lawgivers, prophets, and apostles, and also the records of the words of Christ himself. That they are and were intended to be, by the help of the Holy Spirit, the surest guide to the knowledge of the eternal truths of God, and the "sufficient rule of faith and practice" became the formal principle of the Protestant Reformation, and this is firmly held today among all the reformed Churches of the Christian world. We maintain the *sufficiency* of the Holy Scriptures as a guide in the way of salvation through Christ; but the dogma of "infallibility" is no essential part of the true Protestant principle, but only a cause of confusion and error.

(1) *Involves a Distorted Notion of the Bible.* For this dogma of an "infallible book" involves a distorted and misleading conception of the Bible itself. It is apt to convey to the popular mind the notion of an inerrant, infallible Monarch, uttering nothing but categorical propositions of what is right and what is wrong. It ignores the fact that the Scriptures are a body of various kinds of literature, made up of composite narratives, songs, fables, riddles, parables, allegories, visions, and dreams. In the interpretation of all of these there has never been uniformity of opinion,

nor is there likely to be for ages to come. Strong, sweeping abstract assertions of the equal authority of all portions of this multiform volume go for nothing in the face of opposing facts which appear in the various books, and the contents of many of these books are the farthest possible from the nature of a set of authoritative utterances on matters of doctrine or on questions of conscience. It requires only the slightest attention to the facts to see that the entire Scriptures cannot be accepted in all their parts as so many final and infallible decisions of doctrine, valid alike for all times and for all men. The greater part of the Mosaic legislation, that veritable Holy of holies in Jewish estimation, is obsolete today for the faith and practice of the Christian world.

(2) *Discredited by Discrepancies and Persistent Controversy.* This dogma, moreover, like its twin companion of "verbal inerrancy," is incompatible with the numerous discrepancies of the Scriptures. We have a goodly number of volumes written to harmonize these discrepancies, but their very existence is a fatal witness against the unanimity of the biblical writers. If papal infallibility is effectually discredited by the fact that different popes and councils have widely disagreed on questions of faith and practice, biblical infallibility must for the same reason fall under the same condemnation. For not only have the most eminent Protestant theologians, but famous synods also, and great religious bodies like the Lutherans, the Baptists, the Presbyterians, and the Unitarians have persistently disagreed on matters of doctrine which they all believed to be taught in the Bible. On some doctrines deemed fundamental their divergent interpretations have been the most remarkable. In the face of such age-long controversy over its teaching, wherein consists the infallibility of the book? Obviously there is no such infallibility among men or books. According to 2 Pet. iii, 16, Paul wrote "in all his epistles some things hard to be understood, which the ignorant and the unsteadfast wrest, as they do also the other scriptures, unto their own destruction." Wherein, then, is Paul's infallibility to be seen, and wherefore should we commit ourselves to the needless task of maintaining the infallibility of any such writings? Their everlasting value for instruction in righteousness and in doctrine may be devoutly acknowledged without acceptance of the dogma of their "infallibility."

(3) *The Word itself Irrelevant.* The simple fact, which all who seek the truth should recognize, is that the word *infallibility* has no proper relevancy to a subject in which human judgments and volitions are so largely involved as in this question. All writings known to men are subject to human interpretation. It

is no disparagement of the Scriptures, nor of the power of God, to say that, in all matters which contemplate the exercise of man's intelligence and freedom of will, any assumption of coercion is inept and futile. We may illustrate this by comparison with our concept of the infallibility of God, and the irrelevancy and fallacy of confusing this concept with matters which belong to the province of human responsibility. No man in his right mind will admit that the omniscient Ruler of the world is capable of falling into error. He is absolutely infallible in his judgments and his ways are in large measure past our finding out. But this belief does not rest for its support on any dictum of pope, or Bible, or theologian, although they may all affirm it. We accept it, not because it has been formally declared by a prophet, or apostle, or pope, or council, but rather because of its stronghold in the intuitions of the human soul, in the convictions of the heart, in the necessities of rational thought, and in a consequent impossibility of supposing the contrary. This cannot be said of any man or of any book in the world. And yet, along with this acknowledged infallibility of God, we have the fact that God himself has brought fallible men into his world, and endowed them with powers of free and responsible personality. By reason of being what he is man has through all generations misconceived his Creator and disobeyed his laws. The fallibility and the actual failures are no fault of God, but are charged to the ignorance and perversity of man. When, however, one claims infallibility for a man or for a book we demur, and have the right to demand some incontrovertible proof. It is irrelevant, in answer to such a demand, to be told that God is infallible. The Bible is not God. He is invisible and far beyond us; but the Scriptures are open to our personal inspection and were written by men of various times and of various degrees of culture and knowledge. The real question here is not about God's personal perfections, but whether he has actually given us a book which determines inerrantly and infallibly for mankind all matters of doctrine and morals. We maintain that such infallibility is not found in man or in books. The invisible God is by the necessities of our concept of him infinite in wisdom and knowledge, but we decline to accept, without convincing evidence, the dogma that he has imparted such qualities to any volume written by men. And this position is perfectly compatible with the belief that the Bible, when interpreted in the light of the completed revelation of Jesus Christ, is a unique record of the noblest religious truths and the most perfect standard of morals ever given among men. But being a manifold record of a progressive divine revelation it contains divers portions which represent imperfect standards, as Jesus himself showed, and we refuse to perpetuate the fallacy of affirming of this entire volume of Scriptures what is true of only a part of it. We insist on bringing every doctrine and every question of morals to the final test of the explicit revelation of Jesus Christ. According to his teaching the two commandments of love, as enunciated in Matt. xxii, 37-40, involve the purest concept of religion and the most perfect standard of ethics in the world, and they comprehend the substance of "the whole law and the prophets." But even these most fundamental truths fail to impress some men, and we have too often and too long found men disposed to argue and insist that the morals of the book of Esther are in full harmony with these two commandments!

(4) *Sufficiency Rather than Infallibility.* Over against the dogma of infallibility we maintain the *sufficiency* of the Holy Scriptures as a guide to the knowledge of God and the way of salvation through Jesus Christ. We hold with the apostle to the Gentiles that those who are intrusted with these Scriptures have "much advantage and profit every way" over those who have not been thus favored. But according to Paul God has revealed himself through the visible creation, without the Bible, to the whole Gentile world (Rom. i, 18-20; ii, 14, 15), so that every man is left without excuse for his personal unrighteousness. In the Deistic controversies it was claimed by some that "the light of nature" was of itself quite sufficient for man's moral guidance and for a knowledge of the supreme Ruler. But it was replied that this light of nature is very fallible, and often misleading, and therefore we need the superior light of a written revelation. We admit this plea as valid for the scriptural revelation, but at the same time reject the unwarranted inference that the superior biblical revelation must needs be inerrant or infallible. Paul himself, after affirming the clear revelation of the light of nature to the Gentiles, goes right on in the epistle to the Romans to show that the Jew also, with all his superior advantage of "the oracles of God, and the adoption, and the glory, and the covenants, and the giving of the law, and the promises," failed and fell not only through unbelief but also through misunderstanding of his higher *revelation.* Thus, according to Paul, the written revelation given in the Old Testament, as well as the light of nature, had conspicuously failed to evince any quality that entitles it to the claim of infallibility. The actual failure of the Scriptures to convince and convert thousands of men who read them is a conspicuous fact, but the claim of their infallibility is at best a questionable dogma. To aver that the fallibility is with the reader, not with the book,

does not prove the book infallible. God has never given man a revelation, written or unwritten, that is infallible in securing unity of belief, or uniformity of religious practice. On the contrary, the sufficiency of the biblical revelation as a source of instruction in the knowledge of God and of Christ and the way of salvation is a most wholesome truth, and is verified by the experience of innumerable thousands. Why then hold a dogma which, if not utterly futile, is utterly incapable of proof, and is provocative of constant disputation?

13. Authority as Sources of Doctrine. The authority of the Scriptures as sources of doctrine does not rest upon the basis of a mechanical inerrancy or of a supposed infallibility. Authority in religion is not a matter of ancient sacred records, but of irresistible spiritual convictions. It is analogous to authority in mathematics, in geology, in astronomy, in medicine, and in international law. Whatever has real authority over the judgment and the consciences of men is clearly seen to rest upon indisputable facts. The undisputed and commanding facts in any science are what they are, not because they are written in text-books everywhere accepted as good authority; but the text-book has value and authority according to its acknowledged rank as a full and sufficient guide to the knowledge of the science which it treats. So may we say of the great truths of the Bible that they are what they are, not because they are found in the Bible, but because they are self-evidencing as unquestionable truths of God. For God has revealed some things so clearly to the heart of man that there is no room for real differences of opinion. The chief teachings of Jesus Christ evinced an intrinsic authority that left no place for doubtful disputation. An authoritative revelation must command the honest assent of the reason and the conscience in order to be convincing in its truthfulness. Our claim for the Holy Scriptures is that the Old and New Testaments embody a religious literature of inestimable worth. The various writings are not of equal value in all their parts, but, taken as a whole, they constitute a remarkably self-interpreting book. The well-trained inquirer after heavenly truths finds therein many things both new and old. He perceives how "God spoke in old time by divers portions and in divers manners," and in the later times spoke through Jesus Christ in a manner and fullness that surpassed all other revelations given among men. We make, accordingly, the same relative claim for the Bible that we make for the Christian religion. It consummates and supersedes all other cults ever in force among the various peoples. Such a volume needs no high-flown eulogies, no dogma of inerrancy and infallibility; but having great variety of contents, and written at different times and by many different authors, it has the right to be interpreted rationally and self-consistently. The real value and authority of such a volume are best seen in demonstrable facts which show that this Bible is immeasurably superior to all other religious writings of mankind. The sacred books of other religions have their value; but the scriptures of the Old and New Covenants are preëminently THE HOLY BIBLE, profitable above all other books for teaching, for reproof, for correction, and for discipline in righteousness.

(1) *Superiority in Variety of Contents.* This Holy Bible is superior to all the other bibles of the world in the remarkable variety of its literature. The Rig Veda is a collection of more than a thousand ancient Aryan hymns addressed to many nature-gods; but these hymns are limited in their range of thought, and quite monotonous. The other Vedas are little more than liturgical arrangements of the same hymns, and add nothing of real value to them. So, too, the contents of the voluminous Tripitaka are tedious and tasteless repetitions of Buddhist stories, and minute regulations for the conduct of mendicants. Their doctrines, though relatively few and simple, involve the denial of human personality and the ultimate cessation of our self-conscious being. The Kojiki of the old Shinto cult is a crude mixture of Japanese mythology and traditions, and it possesses no value for religious instruction. The sacred books of China are confessedly non-religious. The Shu King is a collection of historical narratives, the Shih King is a book of poetry, and the other books treat of governmental rites, and ceremonies, and rules of etiquette. None of them claim to be inspired of God, or to embody revelations of heaven. The Avesta is at best the scattered fragments of a warlike cult, which long ago took up the sword for holy wars, and perished by the sword. The prayers, the hymns, the liturgical fragments, and the code of laws are all of one general cast, and the entire collection is more of a prayer book, or a ritual, than a bible. The Koran is a peculiar medley of commandments, admonitions, and narratives dictated by Mohammed, which exhibit numerous blunders in history and chronology, and show in many ways the narrow limits of its author's knowledge of Judaism and Christianity. It is a most wearisome book to read, and seems to be incapable of happy translation into another language. And so we may say, in substance, of all the other religious books which have any corresponding claim to be the bibles of distinct systems of religion. Not one of them is really worthy to be compared with our Holy Scriptures for richness and variety of contents. The annals, proverbs, apocalypses, prophecies, psalms, dramatic

poems, gospel narratives, and epistles which make up the Old and New Testaments speak for themselves in the unmistakable religious character and aim of what they have to tell us. And these divers elements are so interwoven as to command the lively attention and the absorbing interest of the reader. The loftiest concepts of God, the incalculable value of the human soul, the beauty of holiness, and the imperishable permanence of love are truths presented for our instruction in righteousness, and they are made so plain and simple that a little child may understand them.

(2) *Superiority of Historic Outline and Background.* Another aspect of superiority is seen in the strong and clear historic outline in which the progressive character of the biblical revelations is set forth. The oldest Abrahamic traditions contain the germs of the Messianic hope. The divine legation of Moses was narrowed because of the hardness of the people's hearts, and he spoke of a Prophet of God to come after him, like unto him, but greater in the commandments which he should utter in Jehovah's name. David received yet fuller revelations of the advent of his messianic Son, and of the establishment of his throne for ages to come. The prophets and the psalmists after him repeated and enhanced both the ancient promise and the future blessed hope; and when Jerusalem and the throne of David were overthrown by the armies of the king of Babylon, and the princes and the people were carried away into exile, Jeremiah's oracle proclaimed loudly above all the din and ruin and gloom of that sad day the word of Jehovah: "Behold, the days come that I will make a new covenant with the house of Israel." All these successive periods in the progress of Israelite history are so interlinked with the historic records of other peoples that we find them confirmed by several ancient witnesses. Amraphel, incidentally mentioned in Gen. xiv, 1, was a contemporary of Abraham some 2,250 years before Christ. The recovery of a remarkable code of laws enacted by this ancient "King of Shinar" puts the great ancestor of the Hebrew nation in realistic touch with the Babylonia of that date as truly as the mention of Nebuchadnezzar, in the prophecies of Jeremiah, shows a later stage in the history of the seed of Abraham, and confirms the story of their Babylonian exile. The monuments of Egypt and the stones of Palestine give their testimony also to the unmistakable outline of the history of Israel which is clearly traceable in the Hebrew scriptures. No such marks of actual historic intercourse with contemporary nations of world importance are found in the other sacred books that sometimes rank as bibles. These facts remove our biblical narratives from the literature of myth and fable. They show a real historic

background in the gradual development of the religion of Israel, and also a divinely ordered preparation for the coming of the Christ.[1]

(3) *Superiority of the Revelation of Christ.* The crowning glory of the Holy Scriptures appears in the New Testament revelation of Jesus Christ. He is the supreme Prophet and Apostle of our confession, for whose coming all the foregoing revelations given through holy men had prepared the way. He is the Light of the world. The gospels, the epistles, and other New Testament books supply us with the substance of his teaching in a manner too self-evidencing to be misunderstood. When we duly observe that all preceding legislation and prophecy found their fulfillment in him, we shall not be perplexed by the obvious imperfections of Israel's old-time cult. The codes of Moses and of Hammurabi contain evidences of adaptations to the hardness of the hearts of the peoples of those ancient times. Any rational conception of a progress in divine revelation must admit the shortcomings of the former ages. Jeremiah and Ezekiel were gifted above the teachers of an earlier period to declare that the old proverb of setting the children's teeth on edge because their fathers ate sour grapes should be no longer used in Israel (Jer. xxxi, 29; Ezek. xviii, 2). But Jesus Christ fulfilled every jot and tittle of the law and the prophets, so that the entire Old Testament must now be studied and tested by the light of the gospel of Jesus. Had this important truth received due attention, we might have been spared the lamentable spectacle of men strenuously maintaining, on biblical grounds, the righteousness of polygamy, and human slavery, and easy-going divorce, and capital punishment for witchcraft, and the vindictive cursing of enemies. Jesus introduced new thought, new life, and new inspiration. He now "sitteth on the throne, declaring, Behold, I make all things new." If we were not possessed of the profound conviction that the Bible is the divinely treasured literature of a progressive revelation of God in Christ, and that the completed witness and teaching of the New Testament supplies the most authoritative source and

---

[1] We should, in the interests of sound apologetics, abstain from the illogical use sometimes made of these incidental connections of biblical narrative with persons and events of ancient history. The mention of Amraphel, Pharaoh, or any other king is in itself no proof of the historicity of the book of Genesis, or of any other book in which such names may occur. That question must be determined in other ways. A poem, a novel, a parable, or an allegory may make various uses of historical names and facts. No sensible person would argue that the Last Days of Pompeii and Quo Vadis are books of veritable history because they have much to say about famous historical persons and events. And yet it may be added that probably no strictly historical work, compiled from the most trustworthy sources, would supply the common reader with a more truthful picture of Roman life in those days than the celebrated novels named.

means of religious truth within the reach of man, we could never presume to write a Biblical Dogmatics.

14. The Bible and the Word of God. These Holy Scriptures, completed and crowned by the revelation of Jesus Christ, are the treasured result of religious truths spoken in various measures through many generations. Thus they also become for us a most profitable means of discipline in the truth and in all righteousness. By the help of the Spirit, who is given to guide us into all the truth (John xvi, 13), the Bible is a mighty instrument for apprehending and imparting the revelations of God. The real source of all truth and of all revelation in the truth is God himself, and in our search for a knowledge of the mysteries of the kingdom of God we should not confound God and the Bible, as the manner of some is. The heavenly treasure deposited in the biblical records is not identical with the book itself. Like the treasure hidden in the field, and the pearl of great price, the living truth of God has its places of hiding and is not found without search and sacrifice. But when found and made one's own, the heavenly jewel becomes a source of light and comfort and a means of grace and truth. But how are we to distinguish the precious treasure from the field in which it is hidden? Field and treasure both are ours, but some men seem to insist on our saying, The field *is* the treasure; "the Bible *is* the Word of God." This shibboleth, we believe, has been a source of no little confusion and error. It is only in a loose and inaccurate way of speaking that the letter of the Scriptures may be called God's Word, and, when thus designated, it should be seen at once that we are employing a synecdoche, a rhetorical figure of putting the whole for a part. It is like naming the vessel when we mean only the treasure in the vessel. A close examination of all the scriptural texts in which the phrase "word of God," or its equivalent, occurs, will show that there is no warrant in the Bible for the dogmatic shibboleth cited above. It is very easy for a superficial reader of such psalms as Psa. xix, 7-11, and Psa. cxix to imagine that the words *law, testimony, precepts, statutes, commandments, judgments, thy word,* mean the entire scriptures of both Testaments, whereas the real reference of the psalmist is to the Decalogue, and, in his widest thought, to the laws of the Pentateuch. There is no allusion to the Prophets and the Psalms, which as yet formed no portion of the Jewish canon of Scripture. The delusive anachronism of applying the words of such a psalm to the entire Bible ministers not to intelligent study of the Scriptures, but only to ignorance and error. We should observe, further, that the messages of the prophets were usually a word of Jehovah for some person, people, or definite occasion. Not a few of those messages, like that of Isaiah to Ahaz (vii, 3-9), have no natural reference to any other person or time. Others embody helpful promises, or solemn warnings and reproofs, which are profitable for all time, but that which is of permanent value in them is the substantial content of the message, not a written document as such. The word of Jehovah through Isaiah is also called "the vision of Isaiah," and the "burden," or oracle, "which Isaiah saw." But the book of Isaiah contains four chapters (xxxvi-xxxix) out of the book of Kings, and also a "writing of Hezekiah" (xxxviii, 9), which are nowhere called the word of the Lord. But even if the entire book of Isaiah were made up of specific oracles of Jehovah, it would not authorize us to call the books of Samuel, Kings, Chronicles, and Esther "the Word of Jehovah." The phrase "oracles of God" in Rom. iii, 2 is no proper designation of the Old Testament as a whole, but, like the "living oracles" in Stephen's speech (Acts vii, 38), refers more particularly to the Sinaitic decalogue. In 1 Pet. iv, 11, the phrase denotes any utterances of apostle or preacher who declares the living truths of God. In Heb. v, 12, "the oracles of God" are no special portion of the Bible, nor the Bible itself, but the word of the gospel of Christ as preached to them that heard him. In fact, there is no passage of Scripture in which the expression "the word of God" means the biblical writings as a whole. In the New Testament the phrase is often used to designate the content of the gospel message. In Jesus's prayer we have the statement "thy word is truth" (John xvii, 17), but there is no reference here to the Holy Scriptures of the Old Testament, but to the word of the gospel mentioned in verses 14 and 20. Filled with the Spirit of Christ the apostles "spoke the word of God with all boldness" (Acts iv, 31). When persecution scattered them abroad "they went about preaching the word" (Acts viii, 4), that is, the message of salvation through Jesus Christ. "The word" is employed in this sense more than thirty times in the Acts of the Apostles. Paul calls it "the word of faith, which we preach" (Rom. x, 8), "the word of the truth, the gospel of your salvation" (Eph. i, 13), "the word of the message of God, not the word of men, but, as it is in truth, the word of God, which also worketh in you that believe" (1 Thess. ii, 13). In the fullest and deepest sense the Word of God is Christ himself, and it is only as the Holy Spirit of truth takes of the things of Christ and makes them known to us (comp. John xvi, 14), that we can apprehend and appreciate the significance of such a text as Heb. iv, 12: "The word of God is living, and active, and sharper than any two-edged sword, and piercing even to the dividing of soul and spirit, of both joints and marrow, and quick to discern the thoughts and intents of the heart." No writings as such answer to this definition of "the word of God," or satisfy the import of Jesus' saying, "The words that I have spoken unto you are spirit, and are life" (John vi, 63). According to 2 Cor. iii, 15-18, Moses and Isaiah and Paul may be read with such a veil over the heart that the reader himself fails to see that "the Lord is the Spirit." For it is only as we discern the grace and glory of the Lord himself that we can distinguish the hidden treasure from the field, and the pearl of great price from the mother-shell in which it found its setting. The results thus acquired will be no questionable dogma, empty of spiritual content, but intelligible facts of the greatest value for instruction in righteousness.

15. Necessity of Sound Interpretation. Accepting the Bible as the broad field in which lie hidden innumerable treasures of religious wisdom and knowledge, we must at the same time observe that the precious truths are not to be brought forth and employed for teaching and discipline in righteousness except in accordance with sound principles of interpretation. We now reject the former method of catechisms and of other compends of Christian doctrine which was given to citing proof-texts at will from any part of the Bible, without regard to their scope and context. It was assumed, in accord with a current theory of inspiration, that every word of Scripture, whether uttered by poet, chronicler, patriarch, or apostle, was alike the word of God. A saying of Jephthah, a request of Esther, a decree of Cyrus, an oracle of Zechariah, or a parable of Jesus, must needs be equally inspired and useful for doctrine. Such an irrational use of the Scriptures, we may hope, is wellnigh obsolete, but, unfortunately, in some places the evil leaven of it is yet somewhat perceptible. While we accept the entire biblical canon as our great source and means of doctrine, we must study to interpret every relevant text in the light of its context, its authorship, its occasion and its legitimate applications. The facts of a multiform literature in the Bible are never to be lost from sight. We should keep in mind at every step of our procedure that these various scriptures originated at many different times and in different ways. We must study to know whether the words we cite in proof of doctrine are a statement of historic fact, or a fragment of song, or part of an apocalypse, or a proverb or a parable. The words of Jesus are the Holy of holies in the Scriptures, and when we clearly apprehend his teaching on a matter of doctrine we recognize it as the highest authority. But according to Matt. xiii, 10-16, Jesus spoke in parables that the mysteries of the kingdom of heaven might not be too easily grasped. The parables need interpretation, and must be explained on sound and self-consistent principles. The old covenant is fulfilled in the new, and therefore not a jot or a tittle of the Old Testament is to be reckoned as final for instruction in righteousness until tested and confirmed by the gospel of Jesus. Even in the New Testament records we observe some practices of the early Jewish Church which are not intended for the Gentiles or for general acceptance. The apostles had their limitations, and could know and prophesy only in part. It is noteworthy that out of the four "necessary things," which the great Council of Jerusalem required for the peace and unity of the early Church (Acts xv, 28, 29), three have long since ceased to be observed in Christendom. It is only by patient research, by careful discrimination of things that differ, and by the approved methods of critical and historic exposition, that we shall reach results that are trustworthy. We compare scripture with scripture, and honestly endeavor to prove all things and hold fast only that which is good. Every true Protestant and every Church that is true to the principle and spirit of Protestantism must be open and hospitable toward all conscientious research and to whatever new light such research throws upon the Bible and its interpretation.[1]

16. Sufficiency as Sources of Doctrine. Prolonged comparison and study of these Holy Scriptures confirm us in the belief of their superiority and sufficiency as sources of religious instruction. They are conspicuously superior in contents and in style to all the sacred books of other religions, and they contain a sufficiency of doctrine, of helpful precepts, of means for refuting error and for guiding men into the truth and training them in the knowledge and love of God. When the one serious effort is to ascertain the essential religious content of the biblical revelation and its highest expression in Jesus Christ there is found such a solid basis of unquestionable facts and such an organic consensus of belief through the Christian centuries that there appears no place for reasonable doubt. Disputations arise from efforts to exalt matters of secondary and inferior import into the rank of fundamental truths, and questions of this kind will probably never cease to arise while men continue to think and reason. Minds differently

---

[1] Thus Professor J. E. McFadyen writes: "A church which is not willing to welcome new facts, if they be facts; a church which is not willing to respond to new truth, from whatever quarter it comes; a church which binds old forms of truth upon the consciences of men, or refuses to accommodate the truth which they embodied to contemporary modes of thought: such a church, though she will hardly allure within her walls profound and reverent thinkers who stand outside her, may yet be able to do something for others, and especially the more emotional sort of men. But she cannot call herself a Protestant Church."—Old Testament Criticism and the Christian Church, p. 187. New York, 1903.

trained and adjusted to different methods of thinking will always be found to differ in sundry opinions. There are many interesting questions about persons and events mentioned in the Bible and in other books on which we shall never obtain a satisfactory answer. Even on such fundamental doctrines as the nature of God, and of Christ, the resurrection of the dead, and the conditions and modes of future existence, we cannot now learn from the Bible all we would like to know. In the discussion of such themes there has ever been among some theologians a disposition to be wise above what is written in the Scriptures. But aside from such questions, on which there is ample room for many differences of opinion, there is in the Scriptures such a full and unmistakable content of living, convincing, practical religious certainties, that no person of ordinary intelligence need fail to find "the way, the truth, and the life." Into the knowledge of these essentials the Holy Spirit is our assuring Guide. In living fellowship with this abiding Comforter, we need not that any one teach us, for his anointing teacheth us concerning all things, and is true, and is no lie (1 John ii, 27).

CHAPTER III

METHOD OF BIBLICAL DOGMATICS

1. Importance of Method. The fundamental truths of the Christian religion may be studied in almost any relation to each other, but the arrangement of topics in a well-defined logical order is a matter of very great importance. Attention to method and naturalness of procedure in presenting facts or principles is a conspicuous feature of modern scientific discipline, and there is perhaps no department of study that requires the clarifying help of simple and comprehensive method more than that of religious dogma. Real progress and improvement in the treatment of biblical doctrines must not be expected in the discovery of new materials, but rather in the better presentation of the great truths which have been well known for ages. Indeed, no individual, no council, no era of research, may presume to set a final limit to improvement in the formulation and restatement of doctrines which the Church has possessed from the beginning.

2. Lack of System in Ancient Writers. We may accordingly expect modern writers on Christian doctrine to surpass the ancients in scientific method. In the course of the centuries many distinguished theologians have set forth various expositions of fundamental truth, and spirited controversies have at times tended to exalt certain doctrines into undue prominence. Origen's treatise entitled De Principiis is the nearest approach to a comprehensive system of Christian belief to be found among the early fathers; but its four books are without any well-defined order of thought. Gregory of Nyssa's Great Catechism is of much less extent, and is more of an apology for the doctrines treated than an attempt to enunciate a system. The Accurate Exposition of the Orthodox Faith, in four books and one hundred chapters, by John of Damascus, is disproportionate in the treatment of important topics, and gives prominence to some opinions of no value. Augustine's various treatises on Christian doctrine are monumental, but they furnish no good model of scientific method. The celebrated Loci Communes of Melanchthon, published in 1521, and Calvin's Institutes of the Christian Religion, which appeared fifteen years later, attempt no analytic or synthetic arrangement of subject-matter. The Theological Institutes of Francis Turretin, first published in

1679-1685, surpass Calvin's work in logical arrangement; but they follow the catechetical method of question and answer, and discuss the several doctrines in the order commonly found in the confessions of that time. George Calixtus, in his Epitome of Theology, published in 1619, arranged the essential doctrines under three inquiries. He first asks after the object of theological science, and he finds his answer in all those topics which relate to the salvation and ultimate glory of man. Secondly, he finds the subject and the necessity of his doctrines in the facts of creation and human sinfulness. His third inquiry is into the means of securing the salvation of man, under which head he presents the mediation of Christ and the means of grace. This furnishes an analytic method of procedure, and has some attractive features. It moves partly in the line of that dogmatic method which first propounds the great subject of salvation, and then inquires after the causes of the same in the order of (1) the efficient, (2) the meritorious, (3) the instrumental, and (4) the final cause. Much of its substance may be traced back to Peter Lombard's Four Books of Sentences.

3. Federal and Trinitarian Methods. The Federal Theology, so called, produced a method of arranging all the doctrines of Christianity under the two Covenants of Nature and of Grace. But the system compelled its advocates to follow a historical rather than a logical order, and involved no little confusion of thought. Leydecker (in 1682) cast the federal theology in a Trinitarian form by grouping all Christian doctrine under the three headings of Father, Son, and Spirit. He has been followed in recent times by Marheineke and Martensen. The method is attractive for its simplicity, but is incompatible with a proper use of defining terms, and leaves too much room for arbitrary fancies. Martensen, for example, treats the fall of man, human depravity, and guilt under the head of "The Doctrine of the Father"; and Marheineke discusses these same topics under the main caption of "God the Son." Such looseness of construction in methodology is open to obvious objection.

4. Methods of some German Writers. In a study of the methods of treating Christian dogmatics we may profitably observe the courses pursued by some of the most distinguished writers on systematic theology in modern times. The German theologians evince a remarkable genius for analysis and synthesis as well as for breadth of learning and originality of thought. Schleiermacher, in his work on The Christian Faith,[1] treats all evangelical doctrines

---

[1] Der christliche Glaube nach den Grundsätzen der evangelischen Kirche im Zusammenhange dargestellt. 2 vols. 1828.

as so many truths developed out of the feeling of absolute dependence upon God. This feeling is an indwelling element in the nature of man, and the creeds and confessions of Christendom are so many outward expressions of the Christian consciousness. After an introduction of one hundred and fifty pages he divides his work into two parts, the first of which is devoted to the "development of the religious feeling of dependence," and the second to the "development of the indwelling consciousness of God." He treats the doctrine of the Trinity in an appendix. Lange's comprehensive work on Christian Dogmatics[1] is divided into what its author calls "an organic trilogy" of philosophical, positive, and applied dogmatics. He brings all the topics of positive dogmatics under the three heads of Theology, Soteriology, and Pneumatology. August Hahn's Compendium of the Christian Faith[2] is divided into four main parts as follows: 1. Doctrine of God; 2. Doctrine of Man; 3. Christology; 4. Of the Church. Under the last head he treats the several topics of eschatology. Hase's treatise on Evangelical Protestant Dogmatics[3] presents a condensed and somewhat novel scheme. After a short introduction on the theory and the history of dogmatics, he arranges his material under the two heads of Ontology and Christology. Under the first of these he treats (1) Anthropology and (2) Theology; under the second, (1) Christ in History, (2) Christ in the inner Life, (3) Christ in the Church. Two appendixes were added by the author in which he discusses Eschatology and the Trinity. A still more striking outline of the evangelical faith is given in Karl Immanuel Nitzsch's System of Christian Doctrine,[4] in which we have the three divisions of Agathology, Ponerology, and Soteriology. Under the first, the doctrine of The Good, he treats of God and the creature; under the doctrine of The Bad he treats of sin and death; and under Soteriology there are four subdivisions: (1) Salvation established in the person of the Redeemer, (2) The appropriation of salvation, (3) The fellowship of salvation, (4) The completion of salvation. A more recent contribution to dogmatics is the able and comprehensive treatise of Friedrich A. B. Nitzsch,[5] whose main divisions of the part entitled "Special Dogmatics" are Anthropology, Theology, and Christology.

5. Methods of Five American Divines. Five comprehensive works on Systematic Theology, issued during the last thirty years

---

[1] Christliche Dogmatik. 3 vols. Heidelberg, 1849–1852.
[2] Lehrbuch des christlichen Glaubens. 2 vols. Leipzig, 1857, 1858.
[3] Evangelische-protestantische Dogmatik. 6th ed. Leipzig, 1870.
[4] System der christlichen Lehre. 6th ed. Bonn, 1851.
[5] Lehrbuch der evangelischen Dogmatik. Freiburg, 1892.

of the nineteenth century, deserve a passing notice on account of their methods of systematization.[1] They are all from the hands of American divines, they are all cast in a remarkably similar mold, and the arrangement of material in each is shown in the following outline:

Hodge: 1. Introduction. 2. Theology Proper. 3. Anthropology. 4. Soteriology. 5. Eschatology.

Raymond: 1. Apologetics. 2. Theology Proper. 3. Anthropology. 4. Soteriology. 5. Eschatology. 6. Ethics. 7. Ecclesiology.

Strong: 1. Prolegomena. 2. Existence of God. 3. The Scriptures a Revelation from God. 4. The Nature, Decrees, and Works of God. 5. Anthropology. 6. Soteriology. 7. Ecclesiology. 8. Eschatology.

Shedd: 1. Theological Introduction. 2. Bibliology. 3. Theology. 4. Anthropology. 5. Christology. 6. Soteriology. 7. Eschatology.

Miley: 1. Theism. 2. Theology. 3. Anthropology. 4. Christology. 5. Soteriology. 6. Eschatology.

In these several outlines we observe that Hodge reduces his material to the fewest divisions, but the phrase "Theology Proper," which Raymond also adopts, does not commend itself as a heading. Raymond's plan includes the subjects of Apologetics and Ethics which do not strictly belong to a treatise on doctrine. Strong's outline is open to criticism for introducing the section on the Scriptures as a main division, and placing it after his discussion of the existence of God. All that was important for him to say about the Scriptures might have been incorporated in his Prolegomena. His second and fourth divisions might also have been condensed into one section and put under one title. Shedd introduces the word *Bibliology,* under which he discusses the inspiration, authenticity, credibility, and canonicity of the Old and New Testaments. But an extensive treatment of these topics is no proper part of a system of doctrine. The division entitled "Ecclesiology," by Raymond and Strong, includes subjects that do not strictly belong to systematic theology, and the word itself is objectionable because of its very common usage in designating the science of church architecture and decoration. In Miley's outline one may reasonably question the necessity and the propriety of treating Theism and Theology under separate and coördinate divisions.

---

[1] By Charles Hodge (3 vols. 1871–1873); Miner Raymond (3 vols. 1877–1879); Augustus H. Strong (1886); William G. T. Shedd (2 vols. 1888, and a supplementary volume in 1894); John Miley (2 vols. 1892–1894).

6. Outlines of Other Writers. There are many other modern works on Christian doctrine that deserve notice for originality of method or for intrinsic value as contributions to theology. Henry B. Smith labored to construct a system of theology that would be formally Christocentric, and he arranged his entire subject-matter about the person and work of the Redeemer under the main divisions of (1) Antecedents of Redemption, (2) Redemption Itself, and (3) Kingdom of Redemption.[1] Whatever originality of method here appears, it is open to remark that the terminology does not commend itself as either clear or discriminating; the doctrines of God, cosmology, and anthropology are infelicitously styled "antecedents of redemption"; predestination, election, and justification are set forth as operations of grace under the third caption, apart from "the redemption itself," and apart from the "work of the Mediator," which topics fall to the second division of the volume. W. L. Alexander's System of Biblical Theology[2] adopts a fourfold division of parts: 1. Theology; 2. Anthropology; 3. Christology; 4. Soteriology. The less extensive work of John Macpherson[3] has six divisions: 1. Doctrine of God and the World. 2. Doctrine of Man and Sin. 3. Doctrine of Redemption. 4. Application of Redemption. 5. The Means of Grace. 6. The Last Things. The three divisions last named traverse what might have been incorporated with the third, and the brief discussion of the "Last Things" is quite disproportionate in comparison with the other sections of the book. In 1900 Nathaniel Burwash published his Manual of Christian Theology on the Inductive Method.[4] His method of three parts is as follows: 1. The Investigation of True Religion in Historic Form. 2. The Nature and Process of Revelation and the Formation of the Word of God. 3. The Doctrinal Contents of the Word. This third part comprises the larger part of the work and has eight divisions: (1) Of God, (2) The World as Related to God, (3) Man as Naturally Related to God, (4) Human Responsibility and Sin, (5) Redemption, (6) Personal Salvation, (7) The Offices and Agencies of the Christian Church, (8) The Consummation of Christ's Kingdom and the Last Things. William N. Clarke's Outline of Christian Theology[5] is arranged in six parts: 1. God. 2. Man. 3. Sin. 4. Christ. 5. The Holy Spirit and the Divine Life in Man. 6. Things to Come. Henry C. Sheldon's System of Chris-

---

[1] System of Christian Theology. New York, 1884. The volume was compiled by W. S. Karr from the author's unpublished lectures and sermons.
[2] 2 vols. Edinburgh, 1888.
[3] Christian Dogmatics, Edinburgh, 1898.
[4] 2 vols. London.
[5] Cambridge, 1894.

tian Doctrine[1] has the following five parts: 1. Leading Presuppositions of the Christian System. 2. The Doctrine of God and his Relation to the World at large. 3. The Subjects of God's Moral Government. 4. The Person and Work of the Redeemer. 5. The Kingdom of Redemption, or the Practical Realization of the Redemptive Purpose. One of the latest works of this kind to appear is by Olin A. Curtis, whose racy and readable volume[2] is cast in two principal sections of an Introduction to the System of Doctrine and The System of Doctrine. The Introduction has two parts: (1) Man, (2) The Christian Religion. The System shows six doctrinal divisions: (1) Man's Need of Redemption, (2) Jesus Christ, our Lord and Redeemer, (3) Our Lord's Redemptive Work, (4) Redemption Realized in the New Man, (5) Redemption Realized in the New Race, (6) The Triune God Revealed in Redemption. The method of this treatise is notably unique, but the Introduction takes more than a third of the volume, and contains nothing that might not have been presented under the several doctrinal divisions.

7. Questions of Scope and Terminology. A study of these different outlines shows the importance of method in arranging a system of doctrine. It is equally important that we omit from our topics of inquiry those subjects which stand apart from the scope of dogmatics. The doctrines of the Christian faith are easily distinguishable from that which belongs to apologetics, and to questions of Church government and political economy. It is desirable to employ a clear and simple terminology in the outline of distinctive subjects of discussion, but it would seem as if some writers were too much influenced by a passion for the technical nomenclature exhibited in the sonorous words *bibliology, theology, cosmology, angelology, anthropology, hamartialogy, Christology, soteriology, pneumatology, ecclesiology, eschatology*. A well chosen, definite terminology, such as these words of Greek origin furnish, has an unquestionable value, and a methodology which essayed to treat all Christian doctrine under the eleven heads and in the order of the technical terms just given, might have much said in its favor. On the other hand, it may be affirmed that the persistent use of these terms tends to load the study of simple biblical truths with stereotyped formulas which have become obnoxious to many intelligent readers. It may also be argued that the eleven topics indicated are not coördinate, and some of them are not fairly entitled to a place in a system of dogmatics. Bibliology and ecclesiology should hold at most only a subordinate

---

[1] Cincinnati, 1903.
[2] The Christian Faith, personally given in a System of Doctrine. New York, 1905.

place in a treatise on doctrines. Hamartialogy can be logically treated under the head of anthropology, and soteriology and Christology are so closely allied that they may be brought under one caption, as is done in several of the outlines given above. Cosmology, angelology, and eschatology may also be assigned a subordinate position, so that the eleven topics designated by the high-sounding Greek terms named above might all be treated under three or at most four main divisions.

8. A Priori and A Posteriori Methods. The prevailing method in dogmatics, as seen in most of the outlines given above, is to begin with the doctrine of God and conclude with the various questions of eschatology. There is an obvious logical propriety in this order of procedure. Theology in the broad sense is supposed to treat of God, of man, and of the relations between God and man. With this aim and order in view it seems quite possible to bring a comprehensive treatment of the whole under the three divisions of Theology, Anthropology, Soteriology. It is also desirable to bring an entire treatise under as few heads as possible. But if these three divisions were arranged in the order of Anthropology, Soteriology, and Theology, the same field of study would come under view, and every topic would find its appropriate treatment in its own order.

Whether it be better to begin a study of biblical doctrines with the nature of man or with the nature of God is an open question. Not a little may be said in favor of either method, and in adopting one in preference to the other we do not thereby condemn the other. It accords more with *a priori* habits of thought to begin with the nature and attributes of God, and thence proceed with a study of creation and man and redemption and questions of the future as consequences of the divine activity. A monergistic conception of the universe arises quite naturally from this method of procedure, and, so far as one keeps within the limits of demonstrable truth, the method has its unquestionable advantages. The disadvantages are seen in the fact that one pursuing this method is plunged first of all into the most mysterious subject of human thought, the existence and attributes of the Infinite Being. The doctrine of the Trinity, with its incomprehensible metaphysics, is thus soon thrust upon us, and is of a nature to prejudice many students against "systematic theology." It is, perhaps, possible to escape some measure of such theological odium by adopting the *a posteriori* method of beginning with the simplest facts of our personal consciousness, and thence proceeding to the more difficult subjects of human possibilities, and the mystery of Christ and of God. This method accords with that of scientific research in the realm of nature, and has its obvious advantages. It argues from the known to the unknown. As man was made and exists in the image of God, it is altogether probable that a careful study of human nature and its possibilities will go far to prepare the way for the most satisfactory study of the great mystery of God.

9. The Method of This Work. The method of the present treatise begins with the doctrine of man and concludes with the doctrine of our heavenly Father. The fundamental truths of the Christian religion are so vitally related to each other that it is quite impossible to discuss any one of them fully without the frequent assumption of a general acquaintance with other related doctrines. It is not supposed that any student of theology comes to the reading of a book like this without some knowledge of the subjects to be discussed, nor is it supposable that any theologian begins a formal inquiry into the nature of man without some knowledge of the doctrine of God. Several of the most noteworthy books mentioned above, as, for example, those of Hase, Friedrich Nitzsch, and Curtis, present the doctrines of anthropology at the beginning. Such a beginning easily and naturally avoids the prejudicial habit of *a priori* speculation, and deals at first and as far as possible with demonstrable facts. Our own chosen outline, as is readily seen, brings the whole material of biblical doctrine under the three words, Man, Christ, and the Father. Man's natural constitution, his sinfulness, and the facts of his regeneration are matters of personal knowledge, and may well be treated as such, and also with the infinite possibilities of such a nature, before we take up the study of the person and work of Christ. And as "no one knoweth the Father, save the Son, and he to whomsoever the Son reveals him," it seems altogether proper to approach the study of our Father in heaven through the person, the mediation, and the abiding spiritual ministry of his only begotten Son. The greatest religious truths may be thus set forth, not as so many verbal formulas of an outwardly authoritative *credenda,* but as living inspirations to a holy life. Most of these are thus seen to connect with real experiences of the Christian life and of its blessed and eternal hopes. It may also prove a helpful discipline in theological studies to formulate the facts of personal experience as a preparation for inquiring into the deeper mysteries of Christ and of God.

PART FIRST

THE CONSTITUTION AND POSSIBILITIES OF MAN

SECTION FIRST

THE NATURE OF MAN

CHAPTER I

THE NATURAL CONSTITUTION OF MAN

1. Primary Realities. We begin our study of the doctrines of the Bible with the question, What is man? for there can be nothing more real to a thinking being than his own existence. Along with this unquestionable assurance of one's own personality there comes gradually the unmistakable perception of a world about him which is not himself. He soon discovers that he is one of an innumerable company of beings that exist in conditions and with experiences like his own. He finds also that he can in many ways affect or influence his fellow beings and other things in the world about him, and that they also can in like manner affect him. And thus there comes along with the growing knowledge of his own person and powers a clear sense of his dependence and his limitations. These various feelings, perceptions, and activities are matters of personal consciousness, and they are to every man the most real things in the world. There are also certain convictions, ideas, and truths which find expression everywhere and always as the unanimous verdict of mankind. They command recognition in all our continued processes of thought. They are of the nature of unquestionable facts, and are accepted as having inherent authority over the collective conscience and judgment of all civilized peoples. Whatever contradicts such truths and convictions can have no permanent authority over the human soul. With due recognition of these primary realities we turn to the Holy Scriptures to learn what they have to tell us about the nature and origin of man.

2. The Bodily Form. One of the most obvious facts in the constitution of man is his possession of a bodily form. It is remarkable with what minuteness the biblical writers incidentally mention the various parts of the human body: bones, sinews, marrow, flesh, blood, fat, skin, hair; the head, the neck, the shoulders, the arms, hands, fingers, and nails; the eye, the ear, the nose, the mouth, the tongue;—all these and numerous other parts are familiarly referred to in a manner that would be naturally expected in a literature so extensive and various as that of the canonical books. The psalmist was filled with awe at the thought of his being "fearfully and wonderfully made" (Psa. cxxxix, 14). But none of the sacred writers attempt what we would call a scientific analysis and description of the human constitution. The account of man's creation, in Gen. ii, 7, portrays the formation of the body as preparatory to the impartation of the breath of life. The writer of Eccl. xi, 5, does not presume to know "how the bones grow in the womb of her that is with child," nor the "way of the Spirit," nor "the work of God who doeth all." Ezekiel's vision of the resurrection of the house of Israel from their graves of exile exhibits bones, sinews, flesh, and skin appearing before the breath of life came into them (Ezek. xxxvii, 7-10). In Job iv, 19, Eliphaz speaks of men as dwelling in houses of clay, and having their foundation in the dust. In Dan. vii, 15, the Aramaic word for a sheath (נדנה) is employed metaphorically to denote the body as the material cover of the emotional spirit. In 2 Cor. v, 1, the body is called "the earthly house," a tent that is to be dissolved; and in verses 3 and 4 of the same chapter the figure is changed to suggest the thought of the covering of an outside garment. And so in various ways the human body is conceived as a house or cover of the living soul, the external visible organ of the self-conscious personality that thinks and feels.

3. Life, Soul, and Blood. Within this bodily frame, in some invisible organism of its own, exists the living human soul. Man and beast alike possess this element or principle of animal life, which certain scriptures speak of as present and moving in the blood. But how this subtile, invisible essence is distributed through the delicate organs of the body, and what manner of organic connection it holds with them, man has not yet been able to discover. By means of the processes of breathing and through the circulation of the blood the animal soul seems to be present and more or less sensitive in every fiber, nerve, and organ of the body. The language of Gen. ix, 4, is noteworthy: "Flesh with the life thereof, which is the blood thereof, shall ye not eat." Here the word *blood* is grammatically in apposition with *life,* or *soul,* implying that the writer closely identified the two.[1] The context shows that this prohibition of eating blood is based upon the conception that it is the visible bodily element in which the living soul moves and has its being. It thus represents the God-given life, sacred alike in man and beast, but especially in man who was made "in the image of God." In Deut. xii, 23, the prohibition is equally explicit: "The blood is the life (or soul), and thou shalt not eat the life with the flesh." The same thought is even more emphatically expressed in Lev. xvii, 11, 14: "The life (or soul) of the flesh is in the blood; and I have given it to you upon the altar to make atonement for your souls. . . . For as to the life of all flesh, its blood is in (one with) its life. . . . For the life of all flesh is its blood." This mysterious union of life, soul, and blood is also implied in "pouring out one's soul unto death" (Isa. liii, 12; Lam. ii, 12); "smiting the soul of the blood of an innocent one" (Deut. xxvii, 25; comp. Jer. ii, 34). Hence, too, the significance of the blood of Abel crying from the ground on which it had been poured out (Gen. iv, 10), and John's vision of the souls under the altar crying for the avenging of their blood (Rev. vi, 9, 10). So all the biblical writers appear to regard the life, the soul, and the blood as most intimately connected in the natural constitution of man.[2]

4. The Heart. The heart (לֵב, καρδία) of man is spoken of in the Scriptures as the vital center of each individual life. As the life (or soul) of the flesh is in the blood, and at death issues from the body like the pouring out of water from a vessel, so it has, like the blood, its source or fountain in the heart. As the heart in the body is the fountain of the natural life, the same word is appropriately used to designate the center and source of all the higher conscious activities of the soul. Thoughts, imaginations, purposes, memory, reflection, judgment, belief, and unbelief,

---

[1] Literally the passage reads: "Flesh in its soul, its blood, ye shall not eat." In the Hebrew the one word נֶפֶשׁ is employed to denote either *life* or *soul.*

[2] The process of breathing and nourishment is, by the circulation of the blood, spread over the whole body as one single process, bringing to every organ renewed powers of life and growth. In blood, therefore, the invisible breath of the soul is wedded to the most delicate corporeal matter, and what is invisible passes into visible material life. Soul, since it at once gives life to the body, exists in blood as fleshly soul. Blood in its animated state forms the life of every fleshly soul: in other words, it forms animal life, for blood and breath, wanting in plants, are first met with in animals.—Beck, Outlines of Biblical Psychology, pp. 3, 4. Edinburgh, 1877.

and all emotions of love and hatred, of joy and grief, are predicated of the heart. In this higher sense the word is not employed in speaking of the brute creation. It is common to mention heart and soul together (Deut. xxx, 2, 6, 10; Josh. xxii, 5; 1 Sam. ii, 35; Isa. xxvi, 8, 9; Mic. vii, 1). Man is to love God with all the heart and soul (Deut. vi, 4; Matt. xxii, 37). We read of a wise and understanding heart (Exod. xxxv, 25, 35; 1 Kings iii, 9, 12), a willing heart, a tender heart, a hardened heart, a perverse heart, and great projects and resolutions of heart. The heart is capable of joy and sorrow, of vexation, and pride, and anxiety, and madness and despair. The peace of God may dwell in the heart, as well as holy zeal and boldness. The heart of the innocent may be beguiled (Rom. xvi, 18), and become the seat of many fleshly lusts. A man determines in his own heart the free action of the power of his own will (1 Cor. vii, 37). From all which it is clear that the biblical writers employ the word heart to denote the seat and the faculties of feeling, thought, and action.[1]

5. Reins, Intestines, Breath. Other interior organs of the human body are named by the biblical writers as if, like the heart, they were the seat and center of our emotions and our thoughts. The reins (or kidneys), the intestines, and even the liver (Lam. ii, 11) are thus employed to denote the conditions and activities of the living soul. In Prov. xx, 27, the breath is spoken of as if it were one with the intellect that is capable of perception and of searching:

>A lamp of Jehovah is the breath of man
>Searching all the chambers of the body.

In 1 Cor. xiv, 20, "Be not children but men of full age in your powers of understanding," the word $\varphi\rho\acute{\epsilon}\nu\epsilon\varsigma$ (the *midriff*, or *diaphragm*) is used as in Homer for all the mental powers. And thus by a natural way of thinking of the invisible soul as within, the internal parts of the body are named in all languages, by figure of speech, to denote the various emotions, desires, and operations of the mind.

6. The Head. It is somewhat remarkable that the only biblical reference to the head as the seat of human thought is found in the Aramaic portion of the book of Daniel (ii, 28; iv, 5, 10, 13; vii, 1, 15). The phrase employed in these texts is "visions of the

---

[1] The heart is the laboratory and place of issue of all that is good and evil in thoughts, words and deeds; the rendezvous of evil lusts and passions; a good or an evil treasure. It is the place where God's natural law is written in us, and effectually proves itself, as also the place of the positive law put within by grace. It is the seat of conscience, and all the testimonies of conscience are ascribed to it.—Delitzsch, System of Biblical Psychology, p. 295. Comp. also Weiss, Biblical Theology of the New Testament, vol. i, p. 349.

head," and it accords with the habits of prophetic thought and speech for a seer to "lift up his eyes, and look, and behold" (comp. Zech. i, 18; ii, 1; v, 1). So as "the wise man's eyes are in his head" (Eccl. ii, 14), the head itself might very naturally have been mentioned as the seat of vision. We should also compare the saying, "The lamp of the body is the eye" (Matt. vi, 22), and note how "the eyes of the heart" are mentioned in Eph. i, 18. A comparison of Dan. ii, 28 and 30, shows, furthermore, that the Aramaic writer identified visions of the head with thoughts of the heart. The biblical writers seem to have had no knowledge of the modern view of the brain as the chief organ of the mind. It has been thought, however, that the words for *marrow*, in Job xxi, 24, and in Heb. iv, 12, may denote the spinal marrow, and, by association, the entire nervous system, including the brain and the spinal cord. But these allusions are too incidental, and the inferences from a single word so incidentally used are too far-fetched to be trustworthy.[1]

7. The Mind. Man's intellectual faculty of perceiving, thinking, reasoning, and judging is designated in the New Testament by the words νοῦς and διάνοια. The risen Christ "opened their mind, that they might understand the scriptures" (Luke xxiv, 45). Lydia's heart was similarly opened to receive the teaching of Paul (Acts. xvi, 14); so that mind and heart are used in this sense interchangeably. The mind is described in the Pauline epistles variously, as reprobate (Rom. i, 28); fleshly (νοῦς τῆς σαρκός, Col. ii, 18); unfruitful (1 Cor. xiv, 14); vain and corrupt (Eph. iv, 17; 1 Tim. vi, 5). In Rom. vii, 23, 25, the word appears to mean the seat and organ of intelligence and of sober moral judgment. In 1 Cor. xiv, 15, 19, it means intelligent discrimination as against a mere emotional rapture in worship. In Phil. iv, 7, the peace of God which is to guard hearts and thoughts is said to transcend all mind (πάντα νοῦν), that is, it surpasses every power of reason and understanding. In Rev. xiii, 18, and xvii, 9, the man that has mind, and the mind that has wisdom, are called upon to solve the mysteries of prophecy. The word διάνοια appears to be used in the New Testament in substantially the same sense as νοῦς. It is the term employed in the great commandment as found in the three synoptic gospels: "Thou shalt love God with all thy heart . . . soul . . . mind." Compare also 1 John v, 20; 1 Pet. i, 13; 2 Pet. iii, 1; Eph. iv, 18; Col. i, 21; and the association of heart and mind in Heb. viii, 10, and x, 16. In Mark xii, 33, the word σύνεσις is used as a synonym of διάνοια

---

[1] One may read what is to be said for this notion in Delitzsch, System of Biblical Psychology, p. 275. Edinburgh, 1869.

(comp. ver. 30), but in other passages (Luke ii, 47; 1 Cor. i, 19; Eph. iii, 4; Col. i, 9; ii, 2; 2 Tim. ii, 7) it denotes rather the products or the acquirements of the mind. Such a naming of the faculty of thought for thought itself is a common usage in all cultivated languages. The word νόημα (in 2 Cor. iii, 14; iv, 4; xi, 3; Phil. iv, 7) denotes the mind itself; in 2 Cor. ii, 11; x, 5, however, it has the meaning of thoughts or devices of the mind. But the verb νοέω always designates the conscious activities or states of the understanding. In Luke i, 51, we meet the phrase "imagination (διάνοια) of the heart," where it is seen that the heart is conceived as the source of the thoughts of man. In Luke xxiv, 45, we are told that Jesus opened the mind (νοῦν) of his disciples to understand (συνιέναι) the scriptures. One is to be fully assured in his own mind (Rom. xiv, 5), and brethren are exhorted to be perfectly united "in the same mind and in the same judgment (γνώμη)" (1 Cor. i, 10). All these scriptures assume a faculty of thought in man as a natural element of the human constitution, but it does not appear that any special study of the words for *mind, heart, soul,* and *spirit,* as employed by the biblical writers, is likely to throw important light upon the constituent parts of man's nature, or lead to a scientific and trustworthy analysis of them.

8. The Spirit. The spirit of man is a term often employed to denote that which is noblest and most godlike in the human constitution. It is the vital principle by which all other elements of our being are animated. It is the seat of our self-conscious personality, the subject which exercises the power of reasoning, reflecting, judging, determining action, and putting forth free volitions. But the word is very often used in other significations. Both the Hebrew רוח and the Greek πνεῦμα denote the wind, the vital breath, the quality, disposition, or temper of one's mind. Angels and demons are usually called spirits, mainly because their essential nature is supposed to be without any of the characteristic properties of matter. In the highest sense "God is a Spirit" (John iv, 24), and in the New Testament the word appears in naming or referring to "the Holy Spirit" more frequently than in any other connection. More exceptional, both in the Old Testament and in the New, are those passages in which the reference is evidently to that personal spirit in man which is directly conscious of reason, feeling, and volition. Thus Zechariah (xii, 1) speaks of Jehovah "forming the spirit of man within him." The psalmists speak of the spirit "making diligent search" (lxxvii, 6), and being overwhelmed within them (cxlii, 3). In Eccl. xii, 7, the spirit of man is said to "return unto God who gave it." In the New Testament such return of the spirit to God is assumed in Luke, xxiii, 46, John xix, 30, Acts vii, 59; and in 1 Cor. ii, 11, we read: "Who among men knoweth the things of a man, save the spirit of the man, which is in him? even so the things of God none knoweth save the Spirit of God." This assumption of likeness between the spirit of God and that of man is noteworthy, and gives importance to the biblical teaching that man was originally made in the image of God (Gen. i, 27), and still exists in that same image and glory (1 Cor. xi, 7). The statement of Rom. viii, 16, that "the Spirit himself bears witness with our spirit, that we are children of God," also enhances this divine relationship of God and man.

9. The Doctrine of Trichotomy. The words *spirit* and *soul* are often employed interchangeably, as in Hebrew parallelism, and the same experiences are often predicated alike of each. But there are texts in which soul and spirit are distinguished, notably in Heb. iv, 12 ("the dividing of soul and spirit"), and in 1 Thess. v, 23: "May your spirit and soul and body be preserved entire." In this last cited text, especially, some writers find the doctrine of trichotomy, or the threefold nature of man. It is maintained that the soul is the connecting link between the spiritual and the corporeal natures, and has no distinctive personality of its own.[1] It is also supposed to be a sort of house of the spirit, as the body is the house of the soul, and so serves as the subtile medium by which reciprocal action is sustained between spirit and matter.[2] Soul and spirit, having once become united in self-conscious personality, are thereafter forever inseparable, but man's superior nature is to be seen especially in the personality of his spirit. So far, therefore, as the Scriptures speak of the soul as a personal entity, we are to understand, according to the trichotomic theorists, that it derives its personality from the spirit. Others, however, hold that the spirit is rather a constituent element of the soul, and that individuality and personality lie really in the latter. For the soul originated in a union of spirit with matter, so

---

[1] So Delitzsch: "The Soul, made personal indeed by the spirit, is yet in and for itself impersonal. . . . In Gen. ii, 7, we see that man is not already endowed with soul before the spirit is breathed into him, but that it is even by that inspiration that he is endowed with soul."—System of Biblical Psychology, p. 232. Comp. also pp. 263, 264.

[2] In the soul of man the animal and the spiritual meet and combine in a union so intimate that, after their union, their separate existence may be said to be destroyed. Just as oxygen and hydrogen gas, when uniting in certain fixed proportions, lose all the properties of gas and become water, a substance which seems to have little or nothing in common with its two constituent elements, so the animal and the spirit, combined in certain proportions as definite as those of oxygen and hydrogen, though not as easily described by numerical ratios, produce a third and apparently distinct nature, which we call the soul.—J. B. Heard, The Tripartite Nature of Man, p. 49. Edinburgh, 1868.

that spirit forms in part the substance of the soul and individualizes it.[1]

(1) *Has no Support in Sound Interpretation.* But none of these theories of the invisible relations of soul and spirit find support in a sound interpretation of the Scriptures. Their speculative character is not in accord with the thought or the popular language of the biblical writers, who show no uniformity in the use of these various words. The mention of spirit, and soul, and body, in 1 Thess. v, 23, has no real parallel in any other scripture. The same apostle, in 1 Cor. vii, 34, speaks of "the body and the spirit" in a manner that implies dichotomy as clearly as the other text implies trichotomy, and the language of Matt. x, 28, may be used with equal propriety to prove the dichotomy of soul and body. On such principles of exegesis we may find, in Matt. xxii, 37, a trichotomy of heart, soul, and mind, without at all including the body. The parallel passage in Luke x, 27, has four terms, heart, soul, might, and mind, and the text in Deut. vi, 5, whence the citation comes, reads heart, soul, and might. The same three words appear in 2 Kings xxiii, 25. In Heb. iv, 12, God's piercing word is said to divide soul and spirit, joints and marrow, and to be expert in judging the thoughts and intents of the heart. It is obvious that the use of these various terms is largely rhetorical, and is so conspicuously diverse as to nullify their value as prooftexts of trichotomy. The sacred writers display no such proclivity to subtile theories of ontology, and the words *whole* (ὁλοτελεῖς) and *entire* (ὁλόκληρον in 1 Thess. v, 23) cannot be pressed in the interests of a dogma so as to override all other texts and make that one solitary passage an authoritative dictum on biblical trichotomy. The word ἀμέμπτως, *without blame,* might demand equal attention, and a comparison of James i, 4, should not be overlooked in such a contention. The contrast between the natural or soulish man and him that is spiritual, in 1 Cor. ii, 14, 15, has reference to moral and religious qualities, not to elements of the natural constitution.

(2) *The Words Used Indiscriminately.* It appears, furthermore, that the words for *soul* and *spirit* are employed too indiscriminately in other connections to accord with a consistent doctrine of trichotomy. In many passages the word *soul* is used to

---

[1] So G. F. Oehler: "In the soul, which sprang from the spirit and exists continually through it, lies the individuality—in the case of man his personality, his self, his Ego; because man *is* not *spirit,* but *has* it; he is *soul.*"—Theology of the Old Testament, p. 150. New York, 1883. Thus, according to Oehler, trichotomy is not taught or warranted by the Old Testament. "Rather the whole man is included in the *flesh* and *soul,* which spring from the union of the *spirit* with matter." But even this seems like an over-refinement, such as never entered the thoughts of the biblical writers.

denote the entire person (Gen. xlvi, 27; Josh. x, 28; Jer. xliii, 6; Ezek. xviii, 20). *Flesh,* or "all flesh," is often employed in the same sense (Gen. vi, 12; Psa. lxv, 3; Isa. xl, 5, 6). In other passages the same experiences are predicated alike of soul and spirit. Thus trouble, grief, fainting and reviving, longing, searching, thinking, perception, excitement, and purpose are attributed both to the spirit and the soul, and both alike are conceived as departing from the body at death, or are commended to God in the death struggle.

(3) *Yet with Distinctive Connotation.* Such facts sufficiently disprove the idea that the Scriptures teach the doctrine of trichotomy. But the words *flesh, body, soul, spirit, mind, heart, reason,* have their distinctive meanings. Soul and spirit are not strictly synonymous. Spirit has the higher connotation, for the word is commonly employed to designate the nature of angels and of God. And while it may be shown, as above, that there is no clear doctrine of a threefold nature in man to be found in the Scriptures, it does not follow that he is therefore not possessed of such a nature. How the living spirit, existing in God's image and likeness, is united with an organism of flesh and bones and blood, is a mystery which the Bible does not unfold. That there is a spiritual body, a real invisible organism within the fleshly body, seems to be the conception of Paul in 1 Cor. xv, 44, and 2 Cor. iv, 16; and it may well be that, as an intermediate connective between the body and the spirit, there is a psychical organism, a body or house of the spirit, which God gives it to serve the purposes of its being. But these invisible elements of man's spiritual nature are not made manifest to us, and it behooves the theologian and the biblical exegete to refrain from constructing theories of the human constitution out of the incidental and rhetorical language of biblical writers who follow no uniform usage of the same words.

10. General Result. As a general result of this brief study of the natural constitution of man, as outlined in the Scriptures and defined by particular terms, we may affirm with no little confidence that the nature of man is a composite of visible and invisible elements of a most wonderful character. The body, soul, spirit, heart, mind, reason, conscience, and will-power of man present a being which the psalmist appropriately speaks of as "fearfully and wonderfully made." This "offspring of God" is preëminently distinguished above all other living things that move and act upon the earth. We may by careful study and analysis classify the various states and operations of the human soul, and, however we conceive the essence and qualities of man's superior spiritual nature, we find in the Scriptures numerous illustrative examples of its manifold activities. The human body is a marvelous organism and is conceived as a temple and covering of the invisible spirit. This inner spiritual nature is either designated or implied in the common use of the words *soul, mind,* and *heart,* and whatever elements or capacities these several terms may in different connections represent, the personal faculties implied so subsist and work together in the living agent that, in all other literature as well as in the biblical writings, we find these various terms used interchangeably. We are not to look, therefore, in the Scriptures for a scientific analysis and classification of the faculties of the human soul. The biblical writers appropriate the common language of their time, and employ such words as spirit, soul, mind, heart, affections, and thoughts in a popular way, as they were generally understood. It is a delusion to search the Scriptures with the presumption of finding therein anticipations of modern scientific discoveries. The facts or states of human consciousness, which it is the province of the science of psychology to investigate, naturally find more or less mention in the Bible; for all the noticeable facts of one's self-consciousness, such as those of sensation, attention, feeling, sentiment, memory, imagination, reflection, thought, reasoning, deliberation, and volition, must needs have some sort of popular recognition in a literature so extensive and varied as the canonical Scriptures. But this is something very different from the presumption that we may of right search these Scriptures with the expectation of finding therein ancient revelations and anticipations of the results of modern scientific study. We find nothing in these sacred writings which, rationally interpreted, conflicts with any clear disclosures of scientific research. The most lively oracles of the holy men of old, who spoke as they were moved by the Holy Spirit, are cast in popular and poetic forms, and furnish no certain or authoritative guidance into the facts of physiology and psychology. Continuous investigation of these facts by way of observation, experiment, and all possible appliances of scientific research may yet bring to light many mysteries of the natural constitution of man which were unknown to the biblical writers.

CHAPTER II

THE MORAL ELEMENT IN MAN

1. The Fact of Moral Sense. A faithful study of the constituent elements of man's nature requires that we observe them in their higher activities and moral aspects. This being of flesh and blood and bones, of soul and spirit, of heart, and mind, and might, exhibits in his various relations the elements of a moral nature. He formulates his thoughts in language and communicates them to his fellow men. By means of his organs of sense he has conscious contact with the world about him, and comes to know that he is part of it and holds responsible relations to it. He sees, hears, smells, tastes, touches; he also thinks, reasons, forms judgments, and expresses his feelings and opinions. He chooses or refuses objects which come within his reach, and so he finds himself gifted with power to determine his own course of action. In these various ways he comes at an early period of life to exercise the functions of a moral sense and to distinguish between right and wrong. The existence of such a moral element in man is a fact as universal as our knowledge of the human race.

2. Conscience. This feeling, power, or capacity of moral obligation in man, by which he distinguishes between right and wrong, is called conscience. It shows itself along with the first operations of intelligence as an intuitive perception, imperatively controlling the judgment in deciding what *ought* or *ought not* to be done. A sense of guilt and shame comes to the soul whenever the dictates of this moral judgment are violated. No facts of the intellectual and emotional nature of man are more incontrovertible than these mandatory dictations of conscience, and of this we find abundant witness in the Scriptures.

(1) *Old Testament Illustration.*—We have a graphic picture of conscience sounding its admonition to the soul in 1 Sam. xxiv, 5, where it is said "that David's heart smote him" because of a disrespectful act toward the king. The same expression appears in 2 Sam. xxiv, 10, in describing David's sense of guilt in his willful sin of numbering the people. In Job xxvii, 6, the word חרף denotes the reproach of heart which one feels as the sure consequence of failure to observe righteousness, and in Dan. ix, 7, 8, we find the strong expression, "confusion of face," as a

result of sinning against God. The description of the original sin with its consequences of guilt, shame, confusion of face, and penal judgment, as given in Gen. iii, is a most vivid and instructive illustration of the nature of conscience and its working in every act of human sinfulness.

(2) *New Testament use of* συνείδησις. The Greek word employed in the New Testament to denote this moral intuition is συνείδησις. In Rom. ii, 15, we read that the Gentiles "are a law unto themselves, in that they show the work of the law written in their hearts, their *conscience* bearing witness therewith, and their thoughts one with another accusing or else excusing them." Paul appealed to the testimony of his own conscience (Rom. ix, 1; Acts xxiii, 1; xxiv, 16). In the last named passage he tells Felix of his constant endeavor "to have a conscience void of offence toward God and man." He also speaks of a good conscience (1 Tim. i, 5, 19), a pure conscience (1 Tim. iii, 9; 2 Tim. i, 3), a weak, defiled, and seared conscience (1 Cor. viii, 7, 12; Titus i, 15; 1 Tim. iv, 2). Mention also is made of a good conscience in 1 Pet. iii, 16, 21; and in Heb. xiii, 18, we meet the suggestive expression "a beautiful (καλή) conscience," which accompanies the habitual desire and purpose in all things to behave one's self in an honorable and praiseworthy manner of life. In this same epistle we also find the phrase "conscience of sins" (x, 2), and the idea of being "sprinkled from an evil conscience" (x, 22) and of "purging the conscience from dead works" (ix, 14). In 1 Pet. ii, 19, occurs the phrase "conscience of God," that is, a conscience alive and tender in its sense of God and moral obligation.[1]

(3) *Essential Moral Sense.* According to these scriptures conscience is an essential element in the moral constitution of man. It witnesses an intuition of moral obligation and asserts itself in judgments of guilt or of innocence. Its existence is assumed in the original commandment of Gen. ii, 16, 17, and implied in the picture of original innocence in Gen. ii, 25. And so in every record of transgression and punishment, in every commandment of God, as well as in all manner of rebuke, blame, admonition, exhortation, and appeal to the moral sense, we recognize the fact and imperative sway of the faculty of conscience.

3. Personality and Freedom of Will. A closer study of this subject leads to an analysis of the moral faculties of man and the question of the freedom of the will. The action of conscience and the sense of moral responsibility imply the fact of freedom.

---

[1] So Huther: "A genitive of the object, the duty-compelling consciousness of God."—Meyer's Commentary in loco.

The commandments and exhortations of Scripture together with words of warning and assurances of certain penal judgment in case of disobedience are without moral significance if man is not free to act. The final appeal for the truth of this statement must be taken to one's own personal consciousness. All the constituent elements and activities of man's nature which we have passed in review center in the personality of each individual. Human personality consists in the complex self-conscious unity of intelligence, sensibility, and the power of volition, so that these three, thinking, feeling, and choosing, distinguish man as the highest order of being on earth, "crowned with glory and honor," and bearing the image of God. We shall find in the Scriptures, as well as in the study of our own conscious moral action, that rational intelligence in the perception of right and wrong, and the conditions of human sensibility are often necessarily what they are. That is, they are often controlled by causes exterior to themselves, so that what is thought and what is felt can be no other than that which is realized in consciousness. Matters of fact and truth may be so clearly presented to the human understanding that the man cannot fail to know them; and emotions, desires, inclinations, and passions may also be so stirred by forces from without the soul that one cannot possibly ignore the sensation. But this is not true of volition. Under the ordinary conditions of human life the will is free and competent for self-determination. The individual, whose rational judgment is fully settled as to what is right, and whose deepest feelings are moved in the same way possesses the power of volition by which he may deliberately reject what is right and choose what is wrong. The appeal of Moses in Deut. xxx, 19, assumes this freedom of will in the persons addressed: "I call heaven and earth to witness against you this day, that I have set before thee life and death, the blessing and the curse; therefore choose life, that thou mayest live, thou and thy seed." The personal individuality of this appeal is noticeable in the use of the personal pronoun in the singular. The like assumption of responsible moral agency appears in the appeal of the prophet Isaiah (i, 19, 20): "If ye be willing and obedient, ye shall eat the good of the land: but if ye refuse and rebel, ye shall be devoured with the sword." The wail of Jesus over Jerusalem (Matt. xxiii, 37) involves the doctrine of the power of the human will to resist and reject the highest motives and the most affectionate calls: "How often would I have gathered thy children together, even as a hen gathereth her chickens under her wings, and ye would not!" We note also how Jesus is represented, in John iii, 20, 21, as saying: "Every one that doeth evil hateth the light, and cometh not to the light, lest his works should be reproved. But he that doeth the truth cometh to the light, that his works may be made manifest, that they have been wrought in God." The persecution and martyrdom of Stephen were perpetrated in malicious resistance of the Holy Spirit (Acts vii, 51). Paul's doctrine of rewards and punishments—eternal life for those who do well, and "tribulation and anguish, upon every soul of man that worketh evil" (Rom. ii, 9)—is obviously based upon the assumption of a free and responsible moral nature. Scores of similar appeals, exhortations, warnings, and facts of personal consciousness recorded in the Scriptures assume that, while the intellect and the sensibility may be necessitated to states of perception and of feeling, the power of free and responsible volition is fully recognized in man. Man, the personal agent, determines among conflicting reasons and various motives that one course of action which he himself will follow. And this is what is meant by freedom of the will, which may be treated both as a fact and a doctrine, and is essential to the explanation of the nature of man as a moral being.[1]

4. The Moral Element of Social Relations. The recognition of the ethical nature of man is essential to an understanding of his social relations. The lower animals mate together and beget offspring according to their kind, and many kinds become gregarious; but man alone is capable of organizing and perpetuating social institutions.[2] The Scriptures furnish us in sketches of patriarchal life a faithful picture of the family in its earlier forms and also of the development and growth of families into tribes. Later on we see how the tribes become organized into a powerful nation, and adopt various forms of law and government. The records of earliest family life afford evidence of sundry imperfections. While monogamy is the original and fundamental law, the patriarchs were notably implicated in bigamy and polygamy. The Mosaic legislation on divorce is witness to a prevalent defective moral sense. The profound teaching of Jesus respecting the prohibition of adultery (Matt. v, 28) and the bill

---

[1] Hence Dorner, in defining the relation between dogmatics and ethics, very appropriately says that ethics "has for its subject that world of human morality which is brought about by the acts of human self-determination." System of Christian Doctrine, vol. i, p. 28. Edinburgh, 1888. For a most thorough and exhaustive discussion of the freedom, as against all necessitarian theories of human action, see D. D. Whedon's classic treatise, The Freedom of the Will. New York, 1864. Note especially the definitions and arguments of chapters i, ii, iv and vi of Part First.
[2] Human nature has its existence in an ethical sphere and for moral ends of being. We assume that there is a natural capacity or basis for ethical being and life which in the ascent of nature has been reached at length and is occupied by the human race.—Newman Smyth, Christian Ethics, p. 27. New York, 1892.

of divorce (Mark x, 2-12) presents the purest and noblest ideal. The family institution is thus made to appear the most fundamental and sacred of all human relations. Based upon the primal natural constitution of male and female (Gen. i, 27) the man and wife are united for lifelong companionship, and for the propagation of their kind (Gen. ii, 18, 24). In the growth of families and the formation of clans jealousy, bitter feuds, grievous wrongs, and fearful cruelties appear, as in the history of the tribes of Jacob. In the organization of rival states and nations these wrongs take on displays of wrath and vengeance still more terrible, and the history of most of the great nations is one long series of wars and oppressions. Yet slowly and surely through all the ages of strife the moral sense of man has recognized the fact and the excellency of inalienable human rights, and the necessity of guarding them against violence and oppression. Hence the enactment of various forms of law for the family, the tribe or clan, the larger community, the state, and the nation. The highest moral law enunciated in the Old Testament, which has a necessary bearing on all social relations, is written in Lev. xix, 17, 18: "Thou shalt not hate thy brother in thy heart. . . . Thou shalt not take vengeance, nor bear any grudge against the children of thy people; but thou shalt love thy neighbor as thyself." This principle strikes at the root of every human wrong, but the Jew did not comprehend the full truth and application of this noble law. To him no foreigner could be neighbor, but only one of his own tribe or people. It has required ages of discipline to show mankind that they are all brethren, the offspring of one God, and the lesson is yet far from being fully understood. But here, imbedded in the midst of old Levitical precepts, is the highest law of human brotherhood and rights. Jesus himself recognized it (Matt. xxii, 39), and set it in golden form in the commandment: "All things therefore whatsoever ye would that men should do unto you, even so do ye also unto them" (Matt. vii, 12; Luke vi, 31). Thus we perceive that the moral sense is a constituent element in the nature of man, and manifests itself in the individual, in the family, and in all the organized forms of society. As races and states become more civilized the ethical standards of all human relationship become more exalted and controlling. Men are, accordingly, coming to recognize more and more the universal bonds of brotherhood.

CHAPTER III

THE RELIGIOUS ELEMENT IN MAN

1. Essential in Normal Human Nature. The moral element of man's nature is related most vitally and fundamentally to a religious element, in which, in fact, it roots itself and finds its most thorough explanation. Morality is essentially a part of the social aspect of religion. As the capacity to receive and communicate ideas is unmistakable evidence of man's intellectual nature; as all the varied emotions of love, fear, and sensitiveness to objects of beauty and of ugliness are a certain witness of the existence of a living soul, conscious of itself and of its conditions, so there is in the depths of human consciousness an intuition of God. There are facts in the operations of the spiritual nature of man which find adequate explanation only in the doctrine of a necessary relation between the self-conscious personality of the human spirit and the infinite and eternal Spirit who is the upholder of all things visible and invisible. A profound sense of dependence upon some higher Power, and some kind of formal reverence for that Power, have been manifest among all men. The exceptions, if there be any, are so limited and uncertain in character as rather to enhance the farreaching significance of the general fact. Man is as truly a religious as he is a spiritual being. The consciousness that he is somehow related to an infinite Being above him or beyond him, and at the same time within him, is so firmly seated and persistent in the whole race that it demands recognition in any fair outline of the nature of man.[1]

2. Biblical Words Expressive of Religious Feeling and Action. This religious feeling is represented in the New Testament by the words εὐσέβεια, *piety*, or *godliness,* and θρησκεία, reverential *worship,* or religious service. Both words involve the idea of a sacred personal relationship between man and God. The idea is seen in the Old Testament in the frequent use of the adjective חסיד, one who is *pious* or godly, and in the reflexive form of the

---

[1] In the very notion of a spiritual, self-conscious being there is already involved what may be called a virtual or potential infinitude. The first breath of spiritual life is indeed, in one sense, the realization of this capacity, but in another sense, it is only the beginning of a realization which is itself incapable of limitation. We are rational and spiritual beings only in virtue of the fact that we have in us the power to transcend the bounds of our narrow individuality, and to find ourselves in that which seems to lie beyond us.—John Caird, An Introduction to the Philosophy of Religion, p. 112. New York, 1894.

verb שחה to *bow oneself* in acts of worship. The worship of idols is indicated by the hiphil form of the word עצב (Jer. xliv, 19), and the Aramaic סגד. But aside from any special use or implication of definite words, the scriptures of the Old and the New Testaments abound in teaching and illustrations of the religious nature of man. This element shows itself in every race and nation, and is inseparable from the affectional and rational nature. It has been one of the vital factors in the progress of civilization. There can be no correct knowledge of man and no thorough philosophy of human history without a fair reckoning with the facts of man's religious nature.

3. Earliest Manifestations of the Religious Sense. How religion first manifested itself in human life and thought must needs be a matter of conjecture. That the religious feeling originated in an overwhelming sense of superior power, and a consequent fear arising from the consciousness of human limitations, has been the belief of many. But this hypothesis in its logical analysis virtually concedes that the essential content of religion is a revelation of God himself to the religious sensibility inherent in the nature of man. Though the notion of God thus received be vague and imperfect, it contains in every instance the fundamental concept of man's dependence on a higher Power by reason of some necessary constitutional relationship.[1] All prayers and all forms of worship give expression to this fact.

4. Has due Recognition in Scripture. The religious element in man naturally receives due attention in the Scriptures. The pictures of earliest patriarchal times recorded in the book of Genesis, and those also of later times, recognize the worship of God among all the peoples. Melchizedek appears as a famous priest of El-Elyon (Gen. xiv, 18), and Jethro as a priest in Midian (Exod. iii, 1). God speaks in dreams to Abimelech the king of Gerar (Gen. xx, 3). The Hittites call Abraham "a prince of God" among them (Gen. xxiii, 6). Laban the Syrian worshiped teraphim as his gods (Gen. xxxi, 19, 30), and according to Josh. xxiv, 2, the ancestors of Abraham "served other gods" before his migration from beyond the river Euphrates. We read of the

---

[1] Edward Caird, in his Gifford Lectures, discussing the earliest form of religion, observes that "religion is essentially a consciousness of the infinite presupposed in all the divisions of the finite, a consciousness which, however little it be understood by him whom it inspires, however coarse and imperfect the form in which it presents itself, is yet an integral element of man's mind, of which he can no more rid himself that he can get rid of the consciousness of the object or of himself. And the true nature of this idea, as it is implied in the very constitution of our intelligence, continually reacts against the imperfect form in which it is presented. In this way it is not unnatural that even at the lowest stage of his life man should be visited with occasional glimpses of the highest he can ever attain."—The Evolution of Religion, p. 201. New York, 1894.

sacred scribes and priests of Egypt (Gen. xli, 8, 49; xlvii, 22), and how the God of Israel "executed judgment against all the gods of Egypt" (Exod. xii, 12). The various nations of the land of Canaan had their numerous gods and forms of idolatrous worship. There were gods of the Amorites, the Philistines, the Ammonites, the Moabites, the Syrians, and the Zidonians. The Israelites in Canaan after the conquest chose new gods (Judg. v, 8), and, according to Num. xxv, 2, they ran after the gods of Moab while Moses was yet among them. Solomon's heart was drawn after the strange gods of his numerous wives (1 Kings xi, 2), and later kings of Israel gave themselves to various kinds of idolatrous worship. The frequent mention of the names of foreign deities also witnesses to the religious faith and practices of the ancient nations. There were Baal, Ashtoreth, Rimmon, Molech, Chemosh, Dagon, Nergal, Anammelech, Adrammelech, Bel, Nebo, and Nisroch. Some of these represented very degrading forms of idolatry, and were denounced by the Hebrew prophets as so many abominations. But the lowest as well as the highest cults evinced the common religious nature of the worshipers. When Paul addressed the men of Athens on the Areopagus he observed that they were conspicuously devoted to the worship of higher powers (κατὰ πάντα δεισιδαιμονεστέρους), and his language suggests that their devotions contained some elements of superstition (Acts xvii, 16, 22-25).

5. Was Gradually Developed. An outline of the early manifestations of the religious element in man is given in the book of Genesis, and the subsequent books of Scripture show how the highest and purest form of religion was gradually developed. The first man and his wife are represented as living together in the most simple innocence, as children under the law of obedience (Gen. ii). The violation of that law was followed by penal judgment and removal from the previous Edenic life (Gen. iii). The firstborn sons evince their religious nature by their offerings to God (Gen. iv, 1-5), and after Abel's death and the birth of Seth, "men began to call upon the name of Jehovah" (iv, 26). Enoch and Noah "walked with God" (v, 21; vi, 9), and after men had multiplied on earth and been scattered far and wide Abram was called out of his kindred and country and chosen to be the great father of a people whose special mission was to receive the highest revelations of God, and by treasuring and transmitting them to become a blessing to all the families of the earth.[1] And accord-

---

[1] The following from William N. Clarke is worthy of frequent meditation: "From of old, even in prehistoric days, when men were groping after God, God was already reaching forth to men. As they gained their bodily and mental

ingly, as we read in Heb. i, 1, God spoke unto the fathers through great prophets and teachers and at last by the manifestation of his Son, "who is the effulgence of his glory, and the very image of his substance."

6. Universal in Mankind. It would transcend the scope of biblical dogmatics to go beyond these general statements and enter into the disputed questions of the earliest forms of religion. The facts now fairly stated put it beyond all question that man is essentially a religious being. The great religious systems of Brahmanism, Buddhism, Islam, and others of similar commanding history now wide-spread in the world, as well as the defunct religions of ancient Egypt, Phœnicia, Assyria, Babylon, Persia, Greece, and Rome, might be brought forward for additional testimony to the universal religious element in man.[1] But further specific evidence seems quite unnecessary. The lowest forms of fetishism, the ideas and customs of totemism, and the purest worship of Christianity, all alike bear witness to a relationship between the human soul and God of which men everywhere are conscious, and from which they cannot effectually cut themselves away. And so the essential facts of the spiritual nature of man evince the universal truth that we are offspring of God.

---

powers through the response of life to its environment, so they gained the use of their spiritual and religious powers through response to an environment that was wholly invisible, but not less real on that account—an environment of their Father's forthreaching love and care. All down through the ages of religion, there has been something that bore the nature of revelation, an intentional imparting of outward knowledge or else of inward light, proceeding from God himself, who willed that it should come to pass. This impartation from God, the invisible environment, became more definite and helpful as the possibility on man's side increased. The crown and fullness of the revelation came in the appearance among men of Jesus Christ, through whom the Father of men made his clearest self-expression."—Can I believe in God the Father? p. 155. New York, 1899.

[1] No reader of the Vedas, the Avesta, the Accadian psalms or the Egyptian ritual of the dead can fail to recognize in them the true ring of real religion. And the old form of apology, therefore, which endeavored to establish the truth of Christianity by contrasting it with the falsehood of all previous creeds, has for us become a thing of the past. It lingers, indeed, still in certain quarters, but is no longer really tenable; as being not only contradicted by the obvious facts of history, but also in its very nature suicidal, since it seeks to enhance the importance of a special revelation by discrediting the natural religion, to which such a revelation must appeal; to elevate the supernatural by destroying its foundation. —Illingworth, Personality, Human and Divine, p. 161. London, 1894.

CHAPTER IV

PROPAGATION AND DISPERSION OF MANKIND

1. Unity of the Human Race. The unity of the human race, as having sprung by generation from one original source, is apparently assumed throughout the Scriptures. According to Gen. i, 27, 28, the first man and woman were constituted to "be fruitful, and multiply, and fill the earth, and subdue it." The fifth chapter of Genesis is remarkable as a "book of the generations of Adam," who "begat in his own likeness, after his own image" (ver. 3). This ancient genealogy connects Adam with Noah through a period of nearly two thousand years, and from the three sons of Noah, according to Gen. ix, 19; x, 32, "the whole earth was overspread." Paul declared before the Athenians that God "made from one[1] every nation of men to dwell on all the face of the earth" (Acts xvii, 26), and his great antithesis, represented in Rom. v, 12-19, between Adam and Christ, assumes the propagation of all men from one primeval ancestor. The unity of the race appears to be well attested also by the facts of comparative ethnology, physiology, psychology, philology, and history. But into the detailed arguments, based upon alleged facts, the scope of this treatise does not permit us to enter. It may be observed, however, that, should the polygenous origin of different races of men become a demonstrated conclusion of ethnological science, the interpretation of the Scriptures bearing on the subject would accordingly have to take cognizance of the facts.[2]

2. Propagation of Species. We understand, according to the Scriptures and the best attested conclusions of biology, that the human race, as well as all other orders of organic life, is so constituted as to propagate itself in the earth. To herb, tree, fish, fowl, cattle, beast, and every creeping thing that moves on the earth is the commandment given to be fruitful and multiply each according to its own kind (Gen. i, 11, 12, 21, 24, 25, 28). There is no intimation that man is to be an exception to this

---

[1] The most important three MSS. (ℵ, B, A.) omit the word $α\">ιματος$, *blood* from this text.
[2] The doctrine of Pre-Adamites, as maintained by Peyrerius, McCausland and Winchell, is for many reasons inconclusive and unsatisfactory. For *the Adam* האדם of Genesis is much more naturally understood and explained as referring to the primordial race or races, or even as a generic name for original humanity, than as designating a later development, as, for example, the Caucasian race.

universal law. When it is said that Adam begat a child in his own likeness (Gen. v, 3) it is most naturally understood that his offspring was as completely after his kind as is the offspring of any other order of living creature after its kind. Whatever, therefore, goes to constitute the real nature and properties of the human species, as represented in the primeval man—as body, soul, spirit, heart, mind—all are capable of self-propagation. The procreation of man, in the entirety of his nature, may be as confidently affirmed as we affirm the procreation of every other class of living things upon the earth. The transmission not only of striking physical features but also of notable qualities of mind and spirit from parent to child confirms this doctrine of procreation.

3. Creationism and its Proof-texts. Nevertheless, it has been alleged and widely maintained that the human soul is not propagated from parent to offspring, but is created by an immediate act of God upon the event of each human birth. Human parents thus beget the bodies of their offspring, but God in some mysterious way supplies *ab extra* the living soul, or spirit. It would seem, however, that nothing but the most positive and conclusive evidence, or the most explicit revelation could suffice to show man to be such a remarkable exception to the law which governs the propagation of all other living creatures on the earth. The theory cannot find the slightest support in any facts available in scientific and psychological research. It seems to have had its origin in certain dogmatical assumptions touching "the numerical substance of all mankind" in Adam and the possibility of the division and separation of soul-substance in the propagation of a corrupt human nature—questions which may be said to be obsolete for any serious attention in modern theological study. Some of the principal texts of Scripture in which it seeks support should, perhaps, be briefly considered.

It has been argued that the dual nature of man, as described in Gen. ii. 7, distinguishes clearly between body and soul, and shows the one to be of the dust of the earth while the other is from God. But that passage affirms God to be as truly the Creator of man's body from the dust as he was the author of his soul, and it has nothing whatever to tell us about procreation or generation either of soul or body, but is concerned solely with the original creation of man as man. The incidental statement in Eccl. xii, 7, that at the death of a man "the dust returns to the earth as it was, and the spirit unto the God who gave it," has been cited to show that the spirit is from God in some sense that the body is not. But suppose that be conceded, how does it in the least prove that God creates a spirit independently of the laws of propagation at the event of every human birth? The obvious reference of the text is to the record of man's original creation in Genesis, and like it has nothing to say about the time and manner of the production of each human spirit. The same may be said of Zech. xii, 1, often adduced to support creationism: "Jehovah stretcheth out the heavens, and layeth the foundation of the earth, and formeth the spirit of man within him." This glowing language simply refers to the great truth that God is the creator of heaven and earth and man, but it furnishes no specific information of the time and manner of the formation of each. So again in Isa. xlii, 5, Jehovah is described as

> He that created the heavens and stretched them out;
> He that spread forth the earth, and the things which go out of it;
> He that giveth breath unto the people upon it,
> And spirit to them that walk therein.

So far from proving that each human soul is at birth an immediate creation of God, these poetic parallelisms show rather that the creation of the heavens and the earth and all things in them is in like manner a direct and continuous production of Jehovah. The giving of breath to the people is not essentially different from giving spirit to them that walk in the earth. God is the author and continual support of all the growths of nature as truly as he is the giver and upholder of all the souls of men. He is "the God of the spirits of all flesh" (Num. xvi, 22) because he is creator of mankind. He is represented in Ezekiel (xviii, 4) as saying, "Behold, all souls are mine: as the soul of the father, so also the soul of the son is mine." According to Paul the body is the temple of the Holy Spirit which is in man (1 Cor. vi, 19). God is the creator and former of the entire man, body and soul with all their organs and faculties, and when a biblical writer mentions one part of the human constitution as the offspring or the workmanship of God we are not to conclude that therefore he is not as truly the author of the whole. A general statement that God is the father of the spirits of men cannot therefore decide the question of man's propagating his own species. "Thy hands have made me and fashioned me," says the psalmist (cxix, 73), but his statement is as true of the body as of the soul. The classic text, supposed to be quite decisive on the subject, is Heb. xii, 9: "We had the fathers of our flesh to chasten us, and we gave them reverence: shall we not much rather be in subjection to the Father of spirits, and live?" Here it is argued that we have a striking antithesis between the fathers of our bodies and the Father of our souls; as if God were not as truly the author of the one as of the other. The statement of the New Testament writer is not equivalent to the dogma that God creates *ab extra* a spirit for every human body produced under the law of generation. He simply contrasts the fatherhood of man and the Fatherhood of God. He does not even say, "Father of our spirits," but "Father of the spirits," which includes such spirits as are mentioned in chap. i, 14. It is nothing to his purpose to deliver an opinion about the origin of the human soul as incapable of transmission in the ordinary process of generation, but to enhance the thought of the Fatherhood of God over all spirits. The antithesis is between human fathers and the heavenly Father. That the author of this epistle believed in the procreation of human souls is apparent from chap. vii, 10, where he represents Levi as in the loins of his father Abraham at the time when Melchizedek met him. In none of these texts, therefore, do we find any sufficient warrant for the idea that man differs from all other living creatures on earth in the propagation of his kind. But the Scriptures do make it emphatic that his entire being,—body, life, soul, spirit, mind,—springs from the Fountain of all created life, the living and eternal God. By the same upholding Power all things continue in being. No child is born into this world, no fish, no fowl, no insect, comes into existence but the living God is present and efficient at its coming, and also at its going forth again. Not a sparrow lives or dies without our Father (Matt. x, 29). "He is before all things, and by him all things hold together" (1 Col. i, 17).

4. Dispersion of Races and Tribes. The dispersion of all the nations of mankind from one original family is the teaching of Gen. x, 1—xi, 9. The table of nations there given accords with the well-known facts of the outgrowth of families and tribes, and of their multiplication in the earth. The races of mankind are classified under three great divisions, Japhetic, Hamitic, and Semitic. But the families, tongues, lands, and nations mentioned in this ancient scripture are not sufficiently comprehensive in detail to represent the modern races and distribution of mankind. Great peoples and nations have arisen since the book of Genesis was written, and over continents and islands unknown to the biblical writers there exist today families, tongues, and nations with a civilization immeasurably in advance of any of the ancients. Many peoples and races seem also to have deteriorated and become changed in color, stature, and capability. We look almost in amazement on the various types of mankind as modern research has presented them before us, and we wonder how they all could have sprung from one ancestor. The scientific anthropologist examines the remarkable differences in the size of bodily structure, in the configuration of the skull, in the color of the skin, in the peculiarities of the hair, and in mental traits. He studies to classify the different races according to certain notable characteristics which seem to differentiate them. There are the Caucasian, the Semitic, the Mongolian, the Malay, the Australian, the Negro, and the American Indian races, and if these seven be traced out into their various subordinate families, we must make note of Aryans, Ethiopians, Kaffirs, Zulus, Patagonians, Aztecs, Eskimos, and scores of similar divisions which correspond, in their relation to the leading types, to such biblical names as Canaanites, Hittites, Amorites, and Sepharvites. The task of classifying all these scattered tribes of men into the fewest principal types belongs to the specialist in ethnography.[1] How all these races became dispersed abroad from one original center of population; how changes of climate, varieties of food, and habits of life may have brought about, in the long course of ages, the striking varieties of color and of physiognomy which we now find; how languages were formed, modified, and changed in structure and usage in the lapse of time—these are all questions of permanent interest to man, but demand only a passing recognition in a treatise on biblical doctrine. Whatever future research may determine as to the polygenous origin of different races, there is at present no sufficient evidence in hand to warrant belief in that hypothesis. The biblical teaching and the trend of scientific studies in ethnology show rather that all races of men sprung from one original human pair, and were dispersed abroad over the face of the earth and among the islands of the great sea from one geographical center.

---

[1] Huxley's classification of the principal types into the Mongoloid, the Negroid, the Australoid, and the Xanthochroic has met with much favor. See Journal of the Ethnological Society, vol. ii, p. 404. 1870.

CHAPTER V

THE ORIGIN OF MAN

1. The Definite Modern Question. It remains to inquire into the origin of the human race. Whence came the first man? To answer in the bare language of Genesis that "God created man in his own image; male and female created he them," is not sufficient for the modern inquirer. The more formal statement of Gen. ii, 7, that "Jehovah God formed man of the dust of the ground, and breathed into his nostrils the breath of life, and man became a living soul," fails also to answer the more specific questions which are now put forward. For we are now definitely asked whether this process of creation were the act of a moment, an hour, a day, or a thousand years. Was it an immediate and instantaneous creation, or a long process of evolution?

2. Two Ways of Answering the Question. There are two supposable ways in which this question may be answered. One is by receiving direct information from a supernatural and unquestionable source; the other is by means of such methods of research as man employs in ascertaining facts in any other question of archæology. It has long been supposed, on the one hand, that the first chapters of the book of Genesis are a literal and authoritative historical account of the origin of the world and of man. But critical and rational investigation has largely discounted this traditional view of the biblical narrative. The old idea that the world was "made out of nothing," and that all it contains was brought into existence in one week of ordinary days and nights, has been effectually exploded. No modern apologist of reputation argues for a literal interpretation of the six days of creation; but attempts without number have been made to read into the biblical narrative the findings of scientific research and the suggestions of the nebular hypothesis of the universe. These attempts, however, carried on now for more than a hundred years, are in themselves a striking witness of the failure of the narrative itself to convince intelligent readers that it is a literal historical account of the facts of creation. A supernatural revelation of specific facts which thus fails to commend itself to the judgment and conscience of diligent seekers after the truth would seem to be in itself a manifest absurdity. What possible authority can such a variously interpreted record be for determining the specific questions of modern astronomy, geology, and biology? For reasons elsewhere given[1] we are compelled to regard the opening chapters of Genesis as a series of symbolical or idealistic pictures rather than as records of science and of history. Whatever their origin and composite character, set as they now are at the beginning of the biblical canon, they embody sublime ideas of God and the world which the most simple and unlearned readers have always been able to discern. They are profitable for showing that God is the beginning and end of all things. He bringeth light out of the darkness, and order out of confusion. He is the infinite personal Intelligence back of all phenomena. He governs the heavens and the earth according to well established laws, and determines the times and seasons with unerring wisdom. He is the ultimate source of all life[2], and the all-pervading Force by which through illimitable eons the animal creation culminated in man with his godlike capacity for wisdom, love, and power. We accordingly find nothing in the biblical narrative to forbid the hypothesis of evolution in accounting for the origin of man.

3. Poetical Concepts of Creation. So far as the opening chapters of Genesis convey an ideal of the origin of man on earth, they indicate that he is a product of the earth and of the heavens through the creative energy of God. The revelations given are embodied in poetic pictures rather than in prosaic and realistic details of fact. How long and through what details of method the process of man's creation was brought about are no more clearly revealed than are the processes of development by which the heavens and the earth reached their present conditions. It was a beautiful conception of the sacred writer to portray the entire process under the figure of six days of labor followed by a sabbath rest. The whole picture is in substance but an apocalyptic elaboration of what a psalmist (Psa. xxxiii, 6-9) says in a few lines of Hebrew parallelism:

> By the word of Jehovah were the heavens made,
> And all the host of them by the breath of his mouth.
> He gathereth the waters of the sea together as a heap;
> He layeth up the deeps in storehouses. . . .
> For he said, and it came to pass;
> He commanded, and it stood firm.

---

[1] See my Biblical Apocalyptics, chapter iii. New York, 1898.
[2] It is quite possible that if life began in this world by a miraculous act, the creative power may have operated so gently that an investigating committee of angels would have failed to determine whether it may not have been a case of spontaneous generation.—Macloskie, in the Presbyterian and Reformed Review, 1898, p. 16.

Moreover, the statement of Gen. ii, 7, makes no note of time. It simply says,

> Jehovah God formed man of the dust of the ground,
> And breathed into his nostrils the breath of life;
> And man became a living soul.

This language is as compatible with a long period of evolution as with the concept of an immediate creation. Man's lower nature, which is from the earth and earthy, might have been in process of formation (יצר), slowly evolving from lower to higher forms of life and structure, long ages before the breath of God exalted him into the living human soul. The order of nature and of revelation is "first the natural, then the spiritual." Man has his origin from the dust of the earth and from the breath of God. But how long the natural creature with his human form and animal life continued as such before the moral and religious elements were developed into rational self-consciousness, and under what particular customs and activities he first came gradually to realize his moral capabilities, we have no specific revelation, and of course no man can tell. On the hypothesis of evolution he was a natural being a long time before he became a moral being. For morals like manners are not the creation of a moment, or a day. The word ethics, as its Greek derivation shows ($\mathring{\eta}\vartheta o\varsigma$), implies custom, usage, rules, and habits of conduct far above the range of animal life, and these require time for growth. The development of the human mind and of the moral sense through infancy and childhood into the maturity of a disciplined manhood may be taken as a suggestive outline of the gradual advance of the entire human species from the natural to the spiritual.[1]

4. No Definite Answer in Scripture. The Scriptures, then, do not inform us of the time and manner of man's first appearance on the earth. The way is open, accordingly, for the acceptance of any light upon this subject which archæological and scientific research is able to furnish. The prevailing view of specialists

---

[1] We should guard against the assumption that creation must needs be a work of magical instantaneousness, inconsistent with normal processes of becoming. "It is curious," says Le Conte, "to observe how, when the question is concerning a work of nature, we no sooner find out how a thing is made than we immediately exclaim: 'It is not made at all, it becomes so of itself.' So long as we knew not how worlds were made, we of course concluded they must have been created, but so soon as science showed how it was probably done, immediately we say we were mistaken—they were not made at all. . . . Does it not seem that to most people God is a mere wonder-worker, a chief magician? The mission of science is to show us how things are done. Is it any wonder, then, that to such persons science is constantly destroying their superstitious illusions? But if God is an honest worker, ought not science rather to change gaping wonder into intelligent delight—superstition into rational worship?"—Evolution and its Relation to Religious Thought, p. 287. New York, 1895.

in this department of study is that all forms of creature life upon the earth have been produced by a gradual development of higher out of lower types, and that man is no exception to this plan and order of creation. Into the detailed evidences of this hypothesis it is not the province of biblical theology to enter. We do not assume or argue that the evolution of man from lower forms of animal life has been proven. The most that can be said for this hypothesis is that it has for two generations been gaining favor, and a majority of investigators apparently best qualified to judge of the facts and arguments involved in the discussion accept it as probably true. The thoughtful expositor of divine truths, who has becoming respect for the prevailing opinion of specialists in science, will be slow to assume an attitude of hostility thereto. But on the other hand he should not hasten to adopt an unproven hypothesis and work it into his system of doctrine.

5. Man is the Crowning Work of God. We should be content for the present to leave the question of man's origin where Scripture leaves it, that is, indefinite as to its time and method, but with the positive and definite assertion that his creation is a work begun, continued, and completed by the intelligent agency of God. Back of all forms of matter and of life we posit the creative energy of the all-wise and ever-living Personality whom man's religious consciousness adores as God over all. He has brought man into being and has assigned him his high position as master of all the living things that dwell in the earth. Hence the words of the devout psalmist:

> When I consider thy heavens, the work of thy fingers,
> The moon and the stars, which thou hast set in their place,
> What is a mortal, that thou bearest him in mind,
> Or a son of Adam that for him thou shouldest care?
> Thou madest him but a little lower than God,
> And with glory and honor hast crowned him!
> Thou gavest him rule over the works of thy hands;
> Thou hast placed them all under his feet:
> Sheep and oxen, under him are they all;
> And alike the beasts of the fields,
> The birds of the air, and the fish of the sea—
> Even that which frequenteth the paths of the seas!
> O Jehovah, our Lord,
> How exalted is thy name in all the earth![1]

---

[1] Psalm viii. De Witt's translation. From his Praise Songs of Israel. New York, 1886.

CHAPTER VI

MAN'S PLACE IN THE WORLD

1. Man as the Chief Creation of God. The sentiments of the eighth psalm express the biblical conception of man's relation to the world. He stands at the head of God's creations, "a little lower than God," crowned with the honor of "dominion over the fish of the sea, and over the fowl of the air, and over every living thing that moveth upon the earth"(Gen. i, 28). No matter what the method of his creation, nor how long ago nor how recently in the millenniums of the earth's existence he made his first appearance as man, he now occupies the highest place among all creatures in this world.[1] But the discoveries made by means of the telescope and the microscope have marvelously enlarged man's knowledge of the universe. When he now considers the heavens and the immense spaces of the stars, and learns that a ray of light, speeding at the rate of 186,000 miles a second, would require many years to reach us from the nearest star beyond our solar system; and when in the light of such information he tries to reckon the magnitude of some of those distant heavenly bodies, his mind is bewildered, and with a deeper appreciation he now repeats the psalmist's exclamation, What is mortal man that the Creator of all the heavens should show him special care! When, however, he turns his optic glass the other way, and becomes aware of the universe of infinitesimal forms of life below him; when he learns that a million living things, unseen by the naked eye, are moving about within the space of one tiny vessel of water, he comes to recognize himself as somehow between the marvelous extremes, and gifted with faculties to make all heights and depths subserve his own existence. He finds himself at the head of the whole realm of living things; and if it be true that he has reached this wondrous goal through æonic processes of evolution, guided in all his transformations from lower to higher by the wisdom of the omnipresent and omniscient Spirit of the universe, why should he question the method of such a creation and deem it less miraculous than if it had been wrought in a moment of time?[2]

---

[1] "On the earth," writes John Fiske, " there will never be a higher creature than man."—Destiny of Man Viewed in the Light of his Origin, p. 26.
[2] Science is charged with numbering man among the beasts, and leveling his body with the dust. But he who reads for himself the history of creation as it

2. Ancient Concepts of "the Heavens and the Earth." Whatever his origin and the undetermined history of his development through unknown ages in the past, man has now reached a summit on which he sees himself holding no secondary rank to any other being in the visible world. "The heavens and the earth" mean very much more to the modern observer than they could possibly have meant to the ancient Hebrew. To him the שמים were the visible sky, and the ארץ was the outspread fields of land (אדמה). Even the entire habitable world (תבל), as compared with our present knowledge of it, was but a limited domain. And the corresponding Greek words in the New Testament carried for its first readers no such extensive significance as they have in the scientific language of the present time. Luke speaks of an enrollment of all the world (οἰκουμένη) by a decree of Cæsar (ii, 1), and also of "a great famine over all the world" (Acts xi, 28). Paul speaks of the gospel as bearing fruit and increasing in all the world ἐν παντὶ τῷ κόσμῳ, Col. i, 6), and "in all creation which is under the heaven" (i, 23). But so far as any of these terms imply the universe of earth and heavens, they may be, and they often are, employed in the popular speech of the present time just as they were by the ancients. Their special significance in any one passage must be determined by the context.

3. Not Physical Bulk but Rational Nature Man's Crowning Excellence. The glory and honor with which man is crowned cannot be estimated by standards of physical bulk or strength. One human soul is reckoned of more value than a thousand elephants. A million cubic feet of solid or of gaseous matter is as meaningless in itself as a tiny pebble. It has no glory like that of self-conscious spiritual intuition, or a sublime farreaching thought, or a deliberate act of volition which may change the destiny of a human soul. No discoveries in modern science conflict with the biblical teaching concerning man's high place in nature. It is conceded by all that man occupies the foremost position in the visible creation of God. Among the lower orders of animals we find some that exhibit intellect and affection, and

---

is written by the hand of Evolution will be overwhelmed by the glory and honor heaped upon this creature. To be a man, and to have no conceivable successor; to be the fruit and crown of the long past eternity, and the highest possible fruit and crown; to be the last victor among the decimated phalanxes of earlier existences, and to be nevermore defeated; to be the best that nature in her strength and opulence can produce; to be the first of that new order of beings who by their dominion over the lower world and their equipment for a higher, reveal that they are made in the image of God—to be this is to be elevated to a rank in nature more exalted than any philosophy or any poetry or any theology have ever given to man.—Henry Drummond, The Ascent of Man, pp 115, 116.; New York, 1895. And yet some men will argue that man is not and cannot be in any true sense the offspring of God except by regeneration. How can such offspring of God be other than sons and daughters? Such *creation is begetting.*

are capable of a remarkable degree of education and of domestication. Some animals and insects live in tribes, and seem to have their peculiar forms of social organization. It may be that among the more highly developed animals essential features of sensibility, intellect, and will are perceptible; but the gulf which separates the lowest type of man from the highest species of beast or cattle is incalculable, and, so far, there has not been found a real or natural connecting link between them. The rational and spiritual nature of man has, from the beginning of his creation, placed him far above every other living thing upon the earth.

CHAPTER VII

PRIMITIVE STATE OF MAN

1. Completeness of Natural Constitution. If the summit of creature life on earth was attained by the formation of man, we conceive that the first specimen of his kind was complete in all that constitutes the essentials of a human personality. If this estate of manhood were reached through millenniums of evolution, it does not follow that the first *man* was a savage, or that the first communities must have been beastly and ferocious. Many a modern savage, so called, uncorrupted with the sins and vices which prevail under high forms of "civilization," and living in the simplicity of nature, has been found to be a noble, lordly being. According to the Scripture everything which God made was seen at the beginning to be very good (Gen. i, 31). The statement refers to grass, and tree, and bird, and beast, and cattle as well as to man. But the creation of man in the image and after the likeness of God (Gen. i, 26-28) gave him a rank above all other creations. He alone of all the creatures named possesses personality. He was not a normal man until conscious of his spiritual nature with its capacity for mental, moral, and religious activity. We can conceive the first human being as having a complete, sound, healthy body, and along with it all the natural faculties of sensibility, intellect, and will which we now find in the constitution of every normal human being. We are hardly justified in assuming the wild man of the forests and the most abject of savage tribes now living to be specimens of primitive man. Many of these appear to be the degenerate descendants of ancient vagrants from society. They seem to have wandered to the remotest corners of the earth from more civilized centers, and to have become the savages they are by reason of ages of separation from their better kin. So far from being fair types of original normal humanity, they are rather degenerate offshoots. We may think of the first human pair as loving each other with a pure affection and living together in delightful innocency. The picture of "the garden of Eden," in Gen. ii, is a happy presentation of the conditions of earliest human innocence and love. The statement of Gen. ii, 25, that the man and his wife were both naked and yet not ashamed, indicates a complete innocence and simplicity like that of childhood, and the absence of evil thoughts and desires.

2. Undeveloped in Knowledge and Civilization. Beyond this general conception of the natural simplicity and uprightness of an uncorrupted original constitution we have no knowledge of the primitive state of man. We have elsewhere[1] given reason for believing that the portraiture of man's original estate in Genesis is not a historical record, but an ideal conception much after the nature of allegory. There is no sufficient warrant in Scripture or in reason for the notion, propounded by former theologians, that the first human beings were gifted with knowledge, or with capacities superior to those of later generations.[2] On the contrary, knowledge is in its very nature an acquisition, and requires time and study for its attainment. So, too, there is manifest incongruity in speaking of the first condition of man as one of "civilization," for civilization implies commerce, inventions, social and political organization, and progress in arts, knowledge, and refinements. The fourth chapter of Genesis furnishes us with an ideal of the earliest developments of human society in prehistoric times. The offerings of Cain and Abel show how the religious nature first asserted itself. The keeping of sheep, the tilling of the ground, the invention of musical instruments, and the forging of brass and iron indicate the beginnings and development of civilization among the primitive peoples.

3. Original Goodness. In an inquiry after the religious consciousness of primitive man, and after the positive moral excellencies of his character, it is easy to run into worthless speculation and presumption. The original rectitude of human nature is indicated as being "very good." We find in the narratives of creation and of man's Edenic life no more specific revelation touching the nature and degree of his righteousness and holiness than we find touching the specific manner of his original formation. The goodness of his nature, so far as it can be conceived as concreated along with the essential elements of his constitution,

---

[1] See Biblical Apocalyptics, chap. v.
[2] In one of his sermons the eloquent Robert South declares that "an Aristotle was but the rubbish of an Adam." Bishop Bull maintained that Adam's naming of the animals of Eden evinced a wisdom superior to that of all the philosophers of ancient and modern times, and went far beyond what the "Royal Society durst have undertaken." But old Jewish literature exceeds even this extravagance, and conceives a splendor of God resting upon Adam in such excess of brightness that even his heels darkened the sun, and his image beamed from one end of the earth to the other (Weber, Jüdische Theologie, p. 215). Some of these Jewish writers say that the Edenic state lasted only five hours; others say one day, others several days, and the book of Jubilees says seven years. But from Genesis it seems quite clear that Adam and Eve had at first no clothes, no houses, no knives or forks, no tin or glass ware, and no works of art! Theirs was surely a *primitive* state.

differed from that of the grass and the cattle in the same way that his superior nature differed from theirs. He was brought to the perfection of manhood as a rational, moral, and religious being. The constitutional capacities and appetencies of his nature were normal and intact. So long as he continued to think, feel, and act in harmony with the self-conscious approval of his moral sense he must have remained blameless and pure. Beyond such a general conception and statement it seems utterly useless to inquire.[1] We are in possession of no positive knowledge of the first human being and his earliest associates, and all we can safely say about the primitive moral condition of man is that which is written about every living thing which God made on the earth: "Behold, it was very good."

4. Made in the Image of God. It remains to speak here of that highest distinction of man, according to the Scriptures; that glory and honor which are designated by the oft-repeated statement that he was made in the image of God. In what elements or qualities of man's nature are we to see this likeness of the Creator? Little help to understand this term can come from a study of the two words צלם, *image*, and דמות, *likeness*, as found in Gen. i, 26. The first conveys a somewhat concrete, the second a more abstract conception; but when the two expressions are connected they serve to give emphasis to the idea of similarity. They express the thought of some noteworthy resemblance of God, which distinguished man above all other creatures. Among the ancient Christian fathers we observe differences of opinion on this subject. Theodoret informs us that Audius, a native of Syria, found the image of God in man's body and taught that God himself had a human form and a body consisting of parts. Irenæus maintained that it requires body, soul, and spirit to constitute the full image of God in man, the body being essentially the temple of God and of the Holy Spirit. Others distinguished between the *image* and the *likeness* of God, holding that the former consists in the original constitution and faculties of the soul, while the latter is seen rather in the actual exercises of these powers in harmony with the will of God. Philo located the image of God in the rational soul and connected it with his Platonic notions of archetypal ideas in the divine mind, of which man himself is only a copy. Modern theologians have also differed widely on this

---

[1] "It is unfortunate," says Denney, "that the questions as to man's nature have been usually discussed in theology in connection with what is called his original state. The question, What is man? has been treated as if it were convertible with the question, What was Adam? But it is plain that we do not stand in the same relation to these two questions. Man is before us, or rather in us; we have the amplest opportunity for investigating his nature and constitution, and we have the whole range of Scripture to guide and correct our interpretation of these

question, some placing the image in man's dominion over all other creatures, others in his superior intellectual powers, and others in original moral perfections which were lost by sin.

(1) *No Explanation in Scripture.* It is first of all to be observed that in the five places where the phrase occurs (Gen. i, 26, 27; v, 1-3; ix, 6; 1 Cor. xi, 7; James iii, 9) there appears no explanation of its meaning. It is obvious from all these texts that the image and likeness of God exalt man to a dignity of exceptional character. The words of Gen. i, 26, moreover, assign him "dominion over the fish of the sea, and over the birds of the heavens, and over the cattle, and over all the earth," and the eighth psalm adds somewhat to this statement in its poetic paraphrase:

> Thou hast made him but little lower than God,
> And crownest him with glory and honor.
> Thou makest him to have dominion over the works
>   of thy hands;
> Thou hast put all things under his feet.

But in none of these texts have we anything which is of the nature of a definition of the image of God. One of the texts above referred to, Gen. v, 3, has been strangely perverted in the interests of dogma. It has been maintained that "his own likeness, after his image," in which Adam begat Seth, was not the same image in which Adam was at first created (comp. Gen. i, 26, 27). But nothing in the context supplies the slightest intimation of any other image or likeness than that in which Adam was made. In the first verse of this chapter it is expressly said that Adam was made "in the likeness of God," and the next sentence affirms that he begat Seth in his own likeness. What other likeness or image has been so much as suggested in the connection? To introduce a new and radically different idea by means of the identical words employed in the previous sentence, and without any qualifying statement, is arbitrary and unjustifiable in the extreme. There is not here even a hint that Adam had lost the image of God and had acquired another image of his own.[1] The notion that the image in which man was created could not be transmitted by human generation is a dogma of creationism, which we have already seen to be without support in the Scriptures.

---

accessible facts. But Adam is not within our reach at all; and it is simply exposing ourselves, without any necessity whatever, to refutation by the progress of physical or archæological science, when we advance statements about the primitive condition of man which have not only a religious, but a historical content." Studies in Theology, p. 78. New York, 1895.

[1] It should be observed that, in the critical analysis of Genesis, chap. v belongs to the Priestly narrative (P), and connects with ii, 3. The intervening section, ii, 4—iv, 26, is from a different writer (J). So the reference to the image of God in v, 1-3, followed originally soon after the statement of i, 27, and connected with the creation-narrative of chap. i.

(2) *New Testament Texts in Ephesians iv, 24, and Colossians iii, 9, 10.* There are two passages in the New Testament which have also been often cited as proof that man has lost the original image of God in which he was created. The two texts are Eph. iv, 24, and Col. iii, 9, 10. They present a contrast between a "former manner of life," called "the old man," and a "renewal in the spirit of the mind," which is called "the new man." This new man is said to have been "after God created in righteousness and holiness of truth." The parallel passage in Colossians expresses the same thought in substantially the same terms, but it says that "the new man is renewed unto knowledge after the image of him who created him." In both these texts there is an allusion to the image of God in which man was created, but there is no definition of that image, nor is there any evidence that the writer regarded the image itself as lost. Rather is he speaking of a great change in the "manner of life" (ἀναστροφή) apparent in men who had put away anger, malice, and all such qualities and deeds of "the old man," and had become "renewed in the spirit of their mind," that is, the spiritual nature which is characterized by the possession of the intellectual faculty. The form of expression in Col. iii, 10, is, "renewed unto (or *into,* εἰς) knowledge after the image of him who created him"; that is, a knowledge which accords with the image of God. The putting off the old and putting on the new man involves no creation of new elements in the constitution of any individual man, who, according to Paul (1 Cor. xi, 7), "exists in the image and glory of God." The change is not in the image of God which is essential to his nature as man and as an offspring of God, but in the manner of his life. It consists in the putting off of old habits, and a putting on as new clothing (ἐνδύσασθαι) the righteousness which alone becomes the image of God in which man was made. The renewal into knowledge contemplates the acquisition of a superior knowledge (ἐπίγνωσις) which alone accords with, or is in keeping with, the image of God in man. So it is not the original image of God, lost by sin and recovered by grace, that is contemplated in these texts. It is an old habit of sin, which may become in us a kind of second nature beclouding and defiling the image of the Creator, that is to be put away; and it is a new life and habit of righteousness that is to be put on as the only becoming clothing of one who bears God's image in the constitution of his spiritual nature.

So far as this interpretation of the image of God may be supposed to affect other doctrines it should be observed further that one may stoutly affirm "the corruption of the nature of every man, that naturally is engendered of the offspring of Adam, whereby man is very far gone from original righteousness," and at the same time as stoutly maintain that he still bears in the constituent elements of his spiritual nature and personality the image of God in which he was created, and by which he is distinguished above all other creatures upon the earth. There is not a word in the texts of Ephesians and Colossians, here under discussion, that can be fairly made to teach that man has lost God's image through Adam's transgression. In the Ephesian text there is no mention of the "image," and in Colossians it is a "renewal unto knowledge" that is chiefly emphasized. The great change involved in this renewal is of the nature of a new creation rather than the restoration of something that had been lost. In commenting on Col. iii, 9, 10, J. A. Beet observes that the change from the old into the new man is "so complete that the man himself as he formerly was is spoken of as an old garment laid aside, as though personality itself were changed. . . . The new life is represented as one definite assumption of a character which henceforth is gradually progressing. The word *renewed* does not necessarily mean restoration to a former state. The aim of the renewal is to bring us into full knowledge. *The image of him that created him* is an outward manifestation of the inward reality of God. It is the nature of God as set before the eyes of men. The story of creation teaches that the Creator is himself the archetype of his intelligent creatures. He knows perfectly what he has made, and Paul says that this divine knowledge is a pattern of the knowledge which this renewal aims to impart to men. Knowledge is the aim of the renewal, and the Creator is its pattern; therefore the knowledge aimed at must be a human counterpart of the Creator's infinite knowledge. As the renewal makes progress, we shall in greater measure share God's knowledge of all that he has made and done."

(3) *Interpretation of Wisdom ii, 23.* The author of the apocryphal Wisdom of Solomon (ii, 23) expresses what may be regarded as his interpretation of Gen. i, 26, 27:

> God created man for incorruption,
> And made him an image of his own proper nature.

Instead of the text here followed some manuscripts read ἀιδιότης, *eternity, instead of* ἰδιότης, *peculiar* and *proper nature,* and some Jewish writers held that the image of God in man consists in his incorruptible and immortal nature. But ἰδιότης appears to be the better reading, and points to the incorruptible spiritual nature which is conceived as alike in God and man. Other manuscripts read "image of his own likeness" (ὁμοίωσις; Vulg. *similitudo*). But none of these readings give us a very clear or satisfactory idea of what the writer understood by the proper nature or the likeness of God. The interpretation is as indefinite as the biblical texts themselves in which the phrase, "image of God," is found.

(4) *Spiritual Personality.* In the light of the statement of John iv, 24, that "God is Spirit," we dismiss at once the thought of finding the real image of God in any bodily form. Such an idea, according to Paul in Acts xvii, 24-29, naturally leads to the idolatry of images "graven by art and device of man." His higher concept of God is that of a personal intelligence, invisible, incorruptible, immortal, "dwelling in light unapproachable, whom no man hath seen, nor can see" (1 Tim. i, 17; vi, 16). We accordingly should look for the image of God in those essential elements of spiritual life which are perceptible in the personality of the spirit of man. As the Spirit of God searches and knows all things, so in its own limited range, the spirit of man may know many deep things of God, and "things of the Spirit of God" that have been freely given us of God (1 Cor. ii, 10-14). The study of our inner spiritual life acquaints us with the unmistakable facts of intelligent personal agency. The operations of the human soul in self-conscious intellection, sensibility, and will, exhibit man in his most godlike possibilities, and herein we recognize the essential elements of the image of God in him. These constitute him a being capable of fellowship with God, and account for his rational, moral, and religious nature. Lower orders of being show some form and measure of faith, hope, and love; but in mankind only do we perceive these powers of the spirit exalted into rational permanence and glory. In these heavenly powers and possibilities we behold man made a little lower than God, and crowned with a glory and honor far above all other works of the Creator. This lofty conception of the image of God in man shows why it is that he "has dominion over every living thing that moves upon the earth." The "dominion" is not the image, but it is a reflection and a result of the godlike in man which qualifies him for his headship of the creation.

SECTION SECOND

THE SINFULNESS OF MAN

CHAPTER I

THE FACT AND THE NATURE OF HUMAN SINFULNESS

1. The Awful Fact of Sin. The godlike qualities of spirituality, in which we recognize the image and likeness of the Creator in man, must receive due attention and emphasis in order to understand the biblical doctrine of sin. For sin appears to be no necessary part or quality of the nature of man. We find it to be rather a defilement of the image of God in man. And in proportion as we hold a high concept of man made and existing in the image of God, so are we likely to hold a profound conviction of the awful culpability of marring the heavenly likeness by willful transgression. It is a matter of fact that sin has entered into the world, and is as widespread as is the human race itself. It is a persistent evil too deeply rooted and too terrible to be ignored. The Scriptures represent it as a curse and an unspeakable calamity. The psalmists of Israel describe it as a universal bane.

> Jehovah looked down from heaven upon the children of men,
> To see if there were any acting wisely,
> Seeking after God;
> They all have turned aside;
> They have together become filthy;
> No one is doing good, not even one. Psa. xiv, 2, 3.

> If thou, O Jah, shouldst mark iniquities,
> O Lord, who could stand? Psa. cxxx, 3.

> Enter not into judgment with thy servant;
> For in thy sight no man living is righteous. Psa. cxliii, 2.

The prophets are equally pronounced, and they set forth the sins of men in darkest colors. "Ah, sinful nation," says Isaiah (i, 4), "a people laden with iniquity, a seed of evil-doers, children that deal corruptly! they have forsaken Jehovah, they have despised the Holy One of Israel, they are estranged backward."

"Jehovah hath a controversy with the inhabitants of the land," cries Hosea (iv, 1), "because there is no truth, nor kindness, nor knowledge of God in the land. There is nought but swearing and breaking faith, and killing, and stealing, and committing adultery." "All Israel have transgressed thy law," says Daniel (ix, 11), "even turning aside, that they should not obey thy voice." Such questions as that of Prov. xx, 9, presuppose the answer of a universal negative: "Who can say, I have made my heart clean, I am pure from my sin?" The teachings of Jesus presuppose the universality of human sinfulness, and affirm its source in the heart (comp. Matt. iv, 18, 19; xii, 34-35). Paul's doctrine is that all mankind are under the power of sin (Rom. iii, 9, 23; v, 12), and in Gal. iii, 22, he makes use of the bold statement that "the scripture hath shut up all things under sin." According to 1 John i, 8 and 10, any one who declares "that we have no sin," or "that we have not sinned," deceives himself, utters falsehood, and makes Jesus Christ a liar.

2. Depravity of the Race. Furthermore, according to the Scriptures, a sort of taint and corruption of the moral nature originated with the first human pair, and has been universally propagated in the world. We are accustomed to call this general tendency to sin a common inheritance of depravity, and many consider this depravity congenital with every one that is born of flesh and blood. But no special dogmatic significance should be attached to those poetical statements of psalmists and prophets which portray the wicked as "going astray as soon as they are born, speaking lies" (Psa. lviii, 3). Nevertheless, these hyperboles evince a current popular recognition of congenital depravity (comp. Psa. li, 5), and the words of Jer. xvii, 9, although highly rhetorical, are evidently intended to express a general fact: "The heart is deceitful above all things, and it is desperately diseased." The prophet only affirms what all experience and observation confirm. But none of the scriptures of this class teach that the universal depravity is an inheritance transmitted from the first human sinner; much less that the guilt of Adam's transgression has been imputed to his posterity so as to expose them to eternal punishment. This is a fiction of scholastic speculation.

(1) *Depicted in Genesis.* This depravity and general tendency to transgression are depicted in bold outline in the book of Genesis. Cain, the first born of Adam and Eve, is a murderer, and all his descendants seemed to run into violence and crime. A more hopeful new departure is indicated in the line of Seth, but they also in time fell into similar ungodliness, "and Jehovah saw that the wickedness of man was great in the earth, and every imagination

of the thoughts of his heart was only evil continually" (Gen. vi, 5), and he destroyed man from off the face of the earth by a flood of waters. A new series of generations begins with the sons of Noah, but they also ran into evil, and out of the increasing idolatry and wickedness Abram was called to beget a righteous seed. But subsequent history shows how the descendants of Abraham perverted their way, and were finally cast off as having failed to realize the divine ideal of a holy nation and people.

(2) *Paul's dark Picture in Romans i, 18-32.* The same fact is further shown in the dark picture which Paul gives in Rom. i, 18-32, of the apostasy and degeneracy of the human race. The Jew being no exception to this general fact, he concludes that "all are under sin" (iii, 9, 23), and cites various psalms and prophets in proof of his statements (iii, 10-18). We should observe, however, that the apostle here simply portrays the awful fact of the "ungodliness and unrighteousness of men." He describes the actual transgressions of those who had known God, but who, because of personal disobedience and consequent blindness of heart, had been given over by way of judgment to vile passions. But such universal depravity becomes in its way a means and occasion of perpetuating sin in the world. Man's sensuous nature in the midst of such corrupt environment quite naturally brings forth "a reprobate mind."

(3) *Great Antithesis in Romans v, 12-19.* The great antithesis of representative acts of Adam and Christ, in Rom. v, 12-19, is based upon the fundamental assertion that "through one man sin entered into the world, and death through sin; and so death passed unto all men, for that all sinned." Further on Paul says (ver. 15): "By the trespass of the one the many died," and in verse 19, "Through the one man's disobedience the many were made sinners." The entire passage presents a profound conception, peculiar to Paul, of humanity as sprung from one source and receiving thereby a common judgment of condemnation.[1] But the great antithesis becomes misleading when interpreted in the way of historical or of personal realism. It is only in a mystical sense, or as a hypo-

---

[1] This famous passage has been pressed too far in the interests of polemical dogma. The antithesis is designed to magnify the grace of God in Christ by showing that the grace more than counterbalances the facts of sin and death as they appear in the history of man. "Death passed unto all men, for that all sinned." The first man was not the only sinner; nor can Adam be guilty of the crimes of Cain, or of Jezebel, or of Judas Iscariot. Neither can any child of Adam be held guilty of his sin, or responsible for his transgression. So far as "through the disobedience of the one man the many were set down as sinners, so also through the obedience of the one shall the many be set down as righteous" (Rom. v, 19). Hence the entire race of man is under grace. No child of Adam ever has lived or will live apart from this provision of grace. But this fact does not remove the fact of the universal sinfulness of man. Comp. Ritschl, Rechtfertigung und Versöhnung, vol. iii, pp. 326-330.

thetical concept, that all men may be said to have been represented in the first typical sinner. After the manner of Heb. vii, 10, one may conceive all mankind as seminally existing in the first representative man, and it accords with Paul's rabbinic training and mystic idealism that in his favorite contrast of the first and the last Adam he should give a similar expression to his lofty and farreaching generalization. We find him employing the same sort of mystical expression in Rom. vi, 4, 6; 2 Cor. v, 14; Gal. ii, 20; Col. iii, 1-3, where he speaks of being crucified, dead, buried, and risen with Christ. Such language and concepts are not to be construed into literal dogmatic propositions.

3. Hebrew and Greek Words Indicating Nature of Sin. The general fact of human sinfulness is too conspicuous to call for elaborate statement or proof. But the real nature of sin requires detailed analysis and exposition. An interesting light is thrown upon the subject by a study of the various words employed in the Scriptures to designate the manifold ways in which sinful actions are conceived. One of the most common terms used in the Old Testament to denote the act of sinning is חטא, which means primarily to *miss the mark* (see Judg. xx, 16). The Greek ἁμαρτάνω expresses the same thought, and the figure implied in these words suggests a moral standard which one has failed to reach. The sinner, accordingly, is one who has missed some divinely appointed mark, and is therefore guilty of a reprehensible failure, an error, the coming short of the divine ideal. Another word of similar suggestiveness is עבר, which means to *cross over*, and, when employed metaphorically, denotes the crossing of some line of moral obligation, as the violation of a covenant, or the transgression of a commandment. The same idea belongs to the Greek word παραβαίνω, to *pass over* a defined limit and so commit a transgression (παράβασις). Closely akin in signification is παραπίπτω, to *fall* or *turn aside from* the right path, to err. There is also the word παρακοή, *hearing amiss*, followed generally by an unwillingness to hear and consequent disobedience. The two related words פשע and רשע present two aspects of mischief-making transgression, the first denoting more particularly *revolt*, or rebellion, the latter adding to this the idea of great *disturbance*, or *agitation*. This latter appears in the striking statement of Isa. lvii, 20: "The wicked (הרשעים, *the restless disturbers*, who have made themselves abnormal) are like the troubled sea; for it cannot rest, and its waters cast up mud and mire." The word רע denotes *evil* of any kind, and coming from a root which means to *break* suggests, when applied to moral evil, the wreck and ruin of the moral nature. The word און, commonly translated *iniquity*, often *vanity*, indicates the emptiness of all sinful pursuits, and the deceitful and disappointing character of an ungodly life. The two words עָוֶן and עָוֶל supplement each other in designating the inward and outward perversity of sinfulness. The moral *distortion* of a depraved soul is denoted by both of these terms, but the one points rather to what the sinner *is* in his heart and life, the other to what he *does* in outward visible acts. The word ἀνομία means lawlessness, which may be in the first place a direct violation of law, and then pass into contempt of moral law, and also comprehend all disconformity to law. The two words κακία and πονηρία denote the inner and outer aspects of wickedness when developed in an evil heart and life so that the entire moral nature has become depraved and debased. A still broader view of sin is furnished by a study of the numerous crimes, vices, lusts, inordinate passions and follies attributed to wicked men. It is sufficient for our purpose to refer to the enumeration of the "works of the flesh" found in Gal. v, 19, 20: "Fornication, uncleanness, lasciviousness, idolatry, sorcery, enmities, strife, jealousies, wrath, factious divisions, dissensions of party strife, envying, drunkenness, revelings, and the like of these." In Col. iii, 5, we find the mention of "passion, evil desire, and covetousness which is idolatry." These things, it is said, draw down on the guilty ones the penal wrath of God. In verses 8 and 9 are added "anger, raging passion, malice, slanderous railing, shameful speaking and falsehood against one another." All these are in a general way comprehended under the prohibitions of the decalogue. Portraying as they do the various forms in which sin shows itself in actual life, these words of the Hebrew and Greek scriptures are helpful in describing the nature of sin, and showing how it defiles the spiritual image of God in man.

4. Sin Conceived as Transgression and Lawlessness. If we attempt a synthesis of the chief points in our study of the Hebrew and Greek words for *sin,* we shall find that human sinfulness is conceived as primarily the transgression of a good and holy law. Transgression involves more than open, willful acts of wickedness. According to 1 John iii, 4, "sin is lawlessness" (ἀνομία). This *anomia* includes not only actual transgressions, but all contempt of law and all disconformity to law which involves any measure of blame or any departure from the perfect standard of righteousness. And the "law," in the deepest and truest sense, takes cognizance not only of outward acts, but also of the thoughts and intents of the heart. It searches the emotions, the desires, and all that enters into the moral life of man. Any imperfection which involves opposition to the law, or is a result of sinful action, must fall under the head of *anomia,* and be regarded as exposing one to some measure of condemnation. "All unrighteousness (ἀδικία) is sin" (1 John v, 17). And all such transgression and disconformity to the right must needs place the sinner in a state of separation from God. For the law of God in its highest meaning is but a revelation of the Holy One himself, and any disconformity thereto involves estrangement from God.

5. Sin Conceived as Selfishness. Sin is also to be considered as being in its real essence and nature an impious form of selfishness. The persistent sinner puts himself in the place of his Creator and so begets rebellion and disorder in the moral world. For he "exchanges the truth of God for a lie, and worships and serves the creature rather than the Creator" (Rom. i, 25). Thus he becomes a man of lawlessness and ruptures the moral world. In a very noteworthy way the willful, self-centered sinner makes himself "a man of sin, a son of perdition," a personality who "opposeth and exalteth himself against all that is called God or that is worshipped; so that he sitteth in the temple of God, setting himself forth as God" (2 Thess. ii, 3, 4). These words, apart from any particular designation or description of a person intended by the apostle in the passage cited, are peculiarly well adapted to describe any intense sinner who makes himself an incarnation of selfishness and self conceit. They portray the extremes to which a human soul may go in daring forms of impiety, and they show how one made in the image of God may presume to usurp the throne and temple of the Most High. "The covetousness which is idolatry" (Col. iii, 5) has its sources of inspiration and power in selfishness. One can therefore hardly controvert the proposition of Hopkinsianism that the essence of all sin is selfishness.[1]

6. Concept of Spiritual Blindness. We obtain a further concept of the nature of sin in those biblical texts which speak of it as a blindness of the heart and of the mind. In 2 Cor. iv, 4, mention is made of perishing and unbelieving persons whose minds the god of this world had so blinded "that the light of the gospel of the glory of Christ, who is the image of God, should not dawn upon them." So they are conceived as groping under a heavy veil of darkness. So also in 1 John ii, 11, it is written that "he that hateth his brother is in the darkness, and walketh in the darkness, and knoweth not whither he goeth, because the darkness hath

---

[1] Sin consists in self-love. . . . This is in its own nature opposite to all virtuous, holy affection, to all truth and reason; and it is of a criminal nature, in every degree of it, wherever it is found. . . . Self-love pays a supreme and sole regard to an infinitely small and inconsiderable part of existence and the feeling and language of all the exercises of it is, "I am, and there is none else!" There is no other being worthy of any regard, but *myself*.—Samuel Hopkins, System of Doctrines contained in Divine Revelation, vol. i, p. 348. Boston, 1793.

blinded his eyes." Jesus made a forceful use of this figure in what he said about the simple and the evil eye. "If thine eye be evil, thy whole body shall be full of darkness" (Matt. vi, 23). The evil eye is here to be understood as a diseased, distorted, injured eye, the figure of a perverted mind which prefers darkness to light. Such a damaging of the powers of reason is a sad blemish of the image of God in man, for "God is light, and in him is no darkness at all" (1 John i, 5). The word πώρωσις, which conveys the idea of dull perception and loss of spiritual discernment, suggests the same idea of mental blindness. Jesus was grieved over the callous state of the hearts of the Pharisees (Mark iii, 5), which was the result of their spiritual blindness, and Paul admonished the Ephesians (iv, 18) against the vanity of the mind of the Gentiles who are "darkened in their understanding, being alienated from the life of God, because of the ignorance that is in them, on account of the callous blindness of their heart."

7. Concept of Guilt. In connection with the various forms in which sin manifests itself among men there is also the sense or concept of personal guilt. This comes to the consciousness of every sinner charged with such acts of wickedness, because he knows that the wrong act was the product of his own free will. It is because the sin is in him and of him as the responsible author of his own acts that his reason and conscience accuse him (comp. Rom. ii, 15).

(1) *The Fact Explained.* The fact of guilt has its explanation in man's moral freedom. The power of the will to accept or reject an offered good, to keep or violate a given law, is a fundamental fact of man's spiritual nature. It is implied in every commandment, warning, admonition, rebuke, and invitation to accept the mercy of God.

(2) *Significance of αἰτία.* The use of the New Testament word *αἰτία, cause,* has a very significant relation to the concept of guilt. The fault or crime of which a man is held guilty is thought of as the cause or reason of penalty to be assigned. Observe this usage of the word in John xviii, 38; xix, 4, 6; Acts xiii, 28; xxviii, 18. There is thus indicated the relation of cause and effect between the will, in whose free action the crime is supposed to originate, and the crime itself, which the moral sense of mankind ascribes to the convicted criminal as the responsible cause and author of his own wicked deed. And so in all criminal jurisprudence, when penalty is to be decreed, the author of the crime is sought out and condemned as the guilty *cause* of the evil.

(3) *Significance of ἔνοχος.* We also find the concept of guilt in the Greek word ἔνοχος, applied to one *held in* some bond of obli-

gation or desert. In Matt. xxvi, 66, and Mark xiv, 64, it denotes one's *liability* to the death penalty. In 1 Cor. xi, 27, one who comes to the Lord's table in an unworthy manner "is *guilty* of the body and the blood of the Lord." In Mark iii, 29, the man who blasphemes against the Holy Spirit is said to be *"held fast bound in* eternal sin." The same thought of personal responsibility is involved in the use of the word in Matt. v, 21, 22, where the sinner is said to be justly *liable* to the judgment of the gehenna of fire. Similar is the meaning of ὑπόδικος in Rom. iii, 19. The whole world is so brought under condemning judgment as to owe satisfaction to God for its wrongdoing, and is accordingly *liable* to punishment before him.

(4) *Guilt even in Errors of Ignorance.* Guilt is also the main idea in the Hebrew word אשם. In Lev. iv, 13, it is used in connection with שגה which means to *go astray:* "If the whole congregation err through ignorance, and the matter be hidden from the eye of the assembly, and they have done with one of all the commandments of Jehovah what should not have been done, and *have become guilty."* So even if one go astray unawares, as soon as he discovers his error he feels a consciousness of guilty shortcoming. In the stern exactions of the righteousness of the law ignorance does not excuse the transgressor, but when the sin becomes known a sense of guilt and of personal accountability arises and requires acknowledgment in the אשם, *guilt-offering.* But how much deeper must be the sense of guilt when flagrant sins have been committed? An example is to be seen in Ezekiel's word against "the bloody city," full of abominations: "Thou art become guilty in thy blood that thou hast shed, and art defiled in thine idols which thou hast made" (xxii, 4).

8. Degrees of Guilt and Sin. Different degrees of sin and guilt are recognized in the Scriptures and in the moral sense of mankind. For sin becomes deepened and strengthened in the heart by continuous disobedience and resistance of the calls of God. Degrees of guilt are estimated according to the position, the knowledge of what is right, the personal ability, and the relative responsibility of individuals and of communities. In the teaching of Jesus it is declared as a truth beyond question that "the servant who knew his lord's will, and made not ready nor did according to his will, shall be beaten with many stripes; but he that knew not, and did things worthy of stripes, shall be beaten with few stripes. And to whomsoever much is given, of him shall much be required: and to whom they commit much, of him will they ask the more" (Luke xii, 47, 48). It is also affirmed, in Matt. x, 15, that it will be more tolerable for sinners like those of Sodom and Gomorrah in the day of judgment than for those of the city which rejects the message of the gospel. Jesus also spoke to Pilate of the "greater sin" of those who had delivered him over into his hands (John xix, 11). Pilate's sin was great because of the power and authority which were "given him from above." Power to release or to crucify involved heavy responsibility, and to order the death of one in whom he declared he could find no crime was itself a criminal misuse of official authority; but greater still was the sin of those who had been given more abundant evidences of the blamelessness of Jesus, and who nevertheless clamored for his blood.

(1) *Hardening the Heart.* When a person made in the image of God and gifted with normal powers of understanding, of feeling, and of volition deliberately rejects the truth and impiously persists in disobedience, he inevitably begets within his own moral nature a culpable obduracy. Such obduracy is obviously an aggravated form of sinfulness, and deserves a correspondingly severe condemnation. Hence the many warnings of the Scriptures against hardening the heart. The most notable biblical example of such obduracy is that of Pharaoh, as detailed in the ten chapters of Exodus extending from iv to xiv. Three different Hebrew words are employed to describe the hardening, and there are, altogether, twenty passages in which the hardening is mentioned.[1] In ten of these the hardening is attributed to Jehovah; in six it is merely stated that the heart of Pharaoh became hard or was heavy, and in four places he is said to have hardened his own heart. Nothing of importance attaches to the mere number of times any one of these words occurs. The plain import of the whole description is that, by a perverse resistance of Jehovah's demand to let Israel go, the king's heart became stubborn, and his obstinacy grew more and more culpable. In the vivid and graphic portraitures of the Hebrew writers God is conceived as intensely immanent in all human affairs, and events are often ascribed to him without any attempt at a philosophical analysis of the particular facts involved. But a collation and study of all the statements in the case of Pharaoh and of other relevant teachings of the Scriptures warrant the following conclusions: (1) The hardening of the heart of any sinner is the result of a procedure in which both divine and human agency must be recognized. (2) The process of hardening may be properly said to begin with

---

[1] חזק, to *be strong*, occurs in iv, 21; vii, 13, 22; viii, 19; ix, 12, 35; x, 20, 27; xi, 10; xiv, 4, 8, 17. קשה, to *be hard*, occurs in vii, 3; xiii, 15; כבד, to *be heavy* in vii, 14; viii, 15, 32; ix, 7, 34; x, 1. In xiv, 17 the expression is "the heart of the Egyptians"; but as Pharaoh may be included, we include this text with the others.

some word or manifestation of God to the sinner. For as without law there can be no transgression, so there can be no rejection of light and no hardening of the heart without some foregoing revelation of divine truth. (3) When the revelation and claims of God are made known to a man and he deliberately rejects them, hardness of heart necessarily follows as by a law of our moral nature; and the hardening may therefore be attributed either to God or to the man, according as our thought turns, on the one side, to those divinely ordered conditions under which the individual must either obey or disobey, or, on the other side, to the free and responsible act of the man himself.

(2) *Blasphemy against the Holy Spirit.* The most aggravated manner and degree of sin mentioned in the Scriptures is a settled and unchangeable obduracy of spirit which blasphemously rejects the witness of superior light and truth. In 1 John v, 16, there is mention of a "sin unto death," concerning which the writer does not advise that one should make request. But the nature of the sin referred to is not explained, and it is not said that the sin is absolutely unpardonable. There seems to be an allusion to Num. xv, 30, where the case of a soul that commits offense "with a high hand," thereby "blaspheming Jehovah," despising his word and breaking his commandments, is specified as guilty of capital crime. Such a daring sinner was to be "utterly cut off from among his people." But the "sin unto death" in John's epistle seems to refer not to a public offense that demands the penalty of physical death, but some deeper sin of the soul which involves its hopeless perdition. The reference is probably to some form or kind of sinning rather than to any one particular act of sin. Greater definiteness and importance attach to those passages in the synoptic gospels where Jesus speaks of the blasphemy against the Holy Spirit which shall never be forgiven (Matt. xii, 31, 32; Mark iii, 28-30; Luke xii, 10). There is an explicit distinction made in these texts between the unpardonable blasphemy and all other sins, especially "speaking a word against the Son of man." The words of Jesus were occasioned by the charge of the Pharisees and scribes that he cast out demons by the help of Beelzebub, and hence some have supposed that this particular act of blasphemy against the Lord Jesus was itself the unpardonable sin. But if we maintain the distinction made by Jesus himself, we shall most naturally understand the daring blasphemy of the scribes to be what is meant by "speaking against the Son of man." Jesus uttered his warning "because they said, He hath an unclean spirit" (Mark iii, 30). This absurd charge was not itself the unpardonable blasphemy, but the occasion of Jesus's warning. Such bitter speaking against the

Son of man might be forgiven, but if repeated and persisted in against all reason it would inevitably fasten upon the heart an unchangeable hardness and blasphemous rejection of all possible influences of the Holy Spirit. Hence we understand the unpardonable blasphemy against the Holy Spirit to be the final culmination and fatal result of such defiant resistance to the truth as the sin of the Pharisees on that occasion involved. And this exposition finds additional confirmation in the true text of Mark iii, 29: "Whosoever shall blaspheme against the Holy Spirit hath never forgiveness, but is guilty of (ἔνοχος, *held fast in*) an eternal sin." He thus consummates such obduracy and consequent incapacity for obedience to the truth that no change is possible in the nature of things. His blasphemy is unpardonable, not because God is unwilling to save him, but because he has made himself incapable of meeting the conditions of the salvation of Christ.

(3) *Doctrine of Hebrews vi, 4-8 and x, 26, 27.* The same doctrine of a fixed habit of willful rejection of God's truth, resulting in the consummation of an unchangeably perverse character, appears also in Heb. vi, 4-8, and x, 26, 27. The first of these passages states that "as for those who were once enlightened and tasted of the heavenly gift, and were made partakers of the Holy Spirit, and tasted the good word of God, and the powers of the age to come, and then fell away, it is impossible to renew them again unto repentance; seeing they crucify to themselves the Son of God afresh, and put him to an open shame." We should note that in the last clause the two verbs translated "crucify afresh" and "put to open shame" are, in the Greek text, participles in the present tense, and show the ground or reason of the impossibility affirmed. It is impossible to renew them because they keep right on continually crucifying the Son of God, and so holding him up to infamy. The passage in x, 26, 27, says: "If we sin willfully after that we have received the knowledge of the truth, there remaineth no more a sacrifice for sins, but a certain fearful expectation of judgment, and a fierceness of fire which shall devour the adversaries." Here, too, the hopelessness of the willful sinner's condition is in the absence of any further provisions for his salvation from the devouring penal fire. No more is there in his case a sacrifice for sins remaining. The fearfulness of the sin contemplated in these passages appears, therefore, to consist essentially in the three considerations, (1) that the sinner had been favored with a high state of enlightenment and a full knowledge of the truth; (2) that he willfully rejected the light and fell away from the means and ministries of grace; and (3) that he

persistently closes the door of hope upon himself, keeps crucifying Christ afresh, and daringly accepts the consequences and the "fearful expectation of judgment." Such an aggravated extreme of sinfulness presupposes a large amount of light and revelation from God, so that its consummation passes beyond a *grieving* of the Holy Spirit (Eph. iv, 30) and becomes an utter *quenching* of the Spirit (1 Thess. v, 19).

(4) *Other Biblical Testimony.* Numerous other scriptures witness to the degrees of sin and guilt, and the extremes to which willful disobedience may be carried. In the highly wrought language of Prov. i, 24-31, divine Wisdom makes her appeal to those who set at naught all her counsel, and warns them that their continuous and contemptuous rejection of her words will inevitably place the sinner beyond the reach of divine mercy. Jeremiah's address to the people of Jerusalem (vii, 12-16) teaches the same solemn lesson; and what is true of such a community as a whole is true of every individual guilty of the same persistent wickedness. When the moral and spiritual nature of a man has become corrupted by such persistent sinning, and his clearest convictions of truth have become stifled by daring blasphemy, there is superinduced upon his soul a moral obliquity which is of the nature of a judicial penal consequence of such flagrant sinning. The language of Isa. vi, 10, implies an obduracy and blindness to spiritual things resulting in an incapacity to perceive and understand the truth of God: "Make fat the heart of this people, and their ears make heavy, and their eyes besmear, lest they see with their eyes, and hear with their ears, and with their heart understand, and turn, and be healed." This penal blindness was the result of persistent rebellion against the Holy One of Israel. And so we find that in this life the willful sinner works out in part his own penal judgment and is given over to believe a lie (2 Thess. ii, 11, 12). And thus it appears that man, who was originally created upright, and gifted with godlike faculties of reason, love, and will, may abuse and ruin his personal freedom, sear his conscience, and obliterate his moral sense by blasphemous perversity of heart.

CHAPTER II

THE ORIGIN AND THE PERSISTENT CAUSE OF SIN

1. Adequate Cause Must be Sought. Our study of the nature of man and of the nature of sin has prepared the way for a more detailed inquiry into the cause of human sinfulness. The awful fact is distressfully present and open to inspection, but its primeval origin and the conditions and cause of its first appearance in man are matters not so easily determined. We desire to find, if possible, an adequate cause for so great an evil. It would seem that such a cause must have existed from the first moment of the possibility of sin in the world. There is no other creature of whom we have any personal knowledge that is capable of committing sin but man. Hence the necessity of a broad and clearly defined view of the nature of man and the nature of sin in order to an intelligent discussion of the particular subject now before us. No partial or one-sided view of the facts to be accounted for can be allowed, nor should any relevant facts be ignored or set aside. Sin being a fact of our personal experience we should bring all theories of its origin to the test of facts and judgments derived from such experience. Theories or hypotheses which contravene the moral sense and judgment of enlightened people cannot be accepted as satisfactory or worthy of much attention.

2. Inadequate Theories. Accordingly, those theories which attempt an explanation of the origin of sin and yet ignore the sense of personal guilt and the self-condemnation of the sinner can be neither adequate nor satisfactory to one who fairly reckons with all the facts involved. Hence (1) all theories which rest upon the materialistic philosophy must fail to account for the consciousness of guilt just as they fail to account for the real nature of human intelligence and the moral and religious sense. If the soul of man be only an aggregation of attenuated particles of matter, and if these be necessarily fortuitous and temporary in their relations, there is left no ground for the existence of a rational moral sense, and the notion of guilt is but a delusion. Intelligence, sensation, and volition cannot be predicated of matter without giving the lie to the primary facts of observation, experience, and common sense; still less can we affirm of matter the qualities which belong to the spirit and show themselves in ethics and religion. Likewise inadequate is (2) the theory of sensation, which would find the source of sin altogether in the sensuous nature of man. As the child grows out of infancy into self-conscious life and activity, the sensational appetites make their demands, and external *stimuli* compel action in certain ways impossible to be long resisted. Hence all men have become more or less slaves of sensuous instincts and desires. The large element of fact and truth in these statements should be at once conceded. Man has a strong and conspicuous sensuous element in his nature, and that element is the occasion and stimulant of a large proportion of his misdeeds and immoralities. His contact and constant intercourse with the world are realized by means of the senses of touch, taste, sight, hearing, and smelling. In fact, his entire knowledge of the universe is mainly dependent upon the operation of these powers and organs of sensation. But the facts of sensation do not comprehend all the facts of moral action in man, for many of the worst forms of human sinfulness are in no way connected with sensuousness. The blasphemy of the Holy Spirit, which we found to be the most aggravated form of sin, is not a matter of sensuality. All sins of pride and ambition, of hatred and malice and envy, and, especially, deep malignant concentration of bitterness and hostility and scorn toward all that is called God or is an object of religious worship—all these are facts for which the sensuous theory of the origin of sin fails to furnish any adequate explanation. (3) Another theory essays to find the origin of sin in the essential limitations and imperfection of man. It assumes and affirms that, as God is alone the supreme and absolutely good One in the universe, all that is less than he must needs be negatively evil. It must follow that the only real freedom from sin and evil is in a removal of all limitation. The one sufficient reply to this theory is the fact that sin is not the limitation of any natural or normal being. There are, indeed, some sins and infirmities which are called sins of weakness. Limitation and imperfection may involve conditions of sinful action, but sin itself is a willful and needless doing what is wrong, and the self-condemnation of our conscience is inexplicable if such crimes as murder and theft and perjury are only necessary phases of finite being. (4) The same reply fits also that other theory which holds sin to be one of the essential phases of life which appear in the process of human development. All growth and progress in the world, we are told, require the continuous operation of the laws of action and reaction. Life in all its variegated forms is developed by contrasts, and so the spiritual life of man becomes strong by means of struggle for its highest good. So the good that is in us acquires its most admirable elements by contrast with the evil with which it has had to contend for the mastery. But the very statement of this theory ought to show its weakness and insufficiency to account for the origin and persistent cause of sin. The question is not whether struggle against sin develops strength and virtues in the man who contends and triumphs over the evil. That is a simple platitude of the moral life; but is participation in sin an essential part of the struggle? The righteous man, like God himself, may make the wrath of the wicked eventuate in the furtherance of some great good, but not by originating the wrath and the wickedness. This theory tends to destroy all moral distinctions: evil becomes a good thing, and the good cannot attain its goodness without the help of the evil. Truth thus may be primordially indebted to falsehood, and love to hatred and malice. The theory also may be charged with offering a final rather than the originating cause of human sinfulness. It is presumed that its manifestation is to work some highest good of the world and of man, and, so far as this thought is entertained, attention is diverted from the real cause of its origin. Thus the real nature of sin, as willful violation of the right, is ignored, and it is conceived as a mere contrast to what is good, not as bitter and malignant enmity toward truth and righteousness. (5) The hypothesis of dualism affirms the existence of an eternal principle of evil, and has passed through various historic phases. It calls for no further notice here than the observation that it transcends the limits of knowledge so far as to deny that evil ever had a beginning, and it virtually resolves sin into a kind of physical evil inherent in the nature of things. All these theories are invalidated and seen to be inadequate by attention to the two fundamental fallacies common to them all, namely, (a) that of confounding the cause of sin with the finite conditions of human life which furnish the possibility, occasions and motives for sinning, and (b) that of ignoring the real nature of sin and guilt as witnessed by the Scriptures and the universal moral sense of man.

3. Adequate and Actual Cause in Man's Personality. No adequate cause of the sinfulness of man can be shown without due attention to the facts of his moral nature and his bearing the image of God. Whatever is now found to be the cause of man's persistent sinfulness, age after age, that same cause will probably best account for the first sin that ever disturbed the moral world. The real cause of the first sin as of every other subsequent act of sin, is to be sought in the sinner himself. The free, self-conscious, intelligent, deliberate evil-doer is the author of his own wicked deed. The personality of every normal human being consists in the self-conscious unity of intelligence, sensibility, and the power of volition. These are the qualities, as we have previously shown, which exalt man above all other living creatures on the earth, and they stamp him with the image and likeness of God. But he is a finite being, subject to many well-known limitations and conditions. He cannot avoid perceiving things that are presented to his intellectual vision, nor can his sensitive nature help feeling the actual pressure of external *stimuli*. Perception and sensation furnish numerous motives to action, but the deliberate willing of an evil deed is not a matter of compulsion. It is in the power of every intelligent and sensitive person, with temptations and motives for a wrong course of action making powerful impression upon him, to choose the good and refuse the evil. The first sin and all sins that have followed it in human history are traceable to this free and godlike personality in man. He possesses the volitional power of originating moral evil.[1] The universal conscience of mankind affirms this all-important fact, and we must deal with it as one of the necessary truths never to be lost sight of. Our study of the nature of sin and guilt, as presented in the Scriptures, brought us everywhere face to face with the facts of moral obligation and personal responsibility. Not in metaphysical speculation, but in the field of personal consciousness and actual experience, where we can appeal to facts that are beyond controversy, do we find the responsible authorship and origin of sin.

4. Illustrated in Genesis iii. This subject of the originating cause of sin is set forth and illustrated with remarkable clearness in the story of man's first disobedience as recorded in Genesis. That which is written of the woman as being first beguiled and falling into transgression is equally true of the man, and, in all essential elements of temptation and sin, is a most vivid picture of the operation of the emotions, the intellect, and the will. The goodly sight of the forbidden fruit was a stimulus to fleshly appetite, but the external stimulus had no power to compel or determine the action. Its power of stimulation, however, became more intense as the woman saw that the tree was also "a delight to

---

[1] The possibility of evil lies open in any moral beginning which we can conceive. For a moral beginning is a transcendence of the necessity of natural order. Moral freedom is within finite limits a delegation to created being of something of God's power to have life in himself. A life which is thus divine in its essence, although finite in its range, may be a gift of the Creator beyond recall. Moral creation is in a sense a self-limitation of the Creator. Once having trusted nature with this divine gift of self-conscious will, the faithful Creator will keep his trust. Moral personality may fall from its idea, may alienate itself from its source, may possibly sink even in self-degradation beneath the level of conscious intelligence, becoming dead in sin; but it is not a gift of life to be annihilated by a fiat of omnipotence, or to be put back at God's will into its unmoral preëxistence.—Newman Smyth. Christian Ethics, p. 148. New York, 1892.

the eyes, and to be desired to make one wise." Thus the pressure of temptation deepened both upon the senses and upon the intellectual powers, and supplied the motives and conditions of sinful action. There was no sin in the perception that the fruit was good for food and delightful to the eyes. But there was the commandment of God, "Thou shalt not eat of it." Here was an opposite motive and a warning, and there was no power in either class of motives to determine the choice. Another faculty of the soul must decide which motive shall prevail, and that faculty is the free self-determining power of the will. The woman and the man chose the way of transgression and so sinned against God, and the sense of guilt and shame that ensued evinced the fact that they were the responsible authors of their own fall. Whatever the relative intensity of the motive influences brought to bear on each, they both alike transgressed, fell under condemnation of sin, and suffered the penal consequences. In this graphic outline of temptation and failure to resist we may perceive the possibility of sinning in a being who is at the time without moral spot or blemish. The cause, reasons, and conditions of such initial transgression can be clearly apprehended only by the light of an accurate analysis of the constituent elements of man's personality.

5. Same Efficient Cause Apparent in all Sinning. In the continuous experiences of human life we observe innumerable illustrations of man's free and responsible activity. Every separate act of sin in human life and history is explicable after the manner illustrated by the example of the first transgressor. It is noteworthy that in the temptation of Jesus, as recorded in Matt. iv, 1-11, and Luke iv, 1-13, the same threefold manner of motive influences appears which we observe in the record of the woman's temptation in Gen. iii, 6. There were the same appeals to "the lust of the flesh, the lust of the eyes, and the vainglory of life" (1 John ii, 16). These forms of temptation may be so defined as to be in a general way comprehensive of all the motives to evil which appeal to man. No one commits a deliberate act of sin without some motive, but the motive is not the efficient or sufficient cause of the sinful act. It is rather the object, the reason, the occasion, or the condition which prepares the way for volition; the efficient and sole determining cause is in every instance the will of man. His power of volition is proven to be that constituent faculty of his spiritual nature by which he can be lord over all appeals of sensuous appetite or of mental stimulation.

6. Nature of Volitional Freedom. In the nature and activity of the will we observe something notably different and easily distinguishable from desire, inclination, appetite, emotion, and passion[1]; different also from mental perception, thought, reason, judgment, and knowledge. In most cases of personal experience we cannot help feeling and thinking as we do, for there is usually something in the object presented to us that compels us to particular emotion or thought. But such compulsion is not true of the will. In the self-conscious act of volition we observe a power to choose or to refuse, to obey or to disobey. We are conscious of ability to will and to do in a different manner from that to which even a mighty motive may incline us. The intellect and the feelings are subordinate. Sight, hearing, any possible sensation, may necessarily produce conditions of impulse and desire for that which is not good; the moral sense discerns and approves the good, and the intellect perceives, deliberates, estimates. Neither the sensations nor the intelligent perceptions, so far as they supply motives for a possible choice one way or another, are necessarily evil in themselves. They furnish the requisite conditions for the self-determining activity of the will. To refuse the evil and to choose the good is the specific function of volition, and to this self-conscious power of the human soul we trace the originating and the persistent cause of sin. Any supposed compulsion from without or within which destroys this freedom of will and determines its action in one direction with no power to the contrary, reduces moral conduct to a series of mechanical sequences and is inconsistent and irreconcilable with the facts of personal obligation.

7. Other Resultant Facts of Sin. Having fairly traced the origin and cause of sin to the godlike power of volition inherent in man's personality, we should not fail to notice, further, how evil character once formed, miserable conditions of social life, and communal aggregations of vice and criminal depravity become in turn a fearful source of evil. We can not presume to say precisely when, where, and under what formal or actual conditions sin first made its appearance in the world. Omniscience only could make that known. But the facts of sin are very present for our study and we find them to accord most closely with the facts and teachings of the Scriptures on the subject. Probably the origin of sin in the world was facilitated by reason of the comparative imperfection and ignorance of the first generations of men. The once prevalent notion that the first man was perfect in wisdom and knowledge is now quite obsolete. It arose from the assumption that every creation of God must needs have been every-

---

[1] See Whedon's masterly statement of these distinctions, and his definition of the will as against the fallacies of Edwards and others, in his work entitled, The Freedom of the Will as a Basis of Human Responsibility and a Divine Government, pp. 16-20. New York, 1864. Reprint, 1892.

way perfect from the first, and that man himself was the work of a moment of time. We know man only as a being of birth and growth. We know that by laws of heredity parents transmit certain qualities of good or of evil to their offspring. Some are born with a diseased and abnormal constitution, and no wisdom or power of man is capable of removing a prenatal malady. It is also matter of fact that the natural imperfections of childhood furnish occasions for many kinds of sin and folly, and such imperfections are often put forward in extenuation of the offense although admitted to be no real excuse for it. Certain habits of evil-doing and character resulting therefrom become also a fruitful source of sins, just as good habits and excellent character naturally beget the fruits of righteousness. "Each tree is known by its own fruit. For of thorns men do not gather figs, nor of a bramble bush gather they grapes. The good man out of the good treasure of his heart bringeth forth that which is good; and the evil man out of the evil treasure bringeth forth that which is evil" (Luke vi, 44, 45). But in the interpretation of these facts of life and growth we must not forget that character and habits of life are the product of many distinct and successive acts of the will.¹ In the individual life of man we do not find his first sin to be the greatest. It is impossible to determine just when, where, and how the first conscious act of transgression takes place in any one young life. Habits of sinning come by almost imperceptible degrees; and what is thus true in the individual was probably also true in the earliest life of the race. On such a question we do well to refrain from any dogmatic assumptions.

8. Biblical Records of Apostasy. The same cause which accounts for original transgression and for all subsequent acts of wickedness in the history of mankind is also adequate to account for the numerous examples of apostasy which are mentioned in the biblical records. We have seen that the most aggravated form in which sin manifests itself is that settled obduracy which rejects the clearest light of truth, resists all the counsels of love and wisdom, and hardens the heart against all admonition and reproof. It is notably the sin of those who have been enlightened and made partakers of superior revelations of God.

(1) *Israel's Apostasy in the Desert.* The disobedience and apostasy of the Israelites in the wilderness are typical examples. Lawgivers, prophets, psalmists, and apostles hold them up for

---

¹ So Julius Müller: "As the quality of the fruit depends upon the nature of the tree, so the good and evil acts of man depend upon the good or evil state of the heart; but this very state is itself again dependent upon the primary decisions of the will: *Make ye* [ποιήσατε] *the tree good . . . corrupt*" (Matt. xii, 33).— The Christian Doctrine of Sin. Trans. by Urwick, vol. ii, p. 61. Edinburgh, 1868.

religious instruction and for warning. "Because all those men that have seen my glory, and my miracles, which I did in Egypt and in the wilderness, yet have tempted me now these ten times, and have not hearkened to my voice; surely they shall not see the land which I sware unto their fathers, neither shall any of them that despised me see it" (Num. xiv, 22, 23). These words and other scriptures of similar purport inculcate at least four important doctrines so direct and positive as to be treated as so many matters of fact: (1) The most impressive manifestations of God's love and power do not compel the obedience of those who behold them; (2) an evil heart of unbelief is capable of treating all such displays of divine glory with disrespect and scorn; (3) men who have long followed the leadings of God may at last turn and rebel against him; (4) such rebellion is certain to bring condemnation and ruin upon the guilty offenders.

(2) *Examples of Saul, David, Solomon.* Saul, the son of Kish, is represented as a choice young man, and was anointed prince over Israel. The Spirit of Jehovah came upon him and changed him into another man (1 Sam. ix, 2; x, 1, 6). But after many favors of God, and many lessons from the prophet Samuel, he turned back from Jehovah and failed to keep his commandments (xv, 11). David also was highly honored and called a man after God's own heart; but in an hour of temptation he sinned most grievously and even became guilty of the death of Uriah. His son Solomon also began his reign with marked evidences of piety and wisdom; but when he grew old "his wives turned away his heart after other gods" (1 Kings xi, 4). Later examples of unbelief and apostasy among the kings and people of Israel, persisted in against the urgent messages and warnings of the prophets, resulted in national disaster and exile.

(3) *New Testament Admonition and Warning.* The New Testament abounds in warnings and admonitions against apostasy from the living God, and thus inculcates the freedom and responsibility of the individuals addressed. Paul expresses his astonishment that the Galatian converts should so quickly turn away from the gospel of Christ and become bewitched and misled by men who troubled the Church of God (Gal. i, 6, 7; iii, 1). The epistle to the Hebrews is from first to last a continuous admonition for those who had heard the gospel of salvation in Christ, lest they should somehow "drift away from the things that were heard" (Heb. ii, 1). They are warned against "an evil heart of unbelief, in falling away from the living God" (iii, 12). They are reminded of the "provocation in the wilderness," and are exhorted to diligence "that no man fall after the same example of disobedience"

(iv, 11). They are solemnly told that "it is impossible to renew again unto repentance" such as have fallen away from a high attainment of Christian knowledge, "seeing they keep right on crucifying to themselves the Son of God afresh, and putting him to an open shame" (vi, 4-6). Compare also the solemn statements of x, 26-29. The peril of final and remediless apostasy from Christ is assumed in all these alarming appeals, and we are admonished by them that there is lodged in the freedom of the human will the power of breaking away from the highest and holiest good and plunging into the hopeless ruin of a fiery judgment which shall devour the adversaries of God. The last state of those who make such "shipwreck concerning the faith" (1 Tim. i, 19) is worse than the first, and is well set forth in the language of 2 Pet. ii, 20, 21: "For if, after they have escaped the defilements of the world through the knowledge of the Lord and Saviour Jesus Christ, they are again entangled therein and overcome, the last state is become worse with them than the first. For it were better for them not to have known the way of righteousness, than, after knowing it, to turn from the holy commandment delivered unto them." All these and other similar admonitions witness the power and responsibility attaching to human freedom, and the adequacy of that power to account both for the origin and the persistence of sin in the world.

CHAPTER III

DIVERS ASPECTS OF SIN IN THE VARIOUS BIBLICAL WRITERS

1. Defective Moral Standards of Old Testament Times. A noteworthy variety of moral standards, involving as many distinctive conceptions of the nature of sin, may be observed in different parts of the Scriptures. We cannot fail to note the imperfect ethical system witnessed by certain narratives and laws. The examples of polygamy and falsehood among the ancient patriarchs; the laws of slavery as read in Exod. xxi, 4-21, and of divorce in Deut. xxiv, 1; the outrageous cruelties practiced in the times of the judges; the presumptuous daring and immoralities of the kings of Israel and Judah; these and such like are recorded in a manner which implies not only a low moral sense, but also a low moral standard then prevalent among the leaders of the people and in the community at large. Wickedness and transgression are measured, not so much by a profound conception of sin as "exceeding sinful" through the commandment of God (Rom. vii, 13), as by some general notion of disconformity to a conventional standard. The vilest sinners are spoken of as "sons of Belial," good-for-nothing, worthless fellows (Judg. xix, 22; Deut. xiii, 13), who commit "folly in Israel" (Judg. xx, 6). Willful transgression against God is conceived as great foolishness (1 Sam. xiii, 13; 2 Sam. xxiv, 10). The laws of bondage in Exod. xxi, 4-21, and of personal retaliation in Exod. xxi, 23-25; the horrible punishment of Achan visited not on himself only, but on "his sons, and his daughters, and his oxen, and his sheep, and his tent, and all that he had" (Josh. vii, 24); the mutilation of Adoni-bezek (Judg. i, 6), and the hewing of Agag in pieces by Samuel (1 Sam. xv, 33), are witnessing examples of the relative barbarism which had the supposed sanction of divine law among the people of Israel. The prevalence of such ideas and practices implies a notable lack of fine moral distinctions and a corresponding imperfection in the concept of sin.

2. Imprecatory Psalms. The same is to be said of the spirit which finds expression in the imprecatory psalms.

> Hold them guilty, O God;
> Let them fall by their own counsels;

> In the multitude of their transgressions thrust them out;
> For they have rebelled against thee. Psa. v, 10.
>
> Let their eyes be darkened that they see not;
> And make their loins continually shake.
> Pour out upon them thine indignation,
> And let the fierceness of thine anger overtake them.
> Let their encampment be desolate;
> In their tents let there not be a dweller. Psa. lxix, 23-25.
>
> Set thou a wicked man over him,
> And let an adversary stand at his right hand.
> When he is judged, let him come forth guilty;
> And let his prayer be turned into sin.
> Let his children be fatherless,
> And his wife a widow.
> Let his children be vagabonds and beg;
> And let them seek (their bread) out of their desolate places.
> Let the extortioner catch all that he hath;
> And let strangers make spoil of his labor,
> Let there be none to extend kindness to him;
> Neither let there be any to have pity on his fatherless children.
> Let his posterity be cut off;
> In the generation following let their name be blotted out.
>   Psa. cix, 6-13.
>
> O daughter of Babylon that art to be destroyed;
> Happy shall he be that requiteth thee
> The reward which thou hast rewarded us.
> Happy he who shall seize and dash thy infant children
> Against the rock. Psa. cxxxvii, 8, 9.

The vindictive spirit of these psalms, like Elijah's commanding fire to come down from heaven and consume those sent against him (2 Kings i, 10, 12), belongs to an inferior plane of moral sense as compared with the ideals of Jesus when he rebuked his disciples for the manifestation of a similar feeling (Luke ix, 54, 55), and when he inculcated love for enemies and persecutors (Matt. v, 44). Wherever such defective standards of moral sentiment control, there must necessarily be some lack of keen spiritual insight in the prevailing conceptions of the real nature of sin. The imprecatory psalms accord with the spirit and the letter of the legislation of Exod. xxi, 24, 25, rather than with the gospel of our Lord Jesus. The *lex talionis* has its element of righteousness, but is superseded by the higher lessons of the golden rule.

3. Public and National Sins Overshadow the Individual. The national life and theocratic spirit of the Jewish people tended to absorb the individual in the state, and thus to exalt the idea of public righteousness. The solidarity and perpetuity of the nation were of unspeakably greater importance than any interest of a single and separate person. It is no wonder, then, that the sins of individuals were at times lost sight of in the presence of glaring national wrongs, and public calamities were regarded as sure evidences of the wrath of God against the people as a whole. In harmony with this it was also easy to believe that the sins of the fathers were "visited upon the children, and upon the children's children, upon the third and upon the fourth generation" (Exod. xxxiv, 7). Hence, too, the burden of the messages of the prophets had reference mainly to public affairs, to national sins, and to the failure of the people of Israel as a chosen nation to keep the commandments of their God. Hosea bitterly complains that Israel has "played the harlot," and vilely forsaken Jehovah her God by sacrificing and burning incense to other gods (i, 2; iv, 12; ix, 1). Isaiah arraigns Jerusalem and her rulers in language which emphasizes the public character of their wickedness: "How is the faithful city become a harlot! she that was full of judgment! righteousness lodged in her, but now murderers. Thy silver is become dross, thy wine mixed with water. Thy princes are rebellious, and companions of thieves; every one loveth gifts and followeth after rewards: they judge not the fatherless, neither doth the cause of the widow come unto them" (Isa. i, 21-23). Amos appears as a great preacher of righteousness, and the sins and cruelties which he condemns are conspicuously such as give infamous character to a people. He will not turn back Jehovah's voice of judgment which roars out of Zion against the many transgressions of Damascus, Gaza, Ammon, Moab, Judah, and Israel, and he specifies such acts of cruelty as crushing helpless prisoners under threshing instruments of iron, and grinding the life out of the poor and needy by heartless oppression.

4. Divorcing Morality and Public Service. This prophetic exposure and condemnation of national sins naturally led to public fasting with its accompanying signs of humiliation and contrition. All this in conjunction with the elaborate ritual of public sacrifice and priestly ministrations had the effect of dulling the individual conscience, and of sinking the sense of personal responsibility into a sort of fusion with that of the people as a corporate solidarity. Individual sins were thus lost sight of when one's valor and wisdom advanced the public weal. David's despicable crimes were thus condoned by reason of his heroic services for the nation. His uniform loyalty to the highest interests of Israel procured for him, in spite of his sins, the title of "the man after Jehovah's heart," and enthroned him as an idol in the hearts of the people. Similarly the wisdom of Solomon and his successful administration of the kingdom won for him perpetual glory in the history of the nation, notwithstanding all his flagrant sins and idolatry. Such a tendency logically leads to an unconscious divorcing of morality and religion. Worship becomes an outward form rather than a personal matter of the soul; the ministry of a separated priesthood removes the burden of service from one's self to a proxy; religion and ceremony are confounded, and matters involving individual morality become private affairs not amenable to public concern. Under the prevalence of such a discipline the leaven of Pharisaism spread; fine moral distinctions were obliterated; gathering sticks on the sabbath was deemed as great a crime as murder and was punished with the same severity. There was great effort to "cleanse the outside of the cup and of the platter, but within they were full from extortion and excess."

5. Collective Idea of Sin and Penalty. This habit of magnifying the outward forms of religion and morality, and of viewing the nation rather than the individual as the unit of responsibility, would quite naturally overlook the matter of rewards and punishments after the present life. Whatever may have been thought by individual writers, very little on this subject can be found in the Old Testament. When the judgment of God upon the wicked is spoken of the language employed is usually of the vague and general kind which contemplates a collective body of sinners. Thus in Psa. ix, 16, 17:

> Jehovah hath executed judgment;
> Snaring the wicked in the work of his own hands.
> The wicked shall be turned back unto Sheol,
> Even all the nations that forget God.

Even when the individual sinner is designated, the immediate context will often show that his individuality is confounded with the nation of which he forms a part. Thus in Psa. xliii, 1:

> Judge me, O God, and plead my cause against an ungodly nation:
> O deliver me from the deceitful and unjust man.

These psalmists voice that collective and communal idea of national sin and national punishment, which is conspicuous in Hebrew thought. The individual sinner is necessarily included in the concept, and the penal judgment is sometimes expressed as a personal visitation of wrath (comp. Psa. cix, 6-18), but throughout the book of Psalms the more public, national, and collective concept of sinners and their judgment is the most pronounced.

6. Deeper Concepts of Psalms and Prophets. But in the Psalms and the Prophets we also meet with sayings which evince profound conceptions of personal guilt. The so-called penitential psalms (vi; xxxii; xxxviii; li; cii; cxxx; cxliii) abound in sentiments of deep contrition:

> I acknowledge my transgressions,
> And my sin is ever before me.
> Against thee, thee only, have I sinned,
> And done that which is evil in thy sight.
> Hide thy face from my sins,
> And blot out all mine iniquities.
> Create in me a clean heart, O God,
> And renew a right spirit within me.   Psa. li, 3, 4, 9, 10.

The idea expressed in verse 4 of this psalm, that the sin is against God only, is worthy of note. That which gives it its awful guiltiness and curse is not so much the evil it has caused others as the thought that it was done in the very face and eyes of God himself. The "manifold transgressions and mighty sins" (Amos v, 12) of which the prophets speak in detail are in the specifications given necessarily of a personal character, and while they are charged against the "house of Israel" as a whole, they must needs have been often considered in their individual and personal aspects. Moreover, in the great prophets of the eighth century before Christ we find some of the most notable distinctions made between the outward forms of worship and the true devotion of the heart. Hosea thus expresses Jehovah's judgment (vi, 6):

> I desire goodness, and not sacrifice;
> And the knowledge of God more than burnt-offerings.

In Amos v, 21-24, we read the following remarkable deliverance:

> I hate, I despise your feasts,
> And I will take no delight in your solemn assemblies,
> Yea, though ye offer me your burnt-offerings and meal-offerings.
> I will not accept them;
> Neither will I regard the peace-offerings of your fatlings.
> Take thou away from me the noise of thy songs;
> For I will not hear the melody of thy viols.
> But let judgment roll down as waters,
> And righteousness as a perennial stream.

The prophet Micah speaks (vi, 6-8) in a similar way:

> Wherewith shall I come before Jehovah,
> And bow myself before the high God?
> Shall I come before him with burnt-offerings,
> With calves a year old?
> Will Jehovah be pleased with thousands of rams,
> With ten thousands of rivers of oil?
> Shall I give my first-born for my transgression,
> The fruit of my body for the sin of my soul?

> He hath showed thee, O man, what is good;
> And what doth Jehovah require of thee,
> But to do justly, and to love kindness,
> And to walk humbly with thy God?

A still more sweeping word of Jehovah is found in Isa. i, 10-17; and in 1 Sam. xv, 22, is a prophetic utterance which sets the subject in brief yet striking style:

> Hath Jehovah as great delight in burnt-offerings and sacrifices,
> As in obeying the voice of Jehovah?
> Behold, to obey is better than sacrifice,
> And to hearken than the fat of rams.

7. Individual Responsibility in Ezekiel and Jeremiah. But in Ezekiel, and briefly in Jeremiah, we observe an advance in doctrine touching individual responsibility for sins. Jeremiah foretold a coming day when "they shall say no more, The fathers have eaten sour grapes, and the children's teeth are set on edge. But every one shall die for his own iniquity: every man that eateth the sour grapes, his teeth shall be set on edge" (xxxi, 29, 30). Ezekiel (xviii) is much more positive and explicit: "As I live, saith the Lord Jehovah, ye shall not have occasion any more to use this proverb in Israel. Behold, all souls are mine. . . . The soul that sinneth, it shall die: the son shall not bear the iniquity of the father, neither shall the father bear the iniquity of the son; the righteousness of the righteous shall be upon him, and the wickedness of the wicked shall be upon him." This appears as the result of the Deuteronomic teaching (Deut. xxiv, 16), and is recognized in 2 Kings xiv, 6, and 2 Chron. xxv, 4. But although this doctrine of individual responsibility found an emphatic utterance in these Scriptures, it did not supersede the concept of collective and national guiltiness which was so thoroughly inwrought into the religious thought of the Jewish people.

8. Sin as Represented in the Wisdom Books. In the wisdom literature of the Old Testament we meet with detailed portraitures of sin made from the standpoint of the practical observer of men and things. The voice of the accumulated wisdom, understanding, intelligence, knowledge, reflection, and counsel of the good may naturally be expected to express sound doctrine touching human sinfulness and its mischievous workings in private and public life.

(1) *In Proverbs.* In the book of Proverbs wisdom speaks with the authority of God (comp. i, 20-33), and is conceived as the companion of Jehovah before the foundation of the world, and as a master workman, coöperating with him when he constructed the

heavens and the earth (viii, 22-31). When this divine wisdom contemplates the various forms of wickedness which prevail among men and gives judgment as to their real character, we find in her proverbial teaching that all sin is from her point of observation the veriest quintessence of folly. It is an evil which sets on fire the course of nature, and proves itself a noisome bane of human society and civil government.

> His own iniquities shall take the wicked,
> And he shall be holden with the cords of his sin.
> He shall die for lack of instruction;
> And in the greatness of his folly he shall
> go astray. Prov. v, 22, 23.

From every point of view the wicked are virtually the enemies of true wisdom. They are foolish souls, "simple ones," silly, short-sighted, and culpably lacking in discretion and moral sense; they delight in mischief and in forbidden courses of conduct; they become scoffers and take delight in evil counsels; they follow the seductions of the adulterous woman, whose "house is the way to Sheol, going down to the chambers of death" (vii, 27). Such are compelled to confess, when "flesh and body are consumed,

> How have I hated instruction,
> And my heart despised reproof!
> I obeyed not the voice of my teachers,
> Nor inclined mine ear to them that instructed me. Prov. v, 12, 13.

The man who thus despises correction and hates reproof is spoken of as a brutish soul (בער xii, 1), and the evil-doer "is loathsome and bringeth shame" (xiii, 5). His wisdom, if one call it such, is as we read in the epistle of James (iii, 15), "not that which cometh down from above, but is earthly, sensual, demoniacal." In the more public form of its working, "sin is a reproach to peoples" (xiv, 34); and when a wicked man is in power the people groan (xxix, 2). "He that turneth away his ear from hearing the law, even his prayer is an abomination" (xxviii, 9).

The following passage from Prov. vi, 12-19, is a characteristic example of human sinfulness as set forth in this gnomic poetry:

> A worthless person (man of Belial), a man of iniquity,
> Is he that walketh with perversity of mouth:
> Winking with his eyes, talking with his feet,
> Teaching with his fingers;
> Perverseness is in his heart;
> He is devising evil continually;
> He sendeth forth discords.
> Therefore suddenly shall his calamity come;
> On a sudden shall he be broken without remedy.

> These six things Jehovah hateth;
> Yea, seven are the abomination of his soul:
> Haughty eyes, a lying tongue,
> And hands that shed innocent blood;
> A heart that deviseth counsels of iniquity;
> Feet that are swift to run to evil;
> A false witness who will utter lies,
> And he that sends forth discords among brethren.

(2) *In the Book of Job.* The problem of evil, as presented in the book of Job, is not a discussion of the nature of human sinfulness but rather a poetic presentation of the sufferings of a "perfect and upright man, who feared God, and turned away from evil." The author lived at a time when the obvious prosperity of the wicked in certain marked examples stood out in painful contrast to certain notable instances of bitter affliction falling upon the innocent, and prompting inquiry into the reason of such apparent injustice. The speeches of Job and his friends are acknowledged to be one-sided and mistaken utterances of men who "darkened counsel by words without knowledge" (comp. xxxviii, 2; xlii, 3). Two things, however, are insisted upon by Job, his own consciousness of integrity and innocency (x, 7; xiii, 18; xvi, 17; xxiii, 10, 11; xxvii, 5; xxix, 12-17), and the manifest power and prosperity of the wicked (xxi, 7-13). The answer of Jehovah out of the whirlwind (xxxviii—xli) does not assume to clear up the difficult problem of the patriarch and his disputatious friends, and is in substance a reminder of the limitations of human knowledge and power. But it brings Job into humility and reverent silence (xl, 4, 5; xlii, 1-6), and powerfully suggests that he who "laid the foundations of the earth" (xxxviii, 4), leads forth the constellations of heaven, and orders the ways of every living thing from the young ravens to the huge leviathan, knows well what he is doing and must surely care for all his servants who fear God and turn away from evil. The prologue of the poem is, accordingly, an imaginative apocalypse of the comforting thought that no sorrow or trial is permitted to come upon the servant of God without having been first considered in the gracious counsels of heaven, and a limit set to the hand of the adversary (i, 12; ii, 6). The outcome of the whole discussion (iii—xli) is to show the limitations of human knowledge in the questions of theodicy, and the need of some assuring revelations from on high. The epilogue (xlii, 7-17) shows how "Jehovah blessed the latter end of Job more than his beginning," and thus the whole book affords a lesson in substance like that which Jesus taught in another case of sorrow: "Neither did this man sin, nor his parents"; the affliction was not

a punishment, "but that the works of God should be made manifest in him" (John ix, 3). There are forms of suffering and evil which afflict mankind which are not of the nature of penalty to the afflicted ones, but may test the virtue and exhibit the steadfast piety of the righteous servant of God.

(3) *In the Song of Songs.* If we adopt the shepherd-hypothesis of the Song of Songs, we find in that exquisite drama a condemnation of such unhallowed concubinage as that of David and the fair damsel Abishag, the Shunammite (1 Kings i, 1-4), and of Solomon, whose hundreds of wives and concubines turned away his heart after other gods (1 Kings xi, 3). As the book of Job exhibits the trials and the triumph of an upright man, so the Song of Songs extols the virtue and unchangeable affection of a true woman when put to the severest test. The Shulammite maiden of this drama resists all the blandishments of the uxorious king, rejects all his offers, and abides true to her shepherd-lover who feeds his flock among the lilies. Thus understood the Song is no composition of Solomon, but written rather to arraign and rebuke the flagrant offenses of his polygamy. It celebrates the changeless devotion of two faithful hearts, whom plighted love should unite as "one flesh" for a lifelong companionship. Herein we discern the divinely ordered foundation of the true marriage covenant, and by way of the nefarious contrast a stinging censure upon such sensual life as can talk complacently of "eighty concubines" (vi, 8), and show inordinate desire to add another to the number.[1]

(4) *In Ecclesiastes.* The book of Ecclesiastes furnishes no contribution of much importance to the biblical doctrine of sin. The author's main outcry, repeated more than a score of times, is "vanity of vanities, the whole is vanity." He observes the emptiness of all the pleasures which wealth and power can supply (ii, 1-11). Though wisdom excel folly, the wise man dies like the fool, his labor often goes to benefit another, and so life itself seems like a hateful burden (ii, 12-23). All the conditions of human life present to this writer the aspects of an "evil business" (ענין), a "sore travail which God has given to the sons of men to be exercised therein" (iii, 10). In the mysteries of life he says: "I turned about, and my heart was set to know and to search out, and to seek wisdom and the reason of things, and to know that wickedness is folly, and that foolishness is madness; and I find a thing more bitter than death, even the woman whose heart is snares and nets, and her hands as bands: whoso pleaseth

---

[1] See the Song of Songs: An Inspired Melodrama. Analyzed, translated, and expounded by Milton S. Terry. Cincinnati, 1893.

God shall escape from her; but the sinner shall be taken by her" (vii, 25, 26). Looking at all things on all sides, weighing one against another, human ambitions and pursuits appear to this unknown master of proverbs like empty things (הבלים), and a striving after the wind. Wickedness often seems to triumph; tyrants oppress; as far as human eye can see Sheol is a realm of silence and darkness; the dust returns to dust, the soul to God; but whether to be reabsorbed in universal spirit, to ascend, or to go downward, no man can tell. The book ends as it began: "vanity of vanities—all is vanity!"

(5) *In the Later Jewish Literature.* In the Old Testament Apocrypha and Pseudepigrapha, and in the Targums, the Midrash, and the Talmud we meet with the later elaboration of Jewish doctrine which was current at the beginning of our era and some time before. It is noteworthy that the sin of Adam and Eve, their expulsion from the garden, and the farreaching consequences of their transgression first appear to have great doctrinal significance in this later literature. For vague allusions only appear in such texts as Ezek. xxviii, 13-15, and Job xv, 7, 8, and the phrase "like Adam" (כאדם), in Job xxxi, 33; Psa. lxxxii, 7, and Hos. vi, 7, is better translated "like men," or "after the manner of man." According to Gen. iii, 16-19, a curse was pronounced upon the serpent, the woman, the man, and the ground; but nothing was said about penal consequences destined to come upon any besides the original transgressors. But in Ecclesiasticus xxv, 24, it is written: "From a woman was the beginning of sin, and because of her we all die." In 2 Esdras vii, 48 (118), we read: "It had been better that the earth had not given Adam, or else, when it had given, to have restrained him from sinning. . . . O thou Adam, what hast thou done? For though it was thou that sinned, the evil has not fallen on thee alone, but upon all of us that come of thee." Compare also iii, 7, 21, 22, and iv, 30, 31. In the Wisdom of Solomon ii, 24, we are told that "by the envy of the devil death entered into the world," and this statement seems to have influenced Paul in the composition of Rom. v, 12. Here we also notice that Satan is conceived as the original tempter rather than the serpent. According to the Apocalypse of Baruch xxiii, 4, "when Adam sinned and death was decreed against those who should be born, then the multitude of those who should be born was numbered." The book of Jubilees iii, 28, says that on the same day on which Adam was driven from the garden "was closed the mouth of all beasts, and of cattle, and of birds, and of whatever walks or moves, so that they could no longer speak; for they had all spoken with one another with one lip and with one tongue."

The same book explains Adam's dying on the same day he sinned in that he lacked seventy years of being a thousand years old when he died, and "one thousand years are as one day in the testimony of the heavens." In the book of Enoch, however, the origin of sin is traced rather to the angels who kept not their heavenly habitation, but cohabited with the daughters of men and begat the Nephilim of Gen. vi, 4.[1]

9. Paul's Doctrine of Sin in the Flesh. There appears in Paul's epistles the peculiar doctrine of *sin in the flesh*. "When we were in the flesh," he says, "the sinful passions, which were through the law, wrought in our members to bring forth fruit unto death" (Rom. vii, 5). "I know that in me, that is, in my flesh, dwelleth no good thing" (ver. 18). "I serve with the flesh the law of sin" (ver. 25). He speaks of "likeness of flesh of sin" and of "walking after the flesh" and "minding the things of the flesh" (viii, 3-5). "The mind of the flesh is death; it is enmity against God; for it is not subject to the law of God, neither indeed can it be." "They that are in the flesh cannot please God" (vers. 6-8). "If ye live after the flesh ye must die" (ver. 13). He also speaks of "lusts of the flesh," "filthiness of the flesh," "indulgence of the flesh," "works of the flesh," such as fornication, uncleanness, lasciviousness (Gal. v, 19). "He that soweth unto his own flesh shall of the flesh reap corruption" (Gal. vi, 8). In Col. ii, 11, 18, we read of "a circumcision not made with hands, in the putting off of the body of the flesh," and a "being vainly puffed up by one's fleshly mind" (ὑπὸ τοῦ νοὸς τῆς σαρκὸς αὐτοῦ, *by the mind of his flesh*). The Colossians are exhorted to slay or "make dead the members which are upon the earth; fornication, uncleanness, passion," etc. (iii, 5). In Rom. viii, 13, we are told that spiritual life is to be obtained by mortifying or "putting to death the deeds of the body." In 1 Cor. ix, 27, the apostle says: "I buffet my body, and bring it into bondage." One who is under the dominion of a sinful nature, or is easily influenced by passions of jealousy and strife, is called fleshly, carnal (σαρκικός. Rom. vii, 14; 1 Cor. iii, 1, 3). Notice should also be taken of the phrases "body of sin" (Rom. vi, 6); "body of this death" (vii, 24); "passions of sins" (vii, 5).

In these texts the words *flesh, body,* and *members* (σάρξ, σῶμα, and μέλη) are practically synonymous, although the natural distinction of *flesh* as the material or physical elements, *body* as the organism composed of these elements, and *members* as the various

---

[1] See for fuller account of these later Jewish haggadah, F. R. Tennant, The Sources of the Doctrines of the Fall and Original Sin. Cambridge, 1903. Also Ferdinand Weber, Jüdische Theologie, pp. 218–259. Leipzig, 1897.

organs or parts need not be ignored. In other portions of his writings Paul employs all these words in their ordinary and popular meaning. He speaks of the flesh of men and of beasts (1 Cor. xv, 39); of the human body and its various members (1 Cor. xii, 17-20), and of celestial and terrestrial bodies (xv, 40). In other places the word *flesh* denotes, like בשר in the Old Testament, weak and dependent human nature in contrast with God, and is also often used for men generally or mankind as a whole (comp. the phrases "all flesh," and "no flesh"). There are also other minor shades of meaning apparent in certain forms of expression which are of no importance in our present argument. But in the Pauline texts cited above the word *flesh* denotes the lower sensuous nature of man, dominated by sin, and so exercising control over the spiritual life and the conscience. The apostle does not conceive of sin as *originating* in the sensuous nature; much less does he hold the doctrine of an inherent and necessary sinfulness of the flesh, and think of matter as evil in itself. His doctrine of sin is profound and farreaching. He employs all those Greek terms (ἁμαρτάνω, ἁμαρτία, παράπτωμα, παράβασις) which designate sin as a culpable missing of the mark, a trespass, a violation of known law by personal and willful transgression, and he teaches that sin first entered into the world by the trespass of one man (Rom. v, 12-19). As a result of that original transgression sin has "abounded" and "reigned in death," and human nature universally presents the spectacle of sin so regnant in the mortal body that this writer says: "I delight in the law of God after the inward man: but I see a different law in my members, warring against the law of my mind, and bringing me into captivity under the law of sin which is in my members" (Rom. vii, 22, 23). Thus the flesh (σάρξ) and the body as the organized flesh (σῶμα) have become the seat and citadel of all manner of vile passions. The members (μέλη) present themselves as "instruments of unrighteousness," and sin wields dominion over the whole man (Rom. vi, 13, 14).[1] Rom. vii, 14-24, is a graphic picture of the awakened conscience when it recognizes this wretched bondage of sin, confesses "I know that in me, that is, in my flesh, dwelleth no good thing," and cries

---

[1] This condition and aspect of the matter are accordingly well stated as follows by Caird: "The sensuous appetites and passions acquire a new character when they become constituent elements in the life of a self-conscious, self-determining being. As motives to human action they lose their purely animal characteristics; they cease to be what they are in the animal—blind impulses acting under the law of physical necessity, and pointing to satisfactions which are limited and transient; they have infused into them a new element, or undergo a transforming process, in virtue of which they are raised out of the sphere of nature into that of spirit, and become rivals of the higher desires and aspirations of the spirit on their own ground."—Fundamental Ideas of Christianity, vol. ii, p. 38. Glasgow, 1899.

out, "O wretched man that I am! who shall deliver me from the body of this (spiritual) death?" This conflict between flesh and spirit—between the lower passions as demoralized by sin and error and the nobler moral sense and reason ($νοῦς$)—may be more severe, at crucial moments, in a personality like Paul than in persons of inferior spiritual insight and emotionality. The tremendous struggle depicted in Rom. vii, 14-24, is personally known in full experience only by those gifted natures who have been exceptionally "strengthened with power through the Spirit in the inward man. . . . to apprehend with all the saints what is the breadth and length and height and depth, and to know the love of Christ which passeth knowledge" (Eph. iii, 16-19), but all real saints in Christ Jesus must needs know something of its searching discipline. And thus it is by a power of spiritual insight that one who has been freed from the slavery of "the law of sin and of death" perceives the real nature of that fleshly bondage. Only when one has experienced the saving power of "the Spirit of life in Christ Jesus" (Rom. viii, 2) can he truly apprehend the fearful nature of sin.

The "sin in the flesh," "flesh of sin," "mind of the flesh," and such like terms are, accordingly, with Paul, a special and peculiar designation of the corrupt nature of depraved men, especially the lower passions of selfishness, evil desire, and perverse habits of life. In Eph. ii, 1, 3, he speaks of men in this sinful state as being "dead through trespasses and sins," and "living in the lusts of the flesh, doing the desires of the flesh and of the mind, and being by nature ($φύσει$) children of wrath"; that is, subject by reason of their fleshly sinful nature to the wrath of the all-holy and righteous God. In the inmost center of man's self-conscious being two opposite forces are often seen to clash. "The flesh lusteth against the Spirit and the Spirit against the flesh; for these are contrary the one to the other" (Gal. v, 17). The man who gives himself over to the "lusts of the flesh" and to the practice of the "works of the flesh" becomes the "bond servant of sin," and is "brought into captivity under the law of sin which is in his members." Such a deplorable slavery is in its worst aspect a union of all that is high and noble in man with a "body of death."

10. Pauline Rabbinism. The extent of Paul's rabbinical training is evident from his epistles, and from his own testimony as recorded in the Acts. He was "a Hebrew of the Hebrews," "a Pharisee and the son of a Pharisee," trained after the straitest sect, "brought up at the feet of Gamaliel, instructed according to the strict manner of the law of the fathers," and, as he affirms in Gal. i, 14, "I advanced in the Jews' religion beyond many of mine own age among my countrymen, being more exceedingly zealous for the traditions of my fathers." His rabbinical habits of thought appear in numerous allusions and expositions, as when he builds an argument on the singular of the word "seed" (Gal. iii, 16), puts an allegorical construction on the story of Hagar and Sarah (iv, 22-26), speaks of the rock which "followed" the fathers as related in the Targum of Num. xxi, 16-20 (1 Cor. x, 4), and gives the names of Jannes and Jambres (2 Tim. iii, 8), which appear nowhere in the Scriptures, but are found in one of the Targums at Exod. vii, 11. His doctrine of sin and death as connecting with Adam, in Rom. v, 12-19, has evident logical and historical connection with the beliefs which appear in the apocryphal literature of the later Judaism. But this peculiar feature of Paul's character and teaching is not to be deemed any disparagement, but rather a distinguishing excellency. For this apostle did not follow slavishly in the steps of any human master. He imparted a deeper and more spiritual significance to the current Jewish thought of his time which he found occasion to utilize. If in Rom. v, 12-19, he offers an ideal conception of the solidarity of the race in sin and in redemption, in Rom. vii, 7-24, he sets forth the real psychological origin of sin in every man and the reason of its universality.[1]

---

[1] See Henry St. John Thackeray, The Relation of St. Paul to Contemporary Jewish Thought. London, 1900. Also F. R. Tennant, The Origin and Propagation of Sin. Cambridge, 1902.

CHAPTER IV

THE PENAL CONSEQUENCES OF SIN

1. Physical Death as Penalty. The dreadful results of evil-doing are set forth in the Scriptures in a variety of ways. One of the first to be noticed is that which appears in connection with the Edenic story of the first transgression: "In the day thou eatest thereof thou shalt surely die" (Gen. ii, 17; iii, 3). The death here contemplated is generally understood to be the dissolution of the human body and its return to the dust of the earth; and this seems to have been the thought of the author of Gen. iii, as the language of verse 19 clearly implies. This belief has also been strengthened by our familiarity with the solemn sanction of the death-penalty for capital crime, as found in the books of the Law (Gen. ix, 6; Exod. xxi, 12, 15; Lev. xx, 2, 9; Num. xxxv, 16, 21; Deut. xiii, 9; xvii, 6). So far as physical death is thus adjudged as a righteous penalty for criminal deeds, it is of the nature of capital punishment, and finds its justification in the heinous character of the crime and the rights and exigencies of civil government. The safety of the community and of the state requires that the dangerous offender be put out of the way, and a sound jurisprudence may determine the form and measure of penalty to be exacted.

2. Physical Death as Universal Law. But physical death as a fixed and universal fact, and the dissolution of man's body consequent thereupon, are not to be regarded as the penalty of sin. For the law of decay and dissolution, as truly as that of birth and growth, is part and parcel of the divine order stamped upon the nature of all living organisms, both animal and vegetable. Ages before man appeared on earth this law was working in all bodies endowed with life, and there is no sufficient reason to suppose that, if sin had never entered into the world, man would have been any exception to this universal law. Physical death at times takes on many a form of aggravated pain by reason of the sins of the sufferer against his own body, but in and of itself it need not be regarded as an evil or as a necessary result of sin. The annual growths of the harvest, the century-living oaks of the wood, the fish of the sea, the fowl of the air, and the beasts and cattle of the field have each a normal lifetime. Man has his "three-score years and ten." But all alike fall either by some untimely stroke or else by slow decay and death. This universal law of death does not appear to rest on any law of sin, and there is no good reason to burden Christian theology with such a needless dogma. What we call physical death may be only the terminal crisis of transition into a higher form of organic being. This is suggested in John xii, 24: "Except a grain of wheat fall into the earth and die, it abideth by itself alone; but if it die, it beareth much fruit." Similarly 1 Cor. xv, 36: "That which thou thyself sowest is not quickened except it die." As new organic form is given to that which is sown, and each new seed has a body of its own, so it would seem that a law of physical death is a natural and necessary factor in the production of a new phase of life.

3. Physical Evils not a Penalty for Sin. It should be observed, furthermore, that physical evils, such as plagues, pestilences, famines, earthquakes, and awful calamities, are no longer to be regarded, as they once were, the penal consequences of man's original sin. They may, however, be viewed, as the Hebrew prophets suggest, as the occasional judgments of God upon wicked men and nations because of their evil-doings. So Jehovah speaks, in Ezek. xiv, 21, of his "four sore judgments upon Jerusalem, the sword, and the famine, and the noisome beasts, and the pestilence." The language of Gen. iii, 17, 18, implies that the growth of thorns and thistles is an evidence that the ground from which they spring is cursed because of man's sin, and, according to Jer. xii, 4, the land mourns, and the herbs of the whole country wither, and the beasts and the birds are consumed, because of the wickedness of them that dwell therein. But all such scriptures are easily explained without the assumption that such evils are in themselves a necessary penal consequence of human sinfulness. God often employs them for penal purposes, and a personal consciousness of guilt may recognize the penal visitation and confess that it was justly deserved. There is also the notable concept of Paul, expressed in Rom. viii, 19-22, that the whole creation is subjected to a bondage of corruption, and of painful groaning and travail. But there is no intimation that this subjection is of a penal character, or that it contains and carries with it any element of guilt. On the other hand, the main doctrine of the book of Job is that a righteous and innocent man may be subjected to appalling calamities and sorrow for other reasons than for personal sin. Also the words of Jesus, in Luke xiii, 1-5, condemned the error of those who supposed that the Galileans, whose blood Pilate mingled with their sacrifices, must needs have been sinners above all the

Galileans because they suffered so horribly. Nor were they to suppose that the eighteen men on whom the tower in Siloam fell were offenders above all others then dwelling in Jerusalem. Still more explicit is the teaching of John ix, 1-3, where, in direct answer to a question that assumed as a matter of course that such a calamity as being born blind must needs be the penalty of some previous sin, our Lord declared that the misfortune of the blind man was not a punishment of his own sin or of that of his parents, but was somehow designed to manifest the works of God. How far and in what ways the sufferings and the evils of the natural world subserve the purposes of infinite Wisdom we do not presume to tell. So many of his ways are past finding out. But it is obvious from the Scriptures that many personal afflictions have their place and reasons in God's purposes of good will to men, and that "our light affliction, which is for the moment, worketh for us more and more exceedingly an eternal weight of glory" (2 Cor. iv, 17; comp. Rom. viii, 18, 28; 1 Pet. i, 6; Heb. xii, 5-13).

4. New Testament Doctrine of Death. The death which in the New Testament is represented as the penalty of sin is the alienation of the soul of man from fellowship with God. It is a disruption and ruin wrought in the spiritual nature of man, and a consequent demoralization of the image of God within him. Thus, according to James i, 15, "lust, when it hath conceived, beareth sin; and the sin, when it is fullgrown, bringeth forth death." Hence it is that "he who converteth a sinner from the error of his way shall save a soul from death" (James v, 20). But such conversion does not save any one from physical death. Paul's teaching is to the same effect. He affirms that "the mind of the flesh is death" (Rom. viii, 6). This φρόνημα, *mind,* is the habitual thought and purpose of a man prostituted to vile passions of the lower nature; it holds him in "enmity against God," so that the sinful passions work through the members of the body and result in spiritual death (Rom. vii, 5). Even the commandment of God which is holy and designed to train our spiritual nature in the ways of life, proves rather a minister of death; and sin, in demonstration of its own destructive nature and exceeding sinfulness, so works according to a law deep-laid in the nature of man as to result in his spiritual death (Rom. vii, 9-14). In this way "the law of sin" becomes also a "law of death." For sin, "reigning in the mortal body" (Rom. vi, 12), employs its members as "weapons of unrighteousness," subjects the whole person to miserable slavery, and pays the allowance (ὀψώνια) of such an abject soldier: "The wages of sin is death" (ver. 23). And thus it is seen that death, in the penal sense, is the fatal award of disobedience, the end of all the shameful operations of the depraved sensual nature, "for the end of those things is death" (ver. 21). It is to be "carnal, sold under sin," and imprisoned in a "body of death" (vii, 14, 24). Paul does not conceive it as the separation of soul and body and the dissolution of the latter. He speaks of men while living in the flesh as "dead through trespasses and sins" (Eph. ii, 1, 5; comp. Col. ii, 13).

5. Pauline Conception of Sin and Death. It accords with Paul's profound conception of spiritual death as the wages and end of sin that his portraiture of Adam's transgression outlined in Rom. v, 12-21, presents a reign of death over all the world of men consequent upon the entrance of sin. "Through one man sin entered into the world and death through sin," and, what especially deserves notice is the fact that "sin reigned in death." Sin reigned in the very fact of death and by reason of the death which it introduced into the world. It is also observed that "death reigned from Adam until Moses, even over them that had not sinned after the likeness of Adam's transgression." This does not refer to infants, as some have thought, but to all who lived before the giving of the law by Moses. Sin was in the world before the Mosaic lawgiving, and showed itself in many forms that were not "after the likeness of Adam's transgression." "And so death passed unto all men, for that all sinned" (ἐφ' ᾧ πάντες ἥμαρτον). The apostle conceives all mankind as brought under the universal reign of death by reason of the trespass of the first man, whom he idealizes as the typical sinner. The thought of the universality of physical death would naturally associate itself with the statement, but the death which carries its own penal character along with it is the spiritual lapse from God. This passed upon Adam on the very day he transgressed, and in a mystic and figurative manner Paul thinks of all men as both sinning and dying in Adam (comp. 1 Cor. xv, 22). So on the other hand he also conceives himself and others as crucified, dead, and buried with Christ (Rom. vi, 4, 6, 8; comp. Gal. ii, 20). In the same mystic way he speaks in 2 Cor. v, 14, of *the all* (οἱ πάντες) who *died* with Christ. All mankind, accordingly, sin and die, and "the sting of death is sin." Physical death in itself and as a law of nature is not evil; it is God's way of transmuting a living organism into a new form of existence; but to him that sins death becomes a fearful monster, like a scorpion with a tormenting sting (comp. Rev. ix, 5, 10). It gives a pang of torment to all the sadness, despondency, grief, anguish, and spiritual wretchedness of the ungodly, and so it makes "the sorrow of the world work death"

(2 Cor. vii, 10),[1] altogether the opposite of the "godly sorrow which worketh repentance unto salvation." So far, therefore, as the thought of physical death does suggest itself as a penalty for sin, the penal element is in the fatal sting. The sinner who "repents unto salvation" escapes this sting of death, and "cometh not into judgment, but has passed out of death into life," and "shall never taste of death" (John v, 24; viii, 51, 52; comp. vi, 50; xi, 26; 1 John iii, 13). Herein the Pauline and the Johannean doctrines are the same.

6. Penal Consequences beyond this Life. The curse of death began its baneful operation on the very day of the first transgression. For alienation from God, the condemning judgment of conscience, the sense of shame and guilt, and the subsequent hardening of the heart, are all to be regarded as the penal operation of the poison of the sting of death. But to what extent, we may next inquire, does this deadly operation of sin go on? May the "wrath and indignation, tribulation and anguish upon every soul of man that worketh evil" (Rom. ii, 9) continue beyond this mortal life, and go on forever in other states of being? We know that in this earthly life sinful habits beget fixedness of character. If, then, there be a continuation of personal existence beyond the present life, it would seem altogether probable that the self-conscious personality maintains its character as well as its identity in that future state of being. Unless it can be conclusively shown that the soul of man undergoes some radical change of moral character by reason of its entrance into the new state of being, it would seem inevitable that the depraved nature of the self-condemned sinner must remain the same. So far as we observe and know it never changes the sinful character of a man to pass from a prison to a palace, or from one climate to another.

7. Biblical Doctrine of Retribution. So far as the Scriptures throw light upon this question of future retribution they indicate that the penal consequences of sin may run on eternally. The

---

[1] Some such idea of death as the outcome of a "sorrow of the world" may be traced in those passages of the Psalms and the Proverbs where personal distress and terror are depicted. Thus in Psa. xviii, 4, 5:—

> The cords of death compassed me,
> The floods of Belial made me afraid.
> The cords of Sheol were round about me;
> The snares of death came upon me.

Similar is the language of Psa. lv, 4; lvi, 13; cvi, 3, 8. In Prov. v, 5, it is said of the evil woman:—

> Her feet go down to death;
> Her steps take hold on Sheol.

In such scriptures the allusion is to something more than physical death. It is also written that "righteousness delivereth from death" (Prov. x, 2; xi, 4), and that "in the pathway of righteousness there is no death" (xii, 28). The death here contemplated cannot be the exit of the soul from the body.

most solemn declarations of Jesus on this subject occur in connection with his warnings against the "blasphemy against the Holy Spirit," which "shall not be forgiven, neither in this world (age), nor in that which is to come" (Matt. xii, 32). The soul that is guilty of this unpardonable offense is, according to Mark iii, 29, "held fast in eternal sin" (see above, p. 93). This teaching accords strictly with the idea that a free and responsible moral being may by blasphemous and persistent obduracy fix its own character into a condition of unchangeable enmity against God.

(1) *Old Testament Teaching Vague.* We are unable to trace any clear historical development of this doctrine in the canonical writings. We find much in the Old Testament about the severity of divine judgment on those who disobey God's laws, but the retribution appears mostly if not altogether confined to evils inflicted during the period of earthly life. Thus in Lev. xxvi, 14-21, and in Deut. xxviii, 15-45, we read an enumeration of manifold curses sure to come upon Israel in case they "hearken not unto the voice of Jehovah their God"; but the penalties announced are in every case some form of temporal calamity, such as pestilence, famine, sword, and wild beast (comp. Ezek. xiv, 21). Such examples of judgment cannot be properly adduced to prove either the fact or the nature of retribution in another world. There are also passages in the Psalms which speak of blotting the wicked out of the book of the living (Psa. lxix, 28), "casting them down to ruins" (lxxiii, 18), and to sudden desolation (i, 5, 6; ii, 12; v, 6; lv, 23); but these references appear in the main to be to temporal judgments, and can only in the most general way be applied to punishments in a future state of existence. In like manner the striking passage in Isa. xxxiii, 14, appears to have no direct allusion to retribution in another world. In the thought of the prophet "the breath of Jehovah is like a stream of brimstone" that kindles a funeral pile (xxx, 33); he has "his fire in Zion, and his furnace in Jerusalem" (xxxi, 9); hostile peoples, like Assyria, "shall be as the burnings of lime; as thorns cut down, that are burned in the fire" (xxxiii, 12). "Sinners in Zion" (ver. 14) may also fear these fearful burnings of divine judgment, and "the godless ones" may well cry out, "Who among us can dwell with the devouring fire? Who among us can dwell with everlasting burnings?" The thought seems therefore to be that of a funeral pile which burns all wicked ones after the manner of Assyria, and it turns upon the perpetual fire of Jehovah's righteous wrath rather than upon the eternity of punishment visited upon the sinners.

(2) *Isaiah lxvi, 24.* There are, however, two notable passages in

the Old Testament, which have been supposed to involve the doctrine of penal suffering beyond this life. One of these is the last verse in the book of Isaiah (lxvi, 24), where the prophet, after depicting new heavens and new earth and a restored Jerusalem, speaks of a going forth out of the city and looking upon the dead bodies of those who transgressed against Jehovah. Of these enemies of God he declares that "their worm shall not die, neither shall their fire be quenched; and they shall be an abhorrence (דראון) unto all flesh." How far these words were intended to convey some idea of bodily torment in Sheol (comp. Isa. xiv, 11-19) is difficult to determine.[1] Jeremiah (vii, 31) mentions "high places of Topheth, which is in the valley of the son of Hinnom, for burning sons and daughters in the fire," and according to Joshua the valley of Hinnom (גי הנם) was a well-known gorge on the south side of Jerusalem. Here children were burned in the fire after the manner of the idolatrous abominations of the heathen (2 Chron. xxviii, 3). It is not improbable that these facts helped in some measure to produce the prophetic picture in Isa. lxvi, 24. The signal overthrow of Jehovah's enemies carries the thought of the writer to some such ideal of judgment as is seen in Isa. xiv, 11-19, visited upon the fallen king of Babylon, and along with it are associated a fiery retribution, and worms that never die, and all the abhorrence suggested by the abominations that had been practiced just outside of Jerusalem in the former days.[2] All these ideas seem to have entered into the later concept of the "Gehenna of fire" which finds a place in the teaching of Jesus (Matt. v, 22; Mark ix, 43-48), but they were probably yet vague and visional in the mind of the author of Isa. lxvi, 24.

(3) *Daniel xii, 2.* The other Old Testament passage which points to the penal consequences of sin beyond this life is Dan. xii, 2, where it is said that some of "them that sleep in the dust of the earth shall awake to shame and everlasting abhorrence."[3] Beyond this bare statement the writer says nothing from which we can clearly determine his concept of a resurrection to shame and to being an object of aversion. Some sort of retribution

---

[1] The Targum thus translates it: "Because their souls shall not die, and their fire shall not be quenched, and the ungodly shall be judged in Gehenna, until the righteous say concerning them, 'We have seen enough.'"

[2] The picture of judgment, according to Delitzsch, "looks like eternal punishment raised above the conditions of temporality. The prophet blends temporal and eternal. This world and the next coalesce to his view."—Commentary on Isaiah, in loco. "The details of the description suggest, by their obvious inconsistency, that the terms are symbolic of the tortures of the souls in Hades."—Cheyne, The Prophecies of Isaiah, in loco. Ed. Whittaker, New York, 1890.

[3] The word here rendered *abhorrence* is דראון, identical with that which appears elsewhere only in Isa. lxvi, 24. In both texts it means *an object of aversion* or of abhorrence.

after the body has returned to dust seems to be with him, however, a doctrinal belief, and we can scarcely doubt that it was a current belief of the Jewish people of that time.

(4) *Apocrypha and Pseudepigrapha.* The doctrine of future punishment for the wicked is developed and wrought out in great detail in the Jewish apocryphal and pseudepigraphical literature. Sheol becomes more than a name for the abode of all the dead; it is conceived by some writers as divided into various apartments, and includes Gehenna as the eternal abode of the ungodly. In the Ethiopic book of Enoch Sheol is described as divided into four deep and vast hollow places, one bright and inviting with a clear spring of water in the midst, prepared for the righteous, and three of them gloomy, arranged for different classes of souls, the worst being for the vilest of sinners.[1] The book of Judith says of the enemies of Israel: "The Lord Almighty will take vengeance on them in the day of judgment, to put fire and worms in their flesh; and they shall weep and feel their pain forever" (xvi, 17). In 2 Esdras vii, 36, we read: "The pit of torment shall appear, and over against it shall be the place of rest; and the furnace of Gehenna shall be showed, and over against it the Paradise of delight." Many similar ideas are presented with great variety of detail in these later Jewish writings. The general belief of the Pharisees in the first century of our era is thus stated by Josephus (Antiquities xviii, 1, 3): "They believe that souls have an immortal vigor in them, and that under the earth there will be rewards or punishments, according as they have lived virtuously or viciously in this life; and the latter are to be detained in an everlasting prison, but the former shall have power to revive and live again." Thus Sheol, Gehenna, and Hades became common terms to denote the under-world, in one portion of which the souls of the wicked were destined to suffer endless punishment for the sins committed in this earthly life. Whether they should again be raised up and given bodies wherein to suffer, or whether they should be left in Gehenna without their bodies seems to have been a somewhat unsettled question.[2]

(5) *The New Testament Teaching.* The scriptures of the New Testament are quite explicit on the subject of future retribution for the wicked, and are so generally uniform in their statements as to show no considerable differences of view among the different writers. We have noticed the solemn declarations of Jesus concerning those who blaspheme against the Holy Spirit,

---

[1] See book of Enoch, translated by R. H. Charles, chap. xxii, pp. 93-97.
[2] See more on this subject in R. H. Charles, A Critical History of the Doctrine of a Future Life, p. 302. London, 1899.

and have observed the moral fixedness of character acquired by persistent continuance in a course of moral conduct. This is a consideration not to be lost sight of in our discussion of the penal consequences of sin. Nothing of real value in determining the true doctrine of New Testament writers is secured by a minute study of the terms *Hades, Gehenna, Tartarus, death, punishment, destruction,* and *perdition*. One may use any of these words without thereby endorsing the particular or peculiar opinions maintained by a sect or by a few individuals. One of the earliest epistles attributed to Paul declares that those who know not God and refuse to obey the gospel of Christ "shall suffer punishment, even eternal destruction from the face of the Lord and from the glory of his might" (2 Thess. i, 9). Here the idea of future penalty does not depend upon a single word, or upon any mere form of expression. The entire context touching "the revelation of the Lord Jesus from heaven with the angels of his power in flaming fire, rendering vengeance to them that know not God" may be treated as highly imaginative and rhetorical. There is room for differences of opinion in a minute exegesis of the passage; but one thought which on any rational interpretation stands out conspicuously is the certain penal destruction of the disobedient when the Lord Jesus appears in judgment against them. In another epistle we find the following more general declaration: "We must all be made manifest before the judgment-seat of Christ; that each one may receive the things done through the body, according to what he hath done, whether it be good or bad" (2 Cor. v, 10). However much of metaphor may lie in the phrase "judgment-seat of Christ" (a matter to be elsewhere treated), one main thought is emphasized beyond question, namely, that every man is destined to receive recompense of his deeds after he has completed his earthly life-work in or through the body. If he have done what is bad, penal consequences must follow. This Pauline doctrine is in strict accord with the teaching of Jesus in the Gospels. We cannot mistake the significance of his warning in Mark viii, 38: "Whosoever shall be ashamed of me and of my words in this adulterous and sinful generation, the Son of man also shall be ashamed of him, when he cometh in the glory of his Father with the holy angels." In the sublime picture of judgment in Matt. xxv, 31-46, the unrighteous are represented as driven away from the throne of his glory, pronounced "accursed," and sentenced to "the eternal fire which is prepared for the devil and his angels." In Matt. x, 28, he says: "Be not afraid of them that kill the body, but are unable to kill the soul; but rather fear him who is able to destroy both soul and body in

Gehenna." There can be no doubt as to the obvious import of these texts in their bearing on the future punishment of human sinfulness. In the gospel of John (viii, 21-24), Jesus says to the unbelieving Pharisees: "I go away, and ye shall seek me, and shall die in your sin: whither I go ye cannot come. . . . Ye are from beneath; I am from above: ye are of this world; I am not of this world. I said therefore unto you that ye shall die in your sins: for except ye believe that I am, ye shall die in your sins." To die in their sins was evidently to become separated from Christ and to become incapable of coming unto him. Such hopeless separation goes over with the sinner into the world of personal conscious existence beyond death. And this accords with the teaching of Jesus in his description of the rich man, who "died and was buried, and in Hades lifted up his eyes, being in torments" (Luke xvi, 23). He saw Lazarus afar off in Abraham's bosom, and prayed that he might be sent to cool his tongue and ease his anguish in the flame; but he is admonished that he had received his good things in his lifetime, and that between himself and the abode of Lazarus and the blessed dead "there is a great gulf fixed," so that none are able to cross over from one place to the other. This entire portraiture of the future state of the dead is in noticeable harmony with the idea of different apartments or abodes in Hades, of which we read in the later Jewish apocalyptic writings. A condition of anguish and torments is set over against one of comfort and blessedness, with an impassable chasm between. Thus far Jesus seems clearly to recognize and sanction the current doctrine of his time touching future reward and punishment. Whatever else this account of the rich man and Lazarus may teach, it most obviously sets forth the doctrine of retribution in the manner of conscious personal anguish after the death and burial of the body. Another fearful intimation of the penal consequences of sin beyond the present life is given in the language of Jesus concerning his betrayer, whom he calls in one place (John xvii, 12) "the son of perdition," and of whom he says in another (Matt. xxvi, 24), "good were it for him if that man had not been born." Such language is incompatible with any thought of a possible blissful immortality. It is to be explained rather as confirming the doctrine of irretrievable ruin of the soul by wickedness. This doctrine is stated in unmistakable terms in Rev. xxi, 8: "The fearful, and unbelieving, and abominable, and murderers, and fornicators, and sorcerers, and idolaters, and all liars, their part is in the lake that burns with fire and brimstone; which is the second death." From these various scriptures, as well as from many others of like character not necessary to adduce, it seems impossible to avoid the conclusion that the New Testament writers and Jesus himself held and intended to inculcate the doctrine of future punishment for the sins of this earthly life. The bitter consequences of sin, according to these scriptures, torment the sinner beyond the grave. They are essentially penal and are accordingly conceived as "the judgment of God according to truth against them that practice unrighteousness"; they are a divine visitation of "wrath and indignation, tribulation and anguish, upon every soul of man that worketh evil," the absence and the opposite of "glory and honor and incorruption and eternal life" (Rom. ii, 3-11).

8. Inferences Touching the Nature of Future Punishment. If we inquire further as to the real nature of these penal consequences of sin in the world to come we can only speak by way of inference and suggestion. The popular concepts of "Hell" and "eternal perdition" have been in great measure derived from imaginative pictures of poets and apocalyptists, and contain a vast accumulation of crass notions which are no essential part of true scriptural doctrine.[1] The biblical writers employ striking metaphors and not infrequently indulge in extravagant descriptions when they are simply recording personal experiences of the present life. So the psalmist in his personal trouble and sorrow cries out (cxvi, 3),

> The cords of death compassed me,
> And the pains of Sheol found me.

Even Paul in the midst of peril and persecution cites the language of Psa. xliv, 22, as descriptive of his feeling (Rom. viii, 36):

> For thy sake we are killed all the day long;
> We were accounted as sheep for the slaughter.

He protests in 1 Cor. xv, 31, that he is dying daily. When we find such language employed in describing personal affliction in the present life, we may well presume that in portrayals of future existence and of the fearful expectations of judgment after death, even stronger language would be used. When we separate the real

---

[1] The doctrine of the finality of life's spiritual decisions has no necessary connection with ideas of punishment which were once current, or with those realistic pictures of hell and crude conceptions of the retributive awards of divine justice with which it has been burdened. The harrowing, materialistic ideas of the pains of the lost which were natural to times in which life was rougher and more cruel, are a witness to the deep sense of the perils and terrors of sin. But they form no part of the doctrine itself. It has to be relieved of all such accessories. It has to get the benefit of that finer moral sense, those higher and purer ideas of judgment and punishment, those humaner feelings, that deeper insight into the intrinsic nature of things, which are the results of the gradual informing of men's minds with the spirit of Christianity.—Salmond, The Christian Doctrine of Immortality, p. 662. Edinburgh, 1895.

kernel of thought from the drapery in which the biblical writers present this subject, the nature of future punishment for sin will be conceived as involving a variety of elements. The sure penal consequence of persistent transgression is to harden the heart, sear the conscience, and create a fixedness of evil character which it is impossible to change. Thus the willful transgressor stands committed to eternal sin (Mark iii, 29; Heb. vi, 4-6; x, 26, 27). This involves exclusion from the presence and fellowship of God and of all his holy ones (Matt. vii, 23; xxv, 41; 2 Thess. i, 9), and it implies a sort of communal depravity entailed perpetually by contact and association with spirits of wickedness (Matt. xxv, 41; Rev. xxi, 8). Such conditions must needs be thought of as attended with more or less suffering of anguish and despair (Matt. viii, 12; xiii, 42, 50; xxiv, 51; xxv, 30; Mark ix, 48; Luke xiii, 28). Thus we may interpret such terms as the "unquenchable fire" (Mark ix, 43); the anguish and torment ascribed to the rich man in Hades (Luke xvi, 23, 24), and "the lake that burns with fire and brimstone" (Rev. xxi, 8). For God himself, in the execution of righteous judgment upon the wicked, is spoken of as a consuming fire that fearfully seizes and devours his enemies (comp. Exod. xxiv, 17; Deut. iv, 24; ix, 3; Psa. xcvii, 3; Isa. lxvi, 15; Dan. vii, 10, 11; Heb. xii, 29).

9. Sheol, Hades, Gehenna, Tartarus. The use of the names *Sheol, Hades, Gehenna,* and *Tartarus* in connection with the future punishment of the wicked has naturally led to the belief that there is a local prison in which the criminals of the moral world are to be confined forever. In the later Jewish literature this appears as a doctrine generally accepted, and the local abodes of the righteous and the sinners are divided off into various compartments. The use of these terms in the New Testament accords with this idea. Hades includes a place of torment separated by a great gulf from "Abraham's bosom" (Luke xvi, 23). The "Gehenna of fire" clearly connotes a place as well as a condition of penal woe (Matt. v, 22; xviii, 9; Mark ix, 43-48), and the horrible torment is fearfully depicted in the apocalyptic passage where the idolatrous worshipers of the beast are said to be "tormented in fire and brimstone in the presence of the holy angels, . . . and the smoke of their torment is going up for ages of ages" (Rev. xiv, 10, 11). The concept of locality also attaches to the allusion to Tartarus in 2 Pet. ii, 4, whither it is said the sinning angels were cast down, and committed to pits ($\sigma\epsilon\iota\rho\alpha\tilde{\iota}\varsigma$) of darkness.[1] In Luke viii, 31, the demons dread to go away "into the

---

[1] Here the imagery is derived directly from the book of Enoch where the prison of the fallen angels is similarly described. See Enoch, x, 5, 13; xxi, 7-10.

abyss," which is another name for the abode of evil spirits (comp. Rev. ix, 1, 2, 11; xx, 1, 3). The language employed in all these scriptures is plainly in harmony with the prevalent belief in a place of torment for wicked men and angels, and the words of Jesus in Matt. xxv, 41—"Depart from me, ye cursed, into the eternal fire which is prepared for the devil and his angels"—are to be explained in accordance with the current ideas of the Jewish people of that time. But while this was the common belief of that time, it need not be maintained as an essential element of the teaching of Jesus and of the New Testament that Gehenna is a place, or that the future punishment of sin is physical in its nature, and therefore confined to some definite locality. In using the language of his time a great teacher does not necessarily commit himself to all the ideas which popular imagination associates with certain words and names. The one idea of penal suffering as the certain result of sin is the fundamental thought in all such allusions to Gehenna and its perpetual fires. In Rev. xx, 14; xxi, 8, the state of everlasting torment is called "the lake of fire," and "the second death." As death was the original penalty of sin (Gen. ii, 17), and the condition of a depraved sinner is one of spiritual death (Eph. ii, 2; Rom. vii, 10, 13; 2 Cor. ii, 16; 1 John iii, 14), so the ultimate doom of the wicked is appropriately called the second death. And so, perhaps, the idea of a resurrection unto condemnation and eternal abhorrence (John v, 29; Dan. xii, 2) is best understood as a kind of second sentence and penalty of death. The sinful soul, projected into its own depraved conditions of existence beyond the death of the body, experiences as the necessary result of its own wickedness a second and deeper realization of its spiritual death. Whilst, therefore, we have no sufficient knowledge to deny the possibility and reality of local and physical conditions after death, we are under no compulsion to interpret literally such terms as "fire and brimstone," and "Gehenna, where their worm dieth not." The extensive use of metaphor and symbol in the biblical writings, the large amount of apocalyptic elements therein, and the necessities of figurative speech to convey ideas of the spiritual and unseen admonish us to seek the essential thought that is embodied in these figurative terms rather than adopt a literal method of interpretation which would in many instances involve manifest absurdity.

10. Degrees of Penalty. If, now, we conclude that the penal consequences of sin extend beyond this life, and are in their inmost nature the legitimate result of habits and character fixed on the human spirit by persistent acts of opposition to what is known to be holy and just and good, it follows logically that the penal consequences must needs vary according to the various degrees of guilt. The doctrine of degrees of penalty is as clearly taught in Scripture as is the doctrine of degrees of sin and guilt (comp. above, p. 90). The same passages which establish the one prove the other also (comp. Matt. x, 15; Luke xii, 47, 48; John xix, 11). The appeal to reason in Heb. x, 28, 29, assumes as beyond controversy that he who sins under the superior light of the gospel is "worthy of much sorer punishment" than one who "set at naught a law of Moses." This fundamental principle, that all righteous penalty must be proportioned according to the various degrees of sin and guilt in the different criminals, is a truth so obvious to every reasonable mind and so universally accepted as to require no extended argument.

11. Duration of Penalty Everlasting. The duration of future punishment, so far as the Scriptures indicate, is everlasting. This is the idea naturally conveyed by such a statement as that of Matt. xxv, 46: "These shall go away into everlasting punishment" (κόλασιν αἰώνιον). Here the duration of the doom of the accursed ones (κατηραμένοι, ver. 41), who are sentenced to "the eternal fire which is prepared for the devil and his angels," is designated by the same word which describes the everlasting life of the righteous. In like manner the fearful punishment spoken of in 2 Thess. i, 9, is "everlasting destruction (ὄλεθρον αἰώνιον) from the face of the Lord." But the eternal continuance of the penal consequences of sin may be argued on other grounds than the use of a single word like αἰώνιον. The specific statement that he who blasphemes against the Spirit has no forgiveness, "neither in this age, nor in the age to come" (Matt. xii, 32) seems to exclude all possibility of future pardon. For though "the age to come" be explained as the Messianic age, there is no intimation of any other age (αἰών) to follow which will introduce better or more hopeful conditions for the sinner who goes out of this life as an enemy of God.

(1) *Absence of Hope or Promise.* Perhaps the most impressive argument from the Scriptures on this point is the notable absence of any clear and explicit statement that the penal consequences of sin will ever come to an end. This absence of any sure ground of hope for the wicked in any world or age to come cannot be fairly ignored or set aside as of little import. It is as awfully significant as the fearful language of Rom. ii, 9, concerning the positive visitation of "tribulation and anguish upon every soul of man that worketh evil," set over in contrast with "eternal life" which "the righteous judgment of God renders to them

that by patience in well-doing seek for glory and honor and incorruption."

(2) *Question of Matthew xii, 32.* It is often alleged that the language of Jesus in Matt. xii, 32, leaves it to be fairly inferred that in the world to come there may be pardon for other sins than the blasphemy against the Holy Spirit. Let this be freely acknowledged as a legitimate inference; and yet it by no means sets aside the doctrine of eternal doom for some. Rather, may it be said, this very inference enhances the awful conclusion that those who are guilty of the unpardonable sin have no hope of forgiveness, but are shut up in eternal sin and death (comp. Mark iii, 29). We cannot suppose that our Lord would give utterance to such fearful statements about hopeless perdition if no human soul had ever committed or would or could ever commit a sin whose penal consequences might continue through ages of ages. Our contention here is not about supposable possibilities of grace beyond this life, and about future opportunities of knowledge and change for those who in this life never have the light of the gospel. We are inquiring into the possible consequences of willful transgression, and find that, according to the Scriptures, there is no promise of any future provision for a change of character in incorrigible sinners, "but a certain fearful expectation of judgment, and a fierceness of fire which shall devour the adversaries" (Heb. x, 27).

(3) *Question of 1 Peter iii, 18-20.* It has also been supposed that the preaching to the spirits in prison referred to in 1 Pet. iii, 18-20; iv, 6, is evidence of a provision of saving grace that will be effectual for the salvation of sinners in the world of spirits. But here, as in Matt. xii, 32, we may grant any legitimate inference of possible provisions for some exceptional "spirits in prison" without in the least nullifying the equally legitimate significance of those other scriptures already cited which clearly indicate eternal punishment and perdition as the sure result of willful transgression and sin. A careful criticism of 1 Pet. iii, 18-20, moreover, does not warrant all the inferences which some have drawn therefrom. For if we allow the strictest literal construction, the passage only declares that Christ, "being put to death in the flesh, but quickened in the spirit, went also and preached unto the spirits in prison." There is no revelation of what he preached, or of the results of his preaching; and the entire statement is limited to spirits "who beforetime were disobedient, when the longsuffering of God waited in the days of Noah, while the ark was preparing." There is no intimation that he preached to any other spirits, or that any such preaching ever took place before or will ever take

place hereafter.¹ And if we further infer from 1 Pet. iv, 6, that the purpose of this preaching to the dead was to rescue them from their prison in order that they might "live according to God in the spirit," we are not told that even one individual of them accepted the offer, and obtained the salvation of Christ. All our hopeful inferences, therefore, are at the best presumptions, and lack confirmation in other scriptures. Such presumptions are quite insufficient to be made a ground of hope for any willful sinner. For this same epistle sounds a notable warning to evil-doers, and says that "the time is come for judgment to begin at the house of God: and if it begin first at us, what shall be the end of them that obey not the gospel of Christ? And if the righteous is scarcely saved, where shall the ungodly and sinner appear?" (1 Pet. iv, 17, 18.)

12. Doctrine of Annihilation of the Wicked. Many have sought to explain the penal consequences of sin as issuing in the annihilation of the incorrigible sinner. The "eternal destruction" is understood as eternal in effect, and such terms as *death, perdition, destruction, perishing, cutting off, consuming away,* are affirmed to signify in their most natural import the idea of utter cessation of existence. Some go so far as to maintain that the soul is dependent upon the physical organism for its conscious life and must therefore necessarily cease to exist at the death of the body. But this view is incompatible with such language as we find in Matt. x, 28, which clearly implies that to kill the body is not to destroy the soul. It is also irreconcilable with all those scriptures which imply personal conscious life, memory, and thought beyond the grave, as in the description of the rich man after his death and burial (Luke xvi, 23-31). Scriptures also which involve the doctrine of a blessed heavenly life beyond death are against this view of the soul's dependence on the body for conscious life. The words of Jesus to the dying malefactor (Luke xxiii, 43), the prayer of Stephen (Acts vii, 59), and the language of Paul in Phil. i, 21-24, imply a belief in the immortality of the soul. If conscious personal life of the soul be dependent on physical organization,

---

¹ Perhaps, after all, as J. Rendel Harris has suggested (in the Expositor; London, 1901, pp. 346-349), our whole trouble over this obscure text of 1 Pet. iii, 19, is the result of a careless omission, by some early scribe, of the word ENΩX after KAI. That the book of Enoch was widely read among the Jewish Christians of the first and second centuries is evident from the use made of it in 2 Peter and Jude (Comp. 2 Pet. ii, 4, 5; Jude 6), and as matter of fact, we read in the book of Enoch (xii and xiii) that Enoch did, at the command of the heavenly watchers, go and proclaim to Azazel and his associate fallen spirits that they should find no peace nor forgiveness. Thus it was Enoch and not Christ who "went and preached unto the spirits in prison." But see also the Expositor for 1902, pp. 316-320, and 377-390. This conjecture appears among the various readings of Griesbach's critical edition of the Greek Testament. London 1809.

there is no apparent reason why the righteous more than the wicked should survive the dissolution of the body. Such a doctrine of the annihilation of the wicked, moreover, is clearly inconsistent with the idea of degrees of punishment for sin. Others, however, maintain that the wicked after death may suffer various degrees of punishment, according to their sins, but their personal being and faculties become gradually weakened into helplessness, and finally become utterly ruined by the consuming curse of God and so pass out of conscious existence. Such texts as Psa. xxxvii, 20, are cited in evidence:

> The wicked shall perish,
> The enemies of Jehovah shall be as fat of lambs;
> They shall consume; in smoke shall they consume away.

But this psalm has no necessary reference to the question of existence after death, nor can such poetic utterances have any weight in setting aside the more positive and specific import of such texts as those we have adduced to show the perpetual consequences of sin. The admonition to "fear him who is able to *destroy* both soul and body in Gehenna" (Matt. x, 28) is cited as a proof-text for annihilation; but the mere word *destroy* (ἀπόλλυμι) does not and cannot determine the question, for it is used also in speaking of *lost* sheep and *lost* coins (Matt. x, 6; Luke xv, 6, 8). No positive or satisfactory conclusion touching the future destiny of the soul can be reached by the etymology or the suggestions of any one word. Even the very significant word *eternal*, αἰώνιος, is insufficient in itself to determine such a question. The doctrine of the future annihilation of the wicked is at best only a hypothesis beset with manifold difficulties.[1] It cannot be proven from the Scriptures. While it may seem to fit some texts, and may be a possible meaning of some words, it does not naturally accord with the more obvious import of the teachings of the New Testament touching the endless penal consequences of sin.

13. The Question of Theodicy. Why evil in any form should ever have entered the universe of the blessed God is one of the

---

[1] It does not meet the immediate difficulty, not to speak of the further mystery which is left under all theories. It means that in some cases the victory of sin over man and God is so absolute that nothing remains for God but to get rid of it by a *coup de main*. It has been characterized as the 'most wretched and cowardly of all theories'—a theory which surrenders man's true nobility 'in panic at an objection, and like all cowardice fails in securing its object' (Quarry, Donellan Lectures, p. 31). The judgment is strong, but not without its justification. Surely it is more reasonable, more scriptural, more reverent, either to hope that God will find some better way of using sinful souls than to extinguish them, or else to believe that man is so great a work of God, a being endowed with capacities so vast that no limit can be put to the possibilities of his resistance of the divine will, and, therefore, none to the continuance of the penalties of resistance.—Salmond, The Christian Doctrine of Immortality, p. 627.

most perplexing problems of human thought. In view of the awful facts and penal consequences of sin, one hesitates to accept the belief that the God of infinite wisdom, power, and goodness would permit among his creatures the existence of any intelligent being like himself to whom self-conscious existence would prove an everlasting curse. Some necessitarian divines have affirmed and argued that sin is necessary or in some way conducive to the ultimate highest good of the universe. But so far as this hypothesis admits the tacit assumption that God could have secured a universe of moral beings without sin, it cannot present a satisfactory vindication of the divine government of the world. Far better is the hypothesis which starts from the demonstrable facts of man's free personality, and maintains that the existence of moral beings, made in the image of God, is necessary to the realization of the best possible universe. Such beings are essential in any conception of a moral government, but sin is in no sense necessary to the highest good of any being or of any world. God did not desire it, plan it, or authorize it; but he saw, as we also may see, that it was impossible in the nature of things to have a world of free and responsible moral beings without the accompanying possibility of sin. Whether in the ages of ages to come, by some form of Christly mediation, the penal consequences of sin may be overcome and the universe be purged of its stains, is a question we may meditate but may not presume to answer. We have received no message or revelation as to the possibilities of the future times eternal. It has been thought, however, that the language of 1 Cor. xv, 24-28, suggests a far off goal when all authority and power adverse to Christ shall be abolished. We need not doubt that the everlasting Father would gladly, in any age or in any world, welcome any lost spirit that turned freely from his sin and cried for gracious restoration. But we do not know that any such lost spirit will ever thus freely turn unto God. Meanwhile we hold as a tentative theodicy that God prefers a moral universe of innumerable hosts of holy and righteous spirits made perfect, even though that universe be in some spots forever black with Hell, rather than have no free moral universe at all. The best theodicy ever written is, perhaps, the book of Job. But that poem leaves the problem of evil unsolved, and Jehovah's answer out of the whirlwind (Job xxxviii-xli) is an appeal to human limitations and ignorance in justification of his works and ways. But the appeal is adapted to suggest very powerfully that the Creator and Ruler of the world knows what he is doing, and will look after the consequences as well as the beginnings of all things he has made.

SECTION THIRD

THE REGENERATION AND ETERNAL LIFE OF MAN

CHAPTER I

CONVICTION, REPENTANCE, AND CONVERSION

1. Salvation a Fact of Experience. Having seen that man is a moral and religious being, and that he has fallen under the dominion of sin, our next step is to point out the way of his salvation from sin, and from the spiritual death which results from sin. This great salvation is a fact of human experience, as open to investigation as is the fact of sin, and our inductive method leads us to an examination of these matters of personal knowledge before we inquire more deeply into the character and the redeeming work of our Lord and Saviour Jesus Christ. The man blind from his birth submitted to the treatment of Jesus, obeyed his command to go and wash in the pool of Siloam, and came back seeing. He knew very positively what had occurred to him, and others witnessed the indisputable facts, while as yet he knew little of him who had opened his eyes. So we may know and witness to the facts of the consciousness of sin, repentance, and the blessedness of a new spiritual life before we "attain unto the unity of the faith and of the full knowledge ($\epsilon\pi\iota\gamma\nu\omega\sigma\iota\varsigma$) of the Son of God" (Eph. iv, 13). His divine person and mediation are full of mystery, and they open many questions which are better deferred until after we shall have first examined the actual facts of regeneration. The facts of our sinfulness we know. The teaching of Paul that the power of God is manifest in the things which he has made, and that his "wrath is revealed from heaven against all ungodliness of men" (Rom. i, 18), cannot be reasonably questioned. And God has written his law so deeply in the heart of man that there is no escape from the self-condemnation of wrongdoing. With some men the sense of self-reproach and guilt is at times so pungent as to break out in the cry of despair; with others it is comparatively light and transient. There are many forms and degrees of sinfulness. But whenever the soul of man, convicted of sin and also of the righteousness of God, begins to yearn for freedom from the power of "all ungodliness and unrighteousness of men," there is to be seen in the personal experience of such convictions and desires the mighty inworking of some heavenly force. Our present study is with these facts of human experience as they have been verified in actual life and illustrated in the biblical writings.

2. Blameless Childhood and Youth. It is often seen that pious example in the home and a careful training turn the tender heart toward God, inculcate the habit and sentiments of prayer, and instill a feeling of opposition to sin as soon as the child is able to distinguish between good and evil. Such childhood piety may blossom into beautiful young manhood and womanhood, attain in time an admirable maturity, and through all the stages of its growth exhibit a remarkable separateness from sin and sinners, and a pure devotion to truth and righteousness. And this would seem to be the true ideal of a Christian life. Why should not every member of the Christian home be so "nurtured in the chastening and admonition of the Lord" (Eph. vi, 4) as, like the child Jesus, to advance continuously with the years "in wisdom and in favor with God and men"? (Luke ii, 52.) We would not venture to affirm that any other human life was so holy, harmless, undefiled, and separate from sin as that of Jesus Christ. Only omniscience could assure us of the fact and number of such blameless lives, and of not one of them could it be said as of Jesus that he was "without sin." But it may be said, with some confidence, that there have been, by the grace of God, thousands of beautiful and noble lives, early consecrated, kept apart from the ways of sin, disciplined unto righteousness and purity, and attaining a glorious old age "unspotted from the world." At the same time we must note the fact that thousands of those who have shown from childhood a remarkable freedom from sin confess their consciousness of blameworthy shortcomings and manifold transgressions. The most eminent saints of history were sometime slaves of sin, and many of them have made confession of their deep sense of guilt as well as of their deliverance from the same.

3. Conviction of Sin. We shall, accordingly, begin our inquiry into the origin and development of spiritual life in the individual with a due recognition of his personal consciousness of sin. The sense of guilt, awakened in the soul by a revelation of God's truth and of his "wrath against all ungodliness and unrighteousness of men" (Rom. i, 18), is properly among the very first experiences of the sinner who would have peace with God, and it is appropriately called conviction of sin. It arises from a vivid perception of the nature of sin and of the holiness of God. A living, moving contact of the Spirit of God with the heart of his human offspring flashes strong light upon his understanding, and in that light he sees and feels his personal alienation from Him that is holy and just and good, and he becomes deeply troubled. Such contact of God's Spirit and truth with our spiritual nature may be effected in many unseen ways; we cannot discern the process; but the result is always to compel the man to see himself a sinner before God. The power of this conviction will naturally vary according to the measure of guilt.

(1) *Expressed in the Penitential Psalms.* Some of the clearest expressions of the sense of sinfulness and guilt found in the Old Testament scriptures appear in the penitential psalms. Not infrequently the anguish bewailed appears to be intensified by the belief that the bitter sufferings of mind and body are direct judgments of God, the rebukes of his hot displeasure and chastenings on account of sins. Thus in Psa. xxxviii, 1-4, an agonizing penitent exclaims:

> O Jehovah, rebuke me not in thy wrath,
> Neither chasten me in thy hot displeasure,
> For thine arrows stick fast in me,
> And thy hand presseth me sore.
> There is no soundness in my flesh because of thine indignation;
> Neither is there any peace in my bones because of my sin.
> For mine iniquities are gone over my head,
> As a heavy burden they are too heavy for me.

In Psa. li, 1-3, we note the humble acknowledgment of *transgressions, iniquity,* and *sin.* The three terms may be here regarded as possessing distinctive significance. The first denotes actual trespasses, deliberate acts of sin, among which was some terrible "bloodguiltiness" mentioned in verse 14. The second suggests the inbred corruption of a depraved nature, which the supplicant conceives as cleaving to him from his birth (ver. 5). The third is a more generic word (חטאה), and may here refer not only to the idea of failure, a missing of the mark, but also to the accumulated sinfulness of an impure heart and a long course of wicked conduct. How the awakened conscience abhors such a hideous load! It looks like a mass of broken bones (ver. 8). But the most terrible fact in this poetic picture of a crushed and broken heart is the sinner's knowledge that he has done all this evil in the very eyes of God. "Against thee, thee only, have I sinned" (ver. 4). The most profound conception and conviction of the exceeding sinfulness of sin is that which sees it as open opposition to the Holy One. So in his deep contrition David cried: "I have sinned against Jehovah" (2 Sam. xii, 13).

(2) *Described in Romans vii.* The most remarkable description of conviction of sin found in the New Testament is that which is given by Paul in the seventh chapter of Romans. Verses 7-13 inform us how the law of God operates as a holy revealer of sin, and verses 14-25 are a vivid word picture of the inner struggles of an awakened sinner. The real meaning and purpose of this remarkable passage have been greatly obscured by the bare question of its fitness or unfitness to represent the experiences of a regenerate man. It serves rather to show the power of the holy law of God to reveal the knowledge of sin to human consciousness. This is so obvious in verses 7-13 that no one calls it in question. The statement of verse 9 is suggestive: "I was alive apart from law, once; but the commandment coming (like that which prohibits coveting, ver. 7), sin sprung up into life, and I died." That is to say: There was a former time (ποτέ), which seems now like a far-off blessed memory of childhood innocence, when I had no sense of sin and guilt; but the law said to me, "Thou shalt not covet"; whereupon sin found a base of operation (ἀφορμήν), a great opportunity, and "through the commandment wrought in me all manner of coveting" (ver. 8); and so, to the same extent that "sin sprung up into life," my better nature died. "Did then the good become death to me?" he asks in verse 13. No, no, he answers, but by the operation of the good and holy law sin itself has been displayed as preëminently sinful. Its true nature, its deadly working, is thus brought to light, and the law of God in its inmost essence is recognized as spiritual, divine, possessing the power and character of the Holy Spirit for the work of conviction of sin (comp. John xvi, 8). In verse 14 we notice a change of tense from past to present. It serves the purpose of rhetorical emphasis, and aims to set as in a living picture before the reader's eye the life and death struggle of an awakened sinner. The writer continues the use of the first person, for he undoubtedly is giving his own personal experience as memory and deep emotion combine to make it very present to his thought. The three words employed in verses 15, 18, and 21—"I understand not" (οὐ γινώσκω), "I know" (οἶδα), "I find" (εὑρίσκω), —are suggestive of various aspects of the struggle, and may perhaps be regarded in their connection as involving an enslavement of the understanding, the affections, and the will. For in verses 14-17 he represents his understanding as in some sort of bonds; in 18-20 he shows how the fleshly nature has dominion over him; and in 21-24 the law in his members which wars against the law of his mind keeps bringing him into such a bitter consciousness of captivity to the law of sin that he cries out in agony of spirit: "O wretched man

that I am!" He conceives himself bound fast to a dead body, the body of a sinful human nature, which he has already, in vi, 6, spoken of as "our old man" and "the body of sin."

(3) *Experienced by Millions.* Such an analysis of the conviction of sin in a human soul could be made only by a mind of deep spiritual insight. It is a diagnosis of personal experience which only the most gifted and spiritual among men can fully appreciate. But a similar conviction of sin, wrought in the heart by the Spirit of God, yet varying greatly with different individuals, has been the experience of millions. To some extent it is manifest in the little child when he first comes to know good and evil; it is often very powerful in the wayward youth, when arrested by some call of God and brought to acknowledge his sin and folly; it is sometimes overwhelming in a hardened sinner, who has long stifled convictions of truth and right, and at last comes to genuine repentance. Such great varieties of personal experience are capable, however, in the last analysis, of such a portrayal as that found in Rom. vii.

4. Repentance. When such conviction of sin is accompanied by a real sorrow of heart and strong desire to escape from its condemnation and turn unto God it becomes what is called *repentance*. This term is commonly defined as a godly sorrow for sin, a definition warranted by the language of 2 Cor. vii, 10: "Godly sorrow worketh repentance unto salvation"; although in this statement the apostle has prominently in mind the sadness ($\lambda \upsilon \pi \eta$) and mourning ($\dot{o} \delta \upsilon \rho \mu \dot{o} \varsigma$) which his former epistle had caused the Corinthians. The New Testament word for repentance is μετάνοια, and means a *change of mind;* but in usage it means more than a mere change of opinion or sentiment. It is a moral change, and involves not only a deep sorrow for sin, but also an abhorrence of it; a loathing of its guilt and shame, and a yearning to be delivered from its power. In fact, the usage of the word in the New Testament seems to presuppose that the truly penitent soul always turns to God and finds forgiveness of sin. It may, then, be inferred that as a rule every sinner, in whom God's holy law reveals the damning power of sin, and who truly repents of his sins, experiences a change of mind and of spiritual character. To use words peculiar to John, he "passes out of death into life" (1 John iii, 14; John v, 24). Therefore the change is spoken of in Acts xi, 18, as a "repentance unto life," and in 2 Tim. ii, 25, as "repentance unto a full knowledge of truth." It is a change of heart that at once tends toward life, and leads unto the knowledge of God's truth and love.

5. Conversion. Such turning unto God which accompanies

repentance is called *conversion* (ἐπιστροφή). We observe that the exhortation of Acts iii, 19, is "Repent ye therefore, and turn ye (ἐπιστρέψατε, *be ye converted*), that your sins may be blotted out." The conversion of men to Christ by the ministry of the apostles is called a "turning unto the Lord" (Acts ix, 35; xi, 21; xv, 19). The preaching of Paul, both to Jews and Gentiles was "to open their eyes and to turn them from darkness to light, and from the power of Satan unto God, that they might receive remission of sins." His declaration was "that they should repent and turn to God, doing works worthy of repentance" (Acts xxvi, 18-20). "The conversion of the Gentiles" (Acts xv, 3) means their turning away from their former habits of life, from the sins and immoralities to which they had been addicted, and from the service of idols, to the adoption of a new and better life (comp. 1 Thess. i, 9; Eph. ii, 11-13; iv, 17-25; v, 8; Col. i, 21). Thus conversion, in the full Christian sense, involves repentance and a turning from sin to the service of the living God.

6. Requires Coöperation of God and Man. In Rom. ii, 4, Paul speaks of the goodness of God as leading (ἄγω, in the sense of *moving* and *directing*) unto repentance, and in Acts v, 31; xi, 18; 2 Tim. ii, 25, repentance is referred to as a gift of God. But if it be a gift of God, some one will ask why, then, man should be called on to repent and turn to God. The matter explains itself when we keep in mind the doctrine of conviction of sin as already described. There can be no genuine repentance in the soul without an antecedent conviction of sin by the revealing law and Spirit of God. In thinking of repentance as God's gift we have in mind the indispensable gracious conditions which lead to repentance. God first flashes light upon the darkened understanding; he reveals the knowledge of sin, and by the working of his Holy Spirit begets a longing for deliverance from sin. All this is the necessary preliminary to a godly sorrow for sin, and may well be spoken of as the gift of God. But when all this work of conviction is wrought in the heart it yet remains for the conscious soul with its own freedom of will to respond to such calls to repentance as we find in Matt. iii, 2, 8; iv, 17; Mark i, 15; Luke xiii, 3, 5; Acts ii, 38; iii, 19; viii, 22. After this manner we also see both the self-consistency and the significance of such apparently contradictory statements as those of Jesus in John vi, 44, and v, 40: "No man can come to me, except the Father draw him," and "Ye will not come to me that ye may have life." It is the part of God first to draw and lead by the convicting operations of his Spirit; and after this is done, or rather in connection with it, the penitent sinner must himself repent and turn unto God.

CHAPTER II

THE DOCTRINE OF FAITH

1. Faith Defined. The word *faith* means, in religious experience, an absolute conviction of the reality of unseen things. Faith in God is confidence in God; not a mere belief or acknowledgment that there is a God, but rather a personal self-commitment to his care, and a loving confidence in his grace and truth. Faith also includes an element of mystic fervor; for when a human soul commits itself through deep conviction to a power and personality unseen, but believed to be all-wise and good, there is wont to arise a warmth of emotion like the passion of love. In this way faith in Jesus Christ implies a strong, intelligent, fervid conviction of his grace and power and a loving trust in him as the divine Teacher and Saviour of men. Faith thus becomes a living test of one's hold on spiritual things. It is the response of the human heart to the impressions of the Spirit of God.

2. Doctrine of Paul. There is a doctrine of faith peculiar to the writings of Paul. We read in Eph. ii, 8, "By grace have ye been saved through faith; and that not of yourselves; God's is the gift." Some interpreters here understand the demonstrative τοῦτο, *that,* to refer to the word *faith* immediately preceding; but in that case we surely should have had the feminine αὕτη to correspond with πίστις, which is always feminine. The pronoun refers rather to the idea of *being saved* (the σεσωσμένον εἶναι) *by grace* which is made emphatic in the preceding clause. The foregoing context shows that this gracious gift of salvation is a quickening and raising up into spiritual life of those who were "dead through trespasses and sins." The merit and glory of it all are ascribed to the mercy, love, kindness, and grace of God in Jesus Christ. This way of salvation is spoken of in Eph. iii, 10-12, as an exhibition of "the manifold wisdom of God, according to a purpose of the ages which he purposed in Christ Jesus our Lord, in whom we have boldness and access in confidence through our faith in him." Repentance leads unto this great salvation, but the saving grace must, according to Paul, be appropriated by an act of faith in God. "Repent ye, and believe in the gospel," says Jesus (Mark i, 15). Hence it is obviously improper to call faith a gift of God when the word is used in reference to a responsible act and attitude of an individual.¹ Faith that appropriates the saving grace of God and leads to salvation is a free act of the soul. Man is called upon to "have faith in God," to "believe on the Lord Jesus Christ," and the belief required is not merely an assent of the mind to that which is good, nor the exercise of reason and judgment in approving wholesome doctrines. It is a conscious willing surrender of the heart to the righteous claims of God, and a throwing oneself, so to speak, in full confidence on the divine Saviour. In the highest and holiest sense, faith is TRUST.²

3. Theme of the Epistle to the Romans. The great theme of the epistle to the Romans is the doctrine that the gospel "is the power of God unto salvation to everyone who believes." Having shown that the whole world is fallen under the condemning judgment of God, the apostle announces as a fundamental truth that "now, apart from the law, a righteousness of God has been manifested, being witnessed by the law and the prophets; even the righteousness of God through faith in Jesus Christ unto all them that believe" (iii, 21, 22). Here is presented in substance the whole Pauline idea of the attainment of personal righteousness. It is not by the performance of the works of the law; it comes not by way of merit from anything which fallen man can do; it comes solely by an act of faith in the efficacy of "the redemption that is in Jesus Christ, whom God set forth to be a propitiation through faith in his blood." The faith which is here contemplated is a sort of means and condition of receiving the benefit of redemption. It is an act and also a subjective state or attitude of the soul for which the person hoping to be saved is held responsible.

4. Example of Abraham in Romans iv. In the fourth chapter of Romans this idea of saving faith is illustrated in a number of points by the example of Abraham. It is pointed out (1) that the patriarch's trust in God "was reckoned unto him for righteous-

---

¹ The different concepts and shades of meaning which attach to the word $\pi i \sigma \tau \iota \varsigma$ in the New Testament are worthy of notice. In some passages it may connote the antecedents and consequences of the act of saving faith, and be spoken of as a divine possession (1 Cor. xii, 9; James ii, 1, 14); in others it seems to be used as meaning the substance of the gospel itself (Gal. i, 23; Eph. iv, 13; Jude, vers. 3 and 20; and perhaps 1 Tim. i, 19; iv, i; v, 8); in others it suggests the idea of fidelity (Titus ii, 10; Gal. v, 22). These secondary and modified meanings of the word have no necessary connection with the Pauline doctrine of faith as means and condition of salvation. See Lightfoot's dissertation on "The Words Denoting Faith" in his Epistle to the Galatians, pp. 154-158. London, 1890.

² The term *faith* can scarcely be said to occur at all in the Hebrew scriptures of the Old Testament. It is indeed a characteristic token of the difference between the two covenants, that under the law the *'fear* of the Lord' holds very much the same place as 'faith in God,' 'faith in Christ,' under the gospel. Awe is the prominent idea in the earlier dispensation, trust in the later. At the same time, though the word itself is not found in the Old Testament, the idea is not absent; for, indeed, a trust in the Infinite and Unseen, subordinating thereto all interests that are finite and transitory, is the very essence of the higher spiritual life.—Lightfoot, Epistle to the Galatians, p. 159.

ness." It was, accordingly, not by works, but by an act of faith, that he was accounted righteous before God, and his subjective relation to the judgment of God was clearly a faith-righteousness (vers. 1-5). (2) A confirmation of this doctrine is also found in David's words (Psa. xxxii, 1, 2), where they are pronounced blessed "whose sins are covered," and "to whom the Lord will not reckon sin" (6-8). (3) The apostle next shows that this blessedness came to Abraham before he had received the sign and seal of circumcision, and must therefore be independent of such outward rites (9-12). (4) For the same reason this righteousness of faith is also apart from works of law, for it cannot be attained through that which works wrath by its fearful revelation of the damning guilt of sin (13-17). (5) Abraham's faith, moreover, was an example of unwavering confidence in God's word. "Believing in hope against hope," and having his heart set on God's promise, "he wavered not through unbelief, but waxed strong through faith, giving glory to God, and being fully assured that what he had promised he was able also to perform" (18-22). Finally, (6) he alleges that this sublime example of faith in God stands written in the Scriptures as a monumental witness for all believers in Jesus Christ (23-25). This example of Abraham is also adduced in the epistle to the Galatians (iii, 6-29), and is there made to establish the same doctrine of faith as the means of justification.

5. Doctrine of James. But in the epistle of James (ii, 21-23) the faith of Abraham as shown in his readiness to offer Isaac upon the altar is brought forward to prove that faith is not only essential to initiate the believer in righteousness, but also to carry forward the new life of devotion to God. In this later example written in the history of Abraham it is seen "that the faith wrought with his works, and (as a result issuing) from the works the faith was made perfect." The substance of doctrine in both Paul and James is certainly in accord with the fundamental truth that any and every soul of man who has been convicted of sin, and repents and turns unto God in faith, must also "do works worthy of repentance" (Acts xxvi, 20; comp. Matt. iii, 8; Luke iii, 8). Paul makes it very emphatic that one who becomes dead to sin cannot any longer live therein (Rom. vi, 1). It is not, therefore, in any fundamental way that James and Paul differ in their teaching about faith and justification before God. But they do differ, and each writer is to be studied and estimated by a careful attention to his peculiar point of view. James wishes to give strong testimony against such as are forgetful hearers and not actual doers of the word of truth (i, 22-25), and he insists rightly that the only faith which is genuine and profitable is that which is shown by good works (ii, 14-18). This is an aspect of faith which Paul, according to Gal. v, 6, could certainly not oppose.

6. Doctrine of the Epistle to the Hebrews. Still another concept of faith is set forth in the epistle to the Hebrews, and definitely described as the "substance of things hoped for, a conviction of things not seen" (xi, 1). As the etymology of the Greek word translated *substance* ($\dot{v}\pi\acute{o}\sigma\tau\alpha\sigma\iota\varsigma$) suggests, faith is here conceived as the *underlying basis* of the believer's hopes, and at the same time as a profound inward conviction ($\check{\epsilon}\lambda\epsilon\gamma\chi o\varsigma$, *proof*) of the reality of things not seen by fleshly eyes. This conception of faith, as illustrated by the examples of ancient worthies mentioned in this chapter, contemplates that holy trust in God which leads to active and loving obedience. It is, perhaps, more closely related to the doctrine of James than to the Pauline idea of a faith apart from the works of the law. Nevertheless, the faith by which we apprehend the work of God in creation (ver. 3) is essentially the same as that by which we apprehend the grace of God in Jesus Christ. The faith of Abel is conceived as the means "through which he had witness borne to him that he was righteous" (ver. 4). And all the godly acts and heavenly hopes of the long list of worthies were inspired by a conviction and assurance of invisible realities akin to what the repentant sinner realizes when he accepts the redemption of Christ. In every case "the one who comes to God must believe that he is, and that he is a rewarder of them that seek after him" (ver. 6). Such faith ever tends "to a preserving of the soul" ($\epsilon\dot{\iota}\varsigma\ \pi\epsilon\rho\iota\pi o\acute{\iota}\eta\sigma\iota\nu\ \psi\nu\chi\tilde{\eta}\varsigma$, Heb. x, 39). Whether exercised by the penitent sinner or by the hopeful saint, it unites the confiding soul with God.

7. Doctrine of Faith in the Gospels. The doctrine of faith occupies a prominent place in the teaching of Jesus. His earliest preaching was, "Repent ye, and believe in the gospel" (Mark i, 15), and his latest commission, according to Mark xvi, 16, "He that believeth and is baptized shall be saved; but he that disbelieveth shall be condemned." Here faith is obviously an act and responsible attitude of trust, and is made a condition of salvation. A corresponding passage in John's gospel (iii, 36) is in noticeable harmony with the main elements of the Pauline doctrine: "He that believeth on the Son hath eternal life; but he that obeyeth not the Son shall not see life, but the wrath of God abideth on him." In his works of healing Jesus made much of the faith in him which was exercised by those who sought his help. "O woman, great is thy faith!" he exclaimed before the Canaanitish woman who besought him for her daughter (Matt. xv, 28; comp. viii, 10;

ix, 2, and Luke vii, 9). To another woman he said: "Daughter, be of good cheer; thy faith hath saved thee. And the woman was saved from that hour" (Matt. ix, 22). To the blind men who cried for his favor he said: "According to your faith be it done unto you. And their eyes were opened" (Matt. ix, 29). He taught his disciples that they might remove mountains by faith (Matt. xvii, 20; xxi, 21; Mark xi, 23; comp. 1 Cor. xiii, 2), and said in the same connection: "All things, whatsoever ye shall ask in prayer, believing, ye shall receive." He seems almost to employ hyperbole when he declares, "All things are possible to him that believeth" (Mark ix, 23). Many other examples in the synoptic gospels teach the same doctrine of faith, as a condition and means of obtaining the gracious help of God and of Christ. In the gospel of John, as the one passage already cited shows, faith is essential to salvation in Christ. "The right to become children of God" is given "to them that believe on his name" (i, 12; comp. ii, 23; iii, 18; 1 John iii, 23; v, 13).[1] The great text in iii, 16, affirms that "whosoever believeth on" the only begotten Son of God shall not perish but have eternal life. In v, 24, it is declared that "he who heareth my word and believeth on him that sent me, hath eternal life, and cometh not into judgment." The same truth is reiterated in one form and another so as to be a characteristic formula of this Johannine gospel (comp. vi, 29, 35, 47; vii, 38; ix, 35-38; xi, 25, 26; xiv, 1, 11, 12). In fact this gospel claims to have been written "that ye may believe that Jesus is the Christ, the Son of God; and that believing ye may have life in his name" (xx, 31).

8. Personal Confession. The act of personal confession may also well be mentioned in connection with this doctrine of faith. The two are closely associated in Rom. x, 9, 10: "If thou wilt confess the word with thy mouth, that Jesus is Lord, and wilt believe in thy heart that God raised him from the dead, thou shalt be saved; for with the heart one believes unto righteousness, and with the mouth confession is made unto salvation." Some such confession of Christ is spoken of in Luke xii, 8, 9, as opposed to a denial in the presence of men (comp. Matt. x, 32; 1 John iv, 2, 3, 15). In the initial experience of salvation confession of sins must needs accompany the act of faith and the confession of Jesus Christ as Lord; for "if we confess our sins, he is faithful and righteous to forgive us our sins, and to cleanse us from all unrighteousness" (1 John i, 9; comp. Matt. iii, 6).

---

[1] It is worthy of note that the word faith ($\pi\iota\sigma\tau\iota\varsigma$) does not occur in John's gospel, and appears only once in the epistle (1 John v, 4), where it is called "the victory that overcame the world."

CHAPTER III

FORGIVENESS OF SINS AND RECONCILIATION

1. Greek Words for Remission. According to the words of Acts iii, 19, repentance and conversion are essentially preliminary to the blotting out of sins (τὸ ἐξαλιφθῆναι τὰς ἁμαρτίας), and the personal act of faith is the means whereby this blessed result is realized. But this idea of a removal of sin as a blotting out, wiping off, erasure, or obliteration (ἐξαλείφω) of the sins of a human soul calls for separate examination. There are two Greek words in the New Testament which especially deserve our attention in connection with this subject, namely, ἄφεσις (ἁμαρτιῶν) and δικαιόω. The former may be translated *remission, pardon*, or *forgiveness* of sins; the latter means rather to *justify, acquit, clear from guilt, pronounce righteous*. Both terms contain a measure of forensic and juridical significance, and suggest the idea of a prisoner, a debtor, or a guilty person, whose merited penalty is discharged by order of a competent court. When such an act of pardon restores friendly relations between the offender and the party who has been wronged, it not only remits the penalty, but may also include the further idea of personal forgiveness, so that reconciliation is effected between those who were at enmity. Applying these analogies to the relations between a guilty sinner and the most holy God, we may discern a wonderful depth of meaning in such a statement as that of 2 Cor. v, 19: "God was in Christ reconciling the world unto himself, not reckoning unto them their trespasses." The trespasses are blotted out, removed, reckoned as if they had not been. According to Paul the sinner is freely justified through faith by the grace of God (Rom. iii, 24), and being thus justified he has "peace with God," and access into a state of blessed and glorious hope, having the love of God shed abroad in his heart by the Holy Spirit (Rom. v, 1-4). "We reckon therefore," he says (iii, 28), "that a man is justified by faith apart from the works of the law." He maintains (vii, 6) that "we have been discharged from the law, having died to that in which we were held down, so as to serve in newness of spirit." The wretched captive, whose struggle we saw depicted in Rom. vii, 15-25, accepts by faith the gracious pardon, obtains remission of sins, and "thanks God through Jesus Christ our Lord."

2. Peculiarity of Paul's Doctrine of Justification. The chief peculiarity of Paul's doctrine of justification by faith is the intensity with which he conceives it as proceeding from the saving grace of God. He sees in the example of Abraham that "faith was reckoned unto him for righteousness" (Rom. iv, 3), and the whole gospel of Christ is to him the revelation of "a righteousness of God" (δικαιοσύνη θεοῦ, Rom. i, 17). It is "a righteousness of God through faith in Jesus Christ unto all them that believe" (Rom. iii, 22). The word *righteousness* here is not to be understood as an attribute of God in the sense of his divine justice; it is a righteousness which proceeds from God, and is extolled as a "free gift" (χάρισμα), and a "gift in grace" (δωρεὰ ἐν χάριτι, Rom. v, 15-17). He calls it in Phil. iii, 9, "that which is through faith in Christ, the righteousness from God (ἐκ θεοῦ) on the condition of faith." This righteousness or justification (for both these ideas run together in the word) is the gracious state which results immediately from the acquittal which goes with the forgiveness of sin.[1] If it seem astonishing that the "righteous Judge of all the earth," who revealed himself to Abraham as one who will distinguish between the righteous and the wicked (Gen. xviii, 25), should be declared by Paul to be God who "justifieth the ungodly" (Rom. iv, 5), let it be observed that the divine justification goes forth only "to him that believeth." "The righteousness which is of faith" insists that God's free gift comes not to every sinner; only to him who makes the needful confession, and "with the heart believeth unto righteousness" shall the salvation of God be given (Rom. x, 6-10). To all such "God reckons righteousness apart from works" (Rom. iv, 6, 11) in the fact that he reckons faith for righteousness, as in the case of Abraham. The sinner who "believes unto righteousness" is accordingly treated by God as freed from guilt and "from the law of sin and of death" (Rom. viii, 2). The act of faith on the part of the convicted and penitent sinner is accordingly followed by the gracious act of justification on the part of God.

3. Reconciliation. The result of this divine act of pardon is a state of reconciliation and peace between God and the believer. We have seen that, according to Paul, "the mind of the flesh is enmity (ἔχθρα) against God" (Rom. viii, 7); but "being justified by faith we have peace with God through Jesus Christ" (Rom. v, 1).

---

[1] In the strict legal sense, as Merrill has observed, "pardon differs from acquittal. The latter term is applied where guilt is charged but not established. The innocent man, when found to be innocent, is acquitted. He is not pardoned, but justified as an innocent man. In such case there is no forgiveness. But the sinner is not innocent. The dreadful fact of his guilt is established, and cannot be ignored."—Aspects of Christian Experience, p. 79. Cincinnati, 1882.

Such a peace with God involves the removal of the enmity, and the infusion of holy love and joy within the heart. This blessed result of heavenly grace is called in Rom. v, 11, "the reconciliation" (ἡ καταλλαγή), and in the immediate context the apostle writes: "If, being enemies, we were reconciled to God through the death of his Son, much more, being reconciled, shall we be saved in his life" (ver. 10). This idea of reconciliation finds further expression in 2 Cor. v, 18-20: "All things are of God who reconciled us to himself through Christ, and gave us the ministry of reconciliation; to wit, that God was in Christ reconciling the world unto himself, not reckoning unto them their trespasses, and having placed in us the word of the reconciliation." This "word of the reconciliation" is a sacred deposit in the hearts of those who like Paul had received a commission to preach this doctrine of reconciliation. They became ambassadors of Christ, and went about entreating men to "be reconciled to God." Such a ministry of reconciliation was not different from that "word which God sent unto the children of Israel, preaching good tidings of peace by Jesus Christ," mentioned in Acts x, 36. The preaching of this reconciliation is the preaching of "peace with God through Jesus Christ" which follows the free pardon of sin. This work of reconciliation through Christ is spoken of in Eph. ii, 14-18, as a removal of enmity between Jew and Gentile, and effecting peace between them both and God; thereby Christ "reconciled them both in one body unto God through the cross, having slain the enmity thereby; and he came and preached good tidings of peace to you that were far off (Gentiles), and peace to them that were nigh (Jews); for through him we both have access in one Spirit unto the Father." In a similar way, we are told in Col. i, 20-22, of God's "reconciling all things unto himself, having made peace through the blood of the cross," so that those who were once aliens and enemies in their evil works had become reconciled to him so as to be "presented before him holy and without blemish and unreprovable." This happy reconciliation with God is something to be received (Rom. v, 11: λαμβάνω, *lay hold of;* claim and take into possession as one's own blessed boon). But though appropriated by the act of faith, it is a gracious provision coming from the love of God for his enemies (Rom. v, 10). It is, in personal experience, the result of conviction of sin, repentance, turning to God, believing in Christ, receiving forgiveness of sins and justification before God.

CHAPTER IV

NEW BIRTH AND NEW LIFE

1. Comprehensive of the Other Experiences. But all these personal experiences of conviction, repentance, faith, forgiveness of sin, and reconciliation with God do not exhaust the mighty working of the power from on high whereby sinful man is brought into conscious favor and fellowship with God. Other truths vitally connected with these experiences of the soul appear in the biblical writings and are attested by an innumerable company of Christian believers. Chief among these is that mysterious work of the Holy Spirit which we commonly call regeneration, or the new birth. This must not be thought of as an experience that is subsequent to repentance and conversion. There can be no remission of sins and no sense of justification before God apart from the regeneration of the heart. We treat the subject in this relation because of the deeper and broader significance which it has for the whole Christian life. The new birth and the new life, which are contemplated in the spiritual regeneration of a sinner, will be found to be of the nature of a new creation, and in a broad yet true sense, comprehensive of all the experiences of personal salvation in Christ. Pardon and justification are gracious acts of God *done for us;* regeneration is a corresponding and concomitant work of the Holy Spirit *wrought in us.*

2. Idea of a New Heart in the Old Testament. The idea of a new spiritual life, begotten as by a special creative act of God, appears in various parts of the Old Testament. It is suggested by the metaphor of the circumcision of the heart in Deut. x, 16; xxx, 6; Jer. iv, 4. It seems implied in 1 Sam. x, 9, where God gives Saul "another heart." It finds strong expression in the penitential psalm (li, 10), "Create for me a clean heart, O God, and renew a right spirit within me." It is set forth in language of remarkable spiritual depth and beauty in Ezek. xi, 19, and xxxvi, 26: "I will give you a new heart, and a new spirit will I put within you; and I will take away the heart of stone from your flesh, and will give you a heart of flesh; and my Spirit will I put within you." All these scriptures imply a radical change in the spiritual nature of man; not of course the creation of new substance, but such a quickening of all the forces of spiritual life as to produce another mode of life.

3. **Teaching of Jesus in John iii, 3-8.** The most direct and positive teaching in the New Testament on this subject is found in the gospel of John (iii, 3-8), where Jesus says, "Except a man be born from above (ἄνωθεν), he cannot see the kingdom of God." The word ἄνωθεν in this connection seems to mean *from above* rather than *again,* as frequently translated. It occurs again in verse 31 of the same chapter in the statement, "He that cometh *from above* is above all." In John xix, 11, Jesus says to Pilate, "Thou wouldest have no power against me, except it were given thee *from above."* The word has also this meaning in the epistle of James, where it is said that "every perfect gift is *from above,* coming down from the Father of lights" (i, 17), and where the wisdom is extolled "which cometh down *from above"* (iii, 15, 17). And so we understand that the new birth, of which Jesus speaks in John iii, 3-8, is the originating of a new life in the soul by the infusion of a living germ *from above,* that is, "from God," "from heaven," or "out of heaven," whence Jesus himself came (comp. vers. 2 and 13, and John vi, 38, 41, 42, 50). The mystery of this generation from above is deepened by the statement of verse 5: "Except a man be born of water and Spirit he cannot enter into the kingdom of God." The common interpretation which makes the words *born of water* mean the outward performance of baptism in water has never been able to make itself thoroughly satisfactory. It seems inexplicably strange that our Lord should have thus spoken of Christian baptism to "a ruler of the Jews" at the time and under the circumstances supposed.[1] That he should have aimed to set him thinking deeply on "heavenly things" (τὰ ἐπουράνια, ver. 12), is every way supposable, and accords with his remarkable spiritual language to the woman of Samaria and to others. But for him, in a conversation with Nicodemus, to declare most solemnly that the outward ceremony or rite of baptism with water is essential in order to enter into the kingdom of God, is certainly amazing. It is not only out of harmony with the profound spiritual teaching of John's gospel, but it also stands in conflict with the letter and spirit of Jesus's words against the "blind Pharisee," who seeks only to "cleanse

---

[1] Bernard Weiss, in his edition of Meyer's Handbook on John, affirms that "it is historically inconceivable that Jesus should have spoken to Nicodemus of Christian baptism." In his own exposition Weiss maintains that the two factors, water and spirit, "are simply coördinated, the water being conceived in its essence as a purifying factor, the spirit as the efficient creative principle of the new life." But the main trouble is to recognize the water of ritual baptism as a "coördinate" factor along with the creative power of the Spirit. We would rather regard the words ὕδατος καί, *water and,* in verse 5, as an early interpolation; for they do not occur again in verses 6 and 8, where *of the Spirit* is repeated; and, taken in the sense in which they have generally been explained, they savor of the ritualistic and sacramental sentiment which infected Christian teaching at an early period.

the outside of the cup and the platter" (Matt. xxiii, 25, 26; Luke xi, 39; Mark vii, 4). That baptism with water is indeed a symbol of the "washing of regeneration" (Titus iii, 5) is true enough, but to *coördinate* it with regeneration, so as to make it a necessary condition of entrance into the kingdom of God, is to teach "baptismal regeneration" and a "sacramentarian salvation," which ought to be repudiated by all Protestant Christendom.

4. Significance of Titus iii, 5, and Ephesians v, 26. Post-apostolic connotations of baptism and of other external ordinances have been so long read into words and phrases of the New Testament that to question a current interpretation is to expose oneself to the charge of a lack of candor. So it has come to pass that the phrases, "washing of regeneration" (Titus iii, 5), and "the washing of the water in the word" (Eph. v, 26) are claimed with an air of authority to refer necessarily to Christian baptism.[1] But in the first passage it is said that "God our Saviour, not by works in righteousness which we did ourselves, but according to his mercy saved us through washing of regeneration and renewing of the Holy Spirit which he poured out upon us richly." Now this *washing* of regeneration is no more an outward washing with water than is the *"purifying* unto himself a people for his own possession" by "our great God and Saviour Jesus Christ," in Titus ii, 14, an external act or ceremony. To a New Testament writer the conjunction of the two ideas of *"washing* of regeneration" and *"renewing* of the Spirit" would be far more likely to suggest the language and thought of Ezek. xxxvi, 25, 26, than any form or ceremony of baptism. As little can we believe that there is any direct reference to the outward rite of baptism in Eph. v, 26, where Christ is said to have "loved the church, and to have given himself up for her, in order that he might sanctify her, having cleansed her by the washing of the water in the word, that he himself might present to himself the church glorious, not having spot or wrinkle or any such thing, but that she should be holy and without blemish." Here it is the church ($\dot{\eta}$ $\dot{\epsilon}\kappa\kappa\lambda\eta\sigma\iota\alpha$), not the individual believer, that is held before the mind. Christ himself does the cleansing and the washing, though, according to John iv, 2, "Jesus himself baptized not." To suppose that Christ's own cleansing and sanctifying of his church is done by the water of baptism is to magnify an outward ordinance above the word and the Spirit. Those who suppose "the washing of the water" (Eph.

---

[1] So, for example, Ellicott, Commentary on Eph. v, 26: "The reference to baptism is clear and distinct, and the meaning of $\lambda o \upsilon \tau \rho \acute{o} \nu$, *laver*, indisputable." But the word $\lambda o \upsilon \tau \rho \acute{o} \nu$ is never used in the Septuagint as a translation of the Hebrew word for *laver* (כִּיּוֹר). Again, on Titus iii, 5, he writes: "Less than this cannot be said by a candid interpreter."

v, 26) to refer directly to baptism naturally find great difficulty in determining both the meaning and the connection of the phrase ἐν ῥήματι, *in the word*.¹ But nothing is clearer than that this ῥῆμα is *God's word* (ῥῆμα θεοῦ) which in chapter vi, 17, is called "the sword of the Spirit"; that is, the mighty instrument with which the Spirit works all cleansing and sanctifying. In chapter i, 13, it is called "the word (λόγος) of the truth, the gospel of your salvation." This word is the "power of God unto salvation" (Rom. i, 16), active, sharp, and penetrating (Heb. iv, 12), sanctifying in the truth (John xvii, 17-19). In view of this clear and uniform teaching of the New Testament, the connection of the phrase *in the word* with what precedes it need not seem difficult. Both the sanctifying and the cleansing is wrought in, or by the instrumentality of, the word of truth. This being the fundamental doctrine, the use of the metaphor of *cleansing by the washing of water* no more points specifically to baptism in this connection than does the like metaphor of *sprinkling with clean water* in the language of Ezek. xxxvi, 25. That the metaphor may suggest the analogy of *any kind of external ablution* need not be questioned at all. So in Eph. v, 26, there may be, as some maintain, an allusion to the bathing of a bride before marriage.² But whatever the particular source of the metaphor of *washing* in Eph. v, 26, and Titus iii, 5, the real *sanctifying, cleansing,* and *regenerating* in the word and Spirit of God can be no outward washing of the body. No legitimate inference from these texts can warrant the sacramentarian doctrine of "baptismal regeneration," or of the necessity of baptism in order to enter the kingdom of God.

5. The New Birth a New Creation. Recurring now to the statement in John iii, 5, we inquire after the source and significance of the mystic words, "Except one be born of water and Spirit." The concept of birth, generation, a coming into being and life, involves necessarily to some extent the idea of a new creation. It is noteworthy that in the Pauline epistles this new spiritual life which a Christian believer receives from God through faith is called a new creation (καινὴ κτίσις). In Gal. vi, 15, the apostle exalts this ideal above carnal ordinances by saying that "neither

---

¹ This is the frank confession of Ellicott in his notes on the passage. But he rejects, as "scarcely probable," that meaning of ἐν ῥήματι which he calls "the ancient and plausible reference to the words used in baptism." It is amazing to find him writing in the same note that the "idea" of *sanctifying in the word* "is scarcely doctrinally tenable."

² This was an ancient custom, and the *presentation* mentioned in verse 27, and the *adorning of a bride for her husband* in Rev. xxi, 2, favor the supposition of such an allusion. But the sacramentarian, who insists that λουτρόν must mean *laver* rather than the *washing,* and that the reference is to the basin, font, or baptistry rather than to the idea or the act of cleansing, naturally makes more account of the bath tub than the bathing.

circumcision is anything, nor uncircumcision, but a new creature." In 2 Cor. v, 17, he says that "if any man is in Christ, he is (or there is) a new creature; the old things are passed away; behold, they are become new." In Eph. ii, 10, we read: "We are his workmanship (ποίημα), created in Christ Jesus for good works"; and in iv, 23, 24, we have the exhortation to "be renewed in the spirit of your mind, and put on the new man, which after God hath been created in righteousness and holiness of truth." So again in Col. iii, 9, 10, the constant putting away of all kinds of sinfulness is based upon the consideration "that ye have put off the old man with his doings, and have put on the new man, who is being renewed in knowledge after the image of him that created him."¹ In all these passages the result of the mighty working of God in the soul of man, whereby one is brought from the death of sin into the life of righteousness, is conceived as a new creation.² It is, accordingly, most natural to associate this idea of creation with being "born of God." It may be that the truest, clearest concept of creation in the highest sense is that of a *begetting,* a *genesis,* and to understand the real import of John iii, 5, we should recognize in the mystic and metaphorical language of Jesus an allusion to the primeval creation as read in the first chapter of Genesis. There we have the picture of a series of creative acts set forth as a succession of births produced by the word of God, and they are called "generations of the heavens and the earth." At the beginning "darkness was upon the face of the deep and the Spirit of God was brooding upon the face of the waters." And when "God said, Let there be light; and there was light," we get our first and sublimest concept of a divine creative birth ἐξ ὕδατος καὶ πνεύματος, *from water and Spirit.* As in that primeval creation light came forth out of the darkness by the word of God, begotten as it were from the waters and the Spirit that brooded over them, so the new life and light of God are brought forth in the heart of man by the working of the same Spirit from above. The "being born of water," therefore, in John iii, 5, is not the ceremony of baptism, but a mystic allusion to the brooding of the Spirit over the waters and the breaking of the light out of the "darkness that was upon the face of the deep,"

---

¹ The new creation of the spirit into fullness of knowledge and truth, is regarded by the apostle as analogous to man's first creation. As he was then made in the image of God, so now; but it was then naturally, now spiritually in ἐπίγνωσις. . . . . It is not to restore the old, but to create the new, that redemption has been brought about.—Alford, Greek Testament, notes in loco.

² So in fact many interpreters translate the word κτίσις, which may mean either *creature* or *creation.* According to Schöttgen, *Horæ Hebraicæ,* vol. i, pp. 328, 704, the proselyte who was converted from idolatry to Judaism was called בריה חדשה, *a new creation.*

and the significance of the allusion is in the fact that the new birth from above is like the creation of a new heaven and earth. This seems to have been the thought of Paul when he says that "God, who said, Light shall shine out of the darkness, shined in our hearts to give the light of the knowledge of the glory of God in the face of Jesus Christ" (2 Cor. iv, 6). Here we have a true concept of the new birth and the new creation in Christ Jesus. Such generation, or regeneration, is necessarily a work of God in man. It is the gracious product of the life of the Spirit from above (ἄνωθεν). Conviction of sin, repentance, and faith are essential conditions of this transition into heavenly life, and in all these conditions the human soul coöperates with the life-giving Spirit; and so we read in John i, 12, 13: "As many as received him, to them gave he power (ἐξουσίαν, authority, right) to become children of God, even to them that believe on his name: who were born, not of blood, nor of the will of the flesh, nor of the will of man, but of God."

6. Mystery of Spiritual Life. The mystery of this new birth is recognized in John iii, 8, and compared to the wind[1] which blows where it will, and makes itself heard, but no one knows whence it comes nor whither it goes. There is mystery connected with "that which is born of the flesh," as such scriptures as Eccl. xi, 5, and Psa. cxxxix, 14, 15, confess; much deeper is the mystery of spiritual and heavenly things. This much, however, seems to be beyond contradiction, that in all the world of living things no form or kind of life is known to come into existence except as the outgrowth of some antecedent germ of life. No changing of substances, no modifications of environment, no chemical compounds, no forces of electricity or of any kind of energy known to man, can endow one atom of the material world with the principle of life. And so we may say of any form of inanimate matter in the world, Except some germ of life be imparted to it from above, that is, from some higher power or nature having life in itself, it cannot enter the realm of life at all.[2] In accordance with this analogy, so invariable and universal in the world of nature, there can come no spiritual element of life in man, who is "dead in

---

[1] Bengel (Gnomon of the New Testament, in loco) does not allow the meaning of *wind* to τὸ πνεῦμα in this verse but translates: "The Spirit breatheth where it will, and thou hearest its voice, but knowest not whence it comes and whither it goes; so is every one who is born of the Spirit." The Sinaitic MS. reads in the last sentence: "So is every one who is born of water and Spirit." The fact that πνεῦμα is used, like the Hebrew רוּחַ, both for *wind* and *spirit*, occasions ambiguity. The illustration drawn from the mystery of the wind may have been suggested by Gen. i, 2: "The Spirit of God brooded upon the face of the waters," where some render רוּחַ אֱלֹהִים, *a wind of God*. Comp. Gen. viii, 1.

[2] See Henry Drummond's suggestive chapter on "Biogenesis" in his Natural Law in the Spiritual World, pp. 61-94. New York, 1887.

trespasses and in sins," except it be given him from above. There must be some living germ implanted by a power not ourselves, and it must be nourished by appropriate conditions. The Spirit of God, brooding over the great deep of man's elementary possibilities, quickens his spiritual nature into heavenly life and light, and releases him from the darkness of sin. Thus, to use the metaphor drawn from the first creation, he is "born of water and Spirit," he is "called out of darkness into marvelous light" (1 Pet. ii, 9); he has put off the old man of sin, with the fleshly lusts and passions of the depraved nature, and has become a new creation by power from on high. There is chaos no longer in his soul, but peace with God through Jesus Christ. He is now dead unto sin, but alive unto God (Rom. vi, 2, 10, 11). The germ of new and heavenly life abides and develops into the eternal life of God. And so we read in 1 John iii, 9: "Whosoever is begotten of God, doeth no sin, because his seed (σπέρμα αὐτοῦ; that is, *God's seed,* an element of the divine nature as a creative germ of new and higher life) abideth in him." This idea of being *born* or *begotten* of God, and thereby becoming separate from sin, is peculiarly Johannine (comp. 1 John ii, 29; iv, 7; v, 1, 4, 18). But it is clearly implied in the language of 2 Pet. i, 4: "Ye may become partakers of the divine nature, having escaped from the corruption that is in the world by lust." It is involved in such Pauline expressions as "newness of life" (Rom. vi, 4); "the Spirit giveth life" (2 Cor. iii, 6); "it is no longer I that live, but Christ liveth in me" (Gal. ii, 20); "your life is hid with Christ in God" (Col. iii, 3). In fact the doctrine of divine life begotten in the heart of man by the Spirit of God is so common to all the New Testament writers that it seems needless to point out incidental and favorite forms of expression peculiar to any one author.

7. A Passing out of Death into Life. The new birth, then, is a passing out of darkness into light, and "out of death into life" (John v, 24; 1 John iii, 14). It is a new and heavenly creation by the living "Power from on high," and it is necessary for entrance into the kingdom of God. Heirs of God and partakers of the inheritance of the saints in light must be begotten of God, born from above. In language peculiar to John, "the witness is this, that God gave us eternal life, and this life is in his Son. He that hath the Son hath the life; and he that hath not the Son hath not the life" (1 John v, 11, 12). While, therefore, all men by reason of their religious constitution and personality are "offspring of God" (γένος τοῦ θεοῦ, Acts xvii, 28, 29), no one of these offspring enters into conscious and happy fellowship with God except he be "born from above." There is a new and special impartation of heavenly life, given upon conditions of contrition and turning unto God in faith. This new birth quickens all the spiritual possibilities within man's nature, and, in the mystic Pauline phrase, his life becomes hidden with Christ in God and he is conceived as a new creation. The simple facts, sufficiently recognized in the Scriptures, of man's religious nature and possibilities, would seem to leave no ground for the controversies which have been raised over the bearing of the doctrine of regeneration on the universal fatherhood of God. The terms employed, such as *regeneration, justification, a new creation, passing out of death into life*, contain an obvious figurative element, but describe facts of experience. Too many controversialists go far astray over a mere figure of speech, and assume that a new birth and a new creation must needs involve the production of a new being. But no new person is created by this heavenly change. It is the same individual whose conversion is as life from the dead. It is a prodigal son, who forfeited his right to be called a son, and who made himself a child of the devil, selling himself to work ungodliness, that is restored to his father's love, dead but alive again, lost but at length found again, and the witness of his real sonship is of the nature of an adoption, because he had become an alien by his wicked works. So one may say after the manner of Paul in 1 Tim. iv, 10, that God is the Father of all men, especially of them that believe.

CHAPTER V

ADOPTION, SONSHIP, ASSURANCE, AND SPIRITUAL FREEDOM

1. New Relationship of Adoption. In connection with the doctrine of the new birth and the further development of this new life of God in man, we should also take notice of the New Testament teaching on the subject of the real relationship which such new born children of God sustain to him. This heavenly birth, which is conceived as a new creation, is an introduction to something other and more than natural creaturehood. It is not a relationship which can be propagated from parent to child. It is designated in several Pauline epistles by the word *adoption,* υἱοθεσία, so that it is conceived as a constituted, not a natural, sonship (a son by θέσις, not by φύσις). According to Eph. ii, 1-3, all who are "dead through trespasses and sins" were "sons of disobedience," and "we all once lived in the lusts of our flesh, ... and were by nature (φύσει) children of wrath." Such, though begotten of God by a sort of spiritual resurrection, a "quickening together with Christ" (ver. 5), become beloved children by adoption rather than by generation. Like the prodigal, they are welcomed into the family life, but the reception is not so much a second birth as a new creation, and life from the dead; "the dead is alive; the lost is found" (Luke xv, 32). The new relationship, however, is based upon all that work of repentance and faith and regeneration which we have expounded in the foregoing pages, and in the light of those spiritual experiences we can understand the apostle when he writes: "Ye are all sons of God through faith in Jesus Christ." "God sent forth his Son .... that we might receive the adoption of sons. And because ye are sons, God sent forth the Spirit of his Son into our hearts, crying, Abba, Father" (Gal. iii, 26; iv, 5). Similarly in Rom. viii, 14-16: "As many as are led by the Spirit of God, these are sons of God. For ye received not the spirit of bondage again unto fear; but ye received the spirit of adoption, whereby we cry, Abba, Father. The Spirit himself beareth witness with our spirit that we are children of God." In Eph. i, 5, it is said that God "foreordained us unto adoption through Jesus Christ unto himself, according to the good pleasure of his will." This sonship which enables one to "cry out, Abba, Father," is not, according to Paul, a relationship which comes by common birth or generation. It is a new relation to God which the believer *receives* through Jesus Christ, so that in the good pleasure of the heavenly Father he is placed, set apart, constituted and reckoned as a son (θέσθαι υἱόν). The idea may have been suggested by the divine adoption of Israel as the chosen nation to be unto Jehovah a peculiar possession (comp. Exod. iv, 22; xix, 5); for in Rom. ix, 4, the apostle speaks of the Israelites as God's favored ones, "whose is the adoption, and the glory, and the covenants, and the giving of the law, and the service, and the promises." In all these passages we note the same conception of a God-given boon, a reception into the relationship of sons, graciously bestowed on those who accept and obey the gospel. The person thus received is thenceforth treated as a child in the family of God, entitled to all the rights, privileges, and blessings of the household. "If children," says Paul, in Rom. viii, 17, "then heirs; heirs of God, and joint heirs with Christ." The relationship is constituted after the manner of adoption; the heirship and all related privileges are as genuine and certain as if the sonship itself were that of an only begotten of a father.[1]

2. Sons of God. But while the word *adoption* is peculiar to Paul, and his idea of the relation it implies is somewhat governed by his conception of the relation of the gospel to the law, "sons of God," and "children of God," are terms which appear in other scriptures as describing a true and blessed relationship to God as the heavenly Father. The peacemakers "shall be called sons of God" (Matt. v, 9), and those who love their enemies and pray for their persecutors are praiseworthy sons of their Father who is in heaven (Matt. v, 45). The righteous who "shall shine forth as the sun in the kingdom of their Father" are the good ones who in this world are called "sons of the kingdom" (Matt. xiii, 38, 43). These same are also called appropriately "sons of light" (Luke xvi, 8; John xii, 36; 1 Thess. v, 5) and "children (τέκνα) of light" (Eph. v, 8), and being "imitators of God" they show themselves "beloved children" (Eph. v, 1), "children of God without blemish in the midst of a crooked and perverse generation" (Phil. ii, 15). In such texts the filial relation is thought of in connection with the blessedness which it has in itself, and not with reference to the adoption of sons. In one passage (Rom. viii, 23) Paul uses the word *adoption* with reference to a future and final

---

[1] In contrast with those theologians who study to make fine distinctions between the ideas of divine and human adoption, Ritschl observes that "we ought rather to ascertain the harmony between the two. Such harmony cannot be found in the idea of the establishment of a right of inheritance for a person of alien descent. For those persons who in the Christian sense have been adopted by God as his children attain this rank also only under the presupposition that in a certain real sense they derive their being from God, that is, that they have been created in his image."—Justification and Reconciliation, p. 96. Edinburgh, 1900.

glorification, "the redemption of our body" to which believers look forward in longing expectation, and he says (ver. 19) that "the earnest expectation of the creation is waiting for the revealing of the sons of God." And this accords closely with the beautiful sentiment in 1 John iii, 1-3: "Behold what manner of love the Father hath bestowed upon us, that we should be called children of God; and such we are. For this cause the world knoweth us not, because it knew him not. Beloved, now are we children of God, and it is not yet made manifest what we shall be. We know that, if he shall be manifested, we shall be like him; for we shall see him even as he is. And every one that hath this hope in him purifieth himself, even as he is pure." In this conception of the sonship John is not essentially different from Paul, but in substantial agreement. This sonship is not by nature but of grace and love. Its distinguishing mark is the quality of righteousness; for "he that is begotten of God doeth no sin" (vers. 9 and 10). On the contrary, he that doeth sin is a child of the devil, even like Cain, who "was of the evil one, and slew his brother" (ver. 12).

3. Witness of the Spirit. Coincident with this adoption as sons of God there is the removal of the servile spirit of fear. There is no longer a miserable sense of a "law in my members warring against the law of my mind, and bringing me into captivity under the law of sin which is in my members" (Rom. vii, 23); "for the law of the Spirit of life in Christ Jesus made me free from the law of sin and of death" (viii, 2). This is like an experience of life from the dead, a new creation in Christ, and, according to Paul, the believer receives along with the adoption a twofold assurance of the fact: "The Spirit himself beareth witness with our spirit that we are children of God" (Rom. viii, 16). God's Spirit and man's spirit bear united testimony to the new and heavenly relationship. The mighty work of God which brings about the release from sin and the newness of life carries along with it its own proper and peculiar assurance to the human self-consciousness. Such a passing from death into life cannot remain hidden from the knowledge of the new man in Christ. The living Spirit makes his own unmistakable impression on the soul, and in quick concurrent response thereto the human spirit witnesses its own sense of the heavenly fellowship.[1] These concurrent testimonies resolve them-

---

[1] Paul distinguishes from the subjective self-consciousness: *I* am the child of God, the therewith accordant testimony of the objective Holy Spirit: *thou* art the child of God. The latter is the *yea* to the former; and thus it comes that we cry the Abba in the spirit of adoption —Meyer, Critical and Exegetical Handbook, in loco. But the former is also the yea to the latter. In the nature of things, logically speaking, the divine precedes the human witness, and yet the two are simultaneous. See John Wesley's three sermons on "The Witness of the Spirit," in Sermons, vol. i, pp. 85-107. New York, 1854.

selves into a matter of personal self-knowledge as to one's own spiritual experience. "Who among men knoweth the things of a man, save the spirit of the man, which is in him? even so the things of God none knoweth, save the Spirit of God. But we received, not the spirit of the world, but the spirit that is from God, that we might know the things that were freely given to us of God" (1 Cor. ii, 11, 12).

4. Boldness, Confidence, and Full Assurance. This concurrent witness of God's Spirit and man's spirit, testifying to the believer the fact of his adoption, is a conception peculiar to Paul; but the doctrine of a personal experience which it involves is common to Paul and other writers. It is implied in the steadfast *boldness* (παρρησία) with which the child of God "approaches the throne of grace," and enters into the holy places (Heb. iv, 16; x, 19). In the first epistle of John this boldness is spoken of not only as a present and abiding fearlessness toward God but a like feeling of confidence in view of the day of judgment (ii, 28; iii, 21; iv, 17; v, 14). Paul also writes of our boldness in Christ and "access in confidence through our faith in him" (Eph. iii, 12). The faithful minister gains "great boldness in the faith which is in Christ Jesus" (1 Tim. iii, 13). Still more emphatic is the expression of "all riches of the full assurance of understanding" in the mystery of God, in Col. ii, 2, and the "full assurance (πληροφορία) of hope and of faith" in Heb. vi, 11; x, 22. Such assurance is begotten in the heart by the personal fellowship with God which his true children enjoy. They have the confidence of little children, and every faculty of the feeling, the understanding, and the will attests the heavenly union.[1] Here also belong those confirmations of personal experience of which John speaks: "We know that we have passed out of death into life, because we love the brethren" (1 John iii, 14). "Hereby we know that we are of the truth, and shall assure our heart before him" (ver. 19; comp. ver. 24, and iv, 13, 17). Such assurance is no vain boast of self-delusion, but the simple acknowledgment of an inward trust, a confidence in God whose saving power has been realized in the soul. And this confidence is strengthened by the continuous and unwavering "testimony of our conscience, that in holiness and sincerity of God, not in fleshly wisdom but by the grace of God, we have behaved ourselves in the world" (2 Cor. i, 12). There are

---

[1] The witness of the Spirit is sacred to the person who enjoys it. It is the most precious jewel of the heart. It is the hidden treasure, the pearl of great price. It is the secret of the Lord, committed to the believer in trust, not to be despised, nor to be treated as a common thing. It is, therefore, to be spoken of with carefulness in the presence of those who appreciate it, and not boastfully before the multitude.—Merrill, Aspects of Christian Experience, p. 179.

mysteries of the invisible about these things, but the facts of personal feeling and intelligent conviction bear their own witness to the conscious soul. We may not tell whence the wind comes, nor whither it goes (John iii, 8), but at the same time we may have the most unquestionable evidences of its actual movement and effect; and "so is every one that is born of the Spirit."

5. Christian Freedom. Along with the boldness and assurance which come to the soul in the blessed experiences of pardon, regeneration, and adoption, we must notice also that "liberty in Christ" which Paul and others magnify as a glory of the true Christian life. In Gal. v, 1, it is written, "For freedom did Christ set us free"[1]; and in verse 13, "Ye, brethren, were called for freedom." Also in the allegory of Gal. iv, 24-26, where the two covenants are contrasted, those who are in Christ Jesus and walk after the Spirit are conceived as children of the free and heavenly mother Jerusalem, and not to be "entangled again in a yoke of bondage." They are free citizens of a spiritual and heavenly commonwealth, and not to be thought of as bound fast in any system of servitude other than that of voluntary and most honorable loyalty to Jesus Christ. And so we further read, in 2 Cor. iii, 17, that the Lord Jesus is the living Spirit and power by which the entire work of redemption and of revelation is accomplished, "and where the Spirit of the Lord is, there is liberty." This ideal of spiritual freedom is still further brought out in the epistle to the Romans, vi-viii. We are admonished that one may be a bondservant either of sin or of obedience to God in Christ. If one obeys sin, he is the slave of sin; if he obeys God, he is the servant of righteousness. "Thanks be to God," says the apostle, "that whereas ye were bondservants of sin, ye became obedient from the heart to that form of teaching whereunto ye were delivered; and being made free from sin, ye became bondservants of righteousness" (Rom. vi, 17, 18). Further on he adds (ver. 22), "Now, being made free from sin, and become servants to God, ye have your fruit unto sanctification, and the end eternal life." And after depicting the mighty struggle for deliverance from "captivity under the law of sin," which is so vividly set forth in Rom. vii, he declares in viii, 2, that "the law of the Spirit of life in Christ Jesus made me free from the law of sin and of death." This is the liberty of a free human spirit, that has broken with sin, and laid hold on Christ, and passed into the new life of conscious peace and fellowship with God. "The liberty of the glory of the children of God,"

---

[1] Some render, "With freedom did Christ set us free," on which Alford comments: "That is, *free men* is your rightful name and ought to be your estimation of yourselves, seeing that *freedom* is your inheritance by virtue of Christ's redemption of you."—Greek Testament, in loco.

referred to in Rom. viii, 21, is the same royal estate of Christian freedom, only conceived, perhaps, in a later stage of glorious revelation. This same idea of liberty as realized in a blessed service of God appears in the language of 1 Pet. ii, 16, where those who are notable for well-doing are spoken of as "free, and not using their freedom for a cloak of wickedness, but as bondservants of God." James also speaks of the gospel as "the word of truth," and calls it "the perfect law, the law of liberty" (i, 18, 25). He who looks into this law with a steady, continuous, loving devotion, "being not a hearer that forgetteth, but a doer that worketh, this man shall be blessed in his doing." This spiritual freedom, then, is in its inmost nature the realization of a fast fellowship with God and a loving obedience. It brings the soul aloft out of all sense of groveling bondage to sin, and breaks away from mere forms and ceremonies, as from a bondage of the letter that killeth (comp. 2 Cor. iii, 6). Rites, ritual services, fasts, pilgrimages, all such merely outward forms and a mechanical "observance of days, and months, and seasons and years" (Gal. iv, 10), are comparatively like "weak and beggarly rudiments," and one who is dependent on them or unable to rise above them into a pure personal communion with the living God, is entangled in a yoke of bondage. He knows not the light and the liberty of the sons of God. With him rites are an end rather than a means to an end. Such outward forms are utterly insufficient to release a human soul from the bondservice of sin. He only is the true Christian freeman whom the truth of Christ makes free, and he abides, not as a servant, but as a son in the house of his heavenly Father. He walks and talks familiarly with God. Hence the saying of Jesus in John viii, 36: "If the Son shall make you free, ye shall be free indeed." Compare also the whole context in verses 31-38.[1]

---

[1] According to Ritschl, "Melanchthon enumerates four grades of freedom—freedom from sin and the wrath of God, the freedom of the new life inspired by the Holy Ghost, freedom from the Mosaic law, and freedom from the yoke of human ordinances in the worship of the Church. Calvin omits the first and the third of these, and puts in the forefront another aspect of freedom, to which he was necessarily led from regard to the true nature of justification. It is just the other side of justification by faith, that nothing of law or legal works should play a part in it. To this fundamental principle we must reduce the last of the aspects of Christian freedom, the right, namely, to regard human ordinances in the Church as indifferent."—Justification and Reconciliation, p. 115. Edinburgh, 1900.

CHAPTER VI

PROGRESS IN SPIRITUAL LIFE

1. New Life Involves Growth. Having attained the adoption of sons of God we are at the first only as little children, "babes in Christ," and we have seen that the new birth from above does not produce another personality. The subject of the marvelous change from death unto life is still the same in all the elements of natural constitution. The personal identity attaching to body, soul, intellect, and power of volition remains unchanged; but "the new (νέος) man, who is being renewed unto knowledge after the image of him that created him" (Col. iii, 10), henceforth "walks in newness of life" and "serves in newness of spirit" (Rom. vi, 4; vii, 6). By the regeneration of the Spirit he becomes a "new kind of man" (καινὸς ἄνθρωπος, Eph. iv, 24), a new creature, or a "new kind of creation" (καινὴ κτίσις, Gal. vi, 15; 2 Cor. v, 17).[1] In the early period of this new kind of spiritual life he is without mature knowledge of the things of God, and of course needs instruction in "heavenly things" (John iii, 12). Hence we find in many a scripture exhortations to "go on unto full growth" (τελειότης, Heb. vi, 1), to "grow up into Christ in all things" (Eph. iv, 15), to "increase with the increase of God" (Col. i, 10; ii, 19), that is, with such increase in all spiritual attainments as God in his own ways confers. In 1 Pet. ii, 1, 2, it is written: "Putting away all wickedness, and all guile, and hypocrisies, and envies, and all evil speakings, as newborn babes, long for the spiritual guileless milk, that ye may grow thereby into salvation." In 2 Pet. iii, 18, it is also urged, "Grow in the grace and knowledge of our Lord and Saviour Jesus Christ." The faith of the Thessalonians is spoken of as "growing exceedingly," and their love toward one another as "abounding" (2 Thess. i, 3). In the Old Testament we meet the familiar figure of the righteous man, who is "like a tree planted by streams of water, that brings forth its fruit in its season, and its leaf withers not" (Psa. i, 3). "The righteous shall

---

[1] The distinction between the two Greek synonyms for *new* is interesting and suggestive. The word νέος is used, to designate what is new in time, recent, young, fresh. The νέος man is one who has been recently converted and is fresh and young in Christian experience; the καινός man is new in quality and character, and enjoys a newness (καινότης) of life unknown to him before. See Biblical Hermeneutics, p. 96.

flourish like the palm tree: he shall grow like a cedar in Lebanon" (Psa. xcii, 12). And so of every one who passes out of the death of sin into the life of righteousness it may be said, in the beautiful words of Hosea (xiv, 5, 6) concerning restored Israel: "He shall blossom as the lily, and cast forth his roots as Lebanon. His branches shall spread, and his beauty shall be as the olive tree, and his smell as Lebanon." Such ideals of a vigorous life and a healthy growth and fruitage naturally associate themselves together in the scriptural presentation of Christian character.

2. Elements in Spiritual Growth. The divers elements involved in spiritual growth appear in the New Testament teaching as we cannot expect to find them in the Old. For though the Law, the Prophets, and the Psalms contain expressions and suggestions of the most blessed fellowship with God and of the most profound spiritual struggles, these heavenly truths have a much clearer and richer setting forth in the gospel of Jesus Christ. Hence Paul could speak confidently of this latter as a ministration of the spirit and of righteousness which far surpassed in glory and excellence the older Mosaic ministration which was "written and engraven on stones," and was relatively a ministration of condemnation and of death (2 Cor. iii, 6-11). One of the first things to be realized in the personal growth of the newly adopted child of God is a sloughing off, so to speak, of the tissues of the old sensual "body of sin" (Rom. vi, 6). As the living germ in the grain of seed-corn throws off its outer husk and hull, and as the kernel of the acorn casts off its shell when the new plant shoots forth, so is the putting off of the old man essential to the putting on and development of the new man in Christ. While the new life may be imparted in a moment of time, the getting clear from the old body of sin and of death may not be the work of an hour or a day. In many cases it is the work of years. Along with this breaking away from the old conditions there must be a vigorous putting forth of the new life of righteousness, and this will speedily show its independence of external ritual and superiority to all such "bondage of the letter." There must follow instruction in the way of righteousness, and increase of knowledge and wisdom. The passion of holy love will manifest itself from the first and intensify the hunger and thirst after righteousness and true holiness. Personal sanctity and holiness of heart and life must needs accompany and further this life of God in the soul, and hallow all its stages of advance. The continual working and illumination of the Holy Spirit must needs enhance all possible spiritual attainments in such "children of light," and the activities, discipline, and matured experiences of advancing age work together unto the perfection or practicable completeness of Christian character. Some of these experiences call for a more detailed discussion here.

3. Argument of Romans vi. In the sixth chapter of Romans we have an argument intended to show the incompatibility of sin with the new life of righteousness which is received through faith in Christ. Three most important considerations are advanced which we may briefly state as follows: (1) Death unto sin and life in Jesus Christ involves such a crucifixion of the old man that the former bondage to sin is utterly broken, and the passions and lusts which held the higher nature down like a dead body imprisoning a living spirit (comp. vii, 24) are done away (καταργηθῇ, *annulled, abolished,* put an end to). This means a thorough-going emancipation from the bondage of sin (vers. 1-11). (2) Therefore, the argument proceeds, sin is no longer to reign in the body, and sinful lusts must be no more obeyed, but the members of the body are thenceforth to be consecrated unto God as "instruments of righteousness," just as if the body itself were alive from the dead (vers. 12-14). (3) It follows, then, that, as a matter of logical necessity, servants of righteousness cannot be servants of sin. The servant of sin may indeed be free as regards righteousness (ver. 20; but what a wretched slavery such freedom!), but it is clear that the servant of righteousness is made free from sin. And the outcome of it all is that "now being made free from sin, and become servants of God, ye have your fruit unto sanctification, and the end eternal life" (vers. 15-23). There is no mistaking the main points in this argument. Sin and righteousness are opposites. We cannot live in both at the same time, and therefore deliverance from the one involves subjection to the other. With the new birth the entire life of the individual takes a new trend. There is no burden of condemnation crushing down upon them that have obtained pardon and remission of sins, but, according to Rom. viii, 1-11, the Spirit of heavenly life, by whose potent agency the new birth is accomplished from above (ἄνωθεν), triumphs over the flesh, and the adopted child of God is thenceforth to be led and governed by the Spirit which sanctifies the whole nature and ultimately glorifies it in eternal life.

4. Doctrine of 1 John iii, 9, 10. This same doctrine is written in Johannine style in 1 John iii, 9, 10. The necessary opposition of sin and righteousness is conceived as so complete that the two cannot coexist and control the human spirit at one and the same time. "Whosoever is begotten of God doeth no sin, because his seed abideth in him; and he cannot sin (οὐ δύναται ἁμαρτάνειν), because he is begotten of God." In verse 6 of the same chapter it is affirmed that "whosoever abideth in him (that is, in Christ) sinneth not; whosoever sinneth hath not seen him, neither knoweth him." There is, in this apostle's thought, an irreconcilable antagonism between the life of the sinner and that of the child of God who "abides in the Son and in the Father" (ii, 24; comp. i, 3, and John xiv, 23). It was not in his mind to affirm that a child of God can never under any circumstances fall into sin, and bring condemnation upon himself; nor does he teach that the religious life of all the children of God must needs be uniform in light and power. He elsewhere contemplates the case of a "brother sinning a sin not unto death" and receiving life from God (v, 16), and he declares to his little children (τεκνία), whom he would deter from sin, that "if any man sin, we have an advocate with the Father, Jesus Christ the righteous, and he is the propitiation for our sins" (ii, 1). He admonishes against saying that "we have no sin," and "have not sinned," and says that "if we confess our sins, he is faithful and righteous to forgive us our sins, and to cleanse us from all unrighteousness" (i, 8-10). We cannot suppose, therefore, that this apostle shut his eyes to the great variety of human experiences, and intended to maintain that the believer in Christ, once forgiven of sin and "cleansed from all unrighteousness," could never thereafter grieve the Spirit and lapse into sin again. He simply does not entertain such questions in his epistle, although, as we have just shown, he recognizes a "propitiation for our sins" amply sufficient to meet all special situations. His main contention is the fundamental truth that fellowship with the Father and with Jesus Christ is utterly inconsistent with the doing of sin (ποιῶν τὴν ἁμαρτίαν iii, 4).[1] Whosoever abideth and would continue to abide in the blessed heavenly fellowship does not, must not, cannot commit sin. His sins are supposed to be sent away (ἀφίημι), and his spiritual nature cleansed from all unrighteousness, and, in possession of a blessed hope, he "purifieth himself, even as God is pure" (iii, 3; comp. 2 Cor. vii, 1).

5. Sanctification and Holiness. Such purification from sin is clearly indicated in the scriptural use of the words for sanctification and holiness (ἁγιάζω, ἁγιασμός, ἁγιωσύνη, ὅσιος, ὁσιότης). All who have the life in Christ are regarded as sanctified (Acts xx, 32; xxvi, 18), that is, set apart and consecrated to a holy purpose

---

[1] Verse 6 affirms that "whosoever abideth in him sinneth not; whosoever sinneth hath not seen him, neither knoweth him" (οὐχ ἑώρακεν αὐτὸν οὐδὲ ἔγνωκεν αὐτόν). The perfect tense here employed contemplates, as in ii, 3, the condition described as continuing into the present. It refers to the prevailing character and habit of "every one that sinneth" (πᾶς ὁ ἁμαρτάνων). This habitual sinner is not thought of as a man who has suddenly fallen and turned temporarily from the light, but one who has not seen and does not know the Lord Jesus. To all such the Lord himself can also say, as in Matt. vii, 23, "I never knew you."

in life.[1] And thus in Old Testament thought the sabbath day, the place of worship, the priests, and the people Israel were spoken of as sanctified (קדש). But in the New Testament the word *sanctify,* as applied to believers in Christ, means not only a consecration to a holy purpose but also an inner purifying of the soul. Both ideas may be included in the prayer of Jesus that his disciples might be sanctified in the truth (John xvii, 17). According to Eph. v, 25-27, "Christ loved the church, and gave himself up for her, that he might sanctify her, having cleansed her by the washing of water in the word, that he might present the church to himself as a glorious bride, not having spot or wrinkle or any such thing, but that she should be holy and without blemish." Here obviously the idea of cleansing from all defilement is the prominent thought, and so it is again in the somewhat similar language of 1 Thess. v, 23: "The God of peace himself sanctify you wholly; and may your spirit and soul and body be preserved entire, without blame, in the presence of our Lord Jesus Christ." Such sanctification is a work of the Holy Spirit (2 Thess. ii, 13; 1 Pet. i, 2), and consists in personal holiness of heart and life. The heart of everyone who would "increase and abound in love" is to be "established unblameable in holiness before our God and Father in the presence of our Lord Jesus with all his holy ones" (1 Thess. iii, 13). The believer must "present his members as servants to righteousness unto sanctification" (Rom. vi, 19; comp. verse 22), and "abstain from fleshly lusts which war against the soul" (1 Pet. ii, 11). All this is confirmed by the words of 1 Thess. iv, 3-7: "This is the will of God, even your sanctification, that ye abstain from fornication; that each one of you know how to possess himself of his own vessel in sanctification and honor, not in the passion of lust. . . . For God called us not for uncleanness, but in sanctification." The apostle appeals to his own holy, righteous, and blameless behavior as an example (1 Thess. ii, 10), and in 2 Cor. vii, 1, he admonishes and exhorts in the following strong and significant words: "Having these promises, beloved, let us cleanse ourselves from all defilement of flesh and spirit, perfecting holiness in the fear of God." All this accords with the doctrine of "the new man, who after God has been created in righteousness and holiness of truth" (Eph. iv, 24), and it fits the lofty thought of this same epistle that God "chose us in Christ before the foundation of the world, that we should be holy and without blemish before him in love" (i, 4). All these scriptures imply a thorough clearance from the old sinful life, and the attainment of a state of personal purity. It involves the cultivation and

---

[1] Compare the like use of the word in 2 Tim. ii, 21; Heb. ii, 11; x, 10, 14.

growth of positive virtues, as we shall see; but the main thought in the Spirit's work of "cleansing from all unrighteousness" is rather an ideal of release from the old bondage of the flesh; a freedom from the dominion of sin. This emancipation may not be the work of a few days. The struggle may be a long one. The "cleansing from all defilement of flesh and spirit" may require repeated washings from above. And yet, in some hearts, this great work may be speedily accomplished. Habits, temperament, and training may condition many of the operations of the Spirit.

6. Practical Righteousness. In order, then, that the inner cleansing of the sanctification be genuine and permanent, there must be along with it the positive knowledge and practice of righteousness. A holy life is impossible apart from a righteous life, and it is important that our concept of righteousness be accurate and exalted. "Except your righteousness ($\delta\iota\kappa\alpha\iota\sigma\sigma\acute{\upsilon}\nu\eta$) be something more than that of the scribes and Pharisees, ye shall in no wise enter into the kingdom of heaven." If one may not even enter the kingdom without such superior righteousness, much less can he be reckoned great in the kingdom of heaven without the true knowledge and possession of what Christ means by righteousness. He means no mere outward observance of the letter of the law; no Pharisaic show of worship, and fasting, and sacrificing at the temple; no saying and doing not (Matt. xxiii, 3). No tithing of small herbs, nor even of all one's income (Luke xviii, 12), can be made a substitute for those "weightier matters of the law, justice, and mercy, and faith" (Matt. xxiii, 23). A cleansing of the outside, while the heart is ready for extortion and excess, is like the whited sepulcher, "outwardly beautiful, but inwardly full of dead men's bones and of all uncleanliness" (vers. 25-28). The righteousness of the kingdom of heaven sees in the old prohibition of murder a solemn admonition for "every one who is angry with his brother" (Matt. v, 21, 22; comp. 1 John iii, 15). Not only the act of adultery is a violation of the law, "but every one that looketh on a woman to lust after her hath committed adultery already with her in his heart" (Matt. v, 28). The old law of retaliation is for the individual supplanted by the higher law of non-resistance of evil, doing good for evil, loving your enemies and praying for your persecutors (vers. 38-45). True brotherly love must not grow cold upon forgiving an offender seven times; it will not thus set a limit to its pure affection, not even "until seventy times seven" (Matt. xviii, 22); and such forgiveness must come freely "from the heart" (ver. 35). For, according to the old proverb, "As one thinks in his soul, so is he" (Prov. xxiii, 7). The true, pure inner feeling and purpose give character to the outward act. "The good man out of the good treasure of his heart bringeth forth that which is good" (Luke vi, 45), and God knows the hearts of all men (Luke xvi, 15) and the righteousness which endures his gaze must be no outward show but the genuine feeling and purpose of the soul. The doctrine of righteousness in the epistle of James is in substantial agreement with the teaching of Jesus. "The wrath of man works not the righteousness of God" (i, 20), that is, the kind of righteousness which God wills, and which will be acceptable in his sight. The attainment of such righteousness requires the "putting away of all filthiness and overflowing of wickedness." It is the outgrowth of "the implanted word, which is able to save the soul." The man who exemplifies this righteousness is a faithful doer, not a forgetful hearer of the word of truth by which he was brought forth into the light and life of God (comp. ver. 18). "He that looketh into the perfect law, the law of liberty, and so continueth, being not a hearer that forgetteth, but a doer that worketh, this man shall be blessed in his doing" (ver. 25). This perfect law of liberty is in some sense identical with the "word of truth" (ver. 18), but that "word" is in the writer's thought no other than the Law and the Prophets as summed up, explained, and enhanced in the teaching of Jesus. It embodies the "royal law according to the scripture, Thou shalt love thy neighbor as thyself" (ii, 8). The doing of it is a fulfilling ($\tau\epsilon\lambda\epsilon\hat{\iota}\nu$, $\pi\lambda\eta\rho\hat{\omega}\sigma\alpha\iota$) of the law in the present ethical sense, even as Jesus did (comp. Matt. v, 17); a consummation of the inmost ideals of moral excellence. It is a perfect law, inasmuch as it is, like the word of God's holiest revelations, a discerner of the thoughts and intents of the heart. It allows no stumbling even in one thing; "for whosoever shall keep the whole law, and yet stumble in one commandment, has become guilty of all" (ii, 10). It is a law of liberty to the man who looks into its real spiritual nature, sees the blessedness of doing its commandments from a pure heart, and obeys out of unfeigned love of the truth. In perfect love and obedience of this sort of law the soul enjoys its highest freedom. The righteousness of this law is manifest in the bridling of the tongue (i, 26), in visiting the fatherless and widows in their affliction (27), in showing one's faith by his works (ii, 14-26), and in exercising the heavenly wisdom which is "pure, peaceable, gentle, easy to be entreated, full of mercy and good fruits, without variance, without hypocrisy. And the fruit of such righteousness is sown in peace for them that make peace" (iii, 17, 18). Such a personal righteousness is no empty appearance of piety, like "the leaven of the Pharisees" (Luke xii, 1), but a deep inworking principle of obedience to the truth. Similarly in the first epistle of Peter the life of holiness is inseparable from devout obedience to the word of truth. The "sanctification of the Spirit" operates "unto obedience and sprinkling of the blood of Christ" (i, 2). Christians are regarded "as children of obedience," who are to be "holy in all manner of living" (i, 14, 15). They are to "purify their souls in the obedience of the truth unto unfeigned brotherly love, loving one another from the heart fervently" (i, 22), and showing forth "the excellences (ἀρετάς, *virtues, powers, perfections*) of him who called you out of darkness into his marvelous light" (ii, 9). It is blessed to "suffer for righteousness' sake," and to "have a good conscience" and a "good manner of life in Christ" (iii, 14, 16). Having died unto sin we should, after the example of Christ, live unto righteousness (ii, 24).

7. Doctrine of Christian Perfection. This doctrine of a loving obedience to the truth and a personal uprightness of life is common to all the New Testament writings, but may be further enforced and illustrated by the ideals of perfection in the excellencies of Christian character which meet us here and there. It almost startles us to find Jesus saying, "Ye shall be perfect as your heavenly Father is perfect" (Matt. v, 48). But should it be more remarkable than the commandment, "Sanctify yourselves, and be ye holy, for I am holy"? (Lev. xi, 44; xix, 2; xx, 7, 26; xxi, 8; 1 Pet. i, 16.) We are admonished by Zophar that we cannot "find out the Almighty to perfection" (Job xi, 7), and it would be preposterous in a finite being to presume to equal the perfections of the Infinite. But we may feel assured that the saying of Jesus involves no such unreasonable presumption. There is a perfection predicable of the highest possible Christian life, and its noblest ideals are to be attained by an imitation of God. No defective model is offered by Christ, but rather that of the heavenly Father who is good, and true, and righteous altogether: "As you have a perfect heavenly Father, who sends rain on the just and the unjust, imitate him, love as he loves, that you may be true sons of your Father who is in heaven, perfect sons as he is a perfect Father." The young man who thought he had observed all the commandments lacked something yet. "Jesus said unto him, If thou wouldst be perfect (τέλειος), go, sell thy possessions, and give to the poor, and thou shalt have treasure in heaven; and come follow me" (Matt. xix, 21). Here is the ideal of an attainable perfection, and it involves a perfect surrender of all things that would hinder the complete following of Christ. James employs similar language at the beginning of his epistle (i, 4): "Let patience have its perfect work, that ye may be perfect and entire, lacking in nothing." Every possible grace and virtue is to be acquired, and so a completeness of character, that is not wanting in any good thing, will follow as a blessed consummation. The fact that this ideal is not realized in numerous examples is no proof that the perfection contemplated is unattainable. This very practical "servant of God and of the Lord Jesus Christ" reveals no symptom of fanaticism, and has no liking for a religion or a faith that does not verify itself by works. "In many things," he says (iii, 2), "we all stumble." But he immediately adds, "If any stumbleth not in word, the same is a perfect man, able to bridle the whole body also." Paul does not scruple to speak of perfection as the goal of Christian life, although with him it is mainly a future consummation. He expresses his confidence "that he who began a good work in them would perfect it until the day of Jesus Christ." He prays that their "love may abound yet more and more in knowledge and all discernment," and that they may be "filled with the fruits of righteousness" (Phil. i, 6, 9, 11). He himself disclaims any assumption of having "already obtained" his highest ideal of the excellency of the knowledge of Christ, and of conformity to his death, for that can be consummated only in the resurrection; but he says: "One thing I do, forgetting the things which are behind, and stretching forward to the things which are before, I press on toward the goal unto the prize of the high calling of God in Christ Jesus." The goal ($\sigma\kappa o\pi \acute{o}\varsigma$, *thing looked at*) toward which he pressed on was an object in the distance on which his eye was steadily fixed, and upon reaching which he expected to obtain the reward of his heavenly calling in Christ. The imagery employed is substantially the same as that of 1 Cor. ix, 24-26, and the thought is that of running a race in the games in which only the successful runner receives the prize of a crown. The apostle conceived himself engaged in such a contest, and having "finished his course," he would in due time receive "the crown of righteousness" (2 Tim. iv, 7, 8). Nevertheless, though the goal be yet in the distance, he speaks in Phil. iii, 15 (the verse immediately following the statement of his "pressing on toward the goal") of himself and of those who share his feeling and opinion as being in some sense "perfect," and he exhorts the Philippian brethren to imitate him as an example of Christian conduct. He admonishes them that their citizenship ($\pi o \lambda \acute{\iota} \tau \epsilon \upsilon \mu a$) is in heaven (iii, 20), and further on adds (iv, 8, 9): "Finally, brethren, whatever things are true, whatever things are honorable, whatever things are just, whatever things are pure, whatever things are lovely, whatever things are of good report; if there be any virtue and if there be any praise, think on these things; what things also ye learned and received and heard and saw in me, these things do; and the God of peace shall be with you." Surely, the constant meditation and practice of such things must needs lead to a high state of Christian perfection. The apostle elsewhere calls those who are mature in power and penetration of mind perfect (τέλειοι, *full-grown;* 1 Cor. ii, 6; xiv, 20). It is his ambition and hope to "present every man perfect in Christ," and with that glorious end in view he labors and struggles with all the power which Christ supplies (Col. i, 28, 29). It is the prayer of all the Christian brotherhood that they "may stand perfect and fully assured in all the will of God" (Col. iv, 12). From these various statements it appears that with Paul the goal of Christian perfection is at the end of the Christian race. In that day the persevering saint receives his crown, "the prize of his high calling." Meantime we only know in part; we see in a mirror darkly; "but when that which is perfect is. come, that which is in part shall be done away" (1 Cor. xiii, 10). Love, however, is "the bond of perfectness" (Col. iii, 14), the greatest of all virtues, and is a present and abiding possession of the Christian heart, and he who along with this priceless possession has its associate virtues, may be called perfect, complete, full-grown.

8. Specific Christian Virtues. This relative perfection in Christian excellency is to be further considered in the light of those specific virtues which altogether make up the completeness of full-grown Christian character. In Gal. v, 22, 23, we have a noteworthy list of these graces of character set over against an extensive enumeration of "the works of the flesh," and they are called "the fruit of the Spirit." We observe that the word *fruit* is in the singular (ὁ καρπός), as if to suggest that all the virtues named are one combined and vitally inseparable product of the Holy Spirit, like one bunch or choice collection of fragrant flowers. "The fruit of the Spirit is love, joy, peace, long-suffering, kindness, goodness, faithfulness, meekness, self-control." The possession of all these holy and godlike qualities fills out the ideal of being perfect as our heavenly Father is perfect, and they are represented here as living fruit in contrast with dead works of the flesh. In Eph. v, 8-11, we have a conception of these Christian qualities as "the fruit of the light." The passage reads: "Ye were once darkness, but now light in the Lord: walk as children of light (for the fruit of the light is in all goodness and righteousness and truth), proving what is well-pleasing unto the Lord; and have no fellowship with the unfruitful works of darkness." The fruit of the light must needs be what will bear close inspection without any fear of damaging exposure. In the epistle to the Philippians sincerity and blamelessness of life are commended along with abounding love and knowledge, and a "being filled with fruit of righteousness" (i, 9-11); also steadfastness, and "progress and joy of the faith" (i, 25). The several excellences enumerated in iv, 8, are to be exhibited along with the mind which was in Christ Jesus, the loftiest possible example of brotherly love and unselfish humility (ii, 2-8). The true children of God are thus "blameless and harmless, without blemish, in the midst of a crooked and perverse generation, among whom they appear as luminaries in the world" (ii, 15).

9. Love the Greatest of All. If we were to collect all the passages which mention and extol the graces of Christian character, we might transcribe a large portion of the New Testament. But of all the virtues love is by far the greatest. It is the root and fountain of all excellencies in personal life and character. It is "the bond of perfection" (Col. iii, 14), the heavenly girdle in which all other excellencies unite and are banded together unto perfection. It is the essential element and condition of all healthy development in spiritual life. The first and greatest of all the commandments, because it is the sum of all divine law and revelation, is this, "Thou shalt love the Lord thy God with all thy heart, and with all thy soul, and with all thy mind. And a second like unto it is this, Thou shalt love thy neighbor as thyself" (Matt. xxii, 37; comp. Luke x, 27; Deut. vi, 5; x, 12; xi, 13; Lev. xix, 18). This is that "perfect love," which, according to 1 John iv, 16-19, gives boldness in the day of judgment, and casts out fear and tormenting punishment. For "God is love; and he that abideth in love abideth in God, and God abideth in him." To him who thus abides, "Love your enemies" is not a hard commandment. Faith works through love (Gal. v, 6), and the love of God is perfected in him who keeps his word (1 John ii, 5). In Eph. iii, 14-19, we note the remarkable prayer that "the Father, from whom every family in heaven and on earth is named, would grant you, according to the riches of his glory, to be strengthened with power through his Spirit in the inward man, that Christ may dwell in your hearts through faith, in love being rooted and grounded[1] that ye may be strong to apprehend with all the saints what is the breadth and length and height and depth, and to know the love of Christ which passeth knowledge, that ye may be filled with all the

---

[1] The emphatically prefixed *in love being rooted and grounded* is quite in keeping with the Pauline doctrine of the *faith working through love* (Gal. v, 6; 1 Cor. xiii). Through the strengthening of their inner man by means of the Spirit, through the *dwelling* of Christ in their hearts, the readers are to become established in love, and, having been established in love, are able to comprehend the greatness of the love of Christ.—Meyer, Critical and Exegetical Handbook, in loco.

fulness of God." Of all this perfection in Christian faith and power and knowledge love is the root and foundation and central bond, and herewith agrees the exhortation of v, 1, 2, "Be ye therefore imitators of God, as beloved children; and walk in love, even as Christ also loved you." Such love begets and strengthens the love of neighbor and brethren. So far as inward feelings and outward acts may exhibit perfection of Christian character, we find perhaps the most magnificent portraiture of love in 1 Cor. xiii. All other gifts and powers are declared worthless apart from love. Faith and hope command high admiration, but love is greater still. "Love suffers long, and is kind; love envies not; love vaunteth not itself, is not puffed up, doth not behave itself unseemly, seeketh not its own, is not provoked, taketh not account of evil; rejoiceth not in unrighteousness, but rejoiceth in the truth; covereth all things, believeth all things, hopeth all things, endureth all things. Love never faileth" (vers. 4-8). In this forcible description the word *love* is obviously employed by way of synecdoche for the person in whom this heavenly grace abides, and no comment is needed to make the portrayal more impressive or more intelligible.

10. Continual Cultivation and Growth. The high and holy attainments in spiritual life thus far outlined are experiences that require continual cultivation. The "Power from on high" which originates the new life is indispensable in all the stages and forms of its development, and we may here apply the words of the psalmist in their fullest possibility of meaning: "Jehovah God is a sun and a shield: Jehovah will give grace and glory: no good thing will he withhold from them that walk uprightly" (Psa. lxxxiv, 11). His continuous coöperation may therefore be counted on as matter of course. But the Holy Spirit himself can do no perfect work in the heart of man unless there be deep in that heart a "hunger and thirst after righteousness," and a faithful use of every means available for discipline and "instruction in righteousness." Substantial progress can be made only in conscientious fidelity to the truth, and the pure and earnest heart will be on the constant search for truth. It will seek the wisdom which cometh from above and be not only willing but anxious to be taught. The apostle rejoiced in "the order and steadfastness of the faith in Christ" which the Colossians showed, and he wrote them these significant words of counsel: "As therefore ye received Christ Jesus the Lord, so walk in him, rooted and builded up in him, and established in your faith, even as ye were taught, abounding in it with thanksgiving" (Col. ii, 5-7). By such a steadfast course of life and training one comes to beautiful maturity and strength of Christian character. The babe in Christ may "be holy and without blemish before him in love," but strength, wisdom, and maturity in virtues come through the manifold discipline of a protracted life.

11. The Discipline of Trial. The conflict with evil, the sufferings and persecutions to which the Christian confessor is often subjected, the battle for the right, the constant struggle to propagate the gospel, severe personal self-denial, the increasing knowledge of God and of Christ and of holy things which comes from diligent study of the truth—these all have much to do in developing the virtues of godliness and in strengthening the heart in righteousness. Jesus forewarned his disciples that the world would hate and persecute them (John xv, 18-20; xvi, 33), but he prayed, not that they might be taken out of the world, but rather that they might be kept from the evil (xvii, 15). Exposure to severe trial puts one's faith to the test, and affords occasions of noblest spiritual triumph. Hence the words of James: "Count it all joy, my brethren, when ye fall into manifold trials, knowing that the proof of your faith worketh patience. And let patience have its perfect work, that ye may be perfect and entire, lacking in nothing. Blessed is the man that endureth trial; for when he has been approved (δόκιμος, *proved, tested*), he shall receive the crown of life" (James i, 2-4; 12). Similarly Peter: "Now for a little time, if need be, ye have been put to grief in manifold trials, that the proof of your faith, more precious than gold that perishes though it is proved by fire, might be found unto praise, glory, and honor in the revelation of Jesus Christ" (1 Pet. i, 6, 7). Again in iv, 12, 13: "Beloved, think it not strange concerning the fiery trial among you, which cometh upon you to prove you, as though a strange thing happened unto you; but inasmuch as ye are partakers of Christ's sufferings, rejoice, that also in the revelation of his glory ye may rejoice with exceeding joy." Paul speaks of the churches of Macedonia, "how that in much proof of affliction the abundance of their joy and their deep poverty abounded unto the riches of their singleness of heart," as seen in their ready and liberal contributions (2 Cor. viii, 2). Abraham's faith was most remarkably tested in his offering of Isaac; and the heroes of faith, "of whom the world was not worthy," "had trial of mockings and scourgings and bonds and imprisonment" (Heb. xi, 33-38). Such bitter trial, when one even "resisteth unto blood, striving against sin," serves like paternal chastisement to discipline the sons of God, and makes them "partakers of his holiness" (xii, 4-11). All such chastening seems grievous at the time, "yet afterward it yields peaceable fruit to them that have been exercised thereby, even the fruit of righteousness." These teachings are further enhanced by the suggestions of the apocalyptic vision of the great multitude "coming out of the great tribulation, washing their robes and making them white in the blood of the Lamb" (Rev. vii, 9-17). Thus all trials, all spiritual discipline, all chastisements of the heavenly Father, and all devout personal activity which these may occasion serve to strengthen the moral character, and to develop the graces of Christian maturity and perfection. "Our light affliction, which is for the moment, worketh for us more and more exceedingly an eternal weight of glory" (2 Cor. iv, 17). The moral value of affliction was not unknown to the psalmist, "It is good for me that I have been afflicted, that I might learn thy statutes" (cxix, 71).

12. **Growth and Discipline a Manifold Experience.** We have thus shown that real growth and discipline in spiritual life, according to the Scriptures, can be no one-sided experience. And no one word appears sufficient to designate the manifold operations and results of this spiritual development. Not even the terms *sanctification, holiness,* and *perfection* cover the entire portraiture of that "image of the heavenly" which is the ideal of the blameless children of God. We must recognize the elements of growth, the putting away of all impurity of flesh and spirit, the essential antagonism of a life of sin and the regenerate life, the positive facts of sanctification, holiness, and righteousness, the possession of all Christian virtues, and of perfect love that casts out fear. Nor must we fail to see how all the holy virtues are cultivated by the discipline of trial in order that we may be partakers of the holiness of God and so be without blame before him in love. This broad, full, uplifting view of the manifold possibilities of spiritual life in Christ should leave no room for doubtful and confusing disputations, for all these elements of perfection in the Christian life receive about equal prominence in the teachings of the New Testament.

13. **The Beautiful in Religion.** This ideal of completeness in Christian life and character has also what may fittingly be called its æsthetical aspect. The beautiful has its absorbing influence upon every well-trained soul, so that man, who is created in the image of God, and is "renewed unto knowledge after the image of him that created him" (Col. iii, 10; comp. Eph. iv, 24), must needs have the same appreciation of all real excellence which God himself has. We read in 1 Pet. iii, 4, of "the incorruptible adorning (κόσμος) of a meek and quiet spirit, which is in the sight of God of great price." Every element of moral excellence that goes to make up the godlike character of "righteousness and holi-

ness of truth" is of the nature of a beautiful ornament to "the hidden man of the heart." Such qualities in the human personality are "well-pleasing" in the sight of God.[1] They excite in him the emotion of the beautiful as they do also in the souls of all who love God with a pure heart. The absolutely Beautiful is God himself, and a yearning after the perfection of heavenly excellence on the part of man is itself essentially a thing of beauty. Close fellowship with God develops this ideal of beauty and deepens it into a holy passion. It is the peculiar blessedness of the pure in heart to see God, and communion with his works of wisdom and power and love begets in the human heart a deep, strange sense of the One all-pervading Spirit of the universe.[2] The divine sense of beauty is implied in the Creator when it is written that he "saw everything that he had made, and, behold, it was very good" (Gen. i, 31).[3] In like manner the purified heart of man thrills with emotions of delight in the contemplation of "whatsoever things are honorable, just, pure, lovely, and of good report" (Phil. iv, 8). In Psa. xxvii, 4, the one deep desire of the writer is the threefold blessedness of "dwelling in the house of Jehovah," "beholding the beauty (נֹעַם, *delightfulness*) of Jehovah," and "inquiring in his temple." In Psa. xc, 17, the prayer is: "Let the beauty of the Lord our God be upon us." The ways of wisdom are called, in Prov. iii, 17, "ways of beauty." In Psa. xxix, 2, and xcvi, 9, we meet the phrase הדרת־קדש, *the beauty of holiness,* which is also rendered, in *holy array.* In the sense last named the reference is to hallowed garments worn by those who were engaged in acts of divine worship (comp. 1 Chron. xvi, 29; 2 Chron. xx, 21; Psa. cx, 3), but in this sense the word employed points to the *adornment* of the worshipers who appeared in such holy array. The æsthetic charm of a gorgeous ritual service is a well-known power over the feelings of cultivated observers as well as over those who are relatively without æsthetic taste, and however much we condemn "a form of godliness" apart from the power thereof (2 Tim. iii, 5), we should be keenly alive to that which is outwardly and inwardly beautiful in religion. For there is such a thing as "the beauty of holiness," and it is the beauty of God and of all that is truly heavenly.

---

[1] Note the use of ἀρεστός, *pleasing,* in 1 John iii, 22; and εὐάρεστος, *well-pleasing,* in Rom. xiv, 18; Eph. v, 10.

[2] The eternal trinity—Truth, Goodness, Beauty—is a divine unity of elements not to be confounded with each other, nor can they be sundered. Beauty, physical, intellectual, moral, raises the soul to a consciousness of the infinite Goodness, and awakens in the bosom of man the desire of an eternal future and of a sublime existence. C. M. Tyler, Bases of Religious Belief Historic and Ideal, p. 201. New York, 1897.

[3] The Sept. translates this, καλὰ λίαν, *beautiful exceedingly.* The æsthetic nature of God was thrilled with delightful emotion.

CHAPTER VII

MEANS OF PROMOTING SPIRITUAL LIFE

1. The Fellowship and Ministries of the Church. In connection with such growth and discipline as we have described in the foregoing pages we must notice further those means which have been divinely sanctioned for the purpose of cultivating man's spiritual life, and which have to do directly with personal experiences. And first of all we emphasize the importance of the fellowship of the pure and good. The true religious life, according to the scriptural ideal, is best promoted in connection with societies and communities bound together by a common faith and practice. In such a fellowship and communion of the sanctified we perceive the true ideal of the Christian Church. To such a company it may be said with the greatest solemnity: "Ye are fellow-citizens with the saints, and of the household of God, being built upon the foundation of the apostles and prophets, Christ Jesus himself being the chief corner stone; in whom each several building, fitly framed together, groweth into a holy temple in the Lord; in whom ye also are builded together for a habitation of God in the Spirit" (Eph. ii, 19-22). Here is a conception of the church as comprehensive as it is profound. The saints are citizens of one great commonwealth[1] having heavenly interests and aims (comp. Phil. iii, 20), and hence called family-relations (οἰκεῖοι, *members of the household*) of God. Then the thought passes by a natural transition from the idea of a household to that of the house as a great structure builded by God, of which Jesus Christ himself is the chief corner stone, and with the laying of which the apostles and prophets of the New Testament were identified.[2] This great building of God (comp. 1 Cor. iii, 9) is continually increasing and is destined to "grow into a holy temple [ναός, *sanctuary*] in the Lord," embracing in its communion all the members of God's household in all the world and for all time; but as a part and parcel of this magnificent structure "each several building,"[3] every distinct congregation, or local church, like that at

---

[1] Compare the phrase *commonwealth of Israel* in verse 12.
[2] See on this subject Biblical Hermeneutics, pp. 123-127.
[3] The Greek πᾶσα οἰκοδομή, which is the best authenticated reading here cannot be properly rendered *the whole building*, which would require the article, πᾶσα ἡ οἰκοδομή. The apostle means that *every building* which consists of the members

Ephesus or at Corinth, "is builded together for a habitation of God in the Spirit." Each individual of this "household of the faith" (Gal. vi, 10) is a child of God, born from above, and receiving the spirit of adoption. The great practical purpose of this churchly fellowship is edification in Christian life and truth. In this same epistle to the Ephesians (iv, 11-16) we find a similar concept of the church as a great organism, "the body of Christ," and the different members of this body are knit together and builded up, and thus individually and collectively make the increase of the body.[1] The various ministers and ministries of the church are said to be given "for the perfecting of the saints, unto the building up of the body of Christ: till we all attain unto the unity of the faith, and of the knowledge of the Son of God, unto a full-grown man, unto the measure of the stature of the fullness of Christ: that we may be no longer children, tossed to and fro and carried about with every wind of doctrine, by the sleight of men, in craftiness, after the wiles of error; but speaking truth in love, may grow up in all things into him, who is the head, even Christ; from whom all the body fitly framed and knit together through that which every joint supplieth, according to the working in due measure of each several part, maketh the increase of the body unto the building up of itself in love." This scripture especially declares the great aim of the ministries of the church. Apostles, prophets, evangelists, pastors, and teachers serve at least a sixfold purpose: (1) a correcting and training that will overcome the ignorance, instability, and errors of childhood; (2) the perfecting of the saints for holy service; (3) the promotion of unity in faith and knowledge; (4) the exhibition of truth and love; (5) due attention to each several part of the body; (6) the increase of the body as a whole. The positive value of this holy ministration for the edification of the children of God is so apparent as to call for no extended discussion. In 1 Cor. xii, 4-7, the apostle teaches that "there are diversities of gifts, but the same Spirit. And there are diversities of ministrations, and the same Lord. And there are diversities of workings, but the same God, who worketh all things in all. But to each one is given the mani-

---

of any distinct community is closely joined together with all others of its kind, and thus grows into the one great temple of God. Thus *each several building* here means, as J. A. Beet says, the "various parts of the one great structure. Such were the various churches, Jewish or Gentile. So Matt. xxiv, 1, *the buildings of the temple;* that is, the various parts of the temple at Jerusalem. Frequently a great building is begun at different points; and in the earlier stages its parts seem to be independent erections; but as it advances all are united into one whole. So there were in Paul's day, as now, various churches."—Commentary on Ephesians, in loco.

[1] One may profitably compare the figure of the vine and its branches in John xv, 1-8.

festation of the Spirit to profit withal." The entire chapter is given to explanations of this diversity of gifts and ministrations. All believers are in one Spirit baptized into one body of Christ, and all are made to drink of one Spirit. Each particular member needs the coöperation of every other member, and so apostles, prophets, teachers, powers, gifts of healings, helps, governments, kinds of tongues are set in the church for the edification of the whole body. The same lesson is taught by means of the same figure in Rom. xii, 4-8. The church conceived as the body of Christ and perfected in heavenly beauty and excellence is in itself a glorious ideal, "not having spot or wrinkle or any such thing" (Eph. v, 27), but in the actual conditions of its development and working in this world, it is not an end in itself, but rather a means to an end. As our Lord said of the sabbath (Mark ii, 27) so we may say of the church: it was made for man and not man for it. The same is true of all sacred institutions. They exist for the highest culture and advantage of the children of God. The church is the congregation and communion of those who are "called to be saints" (Rom. i, 7),[1] and the fellowship which the members enjoy together, the solemn vows they take, the worship they observe, the counsels and instruction they give and receive, the "speaking one to another in psalms and hymns and spiritual songs, singing and making melody with the heart to the Lord and giving thanks always for all things" (Eph. v, 19, 20; comp. Col. iii, 16), and all the varied ministries of apostles and prophets and teachers are so many direct means of cultivating the religious spirit, and strengthening every element of Christian character.

2. The Sacraments. The sanctity of this churchly fellowship and the solemnity of the bonds which knit all the members of this body to one another are perpetually evidenced by the two sacred rites of Baptism and the Lord's Supper. These, being regarded as signs and seals of a holy covenant relationship before God, are commonly called *sacraments,* because they involve solemn obligations, like the taking of an oath of allegiance and fidelity. Various forms and ideals of baptism were current among the Jewish people before the time of Christ. The rite took on peculiar solemnity in connection with the ministry of John, the forerunner of Jesus, and the whole teaching and work of that remarkable prophet is called "the baptism of John" (Matt. xxi, 25; Mark xi, 30; Luke vii, 29; xx, 4; Acts i, 22; xviii, 25; xix, 3), and "the baptism which John preached" (Acts x, 37). It is also called "the baptism of repentance unto remission of sins" (Mark i, 4; Luke iii, 3). John baptized great multitudes of the people, who

---
[1] On the word ἐκκλησία, *church,* see Biblical Hermeneutics, pp. 74, 75.

confessed their sins, recognized John as a prophet, and "were willing for a season to rejoice in his light" (John v, 35). But the steadfast testimony of John was that he himself was but a voice in the wilderness to make ready the way of the Lord, and to baptize with water unto repentance; but there was a mightier One coming after him who should baptize with the Holy Spirit.

(1) *Christian Baptism.* Jesus himself did not perform the ceremony of baptism with water, but according to John iv, 1, 2, his disciples made and baptized more converts than John. This they would not have been likely to do without his sanction, although it is noticeable that not a word is said about it in the synoptic records of his appointing and sending forth the twelve to preach the gospel of the new kingdom (Mark iii, 13-15; vi, 7-13; Matt. x, 1-15; Luke vi, 12-19; ix, 1-6; x, 1-16). In the commission recorded in Matt. xxviii, 19, and Mark xvi, 15, 16,[1] however, baptism receives distinctive mention, and the Acts of the Apostles shows an apparently uniform practice of baptizing all Christian converts upon confession of sin and of belief in Jesus the Christ (ii, 38, 41; viii, 12, 38; ix, 18; x, 48; xvi, 15, 33; xviii, 8; xix, 5). A saving significance seems to be given to the water of baptism in 1 Pet. iii, 21, where it is called "an antitype" of the water of the flood, by means of which Noah and his family were saved. But the writer takes pains to say that the baptism of which he speaks is "not a putting away of the filth of the flesh, but a question of good conscience toward God." No ritual washing in water can save a soul from sin, and baptism, in this text as in a number of other places, is best understood of that inner washing and purification of which the outward rite is only a symbolic sign. So, too, in those passages in the Pauline epistles where the main reference is to the death unto sin and the newness of life which the believer realizes in Christ, the allusion to baptism is metaphorical, the formal ceremony being mentioned as the sign and symbol of the work of grace in the soul. "As many as were baptized into Christ put on Christ" (Gal. iii, 27). "In one Spirit we were all baptized into one body" (1 Cor. xii, 13). "All we

---

[1] The last-named passage occurs in the appendix to Mark's gospel, is of uncertain origin, and certainly no part of the original gospel according to Mark. See notes to the critical editions of the Greek Testament by Tischendorf, Tregelles, Alford, Westcott and Hort. Inasmuch, also, as no use of the trinitarian formula for baptism occurs elsewhere in the New Testament, and the common method of reference in the Acts of the Apostles is to baptism "into the name of the Lord Jesus" (ii, 38; viii, 16; x, 48; xix, 5), it is believed by some scholars that the language of Matt. xxviii, 19, is not an exact version of the words of Jesus himself, but a clothing of them in the words of a formula which came into early use in the church. Similarly, the doxology of the Lord's Prayer in Matt. vi, 13, came to be interpolated, probably, from the common prevalence of such formulas in acts of public worship. But these facts do not in the least take from the value of the prayer, or from the nature and purpose of the rite of baptism.

who were baptized into Christ Jesus were baptized into his death. We were buried with him through baptism into death" (Rom. vi, 3, 4; comp. Col. ii, 12). As a suggestive symbol of this profound conception of entrance into the new life of Christ the rite of baptism in water was divinely significant in the mind of Paul; but apart from the spiritual reality of which it is the sign the ceremony in itself would be an empty form. The "one baptism" referred to in Eph. iv, 5, is the one genuine baptism "into Christ," and so necessarily supposes the baptism of the Holy Spirit, for no immersion of the body in water, and no pouring or sprinkling of clean water on the body, can effect a change of heart, or bring the soul into fellowship with Jesus. Paul's mystic nature apprehended the deep spiritual truth figured in baptism, but he was so far from exalting this rite above the ministry of the word, that he declares that Christ sent him "not to baptize, but to preach the gospel" (1 Cor. i, 17). The rite of baptism has been regarded as in some sense taking the place of the older rite of circumcision. Abraham "received the sign of circumcision, a seal of the righteousness of the faith which he had while he was in uncircumcision" (Rom. iv, 11; comp. Gen. xvii, 10, 11), and the ceremony obtained formal recognition in the Mosaic legislation (Exod. xii, 48; Lev. xii, 3). It was also conceived as a symbol of the purification of the heart before God (Deut. x, 16; xxx, 6; Jer. iv, 4; Rom. ii, 29). So far, therefore, as both these rites symbolize heart-purity, and are signs and seals of a covenant relation, and tokens of formal union with the people of God, they serve to illustrate each other. But the older rite of circumcision has been abrogated by the gospel of Christ, and all the purpose it may have served as the sign and seal of covenant relations and of sanctification of heart is now met by the simpler and more suitable rite of baptism in water. Specific confirmation of this is, perhaps, to be recognized in the language of Col. ii, 11, 12: "Ye were circumcised with a circumcision not made with hands, in the putting off the body of the flesh, in the circumcision of Christ; having been buried with him in baptism, wherein ye were also raised with him through faith in the working of God, who raised him from the dead." The deep spiritual experience expressed by these figures of death and resurrection in Christ supersedes all the carnal ordinances of Judaism. The rite of baptism has received almost universal recognition in the Christian Church, and even without the authority of a specific commandment of the Lord, would be a beautiful and appropriate form of public initiation into the covenants and fellowship of the children of God. But it is the more impressive and binding by reason of the sanction it received from Christ and the apostles, and the reverential observance it has commanded through all the Christian centuries.[1]

(2) *The Lord's Supper.* As the rite of baptism in the Christian Church takes in some measure the place of circumcision in the Jewish community, so the Lord's Supper (κυριακὸν δεῖπνον; 1 Cor. xi, 20) takes the place of the Jewish feast of Passover. According to Paul, Christ has become the Christian's paschal lamb (1 Cor. v, 7), and in the mystic symbolism of the Lord's Supper the believer signifies in a formal way the vital union he enjoys with Christ. This blessed union is forcibly expressed in the words of Gal. ii, 20: "I am crucified with Christ; and it is no longer I that live, but Christ liveth in me: and that life which I now live in the flesh I live in faith, which is in the Son of God, who loved me and gave himself up for me." In the light of this confession we perceive the deep spiritual import of 1 Cor. x, 16, 17: "The cup of blessing which we bless, is it not a communion (κοινωνία) of the blood of Christ? The bread which we break, is it not a communion of the body of Christ?—seeing that we, who are many, are one bread, one body: for we all partake of the one bread" (ἐκ τοῦ ἑνὸς ἄρτου: *share from the one common bread*), and so participate in the one common life of one great organism. The spiritual unity of all believers is thus most plainly affirmed, as also the fact that they all derive their spiritual subsistence from one common source. Paul himself has given us the earliest record we possess of the institution of the Lord's Supper (see 1 Cor. xi, 23-26), and it agrees in substance with that of the synoptic gospels (comp. Matt. xxvi, 26-29; Mark xiv, 22-25; Luke xxii, 14-20). The Passover was a memorial of Israel's deliverance out of the bondage of Egypt; the Lord's Supper is a memorial of our redemption "with the precious blood of Christ, as of a lamb without blemish and without spot" (1 Pet. i, 19). In the observance of this sacred rite the believer recognizes a divinely ordained means of showing forth his faith in the atoning death of Christ, and his abiding spiritual fellowship with him. In the mystic way of

---

[1] The age of serious controversy over the questions of time, place, subjects, and mode of baptism seems to be past. The allusions to immersion, affusion, and sprinkling are numerous in the Scriptures, and all these modes of ceremonial purification have their sufficient warrant to justify the personal choice of the individual believer. In the Teaching of the Twelve Apostles (chap. vii) it is commanded to baptize in running water; but if that is not at hand, other water may be used, either cold or warm. It is also permitted to perform the rite by pouring water on the head. The practice of infant baptism is without any specific commandment, and also without the record of any clear example, in the New Testament. It has, however, been inferred from the mention of household baptisms, and from the analogy of circumcision, and may find a sufficient reason for itself in the obvious propriety of a public and formal consecration of children to God. We hold, accordingly, that, with or without scriptural warrant, it "is to be retained in the church."

stating it, he eats the flesh and drinks the blood of the Son of man, and so comes to have life in himself (John vi, 53).

3. The Ministry of the Word. The fellowship and communion, which are enhanced by these symbolic signs of the new covenant, must needs be very helpful in developing the spiritual life of the children of God. But far more important than the formal observance of any outward rites is the faithful ministry of the word of God, a preaching and teaching of the great eternal truths which have to do with the moral and religious nature of man. Many of these are treasured in the scriptures of the Old Testament, and, according to Paul, "were written for our learning" (Rom. xv, 4). "Every scripture inspired of God is also profitable for teaching, for reproof, for correction, for instruction which is in righteousness; that the man of God may be complete, furnished completely unto every good work" (2 Tim. iii, 16, 17). The Law, the Prophets, and the Psalms may therefore be profitably searched for religious instruction and edification. The record of creation in Genesis is full of richest suggestions touching the personality and power of God, and implies his immanence in all the world. The promise to the woman (iii, 15), and the symbols of judgment and mercy in flaming sword and cherubim (iii, 24) are prophetic of a divine purpose to redeem from sin and death. The familiar story of Cain and Abel is freighted with moral lessons of imperishable value. The covenant with Noah and its symbolic sign of the bow in the cloud (ix, 9-17) illustrate the ancient ideas of divine compassion and the doctrine of communion between God and man.[1] The various rites of the Levitical worship, the vows and the purifications, the sabbath, the new moons, the sacred seasons and pilgrimages and fasts, the solemn assemblies and the sacrifices, all witness to the religious culture of the Israelitish people, and along with the lively oracles of the prophets and the spiritual songs of the psalmists furnish numerous lessons for instruction in righteousness. Or if we look for special illustrations from individual life and character, we may cite the examples of Enoch, who walked with God; of Abraham, the friend of God; of Jacob and his wrestling with the angel; of Joseph, the honored servant of God; of Moses, who spoke face to face with Jehovah; of Samuel, the venerable prophet, and David, the man after God's own heart. The Psalms and Prophets abound with pious utterances which show that at various periods of the Old Testament history human hearts in Israel were led through remarkable experiences of conviction of sin, repentance, faith, and turning unto

---

[1] See these lessons more fully indicated in Biblical Apocalyptics, pp. 38-67.

God. The symbolical rites and the laws for personal purification inculcated the doctrine of holiness, and the necessity of "clean hands and a pure heart" in everyone who would approach unto God (Psa. xxiv, 3, 4). In these and many other ways the scriptures of the Old Testament afford instruction in divine truth; but we find the teaching embodied in the New Testament a still fuller and clearer revelation of the word of God. Jesus himself is the supreme Teacher. His parable of the sower and the seed illustrates the nature of the "word of the kingdom," and how differently it is received by different human hearts. His parable of the good seed and the tares is even more suggestive. "He that soweth the good seed is the Son of man," and his coming into the world was a going forth to sow. The enemy sows evil seed, and the different sowings produce "sons of the kingdom," and "sons of the evil one." It is, therefore, a matter of the greatest possible moment how we hear and what we hear and receive as the word of God. The incarnation, life, teaching, ministry, miracles, death, and resurrection of Jesus are a revelation of "the good word of God and the powers of the age to come" (Heb. vi, 5). Every manifestation of divine truth from the beginning is in some sense the word of God, who has spoken at sundry times, in diverse manners and by different portions (Heb. i, 1). Thus the gospel, the word of the kingdom, the truth as it is in Jesus (Eph. iv, 21), who himself is "the way and the truth and the life" (John xiv, 6)—even the eternal WORD who was in the beginning with God and was God—this word of God, so inexhaustible in depth and fullness, is the light of the world, and a most efficient instrument for building up the child of God in righteousness and in all virtues. Great zeal in religious life may often display itself without correct knowledge of the truth (Rom. x, 2), and a fervent piety is often seen in persons who are lamentably deficient in their acquaintance with "the word of the kingdom." But such facts admonish us the more that all sound and commendable Christian growth must be according to faithful instruction in the truth. The ancient priests of Israel were required to teach the statutes which Jehovah had spoken (Lev. x, 10, 11). "The priest's lips should keep knowledge, and they should seek the law at his mouth" (Mal. ii, 7). Wise and useful proverbs were sought out and set in order that men might "know wisdom and instruction, and discern the words of understanding" (Prov. i, 2). In accordance with the great Teacher's example and counsels the apostles of the early church gave great attention to teaching (Acts ii, 42) and "the ministry of the word" (vi, 4). "Paul and Barnabas tarried in Antioch, teaching and preaching the word of the Lord" (xv, 35). Paul in founding the church of Corinth "dwelt there a year and six months, teaching the word of God among them" (xviii, 11), and for the space of three years he labored in Ephesus, "teaching publicly and from house to house," and "shrinking not from declaring the whole counsel of God" (xx, 20, 27). He wrote the Corinthians about his supreme desire to profit them by speaking to them "either by way of revelation, or of knowledge, or of prophesying, or of teaching" (1 Cor. xiv, 6). He admonished the churches of Galatia that he received the gospel through revelation of Jesus Christ, and made the same known unto them in the ministrations of his divine apostleship, and he emphasized the work of religious instruction by saying, "Let him that is taught in the word communicate unto him that teacheth in all good things" (Gal. vi, 6). He wrote Timothy and Titus that the minister of Christ must be "apt to teach," "speak the things which befit the sound teaching," "hold to the faithful word which is according to the teaching, that he may be able both to exhort in the sound teaching, and to convince the gainsayers" (1 Tim. iii, 2; 2 Tim. ii, 2; Titus i, 9; ii, 2). Luke wrote his gospel that Theophilus might be informed "concerning all that Jesus began both to do and to teach," and "might know the certainty concerning the words wherein he had been instructed" (Acts i, 1; Luke i, 4). And thus it appears that without diligent instruction and study in the truth of God there can be no healthful growth "in the grace and knowledge of our Lord and Saviour Jesus Christ" (2 Pet. iii, 18).

4. Exercises of Practical Godliness. Numerous forms of religious activity may be viewed as means of promoting spiritual life and cultivating the virtues of Christian character. A vigilant guarding of oneself against all kinds of evil is an essential accompaniment of the petition, "Lead us not into temptation but deliver us from evil." Such vigilance should care to keep the body from all defilement (1 Cor. vi, 19, 20; ix, 27; 2 Cor. vii, 1; 1 Pet. ii, 11); to practice faithfulness with an erring brother (Matt. xviii, 15-17; Gal. vi, 1), to bear the infirmities of the weak (Rom. xv, 1; Gal. vi, 2), to give of one's means liberally and distribute readily according as one is prospered (1 Cor. xvi, 2; 2 Cor. vii, 2, 7; 1 Tim. vi, 18), to show love and hospitality to the stranger (Heb. xiii, 2; Rom. xii, 13), to redeem the time and observe diligence in business (Eph. v, 16; Col. iv, 5; Prov. xxii, 29), and to be faithful in the discharge of all duties in the family and household (Eph. v, 22—vi, 9; Col. iii, 18—iv, 1; 1 Pet. ii, 18—iii, 7). All these and other like activities of practical godliness are essential to a strong and beautiful development of the Christian life; but they are all implied in what has already been said of the elements of growth and the cultivation of every personal excellency in Christian perfection.

5. Prayer. But among all the means of grace the direct personal approach of the soul to God in prayer is preëminent. It is a sort of instinct in the religious nature of man to "cry out unto the living God," and this fact is an evidence that we are the offspring of God. The Scriptures abound with examples of prayer, and no ritual of worship, no offering of sacrifices, no intercession of priests ever seem to have proved sufficient to release the individual heart from the sense of need and of obligation to seek personally unto God. Prayer in the broadest sense includes acknowledgment of past mercies and thanksgiving for all divine favors, confession of sin and unworthiness, supplication for all manner of temporal and spiritual benefits, and ascription of praise to God. In the Hebrew Psalter we meet with all these forms of prayer and praise, and not a few of them are examples of the deepest and most thorough searching of heart before God. The supplications of Moses, as recorded in Exod. xxxiii, 12-16, and Num. xi, 11-15, are remarkable for the boldness of their appeals to Jehovah. Abraham's intercession for Sodom (Gen. xviii, 23-32) is no less notable. The struggle of Jacob at Peniel is unsurpassed as a picture of prevailing prayer alone with God (Gen. xxxii, 24-30). Jesus taught his disciples to pray and enhanced his teaching by his own example. He supplied a model prayer, and uttered parables to show that men ought always to pray. "What man is there," he argued, "who, if his son ask him for a loaf, will give him a stone; or if he ask for a fish, will give him a serpent? If ye then, being evil, know how to give good gifts unto your children, how much more shall your Father who is in heaven give good things to them that ask him?" Hence his own command: "Ask, and it shall be given unto you; seek, and ye shall find; knock, and it shall be opened unto you" (Matt. vii, 7-11; comp. xviii, 19; xxi, 22; Mark xi, 24; Luke xxi, 36; John xv, 7; xvi, 23, 24). The apostolic teaching on this subject is no less explicit. According to James, "If any of you lack wisdom, let him ask of God, who giveth to all liberally and upbraideth not; and it shall be given him. But let him ask in faith, nothing doubting." "Confess your sins one to another, and pray one for another, that ye may be healed. The supplication of a righteous man availeth much in its working" (i, 5; v, 16). "Be ye of sound mind," says Peter, "and be sober unto prayers" (1 Pet. iv, 7). And John writes: "This is the boldness which we have toward him, that, if we ask anything according to his will, he heareth us" (1 John v, 14). "Brethren, pray for us," says Paul;

"pray without ceasing; in nothing be anxious; but in everything by prayer and supplication with thanksgiving let your requests be made known unto God; praying at all seasons with all prayer and supplication in the Spirit, and watching thereunto in all perseverance and supplication for all the saints" (1 Thess. v, 17, 25; Phil. iv, 6; Eph. vi, 18). From these scriptures and others of a like nature it is evident that God is a living presence in the world. He even notices the sparrow that falleth on the ground and numbers the hairs of our head (Matt. x, 29). The uniformities we see in nature can offer no valid objection to the doctrine of prayer, for those uniformities are themselves of his ordaining and have in him their permanent support. His infinite wisdom and power are doubtless competent to make all things work together for good to them that love him and are called according to his purpose (Rom. viii, 28). We may often pray unwisely; "we know not how to pray as we ought, but the Spirit helpeth our infirmity" (ver. 26). David prayed for the life of the child, and his desire was not granted him (2 Sam. xii, 16-18). Jesus prayed in Gethsemane that the cup might pass, but he drank it in amazement of soul, sweating drops of blood. Paul besought the Lord thrice that the thorn in his flesh might depart (2 Cor. xii, 8), but the weakness remained. Yet no such intensely fervent prayer of the heart to God goes without some blessed answer. The child is not spared, but comfort of soul is given. The cup of Gethsemane is not taken away, but an angel comes to strengthen. The thorn in the flesh remains, but there comes the sweet assurance, "My grace is sufficient for thee: for my power is made perfect in weakness." The true idea of prayer implies that in the nature of the act we defer to an infinite intelligence above us, whose wisdom and goodness may often answer our supplication in ways we thought not of. The thing for which we ask may be conditioned on other wills whose free action we cannot influence, and God himself will not coerce. Or we may ask for a seeming and real good which, if given, would effectually prevent our subsequent attainment of a higher boon. And so the human heart, with its ineradicable impulse to pray, may come to God in boldness, and in confidence, nothing doubting, and may ask for any good thing. No such earnest "supplication in the Spirit" goes unanswered. It may not be the specific answer we desire; for the Infinite Wisdom has his ways and his thoughts, which are far above ours (Isa. lv, 9). But the Infinite Wisdom is also the Infinite love, who "withholdeth no good thing from them that walk uprightly" (Psa. lxxxiv, 11). If that good thing for which we pray seems to be withholden, some other and greater good is given in ways we do not comprehend. The spiritual nature that seeks the presence and help of God with a pure longing must needs receive of the infinite fullness, for such the Father seeks to be his worshipers (John iv, 23). And thousands of thousands of such true worshipers have received most blessed answers to their prayers. The heart is enlarged in its sympathies by the habit of prayer. Its hunger and thirst after righteousness receive thereby the deeper satisfaction. The consciousness of a personal fellowship and communion with the living God exalts the spiritual life and prepares it for the fuller vision of God.

6. The Sevenfold Exhortation of Hebrews x, 19-25. In all these means of grace we surely recognize a divine provision for the cultivation of the spiritual life of man. The child of the kingdom, born from above, a new creation in Christ, receiving the spirit of adoption, holy and without blame, perfected in love, is certainly an ideal worthy of all possible struggle to attain. The exhortation of Heb. x, 19-25, in which the writer passes from the doctrinal to the practical part of his epistle, contains a sevenfold admonition. Those who would enter into what this writer conceives as the heavenly Holy of holies in the house of God must have (1) a true and purified heart, (2) a body washed from all defilement, (3) a full assurance of faith, (4) an unwavering confession of hope, (5) a watching of one another for good, (6) assembling together for worship and fellowship, and (7) faithful exhortation. "Having therefore, brethren, boldness to enter into the holy place by the blood of Jesus, by the way which he dedicated for us, a new and living way, through the veil, that is to say, his flesh; and having a great priest over the house of God; let us draw near with a true heart in fulness of faith, having our hearts sprinkled from an evil conscience, and having our body washed with pure water, let us hold fast the confession of our hope that it waver not; for he is faithful that promised; and let us consider one another to provoke unto love and good works; not forsaking our own assembling together, as the custom of some is, but exhorting one another; and so much the more, as ye see the day drawing nigh."

CHAPTER VIII

ETERNAL LIFE

1. Meaning of the Phrase. Our studies thus far into the origin and development of new spiritual life in man have prepared the way for further inquiry into the heavenly nature and destination of this life. The phrase *eternal life* (ζωή αἰώνιος), which is conspicuous in the writings of John but by no means confined to them, demands our first attention. It has become so much associated in Christian thought with the doctrine of future existence that an important part of its significance is overlooked. The new birth from above introduces the believer into a new element of spiritual life, and is spoken of as a passing out of death into life, so that "he that hath the Son hath the life, and he that hath not the Son of God hath not the life" (1 John v, 12). Here "the life" is contemplated as a present actual possession; "God gave unto us eternal life, and this life is in his Son" (ver. 11); and the statement is strictly parallel with John iii, 36: "He that believeth on the Son hath eternal life; but he that obeyeth not the Son shall not see life, but the wrath of God abideth on him." Equally explicit and unmistakable is the language of John v, 24: "He that heareth my word and believeth him that sent me, hath eternal life, and cometh not into judgment, but hath passed out of death into life." In John vi, 54, we meet with this declaration of profound mysticism: "He that eateth my flesh and drinketh my blood hath eternal life; and I will raise him up at the last day." In xvii, 3, we read what bears to some extent the manner of a definition: "This is eternal life, that they should know thee, the only true God, and him whom thou didst send, Jesus Christ." The eternal life which is thus contemplated as a present possession is no other than the blessed life of God in the soul begotten by the heavenly birth and nourished by living communion with God. It is not merely the knowledge of God and of Christ; it is rather vital union with them, as that of the branches with the vine, so that the disciples "shall know that I am in my Father, and ye in me, and I in you" (John xiv, 20). The knowledge of God that comes of such vital union and fellowship is a partaking of the divine nature, and, to use a Pauline expression, the "life is hid with Christ in God" (Col. iii, 3). This eternal kind of life is also closely associated with the idea of light shed abroad through all the spiritual and intellectual faculties of men. "In him was life, and the life was the light of men" (John i, 4). That is, the impartation of new life from above brings along with the life a heavenly illumination. He who is begotten of God should be quick to learn that "God is light, and in him is no darkness at all. And if we walk in the light, as he is in the light, we have fellowship one with another, and the blood of Jesus his Son cleanseth us from all sin" (1 John i, 5, 7). Such are true "children of light," and such divine illumination develops the eternal life as the light of the sun promotes the growth of many living things in the natural world.

2. Paul's View of Life, Light, and Liberty. The mystic element in the writings of Paul is scarcely less noticeable than that of the Johannine books. No New Testament writer exhibits profounder conceptions of spiritual life and fellowship with God. He thinks and speaks of believers as risen with Christ, and seeking things above where Christ is seated on the right hand of God (Col. iii, 1). Their citizenship is in heaven (Phil. iii, 20), and they sit with Christ in the heavenlies ($\dot{\epsilon}\nu$ $\tau o\hat{\iota}_{S}$ $\dot{\epsilon}\pi o\nu\rho a\nu \acute{\iota}o\iota_{S}$, Eph. ii, 6).[1] He, too, knows the power of heavenly illumination, "seeing it is God that said, Light shall shine out of darkness, who shined in our hearts to give the light of the knowledge of the glory of God in the face of Jesus Christ" (2 Cor. iv, 6). "Ye were once darkness, but are now light in the Lord; walk as children of light" (Eph. v, 8). This surpassing light which accompanies the knowledge of the glory of God in Christ is conceived by Paul as a product of the Spirit of the Lord, and a reflection of the glory of the Lord Christ as seen in the mirror of the gospel. The highest liberty of the soul is attained in this transforming light. It is the freedom of which Jesus speaks in John viii, 32, 36: "Ye shall know the truth and the truth shall make you free. If the Son shall make you free, ye shall be free indeed." This holy spiritual liberty exalts the soul above all slavish fear, and enables one to apprehend the living Christ as the light of the world. Paul puts it in contrast with the bondage and darkness which so blinded the spiritual insight of the heart of Israel in his time that they could not apprehend "the illumination ($\phi\omega\tau\iota\sigma\mu \acute{o}_{S}$) of the gospel of the glory of Christ, who is the image of God" (2 Cor. iv, 4). Spiritual illumination dispels the darkness of sin and error, and brings the real freedom. Accordingly we read (2 Cor. iii, 17, 18): "Where the Spirit of the Lord is, there is liberty. And we all, with

---

[1] Compare Biblical Hermeneutics, p. 276.

unveiled face (that is, not veiled as was the heart of Israel, verses 14-16), beholding as in a mirror the glory of the Lord, are transformed into the same image from glory to glory." The believer who receives this liberty-giving Spirit of the Lord beholds the glory of his Lord as it is reflected in the mirror of the gospel, which he calls in this same connection (iv, 4) "the gospel of the glory of Christ." This vision of Christ is a present experience of the soul, and consists in devout and appreciative contemplation of the person and glory of the Lord Jesus. Such a vision of glory has the effect of transforming the devout beholder into the same likeness. He becomes Christlike. He "puts on the new man, who is being renewed unto knowledge after the image of him that created him" (Col. iii, 10). The transformation is not the work of a moment, but may be a long-continuing process, as is suggested by the words *from glory to glory*. The eternal life in Christ of which he has "laid hold" (1 Tim. vi, 12) becomes in him an increasing spiritual power, and advances from one degree of glory to another. It is also a transformation from the vision of glory which one sees in the mirror of Christ's gospel into a glory of personal fellowship with God, which is "as the dawning light that shineth more and more unto the perfect day" (Prov. iv, 18).

3. Eternal Life a Present Possession. Eternal life, then, is to be understood primarily of the free, pure, permanent, and ever-increasing spiritual life of Christlikeness. It is a present possession and a glorious reality to the believer, who can say with Paul, "The law of the Spirit of life in Christ Jesus made me free from the law of sin and of death" (Rom. viii, 2). As spiritual death is the direct penal consequence of sin, so is spiritual life the direct product of the work of the Holy Spirit in the believer's heart; and as the one is a reality of positive knowledge and conviction, so is the other. "The wages of sin is death; but the free gift of God is eternal life in Christ Jesus our Lord" (Rom. vi, 23). We have already observed (p. 120) that the penalty of sin is a ruin of the spiritual nature of man, the blighting of religious life, the self-destructive alienation of the soul from the fellowship of God. When this condition becomes fixed and permanent the blighted nature is guilty of eternal sin. Such fixedness in evil character is in itself a penal consequence of persistent sinning. On the other hand, eternal life may be viewed as a fixedness of opposite character. The children of light have laid hold of the eternal life which is God's free gift; and "the fruit of the light is in all goodness and righteousness and truth" (Eph. v, 9).

4. Endless Permanence in Life. But in the gospel of John we find eternal life contemplated also as an ultimate reward, a future glory, as well as a present possession. The life in Christ is eternal in that it endures in eternal permanence. It has a destination that runs on not only "from glory to glory" but also from eon to eon. Jesus speaks of the water of life which becomes in him who drinks thereof "a fountain of water springing up unto eternal life" (iv, 14). Again in verse 36 he speaks of "gathering fruit unto life eternal," and in vi, 27, of food "which abideth unto life eternal." In xii, 25, we have the strong and peculiar words which remind us both of Matt. xvi, 25, and Luke xiv, 26: "He that loveth his soul loseth it; and he that hateth his soul in this world shall keep it unto life eternal." The eternal life is so exalted in thought that everything which stands in the way of its attainment seems in comparison so mean and despicable as to be an object of hatred. The sordid soul-life, animal life ($\psi v \chi \acute{\eta}$), which seeks all its good in this world is hateful when seen in its antagonism to the life eternal which aims at permanent satisfaction, and seeks things above this world "where Christ is seated on the right hand of God" (Col. iii, 1). In all these passages in John's gospel the eternal life contemplated is some future glorious boon, an endless permanence in the life and light of God.

5. Eternal Life in Synoptic Gospels. In the synoptic gospels the phrase *eternal life* also connotes a future reward or inheritance. In Mark x, 29, 30, Jesus says: "There is no man that hath left house, or brethren, or sisters, or mother, or father, or children, or lands, for my sake and for the gospel's sake, but he shall receive a hundred fold now in this time, houses, and brethren, and sisters, and mothers, and children, and lands, with persecutions; and in the age to come life eternal." The parallel passage in Matt. xix, 29, reads, "shall receive manifold, and shall inherit life eternal." In Luke xviii, 30, the reading is, "Shall receive manifold more in this time, and in the age to come life eternal." Furthermore, in Matt. xix, 16; Mark x, 17; Luke x, 25; xviii, 18, eternal life is spoken of as an inheritance, and this word involves the idea of a property or blessedness to be received at some future time. The phrases *in this time, in this world,* and *on the earth* as contrasted with *in the age to come* imply experiences of life in some other world or age beyond the present. In the picture of eternal judgment, which is written in Matt. xxv, 31-46, the righteous who go "into eternal life" "inherit the kingdom prepared for them from the foundation of the world." That inheritance is an entrance into the joy and glory of the King himself.

6. Eternal Life in the Epistles. In the various epistles the ideal of a glorious inheritance in eternal life is frequently presented. No unrighteous person can inherit the kingdom of God

(Gal. v, 21; 1 Cor. vi, 9, 10; Eph. v, 5), but those who "by patience in well-doing seek for glory and honor and incorruption" shall receive eternal life as reward rendered by the righteous judgment of God (Rom. ii, 7). Grace reigns through righteousness unto eternal life (Rom. v, 21), and they who are "made free from sin and become servants to God, have their fruit unto sanctification, and the end (final result and consummation) life eternal" (vi, 22). So, too, "he that soweth unto the Spirit shall of the Spirit reap eternal life" (Gal. vi, 8). In the Acts of the apostles (xx, 32; xxvi, 18) Paul speaks of "the inheritance among all them that are sanctified." In the epistle to the Hebrews we read of "them that shall inherit salvation" (i, 14), and of them that "receive the promise of the eternal inheritance" (ix, 15). In 1 Pet. i, 4, the writer tells his readers that God has begotten them unto a living hope, "unto an inheritance incorruptible, and undefiled, and that fadeth not away reserved in heaven for them." In Col. i, 12, the apostle "gives thanks unto the Father who made us meet (that is, fit, sufficient, competent) to be partakers of the inheritance of the saints in light"; and in Eph. i, 13, 14, he speaks of "being sealed with the Holy Spirit of promise, which is an earnest (ἀρραβών,= *pledge and part payment*) of our inheritance, unto the redemption of God's own possession"; that is, unto the final consummation of the redemption of all those whom God claims as his peculiar treasure and the people of his own possession (comp. 1 Pet. ii, 9; Exod. xix, 5; Deut. vii, 6).

7. A Glorious Inheritance, Now and Forever. From all these scriptures it becomes apparent beyond controversy that the spiritual life begotten in the heart of man by the power of the Holy Spirit is part and parcel of a glorious inheritance. It is a possession of manifold fullness, and is conditioned in a fitness of character, a godliness (εὐσέβεια, *reverent piety and beautiful religious conduct*) which "has promise of the life which now is, and of that which is to come" (1 Tim. iv, 8). There can be no living this life apart from God, for it is begotten in the soul by a heavenly birth and is continually nourished and strengthened by the Spirit of God. The child of God receives the spirit of adoption, is made a partaker of the divine nature, and cries out, Abba, Father. This heavenly relationship, vitally uniting the soul of man with the eternal Spirit, is of the nature of eternal life. It brings great blessedness in this life and in this world; but it is as abiding as the nature of God. It is continually springing up into eternal life. It is, in a Johannine way of thinking, a life unlimited by time and place, but ever abiding in fellowship with the Holy One, and with his Son Jesus Christ. But in no way inconsistent with this concept it is also thought of as an everlasting inheritance. "If children of God, then also heirs of God, and joint-heirs with Christ" (Rom. viii, 17); and if "sufficient to be made partakers of the inheritance of the saints in light" (Col. i, 12), their portion is an ever-continuing fellowship with the Eternal One. And so by every inference and suggestion of these scriptures each individual life, whose "fellowship is with the Father, and with his Son Jesus Christ" (1 John i, 3), continues eternally in that blessed companionship. Both in this age and in that which is to come, in this world or in any other to which he may depart, on the earth or in the heavens, the child of God abides in life, and in love, and therefore in endless conscious bliss. We may accordingly add one word to the beatitude, and say, "Blessed are the pure in heart, for they shall eternally see God."

CHAPTER IX

THE DOCTRINE OF IMMORTALITY

1. The Fact and the Doctrine. In discussing the penal consequences of sin we were naturally led to inquire into the nature and possibilities of a future existence. Every argument bearing on the subject, whether by way of analogy, or of reason, or of scriptural investigation, resulted in the conclusion that man's conscious existence does not end with physical death, and that his personal identity and moral character, whether it be good or whether it be evil, projects itself as by a law of nature into the new state of existence which follows the present mortal life. Aside from the narrow limits of that discussion, our study thus far has been directed mainly to facts of actual experience and of positive knowledge. The nature and moral condition of man as he exists in this world, his sinfulness and his consciousness of guilt, and the varying experiences of repentance, faith, regeneration, sanctification, and eternal life are made familiar to us by the testimony of innumerable witnesses who confirm the biblical teaching concerning these subjects. But coming now to inquire more directly into the nature and possibilities of spiritual life beyond this present world, we enter a realm of mystery. We may distinguish between the fact or certainty of a future life for man and the biblical doctrine of immortality. As a matter of fact, the belief in some form of future existence is well nigh, if not absolutely, as universal as the human race. Our concept of God, our moral sense, our spiritual intuitions, our native longings and hopes, and our growing rational conviction of the conservation and survival of all that is highest and best in the world combine into a sort of *a priori* assurance of immortality. But when we attempt to formulate our doctrine of the future state, and study the numerous and varying ideals that have been constructed by poetic fancy, we find it difficult to distinguish between what is fact or evident truth, and what is the product of imagination. It is an interesting and not unprofitable study to gather up and compare the different views touching a future life which have been held among the different nations and tribes of men; but the scope of our inquiries is limited to the teachings of the Old and New Testaments. These teachings, however, comprehend the most and the best that has ever anywhere been spoken. What is the biblical doctrine of immortality?

2. Human Limitation and Doubt. The concepts of time and of eternal duration arise from the necessary limitations of our human thought. There is a remarkable statement made in Eccl. iii, 11, which may well receive a passing comment here. The writer says that God "has put eternity (העלם, *the everlasting*) in their heart, so that man may not find out the work which God has done from beginning to end." His meaning seems to be that God has put in the soul of man the concept of eternal duration, and the result with the wise man is that he perceives and acknowledges the necessary limitations of his finite nature. Beginning and end are alike wrapped in mystery, but the idea of eternity is set in his heart and cannot be put away. In Eccl. xii, 5, it is said that man in dying "goes to his eternal house." He passes into the hidden (comp. נעלם in ver. 14), silent, mysterious realm of the dead. "Who knoweth the spirit of the sons of men whether it goeth upward, and the spirit of the beast whether it goeth downward to the earth?" (iii, 21). Doubt and perplexity seem to trouble the soul of this debater, to whom all human pursuits end in "vanity of vanities." With him at least one thing is sure: "The dust [of man's body] shall return to the earth as it was, and the spirit shall return unto God who gave it" (xii, 7). These words are an obvious allusion to what is written in Gen. ii, 7, and iii, 19, and the bare statement that the spirit returns unto God throws no light upon the nature of the future state of existence. It is as perfectly compatible with a pantheistic conception of absorption into the Infinite as with the belief in a personal future existence of conscious fellowship with God in the heavens.

3. Doctrine of the Old Testament. In a study of the Hebrew scriptures we find a number of allusions to a current doctrine of the continuance of personal life beyond its present state, but all of them together are insufficient to make up a clear or satisfactory revelation touching the life to come. Little, if anything, can be found in the most ancient portions of the Old Testament literature. It is remarkable that the appeal which is employed to awaken faith and hope in Israel is not to the thought or motives of a future existence and a judgment to come, but to the living God, "who brought them out of the land of Egypt, out of the house of bondage." In that land of the Nile the Israelites must have come more or less in contact with the Egyptian doctrine of the underworld, and of the solemn judgment to be passed before Ra and Osiris and Ptah. It may be that the absence of any corresponding doctrine among the emancipated Hebrews was a designed reaction from excess of that subject brought to their attention in their house of bondage. They went forth to emphasize rather the laws of righteous judgment in the present world, "to keep the commandments of Jehovah, to walk in all his ways, to serve him with all the heart and soul; for he is the great God, who doth execute justice for the fatherless and the widow, and loveth the sojourner" (Deut. x, 12-18).

(1) *Sundry Intimations.* Nevertheless there are various intimations of belief in a future life noticeable in the Old Testament. The theophanies and angelophanies, whether they be regarded as historical facts or matters of vision and dream and ideal description, suggest another and higher realm of spiritual beings. To the Hebrew seer this world was all alive with God and his angels. It would seem, in fact, that the doctrine of immortality among any people becomes definite and positive according as the doctrine of God becomes clearly defined and exalted. The statement that a patriarch died in a good old age, and "was gathered to his people" (Gen. xxv, 8, 17; xxxv, 29; xlix, 29, 33), appears to mean something different from burial in the ancestral tomb, but is too vague to furnish anything more than the general idea of a gathering in the realm of the dead. The grave itself seems in some way to connect with a vast underworld of departed souls. The superstitions of necromancy imply a belief in the continued life of those who had disappeared from the world. The story of Saul's interview with the witch of Endor (1 Sam. xxviii) shows a current belief that a prophet like Samuel might be summoned back from the underworld to speak with the king of Israel. And the traditions of Enoch and Elijah, and their translation without seeing death, necessarily involve some notion of a heavenly state where godly men may continue to hold exalted fellowship with God.

(2) *Expressed in Many Psalms.* The psalms and hymns and spiritual songs of a nation usually express their belief in a future life, if any such belief exist at the time of their composition. In Psa. lxxiii, 23-26, it is easy to see an outgrowth of the idea of Enoch walking with God:

> I am continually with thee;
> Thou hast holden my right hand.
> Thou shalt guide me with thy counsel,
> And afterwards receive me to glory.
> Whom have I in heaven but thee?
> And there is none upon earth that I desire beside thee.
> My flesh and my heart faileth;
> But God is the strength of my heart and my portion forever.

In these lines we observe how an elevated theism accompanies and enhances the idea of a heavenly life with God, a life that must needs continue beyond this earthly state of being. A similar sentiment is conspicuous in the language of Psa. xvi, 10, 11:

> Thou wilt not abandon my soul to Sheol;
> Nor give up thy pious ones to see the pit.
> Thou wilt show me the path of life;
> In thy presence is fulness of joy;
> In thy right hand there are pleasures forever.

This devout singer is evidently smitten with the conviction that he is absolutely safe in the hand of his God. He expresses his calm assurance and joyful expectation that the pathway of life will open before him as he goes onward, and he has a blessed security for the present and the future because Jehovah is always before him, or at his right hand (ver. 8). His pathway to the life eternal might lead him through "the valley of the shadow of death" (comp. Psa. xxiii, 4), and down into the darkness of Sheol, but then with another psalmist he could say: "God will redeem my soul from the hand of Sheol; for he will take me" (xlix, 15). Here, as in Psa. lxxiii, 24, there is an obvious allusion to the translation of Enoch, whom "God took" (לקח, Gen. v, 24), and the thought may be that he will not enter into the realm of Sheol at all, but that God will come to his rescue and take him away to himself, as he did the ancient father of Methuselah. The same living trust in God and the idea of continuous dwelling with him are apparent in many other psalms:

> God is our refuge and strength,
> A very present help in trouble;
> Therefore will we not fear though the earth change,
> And though the mountains be moved in the heart of the seas.

> Thou art my hiding place; thou wilt preserve me from trouble;
> Thou wilt compass me about with songs of deliverance.

> Be thou to me a rock of habitation,
> Whereunto I may continually resort.

> He that dwelleth in the secret place of the Most High
> Shall abide under the shadow of the Almighty.
> He is my refuge and my fortress;
> My God in whom I trust.

All such metaphors of secure abode, secret intercourse and abiding trust in the eternal and invisible God evince a strong faith in these sweet singers of Israel, and are not compatible either with ignorance of a future life or of disbelief in it. For who but those who possess confident hope of everlasting fellowship with God can properly employ such language as that of Psa. xxvii, 1?

> Jehovah is my light and my salvation;
>   Whom shall I fear?
> Jehovah is the stronghold of my life;
>   Of whom shall I be afraid?

(3) *Job xix, 25-27.* To this same class of composition belongs that impassioned outburst of divine inspiration which we read in Job xix, 25-27:

> And I, I know that my Avenger lives,
> And afterwards shall he upon the dust arise,
> And after my skin—they have struck this off—
> Even without my flesh shall I behold Eloah:
> Whom I, I shall behold for myself,
> And mine eyes shall have seen, and not a stranger.

There is no little obscurity attaching to particular words in this passage, and it may be attributed to the fact that they are the broken utterances of extreme emotion. The poet represents Job, at a moment of his deepest anguish, expressing his confident expectation of a final vindication. He seems to have no very definite idea of the time or the manner in which it will take place. His Avenger may come after he himself shall have returned to dust, and may rise up over his dust to vindicate his cause. But one thing he knows and boldly declares, that, whether in the body or out of the body, whether in this life or in some other life to come, the living God will surely avenge his wrongs, and show forth his innocence.

(4) *The Realm of Sheol.* Other Old Testament texts connected with this subject relate more directly to the doctrine of the resurrection, and will be noticed in our discussion of that doctrine. The word *Sheol,* as a common designation of the abode of the dead, is often employed in a way that assumes a general belief in personal existence after death, but it supplies no clear or positive revelation as to the real nature of the future life. The ideas of reward or of penalty are gathered from what is said in the connection rather than from anything of special significance in the word itself. In his bitter sorrow over the loss of Joseph the aged patriarch Jacob cries: "I will go down into Sheol unto my son mourning" (Gen. xxxvii, 35). In Job xi, 8, Sheol is

spoken of as if it were the opposite of the high heaven, a deep, dark, subterranean abyss; and in Job xvii, 13-16, we read:

> If I look for Sheol as my house;
> If I have spread my couch in the darkness;
> If I have said to corruption, Thou art my father;
> To the worm, Thou art my mother and my sister;
> Where then is my hope?
> And as for my hope, who shall see it?
> It shall go down to the bars of Sheol,
> When once there is rest in the dust.

Here certainly there is no light or hopeful picture.[1] The realm of the dead is but dimly distinguishable from corruption, worms, and dust. The same close association of Sheol and the grave appears in Isa. xiv, 9-11, where in a highly wrought poetic description the shades of departed princes address the king of Babylon upon his coming down among them and say to him:

> Art thou become weak as we? Art thou become like unto us?
> Thy pomp is brought down to Sheol, and the noise of thy cymbals;
> The worm is spread under thee, and the worms cover thee.

The entire passage assumes a current belief in the continued existence of the human soul after death, but the vision is a vague and gloomy one, and has its basis in the poetic fancies of a heathen eschatology. The word רפאים, *shades* (ver. 9), belongs to the same realm of thought, and might be translated "powerless shades," implying souls of fallen heroes.[2] In Job xxvi, 5, 6, the three words, *Rephaim, Sheol,* and *Abaddon* occur together:

> The powerless shades tremble beneath the waters and their inhabitants;
> Sheol is naked before him [God], and Abaddon hath no covering.

The use of the word *Abaddon* in this connection, as in some sense a further characterization of Sheol, indicates that in the writer's mind Sheol is the abode of the helpless dead, deep down underneath the waters, and it is a region of destruction and ruin

---

[1] It is not a whit better than the doleful view of the state of the most honored dead which Achilles expresses to Ulysses in Homer, Odyssey, xi, 487-491:
> O do not thus to me make light of death,
> Glorious Ulysses; I would be a serf
> And toil along with any other man
> Who has no share, and whose life is not much,
> Rather than reign o'er all the wasted dead.

[2] The word is used in both singular and plural to designate a man or men of great size (e. g., 1 Chron. xx, 6, 8; Deut. ii, 11, 20), but as referring to souls of the dead it is always used in the plural (Job xxvi, 5; Psa. lxxxviii, 10; Prov. ii 18; ix, 18; xxi, 16; Isa. xiv, 9; xxvi, 14, 19). The word עתודים, here used poetically for *princes*, means *he-goats*, or *bell-wethers*. See Kay and Cheyne on Isa. xiv, 9.

(אבדון), where the souls of the mighty princes are affected with a sense of fear. It appears, therefore, that no study of the word *Sheol*, as employed in the Old Testament, will bring to light any definite idea of the condition of departed souls. Its use shows that the doctrine of a future life was a current belief, but it affords us little or no help for the elucidation of the doctrine. In some scriptures Sheol is mentioned as if it were the abode of all the dead, both righteous and wicked; in other passages it would seem to be the prison of the ungodly; and yet in others it is referred to as a place or condition from which God will rescue his own devout servants who delight in him and keep his law. In most instances the word occurs in poetic compositions.

(5) *The Greek Word Hades.* We find the same indefiniteness attaching to the Greek word *Hades* ("Αιδης, *invisible* land or realm). In nearly every passage in the Old Testament where the word *Sheol* occurs it is represented in the Septuagint version by *Hades.* The word appears eleven times in the New Testament, but in only one or two passages do we find anything in the context to throw light upon its meaning. One of these occurs in Peter's discourse (Acts ii, 27, 31), where he comments on a quotation from Psa. xvi, 8-10; but the apostle's comment adds no new significance to the word. He applies the psalm to the resurrection of Christ, arguing that it does not fit the fact that David, the assumed author, died and was buried, and his tomb was among them at that day. Jesus, on the contrary, "was not left in Hades, neither did his flesh see corruption."[1] Hades here, as Sheol in the Hebrew psalm, stands simply as the current designation of the invisible realm of the dead. Much more suggestive is the passage in Luke xvi, 23, where it is written: "The rich man died, and was buried; and in Hades he lifted up his eyes being in torments, and he seeth Abraham afar off, and Lazarus in his bosom." Here we have something more than the indefinite use of a word; we have a word-picture of the unseen world. The Hades of this picture seems to include "Abraham's bosom" as well as a region of torment, but the two are separated by "a great gulf" (ver. 26), over which none may cross from one place to the other. The entire word-picture is drawn after the manner of a parable, and we are not at liberty to assume all the details of the description, with the conversation between Abraham and the rich man, to be so many prosaic statements of an actual occurrence. Else might we argue with equal assurance that the good and the bad dwell forever in sight of each other in Hades, and hold conversations like the one

---

[1]Peter uses the Septuagint translation which renders the Hebrew שחת, *pit*, by διαφθορά, *corruption*.

here recorded. Equally futile is the notion that, according to this scripture, poverty like that of Lazarus gains one admission to heavenly comfort and fruition; for this father Abraham, during his earthly life, was a rich man. The main lessons of the parable point to the responsibilities of mortal men to one another in this life. He who fares sumptuously in this world and allows an unfortunate brother to die in abject poverty at his door, is tormented in his existence after death; while the poor unfortunate may appear in the other world to be a friend of God, and a fit companion of him who was noted as the "friend of God" (Isa. xli, 8; 2 Chron. xx, 7; James ii, 23). This portraiture of existence after death, however, belongs rather to the doctrine of the New Testament.

4. Doctrine of the New Testament. Recurring now to the doctrine of eternal life, as set forth in the preceding chapter, we proceed to show what the Christian Scriptures have to say about the future blessedness of the righteous. The foundation of the Christian's hope is in knowing that his "life is hid with Christ in God" (Col. iii, 3). It appears that one's personal and conscious existence may continue beyond death in a condition far apart from fellowship with God and his saints. "He that obeyeth not the Son shall not see life, but the wrath of God abideth on him" (John iii, 36). Without the heavenly life implanted in him by the birth from above he cannot see the kingdom of God (vers. 3 and 5). And in the highest teaching of the Old Testament as well as in the New the main ground of confidence in a blissful immortality is living fellowship with the eternal God. The fundamental thought in all the symbolism of the temple and the tabernacle of Israel was that God would condescend to dwell with man, and sanctify Israel in his glory (Exod. xxix, 42-46); and the ultimate consummation of the kingdom of God is a "reigning in life" (comp. Rom. v, 17), which, in corresponding apocalyptic symbolism, is portrayed by the vision of the tabernacle of God with men, God himself dwelling among them and wiping away every tear from their eyes (Rev. xxi, 3, 4). Then, it is said (Rev. xxii, 5), "There shall be night no more; and they need no light of lamp, neither light of sun; for the Lord God shall give them light: and they shall reign forever and ever." In presenting the New Testament doctrine of immortality and the heavenly life we shall accordingly begin with the Apocalypse of John, and thereafter study the teachings of the epistle to the Hebrews, the Pauline epistles, and the gospels in the order here named. We may the more appropriately begin with the Apocalypse, inasmuch as that book connects closely with the ideas of heavenly life and activity which are peculiar to this class of writings in the Old Testament and in the later apocryphal literature of the Jews.

(1) *In the Apocalypse of John.* We must keep in mind that the Apocalypse of John is cast in the highest forms of biblical symbolism, and that its various statements may not be taken as prosaic declarations of fact or of doctrine. Its elaborate visions of the heavenly world are not realistic but ideal. Nevertheless, it is not difficult to discern under the various figures and symbols a substratum of current beliefs which the author accepted as his own, and which he has enhanced with all the embellishment which his style of composition would naturally appropriate. His ascription of glory and dominion "unto him that loveth us, and made us to be a kingdom and priests unto his God and Father" (i, 6; v, 10) carries with it as an essential thought the fundamental truth that Christ's followers constitute a peculiar possession of God, destined to live and reign with him forever (comp. 1 Pet. ii, 9). We also find in the epistles to the Seven Churches, among the promises "to him that overcometh," language which has significance only when understood to refer to heavenly rewards. Thus "eating of the tree of life which is in the Paradise of God" (ii, 7), receiving the hidden manna and the new name (ii, 17), the name in the book of life (iii, 5), becoming a pillar in the temple of God and going out thence no more (iii, 12), and finally the remarkable words, "He that overcometh, I will give to him to sit down with me in my throne, as I also overcame, and sat down with my Father in his throne" (iii, 21)—these all point to the triumphs and eternal blessedness of those who cleave to the truth and abide faithful to Christ in every trial that may come to test them. There can also be no doubt that when the writer, in chapter iv, describes in glowing style what he saw and heard through "a door opened in heaven," he intends to impress his readers with a sublime conception of a supernatural world, in which God rules in unspeakable majesty. At this point we observe a very obvious connecting link between Old and New Testament revelations. The vision of God's throne in the heavens is modeled after what is written in Isa. vi and Ezek. i, and with these we should also compare the magnificent apocalyptic picture of Dan. vii, 9-14. Such ideals of the King of glory and of his associates, and ministers, and servants become impressively significant of the future glory of all the children of God, who are also "heirs of God and joint heirs with Christ; if so be that we suffer with him, that we may be also glorified with him" (Rom. viii, 17). The significance is the more direct and unmistakable when we read in Daniel that "the kingdom and the dominion shall be given to the

people of the saints of the Most High" (vii, 27), and in Rev. v, 9, that people "of every tribe and tongue and nation are made a kingdom and priests unto God; and they reign upon the earth," and "they shall reign for ever and ever" (xxii, 5). It is evident that in the thought of the apocalyptist the redeemed saints of God, who triumph in Christ, shall be partakers eternally in his heavenly kingdom and glory. In some sense they are to reign with him on the earth and in the heavens, for eternal life in Christ insures all this. The vision of "the souls of them that had been slain for the word of God, and for the testimony which they held," to each of whom was given a white robe and a comforting assurance of righteous judgment (vi, 9-11), would be meaningless and inexplicable apart from the current doctrine of immortality. Still more magnificent and impressive is the vision, in vii, 9-17, of the "great multitude which no man could number, out of every nation, and of all tribes and peoples and tongues, standing before the throne, arrayed in white robes and palms in their hands. . . . They serve God day and night in his temple; and he that sitteth on the throne shall spread his tabernacle over them. They shall hunger no more, neither thirst any more. . . . The Lamb shall be their shepherd and shall guide them unto fountains of waters of life: and God shall wipe away every tear from their eyes." Similar portraitures of a glorified existence in a higher realm are furnished in Rev. xiv, 1-5; xv, 2-4; xx, 4-6; but, as the interpretation of these passages is involved in questions of the plan and scope of the book as a whole, we pass them by with this bare reference,[1] and proceed directly to the vision of the New Jerusalem in chapters xxi and xxii, 1-5. This picture of the holy city of God, coming down out of heaven, arrayed in beauty as a bride adorned for her husband, is a symbol of the coming and kingdom of Christ and of its predestined renovation of all things. He who sits on the throne says: "Behold, I am making all things new. . . . He that overcometh shall inherit these things, and I will be his God and he shall be my son" (xxi, 5, 7). The composite symbolism of the entire vision presents us a picture of the church and kingdom of Christ in time and eternity, but with the ideals of ultimate glorification especially in view. In these visions of glory and triumph no note of distinction is made between those who are in the flesh and those who are perfected in the heavenly places, for they all constitute one body in Christ. Once united in living fellowship with him these children of God inherit all the riches and triumphs and glory of his kingdom in time and eternity. He who thus

---

[1] On the exposition of all these passages, see my Biblical Apocalyptics.

lives and believes in Christ never dies (John xi, 26). The inhabitants of this heavenly Jerusalem dwell with God and God abides with them. Death has no more dominion over them, nor shall they know mourning and crying and pain any more. They shall see God's face, and his name shall be on their foreheads. They shall abide by the river of the water of life, eat freely of the tree of life, and "the Lord God shall give them light, and they shall reign forever and ever." All these exquisite ideals most assuredly contemplate a blessed immortality of conscious personal existence.

(2) *In the Epistle to the Hebrews.* The epistle to the Hebrews magnifies "the great salvation" provided in Jesus Christ, and the salvation cannot be fairly and fully explained except it be made to include the heavenly blessedness that is consequent upon obedience to Christ, the great high priest over the house of God. The angels are ministering spirits unto such as shall inherit the great salvation (i, 14). The suffering and death of Christ are for the purpose of bringing many sons into glory (ii, 10), and through his leadership, more potent than that of Joshua, the people of God look for a blessed sabbath-rest in heaven (iv, 9). Such blessed hope is "as an anchor of the soul, both sure and steadfast, and entering into that which is within the veil; whither as a forerunner Jesus entered for us" (vi, 19). The ancient fathers died in faith and expectation of a heavenly country, for God has prepared for them a city (xi, 13-16). In xii, 22, 23, it would seem that the writer had read the visions of Rev. xiv, 1, and of the New Jerusalem, for he speaks of an entrance into those heavenly places as a possible present experience: "Ye are come unto mount Zion, and unto the city of the living God, the heavenly Jerusalem, and to innumerable hosts of angels, to the general assembly and church of the firstborn who are enrolled in heaven, and to God the Judge of all, and to the spirits of just men made perfect." Once in living fellowship with "the people of the saints of the Most High," the true child of God has entered upon the inheritances of the heavenly life, and receives an earnest of the redemption of his glorious possession. He boldly enters the holy place by the new and living way which his adorable high priest has opened for him, even into heaven itself (comp. ix, 11, 24; x, 19).

(3) *In the Epistles of Paul.* There is ground for the opinion now widely prevalent that the Pauline epistles are not uniform in their treatment of questions of eschatology. But this want of clearness and harmony appears chiefly in the apostle's statements touching the coming and kingdom of Christ, and the resurrection of the dead. Reserving these subjects for separate discussion, we here inquire only after his teachings concerning a future life.

Whatever his belief in the coming of the Lord and the resurrection of the saints, he comforts the Thessalonians with the assurance that those who have fallen asleep in Jesus are with God and will, along with the saints yet living, be finally and forever with the Lord in the heavens (1 Thess. iv, 14, 17), and he admonishes them that, "whether we wake or sleep, we should live together with him" (v, 10). He never seems to lose sight of the blessed truth that the future inheritance of the saints in the heavenly kingdom, whatever the order and manner of its realization, is the certain salvation of "God our Father, who loved us and gave us eternal comfort and good hope through grace" (2 Thess. ii, 16). One great thought emphasized in the epistle to the Romans is that the believer is "dead unto sin but alive unto God in Christ Jesus," and in some sense he so lives in and with Christ that, as in the case of his risen Lord, "death hath no more dominion over him" (vi, 6-11). Hence he is "persuaded that neither death, nor life, nor angels, nor principalities, nor things present, nor things to come, nor powers, nor height, nor depth, nor any other creation shall be able to separate us from the love of God, which is in Christ Jesus our Lord" (viii, 38, 39). This vital union with God in Christ is the power of an imperishable life, and the apostle therefore has no fear of earthly trials. "For I reckon that the sufferings of this present time are not worthy to be compared with the glory which shall be revealed to us-ward" (viii, 18). And so "the God of hope" enables his children to "abound in hope" (xv, 13). He who has the mind of the Spirit, loves the truths of God, and seeks to scatter them abroad so as to promote the work of the Holy Spirit among men, shall surely "reap eternal life" as his reward (Gal. vi, 8). In 2 Cor. v, 1-8, we are taught that the dissolution of "the earthly house of our tabernacle" is to be immediately followed by a "clothing upon with our habitation which is from heaven," so that "what is mortal is swallowed up of life," and the apostle declares that he is "willing rather to be absent from the body and to be at home with the Lord." Here the putting off of the mortal flesh is but to pass into closer fellowship with the Lord, and to be more at home with him. In Phil. i, 21-24, the same apostle speaks of his confidence that Christ will be magnified either by his life or by his death. "For to me to live is Christ, and to die is gain. . . . I am in a strait betwixt the two, having the desire to depart and to be with Christ; for it is far better: yet to abide in the flesh is more needful for your sake." In this passage "living in the flesh," and "abiding in the flesh" are phrases equivalent to "being at home in the body" (2 Cor. v, 6), and in both places the writer clearly implies his belief and confidence that upon the termination of his life in the fleshly body he will at once "depart and be with Christ." This latter would with him be "very far better" than to abide in the flesh. To die would be inestimable gain, but for the sake of the brethren and the church it was needful for him to live in the flesh and seek "fruit from his work." In 2 Tim. i, 10, he speaks of "the appearing of our Saviour Jesus Christ, who abolished death and brought life and immortality to light through the gospel." He cheerfully "suffers hardship unto bonds," and "endures all things for the sake of the elect, that they may obtain the salvation which is in Christ Jesus with eternal glory" (ii, 10). And then he cites by way of confirmation what seems to be a portion of a Christian hymn already familiar to the church when this epistle was written:

> For if we died with him,
> We shall also live with him:
> If we endure,
> We shall also reign with him.

Further on in this epistle (iv, 6-8) he speaks calmly but triumphantly of his own death and of the glory which awaits him beyond: "I am already being offered, and the time of my departure is come. I have fought the good fight, I have finished the course, I have kept the faith; henceforth there is laid up for me the crown of righteousness, which the Lord, the righteous judge, shall give to me at that day: and not only to me, but also to all them that have loved his appearing." Whatever other ideas were entertained by Paul in connection with this doctrine of immortality and heavenly blessedness, this much is clear from the passages cited above from his epistles, that this earthly life, with all its opportunities of faith, and love, and good works, and self-denial, and sufferings, is with the Christian a life hidden in Christ and imperishable; and when he puts off the mortal flesh he only passes on into a closer fellowship with Christ, attains to glory unspeakable, and lives and reigns with his Lord, with whom, indeed, he is evermore at home.

(4) *Teaching of Jesus in the Synoptics.* Much of the teaching of Jesus concerning the future life stands in such close connection with his doctrine of the kingdom of heaven that the one subject cannot be well separated from the other. In the synoptic gospels the kingdom of God is often mentioned in a manner that implies permanent blessedness. The poor in spirit, and those who are willing to suffer persecution for righteousness' sake, shall inherit the kingdom of heaven. They are called upon to rejoice and be exceeding glad because their reward in heaven is great (Matt. v, 12).

Men should not lay up treasures upon the earth, but in heaven, "where neither moth nor rust doth consume, and where thieves do not break through nor steal" (vi, 20). The righteous who make real sacrifices and suffer losses for Christ's sake "shall inherit eternal life" (xix, 29); they are called by their king in the judgment the "blessed of my Father," and are given to "inherit the kingdom prepared for them from the foundation of the world" (xxv, 34). They "shall shine forth as the sun in the kingdom of their Father" (xiii, 43). All these sayings manifestly contemplate a reward and a glory not of this world. We find much of this same teaching recorded also in the gospels of Mark and Luke. And all these synoptists put on record the transfiguration of Jesus, and declare that "there talked with him two men, who were Moses and Elijah, who appeared in glory, and spake of his decease (ἔξοδος, *departure*) which he was about to accomplish at Jerusalem" (Luke ix, 30). Whether this record be explained as a real event, or as a dream, or as a vision (ὅραμα, Matt. xvii, 9), it presupposes from first to last the personal immortality of such saints as Moses and Elijah. They are conceived as existing and capable of appearing in glory, and of communicating with each other.

(5) *Teaching of Jesus in John's Gospel.* In the fourth gospel the doctrine of eternal life, both as a present possession and an everlasting inheritance, receives, as we have already shown, peculiar emphasis. The new life implanted from above is like a new creation; it becomes in the receptive heart a fountain of water springing up unto eternal life. Christ coming down from heaven becomes to those who believe in him the bread of life, of which they eat and live forever (vi, 50, 51). Such "never taste of death" (viii, 52), for Jesus says: "I am the resurrection and the life: he that believeth on me, though he die, yet shall he live: and whosoever liveth and believeth on me shall never die" (xi, 25, 26). Such language becomes him who "knows that the Father had given all things into his hands, and that he came forth from God, and goeth unto God" (xiii, 3). He is acquainted with both worlds of being, and declares with the positiveness of personal assurance: "I came out from the Father, and am come into the world: again, I leave the world, and go unto the Father" (xvi, 28; comp. viii, 14, 42; xiv, 12; xvii, 11). Coming from One who speaks with such heavenly consciousness and light, the memorable saying in John xiv, 1-3, is perhaps the most explicit teaching of our Lord on record touching the blissful immortality and heavenly life of believers: "In my Father's house are many mansions; if it were not so, I would have told you; for I go to prepare a place for you. And if I go and prepare a place for you,

I come again, and will receive you unto myself; that where I am, there ye may be also." There are two other passages in this Gospel which we do well to study in connection with the one last cited. In vi, 38, 39, Jesus says: "I am come down from heaven, not to do mine own will, but the will of him that sent me. And this is the will of him that sent me, that of all that which he hath given me (πᾶν ὃ δέδωκέν μοι; observe the neuter singular, and the concept of the whole vast body of believers as one gift) I should lose nothing, but should raise it up at the last day." In the intercessory prayer he again thus refers to this gift of the Father: "Father, that which thou hast given me (ὃ δέδωκάς μοι), I desire that, where I am, they also may be with me; that they may behold my glory, which thou hast given me; for thou lovedst me before the foundation of the world." In the preceding verses he has prayed "that they may all be one," and "that they may be perfected into one." The one great body of Christ's inheritance is here evidently contemplated as a unit, and this thought is prominent at the beginning of verse 24; but when the idea of "beholding his glory" finds expression, each individual believer is thought of as seeing for himself and not for another; for they are all to be with him, and the plural (κἀκεῖνοι, *they also*) is employed in spite of the apparent grammatical impropriety.[1] Thus each one and all of those whom the Father gives the Son as a glorious possession, and who thus become joint heirs with Christ (comp. Rom. viii, 17) are conceived as beholding the ineffable glory of his heavenly abode. He prepares a place for them among the mansions of his Father's house, and there he will receive them unto himself. They shall be like him and see him as he is (1 John iii, 2).

---

[1] Alford's note on John xvii, 24, is discriminating and appreciative: "The neuter has a peculiar solemnity, uniting the whole church together as *one gift* of the Father to the Son. Then the κἀκεῖνοι resolves it into the great multitude whom no man can number, and comes home to the heart of every individual believer with inexpressibly sweet assurance of an eternity with Christ."—Greek Testament, in loco.

CHAPTER X

THE DOCTRINE OF THE RESURRECTION

1. A Doctrine Variously Apprehended. The biblical doctrine of immortality and eternal life cannot be fully presented without a careful study of those scriptures which speak of the "resurrection of the dead." The fact or reality of resurrection, in some sense, is conceded to be a positive doctrine of the Scriptures, and Paul's argument, in 1 Cor. xv, 1-19, makes this doctrine fundamental to Christian faith and hope. But centuries of experience, observation, and controversy, since Paul wrote, have shown that a great doctrine may be generally and even universally accepted, while the modes of conceiving and stating it may vary to extremes which are quite irreconcilable. It may also be found upon careful investigation that the different biblical writers who deal with this subject are not in exact accord with one another.

2. Vaguely Expressed in Old Testament. It is not strange that the idea of a complete restoration of the dead body should become associated with the doctrine of a future life. But the idea seems to arise in the later elaborations of the doctrine, and in attempts to answer the question, "In what form and manner do the dead ones live hereafter?" Thus in the Zoroastrian doctrines of the future we find in the older portions of the Avesta only a general affirmation of the renovation of all things, but in the later literature the resurrection of the body is shown to be as credible a thought as the creation of any bodily form at the first.[1] In like manner the Hebrew scriptures contain no very certain indications of this doctrine before the time of the Babylonian exile, and all that is found is of a vague and general character, and usually expressed in the poetic and apocalyptic style.

(1) *Psalm xvii, 15.* As an example of vagueness and uncertainty in a text often cited in proof of bodily resurrection we may note the different interpretations of Psa. xvii, 15. The common version is most familiar: "As for me, I will behold thy face in righteousness: I shall be satisfied, when I awake, with thy likeness." On this Adam Clarke thus comments: "I do not think that he refers to the resurrection of the body, but to the

---

[1] Compare Yasna xxx, 9; Vendidad xviii, 51, and the more elaborate argument of the Bundahish xxx.

resurrection of the soul in this life; to the regaining of the image which Adam lost." The Anglo-American revisers carry the idea of beholding God, given in the first member of the parallelism, into the second member thus: "I shall be satisfied, when I awake, with beholding thy form." But the Polychrome Bible renders it, "I shall be refreshed at thine awaking, with a vision of thee." This follows the Septuagint and the Vulgate, which read, "I shall be satisfied when thy glory appears." Thus the awaking is understood of the awaking of Jehovah, not of the psalmist. The writer of the psalm is one in great trouble because of "deadly enemies that compass him about" (ver. 9), and he calls on Jehovah to arise and deliver him from their power (ver. 13), confident that when God's glorious form appears, he himself will behold it and be satisfied. All these are possible explanations of the text, and show that the thought intended is too uncertain for the passage to be of any value as a proof-text of the doctrine of resurrection.

(2) *Language of Other Poets and Prophets.* In Deut. xxxii, 39, we read: "I put to death and make alive again." Similarly the parallelism in 1 Sam. ii, 6:

> Jehovah puts to death and makes alive;
> He brings down to Sheol, and he brings up.[1]

A similar thought is also expressed in Isa. xxv, 8: "He hath swallowed up death forever; and Jehovah will wipe away tears from off all faces." But such a statement determines nothing as to a resurrection of bodies from the grave, neither can we make the language of Hos. xiii, 14, mean more than a recognition of Jehovah's absolute power over death and the whole realm of the dead:

> I will ransom them from the power of Sheol;
> I will redeem them from death.
> O death, where are thy plagues?
> O Sheol, where is thy destruction?

Nevertheless, it is not difficult to recognize in this language some idea of resurrection from death. The earliest readers of these poets and prophets might easily have supposed that the mighty God, who has all power over the realms of the dead, and who is himself the author of life, could rescue his people from the bands of Sheol and restore them to a life more glorious than they had known before. Certain it is that the readers of a later time have

---

[1] These lines are repeated in Tobit xiii, 2:—"He leads down to Hades, and he leads up again." Also in a slightly changed and enlarged form in the Wisdom of Solomon, xvi, 13: "Thou hast authority over life and death, and thou leadest down to the gates of Hades and leadest up again."

thought the words appropriate to the doctrine of a personal resurrection from the dead, and Paul so cites them in his discussion of the doctrine (1 Cor. xv, 54, 55).

(3) *Hosea vi, 1-3.* The following language from Hos. vi, 1-3, has been variously understood and applied:

> Come and let us return unto Jehovah;
> For he hath torn, and he will heal us;
> He hath smitten, and he will bind us up.
> After two days he will revive us:
> On the third day he will raise us up,
> And we shall live before him.
> And let us know, let us follow on to know Jehovah;
> His going forth is sure as the morning:
> And he shall come unto us as the rain,
> As the latter rain that watereth the earth.

Whether we understand these words as the language of smitten Israel exhorting one another to turn to Jehovah, or the utterances of the prophet himself appealing to the fallen people of Israel and urging them to return to their God, the idea of a resurrection attaches to the words *revive us,* and *raise us up.* But the entire context shows that the persons addressed are not physically dead, and therefore there can be no thought here of a resurrection of dead bodies, or of a calling back departed souls to life in the flesh. The other metaphorical allusions employed in the passage indicate a spiritual and national quickening, a restoration to God's favor, a healing of that which had been torn (comp. v, 14), a binding up of that which had been smitten by divine judgments, and a refreshing such as the morning brings and such as comes with the welcome rain. So the metaphor of resurrection is to be spiritually taken, and cannot be cited to prove that this prophet or the Israelites of his time believed in the doctrine of a resurrection of the body.[1]

(4) *Isaiah xxvi, 19.* The concept of a physical resurrection is much more definitely expressed in Isa. xxvi, 19. The entire context (vers. 12-21) must be studied in order to grasp the author's range of thought. He represents the people of Jehovah as having been under the rule of other lords; in their distress they call upon him, writhe as in labor-pains, and confess their helplessness to

---

[1] Many of the older expositors, however, insisted that verse 2 contains an express prediction of the resurrection of Jesus on the third day. Some displayed a disposition of bitter hostility towards those who could find no such specific prediction. Such facts admonish us that not only have predictions of Christ been discovered in Old Testament texts where no sound exegesis finds them, but also that ideas of a physical resurrection have been evolved out of poetic metaphors, which, when first used by the biblical writer, were not at all designed to inculcate such a dogma, nor to affirm it as a fact.

THE RESURRECTION

save their land or multiply their nation. The prophet impersonates the penitent and prayerful people, and referring to the lords who had oppressed them, he says (ver. 14): "The dead ones shall not live; the shades shall not rise up; therefore didst thou visit and destroy them, and cause all memory of them to perish." Then, after telling how Jehovah had multiplied the nation that kept pouring out prayers even while he was chastening them, he breaks out in the following poetic strain:

> Thy dead shall live; my body—they shall rise;
> Awake and sing, O dwellers in the dust;
> For the dew of lights is thy dew, and the earth shall cast
>   forth her shades.

These dead ones who shall live are the deceased ones of Jehovah's people and nation; they are conceived as one body, the collective Israel, of which the prophet considers himself a part and calls it "my body." Each individual of this collective body is destined to live again, and he uses the plural "they shall rise." The divine power which shall bring them forth is called "the dew of lights"[1]; not earthly dew which quickens perishable vegetation, but the dew of heavenly luminaries, which starts forth into life the spirits of the dead, "the shades." So enrapturing is the thought that the prophet breaks out with emotion, and calls upon the dwellers of the dust to awake and sing for joy. But this highly wrought poetic scripture cannot be legitimately construed to support the doctrine of a universal physical resurrection. Jehovah's dead ones live again, but the shades of the lords who oppressed Israel shall not live nor rise (ver. 14). This statement is as positive as that in Job xiv, 10-12:

> The strong man dies and is laid low;
> Yea, man breathes out his life, and where is he?
> As waters go off from the sea,
> And the river wastes and dries away:
> So man lieth down and shall not rise;
> Till the heavens be no more they shall not awake,
> Nor shall they be roused up from their sleep.

No future resurrection is compatible with these assertions, and the language in Isaiah is equally explicit touching the dead oppressors of Israel. But the dead body (נבלה, *carcass*) of God's people shall live and rise again; the dwellers in the dust may

---

[1] Some understand אורות, *lights*, here as in 2 Kings iv, 39, to signify *herbs*; but this interpretation seems to miss the true and deeper thought of the prophet. "The prophet means to say," says Cheyne, "Thy dew, O Jehovah, is so full of the light of life that it even draws forth the shades from the dark womb of the underworld."—Commentary on Isaiah, in loco.

awake and sing for joy. All this may be understood literally or figuratively. If taken in the strict literal sense, we have the positive assertion that there is no future resurrection for the enemies of Jehovah and his people. They are utterly destroyed and their memory is made to perish. But the dead among God's people shall live again, and their dead bodies shall be raised up out of the dust of the earth. If taken figuratively, we have a poetic prophecy of the certain destruction of Israel's enemies, and the salvation of the people of Jehovah. The oppressors shall cease; they shall perish and be known no more. But Jehovah's chosen nation is an imperishable body. Though they fall, "they shall rise again." In exile and oppression, and vainly writhing in labor pains to bring forth children, they are assured that Jehovah will increase the nation in his own supernatural way. He will multiply the people and even enlarge the borders of their land (ver. 15), and his marvelous work will be like a resurrection of the dead. Israel, thus divinely rescued from oppression and exile, will be like a prodigal reclaimed, of whom the joyful father says: "This son was dead, and is alive again; he was lost, and is found." Thus interpreted, the imagery of a physical resurrection is employed to denote a national restoration.

(5) *Ezekiel xxxvii, 1-14.* The figurative interpretation of Isa. xxvi, 19, is strengthened by comparison with Ezek. xxxvii, 1-14, where the same imagery is carried out in much greater detail to portray the restoration of the exiled house of Israel to their own land. The prophet had a vision of an open valley full of dry bones, and the whole process of resurrection to life is pictured before us. There was a noise, and an earthquake, and the bones came together, and then sinews and flesh and skin covered the bones, and finally breath came into them, and they lived, and stood upon their feet, an exceeding great army. Here certainly we have the unmistakable details of a resurrection of bodies to life again. But the entire vision is a symbolical picture, and not to be literally understood. The true interpretation is recorded by the prophet as a part of the visional revelation. "These bones are the whole house of Israel." They represent the people of God in their Babylonian captivity, crying out as from the misery of a living death: "Our bones are dried up, and our hope is lost; we are clean cut off." But the Lord Jehovah says to them: "Behold, I will open your graves, and cause you to come up out of your graves, O my people; and I will bring you into the land of Israel. And I will put my spirit in you, and ye shall live, and I will place you in your own land." Thus the spiritual quickening of the people, who regarded themselves as ruined, dead, and buried, and

their restoration to their own fatherland, are the things symbolized by the vision of the resurrection of dry bones. Whether Ezekiel believed in a future resurrection of all the dead, or in the literal resurrection of the bodies of any of those who were dead and buried, is a question which this scripture does not answer.[1] No true prophet of Israel, however, could well doubt the power of God to raise up out of their graves whomsoever he would, but we must not affirm as a fact, or a positive doctrine, what is simply assumed as a possibility.

(6) *Daniel xii, 2, 3.* Another Old Testament passage bearing on the doctrine of the resurrection is Dan. xii, 2, 3: "Many from the sleeping ones of earth-dust shall awake, these to life eternal, and those to reproaches and contempt eternal. And they that are wise shall shine as the brightness of the expanse, and they that turn many to righteousness like the stars for ever and ever." What is specially notable in this passage is a resurrection both to eternal life and to eternal contempt (דראון, *abhorrence*). It is mentioned among the things which are to come to pass at the time when the Jewish "people shall be delivered, every one that shall be found written in the book." It seems to occur in connection with "a time of trouble, such as never was since there was a nation even to that same time." This time of unparalleled distress is apparently the same as that which is mentioned in ix, 26, 27, of this same book.[2] It follows the overthrow of the impious enemy of the people of God, and the apocalyptic seer is assured that no member of the true Israel shall finally perish. Those enrolled in the book of life shall find glorious "deliverance" (ver. 1), and the wise and useful who turn many to righteousness shall enjoy various degrees of heavenly reward. But the resurrection referred to is not general or universal. Not all of those who sleep in the earth-dust shall awake, but "many of them" shall, and of these many, some awake to life eternal, and some to reproaches and

---

[1] It is not properly a similitude that Ezekiel uses in this vision, if from the certain fact of a general future resurrection he would fortify Israel in the belief and expectation of their own political resuscitation; but it is this resuscitation itself exhibited now in vision, that they might be prepared to look for it afterwards in reality. The mere circumstance of such a resurrection-scene being thus employed by the prophet, for such a specific purpose, could not of itself prove the doctrine of a future general resurrection of the dead, no more than his employing the machinery of cherubim and wheels of peculiar structure in his opening vision is a proof of the actual existence of such objects, either in the past or the future, in heaven or on earth. In both cases alike, what was exhibited in the vision was a representation in symbol of something corresponding that might be expected in the transactions of life, and the events of providence; but whether that symbol might have any separate and substantial existence of its own was not determined by such an employment of it, and in fact was quite immaterial as regarded the end in view.—Fairbairn, Exposition of Ezekiel, in loco.

[2] How all this accords with the bitter persecutions of Antiochus Epiphanes is shown in my Biblical Apocalyptics, pp. 190-194, 199, 205-207, 210-212.

contempt eternal.¹ Such a vague and mystic apocalyptic picture cannot be made to serve any definite dogmatic purpose in the exposition of the doctrine of the resurrection. It gives an ideal of future calamity for the enemies of God and of future triumph and blessedness for the righteous. It affirms an awakening of many of those who sleep in the dust, and so far it accords with Isa. xxvi, 19; but it differs very noticeably from Isa. xxvi, 14, in affirming the resurrection of some to eternal reproach and contempt. The writer is probably not referring to a resurrection of the wicked generally, but to apostate Israelites, like those mentioned in xi, 30, 32, who are destined to be an eternal abhorrence. He does not say that all the dead shall rise; he does not even say that all the people of Israel will awake from the dust of the earth. The words contain no answer to the question how the dead are raised up, and with what sort of a body they return to life. The awaking from the dust may be only an apocalyptic figure designed to indicate some special restoration in Israel in which eternal destinies of opposite character are recognized. The passage stands alone in the Old Testament, having no real parallel in affirming a partial resurrection, and indicating a resurrection of some to a condition of perpetual abhorrence.

(7) *Variety of Later Jewish Opinions.* These Old Testament scriptures furnished a sufficient basis for subsequent elaborations of the doctrine of the resurrection. How far this doctrine may have been derived or developed from the contact of the Jewish people with men of other religions we may not with any certainty affirm. The doctrine was held by the disciples of Zoroaster and formed a part of the Mazdean faith, as is shown from portions of the Avesta.² The apocryphal and pseudepigraphical books of the later Judaism indicate the various speculations of their time. The Alexandrian writers seem to have discarded the idea of a physical resurrection and to have adhered rather to the doctrine of a spiritual immortality and eternal life.³ But the resurrection of the body was quite generally believed, and some of the Jewish books affirm a restoration of the body without change of form.⁴ Some teach a resurrection of all the dead,⁵ while others declare

---

¹ No writer who wishes to make himself understood would employ the word *many* if he intended *all.* "Many from the sleeping ones" cannot mean all the sleeping ones. The expression *the many,* οἱ πολλοί, in Rom. v, 15, is not parallel, and cannot be cited to prove that רבים in Dan. xii, 2, may have the sense of all mankind. In Paul's epistle the word is qualified and limited by the article, and serves a special purpose in a hypothetical argument.
² Yasht xix, 11, 12, 89, 90.
³ Wisdom of Solomon iii, 1-9; v, 16.
⁴ Apocalypse of Baruch l, 2; Judith xvi, 17; Sibylline Oracles iv, 181.
⁵ Fourth Ezra vii, 32. Test. xii Patriarchs, Benj., x.

that the righteous only will be raised.[1] The Sadducees held that the human soul dies with the body and knows no other life.[2] The Essenes believed in the immortality of souls,[3] and the Pharisees, who constituted the majority of the Palestinian Jews, maintained both the immortality of the soul, and the resurrection of the body (comp. Acts xxiii, 8). But even among the Pharisees themselves there seem to have been some differences of opinion, some believing in the resurrection of the righteous only, while others "looked for a resurrection both of the just and unjust" (Acts xxiv, 15).[4] The Alexandrian Jews seem, however, to have imbibed the Greek philosophy so far as to accept the notion that matter is essentially evil; they, accordingly, would naturally discard the doctrine of a restoration of the flesh. Such remarkable variety of Jewish opinion, prevalent at the beginning of the Christian era, is a fact to be carefully observed, and should admonish us against assuming, without specific evidence, that our Lord or any of his apostles accepted or endorsed any one of these current opinions.

3. The Fuller Teaching in the New Testament. The doctrine of the resurrection of the dead finds a fullness of treatment in the New Testament which is in notable contrast with the vagueness of allusions in the Old. The apostles of our Lord, and all who were familiar with the religious opinions current in their time, must have come in contact more or less close with the different views on this subject which appear in the later Jewish literature just referred to. The Greeks who lived at the centers of philosophical thought and culture were disposed to treat the doctrine with indifference, and even with contempt (Acts xvii, 32), and Paul found among the Corinthians some who said, "There is no resurrection of the dead" (1 Cor. xv, 12). It is now impossible to tell precisely what was the error of Hymenæus and Philetus, for the only indication left us is that they affirmed the resurrection, or "a resurrection," to be already past (2 Tim. ii, 18). The statement is too vague to afford us any certain information of the meaning they put upon the word *resurrection* (ἀνάστασις).

---

[1] Book of Enoch li, 1, 2; lxii, 15, 16; xci, 10; xcii, 3.
[2] Josephus, Antiquities xviii, i, 4. Comp. Acts xxiii, 8.
[3] Josephus, Antiquities xviii, i, 5.
[4] See Josephus, Antiquities xviii, i, 3; Wars ii, viii, 14. In the last named passage it is said, as a belief of the Pharisees, "that all souls are incorruptible, but the souls of good men are only removed into other bodies; but the souls of bad men are subject to eternal punishment." The fourth book of the Sibylline Oracles belongs probably to the latter part of the first century, and expresses, in lines 181 and 182, a widely accepted Jewish opinion of that time, namely, that God will again raise up and fashion anew "the bones and ashes of men as they were before." How this belief passed over into patristic doctrine may be seen in Tertullian's treatise, De Resurrectione Carnis, and in Augustine's De Civitate Dei, where it is maintained (xxii, 19) that the hair and the nails shall be restored, inasmuch as Jesus said, "Not a hair of your head shall perish" (Luke xxi, 18).

4. No Help from Etymology of Greek Words. The Greek word employed in the New Testament to express resurrection of the dead is ἀνάστασις, which means a *rising up,* and implies some manner of exaltation of the dead. They rise or stand up again in some new form and power. But we obtain no particular assistance in determining the nature of the resurrection by means of the etymology of this word or of any other. Two Greek words appear in the New Testament in connection with this subject, the verbs ἐγείρω and ἀνίστημι, and their derivatives, ἔγερσις and ἀνάστασις. Both these words convey the idea of *rising up,* but the former is often used in the sense of arousing one from sleep; when it is used in connection with the awaking and raising one from the dead, ἐγείρω sheds no light upon the manner of the awaking and the raising of the sleeper. In Acts iii, 15; iv, 10; v, 30, it is said that God raised up Jesus from the dead, and the same word appears in the gospels in a number of passages where the resurrection of the Lord is mentioned. The verb ἐγείρω is employed by Paul throughout the fifteenth chapter of first Corinthians and also in his other epistles to denote the rising from the dead. But the same word is also often found in many passages where there is no reference to the idea of resurrection. It is used four times in Matt. ii (vers. 13, 14, 20, 21) in reference to Joseph *arising* and taking the infant Jesus into Egypt and out of Egypt. In Matt. viii, 15, it is said that Simon Peter's wife's mother *arose* from her couch, and ministered to those about her, and in verses 25 and 26 of the same chapter the word is used to describe the *awaking* of Jesus out of sleep and of his *arising* and rebuking the winds and the sea. Jesus himself said to the three disciples, when they beheld his transfiguration and were prostrate through fear: "*Arise* and be not afraid" (Matt. xvii, 7). This general sense appears again and again from the common usage of the verb in the gospels and the Acts. The noun ἔγερσις occurs only once in the New Testament (Matt. xxvii, 53), and in this case refers to the resurrection of Jesus. An examination of the verb ἀνίστημι and the noun ἀνάστασις results in disclosing the fact that the verb is oftener used in the more general sense of any rising or standing up, while the noun is always found in connection with the resurrection from the dead. But while in New Testament usage the nouns ἔγερσις and ἀνάστασις always refer to the resurrection, and the corresponding verbs are often employed in the same sense, though quite as often in a more general way, in no case does any one of these words assist us in understanding the mode or the nature of the resurrection of the dead. They indicate a fact, or a general idea, but they cannot be made to serve the interest of any special theory of the resurrection. In like manner, it should be added, the references to a resurrection of the dead in the Old Testament speak of *living again, standing up,* and *awaking out of sleep,* but the words used determine nothing of themselves as to the new mode of life and the nature of the new body which is to die no more.

5. The Teaching of Jesus Christ. In our study of the New Testament doctrine of the resurrection we shall first of all inquire into the teaching of Jesus Christ, and examine in detail the fact and significance of his own resurrection and ascension, the mystery of his forty days' sojourn after the day of his resurrection, the fact of his raising others from the dead, and his teaching on the subject as recorded in the gospels. The fact of the resurrection of Jesus is primary and fundamental to the New Testament revelation of our Lord. No statements of his are better authenticated than his repeated assurances to his disciples that he must suffer death at Jerusalem, and rise again on the third day (Matt. xvi, 21; xx, 19; xxvii, 63; Mark viii, 31; ix, 31; x, 34; Luke ix, 22; xviii, 33). No fact of the New Testament is better attested than that Jesus fulfilled his own predictions, died on the cross, was buried, and rose again on the third day. And this fact, or series of facts, cannot be properly separated from a study of our Lord's doctrine of the resurrection of the dead.

(1) *Significance of Christ's own Resurrection.* The significance of this fact cannot be well overestimated in its bearing on the doctrine, nor should we fail to note the prominence it had in the first preaching of the apostles (comp. Acts ii, 24, 32, 33; iii, 15; iv, 10; x, 40; xiii, 30; xvii, 31; 1 Cor. xv, 12-17). This universal and uniform testimony of the disciples and the early Church is at once a proof and illustration of Jesus's saying in John x, 18: "I have power (ἐξουσίαν, *right, authority*) to lay down my life, and I have power to take it again." Such sayings and the fact of his resurrection entitle him to be called the "Prince of life" (Acts iii, 15), and the "Author of eternal salvation to all them that obey him" (Heb. v, 9). The Son of God has life in himself, and raises up and makes alive whom he will (John v, 21).

(2) *Significance of the Ascension.* Another fact that stands in very significant relation to the resurrection of Jesus, though less fully attested, is that forty days after his resurrection Jesus "was received up into heaven and sat down at the right hand of God" (Mark xvi, 19). The record in Luke xxiv, 51, is that while Jesus was blessing his disciples "he parted from them, and was carried up into heaven." The last statement is wanting in a few ancient

manuscripts,[1] but in Acts i, 1-11, the ascension is made a matter of ample record and more minute detail. It is repeatedly assumed or referred to in the apostolic preaching and in the epistles (Acts ii, 33; vii, 55; Rom. viii, 34; Eph. i, 20; iv, 8-10; Col. iii, 1; 1 Pet. iii, 22; Heb. i, 3; iv, 14; vii, 26; viii, 1; x, 12; xii, 2; Rev. iii, 21. Comp. John vi, 62; xx, 17). The resurrection and ascension are looked upon as essential parts in the one great fact of the glorification of the Son of God, so that the resurrection apart from the ascension was not an end or complete consummation in itself, but required the exaltation to the right hand of God to perfect the glorification.

(3) *Rationale of the Forty Days.* The rationale of the forty days' sojourn of the Lord is given in Acts i, 3, as affording him opportunity to show himself to his disciples, and furnish them *indubitable evidences* (τεκμήρια) of his having truly risen from the dead. In Acts x, 40, 41, Peter says: "God raised him up the third day, and gave him to be made manifest, not to all the people, but unto witnesses that were chosen before by God, even to us, who did eat and drink with him after he rose from the dead." His different appearances to individuals and to assembled groups of the disciples are recorded in the four gospels and briefly referred to in 1 Cor. xv, 5-8. The discrepancies apparent in the several accounts are not of the nature of any irreconcilable contradictions, but are rather incidental evidences of the reality of the great fact which they all witness. We may not be able to harmonize the accounts satisfactorily, or to explain the exact order of events, but the obvious independence of the different narratives, and their agreement in the main, afford a surer proof of their fidelity to fact than would a set of narratives so uniform as to suggest artifice and collusion.

(4) *Forty Days in the Flesh.* During the forty days Jesus retained the fleshly body which after his resurrection still showed the print of the nails in his hands and of the spear in his side (John xx, 27). When the disciples were terrified and affrighted at his presence in the midst of them, and imagined that they beheld a spirit, or an apparition, as when once they saw him walking on the sea (Matt. xiv, 26), he went to pains to convince them of their error, and to prove to them that he had flesh and bones (Luke

---

[1] Hort calls it "a Western non-interpolation. The text was evidently inserted from an assumption that a separation from the disciples at the close of a gospel must be the Ascension. The Ascension apparently did not lie within the proper scope of the gospels, as seen in their genuine texts: its true place was at the head of the Acts of the apostles, as the preparation for the day of Pentecost, and thus the beginning of the history of the Church."—New Testament in Original Greek; Appendix, Notes on Selected Readings, p. 73.

xxiv, 39). He called upon them to handle him, and he called for food and ate it in their presence. Peter affirms in Acts x, 41, that the disciples "ate and drank with him after he rose from the dead." In view of these unmistakable evidences that he arose with the same body of flesh and bones that was put in the tomb, we cannot accept the notion widely current that Jesus arose with a new and glorified body. There were reasons why Jesus should retain for the forty days before his ascension the identical body that was buried. Thus could he best furnish indisputable proofs of the reality of his resurrection, and the records show that such physical evidence was demanded by the unbelief of his own disciples. His sudden vanishing from sight at Emmaus (Luke xxiv, 31) is no proof that he possessed a different kind of body, for he had repeatedly done much the same thing before his crucifixion (Luke iv, 30; John viii, 59; x, 39; xii, 36).[1] His coming into the room among the disciples "when the doors were shut for fear of the Jews" (John xx, 19, 26) is no convincing evidence that his body was no longer fleshly. As well might we argue that his walking on the sea of Galilee is proof that he had not at that time his natural body. It is not said either that he entered the room or that he vanished miraculously. That is an unwarranted inference of expositors. But if he did enter the room miraculously, such fact would not prove that his body had undergone essential change of nature since the time he walked on the sea, for he was certainly as capable of the miraculous after his resurrection as before.

(5) *Not Glorified During the Forty Days.* According to the records, then, Jesus arose with the same fleshly body which was laid in Joseph's tomb. This resuscitated body he retained for forty days that he might convince his disciples of the reality of his resurrection, and might the more naturally fulfill his teaching "concerning the kingdom of God" (Acts i, 3). His own manifestation of himself to men in the flesh must needs be, after this resurrection as before, by means of actual incarnation. There is not the least intimation in any of the records that he showed himself during the forty days in a supernatural glory. Before his death he took three of his disciples up into a mountain, "and was transfigured before them: and his face did shine as the sun, and his garments became white as the light" (Matt. xvii, 2). "His

---

[1] The language of Luke xxiv, 31, "he vanished out of their sight," favors the idea of an intangible and ghost-like appearance of Jesus, as if his entire showing himself to the two disciples up to that point had been only Docetic or apparitional. But how he ἄφαντος ἐγένετο ἀπ' αὐτῶν, *became invisible from them*, is not told any more definitely than how he ἐκρύβη, *was hidden*, or hid himself, and went out of the temple unseen by those who took up stones against him, according to John viii, 59. Imagination easily reads into such statements some things which the words do not clearly warrant.

garments became glistering, exceeding white; so as no fuller on earth can whiten them" (Mark ix, 3). "The fashion of his countenance was altered, and his raiment became white and dazzling" (Luke ix, 29). But no such glory distinguished the form of the risen Jesus. If only the transfiguration and the strange walking on the sea had occurred during the forty days after the resurrection, how would they have been put forward as proofs of "his new glorified body"! The appearance of the angel that rolled away the stone and addressed the women at the tomb "was as lightning, and his raiment white as snow" (Matt. xxviii, 3). According to Mark (xvi, 5) the women "saw a young man sitting on the right side, arrayed in a white robe; and they were amazed." Luke says that "two men stood by them in dazzling apparel" (xxiv, 4). But nothing of this supernatural character is said to have appeared in the countenance or apparel of the risen Christ. He avoided any display that would tend to terrify his disciples, and he assured them that his resuscitated body was the natural body of flesh and bones, and retained the marks of its recent wounds.

(6) *Glorified at the Ascension.* We conclude that the Lord Jesus was perfected in the glory of his resurrection when he was "received up into heaven, and sat down at the right hand of God." Not until after the "cloud received him out of the sight" of his earthly followers (Acts i, 9), was he "received up into glory" (1 Tim. iii, 16). His subsequent appearance unto Saul (1 Cor. xv, 8) was after this glorification, and necessarily unlike his appearances on earth during the forty days. It was accompanied by "a light from heaven above the brightness of the sun" (Acts xxvi, 13), and Saul was blinded by "the glory of that light" (xxii, 11). Such a revelation of the ascended Lord was everyway befitting, and Ananias might well speak of it to Saul as a "seeing of the Righteous One, and hearing a voice from his mouth" (xxii, 14; comp. ix, 17). The resurrection, ascension, and heavenly glorification of Christ are thus to be taken together in order to apprehend his personal exhibition and example of resurrection, and an unspeakable significance must needs be recognized in these transcendent facts. For it is thus that "our Saviour Jesus Christ has abolished death, and brought life and immortality to light through the gospel" (2 Tim. i, 10).

(7) *Jesus's Raising Others from the Dead.* The fact that Jesus, during his earthly ministry, raised a number of persons from the dead, has also its bearing on the doctrine of the resurrection. But such raising of the dead was only one among many signs of his heavenly mission: "The blind receive their sight, and the lame walk, the lepers are cleansed, and the deaf hear, and the

dead are raised up, and the poor have good tidings preached unto them" (Matt. xi, 5). The wisdom and power that can restore sight to the blind are equally competent to raise the dead to life. The three notable examples of such resurrection are the daughter of Jaïrus (Mark v, 22-24, 35-43; Matt. ix, 18, 19, 23-25; Luke viii, 41, 42, 49-56), the son of the widow of Nain (Luke vii, 11-16), and Lazarus (John xi, 1-44). These examples verify the saying of Jesus recorded in John v, 21: "As the Father raises the dead and makes them alive, even so the Son makes alive whom he will." They also give force to such sayings as John vi, 40: "This is the will of my Father, that every one that beholdeth the Son and believeth on him, should have eternal life; and I will raise him up at the last day." It is unspeakably significant that he, who raised others from the dead, and who himself laid down his own life and then took it again, affirms so positively: "The hour cometh in which all that are in the tombs shall hear his voice, and shall come forth" (John v, 28). All this will appear the more clearly as we study the teaching of Jesus concerning the resurrection.

(8) *Jesus's Teaching in the Synoptic Gospels.* In Luke xiv, 14, Jesus speaks of a divine recompense to be made "in the resurrection of the just"; but aside from what this form of expression suggests, the only teaching of our Lord, found in the synoptic gospels, and bearing on the nature of the resurrection, is what he said in answer to the question of the Sadducees, and which appears with a few verbal differences in all these gospels (Mark xii, 18-27; Matt. xxii, 23-33; Luke xx, 27-38). It seems somewhat strange that he should have said so little on a subject of so much interest and importance; but we are told, in Mark ix, 10, that when Jesus spoke to some of the disciples about his own rising again from the dead, they "questioned among themselves what the rising again from the dead should mean." They were not in a condition of mind to understand how their Lord and Messiah was to die and afterwards to rise again, though on the current doctrine of the resurrection they all probably shared the more common belief of the Pharisees. In the reply which Jesus made to the Sadducees, who sought to puzzle him with the supposable case of seven brethren, who, according to the levirate law of Deut. xxv, 5-10, were all married to one and the same wife, but who could not all have her in the resurrection, we observe a number of statements which indicate a deeper and more spiritual apprehension of the resurrection than seems to have been held among the Pharisees in general. From the several synoptic records we may learn: (1) The position of Jesus is clearly one of opposition to the doc-

trine of the Sadducees. He maintains that the dead are raised and live unto God, and he thereby condemns the Sadducean opinion that the soul and body perish alike at death. (2) He boldly charges the Sadducees with ignorance of the Scriptures and of the power of God. He shows that they were superficial readers of the book of Moses, and discerned not the depth of meaning and the suggestiveness of the language recorded therein. A defective knowledge of the power of God hindered their spiritual insight, and naturally led to disbelief of angels and spirits. (3) He condemned their crass notion of a physical or bodily resurrection, which was evinced in the question of the Sadducees. They obviously assumed that in the resurrection the same fleshly body, with all its adaptations to the conditions of human life on earth, must needs be perpetuated without change. (4) He positively declares that in the resurrection-life these human relationships do not exist. "They neither marry, nor are given in marriage," and therefore do not beget offspring, nor continue the family relationships of this world. "They are sons of God, being sons of the resurrection." (5) He teaches, further, that the risen saints are like the angels of God in heaven. They become spiritual beings in a loftier manner than the physical conditions of this mortal life permit. Mortality is so swallowed up of life that they "cannot die any more, for they are equal unto the angels." (6) His citation and exposition of Exod. iii, 6, shows his conception of Abraham, Isaac, and Jacob as living and immortal. The words, "I am the God of Abraham, and the God of Isaac, and the God of Jacob," could not, in his way of reading the Scriptures, allow us to suppose that those patriarchs were not at that very moment alive. "He is not the God of the dead, but of the living." Any other inference would be a great error in understanding the Scriptures. (7) The gospel of Luke contains a few statements not found in Matthew and Mark. His language concerning the matter of marriage is as follows: "The sons of this world (age) marry, and are given in marriage: but they that are accounted worthy to attain to that world (age) and the resurrection from the dead, neither marry, nor are given in marriage." He also adds the words, "Neither can they die any more," "They are sons of God, being sons of the resurrection," and "all live unto him." These statements show that only the resurrection of the just is here contemplated, and nothing in any of these gospels appears to favor the doctrine of the resurrection of all men, good and bad. Not all men, but only those who are accounted worthy, attain the resurrection from the dead. What becomes of the unworthy is a question not here entertained. (8) It is obvious to the unbiased interpreter that there is nothing in all this teaching of Jesus which either affirms or implies a resurrection of the flesh. On the contrary, the risen ones are like the angels of God. They are incorruptible and immortal. They are deathless, and so inherit the eternal life of the world to come, of which we read in Luke xviii, 30. What sort of bodies the angels of God in heaven possess is nowhere revealed to us. (9) The citation and comment on Exod. iii, 6, would seem to be without cogency in an argument touching the resurrection if the patriarchs named were not already risen and living unto God at the time of Moses. There is no intimation that Abraham, Isaac, and Jacob are merely living in Sheol (Hades), waiting for a future resurrection. Some men have imported this idea into their expositions, but Jesus utters no word that clearly warrants such a thought. (10) From all these considerations it is obvious that, according to Jesus, the resurrection of the dead is no restoration of fleshly bodies, but an exaltation and glorification of the living spirit of man. The true sons of God in their resurrection become not mere resuscitated human beings, with bodily natures adapted to the marriage relations of earth, but are equal unto the angels and become possessed of spiritual powers like them. That Abraham, Isaac, and Jacob had attained that age and world of life is implied in the argument of Jesus, who, in all this scripture, utters no word about the simultaneous resurrection of all the dead at any one future time. If at death, or soon after, the spiritual nature of man is exalted and glorified into heavenly life, and becomes a living spirit like the angels of God, incapable of dying any more, then the language and teaching of Jesus in reply to the Sadducees is intelligible, cogent, luminous, and full of force and comfort for the righteous.

(9) *Jesus's Teaching in John's Gospel.* In the gospel of John we find one passage that affirms without qualification the future resurrection both of the just and of the unjust: "The hour cometh in which all that are in the tombs shall hear his voice and shall come forth; they that have done good unto the resurrection of life; and they that have practiced evil unto the resurrection of judgment" (v, 28, 29). This corresponds with Dan. xii, 2, in declaring a resurrection of the two classes, the good and the evil; but it differs from Daniel in making the resurrection universal —"all who are in the tombs"—not merely "many from among them that sleep in the dust." This notable difference between the two texts must be fairly recognized: one teaches a partial, the other a universal resurrection of the dead. And this fact shows that the different biblical writers entertained distinct and divergent conceptions of the resurrection, or contemplated the subject

from different points of view. In John's gospel, in the immediate context of the passage just quoted, Jesus makes three distinct statements about resurrection. In verse 24 he says: "Verily, verily, I say unto you, He that heareth my word, and believeth him that sent me, hath eternal life, and cometh not into judgment, but hath passed out of death into life." This language describes the spiritual experience of one who is awakened by the truth of God, quickened into newness of life by the Spirit, raised, so to speak, out of his deathlike bondage to sin, and made a partaker of the "eternal life" which is a present possession of Christian believers. But that which immediately follows in verse 25 adds another and distinct conception: "Verily, verily, I say unto you, the hour cometh, and now is, when the dead shall hear the voice of the Son of God; and they that hear shall live." Here we observe that specific mention is made of an hour both present and yet coming, when "the dead (οἱ νεκροί) shall hear the voice of the Son of God, and shall live." This "hearing the voice" is not identical with "hearing my word, and believing him that sent me" in verse 24. This latter is hearing and accepting the message of salvation brought by Christ; but hearing his voice (comp. ver. 28 and xi, 43) is hearing the life-giving summons which calls one forth out of the domain of death and of the tomb, as in the case of Lazarus. We accordingly understand our Lord to refer in verse 25 to those instances of resurrection of the dead which occurred in his own time, such as the raising of Jaïrus's daughter, the son of the widow of Nain, and Lazarus. These examples belonged to that period which was well spoken of as "the hour that cometh and now is" (comp. iv, 23). But in verse 28 Jesus affirms the resurrection of "all that are in the tombs," and he speaks of it as occurring at "an hour that is coming" (ἔρχεται ὥρα). The phrase *all that are in the tombs* may be regarded as clearly connoting the idea of a resurrection of bodies from the grave; and yet a rigid literal interpretation may be seen to be inconsistent with the thought that all the dead are referred to. For the dead are not all *in the tombs* (ἐν τοῖς μνημείοις); thousands were never buried, and other thousands are in the depths of the sea.[1] And if the strict literal meaning of the word *tombs* cannot be insisted on, the phrase may be best understood as comprehending all the dead, and equivalent to "all that have passed out of this mortal life and are in the domain of death," and all who shall in their own times thus pass away. In John vi, 39, 40, 44, 50, 51, 54, 58, Jesus speaks repeatedly of giving eternal life to them that believe on him; he declares they

---

[1] The word μνημεῖον always means a *sepulcher*, or *tomb*, constructed for respectful interment of the dead, and for a memorial of them.

shall not die, but live forever; and he says again and again that he "will raise them up at the last day." But there is nothing in any of these passages to determine the nature of the resurrection, save that it obviously involves eternal life and glory. In the lips of Jesus the phrase *at the last day* may or may not have designated the same thought that it conveyed to the minds of others. In the lips of Martha (xi, 23), "the resurrection of the last day" probably meant a future simultaneous resurrection of all the dead, or at least of all the righteous dead; for that was a current belief among many of the Jewish people of that time. But it was not the habit of our Lord to correct or antagonize all the erroneous opinions of the common people, and when at times he did assume the delicate task, he sought to suggest a deeper and richer significance for current phrases. In John xi, 25, 26, we have a remarkable series of statements addressed to Martha, which show that with him the resurrection meant something quite different from what she had supposed. "Jesus said unto her, I am the resurrection, and the life: he that believeth on me, though he die, yet shall he live: and whosoever liveth and believeth on me shall never die." This, in its connection with Martha's words, is equivalent to saying: "Think not of a far-off time of general resurrection. The power to raise the dead and to make them live again is here in me. What I can do 'at the last day' I can also do at the present hour.¹ I am the resurrection in this deep sense, that 'whosoever believes in me and lives in me shall never die.'" So far as these words correct the thoughts of Martha and others of like opinion, they suggest that the power of the resurrection is in Christ, and is an abiding, ever-present power. Accordingly, in his deeper thought, "the last day" would mean the day of ultimate glorification; not necessarily one particular day or hour in which all believers are to be simultaneously glorified. Every individual believer must come personally to his own last day.

(10) *Jesus Absolutely Assures Immortality, but Offers no Theories.* The passages we have now examined include all that our gospels have to say of the teaching of Jesus concerning the resurrection. One may naturally wish to have learned more than this from the Great Teacher. We cannot construct from his words a convincing argument for the resurrection of the fleshly body that returns to dust. Nor can we prove from his teaching that all the

---

[1] It is well in this connection to observe also a similar word of Jesus to the crucified malefactor, who prayed, "Lord, remember me when thou comest in thy kingdom." Jesus replied: "Verily I say unto thee, To-day shalt thou be with me in Paradise" (Luke xxiii, 42, 43). The supplicant thought of a distant time, a future kingdom; but Jesus emphasizes the words *to-day:* not at a remote period, but this very day thou shalt be with me in a blessed Paradise.

dead are to be raised simultaneously. But the things he does declare in his teaching about the resurrection, his raising up of Lazarus and others from death, and his own resurrection and ascension into heaven, taken altogether, are as absolute assurances of immortality and eternal life for the obedient children of God as we may expect in this life to receive. The manner of the resurrection is left in much uncertainty; the mode and conditions of immortality are not made manifest to us; but the truth of the doctrine is placed beyond all reasonable doubt or controversy.

6. Doctrine of the Apocalypse of John. In passing now to examine what the other New Testament books have to say about the resurrection of the dead, we turn first to a passage in the Apocalypse of John (xx, 4-15) which contains some things noticeably parallel with John v, 28, 29. There are two classes of the dead portrayed after the manner of apocalyptic symbolism, one of which is pronounced "blessed and holy," and the other is brought before "a great white throne" for judgment. The blessed ones are "the souls of them that had been beheaded for the testimony of Jesus, and for the word of God, and such as worshipped not the beast, neither his image, and they lived and reigned with Christ a thousand years." They are said to "have part in the first resurrection," and over them "the second death has no power." They represent the glorified martyrs and those who kept themselves pure from all manner of idolatry. They are the same souls that in vi, 9-11, cry from the altar, and are given each a white robe; they belong to the same class as the two witnesses who were killed, but afterward went up to heaven in a cloud (xi, 3-12). In this blessed and holy resurrection they have fulfilled in them the promise of iii, 21: "He that overcometh, I will give to him to sit down with me in my throne, as I also overcame, and sat down with my Father in his throne." This first resurrection is a living and reigning with Christ a thousand years. "The rest of the dead," according to the vision, belonged to a different class, and they came forth unto a resurrection of judgment. "The sea gave up the dead that were in it; and death and Hades gave up the dead which were in them; and they were judged every man according to their works." We may note that nothing is here said of the dust of the earth giving up its dead, but "death and Hades" are put in the same category with "the sea." And nothing is said in any part of the vision of a resurrection of fleshly bodies. No mention is made of a second resurrection, but "the second death, the lake of fire," appears to be set in contrast with "the first resurrection."[1] This

---

[1] For a fuller exposition of Rev. xx, see my Biblical Apocalyptics, pp. 450-459.

apocalyptic vision accords in a general way and in its fundamental teaching with the sublime portrayal of judgment found in Matt. xxv, 31-46, in which the King, who acts also as Judge, welcomes the blessed ones of his Father to a joint inheritance in the kingdom of glory, but sends the accursed ones away into eternal punishment. Both of these passages of Scripture are obviously symbolic representations of most important truths, but they afford us no solid ground for inferences touching the nature of the resurrection of the dead. They are concerned with questions of eternal destiny rather than with modes of existence in the future.

7. Paul's Doctrine of the Resurrection. We find in the writings of Paul our fullest New Testament elaboration of the doctrine of the resurrection of the dead, and in one chapter he discusses the particular question, "How are the dead raised up, and with what manner of body do they come?" But it is noteworthy that he did not answer this question in so clear a way as to prevent expositors, from his time until now, differing most remarkably in their attempts to interpret his meaning. Such differences among expositors, however, should not excuse us from an honest endeavor to ascertain what the apostle meant to teach. Diversity of opinion on a great subject, so far from detracting from the importance of the subject itself, is rather a strong witness to the deep fundamental character of that which is involved in the discussion.

(1) *Acts xxiv, 15*. According to Acts xxiv, 15, Paul declared before Felix his belief "that there shall be a resurrection both of the just and unjust"; but apart from this one statement we find nothing in his addresses or his epistles which recognizes the doctrine of a resurrection of the unjust. This is a noteworthy fact, and yet it does not follow that he made little of the doctrine, or ever discarded it. We can prove nothing from his silence on that point, though it would seem that the scope of his various epistles afforded as much occasion to speak of the resurrection of the unjust as of the just. Perhaps, however, in Paul's way of thinking, as in the Johannine Apocalypse, the resurrection of the unjust was conceived rather as a future coming unto judgment. The idea of resurrection was comprehended or presupposed in that "manifestation before the judgment seat of Christ," when "each one" and "all" "receive the things done in the body, whether good or evil" (2 Cor. v, 10).

(2) *1 Thessalonians iv, 13-18*. The epistles to the Thessalonians are believed to be the earliest of Paul's writings, and in one passage of the first epistle (iv, 13-18) the apostle speaks with great assurance about the resurrection of "them that are fallen asleep in Jesus," whom he also calls "the dead in Christ." He would fain

comfort his Thessalonian brethren by assuring them that those who fall asleep do not perish, but really precede the living in the presence of the Lord. "For if we believe that Jesus died and rose again, even so them also that are fallen asleep in Jesus will God bring with him. . . . For the Lord himself shall descend from heaven with a shout, with the voice of the archangel, and with the trump of God; and the dead in Christ shall rise first; then we that are alive, that are left, shall together with them be caught up in the clouds, to meet the Lord in the air: and so shall we ever be with the Lord." This is usually understood as implying an expectation on the part of the apostle that he and his Thessalonian brethren would most of them live to see the descent of the Lord Jesus from heaven, but before they should be "caught up in the clouds to meet the Lord in the air," the dead in Christ were to be raised from their graves; then those thus raised would together with the living be caught up into the heavens. This snatching away of the living along with those risen from the dead involves the idea of a sudden translation without seeing death, and is parallel with what is written in 1 Cor. xv, 51, 52: "Behold, I tell you a mystery: we all shall not sleep, but we shall all be changed, in a moment, in the twinkling of an eye, at the last trump; for the trumpet shall sound, and the dead shall be raised incorruptible, and we shall be changed." The translation of Enoch (comp. Heb. xi, 5) and of Elijah, and the ascension of Jesus in the clouds (comp. Acts i, 9, 11) may have furnished the imagery of this rapture of living saints.

When these several statements are subjected to critical analysis, and we question the import and inferences which a number of the words and phrases suggest, we are left in no little uncertainty as to the exact meaning of the apostle. The one positive assurance, very full of comfort and unmistakable in its main thought, is that both the saints who had fallen asleep in Jesus, and those who were at the time alive and waiting for the coming of the Lord, were all of them together to be ultimately caught up to be forever with the Lord in the heavens. But if Paul expected that he himself and most of his contemporaries would be alive at the coming of the Lord, it would seem, unless the mortality of the Christians of that generation were exceptional, that "the dead in Christ" would constitute but a small minority of those who were to be glorified at his coming. Then when it is said that "God will bring them that are fallen asleep in Jesus with him," one naturally asks *from whence* will he bring them? If he leads or brings them along with him, must they not be already "with the Lord"? Nothing is intimated of a bringing them from Hades, or from some receptacle of souls where Christ himself is not. We cannot well understand the apostle to assume the unconscious sleep of the soul in the grave. But if we suppose that he brings the disembodied souls out of Hades to be restored again to their former bodies, the resurrection of the bodies follows upon the Lord's descent from heaven, and precedes the change and rapture of the living saints. The dead in Christ thus rise first and anticipate the living by a few moments (or hours?). Such a brief precedence of their brethren in the flesh would seem to be no remarkable advantage, and we fail to see how such a thought could be of any special comfort to the bereaved Thessalonians. The Lord's descent from heaven, the shout, the archangel's voice, and the trump of God, are part and parcel of the imagery of Jewish apocalyptics, and will be discussed in connection with the doctrine of the coming of Christ and his kingdom. We are concerned with this passage now only so far as it helps us to understand Paul's doctrine of the resurrection of the dead. Nothing is here said as to the nature of the body in the resurrection. The dead in Christ rise and are caught up to meet the Lord on high, and abide forever with him. Eliminated from the apocalyptic imagery in which it is cast, the one great fundamental lesson, full of comfort for all readers, is the assurance of ·eternal fellowship with Christ in the heavens. This is the blessed hope of the living saints and the glorious fruition of "them that are fallen asleep in Jesus." This is in substance no other than the inheritance in eternal life in conscious, living fellowship with God, already expounded in foregoing pages.

(3) *The Fifteenth Chapter of First Corinthians.* By far the most thorough and elaborate discussion of the resurrection to be found in the New Testament is that of the fifteenth chapter of first Corinthians, but that which deals directly with the nature of the resurrection-body is confined mainly to the last part of the chapter (vers. 35-58). The entire passage, however, demands our most careful study. It may be arranged in six paragraphs, expressive of so many distinct considerations in the apostle's argument.

Verses 1-11. The fact of Christ's actual resurrection from the dead is first of all emphatically affirmed and confirmed by reference to numerous witnesses to whom he appeared. Of the six appearances of Christ here mentioned only two or three correspond clearly with those narrated in the gospels. No allusion is made to the testimony of the women who were first to see him, nor to that of the two disciples on the way to Emmaus; but it is notable that Paul ranks his own vision of Christ in the same category with those of Peter and James (comp. 1 Cor. ix, 1). But his sight of the Lord Jesus, on his way to Damascus (Acts ix, 3-9, 17), was certainly quite different in character from any of those recorded in the gospels, for it was a vision of the glorified Christ. It occurred at midday, and in the midst of "a light from heaven above the brightness of the sun" (Acts xxvi, 13). It was therefore more like that which Stephen beheld when "he looked up stedfastly into heaven, and saw the glory of God, and Jesus standing on the right hand of God" (Acts vii, 55). But to Paul this sight of the risen and glorified Lord was as real as any fact of his life, and was entitled to as much credit as the testimony of Cephas or of James. The vision, moreover, contemplated the risen Christ as having entered into his heavenly glory, and not, as during the forty days, lingering a while with flesh and bones to give tangible proofs to disheartened and faithless disciples that he was actually risen. In this respect his exceptional vision of the ascended Christ had a special relevancy to this argument for a glorious resurrection of the dead in Christ.

Verses 12-19. In view of these irrefutable witnesses the apostle argues in his next paragraph that denial of the resurrection of the dead must needs involve denial of an authenticated fact, and with it a repudiation of the Christian faith, the apostolic ministry, the forgiveness of sins, and all hope of a future life.

Verses 20-28. He then proceeds to teach that the resurrection of the dead is the triumphal consummation of the divine order of the kingdom of God and of Christ. Death is the last great foe to be annihilated. "For as in Adam all die, so also in Christ shall all be made alive." This statement, when compared with that of Rom. v, 17-19, appears to make the resurrection as universal a fact as human sinfulness, but there is no mention in the entire chapter of a resurrection of the ungodly. It may be, however, that the apostle counted these among the "enemies" who are to be ultimately "put under his feet" (ver. 25), and he felt the incongruity of speaking of them as being made alive in Christ. The most remarkable teaching in this paragraph is that which affirms distinctive orders (τάγματα, *ranks, classes, companies,* or *divisions,* as of an army) in the resurrection. Christ himself is called the first fruits (ἀπαρχή). Next in order after him are "those who are the Christ's at his coming." How large this company may be, and just what persons may have been included or excluded by the designation οἱ τοῦ χριστοῦ ἐν τῇ παρουσίᾳ αὐτοῦ, *those of the Christ in his coming,* is left for the reader to infer. For without any explanation he proceeds: "Afterwards (εἶτα, not τότε. *then*) the end, when he shall have abolished all rule and all authority and power." This end is obviously the goal or consummation of the reign of Christ when he shall have "put all things in subjection under his feet," and shall have abolished death. If we should understand the coming (παρουσία) of Christ to be a continuous process, going on during the entire period in which he is putting all things in subjection unto himself, it would naturally follow that the resurrection of those who are Christ's is also to be understood as a process continuing to the end of his reign.

Verses 29-34. The fourth paragraph corresponds to the second in again showing what serious and deplorable consequences must follow a denial of the resurrection of the dead. Baptism for the dead, and exposure to constant peril of death, signify nothing for the Christian confessor "if the dead are not raised at all." It ought not to be overlooked, however, that both these paragraphs touching the absurd consequences of denying the resurrection of the dead are without force against the doctrine of a happy future life without the body. That is, if one deny the resurrection of the flesh, but maintain a purely spiritual and eternal life to come, these protests of the apostle would be obviously without point.

Verses 35-49. The apostle next takes up the question, "How are the dead raised, and with what manner of body do they come?" These two interrogative sentences are not identical in meaning, but seem rather to present two closely related queries: (1) How is it possible for the dead to arise? and (2) With what kind of a body do they arise? But the two questions are not answered separately. The answer to the first is essentially involved in that of the second and is seen in the wisdom and power of God which govern the whole visible creation. We have been already admonished (vers. 23-28) that the resurrection itself is a part of the preëstablished order of the kingdom of God, and now this thought is expanded so as to show that it is in conspicuous analogy with other arrangements in the world of nature, in which God gives to every kind of seed, and to each one of the particular seeds, a body of its own. The man, therefore, who blindly puts the double question is ἄφρων, one who lacks intelligence and reason. For (1) the sowing and quickening of all kinds of seeds shows that throughout the vegetable world life is perpetuated through death. The bare grain of wheat that is sown is not made alive except it die, and the particular grain that is sown is not the body that shall be, "but God giveth it a body even as it pleased him." And it has pleased God to ordain that each individual seed shall produce its own kind and not another. The grain of wheat is made to produce a new body of wheat, not of some other kind of grain. But the new body that is made alive is not the dust of the old body quickened into a new life, but a God-given body, the particular substance of which is not defined (vers. 36-38). And so far as this applies to the question in hand, we are left to infer that the body of the resurrection is not constituted out of the dust of the old body of flesh, but is a perpetuation of the personal life that was in the body of flesh in a new body of its own, supplied according to a divine order of things in the kingdom of God. But the analogy of the grain is not carried out by the apostle in further detail, for he (2) passes on to call attention to the fact that "all flesh is not the same flesh." Here in this earthly life the flesh of men and beasts and birds and fishes is noticeably different. Who, then, shall presume to limit the possibilities of change in the organic forms of life? He goes on to say (3) that "there are also celestial bodies, and bodies terrestrial." Just what bodies in the heaven and upon the earth (ἐπουράνια and ἐπίγεια) are here intended is not altogether clear. In view of the fact that sun, moon, and stars are separately mentioned in the next verse, and since masses of inorganic matter could hardly be called *bodies* in the sense which the apostle's argument requires,[1] it seems that allusion is made to such bodies as properly belong to the heavenly regions. Since no specification is made, we need not insist that the allusion is to bodies of the angels; and yet the saying of Jesus that "in the resurrection they are as angels in heaven" (Matt. xxii, 30) goes far to persuade us that angelic natures are intended. These might be naturally put in contrast with such bodies as properly belong to the earth, the fleshly bodies of men and of beasts. Thus it is pleasing to God to provide appropriate bodies for all living creatures upon earth. And each has a glory of its own: "The glory of the celestial is one, and that of the terrestrial is another." Whereupon it is added, without a connective particle, as a further illustration and suggestion: "There is one glory of the sun, and another glory of the moon, and another glory of the stars; for star differs from star in glory" (ver. 41). These facts are simple matters of observation, and show the diversities that it pleases God to incorporate in his entire creation. And so this whole paragraph (vers. 35-49), like that of verses 20-28, indicates an obvious divine order of the world and of all things in it. For evidence of this we have only to look at great suggestive facts. Throughout the rest of this paragraph (vers. 42-49) the apostle applies his suggestive analogies to the resurrection of the dead. First we have a series of contrasts between the body as it is sown and as it is raised (42-44), and then the wonderful differences are shown to correspond to the

---

[1] "The whole connection requires," says Meyer, "that σώματα should be *bodies* as *actual organs of life*, not inorganic things and materials." He also observes that to explain "heavenly bodies" as meaning sun, moon and stars would be to attribute to the apostle a modern and nonbiblical use of words.—Exegetical Handbook, in loco.

earthly and the heavenly as represented in the first Adam and the last (45-49). There is no subject formally expressed in verses 42 and 43: "It is sown in corruption; it is raised in incorruption: it is sown in dishonor; it is raised in glory: it is sown in weakness; it is raised in power." It is as if we should say: "There is a sowing in corruption; there is a raising up in incorruption"; but there is scarcely room to doubt that σῶμα, the *body,* is the subject to be understood in all these sentences, and this is confirmed by verse 44, which declares that "it is sown a natural body; it is raised a spiritual body." A more important question arises over the meaning of *sowing* the body. Does the foregoing figure of sowing the grain (vers. 36, 37) so essentially involve the sense of burying it in the earth that we must in analogous consistency of thought understand the *sowing of the body* as the interment of the lifeless corpse in the grave? Perhaps the somewhat similar saying of Jesus in John xii, 24, has helped to strengthen this idea: "Except a grain of wheat fall into the ground and die, it abideth by itself alone; but if it die, it beareth much fruit." But the point and purpose of these words in John are quite different from that which the apostle has especially in view, and nothing is said about *sowing* the grain of wheat. The placing of a seed in the ground is planting, not sowing; the sowing is one thing, and the covering of the seed with the soil on which it falls is another. That the apostle is not referring, in verses 42-44, to the burial of the body in the earth is evident from the following considerations: (1) The word σπείρω, *sow,* does not mean to bury anything in the ground, but designates rather the act and process of scattering the naked grain. The use of this word in 1 Cor. ix, 11; Gal. vi, 7, 8; James iii, 18, and in many other passages, suggests no thought of burying a lifeless body in the earth. Had the writer intended to express the idea of burial, there is no reason why he should not have used the word θάπτω, which always means to *inter a corpse* (e.g., Matt. viii, 21; Luke xvi, 22; Acts ii, 29), and is so employed in verse 4 of this same chapter in reference to the burial of Christ. (2) The qualifying phrases, *in corruption, in dishonor,* and *in weakness* are not appropriate for describing the lifeless body that is put in the grave. Although in our modern usage "corruption, earth, and worms" are terms commonly associated with the grave, the word for *corruption*[1] in this text has no such connotation in the New Testament, but denotes

---

[1] φθορά bears the general idea of *ruin, destruction,* failure to attain certain possibilities, and so applies commonly to moral corruption; but διαφθορά is the proper word to denote *bodily corruption,* and should have been employed here by Paul if he had intended to designate sepulchral decomposition. Comp. Acts ii, 27, 31; xiii, 34-37.

rather the natural condition of humanity during the present life, together with the destructive effects which sin carries with it into the entire human organism. So in Gal. vi, 8: "He that soweth unto his own flesh shall of the flesh reap corruption." This $\phi\theta o\rho \acute{a}$ which is reaped out of the flesh ($\grave{\epsilon}\kappa\ \tau\tilde{\eta}\varsigma\ \sigma\alpha\rho\kappa\acute{o}\varsigma$) is not the corruption of the sepulcher, but a moral and spiritual destruction, the opposite of "eternal life" which those reap who sow unto the Spirit. So also in Rom. viii, 21, the creation groans and travails in expectation of deliverance "from the bondage of corruption into the liberty of the glory of the children of God." Here the corruption is surely not the decay which follows the burial of a corpse, but a conscious condition in which one groans in pain. In 2 Pet. ii, 19, we read that those who are given to the lusts of the flesh "are themselves slaves of corruption"; and in i, 4, we are told of the possibility of "becoming partakers of the divine nature, having escaped from the corruption that is in the world by lust." From this common usage of the word it appears that by *sowing in corruption* the apostle does not mean the interment of the dead body in the grave, but rather the decaying process through which it is constantly passing from the cradle to the grave. And this is precisely what he says in 2 Cor. iv, 16: "Though our outward man is passing through a process of corruption ($\delta\iota\alpha\phi\theta\epsilon\acute{\iota}\rho\epsilon\tau\alpha\iota$), yet our inward man is renewed day by day." Hence we interpret the words *it is sown in corruption* as meaning that the human body, conceived as the outward organism of the living soul, is, by reason of its mortal nature, constantly subject to corruption and decay. But for the continual renewal which it receives in the order of God it would quickly fall into ruin. And, so far as the imagery of verses 36-38 here applies, we may add that this body will not be quickened into immortal vigor and incorruption "except it die." After the final ruin reached at death it is raised in incorruption, in glory, and in power, and God gives each one a body of his own as it pleases him. The other phrases, *in dishonor*, and *in weakness*, are still less appropriate to a dead body than *in corruption*. Many corpses have, indeed, been shamefully treated by barbarous enemies, and in that sense may be said to have been "sown in dishonor"; but it is only by farfetched and irrelevant fancies that the body is thought of as buried in dishonor. On the contrary, it is the universal practice of mankind to honor their dead in the burial. It is a sad but faithful comment on these words of Paul that men sin against their own bodies more in life than in death. Multitudes of those of corrupt minds defile the body and treat it with all manner of dishonor and infamy in the lusts of the flesh, but they will have the defunct corpse most honorably embalmed and interred in a costly mausoleum. Furthermore, to speak of a dead body as being buried *in weakness* seems little else than a stupid misuse of words. The weakness and infirmities of the flesh during the present life are conspicuous facts of experience, but who that appreciates intelligible speech would ever write about the weakness of a corpse! (3) The defunct corpse which is deposited in the grave cannot be properly called a *psychical body* (σῶμα ψυχικόν, ver. 44).[1] A psychical body must incorporate a living soul. "The first man Adam," whom the apostle immediately (ver. 45) cites for illustration, did not "become a living soul" until God "breathed into his nostrils the breath of life" (Gen. ii, 7). A dead body may, perhaps, be called a σῶμα φυσικόν, but not a σῶμα ψυχικόν. The natural, psychical, or soulish body is an outward and visible organ of the human soul, fitted to the conditions of this earthly life, and it is here put in contrast with the spiritual body (σῶμα πνευματικόν) which is the heavenly organ of the spirit, adapted to the conditions of heavenly life. In the following verses (48 and 49) it should be observed that the words *psychical* and *spiritual* interchange with *earthy* and *heavenly*. (4) It appears, furthermore, that the scope of the apostle's argument in this passage involves a contrast between the manner and conditions of our earthy life in the body and those of the heavenly life of incorruption, and glory, and power. It is not a contrast of the lifeless corpse as it appears the hour it is put in the grave and the same identical body as it appears resuscitated and brought up out of the dust in a moment of time. The analogy of the dying seed (ver. 36) does not fit this last conception; for it is sown in its full life and vigor, and dies after it has fallen to the soil, and only an invisible germ sprouts forth into new life, while the old body remains in the earth and is not made alive again at all. But in this argument the conditions of human life on earth are put in striking contrast with the conditions of spiritual and heavenly life after the resurrection. We accordingly understand the series of contrasts stated in verses 42-44 as designed to enhance the unspeakable glory of man's spiritual organism after the resurrection by declaring its remarkable difference from the corrupt, dishonored and infirm conditions of his mortal life on earth. For, having thus stated his striking contrasts, he proceeds (vers.

---

[1] Thus Whitby: "It seems probable that the word *sown* doth not relate to the body's being lain in the earth, but rather to its production in the world; for when it is interred, it is no more an *animal* body, but a body void of life. The apostle doth indeed (verses 36, 37) speak of seed sown in the earth, but then he speaks of it as still alive, and having its seminal virtue, or animal spirit in it, and dying afterwards; whereas our bodies first die, and then are cast into the earth."—Commentary on the New Testament, in loco. London, 1744. Similarly Calvin, Neander, Hengstenberg, Heinrici, T. C. Edwards, Beyschlag, Charles, Schmiedel.

45-49) to show that these differences between the earthly and the heavenly state correspond to the opposite natures of the Adam and the Christ. This form of illustration was suggested by the contrast between a psychical body and a spiritual one. "The first man Adam," according to Gen. ii, 7, "became a living soul" (ψυχή), but according to Paul's gospel and the highest New Testament teaching, Christ, "the last Adam, is a life-giving spirit" (πνεῦμα). And this arrangement follows a divine order, "first, the psychical; afterwards the spiritual." The sowing occurs in the first state; the fruitage and glory in the second. "The first man is from the earth, earthy; the second man is from heaven." The outcome of this part of the discussion is that, in the divine order, man's destiny is to become something far beyond a mere living soul. Everything that is earthy must have its adaptations to earthly environment, and while man continues his life in the flesh on earth, he must needs be earthy, and be sown, as we have seen, in corruption, in dishonor, and in weakness. But, in the resurrection, the earthy is to be superseded by the heavenly in incorruption, in glory, and in power. Whereupon, the apostle concludes this paragraph with the exhortation: "As we have borne the image of the earthy, let us also bear the image of the heavenly."[1] And so, in answer to "With what manner of body do they come?" (ver. 35) we are told that we are to exchange the psychical and earthy for the image of the heavenly.

Verses 50-58. It remains for the apostle to add a number of concluding observations, although with them he adds nothing in substance to his doctrine of resurrection. It follows as a logical consequence from the foregoing discussion, and is now formally stated as a positive conclusion "that flesh and blood cannot inherit the kingdom of God." The psychical body, therefore, cannot partake of the spiritual and heavenly "inheritance of the saints in light," neither is it possible for the earthy to retain its earthy conditions, and bear the image of the heavenly. There must, accordingly, be a change from the earthy state of corruption to the heavenly state of incorruption. But at this point the apostle recalls the thought of remaining alive in the flesh unto the coming of the Lord, and being "caught up in the clouds to meet the Lord in the air," as he had written the Thessalonians,[2] and now he writes the Corinthians this similar form of doctrine: "Behold, I tell you a mystery: we shall not all sleep, but we shall all be changed, in a moment, in the twinkling of an eye, at the last trump: for the trumpet shall sound, and the dead shall be raised

---

[1] The subjunctive reading, φορέσωμεν, seems to be the best attested.
[2] See 1 Thess. iv, 15-17, and our comments above on pp. 231-233.

incorruptible, and we shall be changed." Here, as in first Thessalonians, we naturally infer from the language employed that the apostle expected to remain alive unto the coming of the Lord, and he assumes that many of his Corinthian brethren would also thus remain. Some would doubtless fall asleep before that grand event of the Lord's descent from heaven, but not all. In Thessalonians he says nothing about the change which the living must undergo in order to inherit the incorruptible kingdom, but simply affirms that they "shall be caught up in the clouds unto a meeting of the Lord in the air"; but here, in writing to the Corinthians, having declared "that flesh and blood cannot inherit the kingdom of God," it behooves him to show that, even in the event of a translation into heaven without falling asleep in death, there must be a change from the corruptible to the incorruptible. For without such change the earthy could not "bear the image of the heavenly." Hence the conclusion announced in verse 53: "This corruptible must put on incorruption, and this mortal must put on immortality." This accords with his previous argument and confirms it; from all of which it is to be understood that the body of the resurrection, the one which is adapted to the heavenly kingdom, is not and cannot be a body of flesh and blood. It must be changed so as to be incorruptible and immortal. The image of the earthy must be exchanged for the image of the heavenly. So enrapturing is the thought of such heavenly glorification that the apostle closes his discussion with exclamations of victory and thanksgiving, and an exhortation to steadfastness in the faith and work of the Lord (vers. 55-58).

(4) *Second Corinthians iv, 16—v, 10.* Another important expression of Pauline doctrine on the resurrection and the heavenly life is found in 2 Cor. iv, 16—v, 10. The first statement in this passage affirms that a process of decay and a process of renewal are going on simultaneously every day. The one process is virtually identical with the sowing in corruption, and the other with the raising up in incorruption, which is asserted in 1 Cor. xv, 42. In verse 14 preceding Paul has said "that he who raised up the Lord Jesus shall raise up us also with Jesus, and shall present us with you." Hence the idea of resurrection and glorification in the presence of Christ is in the apostle's mind, and with it he associates the thought of being made perfect through sufferings (comp. Heb. ii, 10, and 2 Tim. ii, 8-12). In accordance with the order of God, and the provision for continual renewal to counteract the process of decay, he declares that our temporary afflictions do in an abundant manner bring about for us "an eternal weight of glory." The contrast is so great that he speaks of the affliction

as a "momentary lightness," and the glory as an "eternal weight"; and then, by way of further explanation, he adds, "while we look not at the things which are seen, but at the things which are not seen: for the things which are seen are temporal; but the things which are not seen are eternal." This looking at (σκοπεῖν, *contemplating, turning attention to, fixing the mind's eye on*) the things which may not be seen with the natural eye (τὰ μὴ βλεπόμενα) is noticeably relevant and suggestive. The unseen and eternal things are more real and substantial than those which appear to fleshly eyes, and we need not doubt or wonder when it is thus plainly intimated that the resurrection body must needs be invisible to mortal gaze. In immediate connection with this reference to the unseen and eternal it is written: "For we know that if the earthly house of our tabernacle be dissolved, we have a building from God, a house not made with hands, eternal, in the heavens." The earthly house is here obviously a designation of the human body, called "our outward man" in iv, 16, above, which is subject to decay and dissolution. But upon the event of its dissolution, "we have a building from God, a house not made with hands." This building is not heaven itself, but the new body which God gives in place of the earthly, temporary, visible tabernacle of the fleshly body, which is dissolved and put off in death (comp. 2 Pet. i, 13, 14). This appears also from the following verse: "For verily in this (earthly house) we groan, longing to be clothed upon with our habitation which is from heaven." This building from God, not made with hands, accords with the figure of the grain in 1 Cor. xv, 36-38, and here as there it might be said, "The house which is dissolved is not the building that shall be, but God gives it a new habitation even as it pleases him." The word *tabernacle* (σκῆνος, *tent*) is applied to the earthly house, but the heavenly structure is called a *building* (οἰκοδομή) and a *habitation* (οἰκητήριον), words that denote permanent abode. This house, moreover, is said to be "eternal, in the heavens," and "from heaven," and so it belongs to the category of "the things which are not seen and are eternal." In connection with the word *habitation* the apostle introduces another but similar figure of "being clothed upon" and "being clothed" (ἐπενδύσασθαι, and ἐνδυσάμενοι; comp. 1 Cor. xv, 53, 54). He seems to have no liking for the doctrine of a separate disembodied condition of the soul, nor does he entertain the Greek conception of a naked, wandering ghost, flitting here and there without shelter or clothing. "We are longing," he says, "to be clothed upon with our habitation which is from heaven; if so be that being clothed we shall not be found naked. For indeed we that are in this tabernacle do groan, being burdened; not for that we would be unclothed, but that we would be clothed upon, that what is mortal may be swallowed up of life." Here there is no conception of an intermediate state of possible long continuance between death and the resurrection.[1] The apostle seems to have had in mind the being "changed in a moment, in the twinkling of an eye," even as he wrote in 1 Cor. xv, 52. His longing for the clothing of the heavenly habitation is acknowledged in verse 2, and in verse 4 he expresses his antipathy to being unclothed, and his wish rather to remain alive and to be so clothed upon by his heavenly vesture "that the mortal ($τὸ\ θνητόν$, *that which is liable to death*) may be swallowed up of life." But at the time of this writing Paul appears to have felt, as Peter in 2 Pet. i, 14, that "the putting off of his tabernacle was coming swiftly on," and hence his language in verses 6-8: "Being always of good courage, and knowing that, whilst we are at home in the body, we are absent from the Lord (for we walk by faith, not by sight); we are of good courage, I say, and are willing rather to be absent from the body, and to be at home with the Lord." The doctrine and sentiment of this confession are in complete harmony with Phil. i, 20-24, which may well be cited here as both parallel and explanatory: "Christ shall be magnified in my body, whether by life or by death. For to me to live is Christ, and to die is gain. . . . I am in a strait betwixt the two, having the desire to depart and be with Christ; for it is far better." According to this faith one need have no fear of death and dissolution of the body. For if the earthy tabernacle be dissolved, we have a building from God; it is not made with hands; it is in the heavens and from heaven; and it may therefore become our actual possession ($ἔχομεν$, ver. 1) immediately after the dissolution of the earthly and the mortal. So by dissolution of the mortal and reception of the immortal, whether through death or by a sudden translation, "death is swallowed up in victory." The writer of these scriptures evidently does not expect to "be found naked" at any time. He expects even in the event of death to be clothed upon by an invisible, eternal vesture from God, and so he continually walks by faith and not by sight. He makes it his aim, as a matter of honorable ambition, "whether at

---

[1] The dogma of "the Intermediate State," an outgrowth in part of the rabbinical theories of "the underworld," has no valid foundation in the Scriptures, finds not a word of support in the teaching of Jesus, and furnishes the logical basis of the Romish doctrine of purgatory and also of various doctrines of a future probation of souls that made a failure of this present life. It depends for all the support it has upon a foregone conclusion touching the nature of the body of the resurrection and the time of its being raised up. Assuming that a long period must elapse between death and the resurrection of the identical fleshly body that is put into the grave, it speculates on the vague possibilities of such a "disembodied state." But from beginning to end it is wholly speculative and imaginary.

home or absent, to be well-pleasing unto the Lord" (ver. 9). In such a state of life and action one experiences the inner working of God himself, and has "the earnest of the Spirit" (ver. 5) which is a conscious foretaste of the heavenly inheritance (comp. Eph. i, 14). As a motive for such honorable ambition to be always well-pleasing to Christ, the apostle concludes this passage with the solemn statement: "For we must all be made manifest before the judgment-seat of Christ; that each one may receive the things done in the body, according to what he has done, whether good or bad." In these words we may discern an implied reference to a resurrection as well as a judgment of the unjust (comp. Acts xxiv, 15); but, if so, it did not accord with the scope of the epistle to enlarge on that particular subject, or to show how it might be adjusted to the doctrine of the resurrection as elsewhere explained to the Corinthians.

(5) *In Romans and Philippians.* We find nothing elsewhere in this apostle's writings to supply other or additional information touching the resurrection of the dead. Such teaching as that of Rom. vi, 5-14, simply affirms the "newness of life" and holy fellowship which the believer enjoys in Christ. It involves death unto sin and life unto God, so that when sin is not allowed to reign in the mortal body, and the members are presented as instruments of righteousness, one is, so to speak, "as alive from the dead." So again in Rom. viii, 11: "If the Spirit of him that raised up Jesus from the dead dwelleth in you, he that raised Christ Jesus from the dead shall quicken also your mortal bodies through his Spirit that dwelleth in you." This quickening we observe is of "mortal bodies" ($\vartheta\nu\eta\tau\grave{a}\ \sigma\acute{\omega}\mu\alpha\tau\alpha$), that is, bodies liable to death, not dead bodies, or lifeless corpses. The process by which these mortal bodies are to be made alive is not stated. The time is equally indefinite. It may be by the sudden rapture, referred to in 1 Cor. xv, 51, 52, at the coming of the Lord; or it may be immediately after the dissolution of the earthly house, as expressed in 2 Cor. v, 1. In Phil. iii, 10, 11, Paul speaks of his ambition and longing to know Christ, "and the power of his resurrection, and the fellowship of his sufferings, becoming conformed to his death, if by any means I may attain unto the resurrection from the dead." The exact concept which is here to be formed of "the resurrection from the dead" is not altogether clear. The reference seems to be to some particular order or class of the dead, like "those of the Christ, at his coming" (1 Cor. xv, 23). In verses 20 and 21 of the same chapter it is also written: "Our citizenship is in heaven; from whence also we wait for a Saviour, the Lord Jesus Christ; who shall fashion anew the body of our humiliation, that

it may be conformed to the body of his glory, according to the working whereby he is able to subject all things unto himself." This also accords with the teaching of 1 Cor. xv, 53. The corruptible, dishonorable, and weak mortal must put on incorruption. Flesh and blood cannot inherit the kingdom of God, and hence this mortal body must be changed and fashioned after "the image of the heavenly."

(6) *In Colossians, Ephesians, and Second Timothy.* In Col. iii, 1-4, we have a beautiful expression of Pauline doctrine, and one that seems to have been of special comfort and inspiration to the apostle in his last years: "If then ye were raised together with Christ, seek the things that are above, where Christ is, seated at the right hand of God. Set your mind on the things that are above, not on the things that are upon the earth. For ye died, and your life is hid with Christ in God. When Christ, who is our life, shall be manifested, then shall ye also with him be manifested in glory." Here the confidence of union with Christ has begotten the faith and experience of "eternal life," which knows no death (comp. John xi, 26), and no separation from Christ, but abides in joyous expectation of a manifestation with him in glory at no distant day. The same inspiring thought is set forth in Eph. i, 20, and ii, 6, where "the Father of glory" is said to have raised up Jesus Christ from the dead, "and made him sit at his right hand in the heavenlies," and has also "quickened us together with Christ, and raised us up with him, and made us sit with him in the heavenlies in Christ Jesus." This living fellowship with Christ and God is in great part, as we have previously shown, a present possession. The Christian believer has already "passed out of death into life" (John v, 24), and his body is a temple of the Holy Spirit which is in him (1 Cor. vi, 19), but immediately upon his putting off the fleshly tabernacle he receives his building from God, eternal, in the heavens. Accordingly Paul, in prospect of martyrdom, said: "I am already being offered, and the time of my departure is come. I have fought the good fight, I have finished the course, I have kept the faith: henceforth there is laid up for me the crown of righteousness, which the Lord, the righteous judge, shall give me at that day; and not to me only, but also to all them that have loved his appearing" (2 Tim. iv, 6-8). That day of the Lord's "appearing" was evidently for him in the near future, at the time of his departure from his earthly life. At that day he expected to receive the crown from the heavenly righteous Judge and Lord. The glorified Christ, reigning and judging "at the right hand of the Majesty on high," and enthroned in the glory of his Father which he had before the world was, is

doubtless capable of "appearing" to every one of his saints at the time of their departure, somewhat, perhaps, as he did to Stephen at the time of his martyrdom. Thus he comes again and receives them unto himself (John xiv, 3), and unto each one will he give, in his own time and manner, his spiritual body as it shall please him. And so, each in his own order and time, shall we all "be clothed upon with our habitation which is from heaven."

8. Various Types of Biblical Doctrine. One result of our examination of what the different biblical writers say about the resurrection of the dead is that their statements, taken as a whole, are not altogether uniform or harmonious. Different types of doctrine appear in the canonical as well as in the apocryphal books. But in the main the various types of doctrine are not so divergent as to be pronounced inconsistent with each other. The Old Testament references are so few and vague that we cannot put them forward as conclusive on any one phase of the subject. The New Testament teaching is very much fuller, but neither Christ nor his apostles have told us all we desire to know about the nature and the conditions of those who attain to the resurrection from the dead. From what is written we may reasonably infer that the change from mortal to immortal modes of life is such that no revelation and no language can clearly impart to the human mind the actual realities. We should not, therefore, think it strange that differences of conception and statement, characteristic of individual modes of thought, appear among the different writers on a theme like this. The teaching of Jesus was suggestive and corrective rather than formal and discursive. He nullified the objections of the Sadducees by exposing their false notions of the resurrection life, but he offered no revelation on the subject beyond a few remarkable statements, partly negative, partly suggestive, but notably adapted to correct the current belief in a literal restoration of the fleshly body.

9. No Basis for Many Prevalent Theories. In a careful study of all that is written in the Scriptures touching the resurrection we are not able to find evidence sufficient to warrant most of the fancies and theories which have widely prevailed. That the body of the resurrection is to be a reconstruction of the same particles of matter which are buried in the grave is a dogma which has no support in the teaching of Christ or of his apostles. That it is constructed out of some indestructible germ, that belongs to the body and is buried with it, has been elaborately argued from Paul's figure of the grain (in 1 Cor. xv, 36-38), and from certain speculations of Jewish rabbis. But the conjecture is entitled to no serious consideration, for Paul's allusion to the grain that is sown is not of a nature to give endorsement to the peculiar rabbinical fancy, and his entire argument throughout that chapter is conspicuously different from the style and the thought of the Jewish schools of that time. The apostle, moreover, positively denies that flesh and blood can inherit the kingdom of God, and his concept of a new, spiritual, and heavenly organism is totally incompatible with the idea of a material body developed out of an infinitesimal germ. Some writers have enlarged upon the supposable impossibilities of restoring the bodies of the innumerable dead. They have cited the fact of one human body going to form some part of another, as when devoured by cannibals. The different members of one and the same body have in some cases been scattered far apart, and separated by intervening oceans. Some have argued that all the dust of the earth would be insufficient to reconstruct the material bodies of all men who have lived and died, and others have alleged that, if all who have ever lived were to stand up at one time, there would not be room enough on the entire surface of the earth to place them. These crass conceptions and the supposed impossibilities are all irrelevant and futile, and they have grown out of the notion of a resuscitation of the mortal body of flesh and blood. That several Old Testament writers entertained some idea of a future resurrection of the physical body, and cast their utterances in the forms of popular expression, may be true. But so far as they have done so, their utterances do not prove the truth of any particular dogma or theory. Incidental allusions are not proofs. Nearly all the issues of controversy on this subject have arisen over attempts to dogmatize on questions which the Scriptures have left undetermined.

10. The Main Idea is a New Organism. So far as the concept of the resurrection of the dead differs from that of the "immortality of the soul," it seems to consist mainly, according to the Scriptures, in some new and more enduring organism of the conscious personal life. It is the projection of that life, in the order of God, and with all that constitutes its spiritual nature and character, into the unseen and eternal future. This change from a condition of corruption to one of incorruption is conceived as a restitution of the individual who dies and is buried. He does not perish in the dust, but rises up in a new and imperishable body such as it pleases God to give to every one. A few very explicit declarations of Scripture affirm a resurrection both of the just and the unjust. The wicked awake to shame and contempt, and come forth to a resurrection of judgment, which is of the nature of a second death. But the righteous are clothed in light as with a garment. They shine as the stars forever, and like the sun in the kingdom of their Father. They put off the earthly tabernacle, but immediately receive from God their new house, not made with hands, eternal, in the heavens.

11. All the Dead Not Raised Simultaneously. It has been common with theologians to speak of "the general resurrection of the last day" as if all the dead were to be simultaneously raised up out of their graves at some future day or moment of time. But our study of the Scriptures has failed to find sufficient warrant for this dogma. On the contrary, we find numerous intimations that the resurrection of different persons and orders occurs at different periods of time, and indeed may be a process ever going on, although we know not how. The incidental use of such a phrase as *at the last day* cannot determine such a question, for every individual may and must in a very obvious sense have his own last day, whether it be simultaneous with that of others or not. The statement of John v, 28, 29, is not equivalent to saying that all who are in the tombs shall come forth at one and the same instant, for the context shows, as we have seen, that such a thought is not in the mind of the speaker, but rather a succession of resurrections. And when Paul writes that "as in Adam all die, so in Christ shall all be made alive," he does not say that they shall all be made alive at once. As well might one insist that when Jesus says, "If I be lifted up, I will draw all men unto me," he means that all this drawing unto himself is the matter of an hour or a day. The language of Dan. xii, 2, clearly conveys, as we have seen, the idea of a partial resurrection. So too, in 1 Cor. xv, 20-26, Paul speaks of different orders and successive periods of the resurrection. The language of Phil. iii, 10, 11, seems also to imply a partial and special resurrection from among the dead, for why should the apostle have such longing and struggle "to attain unto the resurrection from the dead" if all the dead are necessarily and as a matter of course to be raised up in one general resurrection of the last day? The same comment may be made on the language of Jesus in Luke xx, 35, "they who are accounted worthy to attain the resurrection from the dead," for if all the dead are to be raised up in one general resurrection, what is the sense of being counted worthy of obtaining a part in the inevitable?[1] It may be that in passages like the last two cited the reference is to the "resurrection of the just" (Luke iv, 14). We may conceive the righteous and the wicked as two great companies, and that Paul

---

[1] According to Godet, "the resurrection *from the dead* is very evidently, in this place, not the resurrection of the dead in general. What is referred to is a special privilege granted only to the faithful who shall be accounted worthy." Commentary on Luke, in loco.

was anxious to obtain a part in the resurrection of the righteous, and that Jesus also means the resurrection of the just when he speaks of being worthy to attain unto it. But even if we allow this interpretation of the language in Luke and Philippians, it will not fit the doctrine of successive orders and times as stated in 1 Cor. xv, 23. But if we suppose that the just and the unjust form the two classes to whom allusion is made, it is nowhere affirmed that all the individuals of either of these two classes are raised up simultaneously. What we have been accustomed to think of as a single and instantaneous event may be in the wisdom and power of God a continuous process, or it may have various times and seasons "which the Father hath set within his own authority." We deem it highly important for the expositor of this class of Scriptures to refrain from positive assertions where the sacred writers are not unquestionably clear. On these mysterious questions of the time and manner of resurrection we see at best but "in a mirror, darkly." We know only in a very small part, and we can at most explain only in part.

12. The Subject Belongs to the Unseen. It is worthy of special remark that in Paul's teaching in 2 Cor. v, 1-8, the new organ of the spirit, the building or habitation which we have in the heavens in place of the dissolved tabernacle of the flesh, is not a natural product out of the elements of the earthly house, but is from God and from heaven. How and from what he fashions it, we are not told. The most obvious import of the apostle's words is that, upon the dissolution of the mortal frame, God immediately clothes the spirit with a bodily organism, invisible as the spirit itself, immortal, eternal, glorious. How much of the mortal body is utilized for the immortal we cannot know. As the eternal things are declared in this context to be invisible, we ought not to err in assuming that the substance of the heavenly body is of a nature to be seen by mortal eyes, or touched by fleshly hands. There are millions of living creatures about us in this world which even the microscope reveals but imperfectly; much less can they be discerned by the naked eye. In the realm of the unseen and eternal mysteries of spiritual life there are many things which we must accept by faith and not by sight. John writes that it is not yet manifest what we shall be, but if he shall be manifested, we shall be like him and see him as he is. When the Lord was transfigured before the three disciples "his face shone as the sun, and his garments became white as the light." We may well regard that transfiguration as an ideal of the image of the heavenly which those who are risen in Christ shall ultimately bear. For aught that anyone can prove to the contrary, the resurrection of the dead may be a process that is continually going on, like all the other gracious work of the salvation of Jesus Christ. The great comprehensive announcement of our Lord, "If I be lifted up from the earth, I will draw all men unto myself" (John xii, 32), is quite analogous with the statement of Paul, "As in Adam all die, so also in Christ shall all be made alive" (1 Cor. xv, 22). But neither of these general statements implies that the drawing unto Christ and the making alive of all men are to be accomplished at one last period or point of time. The mighty work is better conceived as going on during the whole time that the enthroned and reigning Christ is putting all his enemies under his feet (1 Cor. xv, 25). The new life of God, which is implanted by spiritual regeneration, develops day by day into eternal life, and whenever its mortal tabernacle is dissolved, the living soul receives its new building from God which is fashioned after the image of the heavenly and eternal. But on all these mysteries of the invisible world we must be content not to know all that we may very much desire to ascertain.

13. Summary of the Biblical Teaching. Recapitulating now, we may briefly sum up the results of the foregoing discussion in the following statements:

1. Jewish and Christian interpreters have read into certain poetical passages of the Old Testament a crass conception of a resurrection of fleshly bodies, and these notions have taken on various materialistic forms in popular thought. It is natural for the popular imagination to clothe all concepts of a future life in materialistic forms.

2. There was no uniformity of opinion on this subject among the Jewish people. Some of the Jews denied the resurrection altogether, and rejected the doctrine of angels and spirits. Those who affirmed the doctrine of a future resurrection differed among themselves as to its nature and extent: some believing in the resurrection both of the just and unjust, others only of the just.

3. The teaching of Jesus in the synoptic gospels does not favor any theory of the resurrection of the natural body. In his reply to the Sadducees he declared that in the resurrection they are not fleshly but spiritual beings like the angels in heaven.

4. In the fourth gospel Jesus affirms in one passage the resurrection of "all that are in the tombs," both the good and the evil; but in the same connection he outlines three kinds of resurrection, and in other parts of this gospel teaches that they who partake of his life and spirit shall never taste of death.

5. The Apocalypse accords with the fourth gospel in presenting the idea of a "first resurrection" and a "second death," but the doctrinal content is uncertain by reason of its setting in a composi-

tion so mystical and visional that interpreters differ widely among themselves as to its meaning.

6. Paul is much more explicit and detailed in his treatment of the subject, and his teaching involves the following propositions: (1) The resurrection of the dead is a fundamental article of the Christian faith. (2) It is conceived as in some sense a quickening of the mortal body and making it alive with immortal vigor. This thought attaches especially to the mystery of a sudden change which those experience who remain alive unto the coming of the Lord from heaven. (3) The apostle gives no place for the doctrine of an intermediate state of long duration between death and the resurrection. The heavenly body is given immediately after the dissolution of the earthly house, and is as truly an organism as is the earthly body. (4) The body of the resurrection is not the body that is sown during the earthly existence; it is not a body of flesh and blood, but is to exist in striking contrast to the corruptible, dishonored, and weak conditions of this mortal life, and to abide in incorruption, glory, and power. (5) The dead are not all raised simultaneously, but each in his own order and in his own time. (6) Since flesh and blood cannot inherit the kingdom of God, the mortal body must be put off by death, or by some transmutation and transfiguration, and be so changed as to be adapted to the conditions of heavenly life with our glorified Lord. There must be a new spiritual organism for each risen and glorified human personality.

CHAPTER XI

VARIOUS ASPECTS OF THE HEAVENLY GLORY

1. The General Conception. The significance of the biblical doctrines of eternal life, immortality, and resurrection is of unspeakable moment. The truths set forth in the foregoing chapters contemplate citizenship in heaven so positively assured to the Christian in his earthly life that he reckons himself as already a member of the commonwealth which is in the heavens (Phil. iii, 20). He is in some sense already risen with Christ; he has his heart set on things above where his Lord is enthroned, and indeed he is made to sit with him in the heavenly places (Eph. ii, 6). The prayer of Jesus, in John xvii, 24, for all those who are to make up his peculiar treasure is that they may be with him where he abides, and that they may behold his glory. We may, then, appropriately inquire, before leaving this general subject, What are the things that make up the various aspects of this heavenly glory? We have been admonished that amid the limitations of this present life we can at best see only as in a mirror and learn by means of enigmatic language and symbolism, and can accordingly know only in part (1 Cor. xiii, 12). But this fact serves only to enhance in our minds the unspeakable glory which is yet to be revealed, and while we seek to gather up and state the various ideals of heavenly life which the Scriptures suggest, we must still keep in mind, what has previously been made emphatic, that the essence of eternal life is loving fellowship with the Father and with Jesus Christ. This fellowship is one that never faileth. It grows deeper and stronger with increase of divine knowledge, and passes on from glory to glory, both in this age and in that which is to come—in this world and in any other to which the risen child of God may go—so that the pure in heart shall be forever blessed, inasmuch as they shall eternally see God.

2. Heavenly Recognition. One of the first things to invite our thought, when we contemplate this heavenly life, is the question of recognition and reunion. It is fundamentally the simple question of the perpetuation of conscious personal identity. When we ask, Shall we know each other in the future state? we should first inquire, Shall we know ourselves? It would seem to be beyond reasonable controversy that if there be any future life of man at all, it must needs be a life that would recognize itself as having had a previous existence.

(1) *Doctrines of Absorption and of Transmigration.* There are, indeed, two distinct concepts of the destiny of the human soul which have a place in certain systems of religious belief. One is the doctrine of absorption, which affiliates with a pantheistic conception of the universe. All human souls are conceived as but so many emanations from the one universal Essence, and to it all ultimately return. The conscious personal life ceases when the soul is thus received back into the impersonal unconscious essence of the world. This doctrine, of course, involves the annihilation of all personal self-consciousness and is essentially materialistic. Another concept of the soul's future state is found in the doctrine of transmigration, according to which the soul at death passes into the body of some animal, reptile, or insect. The soul may thus pass through innumerable forms of life, and become again and again incarnate in a human body, and yet retain no recollection of any of its former states. But neither of these conceptions is compatible with the biblical doctrines of eternal life and the resurrection of the dead, for our Scriptures are utterly misleading if they do not clearly teach the conscious, blissful immortality of the children of God.

(2) *The Biblical Suggestions.* The thought of being gathered to one's people (Gen. xxv, 8; xlix, 29, 33), and the saying of David (2 Sam. xii, 23) that he should some time go to his dead child, carry with them an idea of personal reunion. Burial in a common grave, or in the ancestral tomb, does not satisfy the import of the language employed. And so with all the scriptures previously cited to show the immortality of the soul and the resurrection of the dead, there in an implied assumption of personal identity and reunion after death. If Abraham, Isaac, and Jacob are not dead, but live unto God (Exod. iii, 6; comp. Luke xx, 37, 38), they are no other than the same personal beings they were upon earth. The language of Isa. xiv, 15, 16, implies a recognition of the king of Babylon in Sheol, and the same statement holds good of our Lord's picture of the rich man and of Abraham and Lazarus in Hades (Luke xvi, 23). How, moreover, could the Lord Jesus have said to his disciples, "I go to prepare a place for you, and I come again and will receive you unto myself, that where I am, there ye may be also," if personal recognition, reunion, and blessed fellowship are not presupposed? But aside from the numerous scriptures of this class, which unmistakably imply heavenly recognition and fellowship, we have more direct suggestions in the narratives of the transfiguration of Jesus where Moses and Elijah,

who "appear in glory," obviously know each other and commune with Christ, and are also by some means recognized by Peter, who calls them each by name. The words of Jesus to the dying malefactor, "To-day shalt thou be with me in Paradise" (Luke xxiii, 43), are meaningless without the concept of personal reunion and fellowship beyond death; and Stephen's prayer, "Lord Jesus, receive my spirit," involves the hope and expectation of a conscious transition of the personal spirit to the presence of Jesus at the right hand of God (Acts vii, 56-60). Many interpreters also understand the friends, who receive the faithful and wise stewards into the eternal tabernacles (Luke xvi, 9), to be those persons whom they have befriended on earth by means of the mammon of unrighteousness. These, going on before them into the heavenly abodes, receive and welcome them there into the eternal glory. But if the subject of δέξωνται, *may receive,* be understood of the angels, or of Christ and of God, the idea of heavenly recognition and eternal fellowship is clearly involved. One may naturally wonder that the doctrine of heavenly recognition should ever be questioned by a believer in the soul's immortality. "They who are accounted worthy to attain that world, and the resurrection from the dead, neither marry, nor are given in marriage: for neither can they die any more: for they are equal unto the angels; and they are sons of God, being sons of the resurrection" (Luke xx, 35, 36). Here it is clearly taught that marriage, the propagation of offspring, and the family relations which arise thereby in this world, are not perpetuated in the life to come; but it by no means follows that any hallowed and beautiful friendship of earth must be broken off in the heavens, or become any less in personal affection. True knowledge must enlarge, and heavenly acquaintances unknown on earth may come to be esteemed above all that were ever known in the body of flesh and blood.[1] What home-gatherings must there be in the Father's house of many mansions! What unspeakable possibilities of bliss in the heavenly Jerusalem, among innumerable hosts of angels, and with the spirits of just men made perfect, who compose the general assembly and church of the firstborn who are enrolled in heaven! (Heb. xii, 22, 23.) What incalculable treasures in heaven must they have who are "meet to be partakers of the inheritance of the saints in light" (Col. i, 12), "children and heirs of God, and joint-heirs with Christ"! (Rom. viii, 17.) But all these ideals would be without

---

[1] Even Socrates is represented as saying: "What would not a man give if he might converse with Orpheus, and Musæus, and Hesiod, and Homer? Nay, if this be true, let me die again and again. I shall have a wonderful interest in there meeting and conversing with the heroes of old."—Plato, Apology, 41.

significance apart from belief in personal identity continuing in the heavenly life along with recognition of saints, and blissful intercourse. In John's beatific vision of the great multitude before the throne of God, arrayed in white robes and with palms in their hands (Rev. vii, 9-17), a large part of what most deeply affects the heart is the implied knowledge of the past which those who come out of a great tribulation must have, and the comfort, communion, and fellowship which must needs attend the guiding of them unto fountains of waters of life, and having every tear wiped from their eyes. The essential facts of self-conscious personality show that man is constituted for intelligent fellowship and love, and personal recognitions, reunions, and blissful associations are to be gloriously perfected rather than abolished in the life to come.

3. Absence of All Evil. The blessedness of the heavenly life is further enhanced in our thought by the assured absence of all that involves pain and trouble. In the scripture last cited it is said that the glorified ones hunger no more, nor thirst, nor suffer any evil stroke. "There shall be no night there, and there shall in nowise enter anything unclean, or he that maketh an abomination and a lie: but only they that are written in the Lamb's book of life" (Rev. xxi, 25-27). There "thieves do not break through nor steal" (Matt. vi, 20). Such absence of all that can cause trouble or distress does not, however, as in the Buddhist concept of Nirvana, involve extinction of self-conscious personality, but rather a higher and more perfect activity of the sensibility, the intellect, and the will.

4. A Sabbath Rest. In Heb. iv, 9, we have the future blessedness of the saints conceived as "a sabbath rest ($\sigma\alpha\beta\beta\alpha\tau\iota\sigma\mu\delta\varsigma$) that remaineth for the people of God." A greater than Joshua leads the true Israel into such blessed heavenly rest as God himself enjoys. It is attained in a higher and holier land than the Canaan which was promised to the fathers of the Hebrew people, and it is obtained through faith and holiness. Even those ancient Hebrew fathers "confessed that they were strangers and pilgrims on the earth. For they that say such things make it manifest that they are seeking after a country of their own. And if indeed they had been mindful of that country from which they went out, they would have had opportunity to return. But now they desire a better country, that is, a heavenly: wherefore God is not ashamed of them, to be called their God: for he hath prepared for them a city" (Heb. xi, 13-16). And thus according to this writer the sabbath rest that remains for God's people is the possession of a heavenly fatherland ($\pi\alpha\tau\rho\ell\delta\alpha$), and a city which God himself has prepared for them.

5. Advance in Knowledge and in Heavenly Vision. Another element of the heavenly glory will be advancement in knowledge beyond all that is possible to man in this earthly life. "Now I know in part," says Paul (1 Cor. xiii, 12); "but then shall I know fully even as also I was fully known." John assures us, as children of God, that at the heavenly manifestation of God "we shall be like him; for we shall see him even as he is" (1 John iii, 2). And in Rev. xxii, 4, 5, it is written that the servants of God "shall see his face, and his name shall be on their foreheads. And there shall be night no more; and they need no light of lamp, neither light of the sun; for the Lord God shall give them light." All this is significant of mental and spiritual illumination. "God is light, and in him is no darkness at all. If we say that we have fellowship with him, and walk in the darkness, we lie, and do not the truth: but if we walk in the light, as he is in the light, we have fellowship one with another" (1 John i, 5-7). Hence those who enjoy fellowship with God and with one another are fittingly called "children of light" (Eph. v, 8; 1 Thess. v, 5), for, according to 1 Pet. ii, 9, they have been called by God himself "out of darkness into his marvellous light." Jesus himself said: "I am the light of the world: he that followeth me shall not walk in darkness, but shall have the light of life" (John viii, 12). This light of life comes to every soul that is begotten of God, and, according to the ancient proverb concerning the path of the righteous, it is "like the dawning light, that shineth more and more unto the perfect day" (Prov. iv, 18). But the light of the heavenly glory connotes a range and perfection of knowledge that far transcends the highest possibilities of attainment on earth. God "dwells in light unapproachable; whom no man hath seen, nor can see" (1 Tim. vi, 16). For it is as true now as in the time when Moses prayed that he might behold the glory of Jehovah: "Thou canst not see my face; for man shall not see me and live" (Exod. xxxiii, 20). But when "that which is mortal is swallowed up of life" (2 Cor. v, 4), the saints in light shall see God face to face. "When that which is perfect is come, that which is in part shall be done away" (1 Cor. xiii, 10). The limitations of this mortal life will be removed. In the fullest sense will it be made to appear that "there is nothing hid, save that it should be manifested; neither was anything made secret, but that it should come to light" (Mark iv, 22). Of a thousand thousand mysteries the Lord may say to us, as he said to Simon Peter: "What I do, thou knowest not now; but thou shalt understand hereafter" (John xiii, 7). Now we can see but parts of his ways, but in the heavenly light we shall not only see him as he is, but understand his creation, his providence, his power, and all his universe as we can not understand them now.

6. Increase of Capacity. Along with such marvelous increase of knowledge we also associate personal fellowship in the glory of God, and a corresponding increase of capacity and power for all heavenly activity. All that is now realized in the richest religious experiences of saints is to be intensified in and after the resurrection of the just. The worship of God in the holy heavens of light must needs be a far more intelligent one than we may now offer. For the God of life and light, who has already "shined in our hearts, to give us the illumination of the knowledge of the glory of God in the face of Jesus" (2 Cor. iv, 6) will assuredly increase our capacity for divine illumination in his house of many mansions, and what the apostle prays for, in Col. i, 9-13, will be carried to a perfection which it is now impossible for man to estimate: "That ye may be filled with the knowledge of his will in all spiritual wisdom and understanding, to walk worthily of the Lord unto all pleasing, bearing fruit in every good work, and increasing in the knowledge of God; strengthened with all power, according to the might of his glory, unto all patience and long-suffering with joy; giving thanks unto the Father, who made us meet to be partakers of the inheritance of the saints in light; who delivered us out of the power of darkness, and translated us into the kingdom of the Son of his love." According to verse 20, we may apply all this both to "things upon the earth, and things in the heavens."

7. Reigning with Christ. We can now apprehend but dimly, at best, what it is to "reign with Christ." We read in Rom. v, 17, that "they who receive the abundance of grace and of the gift of righteousness shall reign in life through Jesus Christ." In 2 Tim. ii, 12, it is said, "If we endure, we shall also reign with him." In Rev. iii, 21, it is written: "He that overcometh, I will give to him to sit down with me in my throne, as I also overcame, and sat down with my Father in his throne." In Rev. xx, 6, we are told that the second death has no power over the blessed and holy ones who have part in the first resurrection, "but they shall be priests of God and of Christ, and shall reign with him a thousand years."[1] In Rev. xxii, 5, it is said of those who shall see the face of God and have his name on their foreheads, that "they shall reign forever and ever." All these scriptures imply a superior association with Christ in the administration of the affairs of his kingdom. His triumphs are their triumphs, and of all his pos-

---

[1] For exposition of these apocalyptic passages, see Biblical Apocalyptics, in loco.

sessions they are joint heirs. So also in the visions of Daniel (vii, 18), "the saints of the Most High shall receive the kingdom, and possess the kingdom forever, even forever and ever." Behind all this symbolism of throne, and reign, and kingdom, we recognize the assurance of unspeakable honor and exaltation in the manifold operations of the eternal Ruler. His enthroned kings and priests participate, so to speak, in his state counsels, and are set in authority over all that he hath (comp. Matt. xxiv, 47; xxv, 21; Luke xix, 17). Some such ideal of heavenly glory and power and dominion is evidently intended in the Lord's promise to his twelve disciples: "When the Son of man shall sit on the throne of his glory, ye also shall sit on twelve thrones judging the twelve tribes of Israel" (Matt. xix, 28).

8. Glory Through Ages of Ages. Finally, the inconceivable ages of ages through which the heavenly glory evermore intensifies give all other aspects and ideals of it an overwhelming impressiveness. The Hebrew and Greek phrases usually translated *forever and ever* are strikingly expressive. לעולם ועד may be rendered *to eternity and beyond;* or *forever and onward.* In Eph. iii, 21, the Greek expression is, literally, "unto all the generations of the age of the ages." In Rev. xxii, 5, and often elsewhere we meet the phrase *unto the ages of the ages.* Æons, and dispensations, and illimitable sweep and progress of all that is ennobling in the heavens of God are naturally associated in thought with these suggestive indications of inconceivable duration. And we may well believe that every thousand years of the heavenly life will be an "intermediate state" between the preceding and the next following thousand years, so that through all the ages of ages one period of heavenly blessedness will prepare the way for something still more blessed and glorious beyond, and the modes and possibilities of eternal life may vary with the successive millenniums. Such a concept is hospitable toward any theory of the future state which makes for blessedness. It need have no controversy with any rational ideal of being at home with Christ, "forever with the Lord," and beholding him as he is. All the hymns of the Christian ages which celebrate the eternal union of God, and Christ, and angels, and the spirits of just men made perfect, accord with this illimitable outlook. Now we know only in part; it does not yet appear what we shall be, or what we may become. But the human mind, in our present mortal life, becomes bewildered in its attempts to grasp the possibilities of the life and growth of the ages of ages.

PART SECOND
THE MANIFESTATION OF CHRIST

SECTION SECOND

THE PERSON OF CHRIST

CHAPTER I

FACTS OF HIS EARTHLY LIFE

1. Born of the House of David. In the opening chapters of the gospels of Matthew and Luke we read that Jesus was born at Bethlehem, in Judæa, whither his parents had gone from their home in Galilee. He was the firstborn son (ὁ πρωτότοκος, Luke ii, 7) of Mary, the wife of Joseph, whose genealogy is recorded in two different ways in Matthew and Luke. Some have inferred from the language of Luke i, 32, that Mary was also a descendant of the house and family of David, and it has been maintained that Matthew has preserved the genealogy of Joseph, and Luke that of Mary. This hypothesis, however, has not commanded general acceptance, for Joseph is expressly named in Luke iii, 23, and there is no mention of Mary in that connection; a fact inexplicable if the writer had intended to make a record of Mary's lineage. It is probably impossible at this day to harmonize these different genealogies,[1] but the discrepancies in the lists of names are not sufficient to discredit the main fact which the two records attest, namely, that Jesus was an offspring of the house of David. There seems to have been no question, from the times of the earliest apostolic tradition, "that our Lord hath sprung out of Judah" (Heb. vii, 14). Paul speaks of him as "born of the seed of David" (Rom. i, 3; comp. 2 Tim. ii, 8; Acts xiii, 23). Matthew's gospel begins with the title, peculiarly Hebraic, "Book of the generation of Jesus Christ, the son of David, the son of Abraham." The descent from the royal house of David is noteworthy as making

---
[1] See Biblical Hermeneutics, pp. 411-413.

for him an external claim that fitted current Jewish beliefs concerning the Messiah.[1]

2. Record of the Virgin Birth. The opening chapters of Matthew and Luke also record the fact that this firstborn son of Mary was supernaturally conceived in her virgin womb by the power of the Holy Spirit. The gospel according to John contains no parallel narrative of the miraculous birth of Jesus, but seems clearly to imply it by saying that the Logos, or Word, who was in the beginning with God, and without whom no work of creation was made, "became flesh, and dwelt among us." Three of the gospels thus concur in witnessing this fact of a supernatural incarnation of Jesus as the Son of God, but they differ in their record of details. The prologue of John's gospel is cast in the style of Alexandrian-Greek thought, gives no details of Jesus's birth or childhood, but carries our concept of his origin aloft and afar, "in the bosom of the Father." In Matthew's narrative the special dreams and revelations touching the miraculous conception come to Joseph; but in Luke the revelation is made to Mary by the salutation and direct announcement of the angel Gabriel. Matthew tells us nothing of the earlier residence of Joseph and Mary at Nazareth, but informs us of their going down into Egypt to escape the wrath of Herod, and says that, when they returned and heard that Herod's son Archelaus was reigning over Judæa, they were afraid to go thither and withdrew and went to Nazareth in Galilee. This tradition varies from that of Luke, who explains how the birth of Jesus occurred somewhat unexpectedly at Bethlehem, makes no mention of a journey to Egypt, nor of the visit of the wise men from the East, but records the appearance and words of the angels to the shepherds near Bethlehem, and the visit of the shepherds to "the babe lying in the manger," the circumcision and naming of Jesus "when eight days were fulfilled," and his presentation in the temple at Jerusalem, after forty days, as the Levitical law of purification required. Luke's narrative also contains many details of the birth of John the Baptist, the visit of Mary to Elisabeth, and the poetic utterances of Mary, Zacharias, and Simeon. However we may account for these differences between Matthew and Luke, they cannot be shown to involve any real inconsistency or contradictions of statement. Rather do they supplement each other, and evince the fullness of the early traditions, of which Luke affirms that "many had taken in hand to draw up a narrative." One may also regard the literary form of a narrative and the insertion of prophetic songs as marks of a later

---

[1] See Matt. ii, 5, 6; John vii, 42; and comp. Mic. v, 2; Jer. xxiii, 5, 6; Isa. ix, 7; xi, 1, 10; 2 Sam. vii, 16; Psa. lxxxix, 3, 4.

strata of tradition, and the embellishments of composition peculiar to the writer without thereby disparaging the main facts of the record.[1]

3. Childhood and Growth. According to Matthew's gospel, Herod became furiously angered because the Magi did not return to bring him word about the newly born babe of Bethlehem, but went back by another route to their own country in the far East. Advised of his cruel edict for the slaughter of all the children in and about Bethlehem who were less than two years old, Joseph took the child Jesus and his mother into Egypt and remained there until after Herod's death. Then they all returned to Galilee, and dwelt at Nazareth, where Jesus grew up and spent the first thirty years of his life. He became known as "the carpenter's son," and is called "the carpenter, the son of Mary, and brother of James, and Joses, and Judas, and Simon" (Mark vi, 3). Several sisters are also mentioned, from which it appears that Mary became the mother of other children besides Jesus, "her firstborn Son."[2] But the child Jesus early showed his exceptional strength of character and wisdom. When he was twelve years old he went up with his parents to Jerusalem, and amazed the Jewish teachers in the temple by his understanding and the superior wisdom with which he asked and answered questions. But he returned to Nazareth with Joseph and Mary, and was subject unto them as a dutiful child until he was about thirty years of age. It is said of him that, during these years, he "advanced in wisdom and stature, and in favor with God and men" (Luke ii, 52; comp. 1 Sam. ii, 26).

4. His Baptism and Temptation. When Jesus was about thirty years old he left Nazareth and went to the river Jordan at some

---

[1] A full critical discussion of the questions of "the virgin-birth" is quite beyond the purpose and the limits of this volume. Those interested in these questions are referred to the following literature. Charles Gore: Dissertations on Subjects connected with the Incarnation. Dissertation i, pp. 3-68. London and New York, 1895. Percy Gardner: Exploratio Evangelica. Chapter xix. London and New York, 1899. James Thomas: Our Records of the Nativity and Modern Historical Research. London, 1900. P. W. Schmiedel, in Encyclopædia Biblica; Article, "Mary." H. Usener: in same Encyclopædia; Article, "Nativity-Narratives." W. Sanday, in Expository Times, of April, 1903. Alexander Brown, in London Quarterly Review of April, 1903. M. S. Terry, in Methodist Review of November, 1901. T. Allan Hoben, in American Journal of Theology of July and October, 1902, and Bacon, Zenos, Rhees and Warfield in same Journal of January, 1906. C. A. Briggs: The Incarnation of the Lord. Sermon x. New York, 1902. Paul Lobstein: The Virgin Birth of Christ; trans. by V. Leuliette. London, 1903. W. M. Ramsay: Was Christ Born at Bethlehem? London, 1898. Soltau: Birth of Jesus Christ. Eng. trans. London, 1903. G. H. Box: The Gospel Narratives of the Nativity and the Alleged Influence of Heathen Ideas; in Zeitschrift für die neutestamentliche Wissenschaft for 1905, Heft i. R. J. Cooke: The Incarnation and Recent Criticism, New York, 1907.

[2] These brothers and sisters of Jesus might have been children of Joseph by a former marriage, and so many have believed. But if this were the case, it is quite strange, not to say inexplicable, that such a fact is nowhere mentioned or even intimated in the gospels. On the other hand, the mention of Jesus as Mary's "firstborn son" most naturally implies that she had other children born after him.

place in the wilderness of Judæa where John was baptizing. When he presented himself for baptism John hesitated, feeling that he had need rather to be baptized by Jesus; but immediately after the baptism Jesus "saw the heavens rent asunder, and the Spirit as a dove descending upon him; and a voice came out of the heavens, Thou art my beloved Son, in thee I am well pleased" (Mark i, 10, 11). Thereupon he withdrew into the wilderness, and for forty days passed through a severe struggle of temptation over the manner in which he should show himself to be the Son of God. He triumphed over the evil one in that conflict, and "returned in the power of the Spirit into Galilee; and a fame went out concerning him through all the region round about. And he taught in their synagogues, being glorified of all" (Luke iv, 14, 15).

5. His Public Ministry and Death. Soon after his return to Galilee he chose twelve disciples to be intimately associated with him in his ministry, and to witness his mighty works and his teaching. He subsequently appointed seventy others to go out into the various cities and places of the land and to proclaim that the kingdom of God was nigh at hand. The mention of three passovers in the gospel of John (ii, 13; vi, 4; xii, 1) justifies the prevailing belief that the public ministry of Jesus extended over at least three years.[1] These years were filled with the performance of many wonderful works, especially of healing, and with the inculcation of the truths and mysteries of the kingdom which he came to establish in the world. His teaching and his works provoked the bitter opposition of the Jewish leaders of that time, and he was arrested, condemned, and crucified. But his life and work made an indelible impression upon some men in high positions. He was buried in the tomb of a rich man of Arimathea, who had been deeply affected by his teachings, and had secretly become a disciple.

6. A Man Among Men. From all the traditions and records, Jesus appears to have been in every way a man among men. He passed like other children through the period of helpless infancy and dependent childhood. The lowly estate of his parents is inferred from their offering "a pair of turtle-doves, or two young pigeons" on the occasion of the purification (Luke ii, 24), a provision allowed for such as had not sufficient means to offer a lamb (Lev. xii, 8). But the family of Joseph and Mary at Nazareth, though belonging to the class of the poor, do not seem to have

---

[1] The idea that it was only one year in duration seems to have arisen from the mention of "the acceptable year of the Lord," in Luke iv, 19, and also from the fact that the first three gospels mention but one passover. But this inference is entitled to no more credit than that of Irenæus from John viii, 57, that Jesus at that time must have been nearly fifty years old.

suffered from poverty, but were in a way to earn for themselves a respectable livelihood. At a subsequent time Jesus said to one who wished to become his disciple: "The foxes have holes, and the birds of the heaven have nests; but the Son of man hath not where to lay his head" (Matt. viii, 20). Like other men he was often hungry and thirsty, and he wept and prayed. According to Heb. iv, 15, he was subject to human infirmities and was "in all points tempted like as we are." He spoke of his own trials (Luke xxii, 28). His sense of human limitation was manifest in many ways, and he declared, when speaking prophetically of a great event to come, that he did not know the time when it should come to pass (Mark xiii, 32). The tenderness of his affections appeared when he took little children in his arms, and blessed them. His amazement and sore trouble of soul in Gethsemane, and the words of his prayer that the bitter cup and hour might pass from him, reveal a depth of human emotion that is most remarkable; and his words and agony on the cross show that he was human to the last.

7. A Man of Transcendent Greatness. But while the evidence is abundant that Jesus of Nazareth was very human and subject to all those feelings of pain, emotion, anxiety, shrinking from trial, and exultation in hope and spiritual comfort, there is even more abundant evidence that he was a man of transcendent greatness. His personal influence over those with whom he came in contact was of a most marvelous character; and the fact that to-day, after nearly two millenniums, the name and teachings of Jesus Christ command the reverence of the civilized world, and seem in a fair way to be the most important force in developing the highest possible civilization among all nations, indicates that this remarkable personage is second to no other that has ever appeared among men. This fact is the more astounding when we consider the obscurity of his early life; his associations with the poor and lowly, and his utter lack of friends in high places of influence who dared to show themselves in his favor; also his persistent refusal to court notoriety, or allow his mighty works to be published abroad during his lifetime. The shortness of his public career would seem to have been fatal to a successful introduction of his gospel to the world. Confucius and Buddha lived nearly half a century to formulate and propagate their doctrines, but Jesus less than four years. Furthermore, the shame and ignominy of public crucifixion would seem to have gone far to cover up the whole work of his life in reproach and oblivion. But in spite of all these adverse conditions, the teaching of Jesus has gone out into all the earth, and his personality is recognized as the most adorable of all that have ever been honored as founders of new systems, or as opening a new era in the history of the human race.¹

8. Manner and Matter of his Teaching. This personal superiority of Jesus becomes the more impressive when we observe the remarkable manner and matter of his teaching. His method seems to have been that of simplicity itself, and there is no proof that he ever sought to thrust himself into public notice. Much of his teaching was imparted privately to his chosen disciples. Proverbs and parables and allegories fell from his lips, and were caught up by his hearers and repeated until they formed an extensive body of λόγια, *sayings;* and these have been incorporated in our written gospels and remain as jewels in the religious literature of the world. So potent and self-evidencing are his statements of truth that they need no arguments to make them more convincing.² This fact explains how it was that he "taught as one having authority, and not as the Jewish scribes" (Matt. vii, 29), and the officers of the chief priests and Pharisees were compelled to acknowledge, "Never did man so speak" (John vii, 46). His sermon on the mount, his response to various questions put to him, and the contents of his discourses in John's gospel, though they be there cast in the peculiar style of a disciple writing long afterward, all breathe an authority and a spirituality of thought which have no parallel among the original teachings of men. So commanding is his authority as a teacher of the truth that when upon any subject it is made clear to us what Jesus said and thought, that testimony is the end of all controversy.

9. His Marvelous Self-Expression. No less marvelous is the calm self-expression of superior authority which often appears in the sayings of this great teacher. He calls himself "the Son of man," and declares that he has power on earth to forgive sins (Luke v, 24; Matt. ix, 6). He assumes an authority in lawgiving above that of Moses (Matt. v, 21-32), and declares that his mis-

---

¹ See these facts admirably constructed into an argument for the superior personality of Jesus by Dr. John Young, of Edinburgh, in his work entitled, The Christ of History: An Argument Grounded on the Facts of his Life on Earth. New York, 1866.

² Harnack notes the fact that there appears nowhere in the first thirty years of Jesus's life any evidence of violent soul-struggles, crises, and storms, and breaking with the past. "Everything seems to pour from him naturally, as though it could not do otherwise, like a spring from the depths of the earth, clear and unchecked in its flow. Where shall we find the man who at the age of thirty can so speak, if he has gone through bitter struggles—struggles of the soul, in which he has ended by burning what he once adored, and by adoring what he burned? Where shall we find the man who has broken with his past, in order to summon others to repentance as well as himself, but who through it all never speaks of his own repentance?" Das Wesen des Christentums, p. 21. Eng. trans. by T. B. Saunders, p. 36. New York, 1901.

sion is to perfect (πληρῶσαι, *complete, fulfill, consummate*) the law and the prophets (Matt. v, 17). He assumes to be greater than Solomon, greater than Jonah, greater than the temple, and to be Lord of the sabbath (Matt. xii, 6, 8, 41, 42; Mark ii, 28). And what shall we think or say of one who quietly and calmly employs such self-expression as the following texts contain? "All things have been delivered unto me of my Father: and no man knoweth the Son, save the Father; neither doth any know the Father, save the Son, and he to whomsoever the Son willeth to reveal him. Come unto me, all ye that labor and are heavy laden, and I will give you rest" (Matt. xi, 27, 28; comp. Luke x, 22-24). "Take and eat this bread, and drink of this cup, for these are my body and my blood of the covenant, which is shed for many" (Mark xiv, 22-24; Luke xxii, 19, 20). "Except ye eat the flesh of the Son of man and drink his blood, ye have not life in yourselves" (John vi, 53). "I am the bread of life" (John vi, 35, 48). "I am the way, and the truth, and the life" (John xiv, 6). "If I be lifted up from the earth, I will draw all men unto myself" (John xii, 32). "Before Abraham was born, I am" (John viii, 58). "I am the resurrection and the life. . . . Whosoever liveth and believeth on me shall never die" (John xi, 25, 26). Such superhuman claims would seem in any other person like the extravaganzas of insanity, but in Jesus Christ they have come to be regarded as perfectly befitting and natural.

10. His Sinlessness. Another quality of this transcendent personality is his sinlessness. All tradition and testimony unite to pronounce him "holy, guileless, undefiled, separated from sinners" (Heb. vii, 26); "in all points tempted like as we are, yet without sin" (Heb. iv, 15). He "did no sin, neither was guile found in his mouth" (1 Pet. ii, 22); "in him is no sin" (1 John iii, 5); and he "knew no sin" (2 Cor. v, 21). He is spoken of "as a lamb without blemish and without spot" (1 Pet. i, 19), and as "the holy and Righteous One" (Acts iii, 14). Pilate declared to the priests and to the multitudes, "I find no fault in this man" (Luke xxiii, 4), and both he and his wife referred to him as "that righteous man" (Matt. xxvii, 19, 24). Even the demons address him as "the Holy One of God" (Mark i, 24). One of his own most memorable sayings is, "Which of you convinceth me of sin?" From his childhood up to the close of his life he maintained the record of a spotless character, and while assuming authority to forgive the sins of others, he never acknowledged a need of repentance or of remission of sins on his own part. He stands sublimely apart as the one transcendent sinless personality among men.

CHAPTER II

THE TITLES, "SON OF GOD" AND "SON OF MAN"

1. The Title, "Son of God." The sinlessness of Jesus Christ, when contemplated in connection with the remarkable matter and manner of his teaching and the marvelous self-expression of his inner consciousness, comports very noticeably with the announcement of the angel in Luke i, 35: "The Holy Spirit shall come upon thee, and the power of the Most High shall overshadow thee; wherefore also the holy thing which is begotten shall be called the Son of God." This last sentence may also be translated, "That which is to be born shall be called holy, the Son of God." The voice out of the heavens which came to Jesus after he had been baptized declared him "my beloved Son, in whom I am well pleased." This language is in substance the same as that addressed to "my servant, my chosen," in Isa. xlii, 1, which is believed to have Messianic significance. The language of the temptation, "If thou art the Son of God" (Matt. iv, 3, 6), implies some unique and supernatural relation to God. It is worthy of note that, in the synoptic gospels, Jesus does not call himself the Son of God, although the title is ascribed to him by others, and he allows himself to be thus addressed (see Matt. viii, 29; xiv, 33; xxvi, 63; xxvii, 54; Mark iii, 11; xv, 39; Luke iv, 41; viii, 28).

(1) *Old Testament Origin and Messianic Significance.* The title was evidently understood both by Jesus and his contemporaries to denote not only a unique relation to God, but also a claim to be the Messiah who was to come into the world and fulfill certain oracles of the Old Testament prophets. Its origin may be traced to such scriptures as 2 Sam. vii, 14, where Jehovah promises to be a father to David's future son and to establish his throne forever. The second psalm represents Jehovah setting his king on the holy hill of Zion, and saying unto him, "Thou art my Son; this day have I begotten thee"; and the psalm has obvious relation to the promise made to David. When the high priest asked, "Art thou the Christ, the Son of the Blessed?" he evidently assumed that the claim to be the Messiah was involved in a self-appropriation of the title, "Son of God" (comp. Mark xiv, 61; Luke xxii, 67-71), and he and the people construed it as blasphemy. On the other hand, Nathaniel's exclamation, "Thou art the Son of God; thou

art the King of Israel" (John i, 49) was a devout acknowledgment of the Messiahship of Jesus.

(2) *His Knowledge of the Father.* A deeper conception of the divine Sonship of Jesus appears in his unique claim of personal acquaintance with God: "No one knoweth the Son, save the Father; neither doth any know the Father, save the Son, and he to whomsoever the Son willeth to reveal him" (Matt. xi, 27). Here, certainly, is the expression of a consciousness of God, a knowledge of the Father, and a power to make him known to others, which are more than human. The divine mysteries are matters of everyday life with this Son of God, this beloved of the heavenly Father. The language is in vital harmony with that of John x, 38: "Ye may know and understand that the Father is in me, and I in the Father"; and also that of xiv, 10, 11: "I am in the Father, and the Father in me." Where else among all prophets or teachers can we find any other such witness of conscious life in God? He speaks as if he were in some sense one with God, knowing him intimately as a beloved son knows his affectionate father, and so partaking of his divine nature and fellowship as to call him in an exceptional manner "My Father" (comp. Luke ii, 49; xxii, 29; xxiv, 49; Matt. vii, 21; x, 32, 33; xvi, 17; xviii, 10; John ii, 16; v, 17; xiv, 2, etc.). These various expressions imply something more than a mere inner moral likeness to God; they point to an essential spiritual relationship, unique in itself, and superior to that of any other man. In the language employed in Mark xiii, 32, and Matt. xxiv, 36, we also observe that, while affirming a limit to his own knowledge, Jesus assigns "the Son" a rank above men and angels.

(3) *The Only Begotten Son.* Another form of this title peculiar to the writings of John is "the only begotten Son" (John i, 14, 18; iii, 16, 18; 1 John iv, 9). The only begotten child in any family is naturally thought of as a special treasure in the affection of the parents (comp. Heb. xi, 17; Luke vii, 12; viii, 42; ix, 38), and this fact is a matter of common remark. But as men and angels are called "sons of God," the title, "only begotten Son" of God must be intended to express an exceptional and superior relationship. In this unique relation to God he can have no brethren and no sisters. The title being found only in John, we may with good reason believe that it holds a close ideal relation to his doctrine of the Logos who became flesh and thus manifested the grace and truth of the eternal Father. He who was in the beginning with God (John i, 1), and who in the days of his incarnation spoke of "the glory which he had with the Father before the world was" (xvii, 5), was preëminently "the Son of

God," ὁ υἱὸς τοῦ θεοῦ, and "the only begotten from the Father." In bringing many sons into glory, and making them all one in the fellowship of God, "he is not ashamed to call them brethren" (Heb. ii, 11), but he himself, by reason of his premundane existence in the glory of God and his supernatural incarnation, is "the only begotten Son who is in the bosom of the Father" (John i, 18), and who is therefore alone competent to reveal the everlasting Father unto men. He hath seen him and declared him.

2. The Title, "Son of Man." The title, "Son of man," however, is the one which Jesus most frequently employs when speaking of himself, especially as we read in the synoptic gospels. Except in Acts vii, 56, where Stephen says, "I see the heavens opened, and the Son of man standing on the right hand of God," this title of our Lord is found only in his own discourses. He seems to have chosen it as one full of meaning and well adapted to suggest the profound significance of his incarnation and his messianic ministry, while at the same time the common use of it as a title did not expose him to collision with his enemies who were watching to catch him in his talk (Mark xii, 13; Luke xi, 54); for "Son of man" does not appear to have been understood by the Jews as a messianic title.

(1) *Its Usage in the Old Testament.* The phrase is not an uncommon one in the Old Testament. It often appears in poetic parallelisms as synonymous with "man," as in Psa. viii, 4:

> What is man that thou art mindful of him?
> And the son of man, that thou visitest him?

In Ezekiel (ii, 1, 3, 6, 8; iii, 1, 3, etc.) it appears as the characteristic designation of the prophet himself when addressed by Jehovah, and it has been thought to have some peculiar significance as coming from one who was upon "the likeness of a throne," and had "a likeness as the appearance of a man" (i, 26). The title, "Ben-Adam" was adopted to impress the prophet with the thought that he was a man among men, and his readers would be made to feel that the heavenly messages he bore were evidences of Jehovah's interest in the creatures who had been made in the image and after the likeness of God. Daniel's vision of one "like a son of man coming with the clouds of heaven" (vii, 13) has obvious connection with the words of Jesus in Matt. xxiv, 30; xxv, 31; xxvi, 64, and Luke xxi, 27. It matters not that in Daniel the expression is indefinite, "like a son of man," and that it stands in a noticeable contrast to the symbols of beasts, "like a lion," "like a bear," "like a leopard." Nor need we dispute the statement that the "son of man" in Daniel's vision is a collective term, and identical in meaning with "the people of the saints of the Most High" (ver. 27). If we believe that the language ascribed to Jesus in the passages cited above (and also in Matt. xvi, 27, 28; Mark viii, 38; Luke ix, 26) implies a conscious allusion to Daniel's words, we may also believe that that Messianic prophecy had something to do with Jesus's choice of the title, "Son of man." As truly as in the case of Ezekiel our Lord was a man among men, and inasmuch as one great purpose of his mission in the world was to teach the world that humanity is a lost child of God which he would fain restore to its heavenly Father, so much the more significant are the allusions to the words of Daniel and Ezekiel. He came forth from God, and he knows the Father as no man knoweth him (Matt. xi, 27), yet he desires to emphasize his identification with the humanity he came to save. For "it became him, for whom are all things, and through whom are all things, in bringing many sons unto glory, to make the captain of their salvation perfect through sufferings. For both he that sanctifieth and they that are sanctified are all of one (Father): for which cause he is not ashamed to call them brethren. . . . Since then the children are sharers of flesh and blood, he also himself in like manner partook of the same, that through death he might bring to naught him that had the power of death, that is, the devil; and might deliver all them who through fear of death were all their lifetime subject to bondage. For verily not of angels doth he take hold for the purpose of helping (ἐπιλαμβάνεται), but he taketh hold of the seed of Abraham. Wherefore it behooved him in all things to be made like unto his brethren" (Heb. ii, 10-17). This is an excellent and impressive rationale of the manifestation of Christ in the flesh, and by way of comment on the passage we observe four things: (1) the common origin of Christ and his sanctified followers as children of one heavenly Father, so that our Lord may call us brethren; (2) the necessity of Christ's incarnation, for in no other way could he abolish death and deliver man from the fear of it; (3) hence the fitness of Christ's perfect human nature, "like unto his brethren," for he came to save men in the flesh, not angels; (4) and so the perfection of Christ's sanctifying and saving work is attained through sufferings. How fitting, then, and how significant that our Lord should bear the title, "Son of man," and thus identify himself with the humanity he came to sanctify and save!

(2) *"Son of Man" in the Book of Enoch.* The use of the title, "Son of man" in the book of Enoch is too remarkable to be overlooked. In chapter xlvi, 1-3, we read: "I saw one whose head was white like wool, and with him was another being whose coun-

tenance had the appearance of a man and his face was full of graciousness, like one of the holy angels. And I asked the angel, who showed me all the hidden things, concerning that Son of man, who he was, and whence he was, and why he went with the Head of days? And he answered, This is the Son of man who hath righteousness, and who reveals all the treasures of that which is hidden, because the Lord of spirits hath chosen him, and his lot before the Lord of spirits hath surpassed everything in uprightness for ever." Again in xlviii, 2-7, we read that "the Son of man was named in the presence of the Lord of spirits, and his name was before the Head of days. And before the sun and the signs were created, before the stars of the heaven were made, his name was named before the Lord of spirits. He will be a staff to the righteous on which they will support themselves and not fall, and he will be the light of the Gentiles and the hope of those who are troubled in heart. All who dwell on earth will fall down and bow the knee before him, and will bless and laud and celebrate with song the Lord of spirits. And for this reason has he been chosen and hidden before him before the creation of the world and for evermore. And the wisdom of the Lord of spirits hath revealed him to the holy and righteous, for he preserveth the lot of the righteous." Still further, in lxii, 5-7, we have a picture of "the Son of man sitting on the throne of his glory. And the kings and the mighty and all who possess the earth will glorify and bless him who rules over all, who was hidden; for the Son of man was hidden before him, and the Most High preserved him in the presence of his might and revealed him to the elect." Another passage, in lxix, 27, 29, speaks also of the Son of man sitting on the throne of his glory and executing judgment upon sinners; "for the Son of man has appeared and sits on the throne of his glory, and all evil will pass away before his face and depart; but the word of the Son of man will be strong before the Lord of spirits." All these citations are from that section of the book of Enoch which is called "The Similitudes." The author evidently derived his idea of the Son of man from the book of Daniel, and added to it ideals drawn from the Wisdom-literature of the Hebrews. With him this Son of man is the Messiah, and is repeatedly called "the Anointed One," "the Elect One," "the Righteous One." But he is conceived as a supernatural being, who "stands before the Lord of spirits, and his glory is for ever and ever, and his might unto all generations" (xlix, 2). He was with the Most High before the creation of the sun and stars, sits upon the throne of his glory, executes judgment, and reigns in righteousness forever. So strikingly do these expressions conform to well-known teachings of the New Testament touching the person of Christ that there is reason to suspect that they are not the words of the original writer, but Christian interpolations which found their way into the Ethiopic version of the book of Enoch. But, accepting them as pre-Christian, it is not difficult to believe that a late Jewish writer, after the times of the Maccabees, might have constructed out of the sublime suggestions of the book of Daniel (vii, 9-14), and from such portrayals of Wisdom as we read in Prov. viii, 20-31, all these heavenly conceptions of the Messiah as the Son of man. Whether Jesus himself ever read these Similitudes of the apocryphal Enoch, we may not say; but many interviews with wise men of his nation and with teachers of the law, like the one recorded in Luke ii, 46, were possible to him during the eighteen years which passed between that event in the temple and the time of his baptism at the Jordan; and from such conversations he might have gathered up all the various ideals of the Messiah which were entertained among the Jewish people of that day. He may have added to them in his own thought the conception of "the Servant of Jehovah" from Isa. lii, 13—liii, 12.[1] The "one like unto a son of man" in the apocalypse of Daniel (vii, 13), whether understood personally or collectively, "came with the clouds of heaven to the Ancient of days, and there was given him dominion, and glory, and a kingdom, that all the peoples, nations, and languages should serve him: his dominion is an everlasting dominion, and his kingdom shall not be destroyed." This magnificent conception embodies in substance all the supernatural elements which appear in the Son of man as presented in Enoch. The idea of preëxistence, as suggested in Prov. viii, must have been as familiar to Jesus as it was to any of the later Jewish writers, and his own profound interpretations of Scripture, of which we possess not a few examples in the gospels, leave no room for us to question that in the course of his "advance in wisdom and in favor with God and man" (Luke ii, 52) he selected from his own abundant stores of the knowledge of the Scriptures and of all sacred things such forms of expression as would best suit his deep spiritual understanding of the kingdom of God and the mission of God's Anointed One. His increase in wisdom was as normal as his bodily growth.

---

[1] This view is maintained by Charles in his annotated translation of the book of Enoch (Oxford, 1893), Appendix B; pp. 314-316: "While retaining its supernatural associations, this title underwent transformation in our Lord's use of it. . . . And just as his Kingdom in general formed a standing protest against the prevailing Messianic ideas of temporal glory and dominion, so the title, 'Son of Man' assumed a deeper spiritual significance; and this change we shall best apprehend if we introduce into the Enoch conception of the Son of man the Isaiah conception of the Servant of Jehovah."

(3) *The Lord's Own Favorite Title.* "Son of man" is, accordingly, our Lord's own favorite Messianic title. He deliberately assumed it because of its scriptural connotation, and also because it most appropriately designated his Christly manifestation in the flesh. Paul's doctrine of the first and the last Adam seems to be a further elaboration of this Messianic concept. The first Adam was made in the image of God; the second in the likeness of men; and as by the transgression of the first man death passed upon all men, so by the redemptive Messianic ministry of "the second man from heaven," those who have borne the image of the earthy shall also bear the image of the heavenly. Our Lord's chosen title is one which magnifies his own humiliation by suggesting the great purpose for which he came into the world.[1] Others may call him the Son of God; he does not forbid them. But it is at least interesting to note that when, according to Matt. xvi, 13-20, Jesus asked his disciples, "Who do men say that the Son of man is?" Peter answered, "Thou art the Christ, the Son of the living God." Whereupon Jesus pronounced a remarkable blessing upon Peter, and yet "charged the disciples that they should tell no man that he was the Christ."

(4) *A Person Sublimely Unique.* Our conclusion is that the title, "Son of man," as well as "Son of God," served of design to point him out as the very Christ of God. His person was sublimely unique, and he and those who were nearest to him felt that in him were fulfilled, or soon to be fulfilled, the Messianic hopes of Israel. He was divinely commissioned and manifested for effecting "the consolation of Israel and the redemption of Jerusalem" (Luke ii, 25, 38). But this redemption was to be accomplished in a more profoundly spiritual manner than the Jewish people of that day were able to apprehend. His exaltation to the right hand of God, and his exercise of all power in heaven and on earth until he shall have put all things under him, imply a sovereignty of the world, and a participation in the glory of his Father which we shall treat in another connection.

---

[1] So Beyschlag: "The Son of man is the God-invested bearer of the kingdom that descends from above, that is to be founded from heaven; it is he who brings in the kingdom of God."—New Testament Theology, vol. i, p. 64. Edinburgh, 1895.

CHAPTER III

THE SUPERNATURAL IN THE PERSON OF CHRIST

1. The Supernatural Birth. The supernatural birth of Jesus Christ is unmistakably attested by the gospels of Matthew and Luke, and clearly implied in the gospel of John. The criticism which questions the credibility of the first chapters of these gospels is conspicuously negative in its character and has not been able to show any real contradictions in the varying narratives. These narratives of the birth and childhood of Jesus are apparently from another source of tradition than that from which the main portions of the synoptic gospels arose, but they must have originated too near the time of the facts recorded to be arbitrarily cast aside as untrustworthy. Matthew's record embodies the secret of Joseph, and Luke has preserved the secret of Mary, and we cannot allow the noteworthy variations of the two traditions nor any *a priori* assumptions in denial of the supernatural to prejudice the main testimony which they bear to the virgin birth of Jesus. Luke's gospel has been regarded as in some sense, or to some extent, embodying the gospel according to Paul,[1] and his narrative of the birth of Jesus may be taken as in full accord with what Paul meant by "God's sending forth his Son, born of a woman, born under the law" (Gal. iv, 4). There is also a suggestion of preëxistence in the words, "God sent forth his Son," as truly as there is a witness of the supernatural "Spirit of his Son" in verse 6, immediately following. This is in deep harmony with the words of Luke i, 35: "The Holy Spirit shall come upon thee, and the power of the Most High shall overshadow thee." The birth of Jesus is to be regarded as the product of a supernatural agency like the creation of the first Adam, who in Luke's genealogy (iii, 38) is called "the son of God." If we believe that vegetable and animal life in the cosmos originated, not in nonliving matter, but in a principle of life imparted directly from the ever-living God, it ought not to be difficult for us also to believe that the human life of the immaculate Son of God was supernaturally begotten of the same eternal Source of life. Luke's record calls both Jesus and Adam son of God and has a perceptible relationship with Paul's

---

[1] This belief is as old as the time of Irenæus and is repeatedly mentioned in Eusebius, Ecclesiastical History, book iii, chaps. iv, xxiv; book v, chap. viii; book vi, chap. xxv.

habit of contrasting the first Adam and the last. The mystery of the origin of the first man is beyond our ken, and the incarnation of "the second man from heaven" (ὁ δεύτερος ἄνθρωπος ἐξ οὐρανοῦ; 1 Cor. xv, 47) is even more impenetrable. But all that is exceptional and marvelous in the subsequent career and the exaltation of Jesus is in perfect harmony with the story of his supernatural birth. It was fitting that the advent of such a personage should be celebrated by a choir of angels (Luke ii, 8-14), and that prophetic words should be spoken over the Child by the aged Simeon and Anna (ii, 25-38). It was very appropriate that wise men from the far East should be guided to his cradle by a conspicuous star (Matt. ii, 1-12), for this "root and offspring of David" was himself "the bright, the morning star" (Rev. xxii, 16), destined in the great future to draw all the truly wise ones to himself, and lift them up into the holy heavens. And it accords with all this that the public ministry of Jesus was heralded by a Levitical prophet, who appeared as his forerunner "in the spirit and power of Elijah" (Luke i, 17; comp. Matt. xi, 14), and proclaimed the coming of one far mightier than himself, the latchet of whose shoes he was not worthy to stoop down and unloose, and who would baptize with the Holy Spirit and execute judgment as with the purging fire of God (Mark i, 7, 8; Matt. iii, 11, 12; Luke iii, 16). When Jesus received baptism at the hand of this prophet, of whom he testified that none greater had ever been born of woman (Matt. xi, 11), the heavens opened above him, the Spirit descended upon him, and a voice out of heaven declared: "This is my Son, the beloved, in whom I am well pleased" (Matt. iii, 16, 17).

2. The Baptism, Temptation, and Triumph. The baptism of Jesus and the descent of the Spirit upon him were of the nature of an inauguration to his public ministry. There followed immediately the temptation in the wilderness, which is made prominent in all the synoptic gospels. This trial corresponds and contrasts with the temptation of the first Adam, who miserably failed when beset with the wiles of the devil (Gen. iii, 1-7). The second Adam proved himself worthy to be called the Son of God, was tempted in the threefold manner of the lust of the flesh, the lust of the eye, and the lust of dominion, but he put the adversary to flight and came off more than conqueror. Whatever interpretation be put upon the narratives of this temptation and the whole subject of demonology as presented in the New Testament, the early triumph of Jesus over Satan is significant of a purpose to overcome the dominion of evil. The power of sin and its appalling consequences among men may well be conceived as a kingdom of wickedness, and the ministry of Jesus Christ, as told in the New Testament, treats it as a tremendous fact. According to 1 John iii, 8, "he that doeth sin is of the devil, and the Son of God was manifested that he might destroy the works of the devil." And so the Son of God might well have asked himself at the beginning of his ministry, "How can one enter into the house of the strong man, and spoil his goods, except he first bind the strong man? And then will he spoil his house" (Matt. xii, 29). His manifestation in the flesh had for its high aim the salvation of man from the evil forces of the world; his signal victory, at the beginning of his career, over the prince of darkness evinced his ability to despoil the principalities and powers, and it was prophetic of an ultimate putting of all his enemies under his feet. There is, accordingly, peculiar significance in the language of Luke iv, 13, 14: "When the devil had completed every temptation, he departed from him for a season. And Jesus returned in the power of the Spirit into Galilee; and a fame went out concerning him through all the region round about." Thereupon he began that series of wonderful works which were in themselves a conspicuous sign of the ultimate overthrow of the kingdom of Satan and of the coming of the kingdom of God (comp. Luke x, 18; Matt. xii, 28). Hence we regard the baptism and the temptation of Jesus Christ as charged with an element of supernaturalism. By means of these extraordinary experiences he came into conscious contact with what are called in Eph. vi, 12, "the world rulers of this darkness, spiritual hosts of wickedness in the heavenly places." From that time onward he was to act "in the power of the Spirit," and to cope with infernal forces, as he had not done before.

3. **The Miracles of his Ministry.** The supernatural element in the person and work of Jesus is a very conspicuous feature of the gospel narratives. Nothing is more certain than that the earliest reports of the life of Jesus teemed with the accounts of his miracles. The oldest written sources from which our present gospels derived their contents of the words and works of Jesus were evidently records of the numerous "signs and wonders" which were performed by him. The gospel of Mark, now generally believed to be the oldest of the Synoptics, and containing much that seems to have been derived directly from disciples and contemporaries of Jesus,[1] has been appropriately called "a miracle-gospel" because of the prominence it gives to the mighty works of the Son of God. According to Matthew (xi, 2-5) and Luke (vii, 18-23) the great prophet who came as the forerunner of Christ fell into a

---
[1] Tradition says from Peter. See Eusebius, Ecclesiastical History, book ii, chap. 15; book iii, chap. 39.

despondency much like that recorded of the ancient Tishbite (comp. 1 Kings xix, 4, 10, 14), and seemed to doubt whether Jesus were indeed the Messiah who was coming; and "in that hour he (Jesus) cured many of diseases, and plagues, and evil spirits; and on many that were blind he bestowed sight"; and then he sent word to the desponding prophet: "Go and tell John the things which ye have seen and heard: the blind receive their sight, the lame walk, the lepers are cleansed, the deaf hear, the dead are raised up, and the poor have the gospel preached unto them." One who was so familiar with the Law and the Prophets as John the Baptist (comp. Luke iii, 3-19; Matt. iii, 3; xiv, 4) would, on receiving such a message from Jesus himself, at once perceive that these mighty works were the sure tokens of Messiah's day. The prophecies of Isaiah (xxxv, 5, 6; lxi, 1-3) thus received significant fulfillment.

4. Miracles Natural with Christ. The miracles of Jesus Christ are accordingly to be regarded as a natural and appropriate accompaniment of his unique personality, and also of his Messianic office and ministry. They are rationally explicable when thus viewed as signs and wonders caused by the manifestation of a supernatural person upon earth. In his adorable personality, as we shall further see, this "Christ of God" is immeasurably greater than all his miracles, and to one who accepts him as the "only begotten of the Father," "the light of the world," "risen from the dead," "received up into heaven," and enthroned "at the right hand of God" it is utterly superfluous to offer any apology for the reported miracles of his earthly life. It would rather have been a greater marvel if such a transcendent personality, appearing at the time he did, had wrought no miracles. If, indeed, he were supernaturally begotten of the Holy Spirit, if the gospel records of his infancy and early life be true, if the descent of the Spirit upon him at his baptism and the accompanying voice from heaven be accepted as veritable facts, then certainly all his miracles recorded in our gospels would but naturally fill out the legitimate sequel of a beginning so exceptional. His casting out of evil spirits, and healing all manner of sickness and diseases most appropriately follow his far-reaching triumph over the prince of darkness when tempted in all points as other men. It is worthy of note that a large proportion of his mighty works were miracles of healing, and in an age and generation that conceived "the whole world as lying in the evil one" (1 John v, 19), and regarded bodily infirmities as the bonds of Satan (Luke xiii, 16), such displays of his wisdom and power were strikingly significant of his divine purpose to subdue the entire realm of evil. How fitting that the world's

Redeemer should heal the sick, cleanse the leper, give sight to the blind, multiply the loaves and the fishes, walk upon the waters of the sea, and calm the raging storm, and show himself the Prince of life by raising the dead!

5. No Ostentatious Display of Miracles. Yet never did Jesus make an ostentatious display of his miraculous power. His manner was utterly unlike those wizards who go about performing strange feats to awe and confound the vulgar crowd. He would not exhibit a sign from heaven to gratify a morbid curiosity. It is rather with a sigh of pity over human weakness and lack of spiritual insight that he says, "Except ye see signs and wonders ye will not believe" (John iv, 48). To men like the scribes and Pharisees of his time, who would see a sign from heaven, he said: "An evil and adulterous generation seeketh after a sign" (Matt. xii, 39). It was foreign to his mission to work a prodigy. His miracles were all of them remarkable manifestations of love and mercy, and stand forth in the gospel records as so many types of what he is perpetually aiming to accomplish in the salvation of mankind. Profound spiritual lessons, most profitable for religious instruction, may be derived from them as truly as from his inimitable parables. Even his cursing of the barren fig tree has a most solemn admonition to men of every age.

6. Miracles Proofs of Divine Wisdom and Power, but Not of Omnipotence. The miracles of Jesus, however, should be studied as exhibitions of his divine wisdom as well as proofs of his power. These mighty works of healing and of raising the dead are no sufficient evidence of omnipotence, nor of omniscience; nor should they be construed and appealed to as a demonstration of the deity of Christ. For the disciples were able to perform like miracles, and no one would presume to construe their exercise of such power as a proof of their omnipotence. Jesus himself made no such claim, but on the contrary declared most positively that "the Son can do nothing of himself, but what he seeth the Father doing. . . . I can of myself do nothing. . . . The works which the Father hath given me to accomplish, the very works that I do, bear witness of me (not that I am omnipotent, but) that the Father hath sent me" (John v, 19, 30, 36). Miracles, whether performed by Jesus, or by his disciples, or by any other true prophet or teacher, are manifestations of the supernatural, and God is glorified thereby. But while Jesus so positively affirmed that his mighty works were wrought by a power given him from the Father, he exercised that power in a manner which no prophet or apostle presumed to imitate; for he spoke with an authority and wisdom so commanding that we recognize in him a conscious relationship to God superior to that possessed by any other. They performed miracles in the name of Jesus, but he performed them in a way that commanded astonishment "at the majesty of God" (Luke ix, 43). He possessed the secret of God, and real miracles are the exercise of such a knowledge of the secrets of the world as will secure effects desired without any violation of natural law. Other and inferior servants of God may be gifted to perform such works without full knowledge of the secrets of the Almighty, but to Jesus was given the wisdom as well as the power of God (Mark vi, 2).

7. The Resurrection and Ascension. The mighty works of the ministry of Jesus Christ were consummated, in a manner worthy of the wisdom and power of God, by his resurrection from the dead and ascension into heaven. According to the gospel of Paul (Rom. i, 4), he was thereby "declared to be the Son of God with power." He was marvelously "manifested in the flesh"; he was also as marvelously "received up in glory" (1 Tim. iii, 16). The resurrection of our Lord and his ascension and session at the right hand of God are events which connect essentially with each other, and together indicate his heavenly glorification. This supernatural ending of his Messianic career accords most fittingly with its supernatural beginning. It is the appropriate sequel and the consummation of the incarnation of the only begotten Son of God. "No one hath ascended into heaven, but he that descended out of heaven" (John iii, 13). "He that cometh from above, from heaven, is above all," and he calmly says: "I am not of this world" (John iii, 31; viii, 23). No facts of the New Testament are more firmly attested than the resurrection of Jesus and his exaltation to the throne of God. He foretold these things to his disciples, but they were slow to comprehend his words and "questioned among themselves what the rising again from the dead should mean" (Mark ix, 10). Immediately after the crucifixion they were smitten with terror and concealed themselves; but after the third day they all declared that they had seen their risen Lord, and they gave minute details of his various appearances. The variations in their reports evince the unspeakable awe and reserve which those appearances inspired. For forty days he showed himself alive after his passion, and did eat and drink in the presence of the disciples, and furnished them many proofs of his identity. "See my hands and my feet, that it is I myself," he said to them; "handle me and see, for a spirit hath not flesh and bones, as ye behold me having" (Luke xxiv, 39; comp. John xx, 27). He thus retained his fleshly body for the forty days, but when he was parted from them and ascended far above all the heavens, that he might fill all things" (Eph. iv, 10), he was glorified "with the glory which he had with the Father before the world was" (John xvii, 5). Paul was well acquainted with Peter, and spent fifteen days with him at one time in Jerusalem (Gal. i, 18). He testifies that the risen Christ was seen by Peter, and James, and the twelve, and also by more than five hundred at once, most of whom were living at the time he wrote to the Corinthians (1 Cor. xv, 5-7). During all the generation following their Master's ascension the disciples went everywhere "preaching Jesus and the resurrection," and were ever ready to seal their testimony with their blood. And the ascension is attested as positively as the resurrection. Jesus said to Mary Magdalene, "I ascend unto my Father and your Father, and my God and your God" (John xx, 17). The appendix to Mark's gospel says that "the Lord Jesus was received up into heaven, and sat down at the right hand of God" (Mark xvi, 19). Luke's gospel states that after his various appearances to the disciples, "it came to pass, while he blessed them, he parted from them," and most of the ancient manuscripts add, "he was carried up into heaven" (Luke xxiv, 51). In Acts i, 9, it is written that "as they were looking, he was taken up, and a cloud received him out of their sight." In Acts ii, 32-34, Peter declares that God raised up Jesus from the dead and exalted him by his right hand. Paul affirms, in Rom. viii, 34, that "Christ Jesus was raised from the dead, and is at the right hand of God." In Heb. iv, 14; vii, 26; viii, 1, it is said that "Jesus, the Son of God, hath passed through the heavens," "was made higher than the heavens," and "sat down on the right hand of the throne of the Majesty in the heavens." These and other similar statements place the ascension into heaven on as positive a testimony as the fact of the resurrection; and while Luke alone records that the disciples were looking on Jesus when he was parted from them and taken up, the whole New Testament is practically a unit in affirming his ascension and sitting at the right hand of God.

CHAPTER IV

THE SELF-CONSCIOUSNESS OF JESUS CHRIST

1. The Mighty Works and Mighty Words of Jesus Inseparable.
The supernatural in the person of Christ appears in a striking manner in his own self-expression in connection with the work of his ministry. It is impossible to separate the mighty works of Jesus from his mighty words. There is the record of his virgin birth with its unquestionable basis in the belief of a supernatural beginning of his incarnate life; the testimony of his resurrection and ascension evinces a like faith in his miraculous exit from the world, and the records of his ministry teem with accounts of his going about working miracles of goodness. Thus the entire manifestation of this Messianic Son of man and Son of God is compassed about with miracle. It seems utterly futile to accept a part of this record as true and another part as untrustworthy. Like the seamless coat which Jesus wore, the self-consistent witness of the apostolic tradition to his supernatural career cannot be rent. If we dispute the records of his miraculous entrance into the world on grounds of critical conjecture and doubt, we do not see how the accounts of his miraculous exit from the world can be consistently maintained. And if these be given up, with what better reason shall we accept the miracles of his public ministry? All these, moreover, stand in such vital relation to his words of grace and truth that we cannot fairly hold to the one and reject the other.

2. His Consciousness of God. One of the first things to be noticed in the self-expression of Jesus is his consciousness of God. According to Matt. xi, 27, he possesses an immediate knowledge of the Father such as no one else enjoys. This superior knowledge found significant expression when he was twelve years old and began to feel the necessity of being engaged in the affairs of his Father (Luke ii, 49). It spoke out in his utterance of the beatitudes, and of the other profound teachings in the Sermon on the Mount and elsewhere, and it gave the impression of authority not to be found in other teachers (Matt. vii, 29). How intimate the acquaintance with the heavenly Father that speaks so confidently of his immanence and love as to assure us that the hairs of our head are all numbered, and not even a sparrow falleth on the ground without his sympathetic notice! (Matt. x, 30.) He knows of the "joy in the presence of the angels of God over one sinner that repenteth" (Luke xv, 10), and of the Father's will that not one of his little ones perish, and how their angels are ever looking on the Father's face in the heavens (Matt. xviii, 10, 14). He tells the disciples how the heavenly Father, "who seeth in secret," will surely reward the good, how he knows and cares for all their needs, and that it is his good pleasure to give them the kingdom (Luke xii, 32). His intimacy with God is also evinced in his rising up at times a great while before day, and going apart into a desert place to pray, and sometimes continuing all night in prayer to God (Mark i, 35; Luke vi, 12). The gospel of John is especially rich in its record of the God-consciousness of Jesus, and while it is admitted that the record is cast in a style peculiar to the writer, the content is essentially the same as that of the synoptic gospels on this subject. So one cannot but feel that the language of the marvelous prayer in John xvii discloses a consciousness of intimacy and fellowship with God that has no parallel. But many other passages in this gospel express the same consciousness of God: "The Son can do nothing of himself, but what he seeth the Father doing. For the Father loveth the Son, and showeth him all things that himself doeth" (v, 19, 20). "I do nothing of myself. . . . He that sent me is with me; he hath not left me alone; for I do always the things that are pleasing to him" (viii, 29). "I am not alone, but I and the Father that sent me" (viii, 16). "The living Father sent me, and I live because of the Father" (vi, 57). "Not that any man hath seen the Father, save he that is from God, he hath seen the Father" (vi, 46). "The Father knoweth me, and I know the Father" (x, 15). "I and the Father are one. The Father is in me, and I in the Father" (x, 30, 38). In view of such expressions of his conscious oneness with God his Father, well might the officers sent to arrest him declare, "Never man so spake" (vii, 46), and well might the author of the fourth gospel write: "No man hath seen God at any time; the only begotten Son, who is in the bosom of the Father, he hath declared him" (i, 18).

3. His Sense of Subordination. It is perhaps no less striking that this consciousness of God is accompanied also with a sense of subordination, limitation, and dependence. It is remarkable that the fourth gospel, which abounds in the loftiest teaching of his preëxistence, his oneness with God, and his authority to judge the world, contains the most positive assertions of this subordination. "I can of myself do nothing"; "The Son can do nothing of himself, but what he seeth the Father doing" (v, 19, 30). "As the Father hath given me commandment, even so I do." "The

Father is greater than I" (xiv, 28, 31). He acknowledges the limitation of his knowledge in Mark xiii, 32, and Matt. xxiv, 36. He tells the ambitious sons of Zebedee that "to sit on my right hand, and on my left hand, is not mine to give; but it is for them for whom it hath been prepared of my Father" (Matt. xx, 23). His praying unto the Father, his agony and strong crying in Gethsemane, his wail of abandonment on the cross, and his final commending of his spirit to the Father (Luke xxiii, 46), all imply a noteworthy subordination and dependence, which are the more remarkable by reason of his many other expressions of the consciousness of superhuman power. Could he not beseech the Father and obtain the help of "more than twelve legions of angels"? (Matt. xxvi, 53.)

4. Consciousness of Commitment to a Purpose of the Ages. This last citation, however, connects with the intimation of a conscious self-commitment to fulfill a divine purpose of the ages already written in the Scriptures: "How then should the scriptures be fulfilled, that thus it must be?" The same chapter of Matthew (vers. 24, 56) records as sayings of Jesus, "The Son of man goeth, even as it is written of him," and "all this is come to pass, that the scriptures of the prophets might be fulfilled." This consciousness of his personal connection with a divine, eternal purpose of God finds repeated expression in the gospels. While yet only twelve years old he was feeling the pressure of some kind of a necessity ($\delta\epsilon\tilde{\iota}$) to be about his heavenly Father's business (Luke ii, 49). Later he declared to the multitude: "I *must* preach the gospel of the kingdom of God to the other cities also" (Luke iv, 43). Over and over again he repeated the word, "The Son of man *must* suffer, be rejected, be killed, and after three days rise again" (Mark viii, 31; comp. Luke ix, 22; xiii, 33; xvii, 25; xxii, 37; xxiv, 7, 26, 44, 46; John ix, 4; xx, 9). A self-commitment to the conditions of an eternal purpose of love involved no compulsion, as from without, or any infringement of the pure personal freedom of the Lord Jesus. He freely accepted the mission of the accomplishment of the blessed work, and his oft-expressed consciousness of the holy obligation is as marvelous as his obedience unto the death of the cross.

5. Consciousness of Preëxistence. The consciousness of his commitment to the great purpose of the ages accords with all the sayings of Jesus that imply preëxistence. These sayings are peculiar to the fourth gospel, and have a logical connection with the doctrine of the Logos, who became flesh, and manifested a "glory as of the only begotten from the Father" (i, 14). The Son of man speaks of his descending out of heaven, as one "whom the

Father sanctifieth and sent into the world" (iii, 13; x, 36). "I am come down from heaven," he says (vi, 38); "I am from above; I am not of this world; I came forth and am come from God; before Abraham was born, I am; I came out from the Father, and am come into the world; again, I leave the world and go unto the Father" (viii, 23, 42, 58; xvi, 28). When some of his disciples questioned his mystic sayings he said to them: "Does this cause you to stumble? What then if ye should behold the Son of man ascending where he was before" (vi, 62). Most remarkable are those passages in his prayer where he says, "Glorify thou me with the glory which I had with thee before the world was; thou didst send me into the world; thou lovedst me before the foundation of the world" (xvii, 5, 18, 24). All these utterances express a consciousness of heavenly life and glory with the Father before his manifestation in the flesh. And they also add significance to the words addressed to Philip, in xiv, 9, 10: "He that hath seen me hath seen the Father; I am in the Father, and the Father in me"; and to the similar utterance in xii, 45: "He that beholdeth me beholdeth him that sent me." Whatever element of theosophic mysticism, or of idealism is recognized in this language, none can ignore the transcendent consciousness of æonic union with God which it implies.

6. Conscious Freedom from Sin. Here should be mentioned also our Lord's unbroken consciousness of complete freedom from sin. This appears not alone from the open challenge to his enemies, "Which of you convicteth me of sin?" (John viii, 46.) It is a standing feature of his whole life from the beginning. His manner, his words, his works, his exposure of the evil leaven of the Pharisees, his disclosure of the real depths and extent to which the prohibitions of murder and adultery in the decalogue penetrate, his showing that all evil thoughts and deeds originate in the heart of man and defile him, his extolling of the blessedness of the pure in heart, the utter failure of all the efforts of his enemies to prove him guilty of any fault whatever—all these facts are indicative of his sinlessness and of his consciousness of the same. All this accords perfectly with the testimony of his one supreme purpose and desire to accomplish the will of the holy and righteous Father. The words of Psa. xl, 8, as construed in Heb. x, 7-9, are a beautiful and striking statement of the fact itself: "Lo, I am come to do thy will, O God." And so we read in John v, 30: "I seek not mine own will, but the will of him that sent me." And again in vi, 38: "I am come down from heaven, not to do mine own will, but the will of him that sent me." This exalted devotion to the will of God and ever-present consciousness of doing that will, place the whole life work of the Son of God in a glory peculiarly sublime.

7. Consciousness of Being Saviour of Men. Deserving of particular notice are also those sayings of Jesus which express his consciousness of being the Saviour of men. The angels announced him as "a Saviour, who is Christ the Lord" (Luke ii, 11), and his name Jesus implied "that he shall save his people from their sins" (Matt. i, 21). His own words are, according to Luke xix, 10, "the Son of man came to seek and to save that which was lost." All his mighty works of healing were especially illustrative of his gracious purpose in coming into the world, and the record of them in our gospels enables us to study them as so many typical examples of what he is continually doing through the ministry of his Spirit in the salvation of men from sin and spiritual death. How wonderful his consciousness of power over nature when "he arose and rebuked the winds and the sea; and there was a great calm"! (Matt. viii, 26) or when he stood over Simon's wife's mother "and rebuked the fever, and it left her"! (Luke iv, 39.) In like manner he rebuked the demons (Luke iv, 35, 41; ix, 42). Where can we find anything more touchingly sublime than his manner toward the leper who kneeled down to him and said, "If thou wilt, thou canst make me clean. Being moved with compassion, he stretched forth his hand, and touched him, and said unto him, I will; be thou made clean"! (Mark i, 41.) How he silenced the narrow, sabbatic notions of the Pharisees by the majestic challenge, "Is it lawful on the sabbath day to do good, or to do harm? to save a life, or to kill?" (Mark iii, 4.) His words, his action, and his manner all breathed the consciousness that he was "lord even of the sabbath day." We discern the evidence of like superhuman consciousness when he says to the critical scribes, "The Son of man hath authority on earth to forgive sins" (Mark ii, 10). In perfect accordance with this lofty assumption of authority are those sayings in the fourth gospel in which he declares himself the life and the light of the world. "This is the will of my Father, that every one that beholdeth the Son and believeth on him, should have eternal life; and I will raise him up at the last day. . . . I am the living bread which came down out of heaven: if any man eat of this bread, he shall live forever" (vi, 40, 51). "I am the light of the world: he that followeth me shall not walk in the darkness, but shall have the light of life," "When I am in the world I am the light of the world," "I am come a light into the world, that whosoever believeth on me may not abide in the darkness" (viii, 12; ix, 5; xii, 46). "I am the resurrection and the life: he that believeth on me, though he die, yet shall he live; and whosoever liveth and believeth on me shall never die" (xi, 25, 26). The personality that was thus "anointed with the Holy Spirit and with power, and went about doing good" (Acts x, 38), and time and again gave expression to such marvelous words, transcends immeasurably all other men. The self-consciousness that speaks calmly and naturally of such relations to God, and of such a heavenly power to save men from darkness and sin and death, and bring them into the life and light of God himself, is truly awe-inspiring. Such a revealer of God might well say, "He that hath seen me hath seen the Father" (John xiv, 9). Such a "Son of the Blessed" might well speak of himself as we read in Matt. xi, 27, and then add the words that imply a consciousness of power to give heavenly comfort and peace: "Come unto me, all ye that labor and are heavy laden, and I will give you rest."

8. Consciousness of His Messiahship. Finally, we observe the consciousness of his Messianic dignity and destiny which finds great variety of self-expression in the gospels. It has long been a question among the theologians when and how Jesus first came to know himself the Christ of God. Many have inclined to believe that the revelation first came to him at the time of his baptism, when the voice out of heaven pronounced him the beloved Son, in whom the Father was well pleased. We doubt, however, the wisdom of attempting so definite an answer to the question. In the absence of any testimony of Jesus himself on this point it seems presumptuous to say when and how such a conviction arose in his soul. It would seem that already, at twelve years of age, he was divinely gifted to discern that he "must be about his Father's business," and it is reasonable to suppose that, as he advanced in wisdom and in the grace of God, he came by degrees to know more and more clearly the significance of his coming into the world. The Messianic consciousness of Jesus may be conceived as including all the various forms we have so far mentioned, namely, a living consciousness of God, and of subordination to the will of the Father, in harmony with an eternal purpose of accomplishing the regeneration of the world. Along with this came out occasional intimations of preëxistence in the bosom of God, of conscious freedom from all taint of sin, and of being the Saviour of the world.[1] These all enter into the Messianic work, as conceived by Jesus

---

[1] Such convictions are not to be regarded as results reached after a process of reflection. Rather, as Baldensperger has observed, "the Messianic resolution of Jesus was not called forth by means of intellectual reasonings; on the contrary, it was rather a direct revelation within the marvelous depths of his religious spirit-life, by which his person was overwhelmingly and immediately smitten as by an electric shock." Das Selbstbewusstsein Jesu, p. 164. Strassburg, 1888.

himself, and all these facts together give the greater significance and propriety to his chosen title of Son of man. He knows himself as having come from heaven, and as being so identified with the highest interests of man, as those interests can only be secured in accordance with obedience to the truth, that he can say, "Whosoever shall do the will of God, the same is my brother, and sister, and mother" (Mark iii, 35).

(1) *Assumed in his Fulfilling Law and Prophets.* The consciousness of Messianic authority speaks out in those sayings in which he assumes to fulfill the Law and the Prophets, and to show that even the weightiest commandments of the decalogue are not fully obeyed in the mere observance of the letter. He gave to murder and adultery and swearing a profounder definition than any Jew of his time had thought, and he positively set aside the old Mosaic statutes of retaliation, and proclaimed the higher law of "Love your enemies." He assumes to be a preacher and prophet greater than Jonah, and gifted with a wisdom greater than Solomon (Matt. xii, 41, 42). He showed himself greater than Elijah when he rebuked the disciples who would have called down fire from heaven to consume the inhospitable Samaritans (Luke ix, 54, 55). The tone of authority which characterized all his teaching was that of the Messenger of a new covenant, who said, as if expressing a thought that was ever present with him, "The Father loveth the Son, and hath given all things into his hand" (John iii, 35).

(2) *Directly Acknowledged.* The direct expression or acknowledgment of his Messiahship appears in those texts in which he asks his disciples the opinion of the people concerning himself. When Simon Peter confessed him as "the Christ, the Son of the living God," he anwered with no little emotion: "Blessed art thou, Simon Bar-Jonah; for flesh and blood hath not revealed it unto thee, but my Father who is in heaven" (Matt. xvi, 17). He thus declared Simon a partaker of divine revelation on this question, and a living stone or rock on which his Church was to be builded. In Luke's gospel (ix, 20) he is pronounced "the Christ of God," and in a passage of John's gospel (vi, 69), Peter says, "We have believed and know that thou art the Holy One of God." In the same chapter (ver. 27) Jesus speaks of himself as "the Son of man, whom the Father, even God, hath sealed." That is, the Father had confirmed and authenticated his Messianic ministry by the heavenly approval given at his baptism and the many "works of God" which he had performed. This reached a climax when he rode triumphantly into Jerusalem, and the multitude of his disciples saluted him, saying, "Blessed is the King that cometh in the name of the Lord." The Pharisees would have had him

rebuke such noisy demonstration, but he answered: "If these should hold their peace, the stones would cry out" (Luke xix, 40).

(3) *Indicated in his Doctrine of the Kingdom.* His doctrine of the kingdom of God led him again and again to indicate his conscious relation to that kingdom as the Messianic ruler and judge. The mysteries of the kingdom of heaven are familiar to him, and it is his delight to impart them to the inquiring souls who love the truth. His parables illustrative of the kingdom not only show his own knowledge of the mysteries of God, but deeply confirm his right to be acknowledged as the Messianic King, anointed to preach good tidings to the poor, proclaim the release of captives, restore sight to the blind, set the bruised at liberty, and proclaim the year of Jehovah's grace, the beginning of a new era, even as the prophets had written (Luke iv, 18-21). The eschatological element in his doctrine of the kingdom is especially noteworthy. He spoke of the end or consummation of the age when "the Son of man shall send forth his angels, and they shall gather out of his kingdom all things that cause stumbling, and them that do iniquity" (Matt. xiii, 41; comp. xxiv, 30, 31; Mark xiii, 26, 27). He said that some of those who stood by him should "in no wise taste of death, till they had seen the kingdom of God come with power" (Mark ix, 1). In the presence of the high priest, where the scribes and elders of the Jews were assembled, he uttered the memorable words: "Henceforth ye shall see the Son of man sitting at the right hand of Power, and coming on the clouds of heaven" (Matt. xxvi, 63; Mark xiv, 62). He told his disciples that "in the regeneration, when the Son of man shall sit on the throne of his glory, ye also shall sit upon twelve thrones, judging the twelve tribes of Israel" (Matt. xix, 28). What prophetic vision and what majestic consciousness of wisdom and power in his language in Luke x, 18, 19: "I beheld Satan fallen as lightning from heaven. Behold, I have given you authority to tread upon serpents and scorpions, and over all the power of the enemy; and nothing shall in any wise hurt you." The portrayal of the Son of man sitting on the throne of his glory and executing judgment upon all the nations (Matt. xxv, 31-46) accords with the sayings in John's gospel that the Father "has given all judgment unto the Son," and "given him authority to execute judgment, because he is Son of man" (v, 22, 27). In him also is the power of the resurrection, and "all that are in the tombs shall hear his voice, and shall come forth" (v, 28). Especially calm and yet of supernatural import are his words in John xiv, 1-3: "Let not your heart be troubled: believe in God, believe also in me. In my Father's house are many mansions. . . . I go to prepare a place

for you. And . . . I come again and receive you unto myself." He speaks with the consciousness of being Lord of both worlds, and as no one can well be conceived as speaking unless, as he said of himself, he had descended out of heaven and was, even on earth, as one who was also in the heaven (John iii, 13). After his own resurrection, according to Matt. xxviii, 18, 19, he associated his name with that of the Father and the Holy Spirit, and said: "All authority hath been given unto me in heaven and on earth."

9. Significance of This Consciousness. The significance of all these varied expressions of the self-consciousness of our Lord is their witness to his transcendent personality. No other man ever spoke like this, for no other ever possessed such consciousness of immediate fellowship with God and of superhuman relationship to the mysteries of earth and heaven. One might conceive a superior philosopher and poet, gifted with deep religious instinct and with a bold imagination, constructing such ideals of a personal life out of many possible sources; but these self-expressions of the consciousness of Jesus Christ have an unmistakable historic background. They all center in a divine-human personality from which there is no getting away. That the first disciples of Jesus, or those who succeeded them for two or three generations, created such a character out of their own extravagant ideals of what the Christ should be, is a hypothesis utterly inadequate to meet all the facts of the life of Jesus and all these diversified expressions of his Messianic consciousness. In fair view of all the facts such a hypothesis is unthinkable. The only solution which fully accounts for such a marvelous self-revelation of the most influential person that ever appeared in this world is that which the Christian faith of the centuries has acknowledged both in creed and in song. Such words, such thoughts, such calm consciousness of being at home alike in the heavens and in the earth, such sense of subordination as to be able to do nothing without the Father, yet united with a power and authority to lay down his life and to take it again—these and like expressions of transcendent being find rational explanation only in the faith that Jesus Christ was the veritable incarnation of the mystery of God (1 Tim. iii, 16). The earliest confessions and worship of the Christians recognized in that mystery an adorable Personality,

> Who was manifest in the flesh,
> Was justified in the spirit,
> Was seen of angels,
> Was preached among the nations,
> Was believed on in the world,
> Was received up in glory.

CHAPTER V

CHRISTOLOGY OF THE FIRST APOSTLES AND OF THE GENERAL EPISTLES

1. Sources of Information. Thus far our study of the person of Christ has been directed mainly to the facts of his life and to his self-expression as recorded in the gospels, especially the synoptic gospels. Our next step will be to inquire after the earliest apostolic teaching, and our sources of information are a few passages in the Acts of the apostles and in the epistles of James, Peter, and Jude. The date of these writings is a very open question, and most of them are doubtless later than the principal Pauline epistles; but, so far as they present a doctrine of the person of Jesus Christ, they appear to reflect the popular conceptions of the apostolic age. They are, accordingly, a class of witnesses which may be best examined before we proceed to the more elaborate teaching found in other New Testament writings.

2. The Preaching of Peter. The first recorded example of apostolic preaching is Peter's sermon on the day of Pentecost (Acts ii, 14-40). The speaker regards himself and his hearers as living "in the last days," about which Joel had prophesied, and he represents "Jesus the Nazarene" as "a man approved of God by mighty works and wonders and signs which God did by him." The close agreement of this description of Jesus with that made by the same apostle in Acts x, 38, is noteworthy: "Jesus of Nazareth whom God anointed with the Holy Spirit and with power: who went about doing good, and healing all that were oppressed of the devil; for God was with him." It is also worthy of our attention that the gospel according to Mark, which early tradition ascribes largely to Peter, is in striking harmony with this simple but comprehensive statement. When this apostle healed the lame man at the door of the temple, he did it "in the name of Jesus Christ the Nazarene" (Acts iii, 6); and also when he exhorted his convicted hearers to repent and be baptized he assumed and said that it must be done "in the name of Jesus Christ" (ii, 38). It is to be noticed, further, that Peter proclaims this Jesus of Nazareth as crucified, raised up from the dead, and exalted by the right hand of God (ii, 23, 32, 33). Thus he affirms and confirms the great facts attested in the gospels, and makes them fundamental in his preaching. He affirms "that God hath made this Jesus both Lord and Christ" (ii, 36), and he calls him God's glorified Servant (or *Child,* παῖδα) Jesus, "the Holy and Righteous One," "the Prince (or *Author* ἀρχηγός) of life" (iii, 13-15). It was impossible, he says, that this Christ of God should be permanently held fast in the bonds of death (ii, 24). But God raised him up, "and exalted him at his right hand to be a Prince and a Saviour, to give repentance to Israel, and remission of sins" (v, 30, 31). He furthermore declares that the exalted Christ had received of the Father the promised Holy Spirit, and had poured forth that marvelous affusion of heavenly power, whose effects they had themselves witnessed, and which was of a nature to make that day of Pentecost forever memorable in Christian history (ii, 33). He teaches also that the delivering up of Jesus to his enemies and the crucifixion, although accomplished by the hands of lawless men, were in accordance with "the determinate counsel and foreknowledge of God" (ii, 23). It was part and parcel of the divine purpose and mystery of the ages, of which Jesus himself had often spoken. We should observe how this accords with what is written in Luke xxiv, 26, 46-49, that "the Christ must suffer, must rise, must enter into his glory, and send forth the promise of the Father." That all this is part of the great purpose of ages and generations is furthermore declared in Acts iii, 21, where we are told that the heaven must receive this Christ Jesus "until the times of restoration of all things, whereof God spoke by the mouth of his holy prophets that have been from of old." In Acts x, 42, Peter makes the further statement that he and his fellow apostles were "charged to preach unto the people and to testify that this risen Christ is he who is ordained of God to be the Judge of the living and the dead." These various sayings of Peter, as they are reported in the Acts, seem very fragmentary, but it is remarkable how full a presentation they give of the person of Jesus Christ. The Christ whom this apostle preached is identical with the Christ of the gospel of Mark. He is the Messiah in whom God declares himself well pleased. His life is made famous by the wonders and mighty works which he performed. He went about doing good. He was crucified, raised up, and exalted to the right hand of the Father, and made the Prince of life. "In none other is there salvation; for neither is there any other name under heaven, that is given among men, wherein we must be saved" (Acts iv, 12). He is the King and Disposer of the ages, accomplishing the eternal purposes of God, the righteous and holy Judge of the living and the dead. This preaching of Peter, so simple, direct, and comprehensive, amounts to nothing less than a glorification and even a deification of Jesus. He does not call him God, but he proclaims him as the Anointed Son and Saviour who rules in heaven and on earth and does the works of God.

3. The First Epistle of Peter. In the first epistle of Peter we find comparatively little concerning the person of Christ which does not appear in the preaching reported in the Acts. What is written therein on the subject contains no different type of doctrine. The trinitarian element which appears in the first two verses of the first epistle is remarkable: "Foreknowledge of God the Father, sanctification of the Spirit, and sprinkling of the blood of Jesus Christ." These three are mentioned together in Acts ii, 32, 33, but in a less formal manner. The third verse of the epistle is a brief but beautifully comprehensive statement of the apostolic gospel: "Blessed be the God and Father of our Lord Jesus Christ, who according to his great mercy begat us again unto a living hope by the resurrection of Jesus Christ from the dead." Here Jesus is both Lord and Christ, risen from the dead, and begetting a living hope in them that love and obey him. In iii, 22, he is said to be "on the right hand of God, having gone into heaven; angels and authorities and powers being made subject unto him." He is called "the Shepherd and Bishop of souls," and "the Chief Shepherd" (ii, 25; v, 4). Repeated reference is made to the sufferings of Christ, and he is called "a living stone, rejected indeed of men, but with God elect, precious" (ii, 4). He has left us an example to follow as those who walk in the steps of one "who did no sin, neither was guile found in his mouth" (ii, 22). He is also spoken of as "a lamb without blemish and without spot, who was foreknown before the foundation of the world but was manifested at the end of the times" (i, 19, 20). Reference is also made to a future "revelation of Jesus Christ," "the revelation of his glory" (i, 7, 13; iv, 13). Believers are called upon to sanctify Christ in their hearts as Lord (iii, 15), and to "set their hope perfectly on the grace that is to be brought unto them" at the time of that future glorious revelation of the Lord. That revelation involves "eternal glory in Christ" (i, 13; v, 10), "whom not having seen ye love; on whom, though now ye see him not, yet believing, ye rejoice greatly with joy unspeakable and full of glory, receiving the end of your faith, even the salvation of your souls" (i, 8, 9).

4. Second Peter and Jude. The second epistle of Peter and that of Jude contain very little that bears distinctive witness to the person of Christ. They both appear to belong to a later time than that of the first epistle of Peter, and what they say of the

Lord Jesus is of the most general character. The epistle of Jude is generally believed to be the earlier of the two, and forms the basis of second Peter, the second chapter of which is largely fashioned after the more original and vigorous writing of Jude. In this brief letter Jesus Christ is called "the only Master (δεσπότης) and our Lord Jesus Christ" (vers. 4, 17, 21, 25). Those who are "called and beloved in God the Father" are firmly "kept for Jesus Christ" (ver. 1), but must also "keep themselves in the love of God, looking for the mercy of our Lord Jesus Christ unto eternal life" (ver. 21). The ascription of "glory, majesty, dominion, and power to the only God our Saviour through Jesus Christ our Lord" (ver. 25) clearly recognizes God as the Saviour, and Christ as the Mediator of his glory and grace. In 2 Peter we meet with the phrases, *the righteousness of our God and Saviour Jesus Christ, the knowledge of our Lord Jesus Christ, the eternal kingdom of our Lord and Saviour Jesus Christ, the power and coming of our Lord Jesus Christ, and the grace and knowledge of our Lord and Saviour Jesus Christ* (i, 1, 8, 11, 16; ii, 20; iii, 18). These ascriptions of knowledge, salvation, and power to Jesus Christ imply his exaltation at the right hand of God and associate him with God. The old contention that, because the grammatical construction of the words *our God and Saviour Jesus Christ,* in i, 1, is the same as *our Lord and Saviour Jesus Christ,* in iii, 18, therefore this writer calls Jesus God as well as Lord and Saviour, cannot be fairly maintained; for not only is the translation "our God and the Saviour" conceded as entirely proper, and adopted in the American Standard Revision, but the statement, in i, 17, that Jesus "received from God the Father honor and glory, when there was borne such a voice to him by the Majestic Glory, This is my beloved Son, in whom I am well pleased," shows that the author of this epistle conceived the beloved Son as holding a subordinate relation to God the Father. Nevertheless, it must also be conceded that the construction of the words *our God and Saviour* so as to make them both refer to Jesus Christ is grammatically both possible and proper.

5. The Epistle of James. The epistle of James makes only a few references to the person of Christ, but those few are sufficient to indicate the author's thoroughly worshipful devotion to "the Lord Jesus Christ" (i, 1; ii, 1), of whom he declares himself a bondservant. The aim of the epistle is conspicuously practical and finds no occasion to speak particularly of Jesus, but it recognizes "the faith of our Lord Jesus Christ" (ii, 1) as a regulative principle of all true Christian life. This faith centers in the Lord Jesus as "the Lord of glory." The grammatical construction of the genitive τῆς δόξης, *of glory,* in this last clause has puzzled interpreters, and is confessedly obscure; but that adopted in the current English versions seems on the whole the best, and is made emphatic by repeating the word *Lord* immediately before these words. We may, however, understand these last words as an adjectival genitive qualifying the entire phrase preceding, and translate accordingly, "the faith of our glorious Lord Jesus Christ." He is glorious in his exaltation, and like God himself has no respect of persons, but "chooses them that are poor as to the world to be rich in faith, and heirs of the kingdom which he has promised to them that love him" (ii, 5). According to this epistle, "the coming of the Lord is near at hand" (v, 8), whence we infer that the author accepted the current belief of the first apostles that their Lord was enthroned in glory and would soon come again to judge the world. The doctrine of these catholic epistles and of the preaching of Peter is thus seen to be in harmony with the portraiture of Christ found in the synoptic gospels. The preaching of Stephen and of Philip, as may be inferred from Acts vi, 14; vii, 52-59; viii, 12, 35, was of the same general type, and aimed to magnify "the Name" (Acts v, 41, 42). The doctrine of the three epistles of John will be more properly considered in connection with the Johannine Christology.

CHAPTER VI

THE CHRIST OF JOHN'S APOCALYPSE

1. Date and Composition of the Book. One may well hesitate in determining the date and rank of the Christology of the New Testament Apocalypse. The present trend of expert criticism is to recognize a variety of sources and older fragments of a somewhat heterogeneous character out of which the book in its present form has been compiled and wrought over into a perceptible unity of plan. The two passages in the book itself which indicate its date are xi, 1, 2, and xvii, 10, from which one naturally infers that the Jewish temple was yet standing and Nero was emperor of Rome. The riddle of "the number of the beast" in xiii, 18, is also best explained by the numerical value of the Hebrew letters in the name Nero Cæsar (נרון קסר), which when added together make the sum of six hundred and sixty-six. The external evidence, however, has been quite generally understood as fixing the date near the close of Domitian's reign (about A.D. 96), and it is overwhelmingly strong and uniform in assigning the authorship to John, the son of Zebedee, the disciple of Jesus. It is noteworthy that the apostolic origin of no book of the New Testament is better attested by external evidence than that of this Apocalypse of John. But it may be that the work is composite, and that, like most of the numerous Jewish apocalypses dating all the way from B.C. 175 to A.D. 200, it has appropriated elements of earlier writings. The apostle John himself might have done this, and it is a noteworthy fact that there is scarcely a figure or a symbol in this New Testament Revelation which may not be traced to some corresponding idea written in the Old Testament.[1] So far as it represents a distinctive Christology, we shall regard it as an apocalyptic portraiture of the same Son of man who is described in the synoptic gospels as "coming on the clouds of heaven with power and great glory" (comp. Matt. xxiv, 30, and Rev. i, 7). The Christ of this prophecy is the one who was dead, but is risen to the throne of God and "holds the keys of death and Hades." He is "ruler of the kings of the earth," and his throne is the throne of God. In all these conceptions the Christ

---

[1] For what may be said in favor of the apostolic origin and early date of the book, see Biblical Apocalyptics, pp. 253 ff. For the critical discussions see the Encyclopædia Biblica, Art. Apocalypse, and the literature mentioned therein.

of the Apocalypse is identical with the Messiah of the earliest apostolic preaching. But the author's manner of describing the supreme majesty and glory of Jesus Christ is confessedly visional.

2. The Christophany of i, 12-16. The Christophany described in i, 12-16, is a most impressive picture of the Son of man, and its details are appropriated mainly from Dan. vii, 9, 10. His garment and girdle, his forehead and hair white as wool and as snow, his flaming eyes, his feet like burnished brass, his voice like that of many waters, the sword proceeding from his mouth, and his countenance like the dazzling sunlight, are all indicative of a supernatural Being. When, now, this august personage declares himself to be "the first and the last," "the Living One," once dead but now alive for the ages of ages, we cannot mistake the purpose of the writer to honor and glorify this Son even as he would honor the Father Almighty (comp. John v, 23), for he applies to him attributes which the Old Testament prophets apply to Jehovah.

3. The Lamb in the Midst of the Throne. It should also be noted how conspicuously the Christ is associated in the visions of this seer with the throne of God. In v, 6, he appears as "a Lamb in the midst of the throne" (comp. vii, 17). His position was so in the midview of the throne and the Lamb himself was so related to "him that sat on the throne," that the throne itself is called in xxii, 1, "the throne of God and of the Lamb." This Lamb is no other than the "one like unto a son of man" in the Christophany of i, 12-16, and who says in iii, 21, "I overcame, and sat down with my Father in his throne." The symbolism of "a Lamb standing as though it had been slain," has unmistakable reference to the redemptive work of the Saviour of men, whom he "purchased unto God with his blood" (v, 9), but our interest at present is only with his exalted position at the throne of heaven. This conception is most naturally connected with the uniform apostolic teaching that Jesus, the Christ, has ascended into heaven and is enthroned at the right hand of God, where, according to Paul (Rom. viii, 34), he "maketh intercession for us." So the Apocalypse of John, like the preaching of Peter and of others, exalts Christ to the right hand of God, to share his throne, and to be "a Prince and a Saviour" (Acts v, 31). It is also worthy of note that this Lamb of the Apocalypse has seven horns, symbols of perfection of power, "and seven eyes, which are the seven Spirits of God sent forth into all the earth" (v, 6). The seven Spirits of God have been already described as so many "lamps of fire burning before the throne" (iv, 5), and being here identified with the seven eyes of the Lamb, we infer that the writer associated the thought of perfection of wisdom as well as perfection of power with the Lamb. The seven Spirits of God are the Spirit of the Lamb just as the throne of God is the throne of the Lamb.

4. His Titles, Glory, Triumphs, and Worship. This "revelation of Jesus Christ" is remarkable for the number and variety of significant titles ascribed to him. He is "the Alpha and the Omega," "the first and the last," "the faithful and true witness," "the beginning of the creation of God," "the Lion of the tribe of Judah, the Root of David," "the Word of God," "King of kings and Lord of lords," "the root and the offspring of David, the bright, the morning star." He appears also in the visions as a mighty angel coming down out of heaven, arrayed with a cloud and a rainbow, and "his face was as the sun, and his feet as pillars of fire" (x, 1). He is seen standing on Mount Zion with twelve times twelve thousand of his holy ones (xiv, 1), and also sitting on a white cloud, like a son of man, having a golden crown and a sharp sickle (xiv, 14). He appears also as a heavenly conqueror sitting on a white horse, followed by the armies of heaven, wearing many diadems, smiting the nations and ruling them with a rod of iron (xix, 11 ff.). Along with God he receives the worship of all the hosts of earth and heaven (v, 8-13; vii, 9, 10).

5. The Grand Total Impression of the Revelation. It is not necessary to put forward any theory or exposition of this remarkable Apocalypse in order to perceive its witness to the adorable personage, whose name stands at the beginning, and whose relation to the throne of God is made so prominent throughout. Nor need we enter here upon any discussion of peculiar verbal expressions, or of the various symbols employed by the writer. It is quite sufficient to appeal to the grand total impression which this apocalyptical revelation of Jesus Christ must needs make upon any appreciative reader. The transcendent personality, whom the author of this book adored, is exalted into heavenly splendor, is "in the midst of the throne of God," and receives ascriptions of blessing and honor and glory and dominion from "every created thing which is in the heaven, and on the earth, and on the sea, and all things that are in them" (v, 13). But it is his great purpose and desire to restore men to the tree of life and the "Paradise of God" (ii, 7). His messages to the churches are salutations of grace and peace, but he also executes judgment in righteousness. His ultimate aim is to make all things new (xxi, 5); hence his authority is over heaven and earth; he is seated on his Father's throne (iii, 21), and the kingdom of the world is to become his own (xi, 15). This doctrine of the Apocalypse is in essential harmony with Paul's conception of the rule of Christ, "He must reign, till he hath put all his enemies under his feet" (1 Cor. xv, 25).

CHAPTER VII

THE PAULINE CHRISTOLOGY

1. Significance of Paul's Conversion. In the study of the Pauline portraiture of Jesus Christ we are impressed from first to last with the fact that the revelation of Jesus, which came to him at the time of his conversion, was a most decisive inner experience, and the memory of it ever afterward stood forth as a living vision in his soul. The reader should carefully study and compare the narratives in Acts ix, 3-9, 17-19; xxii, 6-16; xxvi, 12-20, with the statements of 1 Cor. ix, 1; xv, 8; Gal. i, 12, 16; and Eph. iii, 3. That revelation worked a radical crisis in his religious nature, and during all his subsequent life Paul seemed "determined not to know anything save Jesus Christ and him crucified" (1 Cor. ii, 2). His uniform testimony was, "It is Christ Jesus that died, yea, rather, that was raised from the dead, who is at the right hand of God, who also maketh intercession for us" (Rom. viii, 34). This revelation was like a voice out of heaven speaking in his soul with an authority he could never question. To his thought thereafter God was in Christ and Christ was a new and deeper revelation of God than he had known before. In all his epistles he associates the names of "God the Father and the Lord Jesus Christ." With slight variations we find these holy names thus placed together both in the salutations with which his epistles open, and in the benedictions with which they close. God and Christ are existing in one superior glory, and are the source of "grace and peace." In 2 Cor. xiii, 14, we have the trinitarian formula: "The grace of the Lord Jesus Christ, and the love of God, and the communion of the Holy Spirit, be with you all." Unlike the formula of Matt. xxviii, 19, the name of the Lord Jesus here precedes that of God, the Father.

2. The Thessalonian Epistles. The Thessalonian epistles make prominent the coming of the Lord Jesus from heaven, and by various allusions they represent him as the Son of God, raised from the dead, having power to deliver men from the wrath to come, and to gather together all who have salvation in him and catch them away to meet him in the heavens (1 Thess. i, 10; ii, 19; iii, 13; iv, 14-17; v, 23). There is to be a "revelation of the Lord Jesus from heaven with the angels of his power in flaming fire, rendering vengeance to them that know not God, and to them that obey not the gospel of our Lord Jesus" (2 Thess. i, 7, 8; comp. Psa. lxix, 6; Jer. x, 25; Isa. lxvi, 14, 15). "He will take away the man of sin with the breath of his mouth (ii, 8; comp. Isa. xi, 4; Job iv, 9; Dan. vii, 11, 26), but he will glorify his saints, establish them, and guard them from the evil one, and direct their hearts into the love of God, and the obtaining of the glory of our Lord Jesus Christ" (ii, 14; iii, 3, 5, 16). From all of which it is evident that the Lord Jesus, as set forth in these earliest epistles of Paul, is Lord of heaven and earth, and exercises divine judgment and power in the administration of the kingdom of God. All this accords perfectly with the doctrine of the earliest apostolic preaching.

3. The Corinthian Epistles. At the beginning of the first epistle to the Corinthians we have "the name of our Lord Jesus Christ" presented as an object of worship to "all in every place who are sanctified in Christ Jesus and called to be saints." Further on (vers. 23, 24) it is said that "Christ crucified is to the Jews a stumblingblock and to the Gentiles foolishness, but unto them that are called, both Jews and Greeks, he is God's power and God's wisdom." To all such he becomes "wisdom from God, and righteousness, and sanctification, and redemption" (ver. 30). The gospel of Christ is "God's wisdom in a mystery," and they who have "the mind of Christ" have a knowledge of "the deep things of God" which worldlings cannot apprehend (ii, 6-16). "There is one God, the Father, of whom are all things; and one Lord, Jesus Christ, through whom are all things, and we through him" (viii, 6), and "Christ is God's" (iii, 23). He would have the Corinthians know "that the head of every man is Christ; and the head of the woman is the man; and the head of Christ is God" (xi, 3). The spiritual rock that followed Israel in the desert was Christ (x, 4). This Lord Jesus Paul recognizes as his own judge, who searches him through and through (ὁ ἀνακρίνων), and who in his own time will "bring to light the hidden things of darkness, and make manifest the counsels of the hearts" (iv, 4, 5). For he has a day of revelation, and before his tribunal every man must be made manifest according to his works (i, 7, 8; iii, 13; comp. 2 Cor. v, 10; Acts xvii, 31). He is the second Adam, the man from heaven, a life-giving spirit, who is to abolish death, and subject all things to God (xv, 22, 24-28, 45, 47). In the second epistle we are told that "the Son of God, Jesus Christ, who was preached among you by us, by me and Silvanus and Timothy, was not yea and nay, but in him is yea. For how many soever be the promises of God, in him (*i.e.*, Christ) is the yea: wherefore also through him is the Amen, unto the glory of God through us"[1] (i, 19, 20). In him the apostle and all saints find an unfailing source of inspiration unto every good word and work (ii, 12, 14, 17; xii, 19; xiii, 3, 4). His grace was shown in the fact "that, though he was rich, yet for your sakes he became poor, that ye through his poverty might become rich" (viii, 9). He is the image of God reflected as in a mirror to the adoring saint, who is thereby "transformed into the same image from glory to glory, even as from the Lord, the Spirit" (iii, 17, 18). That is, as the immediate context shows, the Lord Christ is the illuminating Spirit, through whom the veil of spiritual darkness is taken from the heart, and men are permitted to behold in him the glory of God. For the apostle goes on to say that "the illumination of the gospel of the glory of Christ, who is the image of God," is ready to beam on all such as do not permit their thoughts to be blinded through unbelief. "For it is God, that said, Out of darkness light shall shine, who shined in our hearts for an illumination of the knowledge of the glory of God in the face of Jesus Christ" (iv, 4-6). The glory that shined from the face of Moses by reason of his speaking with God was so overpowering "that the children of Israel could not look stedfastly" thereon (iii, 7; comp. Exod. xxxiv, 29); how much more excessive must be "the glory of God in the face of Jesus Christ"! It is as true now as in the time of Moses that man may not see the face of God and live (Exod. xxxiii, 20), but the doctrine of Paul (as of John i, 18) is that God has graciously provided a heavenly illumination by means of "the gospel of the glory of Christ," in which gospel, as in a mirror, the glory of God as it shines in the face of Jesus Christ is reflected, and we all "with unveiled face," beholding in that mirror the glory of the Lord, receive along with the blessed vision "the light of the knowledge of the glory of God."

4. The Epistle to the Galatians. The epistle to the Galatians, aside from the salutation and the benediction, and a few expressions common to all the epistles, contains little that bears directly on the doctrine of the person of Christ. We may note the emphasis with which its author speaks of the indwelling Christ who enables him to "live unto God. With Christ I have been crucified; and it is no longer I that live, but Christ lives in me: and that which I now live in the flesh I live in faith which is of the Son of God, who loved me and gave himself for me" (ii, 19, 20; comp.

---

[1] According to Meyer the distinction between *the yea* and *the amen* is that *the yea* denotes the certainty and confirmation *objectively* given in Christ, and *the amen* is the certainty *subjectively* existing, and which finds expression through the experience and ministry of the gospel. In Christ and through Christ are all God's promises certified so as to redound through us to the glory of God.

iv, 19). In iv, 4-6, he furnishes the definite concept of the Son of God as "sent forth," "born of a woman," "born under law," and providing that God might "send forth the Spirit of his Son into our hearts, crying, Abba, Father."

5. The Epistle to the Romans. The epistle to the Romans, like the one to the Galatians, deals mainly with the saving mediation of Christ, but there are several passages which refer to the person of Christ in a way that demands our attention. At the beginning of this epistle the apostle declares himself a bondservant of Jesus Christ, whom he describes (vers. 3 and 4) as "born of the seed of David according to the flesh, and declared the Son of God with power, according to the Spirit of holiness, by the resurrection of the dead." Here, as in Acts xiii, 29-39, the humiliation of Christ and his exaltation by the resurrection are designedly contrasted. Paul, like Peter (comp. Acts ii, 29-36), loved to think of his Lord as the son of David and heir of all the promises; not permitted to see corruption in the tomb, but raised up from the dead, and enthroned at the right hand of God (viii, 34). Thus was the Son of God placed beyond the power and dominion of death (vi, 9) so as to be "Lord of both the dead and the living" (xiv, 9). He is descended from the Israelite fathers according to the flesh, and, according to a time-honored punctuation and interpretation of Rom. ix, 5, he is also "over all, God blessed forever." Through him "will God judge the secrets of men" (ii, 16). In v, 12-21, he is set forth as the great antitype of Adam through whom sin entered into the world, for through Jesus Christ shall "grace reign through righteousness unto eternal life." He is "God's own Son, sent in the likeness of sinful flesh" (viii, 3), but he pleased not himself, and submitted to reproaches that he might receive his redeemed ones to the glory of God (xv, 3-7). Paul as his minister unto the Gentiles has great "glorying in Christ Jesus in things pertaining to God" (ver. 17), and he visits the churches "in the fulness of the blessing of Christ" (ver. 29). He begs his brethren "by our Lord Jesus Christ, and by the love of the Spirit" to join with him in "prayers to God" (ver. 30).

6. The Epistle to Philemon. In the short epistle to Philemon we may note the warmth with which Paul twice (vers. 1 and 9) calls himself a "prisoner of Christ Jesus," and also mentions Epaphras as his "fellow prisoner in Christ Jesus" (23). He praises the faith which Philemon has "toward the Lord Jesus" (5), and prays that it may become "effectual unto Christ" (6), and that his own heart may be refreshed "in Christ." He would fain receive profit of Philemon "in the Lord" (20), and he trusts that he will receive Onesimus "no longer as a slave, but more than a slave, a brother beloved both in the flesh and in the Lord" (16). This remarkable ideal of loving fellowship *in the Lord Christ* evinces a vivid concept of the divine and worshipful personality of the Lord, and illustrates the thought elsewhere (Col. iii, 3) expressed by the apostle of spiritual life hidden with Christ in God.

7. The Pastoral Epistles. In the pastoral epistles we find the true humanity of Jesus recognized in the statements that he was "manifested in the flesh" (1 Tim. iii, 16), and sprung "from the seed of David" (2 Tim. ii, 8). His preëxistence seems to be implied in the "faithful saying and worthy of all acceptation, that Christ Jesus came into the world to save sinners" (1 Tim. i, 15). In 1 Tim. ii, 5, we are told that "there is one God, one mediator also between God and men, himself man, Christ Jesus, who gave himself a ransom for all." In Gal. iii, 19, Moses is referred to as a mediator by whose agency the law was delivered to Israel; here the mediator is of a higher order, and the mediator offers himself up as a ransom for all men. When allusion is made, in 1 Tim. i, 11, to "the gospel of the glory of the blessed God," the writer immediately adds: "I thank him who has endued me with power, even Christ Jesus our Lord, because he counted me faithful, appointing me unto service." Here Christ Jesus is recognized as the Lord who is exalted in unspeakable glory, exercises a heavenly authority, and appoints men unto holy ministries. In 2 Tim. i, 1, Paul speaks of "the promise of the life which is in Christ Jesus," and, in verses 9 and 10, of the "purpose and grace, which was given us in Christ Jesus before times eternal, but hath now been manifested by the appearing of our Saviour Christ Jesus, who abolished death, and brought life and immortality to light through the gospel." The fact that Christ Jesus is "our Saviour" becomes the more noteworthy when we study the expressions, "God our Saviour, and Christ Jesus our hope" (1 Tim. i, 1); "our great God and Saviour Jesus Christ" (Titus ii, 13); "God our Saviour" (1 Tim. ii, 3; Titus ii, 10; iii, 4); "Jesus Christ our Saviour" (Titus iii, 6). This general and indiscriminate use of "God our Saviour," and "Jesus Christ our Saviour," shows that in the mind of the writer God and Christ are one in the ministry of salvation. According to 1 Tim. iv, 10, "the living God is the Saviour of all men, specially of them that believe"; but in v, 21, "God and Christ Jesus and the elect angels" are mentioned in holy and reverend association. Christ Jesus is also the final judge of the living and the dead (2 Tim. iv, 1, 8, 14), and his title and power as Lord are repeatedly acknowledged (1 Tim. i, 14; 2 Tim. i, 8; iii, 11; iv, 17, 18, 22). The great "mystery of godliness" (1 Tim. iii, 16) consists in the marvelous facts enumerated in the poetic confession:

> He was manifested in the flesh,
> Was justified in the Spirit,
> Was seen of angels,
> Was preached among the nations,
> Was believed on in the world,
> Was received up in glory.

Thus in the pastoral epistles the glory of Christ transcends that of any other being except the "One God," who, in 1 Tim. vi, 15, 16, is called "the blessed and only Potentate, the King of kings, and Lord of lords; who only hath immortality, dwelling in light unapproachable; whom no man hath seen, nor can see," and who will, in his own times, "show forth the appearing of our Lord Jesus Christ."

8. The Ephesian Epistle. The three Pauline epistles, which more than all others are entitled to be called Christological, are those to the Ephesians, the Philippians, and the Colossians. After the usual salutation the epistle to the Ephesians opens with a reminder that "every spiritual blessing in the heavenlies is in Christ, even as the God and Father of our Lord Jesus Christ chose us in him before the foundation of the world, that we should be holy and without blame before him" (i, 3, 4). The epistle abounds in references to "the mystery of his will," and the "good pleasure of his will," and of his eternal purpose "to sum up all things in Christ, things upon the heavens and things upon the earth" (i, 10). This summing up, or gathering together again for himself under one head (ἀνακεφαλαιώσασθαι, note the middle) all things in heaven and earth must needs involve such a disclosure of the character of "the God of our Lord Jesus Christ, the Father of glory" (i, 17) that one who apprehends and appreciates it will surely be gifted with "a spirit of wisdom and revelation in the knowledge of him." With this uplifting thought in his soul the apostle prays for his readers that the eyes of their heart may be enlightened in order that they may "know what is the hope of his calling, what the riches of the glory of his inheritance in the saints, and what the exceeding greatness of his power to us-ward who believe, according to the working of the strength of his might which he wrought in Christ, when he raised him from the dead and made him to sit at his right hand in the heavenlies, far above all rule, and authority, and power, and dominion, and every name that is named, not only in this world (or age), but also in that which is to come: and he put all things in subjection under his feet, and gave him to be head over all things to the church, which is his body, the fulness of him that filleth all in all" (i, 18-23). According to iii, 18, 19, if anyone is "strong to apprehend with all the saints what is the breadth and length and height and depth, and to know the love of Christ which passeth knowledge," he too "may be filled unto all the fulness of God." Believers are "created in Christ Jesus for good works" (ii, 10), and the Church is conceived as "the household of God, builded upon the foundation of the apostles and prophets, Christ Jesus himself being the chief corner stone; in whom each several building, fitly framed together, groweth into a holy sanctuary in the Lord" (ii, 19-21). As the husband is head of the wife, "so also is Christ the head of the church, being himself the Saviour of the body" (v, 23). The mystery of Christ and of his Church is great (v, 32), but the enlightened heart, described in i, 18, will delight in the study of these sacred truths, and will admire the apostle's revelation and "understanding in the mystery of Christ" (iii, 4). The shining of Christ upon the soul that awakes to spiritual life at his call is able to bring forth into the light all hidden things (v, 13, 14). And thus this epistle is unique in its mystic tone and in profound conceptions of God in Christ gathering unto himself a redeemed and glorious body of saints, and dwelling in them as in a holy habitation. The gospel embodies "the unsearchable riches of Christ," and is a "dispensation of the mystery which from all ages hath been hid in God," and which is to be "made known through the church unto the principalities and the powers in the heavenlies, as the manifold wisdom of God, according to the purpose of the ages which he accomplished in Christ Jesus our Lord" (iii, 8-11). Christ Jesus is thus conceived as central in the glory of this mystery of God, and he is referred to in iv, 9, as having "descended into the lower parts (τὰ κατώτερα)[1] of the earth, and having also

---

[1] According to Meyer this expression means that Christ "descended deeper than the earth, even into the subterranean region, into Hades. The object was to present Christ as the one who fills the whole universe, so that, with a view to his entering upon this his all-filling activity, he has previously with his victorious presence passed through the whole world, having descended from heaven into the utmost depth, and ascended from this depth to the utmost height." Exegetical Handbook, in loco. Eng. trans. of 4th German ed., 1880. This interpretation accords, perhaps, with the most natural meaning of the words, but has nothing in the context that requires or even suggests an allusion to Hades. Yet this interpretation has been adopted by many ancient and modern expositors (e. g., Irenæus, Jerome, Alford, Ellicott, Beet). It is not necessary, however, to say with Meyer that he "descended into the *utmost* depth," for Paul does not use the superlative. Inasmuch as the phrase *lowest parts of the earth* is used in Psa. cxxxix, 15, to denote the womb, Witsius and some others explain it of the descent of the preëxistent Christ into the womb of the virgin. Chrysostom, Theodoret, and others, see in the words an allusion to the death and burial of Christ." But the more widely accepted modern interpretation takes the words τῆς γῆς as a genitive of apposition—"this lower earth," "lower parts of the universe," as contrasted with the height (ὕψος) of heaven.

ascended far above all the heavens, that he might fill all things." This passage is somewhat remarkable for its free appropriation of the language of a well-known psalm (lxviii, 18), and the application of it to Christ. The words of the psalm are addressed directly to Jehovah, the God of Sinai:

> Thou hast ascended on high;
> Thou hast led away captives;
> Thou hast received gifts among men.

The imagery is that of the triumphal return of a conqueror to his fortress in the height ("the mountain which God hath desired for his abode," ver. 16; comp. "the height of Zion," Jer. xxxi, 12), leading in his train a large body of captives whom he has taken (comp. Judg. v, 12), and receiving tributary gifts from among the subject nations (comp. Isa. lx, 5-11). The God of Israel is thus conceived as ascending in triumph to his chosen dwelling in the holy mountain of Zion. But the apostle not only applies this language to the ascension of Christ "far above all the heavens," but he also changes one important word so as to represent his hero as *bestowing* rather than *receiving* gifts among men. The gifts which he bestowed are specified in verse 11, "apostles, prophets, evangelists, pastors, and teachers," and the purpose for which these were given is stated further on. The significance of this passage for the doctrine of the person of Christ is to be seen in its bold application to him of language which the Hebrew scripture employs in describing the triumphs of Jehovah, and also in its assertion that Christ has ascended above all heavens so as to fill all things." In Exod. iii, 7, 8, Jehovah says: "I have seen the affliction of my people who are in Egypt, . . . and I am come down (וָאֵרֵד, *and I descended;* Sept., κατέβην) to deliver them," etc. It is not improbable that this very passage floated before the mind both of the psalmist and of the apostle when they wrote. There is no necessity of assuming that Paul's memory failed him so that he substituted *gave* for *received,* nor that he intended to quote the passage accurately, or to interpret it in its true historical meaning. Nor is it important to determine whether by "the lower parts of the earth" he means Hades, popularly conceived as located under the earth, or the grave, or the earth itself as lower than the heavens. The main thoughts are the descending, and the ascending, and the giving gifts unto men. With that mystic and spiritual insight which discerned so many suggestive figures of Christ in the Old Testament the apostle saw the fitness of the passage under discussion to portray the incarnation, ascension, and triumph of the Lord Jesus. The triumphal ascent of

Christ to the highest heaven implied that he also previously came down from on high, and so far it accords with the teaching of John iii, 13; vi, 62; xvii, 5. Thus a concept of personal preexistence is put forward, for "he that descended is the same also that ascended." It may be alleged in general that one may ascend who has not previously descended, so that ascent into heaven does not necessarily imply a previous descent therefrom. But this allegation is precluded by the imagery of a conqueror ascending to his own native height and leading captives in his triumphal march. Moreover, the ascent "far above all the heavens, that he might fill all things" is an ascription of exaltation to Christ which involves transcendent and most worshipful relation to the throne and dominion of the Most High. The "filling of all things" suggests the divine prerogative of Jehovah, who says in Jer. xxiii, 24: "Do not I fill heaven and earth?" Omnipresence would thus seem to be predicated of the ascended Christ; and yet other uses of this expression in the epistle make it somewhat questionable just how far we are at liberty to press the literal import of the language. For while the statement of this verse is made without any limit or qualification—"that he might fill all things"—it is said immediately afterwards that he gave apostles, and prophets, and pastors, and teachers "for the building up of the body of Christ, till we all attain unto . . . the measure of the stature of the fulness of Christ." Moreover, in i, 23, it is said that the church "is his body, the fulness of him that filleth all in all." This last saying is best explained as meaning that he fills "all things" (τὰ πάντα, i.e., the whole universe,) "with all things" (ἐν πᾶσιν, i.e., with all things which the universe contains, ἐν to be taken with dative of the instrument): he fills the universe of things with all things which are therein. This is in harmony with Col. i, 16-19; 1 Cor. viii, 6; Heb. i, 2, and John i, 3, 10. Unless, therefore, his church be understood to be coextensive with the universe, his fullness extends beyond that of "his body," and permeates all elements and creations of the cosmos. It would seem, therefore, that the absolute omnipresence of Deity is thus attributed to Jesus Christ, and it is expressly said in Col. ii, 9, that "in him dwelleth all the fulness of the Godhead (θεότης, Deity) bodily." And yet this apostle prays that his readers "may be filled unto all the fulness of God" (Eph. iii, 19). What sort of *fullness* can all this mean? Some "measure of the stature of the fulness of Christ" is, according to iv, 13, attainable by all who belong to the body of Christ. They partake of his πλήρωμα, and his fullness seems from iii, 19, to be identical with "all the fulness of God" (πᾶν τὸ πλήρωμα τοῦ θεοῦ). The solution of this mystery is difficult because of our habit of conceiving omnipresence in terms of space and bulk. We think and speak as if a universal spiritual presence were of the nature of a diffused material essence. This was not the idea of Jesus when he said: "Where two or three are gathered together in my name, there am I in the midst of them" (Matt. xviii, 20), and "I am with you alway" (xxviii, 20). And Paul himself speaks of his "being present in spirit" with the Corinthian church though "absent in body" and with them performing an act of authoritative discipline "in the name of the Lord Jesus, ye being gathered together, and my spirit, with the power of our Lord Jesus" (1 Cor. v, 4). This concept of a spiritual as distinct from a bodily presence requires that the "fulness of him that filleth all things with all things" be not defined in terms of material bulk, but be conceived rather as a personal capability of manifesting sympathy, wisdom, and activity wherever and whenever desired. We should think of spiritual ubiquity as we think of love, truth, energy, or efficiency making itself known wherever occasion may demand. God thus fills the universe, and Christ partakes of this divine *pleroma;* and all those who are Christ's are "strengthened with power through the Spirit in the inward man" by that vital relationship. They are filled with like energy and efficiency, and thus become "partakers of the divine nature."

The person of Christ, as presented in the epistle to the Ephesians, is accordingly the central figure in the great purpose of God which runs through all ages and reveals itself in the administration of the world. He descended from heaven; he showed forth the manifold wisdom of God; he ascended above all the heavens; he has given his Church all necessary ministrations and helps; he himself, like the omnipotent Father, is cognizant of all things in heaven and in earth, and his personal spirit and authority are potent throughout the universe. And yet the ultimate source of all this power and wisdom and grace is "the God of our Lord Jesus Christ, the Father of glory" (i, 17). Jesus is the Christ of God.

9. Epistle to the Philippians. The epistle to the Philippians is less mystic in tone and style than the Ephesian epistle, and, like the letter to Philemon, exhibits elements of a more personal and familiar cast, arising out of precious remembrances (i, 3; iv, 1). The apostle speaks of the "tender mercies of Christ Jesus," and of the "fruit of righteousness which is through Jesus Christ unto the glory and praise of God" (i, 8, 11). He has confidence in "the supply of the Spirit of Jesus Christ," and has assurance that "Christ will be magnified in his body," whether he suffer a martyr's death in the near future or be permitted to abide longer in the flesh; for with him "to live is Christ, and to die is gain" (i, 19-22). His personal desire is "to depart and be with Christ," but it seems on the whole more needful for him to abide in the flesh in order to advance the Philippians' progress and joy in the faith. Aside from expressions and references which are common to all the epistles the one most important Christological passage in this epistle is ii, 5-11: "Have this mind in you which was also in Christ Jesus, who, existing in the form of God, counted not the being on an equality with God a thing to be grasped, but emptied himself, taking the form of a servant, becoming in the likeness of men; and being found in fashion as a man, he humbled himself, becoming obedient unto death, yea, the death of the cross. Wherefore also God highly exalted him, and gave unto him the name which is above every name; that in the name of Jesus every knee should bow, of those in heaven and of those on earth and of those under the earth, and that every tongue should confess that Jesus Christ is Lord, to the glory of God the Father."

This scripture has naturally held a very prominent place in all polemic discussions of the person of Christ. Simple as the main purport of the passage is, when considered as an exhortation to self-denial and humility, the phrases *form of God* (μορφὴ θεοῦ), *the being on an equality with God* (τὸ εἶναι ἴσα θεῷ), and *emptied himself* (ἑαυτὸν ἐκένωσεν), have occasioned perpetual controversy, and even now seem as far as ever from final determination.[1] Some writers point out nice distinctions of meaning between the words for *form* (μορφή), *likeness* (ὁμοίωμα), and *fashion* (σχῆμα), and presume to make such distinctions serve the interests of dogma. It is noticeably assumed by others that the word *existing* (ὑπάρχων) means preëxisting from eternity,[2] that "existing in the form of God" is equivalent in sense to "being on an equality with God," and that "emptied himself" must signify something quite different from "humbled himself." But there seems to be no room for serious difference of opinion as to the facts of Christ's exaltation as affirmed in verses 9-11. "Wherefore also (διὸ καί, that is, as the fitting consequence and reward of such emptying and humbling himself) God highly exalted him, and gave unto him the name

---

[1] The word κενόω, here employed, has naturally lent itself to the so-called "kenotic theories" of the incarnation; but it is not said that he emptied himself of any essential equality with God, nor does anything in the passage require us to think here of Christ's preëxistent state. The whole passage, as we show, is capable of a more simple and natural exposition in the recorded facts of the man Christ Jesus in his earthly life.

[2] The following paraphrase of verses 6 and 7 by J. B. Lightfoot is a good example of dogmatic exegesis: "Though existing before the worlds in the eternal Godhead yet he did not cling with avidity to the prerogatives of his divine majesty, did not ambitiously display his equality with God; but divested himself of the glories of heaven, and took upon him the nature of a servant, assuming the likeness of men." Notes on Epistle to the Philippians, in loco. How much soever of truth this paraphrase contains, it takes great liberties with the apostle's language.

which is above every name." This exaltation is no other than the resurrection and ascension of Christ to the throne of God, "far above all the heavens" (Eph. iv, 10), and it is here represented as a meritorious result of his self-humiliation. It is the highest possible illustration of what Jesus himself taught in Matt. xxiii, 12: "Whosoever shall exalt himself shall be humbled; and whosoever shall humble himself shall be exalted." Hence in this notable passage in Philippians we observe a most unquestionable distinction between God and Christ; for God honors Christ, who empties and humbles himself and acts the part of a slave. To affirm that the exaltation of Christ was a *consequence* of his humiliation, but not in any sense a *reward* or recompense, is to allow dogmatic presuppositions to control our exegesis. Why should not the honor and glory of sitting on the right hand of God be considered a reward for his earthly suffering and obedience unto death?[1]

Turning now to the leading words of the passage, we may fairly submit (1) that ὑπάρχων, *existing,* does not necessarily mean *preexisting,* nor does the context require us to import that thought; (2) that the *form of God* does not mean the nature or essence of God (φύσις, or οὐσία), nor is it equivalent to "the being on an equality with God"[2]; (3) that *emptying himself* does not necessarily mean divesting himself of any real quality or attribute of his nature, nor necessarily mean something so very different from *humbling himself* that the one phrase must refer to a preëxistent state while the other refers to what occurred during his earthly life. All this may be said negatively; but when we inquire after the exact meaning and significance of these terms we may well hesitate to pronounce a positive conclusion. For, in the absence of anything essentially determinative, who will presume to say just what is meant by the *form of God?* Aside from this passage the word μορφή occurs nowhere else in the New Testament except in Mark xvi, 12, where it is said that the risen Jesus "was manifested in another *form* unto two of them, as they walked, on their way into the country." Here the reference is to some aspect of his bodily form. In our text the *form of God* is contrasted with the

---

[1] Compare Heb. ii, 9; xii, 2, where this is affirmed.

[2] One may, indeed, understand the one phrase as equivalent to the other, but only by an inference and a construction which may be offset by what others regard as an equally valid interpretation. Thus one may explain: Existing in the form of God (i. e., preëxistent glory) he did not regard *such glorious equality* with God as a prize to be eagerly grasped and held fast, but he laid it aside for a while, etc. But ought not the unbiased interpreter to see that such a construction is not necessary when one so natural as the following can be offered instead of it? Existing in the form of God (i. e., in the image and glory of God like the first Adam, as Paul conceived man in general, 1 Cor. xi, 7) he did not eagerly grasp after a higher equality with God like one ambitious to gain a prize, but took the very opposite course, abased himself, and acted the part of a servant rather than that of a lord and ruler.

form of a servant; but how may we suppose God's *form* differs from a servant's *form?* If any visible aspect or shape be supposed, it may at once be said that the *bodily form* of a servant may be as noble and commanding as that of a king; nay, many a slave has possessed a far more imposing and glorious figure to look upon than his lord. So far as ranks and classes of mankind are distinguished as princes, rulers, lords, and slaves in outward aspect or bodily form, they all alike exist in the form and likeness of men. The word *form,* therefore, does not seem to mean anything essentially different from *likeness* (ὁμοίωμα), and might have εἰκών, *image,* substituted in its place in this passage without changing in the least the lesson which the apostle aims to inculcate. In 1 Cor. xi, 7, it is said that man "is the image and glory of God" (εἰκὼν καὶ δόξα θεοῦ ὑπάρχων), the reference being obviously to Gen. i, 26. In 2 Cor. iv, 4, Christ is called "the image (εἰκών) of God," and in Col. i, 15, "the image of the invisible God." It would seem to follow from all this that the *form* or *image of God* in which Christ Jesus is said to exist need not be understood as the distinctive form in which he existed before he was manifested in the flesh and became in the likeness of men. That is, without denying the preëxistence of Christ, this passage in Philippians does not necessarily set forth that doctrine. In this epistle the word εἰκών, *image,* does not occur, but μορφή, *form,* is employed as its equivalent. In this case the apostle seems to have had his favorite contrast of the first and second Adam in mind, and the several allusions may be explained in some such paraphrase as the following: In self-denial and lowliness of mind, each counting other better than himself and so guarding against faction and vainglory (vers. 3 and 4), imitate the spirit and example of Jesus Christ, who, like the first Adam, was made in the image and after the likeness of God (Gen. i, 26), and as man exists in "the image and glory of God" (1 Cor. xi, 7), yet, when tempted to become like God (comp. Gen. iii, 5) in power and dominion by grasping as a prize the kingdoms of the world and all their glory (Matt. iv, 8; Luke iv, 6), and to rule like the god of this world, he did not regard such an equality with God as a boon or booty to be eagerly grasped; but on the contrary, he set at naught all such selfish ambitions, emptying himself for the time of all assumption of lordship and power, laying hold (λαβών) rather of the outward appearance and figure of a bondservant, even declaring that he came not to be served but to do service for others and to give his life for many (Mark x, 45), for he came in the likeness of men, thus identifying himself with common humanity; and being thus seen and recognized as a man among men, he subjected himself willingly to the humiliation of an obedience so implicit that it did not shrink from the ignominious death of the cross. Wherefore, on account of this lowliness of mind and self-sacrifice for others, God highly exalted and honored him. Such a reference to the well-known facts in the life of Jesus would have been far more natural and cogent than allusions to his preëxistent state and assumed equality with God.

The honor and glory to which this conspicuous self-renunciation led Christ Jesus must be duly emphasized. Some writers seem far more anxious to maintain Christ's preëxistence and his "equality with God" (which he "counted not a thing to be grasped") than to accept the unquestionable fact that "God highly exalted him." That exaltation "gave unto him the name which is above every name," and the word employed here ($\dot{\epsilon}\chi\alpha\rho\dot{\iota}\sigma\alpha\tau o$; comp. i, 29; Rom. viii, 32) clearly affirms that this ennobling gift of God *was graciously bestowed*. But how marvelous that gift of grace which exalted Christ to the intent and purpose "that in the name of Jesus every knee should bow, of things in heaven and things on earth and things under the earth, and that every tongue should confess that Jesus Christ is Lord, to the glory of God the Father." The last phrase here expresses the object aimed at in the confessing that Jesus Christ is Lord. The confession of this blessed truth redounds "to the glory of God the Father," and by its very terms associates the Lord Jesus in the same glory. And thus Christ Jesus is, along with "God the Father," presented as an object of worship before whom all should bow.[1] This adorable Lord is a personality as well as a spiritual power that fills the vision of the apostle's soul. He reckons all things as loss, and is willing to make any sacrifice and undergo any labor "for the excellency of the knowledge of Christ Jesus his Lord"; and with all possible energy and zeal he "presses on toward the goal of the upward calling of God in Christ Jesus" (iii, 8, 14). He reckons himself a citizen of heaven, "from whence we wait for a Saviour, the Lord Jesus Christ, who shall fashion anew the body of our humiliation, that it may be conformed to the body of his glory, according to the working whereby he is able to subject to himself all things" (iii, 20, 21). Such is the magnificent portraiture of the person of Christ, as presented to us in the epistle to the Philippians.

---

[1] The phrase *in the name*, according to Ellicott, "denotes the spiritual sphere, the holy element as it were, in which every prayer is to be offered and every knee to bow."—Commentary, in loco. So, too, Meyer, commenting on this phrase in Eph. v, 20, observes that "what is embraced in the name Jesus Christ is the element, in which a grateful consciousness moves in the act of thanksgiving." Beet comments thus: "A name is personality as known and recognized among men, and as distinguished from others. In the recognized personality of Jesus abides the majesty before which God designs all to bow."—Commentary on Philippians ii, 10.

10. The Epistle to the Colossians. In the epistle to the Colossians the Pauline Christology reaches its highest forms of statement. Here, too, as in other epistles, the apostle speaks of "the mystery which has been hidden from the ages and from the generations, but has now been manifested to his saints" (i, 26), and he affirms that "the riches of the glory of this mystery" consists essentially in the profound thought of "Christ in you, the hope of glory." Great indeed must be "the mystery of God, of Christ, in whom are all the treasures of wisdom and knowledge hidden" (ii, 2, 3). That Christ, who embodies all the treasures of heavenly wisdom, should dwell among and within the converted Gentiles, so as to be to them the hope of eternal glory, is an idea adapted to elevate the Christian heart to heights of spiritual rapture. To lodge this thought in every mind (νουθετεῖν, i, 28) is Paul's high aim and holy ambition, for by admonishing every man and teaching every man he is ever striving to "present every man perfect in Christ." The thrice repeated *every man,* in verse 28, is worthy of special note, as indicating the world-wide aim of Paul's gospel. All perfection in spiritual life, in this world and in the world to come, is to be attained "in Christ." His saving personality is conceived as an all-pervasive element of wisdom, love, and power, apart from which there is no hope of glory.

(1) *Fullness of the Deity.* Not only are "all the treasures of wisdom and knowledge hidden in Christ," but according to ii, 9, 10, "in him dwelleth all the fulness of the Deity (τῆς θεότητος *Godhead;* nature of God) bodily, and ye are filled full in him, who is the head of all principality and power." We should notice the distinction in signification between θεότης here and θειότης in Rom. i, 20. In Romans the apostle speaks of "the eternal power and divinity" of God perceptible in the works of creation, referring to the divine qualities or Godlike attributes of the Creator which may be inferred from the things which he has made. But θεότης means the divine nature, or essence, and is properly translated only by the word *Deity,* or *Godhead.* It appears, therefore, beyond question that this scripture affirms the essential deity of Christ. But it is *Deity dwelling in bodily form* (σωματικῶς), and must therefore be understood as dwelling in Christ after he became manifest "in the body of his flesh" (i, 22), not before his incarnation, when as yet he did not exist σωματικῶς. The thought is accordingly turned to "the body of his glory" (Phil. iii, 21), in which he is "seated on the right hand of God" (iii, 1). By this heavenly exaltation he has become "the head of all principality and power" (comp. Eph. i, 20-23; Phil. ii, 9), and participates not only in the glory of the Father, but also in attributes and prerogatives of Deity.

The *fullness* (τὸ πλήρωμα) of Christ and his *making full* those who "were circumcised in the circumcision of Christ," "buried with him in baptism," and "raised with him through faith in the working of God" (vers. 11, 12), are to be understood in the same manner in which we have explained "the fulness of him that filleth all in all," and "filled unto all the fulness of God" in Eph. i, 23, and iii, 19 (see above, pp. 305, 306).[1]

(2) *Significance of i, 13-18.* But the most important Christological text in Colossians is the passage (i, 13-18), where it is declared that "the Son of his love," who effects our redemption, "is the image of the invisible God, the firstborn of all creation; for in him were all things created, in the heavens and upon the earth, things visible and things invisible, whether thrones, or dominions, or principalities, or powers; all things have been created through him and unto him; and he is before all things, and in him all things hold together. And he is the head of the body, the church: who is the beginning, the firstborn from the dead; that in all things he might have the preëminence." In this classic passage the person of Christ is presented (1) in his relation to God and the whole creation (vers. 13-17), and (2) in his relation to the church (18). In calling him "the image (εἰκών) of the invisible God," the apostle affirms only what is written in 2 Cor. iv, 4; for the addition of the epithet *invisible* merely expresses the uniform teaching of the New Testament that God is not seen by mortal man (John i, 18; 1 Tim. vi, 16). There is nothing in either of these texts to show that the image of God in which Christ exists is essentially different from the image and likeness of God in which the first man was created (Gen. i, 26), and "the image and glory of God" which 1 Cor. xi, 7, makes the distinguishing feature of man in general considered as the highest creation of God. But when it is said that Christ is "the firstborn of all creation," and that all things in the universe, whether visible or invisible, were created *in him, through him,* and *unto him,* we are at once lifted in thought to the concept of Deity. The additional statement that "he is before all things, and in him all things hold together," not only affirms the preëxistence of Christ, but implies his essential lordship over the universe of God. The personification of Wisdom, in Prov. viii, 22-30, contains some ideals which may have floated before the apostle's mind when he wrote this passage; but though wisdom was a possession of Jehovah "before his works of old," and "was brought forth before the hills; while

---

[1] What is stated in Col. ii, 14, 15, might be very appropriately affirmed of Christ; but as the subject of all the verbs and participles in verses 13-15 seems so obviously to be God (τοῦ θεοῦ of ver. 12), I make no further mention of it here.

as yet he had not made the earth, nor the fields, nor the beginning of the dust of the world," and was with God "as a master workman," there is nothing in the highly embellished portraiture of the Old Testament writer which goes so far as to say that all things were created in and through and unto wisdom. Moreover, no reader of Prov. viii, 22-31, fails to see that the description of Wisdom there given is ideal, as is also the somewhat similar passage in the apocryphal Wisdom of Solomon, vii, 24-30; but what is written in Col. i, 13-18, is affirmed of "the Son of his love, in whom we have our redemption, the forgiveness of our sins." Here is a real personality, not an abstract ideal personified; and it is difficult to believe that either Paul or his first readers could have understood the language here employed in any other way than as descriptive of the real person of Christ.

(3) *Firstborn of All Creation.* The exact import of the phrase *firstborn of all creation* is not altogether clear. The Arian interpretation, which makes Christ himself a part of the creation, that is, the first created being in the universe, is not incompatible with the phrase when taken by itself; for the expression *firstborn of all creation* (or *of every creature*) no more forbids our inferring that the firstborn is himself a creature than the phrase *first born from the dead,* in verse 18, or *first born of the dead,* in Rev. i, 5, forbids our inferring that this firstborn was himself once truly dead and buried. Nor need we deny that the title of *firstborn* carries with it here, as in Rom. viii, 29, and Psa. lxxxix, 27, the idea of superior excellence. But the immediate context requires that the word πρωτότοκος be here understood of the Son as *born before all creation,* existing *before all things,* as verse 17 declares.[1] It is not said that he existed *eternally* before all things, nor does the word require us to believe that Paul reckoned Christ among created beings. The word denotes rather a divine *generation* from the Father, and, like μονογενής in John i, 18, designates his exceptional and unique origin as *begotten,* not created. He was begotten of the Father before there was any created thing or being, and so far is he exalted in his nature above every creature that all created

---

[1] Ritschl insists that the preposition πρό in verse 17 points to priority of place rather than of time. "The temporal priority of Christ before the world cannot be the point at issue; that would be a barren thought. Superiority over the world is ascribed to Christ in view of the world which belongs to him in his position as the image of God and the head of the community. It is as the image and revelation of the invisible God (2 Cor. iv, 4) that the exalted Christ is *firstborn of all creation.* In this connection *firstborn* can be understood only in the metaphorical sense in which the corresponding Hebrew word is used, namely, he who is preferred—the same sense in which it is used in Rom. viii, 29, and probably also in Rev. i, 5. Christ is he who is preferred, who belongs to God in contrast with creation as a whole, which is not the image and direct revelation of God." Justification and Reconciliation, p. 402.

things in heaven and earth, visible and invisible, were brought into being by him, or through his agency, and he is the final cause (εἰς αὐτόν), the end and aim of the whole creation of God. He is truly "the first and the last, the beginning and the end."

(4) *His Preëminence.* The remaining statements in this passage only enhance the significance of what has been already affirmed of Christ. Not only have all things been created by him, but in him as a uniting and conserving bond "all things hold together," and are preserved in their orderly arrangements. His headship of the church, which is his body, is a familiar and peculiar thought of Paul, and has been already noticed in Eph. i, 22, 23. He is, moreover, "the beginning" (ἀρχή), not only "the beginning of the creation of God," as we read in Rev. iii, 14, being "before all things," but more specifically the beginning of the new order of things which is introduced by his manifestation among men and by his resurrection from the dead. Hence it is immediately added, as if in part defining this beginning, he is "the firstborn from the dead" (comp. Rev. i, 5), and so preëminently "the Prince of life" (Acts iii, 15), being thus "powerfully declared to be the Son of God" (Rom. i, 4). For, as this apostle elsewhere argues, "Christ being raised from the dead dieth no more; death no more hath dominion over him" (Rom. vi, 9). The purpose of all this is "that in all things he might become himself preëminent." The γένηται in this last clause contrasts with the ἐστιν in the preceding statement, and indicates that his preëminence is the outcome of a divine purpose and order in the manifestation of Christ.[1] The result is that this transcendent Son of the Father's love (comp. vers. 12, 13) holds the first place and highest rank in all points (ἐν πᾶσιν) that he may bring about the reconciliation of all things unto himself. Accordingly, and in confirmation of this truth, we are told in the next verse that God was pleased that "all the fulness" should dwell in Christ.

11. The Pauline Doctrine of Preëxistence. In our study of the Christology of Paul we should here examine the several passages in his writings which have been supposed to teach the preëxistence of Christ. The witness of the Colossian epistle to this doctrine seems unmistakable. In some sense Christ was before all things, and by him all things, visible and invisible, were created and are

---

[1] The final clause indicates that the apostle has a progress of development in his mind—a progress from a beginning to a consummation—and in this the rising from the dead and being head of the body is an essential step. He moves forward in his thought from the preëxistent state, before the creation of all things, to the final result, when the reconciliation of all things shall have taken place. This clause thus points to the eternal divine purpose, which is in process of accomplishment.—T. Dwight, in American ed. of Meyer's Exegetical Handbook of New Testament, in loco.

held together.¹ But the other Pauline texts bearing on this subject are open to some question. We have already seen that the famous kenotic text in Phil. ii, 5-11, is capable of another interpretation than that which it has generally received. But certain other texts demand attention.

(1) *The phrase "sent forth from God."* There are those passages which speak of Jesus as one sent forth from God. One of these is Gal. iv, 4: "When the fulness of the time came, God sent forth his Son, born of a woman, born under law." Another text is Rom. viii, 3: "God, having sent his own Son in the likeness of sinful flesh, . . . condemned sin in the flesh." These statements, however, are not in themselves sufficient to establish the doctrine of a real preëxistence; for any prophet or apostle sent forth into the world by a divine commission may be thus spoken of. John the Baptist was a man thus sent from God (John i, 6). But at the same time it should be admitted that these forms of expression are in harmony with the idea of personal preëxistence.

(2) *Christ the Spiritual Rock.* The real preëxistence of Christ is argued from the statement of 1 Cor. x, 4, that the fathers "drank of a spiritual rock that followed them, and the rock was the Christ." In the verses preceding mention is made of the pillar of cloud which accompanied Israel in their march out of Egypt, and of their passage through the sea and of their eating the manna and drinking water from the rock, which food and drink, being miraculously supplied, are called spiritual ($\pi\nu\epsilon\nu\mu\alpha\tau\iota\kappa\acute{o}\nu$). There is nothing said in the Old Testament narrative about a rock that followed the Israelites in their journey,² but in the early part of the journey Moses smote a rock in Horeb (Exod. xvii, 6), and later, at Kadesh (Num. xx, 1-11), and in each case there came forth water from the rock. In all these miraculous events of cloud, and sea, and manna, and water gushing from the smitten

---

¹ In the Pauline statements touching the preëxistence of Christ Beyschlag observes the striking fact "that the apostle nowhere really establishes or teaches the preëxistence of Christ, but, especially in his earlier epistles, presupposes it as familiar to his readers, and disputed by no one."—New Testament Theology, vol. ii, p. 78.

² The Targum of Onkelos has a curious mistranslation of Num. xxi, 18-20, which the critical reader will perceive to be a singular reading of the Hebrew text, mistaking the proper names for verbs and for common nouns of similar letters. The Targum reads: ' And from the wilderness it (the well) was given to them. And from the time it was given to them it went down with them to the rivers, and from the rivers it went up with them to the height (or to Ramath), and from the height to the valleys which are in the fields of Moab, at the head of the height (or of Ramath) which looks over the face of Beth-jeshimon." From this mistranslation, perhaps, arose the various Jewish legends of the fountain and rock which followed the Israelites in all their journeys through the desert. The various forms of the tradition may be read in Schöttgen's Horæ Hebraicæ, pp. 623, 624. It is probable that this tradition was familiar to Paul, and that it was in his thought when he wrote this letter to the Corinthians. See my article on "The Song of the Well" in the Bibliotheca Sacra of July, 1901.

rock the apostle discerned the immediate presence of the ever-living God, and types (τύποι, ver. 6; τυπικῶς, ver. 11) of spiritual things which were full of suggestion and admonition for himself and for those to whom he was writing. In such typical and spiritual significance he might say "the rock was Christ." For every such manifestation of God's presence and power in Israel's history was a figure of what Christ is and does in his abiding presence with those who truly participate in the communion of the blood and of the body of Christ (vers. 15-17). Accordingly, Paul, might with equal propriety have said that the pillar of cloud and the manna were Christ. The rock was Christ in much the same sense that "Hagar is mount Sinai in Arabia," and Sarah, the freewoman, is "the Jerusalem that is above, which is our mother" (Gal. iv, 25, 26). The statement made twice over in the context that these events of Old Testament story have a figurative significance for us justifies the above interpretation, and removes the passage in 1 Cor. x, 4, from the list of texts which teach the real preëxistence of Christ.

(3) *First Corinthians xv, 45-49.* Another passage is in 1 Cor. xv, 45-49, where the first man Adam is contrasted with the last Adam, who is called "a life-giving spirit," and "the second man from heaven." The first man is said to be ἐκ γῆς χοϊκός, *from earth, earthy,* in allusion to Gen. ii, 7. The earthly origin and nature of his body are here affirmed, for the apostle could hardly have intended to affirm that the soul of the first Adam was from the earth. That was from the breath of God and so far heavenly. In what specific sense, then, is Christ *from heaven*[1] and *heavenly?* He, too, possessed a σῶμα ψυχικόν, *natural body,* as well as the first man. He died and was buried. A reference to the heavenly preëxistence of Christ and to his incarnation as the earthly manifestation of the last Adam would suit the words well enough, but has no relevancy to the context. Emphasis is placed in verse 45 on what each of these contrasted Adams *became* (ἐγένετο εἰς), and the next verse calls attention to the fact that the spiritual does not precede but follows the natural. The heavenly origin and nature of the second man, accordingly, are here thought of in reference to what he became as a life-giving spirit by his resurrection from the dead, not to what he was before he came into

---

[1] The words clearly denote some sort of heavenly origin or derivation, but not necessarily personal preëxistence. So the baptism of John was *from heaven* (Matt. xxi, 25). But in this argument of Paul touching the resurrection Meyer well says that the phrase *from heaven* "applies to the glorification of the body of Christ originating from heaven, i. e., wrought by God (comp. 2 Cor. v, 2, 3), in which glorified body he is in heaven, and will appear at his parousia (comp. Phil. iii, 20). Referring *from heaven* back to the incarnation is contrary to the context and mixes up things that differ."—Exegetical Handbook, in loco.

the world. Hence it is shown that "we, who have borne the image of the earthy, shall also bear the image of the heavenly." There is, therefore, no necessary reference to the personal preëxistence of Christ in this Pauline argument for the resurrection.

(4) *Second Corinthians viii, 9.* The preëxistence of Christ is clearly in accord with the language found in 2 Cor. viii, 9, where "the grace of our Lord Jesus Christ" is extolled in the fact "that, though he was rich, yet for your sakes he became poor, that ye through his poverty might become rich." Accepting or assuming the doctrine of Christ's preëxistence, these words may be regarded as a simple and natural reference to his voluntary relinquishing of the riches of his heavenly glory and living the life of poverty in which he appeared among men. The aorist tense of $\frac{\epsilon}{\epsilon}\pi\tau\omega\chi\epsilon\nu\sigma\epsilon$, *became poor,* is deemed quite decisive of the definite reference to the once-occurring event of his entering upon the state of earthly poverty, and most naturally implies the preëxistent state of heavenly glory, out of which he came forth in order to become incarnate. And yet it must in all fairness be conceded that these statements may be explained by facts which belonged to the historical life of Jesus Christ on earth. In this same epistle (vi, 10) it is affirmed of all the true ministers of God that they commend themselves "as sorrowful, yet always rejoicing; as poor, yet making many rich; as having nothing, and yet possessing all things." According to Eph. iii, 8, Paul preached to the Gentiles "the unsearchable riches of Christ," by which he certainly did not mean the riches of his preëxistence, and when further on (ver. 16) he speaks of "the riches of his glory" he refers to the risen and glorified Christ rather than to any preëxistent riches of glory. The *being rich* and *becoming poor,* in 2 Cor. viii, 9, are not mutually exclusive opposites, nor are the words *rich* and *poor* to be understood alike literally; for while the poverty was outward and manifest, the riches were essentially an inalienable possession and of a spiritual kind. So it was that the Master and Lord could humble himself to wash the disciples' feet and yet remain their Lord and Master. In like manner in the days of his flesh our Lord was both rich and poor; for he was unspeakably rich in heavenly gifts and power, the Son of God and heir of all things, and yet had not where to lay his head. The apostle, writing long after the glorification of Jesus, conceived and spoke of one and all of these facts of the self-humiliation of Christ in the definite aorist tense, for his manifestation in the flesh was then a fact of the past.

12. Pauline Texts which Call Christ God. A study of the Pauline Christology requires us further to examine those texts which have been supposed to speak of Christ as God. Most of these have been appealed to as proof-texts for the deity of Christ, for it has seemed to many that they speak of the Saviour in a form of language which attributes the highest divine title to him. A more minute study of the Greek manuscripts, however, has largely deprived these texts of the dogmatic value they once seemed to possess.

(1) *First Timothy iii, 16.* The reading in 1 Tim. iii, 16, "God was manifested in the flesh," has been proven to be an error. There is no trace of it to be found previous to the fourth century. The oldest manuscripts do not read θεός, *God,* but ὅς, *who,* and this is now accepted in all critical editions of the Greek Testament, in all the recent and revised versions, and by all the leading interpreters. The margin of the Anglo-American Revision informs the reader that the word *God* in this passage "rests on no sufficient ancient evidence." It has been argued, however, that the reading ὅς presents a grammatical difficulty in having no masculine antecedent. This consideration probably led to the ancient correction which some manuscripts contain in the reading ὅ, *which,* so as to make the relative agree with the preceding τὸ μυστήριον, *the mystery.* But as Christ himself is called, in Col. ii, 2, "the mystery of God," the grammatical inaccuracy furnishes no decisive argument.[1] It is clear that Christ is not here called God, but here as elsewhere in the Pauline writings he is called the mystery of God.

(2) *Titus ii, 13.* Another text is Titus ii, 13, where the reference of the words "the great God" turns upon a question of grammatical construction. On this question distinguished interpreters have long disagreed. Shall we read, "the appearing of the glory of our great God and Saviour Jesus Christ," or "the appearing of the great God and of our Saviour Jesus Christ"? The arguments put forth on each side of this question seem to be quite evenly balanced, and leave us, therefore, without positive result. That the language may be legitimately construed so as to make "the great God" an appellative of Christ ought in all fairness to be conceded; but equal fairness of judgment seems to demand that the arguments for this view be not held as decisive. Here, therefore, as in other cases where learned and deliberate opinions are in open conflict, and the opposing arguments are so evenly bal-

---

[1] The following comment of Hort is worthy of note: "Θεός is not a word likely to be chosen deliberately to stand at the head of this series of six clauses, though it might seem to harmonize with the first of the six. . . . The concurrence of three independent data, ὁμολογουμένως, ὅς, and the form of the six clauses, suggests that these clauses were a quotation from an early Christian hymn; and, if so, the proper and original antecedent would doubtless have been found in the preceding context which is not quoted."—Notes on Select Readings, p. 134.

anced, we cannot adduce the text in question as fairly determining any doctrine of importance.

(3) *Romans ix, 5.* We are obliged to express the same judgment on the much-disputed construction of Rom. ix, 5, where a very strong argument can be made to show that the words *who is over all, God blessed forever,* refer to the Christ mentioned immediately before. These words, expressive of the exaltation and divinity of Christ, come in as an appropriate contrast to the preceding phrase *according to the flesh,* after the manner of the similar contrast in Rom. i, 3, 4. The other interpretation, which puts a full stop after the word *flesh* and translates the following words as a doxology to God,[1] is open to strong objection for the reason that the word εὐλογητός, *blessed,* occupies a wrong position in the sentence to be thus construed (comp. Luke i, 68; 2 Cor. i, 3; Eph. i, 3; 1 Pet. i, 3). Similar ascriptions of blessing and praise to the Lord Jesus Christ appear in 2 Tim. iv, 18; 2 Pet. iii, 18; Rev. i, 6; v, 13, and possibly in 1 Pet. iv, 11. On the other hand, it is strenuously urged that Paul commonly distinguishes so definitely between Christ and God that we should naturally hesitate in the presence of such a sentence as the closing portion of Rom. ix, 5, and adopt, if reasonable, any construction which goes to make the apostle consistent with himself. In Rom. i, 25; xi, 36; 2 Cor. xi, 31; Gal. i, 5; Eph. iii, 21; Phil. iv, 20, and 1 Tim. i, 17, we find similar doxologies to the God and Father of the Lord Jesus. After weighing all the arguments, on both sides, we are compelled to acknowledge that either construction is possible, and about as much can be said in favor of one interpretation as the other.

(4) *Ephesians v, 5.* The phrase *kingdom of the Christ and of God* (τοῦ χριστοῦ καὶ θεοῦ), in Eph. v, 5, is too incidental to be made the ground of an argument for the deity of Christ on the plea that the words *Christ* and *God* are here construed as two different titles of the same person. There is nothing in the context to make such a dogmatic construction plausible,[2] and the phrase *kingdom of God* is so common as not to call for a repetition of the article (comp. Gal. v, 21; 1 Cor. vi, 9, 10; xv, 50). The kingdom

---

[1] Thus: "Whose are the fathers, and of whom is Christ as concerning the flesh. He who is over all, God, be blessed forever." This punctuation is adopted by Lachmann and Tischendorf, and appears in the margin of Westcott and Hort and of the American Revisers' Version. A most comprehensive and thorough discussion of both sides of this question, by Timothy Dwight, who refers the doxology to Christ, and Ezra Abbott, who refers it to God, may be found in the Journal of the Society of Biblical Literature and Exegesis, for 1881, pp. 22–55 and 87–154.

[2] Some of the older polemical writers contended that the absence of the article before θεοῦ is a proof that Christ is here called God. But this plea is set aside by such Trinitarian exegetes as Alford, Ellicott, Meyer, and Beet. It may be here noticed that the common reference of ὁ θεός, in Heb. i, 8, to Christ as a vocative appellative is also disputed by high Trinitarian authorities, as will be shown in the next chapter.

of heaven is both Christ's and God's, and this placing of the two names together here, as often elsewhere, is an exaltation of Christ in the glory of God the Father.

(5) *Acts xx, 28.* The language of Acts xx, 28, should also be noticed in this connection, since it is reported as a part of Paul's address to the Ephesian elders. The question is whether we should read "church of God, which he purchased with his own blood," or "church of the Lord" (*κυρίου*). Ancient and excellent evidence for each reading exists, and critics of acknowledged ability and learning have taken opposite sides in the discussion.¹ It is certainly a strange thing to speak of the *blood of God*, and any rational explanation of such language would seem to require an assumption of the fleshly human nature of Jesus as implied in the passage. In that case it is the blood of the Son of God, the human Christ, and not God's blood in any strict sense of the words. For God is a Spirit, and cannot be flesh and blood. According to Paul, in Rom. viii, 32, "God spared not his own Son (*ἰδίου υἱοῦ*), but delivered him up for us all," and we are saved "through faith in his blood" (Rom. iii, 25; v, 9), that is, the blood of Jesus Christ. In view of the conflicting testimony of the oldest documentary evidence for the readings in Acts xx, 28, it is probable that the text is here corrupt,² and because of such conflicting testimony and the high authorities which may be cited in support of each reading, no party is at liberty to employ this scripture as decisive of a doctrinal issue. It ought to be apparent to every unbiased expounder of the apostolic writings that no doctrine of religion can be permanently helped by what has any appearance of dogmatic persistence in the face of strong textual evidence to the contrary. A doctrine of genuine importance ought not to depend on precarious grounds or arguments of doubtful value.

---

¹ For the reading θεοῦ stand the great uncials ℵ and B, the Greek texts of Alford, Wordsworth, Westcott and Hort, and the English Revisers. For κυρίου are the uncials A, C*, D, and E, the Greek texts of Lachmann, Tischendorf, Tregelles, and the American Revisers. For a very discriminating discussion of the subject see Ezra Abbott's article in the Bibliotheca Sacra for 1876, pp. 318-352.

² Instead of διὰ τοῦ ἰδίου αἵματος, *through his own blood*, which is not well supported by ancient evidence, ℵ, A, B, C, D, E, and the texts of Lachmann, Tregelles, Tischendorf and Westcott and Hort read διὰ τοῦ αἵματος τοῦ ἰδίου, *through the blood of his own*, and Hort suggests that the word υἱοῦ, *son*, may have dropped out of the original text "at some very early transcription, thus affecting all existing documents. Its insertion leaves the whole passage free from difficulty of any kind."—Notes on Select Readings, p. 99. Thus emended the revised text would read: "Church of God, which he purchased with the blood of his own Son."

CHAPTER VIII

CHRISTOLOGY OF THE EPISTLE TO THE HEBREWS

1. Character and Scope of the Epistle. The epistle to the Hebrews naturally serves, in the construction of New Testament Christology, as a transition from the doctrine of Paul to that of the writings of John. For its Alexandrian cast of thought is unmistakable, and its portraiture of the heavenly and preëxistent Christ is in striking harmony with that of Col. i, 13-18. The main argument of the doctrinal part of the epistle is to prove Christ superior to the angels, worthy of more glory than Moses or Joshua, superior as a high priest to Aaron, minister of a more perfect tabernacle than that of the Levitical priesthood, and mediator of a new and better covenant.

2. The Facts of the Incarnation. The incarnation and perfect humanity of Jesus are assumed or affirmed in numerous allusions, and the allusions show the author's familiarity with the life and teaching of the historical Christ as it had come to him by direct transmission from "them that heard" (ii, 3). Inasmuch as the saving mission of our Lord was for the redemption of mankind, it behooved him to be made like unto his brethren, and therefore he became partaker of flesh and blood, was in all points tempted as other men are, and is not ashamed to call them brethren (ii, 11-18). He is called "the firstborn" of God (i, 6) which title is equivalent to Paul's phrase, *the firstborn among many brethren* (Rom. viii, 29).[1] He was a scion of the tribe of Judah (vii, 14), touched with sympathy for human infirmities (iv, 15), yet altogether sinless. His miracles, his agony in the garden, his learning obedience through suffering, his enduring the cross and despising its shame, his resurrection from the dead, and his ascension to "the right hand of the Majesty in the heavens," are all referred to in this epistle as familiar facts.

3. Various Designations of Christ. In connection with these familiar facts of his manifestation in the flesh we find in this epistle a series of most remarkable designations of Christ's person

---

[1] The word πρωτότοκος, *firstborn*, in these texts, does not seem to be equivalent to 'the firstborn of all creation" in Col. i, 15, nor to "the firstborn from the dead"? Col. i, 18, and Rev. i, 5. Still less is it the same as μονογενής, *only-begotten*, in the Johannine writings. It here denotes rather the rank of Jesus among his holy brethren, in "the church of the firstborn who are enrolled in heaven" (Heb. xii, 23). Comp. the use of the word in Psa. lxxxix, 27.

and work. In the first four verses, which announce the author's principal theme, we find at least seven distinctive propositions affirmed of Jesus as God's Son: (1) God appointed him heir of all things; (2) through him he made the worlds of time; (3) he is the effulgence of the glory of God; (4) he is the exact likeness of his substance; (5) he sustains all things by the word of his power; (6) he has made purification of sins; (7) he is now enthroned at the right hand of God. A little further on in the same chapter he is presented as an object of the worship of all the angels of God, and psalms are quoted in which it is assumed that he is addressed as God and Lord (vers. 8 and 10). He is also called "the Apostle and High Priest of our confession" (iii, 1). He is the supreme minister of the sanctuary of God in the heavens (viii, 2), the mediator of a new and better covenant than that of Sinai (viii, 6; ix, 15), the author and perfecter of our faith (xii, 2), the great shepherd of the sheep (xiii, 20). Taken altogether, these various designations present a most exalted doctrine of the Christ of God. He is declared at the very opening of the epistle to be the latest and highest medium of divine revelation; for God, who spoke in ancient time to the fathers of the Hebrew people, spoke in the last days of the old dispensation in the person of one who was above angel, prophet, and priest, and who inherited the more excellent name of SON, the constituted heir of all things and maker of the worlds.

4. Doctrine of Preëxistence. Among these designations of our Lord there are statements which seem even to go beyond Col. i, 13-18, in affirming the preëxistence and supreme power of the Son. His agency in the creation of the world is to be understood here as in Col. i, 16, 1 Cor. viii, 6, and John i, 3, and the statement of Heb. xi, 3, that the world-ages "were framed by the word of God," moves in the same realm of thought, and has essential connection with the idea of "upholding all things by the word of his power," as expressed in Heb. i, 3. All this is in notable harmony with the statement of Col. i, 17, that the Son of God "is before all things, and in him all things hold together." The concept of preëxistence is also traceable in the assumption of Heb. iii, 3, that Jesus was the builder of the house of which Moses was but a part. It appears also in the typical illustration from Melchizedek, who is spoken of as "having neither beginning of days nor end of life, but made like unto the Son of God" (vii, 3),[1] thus implying that

---

[1] The Son of God is not said to be made like to Melchizedek, but the contrary; for the Son of God is more ancient, and is the archetype. Comp. viii, 5, where likewise heavenly things are set forth as more ancient than Levitical things. Bengel, Gnomon on Hebrews vii, 3.

Christ is himself the great archetypal model, made such "according to the power of an indissoluble life" (vii, 16). In xiii, 8, we read that "Jesus Christ is yesterday and today the same, and unto the ages," a simple affirmation of the unchangeableness of Christ in the past, the present, and the future; but it cannot be fairly claimed that ἐχθές, *yesterday,* must mean the eternal past. The doctrine of preëxistence, however, is unmistakable in the epistle, and is assumed to be a part of the gospel of salvation which was first taught by the Lord and afterwards confirmed by them that heard him. It is, perhaps, implied in the author's use of Psa. viii, 5; especially if we allow the temporal sense of βραχύ τι, and think of Jesus as "made *for a little while* lower than the angels" (Heb. ii, 7, 9). Thus the incarnation is conceived as a temporary manifestation of one who had existed from times eternal. Also in x, 5, 6, our author employs the Septuagint version of Psa. xl, 6, 7, in a way to suggest the same far-reaching thought. God prepared him a body in which he came to do the Father's will. Here is a concept of divine incarnation.

5. Effulgence of Glory and Image of Substance. Deserving special attention are the words of Heb. i, 3: "Being the effulgence of his glory and the very image of his substance." It is apparent that the writer was influenced, in his selection of these words, by the language of the book of Wisdom vii, 25, 26, where it is said that wisdom "is a breath (ἀτμίς) of the power of God, and a clear effluence (ἀπόρροια) of the glory of the Almighty; an effulgence (ἀπαύγασμα) of everlasting light, an unspotted mirror (ἔσοπτρον) of the working of God, and an image (εἰκών) of his goodness." The Alexandrian cast of the epistle is nowhere more conspicuous than in this passage, and here it is obvious that the older apocryphal writing was made to serve the New Testament writer's purpose. The word ἀπαύγασμα has the same meaning in both books, and χαρακτήρ, *very image,* signifies nothing essentially different from εἰκών *image*. The exact import of ἀπαύγασμα has been much disputed, and some of the best exegetes hesitate over the question whether we should explain it actively, *a streaming forth, radiation, effulgence,* or passively, as a result produced, *reflected radiance, reflection, refulgence.* This nice distinction is not, however, a matter of much importance in ascertaining the real doctrine of the text. Both meanings may be accepted as substantially true in describing Christ as a manifestation of the glory of God, for he is both the effulgence and refulgence of that glory, the active beaming forth and also the reflected brightness of the divine δόξα. The other phrase, χαρακτὴρ τῆς ὑποστάσεως, *very image of his substance,* cannot be properly interpreted in any other sense than that the Son is an exact representation of the essential being of God. The word χαρακτήρ denotes strictly the *stamped impression* which an instrument made for the purpose leaves visible upon the surface that is stamped. Such an impress must needs be the very image of that which produces the mark. The word ὑπόστασις (etymologically, *what stands under,* and so supports) indicates that which is the foundation and support of any thing or being; that without which it could not be what it is. Hence when applied to God it means the *very nature, essence,* or *substance* of the Deity. Jesus Christ, the Son of God, is the exact representation, the image, and likeness, of God's real nature. The phrase is, perhaps, a more striking way of expressing the same truth that inheres in the words *image of God,* in 2 Cor. iv, 4, and *image of the invisible God,* in Col. i, 15. As the "effulgence of his glory," the Son radiates forth into a visible manifestation the glory of his Father; as the "very image of his substance," he bears upon his person and character a perfect representation of the essential nature of God. The ἀπαύγασμα involves and suggests the everlasting source, the "eternal generation," so to speak, of the Son; the χαρακτήρ affirms the exact likeness, and with its following genitive, *of his substance,* indicates the coessential or consubstantial relationship of this only begotten Son to God. It may also be added that both the effulgence and the image of his substance are conceived, in true Alexandrian style, as eternally existent and coexistent, like the eternal Wisdom that is extolled in Prov. viii, 22-30, and in the Wisdom of Solomon, vii, 25, 26.

6. Question of Divine Titles Applied. It remains to notice briefly how divine titles are applied to Jesus Christ in this epistle. The most remarkable example is found in i, 8, in the quotation from Psa. xlv, 6: "Thy throne, O God, is for ever and ever." The grammatical construction of these words is ambiguous. The American Standard Revision presents the marginal reading: "Thy throne is God forever," and the marginal reading of the psalm is, "Thy throne is the throne of God." The nominative form of the word for God, both in the psalm and in the citation (ὁ θεός, not θεέ, comp. Matt. xxvii, 46), seems to favor the marginal reading, which is a perfectly legitimate grammatical construction, and has the support of high Trinitarian authorities.[1] It should also be

---

[1] Tischendorf's and Westcott and Hort's Greek texts adopt the nominative reading, and Dwight in his additions to Lünemann admits that this construction can hardly be denied. Westcott says: "It is scarcely possible that Elohim in the original can be addressed to the king. The presumption, therefore, is against the belief that ὁ θεός is a vocative in the LXX. Thus, on the whole, it seems best to adopt the rendering, *God is thy throne* (or *thy throne is God*); that is, thy Kingdom is founded upon God, the immovable Rock." On the other side, Stuart, Alford, Moll, Bleek, Delitzsch, De Wette, and Ebrard construe ὁ θεός here as a vocative.

observed that the language immediately following, both in the epistle and in the psalm, "Therefore God, thy God, hath anointed thee," is not compatible with a vocative construction; for it would be very strange to read, "Therefore, O God, thy God hath anointed thee." On the other hand, it must be conceded that the nominative of the Greek word θεός may be and is used instead of the vocative, and the common version, "Thy throne, O God," is also perfectly grammatical. It may also be observed that the citation of Psa. cii, 25, and its direct application to Christ in Heb. i, 10, accords with the vocative construction in verse 8 of this same chapter. Such being the facts, all we can say of such a text when cited for purposes of doctrine is that it may refer either to Christ or to God.

A similar question arises in the doxology at the close of xiii, 21. To whom is the ascription of "the glory forever and ever" there applied, to Jesus Christ who is last mentioned in the context immediately preceding, or to "the God of peace," the first and main subject of the entire sentence, the God who brought again our Lord Jesus from the dead? This epistle regards the Son of God as entitled to the worship of all the angels of God (i, 6), and the language of 2 Pet. iii, 18, and Rev. i, 6, ascribes glory to Jesus Christ forever. So there is no question as to the propriety of ascribing such glory to our Lord as well as to our Father in heaven; the only issue here is the grammatical construction of the concluding words of the doxology. On this question interpreters are quite evenly divided,[1] and, therefore, no one can employ the text for dogmatic purposes as if it were incapable of more than one legitimate construction.

---

[1] Bengel, Alford, Delitzsch, Dwight, and Westcott refer the doxology to the God of peace; Bleek, Tholuck, Stuart, and Lünemann refer it to Jesus Christ. See Westcott's Additional Note on the Apostolic Doxologies in his Commentary on this epistle, pp. 464, 465.

CHAPTER IX

THE JOHANNINE CHRISTOLOGY

1. The Johannine Peculiarities. We have had occasion already to make use of the gospel according to John, and have noticed therein the corroborating testimony to many facts which the synoptic gospels record, and to the remarkable expressions of our Lord's self-consciousness. But the fourth gospel contains other things of a peculiar cast, bearing on the doctrine of the person of Christ, which demand a separate discussion. The three epistles of John are so in accord with the gospel on this subject that they may also be cited as like witnesses to the Johannine Christology. The doctrine of the Logos and the entire style and content of the fourth gospel confessedly represent a later and peculiar manner of conceiving the person of Jesus, the Son of God. The philological and historical questions of the authorship, date, and scope of this remarkable idealistic portraiture of Christ are a vast study by themselves, and cannot here be entertained. But we accept both the gospel and the epistles as a truthful presentation of the Christ, the Son of the living God. As compared with the synoptic records this writing of John is conspicuously more philosophical, more ideal, more spiritual, more mystic, but, we think, no less truthful and impressive in its way.[1] The facts and the thoughts which it records bear the impress of a disciple who has long meditated on the significance of the manifestation of his incarnate Lord.

2. The Word, or Logos. Unlike the human genealogies of Jesus which are found in Matthew and Luke, the doctrine of THE WORD confronts us at the opening of John's gospel, and turns our thought at once to the beginning of all things: "In the beginning was the Word, and the Word was with God, and the Word was God." This Word was the life and the light of men, and "became flesh and dwelt as in a tabernacle (ἐσκήνωσεν) among us. In this allusion to the tabernacle we perceive a metaphor drawn from Exod. xl, 34-38, where it is said that the glory of Jehovah came down and filled the tabernacle of meeting, and hung like a cloud

---

[1] We may with all reverence describe it as the history of Jesus read as a chapter in the life of God. . . . The distinguishing feature in the mind of the evangelist is that he read God through Jesus before he attempted to read Jesus through God. The book is a history written from a standpoint which its subject himself had supplied.—Fairbairn, The Place of Christ in Modern Theology, p. 340. New York, 1893.

of glory in the sight of the whole house of Israel; for it is immediately added: "We beheld his glory, glory as of an only begotten from a Father, full of grace and truth"; and in verse 18 it is written: "No man has seen God at any time; the only begotten Son,[1] who is in the bosom of the Father, he has declared him." It seems obvious, from all this, that "the Word" is in some real sense identical with the Son of God, and is here conceived as essentially the highest revelation of God.

3. The Logos in Greek Philosophy and in Philo. This term λόγος, *Word,* was not original with the author of the fourth gospel. Long before any of the New Testament books were written there were divers speculations of a theosophic character about the creation of the world and God's relation to the visible universe. Poets and writers of wise proverbs had made much use of such terms as Logos, and Wisdom, in connection with the idea of God's self-manifestation. Heraclitus of Ephesus (B.C. 500) used the word Logos to designate the underlying, universal principle of the universe, the divine eternal Reason, immanent in all things. The Stoic philosophers reproduced this doctrine of Heraclitus, and conceived the Logos as the soul of the world, working out the all-embracing and eternal order of the universe. In Alexandria Greek thought and Oriental mysticism commingled a century or two before Christ, and we find a remarkable illustration of the mixture in the various writings of Philo, an Alexandrian Jew, contemporary with Jesus. This writer speaks of the divine Logos as the "elder Son of the Father," and his "firstborn." He calls him the "image of God," "the oldest angel," "archangel of many titles," a "second God," and the "archetype and pattern of the light." He is also conceived as the "indwelling Word," and the "uttered Word," the relation of which to each other is like that of thought to speech. Philo's Logos is the sum total of all divine energies, both as they exist in archetypal ideas in the divine mind and as they come forth in the varied forms of creation. He is, in fact, the ideal world as conceived by God, and also the actual world as outwardly existing in all visible products of creative energy. But in view of his numerous epithets and varied forms of statement it is difficult to determine the precise conception which Philo attached to the term

---

[1] The reading *God only begotten,* μονογενὴς θεός, is too well attested to be ignored in the discussion of this passage. It appears in ℵ*, B, C*, L and in ancient versions and patristic citations, and is inserted in the Greek text of Westcott and Hort. The evidence is not, perhaps, sufficient to displace the more common reading, *only begotten Son;* but it is of sufficient importance to suggest the profound and far-reaching significance of the Logos-doctrine in this prologue of John. According to Thayer (Greek-English Lexicon New Testament, under μονογενής), the reading θεός "appears to owe its origin to a dogmatic zeal which broke out soon after the early days of the Church."

Logos. It is a matter of dispute among the learned how far he really hypostatized the divine Logos, for some of his declarations on the subject are hard to reconcile with each other. His ideas are no doubt, to some considerable extent, an elaboration of the teaching of Plato concerning the eternal archetypes of all things which come into being and form in time. But we are not here concerned to expound the various sayings of Philo about the Logos. They represent only an Alexandrian method of conceiving God's relation to the world, and one which is peculiar to Philo himself.[1]

4. Personification of Wisdom in Jewish Writings. In the apocryphal book of the Wisdom of Solomon (vii, 24-26) we find a striking personification of Wisdom, which has close affinity with some aspects of the Logos of Philo:

Wisdom is more mobile than any motion;
Yea, she pervadeth and penetrateth all things by reason of her pureness.
For she is a breath of the power of God,
And a clear effluence of the glory of the Almighty. . . .
She is an effulgence from everlasting light
And an unspotted mirror of the working of God,
And an image of his goodness.

In the same book, ix, 1, 2, we find the following prayer:

> God of the fathers and Lord of thy mercy,
> Who madest all things in thy Logos,
> And by thy Wisdom didst form man.

And again, in xviii, 15, 16:

Thy all-powerful Logos leaped from heaven out of the royal thrones, a stern warrior into the midst of the land doomed to destruction, bearing thy faithful commandments as a sharp sword, and standing, it filled all things with death; and it reached unto heaven while it stood upon the earth.

Similarly the son of Sirach, in Ecclesiasticus xxiv, 3-10, where Wisdom says of herself:

> I came forth from the mouth of the Most High,
> And covered the earth as a mist.
> I dwelt in high places,
> And my throne is in the pillar of the cloud. . . .
> He created me from the beginning before the world;
> And to the end I shall not fail.
> In the holy tabernacle I ministered before him,
> And so was I established in Sion.

---

[1] For discussions of Philo's doctrine of the λόγος see Gfroerer, Philo und die alexandrinische Theosophie, in his Kritische Geschichte des Urchristenthums. Erster Theil, chap. viii, pp. 168-326. Stuttgart, 1831. Also Dorner, History of the Doctrine of the Person of Christ, vol. i, pp. 19-39.

But the older source from which these concepts of Wisdom may be read is Prov. viii, 22-30, where Wisdom thus speaks:

> Jehovah possessed me in the beginning of his way,
> Before his works of old,
> I was set up from everlasting, from the beginning,
> Before the earth was.
> When there were no depths, I was brought forth;
> When there were no fountains abounding with water. . . .
> When he established the heavens I was there, . . .
> When he marked out the foundations of the earth,
> Then I was by him as a master workman.

All these poetic portraitures belong to the so-called "Wisdom literature" of the Old Testament, and partake of its spirit.

5. Creation by the Word of God. The concept of God as Creator carries along with it the thought that all things were first brought into existence through wisdom, for without wisdom none of the objects of creation could have been made and pronounced very good. This lofty ideal of wisdom, as it took shape in the Hebrew mind, may well have started from suggestions of the Elohistic picture of creation in Gen. i, 1—ii, 3. A philosophic and poetic reader of that sublime description of God's work would naturally notice how each creative act is introduced by ויאמר אלהים, *and God said*. Such an omnific word of God as brought light out of primeval darkness was necessarily a manifestation of the unseen personal Power. Hence one of the psalmists gives this profound thought the following poetical expression:

> By the word of Jehovah were the heavens made,
> And all the host of them by the breath of his mouth;
> For he spake, and it was done;
> He commanded, and it stood fast. Psa. xxxiii, 6, 9.

And so it became a common Hebrew conception and an article of faith that all created things which have been brought into manifestation, and continue through the ages, "were framed by the word of God" (Heb. xi, 3).[1] A philosophic mind, moreover, would naturally perceive in such a picture of creation the distinction between God as he exists in his essential nature and as he expresses himself in an outward act of power.

6. Theophanies and Angelophanies. The theophanies and angelophanies of the Old Testament would naturally suggest further modifications of this concept of God as revealing himself in some

---

[1] Here the term employed is $\dot{\rho}\tilde{\eta}\mu\alpha$, not $\lambda\acute{o}\gamma o\varsigma$; but there is no essential difference of thought, as a comparison with 2 Pet. iii, 5, shows, where it is said that heavens and earth were "compacted by the word ($\lambda\acute{o}\gamma o\varsigma$) of God."

visible form. "The angel of Jehovah" that appeared in a flame of fire in the bush, and seems to be identified with Jehovah in the narrative of Exod. iii, 2-6, presents an ideal of divine revelation which receives additional emphasis by comparison with what is written in Exod. xiv, 19; xxxii, 34; xxxiii, 2, 14. In these places the angel of God appears to be identical with the pillar of cloud, and to represent the presence of Jehovah and to bear his name. This manner of thought and speech led to the later substitution of the terms *Memra, Dibbura,* and *Shekina* for the sacred name of Jehovah, as we observe in the Aramaic Targums.¹ The later Judaism shrank from pronouncing the holy name of four letters (יהוה), and so the words *Memra* and *Shekina,* as well as the title *Lord* (אדני), were employed as welcome substitutes.

7. John's Gospel Gave the Logos New and Deeper Significance. From the foregoing outline and references it is evident that λόγος, *Word,* in the fourth gospel, was no new or strange term first introduced into theosophic writing by the author of this remarkable composition. The first apostles of Christianity must have often come into contact with current systems of speculative thought. Paul encountered Stoic and Epicurean philosophies at Athens. The Alexandrian Jew, Apollos, "a learned man (ἀνὴρ λόγιος) and mighty in the scriptures" (Acts xviii, 24), taught in Ephesus before he was thoroughly instructed in the doctrines of Jesus, and it is hardly supposable that he was not familiar with Alexandrian theosophy. But another Alexandrian Jew, Cerinthus, came at a later period to Ephesus, taught a form of Gnosticism that was largely mixed with Jewish and Christian elements, and, according to ancient tradition, came into sharp conflict with the apostle John. It was impossible for the early teachers of Christianity to avoid conflict with the doctrines of that eclectic Alexandrian philosophy which, in one form and another, sought to establish itself in every religious and literary center of the Greek-speaking Orient. It is a notable fact, moreover, that the first apostles of Christianity were obliged to use the Greek language for the propagation of their gospel of salvation, and to employ many a common Greek word to inculcate ideas which were new to the world. Thus old

---

¹ Thus in the Targum of Onkelos, Gen. iii, 8, we read: "They heard the voice of the *Word* (מימרא) of the Lord God walking in the garden." The Jerusalem Targum of Exod. xxxiii, 11, reads: "The voice of the *Word* (דבורא) he heard, but the splendor of his face he did not behold." In Exod. xvii, 7, the Onkelos Targum reads: "Is the *Shekina* (שבינא) of the Lord among us or not?" It is also worthy of note in this connection that the Targum on Isa. ix, 6; Mic. v, 1, and Zech. iv, 7, says that the Messiah is from eternity and to eternity, and, according to the book of Enoch (xlviii, 2, 3, 6), his name was called the Son of man before the sun and stars were made; he was chosen before God, and hidden in him before the world was created; and he will abide before him to all eternity.

and familiar words were turned to new uses and filled with new meaning and significance.[1] The term λόγος, *word*, was seen by the author of the fourth gospel to be admirably fitted to express his lofty conception of the Christ of God. He appropriated it and filled it with a fullness of meaning it had never borne before. It is not a vague and indefinable concept like the λόγος of Philo; nor is it the archetypal idea (ἰδέα and εἶδος) of Plato, nor the Memra of the Targums, nor the personified Wisdom (חכמה) of the book of Proverbs. And yet all of these may have contributed somewhat to the doctrine of the Word as set forth in the prologue of John's gospel. The superiority of John's conception and the originality of his genius appear in the ease and simplicity which he evinces in all this realm of thought. His divine Logos is no mixture of dualistic and docetic fancies; no philosophic portrayal of powers and attributes, now in repose and now again in activity. There is in his language the calm expression of one who knows of what he speaks. The Word of God is to him a living reality. For he tells us at the beginning of his first epistle that he himself had heard, and seen with his own eyes, and even handled the Word of life, which was so manifested in Jesus Christ, the Son of God, that he could personally "bear witness and declare the eternal life, which was with the Father." This heavenly Logos is the "only-begotten from the Father," the "only begotten Son (or God) who is in the bosom of the Father," and has revealed his nature and glory by a personal incarnation among men.

8. Necessity of Incarnation. According to John, all true knowledge of God must come to us through some manner of incarnation. The thoughts of God, the mind, will, wisdom, and feeling of the eternal Father cannot be expressed except by such a manifestation of himself as can be seen, heard, and touched by conscious contact. Hence the necessity of real personality in the divine Logos of revelation. The Hindu mystic has much to tell us about Avatara, incarnation, transmigration of souls, and ultimate repose in the bosom of Brahm, the divine Essence of the Universe. We may discern a profound concept of the truth in all this mystic dreaming, but it lacks the element of personal reality, which is the distinguishing feature of John's doctrine of the incarnation and

---

[1] "The apostolic proclamation," says Delitzsch, "did not scorn the forms of ideas already coined by the Alexandrian philosophy, but it filled them with the contents presented by the history of their New Testament realization. As Christianity withdrew the limits from the spirit of the Old Testament revelation, and separated the imperishable gold of its substance from the dross of its cosmical elements so it became a refining fire for Hellenistic and Hellenic philosophy, the transfiguration and consecration of what was true, and of the forms in use for both in the presentation of the Truth."—System of Biblical Psychology, p. 211. Eng. trans., Edinburgh, 1869.

visible manifestation of the Word. The eternal God revealed himself in the Word which "became flesh and tabernacled among us . . . full of grace and truth." This manifestation is no other than that which is to be seen in the person of Jesus Christ, the Son of God, who "is come in the flesh."

9. Suggestive Words and Phrases. A closer study of the prologue will discover a number of far-reaching suggestions. At the beginning of the creation the Word already *was;* did not begin to be. The statement implies that the Word was without beginning, and is himself no part of God's creation. Then it is added, "and the Word was with God" (πρὸς τὸν θεόν), obviously indicating some manner of distinction between God and the Word; and then it is immediately added, as if to emphasize the unity and substantial identity of the Word with Deity, "and the Word was God."¹ The word θεός is here without the article and occupies the position of emphasis in the sentence, being thus made the emphatic predicate, and affirming the *divine nature* of the Logos. Thus it is shown that this Word is no "second God," like the λόγος of Philo, but of the essential nature of Deity.² The first three verses of the prologue point to the narrative of creation in Gen. i, where it is written over and over again, "God said," and it was done. The creative Fiat was a manifestation of God himself, and the personal Logos of John's gospel is God himself speaking, acting, and bringing all things into being.

10. The Word of Life. That all things were created through the Word or Son of God (ver. 3) is a doctrine we have already found in 1 Cor. viii, 6; Col. i, 16; and Heb. i, 2; xi, 3. He is before all things; without him nothing ever came into existence, and in him all things hold together. But when it is added in John's prologue, verse 4, "In him was life, and the life was the light of men," we advance to another lofty concept of the Logos. In v, 26, we read: "As the Father hath life in himself, even so gave he to the Son also to have life in himself." In xi, 25, and xiv, 6, he is called emphatically "the life." At the beginning of the first epistle of John he is called "the Word of life," and there it is declared that "the life was manifested, and we have seen, and bear witness, and declare unto you the life, the eternal life, which was with the Father, and was manifested unto us." This manifestation of the life was, according to John, specifically and definitely in the historic fact that "Jesus Christ is come in the

---

¹ Comp. Gloag, Introduction to the Johannine Writings, p. 171. London, 1891.
² We may, perhaps, best indicate the import of the anarthrous emphasis of θεός in the sentence καὶ θεὸς ἦν ὁ λόγος by the translation, *and Deity was the very nature of the Word*.

flesh" (1 John iv, 2; 2 John 7), for it was such an unmistakable disclosure concerning the Word of life that it could be heard, seen, and handled (1 John i, 1). Paul taught that "the free gift of God is eternal life in Christ Jesus our Lord" (Rom. vi, 23; comp. Col. iii, 3, 4; 2 Tim. i, 1), but according to John's gospel Jesus declares himself "the bread of life which cometh down out of heaven, and giveth life unto the world" (vi, 33, 35, 41, 48, 50); and according to the epistle (v, 11, 12), "God gave unto us eternal life, and this life is in his Son. He that hath the Son hath the life; he that hath not the Son of God hath not the life."

11. The Word of Light. The Logos of John's gospel is also the light as well as the life of men. This light was no new thing, shining for the first time when the Word became flesh. It was coetaneous with the creation of the world, when God said, "Let there be light," for "God is light and in him is no darkness at all" (1 John i, 5). And this light did not go out when sin entered the world and filled the hearts of men with darkness. The light keeps right on shining in the darkness,[1] whether men regard it or not, and it has been shining from the beginning until now. Here and there, during the long times of darkness, some pious souls have caught gleams of this heavenly light, and have given glory to God (Psa. xxvii, 1; xxxvi, 9; xliii, 3; xcvii, 11; cxii, 4; Prov. iv, 18; Mic. vii, 8), and prophets saw its future shining as a revelation of Jehovah's glory (Isa. lx, 1-3, 19, 20). But the sad, condemning fact remains that "the light is come into the world, and men loved the darkness rather than the light; for their works were evil" (iii, 19). Evil doers hate the light, which convicts them of sin and guilt (iii, 20). Hence it is that while the light is all the time shining in the darkness "the darkness apprehended it not."[2] Even before the Word became flesh "there was coming into the world the light, the true light, which lighteth every man" (ver. 9), and this only genuine light was from the Logos, who was in the beginning with God, and was God. He accordingly declares: "I am the light of the world: he that followeth me shall not walk in the darkness, but shall have the light of life" (viii, 12; comp. ix, 5; xii, 35, 36, 46; 1 John i, 5-7; ii, 8). Thus the Logos of John's gospel has life in himself and is at the same time the fountain of light to men. He is the creative Word and the Word of spiritual illumination. He was all this in the beginning; but, having come in the flesh, he has manifested the life and the light of God in a fullness never known before.

---

[1] Note the force of the present, $\phi\alpha\acute{\iota}\nu\epsilon\iota$, in verse 5.

[2] Οὐ κατέλαβεν; that is, did not *seize hold upon it* so as to make it a possession of its own.

12. Doctrine of Preëxistence. The entire presentation of Christ in the fourth gospel is in strict harmony with this doctrine of the preëxistent Word of God who was manifested in the flesh. He himself says, in iii, 13, "No man hath ascended into heaven, but he that descended out of heaven, the Son of man, who is in heaven."[1] In vi, 62, he speaks of "the Son of man ascending up where he was before." In viii, 58, he says: "Before Abraham was born, I am." In xvii, 5, he prays to the Father: "Now glorify thou me with thine own self, with the glory which I had with thee before the world was"; and in verse 24 he adds, "for thou lovedst me before the foundation of the world." These passages all clearly involve the doctrine of personal preëxistence, and they accord with the statement in the prologue that the Word "was in the beginning with God"; and this has been the interpretation put upon them by the great majority of expositors during the Christian centuries. The profoundly realistic manner in which the doctrine of incarnation is thus conceived is most impressive.

13. The Idealistic Explanation. But there are those who explain all these utterances touching Christ's preëxistence in a purely mystic or ideal way. Appeal is made to the Platonic doctrine of archetypal ideas, to the use of the term Logos in Philo and in the apocryphal book of Wisdom; to the personification of Wisdom in Prov. viii; to the fact that, in Heb. viii, 5; ix, 23, the Mosaic tabernacle is conceived as a copy of heavenly things; and to the ideal of the New Jerusalem of John's Apocalypse, "coming down out of heaven from God" (Rev. xxi, 2). These references are cited to show that the heavenly original of all things which appear in time was, during the first century, an idea very common and current in the widely scattered communities of Greek-speaking Jews. These facts are indeed beyond successful contradiction, and the proofs have been sufficiently given in the foregoing pages. But it does not follow that John's doctrine of the Logos and of the heavenly preëxistence of Christ is identical in meaning with these Platonic and Jewish-Alexandrian conceptions, or was derived from them. On the contrary, it is maintained that the teaching of the fourth gospel, while appropriating current words and expressions

---

[1] The genuineness of the words ὁ ὢν ἐν τῷ οὐρανῷ, *who is in heaven*, is very doubtful. They are not found in the great manuscripts ℵ, B, L, T, C, nor in a number of other ancient authorities, and they are omitted from the text of Westcott and Hort, who say in their Notes on Select Readings: "There are many quotations of verse 13 (in early Christian writers) which stop short at τοῦ ἀνθρώπου; and it is morally certain that most of them would have included ὁ ὢν ἐν τῷ οὐρανῷ if it had stood in the texts used by the writers. . . . The character of the attestation marks the addition as a Western gloss, suggested perhaps by i, 18; it may have been inserted to correct any misunderstanding arising out of the position of ἀναβέβηκεν, *hath ascended*, as coming before καταβάς, *descended*." Notes on Select Readings, p. 75.

of this ideal cast, fills them with a significance they had not borne before. And the various assertions of a personal character, and the emphasis put upon them both in the gospel and in the first epistle of John, are not compatible with a mere ideal existence or preëxistence.[1]

(1) *Does Not Accord with John's Explicit Language.* The language employed in John's gospel is too explicit and personal to be satisfactorily explained after the manner of conceiving Plato's doctrine of archetypal ideas. For Plato's ideas were pure abstractions of thought, the perfect models or forms in which all things intelligible were conceived as eternally existing. He seems to have regarded them as something which human souls might have contemplated in a preëxistent state,[2] so that the process of learning things in this life is a recollection of preëxistent thoughts.[3] So lacking in clearness and consistency are some of Plato's statements on this subject that one may well believe that his views underwent considerable change in the course of his own life and study. But no possible construction of his *ideas* ($l\delta \acute{\epsilon} \alpha \iota$) and *forms* ($\epsilon \acute{\iota} \delta \eta$) can be rationally adjusted to the words of John's gospel.

(2) *Logos Not Synonymous with Abstract Terms.* Equally futile is any attempt to expound the Johannine teaching by means of the various and often contradictory statements of Philo. Nor can the concepts of the Logos in the Wisdom of Solomon be made to fit the specific and sublime utterances of the fourth gospel. If the Logos be explained as *Reason, Intelligence, Wisdom, Power,* or some other like term, it should be said, by way of reply on the other hand, that we may readily perceive a certain simple and intelligible meaning in declaring that God created the world in the exercise of his perfect wisdom; but when one says, "This Power became flesh and dwelt among us," "This Reason shall ascend up where it was before," "Glorify this Wisdom with the glory it had before the world was," we cannot but feel that there is an element of unreality in the entire conception. John's Logos is not an abstract quality or idea hypostatized, but an eternal Person, inscrutably identified with Deity, and manifested in the flesh of Jesus.

---

[1] It is almost amazing that in his special pleading for a purely ideal preëxistence of Christ, Beyschlag should thus comment on John viii, 58: "He does not say, I was; his point is not his having been before, but his eternal being. Abraham is only a transient appearance—he is the appearance of the Eternal in time. Before God thought of the birth of Abraham, he stood before him, through whom he would lead humanity to the goal of its destiny, the Alpha and Omega of his decree" (New Testament Theology, vol. i, p. 254). But if his "eternal being" and preëxistence were real in no deeper sense than the ideas of Plato (comp. Beyschlag, p. 252), he was no more eternal or preëxistent than Abraham. The archetypal Abraham must have been as real and as eternally preëxistent as Jesus Christ. Omniscience would think of the birth of Abraham as occurring long before that of Jesus.

[2] Phædrus, 249, 250.   [3] Phædo, 76.

(3) *More than Memra, Shekina, or Angel.* We may go further and maintain that the use of *Memra, Dibbura,* and *Shekina* in the Targums and what is said of the angel of Jehovah appearing in the bush, and accompanying the Israelites through the desert, are not sufficient to furnish a full or satisfactory interpretation of the Johannine Logos who "was in the beginning with God and who was God." These words of John and those also which relate to Christ's preëxistence, point to a more definite belief, a conception which cannot without unnatural violence be fitted to the vague, fanciful, and abstract ideals of the later Jewish theosophy. John's conception is notably positive and realistic.

14. John's Doctrine Far Above the Current Theosophy. Over against all these attempts to explain the Logos of John's gospel we submit that the apostle presents a doctrine far in advance of the current theosophic speculations of his time. He appropriates a well-known term, long employed with various shades of meaning in Hellenic and in Hellenistic literature, and fills it with a new and higher significance. With him the Logos of God is conceived rather in the light of God's activity and self-manifestation at the beginning of the creation. The Hebrew poets as well as the writer of Gen. i had made it a familiar thought in Jewish circles that God spoke the world into being. John places this idea in a new setting at the beginning of his gospel, appropriates for his purpose the suggestive term Logos, and declares that the Word of God and God himself are one. The Logos is God, the eternal Spirit, speaking, acting, manifesting himself, first in creation and afterward in the incarnate Son of his love. This manifestation of God embodies all that is deepest, highest, and most glorious in the suggestions attaching to the terms Logos, Dibbura, Memra, and Shekina. In him is the perfection of Might, Wisdom, and Love, but not as so many attributes personified or hypostatized after the manner of poetic and philosophic thought. "The only begotten Son, who is in the bosom of the Father,"[1] is the living, conscious embodiment of Deity, and the only one capable of interpreting (ἐξηγέομαι, *explain, unfold, declare*) the invisible God by a visible incarnation.

---

[1] The phrase ὁ ὢν εἰς τὸν κόλπον τοῦ πατρός, *who is in the bosom of the Father,* is equivalent in meaning to *the Word was with God* (ἦν πρὸς τὸν θεόν) in verse 1. The ὤν, however, of verse 18, points rather to the *timeless existence* of the Only Begotten, as the ἦν points to the *preëxistence* of the Logos; and the preposition εἰς in verse 18, as distinguished from πρός in verse 1, may indicate entrance (reëntrance) into the antemundane glory (comp. xvii, 5) consequent upon the historical manifestation in flesh; as if the writer for the moment thought of the fellowship of Father and Son as temporarily interrupted by the necessary conditions of incarnation. The definite historical character of the incarnate manifestation, conceived as a completed fact, is shown by the use of the aorist in ἐξηγήσατο, *he declared.*

15. Erroneous Metaphysical Distinctions. The chief difficulty in conceiving the whole subject of the incarnation of the Logos has been, perhaps, an erroneous notion of the deity of Christ as of something distinct from the deity of the Father. The agelong controversies over metaphysical distinctions between *essence* (οὐσία), *substance* (ὑπόστασις), and *person* (πρόσωπον, Persona) have involved these words in such confusion that it seems desirable to avoid the use of them entirely, and to adopt if possible some other forms of stating the biblical doctrine of Christ and of God. Some distinction must be recognized in John i, 1, between the Logos and God, and some explanation should be given of the love of the Father for the Son before the foundation of the world (xvii, 24).[1] The distinctions here implied point to real facts and experiences in the personality of God, but the mystery is not to be solved by any interpretation which supposes the preëxistent Logos to possess an individual will and intelligence distinct from the will and intelligence of God. Such a dual concept of the nature of Deity is not the doctrine of John's gospel. The Holy Spirit and God himself are one. There is no other Holy Spirit. When it is said that "God is Spirit" (iv, 24) the reference is to the Father who is repeatedly mentioned in the context. And so also, in i, 1, the Logos, who was with God in the beginning, was God. Whatever the distinction intended in the phrase πρὸς τὸν θεόν, *with God*, there is no mistaking the emphatic declaration that "the Logos was God." Our author nowhere attempts to describe or explain the incarnation. His whole portraiture of the Lord Jesus is ideal, mystical, all-comprehensive, and therefore we should not look in his record for accounts of the infancy, growth, and human limitations of the man Christ Jesus. The scope and plan of his writing did not make use of those facts; but it does not follow that he did not know and believe them. He is not so much the annalist as the interpreter of the incarnate Word of God. He thinks the thoughts of the Lord Jesus after him, and gives them mystic expression.

16. Jesus Christ in the Flesh. But while the Christ of the fourth gospel is the preëxistent Word, who both came down from heaven and ascended into heaven, he is also a man, and speaks of himself as such (viii, 40). He is no other than "Jesus of Nazareth,

---

[1] The statement that Christ "was *foreknown* before the foundation of the world" (1 Pet. i, 20) presents no difficulty, for that is a simple truism of the divine prescience, like that of the election of the sojourners to whom Peter's epistle was addressed (i, 1, 2). Any prophet or apostle of God may be spoken of, like Jeremiah (i, 5), as known, sanctified, and appointed in the purpose of God for a holy work before his appearance or existence in the world. But such a statement as "thou *lovedst* me before the foundation of the world," coming from the lips of Jesus himself in the act of prayer, cannot be thus explained as a matter of knowledge or of purpose.

the son of Joseph" (i, 45). That "the Word became flesh" is affirmed as positively as that he "was in the beginning with God." The reality of the incarnation is made emphatic at the beginning of the first epistle: "That which was from the beginning, that which we have heard, that which we have seen with our eyes, that which we beheld, and our hands handled concerning the Word of Life." Here we have unquestionably the same style of thought and expression as in the Johannine gospel, and the language points to a real, tangible personality, not to an abstract idea. It is fundamental in the teaching of this epistle "that Jesus Christ is come in the flesh" (iv, 2). The denial of this fact is a mark of "the deceiver and the antichrist" (2 John, 7). He "came by water and blood" (v, 6), for the baptism in Jordan and the death of the cross attested the reality of his life in the flesh. In 3 John, 7, the word Name is employed with a peculiar emphasis instead of the fuller phrase *name of the Son of God,* in 1 John v, 13. Compare John xv, 21, and Acts v, 41. So these epistles represent the common apostolic preaching and confession "that Jesus is the Christ" (v, 1), and in ii, 1, he is called our "Comforter," or "Advocate with the Father." The fact that Jesus in the flesh was a *manifestation* of God, and of the life and love of God, is affirmed in the gospel (ix, 3; xiv, 9; xvii, 6) and in the first epistle (i, 2; iii, 5, 8; iv, 9). In no part of the New Testament is the subordination of Jesus to the Father so explicitly and repeatedly affirmed as in the fourth gospel. Over and over he declares that "the Son can do nothing of himself, but what he seeth the Father doing." His human sympathy and affection appear incidentally but most significantly in connection with Lazarus and his sisters at Bethany (John xi, 3-5). His weeping at the tomb of his friend gave the Jewish lookers-on occasion to say, "Behold how he loved him!" And he was very human and tender to the last, and commended his mother, standing at the cross, to the disciple whom he loved (xix, 26, 27). It cannot therefore be said, with any reasonable propriety, that the humanity of Jesus is overlooked or disparaged in the Johannine books. On the contrary, it is most positively presented. But the great aim of the writer is not so much that of a reporter of the facts of Jesus's earthly life as of an interpreter of the Saviour of the world, who came forth from the bosom of God. An old disciple, who had intimately known Jesus in the flesh, and had leaned upon his bosom, after more than fifty years of meditation, teaching, and worship, gives his own translation of the thoughts of his Master.

CHAPTER X

SUMMARY OF THE NEW TESTAMENT DOCTRINE OF THE PERSON OF JESUS CHRIST

1. The Divers Dogmas of Historical Christology. Historical theology acquaints us with divers attempts to formulate the various biblical statements touching the person of Christ into one coherent doctrine. A vast literature has grown up around this subject, and in connection with the great ecumenical creeds, known as the Nicene, the Chalcedonian, and the Athanasian, and the later confessions in substantial accord with them, other opinions and theories of the person of Christ became historic under such names as the Arian, Apollinarian, Nestorian, Eutychian, and Socinian Christology. Each one of these represented a strenuous effort to define the relation which Jesus Christ, the Word and Son of God, sustains to the eternal Divine Nature, whom we worship as God, the Father Almighty. Was he of the same identical divine nature (*homoousian*), or of a similar nature (*homoiousian*)? Or was he even of a different nature or essence (*heteroousian*)? Whatever partisan feeling, or whatever dishonesty of procedure appeared at times among any of the different parties in the long conflict of opinion, we should credit all of the great leaders with a profound sincerity in their search for the truth. The one conspicuous fact is that these ancient leaders and teachers in the Church differed in their conclusions concerning the person of Christ. And probably everyone of the dogmas on this subject, maintained in the ancient or in the later times, has its defenders at the present day. Exact unanimity of opinion and uniformity of statement have never universally prevailed since the subject first became a matter of controversy; nor is such unanimity ever likely to prevail among all the disciples who call themselves Christians. All these dogmatists have appealed to the Scriptures in maintaining their particular views, confessedly willing to abide by the unquestionable teaching of Jesus Christ, and of his prophets and apostles. But the fact of their differences of interpretation shows the utter fallacy of the claim that the Scriptures are an "infallible" revelation and means of determining questions of this kind.

2. Divers Types of the Biblical Doctrine. But our study of the Christology of the different New Testament writers discloses the fact that the evangelists and apostles are not all in strict accord.

They represent different types of doctrine when they speak at length about the person of Christ. Biblical theology has in modern times put this fact in such conspicuous light that many of the contentions of former times have become nugatory. The notion that all the biblical writers, being inspired of God, must needs exhibit unanimity of opinion and statement is fast becoming obsolete. It is seen that the greatest and purest men of all the Christian ages have honestly differed on matters of grave importance, and all the evidence in hand goes to show that the first college of apostles was no exception. Paul, and Apollos, and Cephas, and James, and John looked upon Jesus from different points of view; each saw some things which the others did not seem to apprehend or emphasize; to each was given a distinctive message and ministry; and yet they were, in life and spirit, "all one in Christ Jesus." A number of men may differ widely on certain subjects, and yet all be true. Varieties of conception and statement are not necessarily contradictions. By means of the different presentations of Jesus the Christ, as found in the New Testament, we are richer in our spiritual possession than we could have been had we been left shut up to any one writer's report and portraiture of our Lord.

3. One-sidedness of Polemics. In view of these facts it ought to be seen that we do not truly honor our Lord Jesus by suppression of any of the facts reported of him in the gospels, or by magnifying any one aspect of his nature and personality to the neglect of others. Some theologians seem to feel scandalized by the plain statement in Luke's gospel that Jesus grew in grace and in wisdom; also by the fact of Jesus's own positive declaration, according to Matthew and Mark, that he himself did not know the day and the hour of the coming events of which he spoke. The older Christology was in the habit of building an argument for the deity of Christ on the claim that he is repeatedly called God in Paul's epistles and in Heb. i, 8; but textual criticism and the most painstaking exegesis now concede that all the texts on which that claim was founded are capable of another interpretation. One-sided dogmatism has nowhere, perhaps, displayed its partisan bias more notoriously than in reading the doctrine of the preëxistence of Christ and also that of his absolute equality with God into Phil. ii, 5-8, while it has at the same time ignored, or dismissed with few words, the statement of verse 9, immediately following, that "God highly exalted him." Some partisan writers have even displayed confusion and distress over this latter statement. They appear also unwilling to observe that it accords better with the teachings of Christ and his apostles to say that "God was in Christ" than to say that "Christ is God." We may affirm the true biblical interpretation of both these statements, but our Christology will become more scriptural, more impressive, and more worshipful by conforming to apostolic ways of expression than by strenuous adherence to the nonhuman, abstract, metaphysical dogma of Christ's deity as set forth in the Nicene creed and in the later Trinitarian symbols. It is only by exact interpretation of all the relevant scriptures and by a dispassionate comparison and adjustment of them that we escape the one-sidedness of partisan polemics, and recognize the various types of doctrine and peculiar forms of speech which are perceptible among the different biblical writers.

4. The Simplest Facts of His Life. We begin most naturally with a study of the simplest facts of the reported life of Jesus. There is a large body of these facts over which no serious differences of opinion exist. Jesus was truly human, born of a woman, a scion of the tribe of Judah and the house of David. He grew up from dependent infancy and childhood to middle age like other men. He doubtless learned as other children learn, for he advanced in wisdom as he advanced in years and in physical growth. His baptism by John, his subsequent ministry, his conflict with the leaders of the Jewish people, and his crucifixion are familiar facts which no one now disputes.

5. His Subordinate Relation to God. We observe, next, that he became conscious at an early period of his life that he was sent upon a divine mission by his heavenly Father. According to Luke's gospel, when he was only twelve years old he spoke with an understanding of sacred things which astonished the Jewish teachers in the temple. In his later ministry he spoke with a wisdom and authority unparalleled among the great religious teachers of the world. He never claimed or assumed omniscience, but God so possessed him from the beginning to the end of his earthly life, that, though he advanced in wisdom, he never uttered that which was not truthful, never maintained a false opinion, never had to correct an error in his own teaching, and never committed an act of sin. His obedience and subjection to the will of God constitute a conspicuous feature of his life and teaching. In John's gospel, where we find the most remarkable self-expression of superior wisdom and power, we find also the most positive assertions of his subordination to the Father. He calls himself a man who tells the truth which he received from God (viii, 40). He can do nothing of himself, but the Father who sent him and who abides in him is the real doer of his mighty works. His prayers accord perfectly with this acknowledged subordination; his sufferings and his supplications in Gethsemane and the bitter cry on the cross, "My God, why hast thou forsaken me," evince these facts of his dependence in a manner most impressive.

6. His Consciousness of Unique Relationship to God. As he advanced in wisdom the consciousness of his unique relationship to God seems to have deepened and strengthened within him. The heavenly revelation made to him at his baptism in the Jordan (Mark i, 10, 11) marked a distinctive crisis in his life, and drove him for a time into the wilderness of temptation; but, unlike the first Adam in his hour of trial, he "counted not the being on an equality with God a thing to be grasped," but humbled himself and chose the way of obedience. From that day onward Jesus proceeded with his work "in the power of the Spirit" (Luke iv, 14), and more and more his conscious convictions deepened into the knowledge that he came forth from God and was going away to be with God (πρὸς τὸν θεὸν ὑπάγει, John xiii, 3; comp. i, 1). The various recorded expressions of his self-consciousness reveal such transcendent knowledge of the Father Almighty as to exalt him immeasurably above all other prophets and teachers. It became perfectly natural for him to say of himself: "All things have been delivered unto me of my Father: and no one knoweth the Son save the Father; neither doth any know the Father save the Son, and he to whomsoever the Son willeth to reveal him" (Matt. xi, 27). And so, as he neared the end of his earthly ministry, he expressed this heavenly consciousness with an intensified emphasis: "Have I been so long time with you, and thou dost not know me? He that hath seen me hath seen the Father" (John xiv, 9).

7. His Heavenly Preëxistence. This profound inner consciousness of God found at times both a natural and a supernatural expression in allusions to his heavenly preëxistence and his coming forth from God. This doctrine appears unmistakably in the writings of Paul and of John, and is best accounted for as having first found utterance in the teaching of Jesus himself. In the light of this teaching we are led to think of God as existing eternally in the perfection of personal sensibility, intellect, and will. These constituent elements of personality subsist and act in God as in man, who "exists as the image and glory of God" (1 Cor. xi, 7). The greatest and most real Being in the universe is He who speaks of himself in this wise: "I AM WHO I AM." Every intelligent being, bearing the personal image of God, and existing in the glory and power of heavenly life, must needs experience emotional resources of delight within himself, and so this "only begotten Son of God" speaks of a glory and a love of the Father with himself "before the foundation of the world" (John xvii, 5, 24). These facts agree with John's conception of the Logos existing in the beginning with God, and existing as only begotten Son in the bosom of the Father. (The facts and the various expressions indicative of preëxistence find their best explanation in the fundamental truth that "the Word was God." Thus in the depths of the divine nature and personality the Father loved the Son before the foundation of the world; for the eternal Father, Word, and Spirit have, within the Father's bosom, infinite resources of delightful love. So, too, according to Paul, "the Son of his love, who is the image of the invisible God, is before all things, and in him all things hold together" (Col. i, 13-17).

8. Self-Coherence of the Supernatural in Christ. This doctrine of the preëxistent Word is the logical complement and clearest explanation of the supernatural which forces itself upon us in the manifestation of Jesus Christ in the flesh. This adequately explains, so far as we may know it, the mystery of the miraculous birth, and gives intense significance to the incarnation of "the only begotten Son." The mystery of his coming into the world comports uniquely with his resurrection and exit from the world, and with all the miraculous works and the incomparable words of wisdom and truth which appear in the records of his earthly life. His exaltation at the right hand of God places his person and his name far above every name, "that in the name of Jesus every knee should bow, and every tongue should confess that Jesus Christ is Lord, to the glory of God the Father" (Phil. ii, 10, 11). The apostolic salutations, doxologies, and benedictions associate these heavenly names, and teach us to honor and worship the Son even as we worship the Father.

9. A Likeness of Method in Paul and John. Paul's manner of addressing the philosophers of Athens was somewhat like that of John in setting forth a new and higher doctrine of the Logos to the thinkers of his time, whom he would fain persuade to the belief that "Jesus is the Christ, the Son of God." As the apostle to the Gentiles found an altar in Athens inscribed "to an unknown God," and as he appropriated that inscription as a text and starting point from which to turn the thoughts of the men of Athens to the true doctrine of "the God who made the world and all things therein" (Acts xvii, 24), so John appropriated a word, Logos, long common in Greek philosophy, and suggestive of much that was deepest in Hellenic and in Jewish theosophical thought, and filled it with a sublime significance. He gave the term an emphatic personal setting, and made its far-reaching suggestiveness a means of setting forth the true concept of the Son of God in his essential relations to the everlasting Father. In the manifestation of Jesus in the flesh, whom he had personally heard and seen and touched

(1 John i, 1), John beheld the true Word of life and light, a radiation of the real Logos who was in the beginning, who was with God, and who was God. And by his superior witness to the facts with which he was very familiar, he has filled that old philosophical term Logos with a divine significance which it never contained before, and which can never be taken away from it.

10. The Godhead of Christ Jesus. According to Paul's Christology it was the Father's good pleasure that in the Son of his love "all the fulness should dwell," and he affirms that "in him dwelleth all the fulness of the Godhead bodily" (Col. i, 19; ii, 9). He should not, therefore, be conceived as an incarnation of a part of God, as of one element, one πρόσωπον, or one ὑπόστασις, of eternal Deity. In him dwelt and was manifest the totality of Deity, "all the fulness of the Godhead." Somehow he enshrined the fullness of God in a human personality, and now and ever in him the Divine Essence in its fulness permanently dwells. According to John's Christology he is the "only begotten from the Father," and yet "is in the bosom of the Father." The Father is in him, and he is in the Father. The Father dwelt in the beloved Son through every moment of his incarnate life, and withheld not from him the fullness of his Spirit. But this divine indwelling was conditioned by the facts and necessary limitations of his manifestation among men, and when he "ascended where he was before," those temporary limitations were removed. He is at home in the throne of God, and the divine purpose of the ages is to be consummated in him when all who believe on him through the word of his gospel shall behold him in his heavenly glory. The Christological conceptions of Paul and John supplement each other, and when they are fairly combined with all the other New Testament teaching on the subject they present for our meditation and worship a transcendent Personality, filled with the fulness of God. We do not presume to understand or to explain the inner mystery of his being. We deem it wise to abstain from attempting to determine the precise metaphysical relations of the divine and the human in this "only begotten Son of God." But the biblical doctrine of this adorable Personality makes it emphatic that he is of the same nature (*homoousian*), and not, as the Arians held, of a similar nature (*homoiousian*), much less of a different nature from that of the everlasting God.

11. The Mystery of God. When we endeavor to combine all the facts involved, and with them to inquire after the premundane relations of the Father and the Son and the Spirit, we soon find ourselves overwhelmed with the sense of our human limitations. We may with Paul speak of this whole subject as "the mystery of God," and "the mystery of Christ." "God is in Christ," and "Christ is God's." As a theological term, the Logos, or Word, is not altogether synonymous with the Christ. Christ Jesus is a name that always points us to the historical Christ of the gospel; the Logos suggests more directly the supernatural and premundane Being in whom abides the mystery of the ages, but who voluntarily took upon himself the human, fleshly manifestation of Jesus Christ our Lord. But we should not forget that this doctrine of the Person of Christ has been the fruitful subject of controversy through all the Christian centuries, and never was the question, "What think ye of Christ?" more commanding than at the present hour. Such a question cannot be finally settled by any one man or by any council of the churches. Every age will make its own answer, or, rather may we say, Christ himself has his own specific and unmistakable answer for every age. But the answer for ever resolves itself into "the mystery of God," and all they whose lives become hidden with Christ in God may rest in blessed assurance that they shall hereafter behold him in the glory of his Father, and then only shall they "see him even as he is."

SECTION SECOND
THE MEDIATION OF JESUS CHRIST

CHAPTER I

THE MYSTERY OF MEDIATION AND OF INCARNATION

1. Nature of Mediation. The adorable personality of Jesus becomes still more impressive and affecting when studied in connection with his redemptive ministry of mediation. The words *mediator* and *mediation* imply two parties who are at variance, and an efficient mediator is one who can fairly represent the two and make peace between them. The peace thus secured is called a reconciliation. According to 1 Tim. ii, 5, "There is one God, one mediator also between God and men, himself man, Christ Jesus, who gave himself a ransom for all." A competent mediator must be vitally acquainted with the feelings and interests of both the parties whom he would bring together, and when those who are alienated are, as in this case, God and man, the efficient mediator must be at once a partaker of the divine nature and also of flesh and blood. Such was Jesus Christ. Although in glory with the Father and partaking of his love before the world was, he was in the fullness of time born of a woman, grew up as other men from infancy to manhood, was tempted in all points as we are, and suffered and died the death of the cross. Thus "it became him, for whom are all things and through whom are all things, in bringing many sons unto glory, to make the author of their salvation perfect through sufferings." The perfection of this human experience was as essential to the world's Mediator as was his heavenly preëxistence in the bosom of the everlasting Father. Hence it is that, from a New Testament point of view, all the problems of the moral universe center in Jesus Christ, and through his mediatorial ministry they are to find their ultimate solution.

2. Doctrine and Ideals of Incarnation. In the prologue of John's gospel we have a very remarkable presentation of the doctrine of divine incarnation. The eternal Word of God became flesh and dwelt among men in a way adapted to show forth the glory, grace, and truth of the eternal Father. The mediation of Jesus Christ cannot receive a full biblical exposition apart from this fact and doctrine of incarnation, for "God was in Christ reconciling the world unto himself." The idea of incarnation may be shown to have had from the beginning both a cosmical and a personal expression in many different ways. The outward expression of God's everlasting power and divinity may be seen in natural phenomena to which it has not always occurred to man to give a spiritual interpretation. The heavens have declared his glory, and the wonders of creation have made known his wisdom and power, but the vain reasonings of men have too generally perverted the import of these cosmic revelations of God. Even in the myths current among the nations, and in the strange superstitions of the earth, we are able to discern the concepts of divine incarnation written in the heart of man. Some writers maintain that the idea of incarnation is a crude belief of rude society in its earliest stages: uncivilized and ignorant tribes conceive God as a great man, but later and more accurate thinking begets the conviction of an impassable gulf between God and man. We reject this construction of the facts alleged, and submit as a more trustworthy and tenable opinion that this human way of thinking about God is eminently proper. The biblical doctrine is that man is himself the highest visible image and likeness of the invisible God, and surely the heavenly Father may be most properly conceived as partaking of the qualities of his noblest offspring. The various ideas of incarnation traceable in the religious thought and in the mythologies of the nations may be studied as so many different indications of the one great truth that our God and Father thus condescends to make himself known to his human offspring. Zoroaster is said to have received his revelations through an archangel of colossal form, nine times as large as an ordinary man. Hindu mythology is particularly noted for its innumerable stories of incarnation, or descents of the various deities. The god Vishnu is remarkable for his numerous manifestations. Whenever iniquity seems to triumph and religion is exposed to danger he issues forth from the unseen realms in some new avatar.[1] In the older cult of Brahmanism Brahm is conceived as the divine spiritual essence from which all things proceed, and Brahma is his first manifestation, the first lawgiver of India, and the inspirer of the Vedas. The doctrine of transmigration, so conspicuous in all the native religions of India, is essentially a concept of reincarnation. Buddhism furnishes a most remarkable conception of the doctrine of incarnation. Its fundamental tenet is that the successive Buddhas

---

[1] So in the Bhagavad Gita (iv, 7, 8) he says: "I manifest myself from age to age for the defense of the good, for the suppression of the wicked, and for the establishment of justice."

are beings who repeatedly make their appearance in human form, yet only after immense intervals of time. Previous to his incarnation in human form the Buddha is believed to have passed through various births, at one time appearing as a reptile, at another as a bird; but when at last he appears as Buddha, he is always born of a woman, and born under the ordinary laws of human life. The distinguishing qualities of the Buddha are calmness, gentleness, and repose, and these thus become incarnate in their highest manifestation. Here, then, is an ideal of all that is noblest and best in moral attainment set forth before us in the form of a perfected human being. But while the Father has not left himself without witness among the nations, all other manifestations of himself have been eclipsed by the incarnation and mediation of Jesus Christ. Even the superior revelations of God given in the books of Moses and the Prophets and the Psalms are consummated and superseded by the manifestation of the Christ; how much more completely has this manifestation consummated and eclipsed the inferior revelations of the whole Gentile world!

3. Mystery and Purpose of the Ages. It appears from the teachings both of John and of Paul that the marvelous incarnation of God in Christ, reconciling the world unto himself, is the great mystery of the ages, hidden during the times of the eternal past, but disclosed through the personal manifestation and mediation of the only begotten Son of God. We are to conceive this great mystery and purpose of God as a process going on through the ages. These ages have their epochs, and crises, and consummations. The regeneration of mankind is not brought about in one thousand years, nor are human hearts with their many experiences of emotion and intelligence the creation of an instantaneous act of omnipotence. Times and seasons of world-wide significance, and the many modes of his self-revelation are matters which the everlasting Father keeps within his own counsels, but it is his good pleasure to make known to men such blessed truths as make for their well-being. The revelation of God in Christ is often spoken of, especially in the writings of Paul, as a holy "mystery" (μυστήριον). In the twenty-seven passages of the Greek Testament where this word occurs it always denotes some noble spiritual truth, some hidden fact or mystical relation, which, though withheld from the many who care for none of these things, is made known to them that have the Spirit of God. Paul speaks of "God's wisdom in a mystery, that which has been hidden, which God foreordained before the ages unto our glory" (1 Cor. ii, 7). In the doxology with which he concludes the epistle to the Romans he speaks of "the revelation of the mystery which hath been kept in silence through times eternal, but now is manifested and . . . is made known unto all nations unto obedience of faith" (xvi, 25, 26). In Eph. i, 9-11, we read of "the mystery of his will, according to the good pleasure which he purposed in him unto a dispensation of the fulness of times, to sum up all things in Christ, the things in the heavens and the things upon the earth." The same idea finds repeated statement in Eph. iii, 9, 11, and in Col. i, 26. Other epistles witness the same eternal truth. The earth, the world, the universe has its deep mystery and purpose, which comprehends all things in the heavens as well as the things in the earth. The Lord Christ in the continuous ministry of his mediation between God and man is bringing into light this mystery of the ages. His redeeming work and its eternal purpose of love have their origin in the bosom of the Father, and this sublime concept accords notably with all that is highest and best in the theistic arguments of teleology. This universe of being shows manifold evidences of intelligent design, and the divine "purpose of the ages" means that back of all phenomena there exists not only an invisible Energy by which all things are held together, but also a Supreme Intelligence, which sees all things and rules all things from beginning to end. We, who can see but parts of his ways, gladly study what may now be known of him as he reveals himself in the one great Mediator.

CHAPTER II

OLD TESTAMENT IDEAS OF MEDIATION

1. Value of Old Testament Ideas. The scriptures of the Old Testament enable us to see, in great measure, how God's eternal purpose of the ages was gradually unfolded. The everlasting Father made himself known to the Melchizedeks and Jethros of ancient time as truly if not as fully as to Abraham and Moses. The Wisdom from above has cried aloud in the high places and along the pathways of the sons of men (comp. Prov. viii, 1-4), and all nations of men have heard the heavenly voice and have shown "the work of the law written in their hearts." But God bestowed exceptional advantages upon the Jewish people, and chiefly in the fact that they were intrusted with the records of a divine revelation (comp. Rom. iii, 2), which show how God spoke unto the fathers in many different ways. And these Hebrew scriptures are still profitable for us in our study of the ever-unfolding mystery of God and of Christ.

2. Primitive Priesthood and Mediation. It is quite natural for any worshiper of a supernatural Power to resort for assistance to some mediator between himself and the Deity. This fact has been to some extent apparent among the devotees of all the religions of the world. Among savage tribes we note the need and the reverence felt for the medicine man, the soothsayer, or the priest, who is supposed to possess some superior influence with the powers invisible. In the biblical narratives of early patriarchal times the head of the household acted as priest and mediator. Melchizedek is mentioned in Gen. xiv, 18, as "king of Salem" and "priest of God Most High." Noah, Abraham, Isaac, Jacob, and Jethro, priest of Midian, are represented as building altars, offering sacrifices, and calling upon God, as if acting the part of mediators and intercessors. Especially noteworthy is the account of Abraham standing as an intercessor before Jehovah, and pleading for the cities of the plain when their enormous wickedness had exposed them to the sentence of destruction from the righteous Judge of all the earth. The hero of the book of Job is depicted as an ancient patriarch and priest, offering up burnt offerings for the sins of his sons and daughters (Job i, 5). Such mediation, intercession, and sacrifice, whatever their various forms among the different peoples, are an obvious provision for the sense of spiritual need which is deeply felt in the heart of man. For men are the offspring of God, and they come into conscious being possessed of a religious nature that instinctively feels and yearns after the living God. And the most ancient forms of priestly mediation between man and God evince an inborn yearning of the soul for peace and favor with the Author of its being.

3. Moses and Samuel as Mediators. Moses is represented as preeminently a mediator between Israel and God. The people were filled with a deep sense of awe, and they said unto Moses: "Speak thou with us, and we will hear; but let not God speak with us, lest we die. . . . And they stood afar off, and Moses drew near unto the thick darkness where God was" (Exod. xx, 19, 21). We also read that "Jehovah spoke unto Moses face to face, as a man speaketh unto his friend" (Exod. xxxiii, 11; comp. Num. xii, 8; Deut. xxxiv, 10). We find remarkable examples of Moses pleading before Jehovah in Exod. xxxii, 31, 32, and Num. xi, 11-15, and in the first-mentioned intercession he is spoken of as "going up unto Jehovah" to make atonement for the sins of the people. Similarly Samuel the prophet is besought to pray for the sinful people that they may not die (1 Sam. xii, 19-23). He offered burnt offerings to Jehovah, cried out aloud unto Jehovah, and was signally answered in behalf of Israel (vii, 9, 10). In all this he acted the part of a mediator and priest.

4. The Levitical Priesthood. Moses was of the tribe of Levi (Exod. ii, 1), and according to the Levitical tradition he consecrated his brother Aaron to the priesthood, and the sons of Aaron were thereafter set apart by a perpetual statute to execute the office of priest in Israel. According to Exod. xiii, 2, 12, 15; xxii, 29, Jehovah claimed all the firstborn of Israel as his peculiar possession, but he substituted the tribe of Levi for the firstborn of all the people, and ordained that they alone should minister in holy things before him (Num. iii, 12, 41, 45; viii, 16-19). The trustworthiness of this Levitical tradition has been questioned, for subsequent to the times of Moses we read of such men as Gideon and Samuel and David and Solomon and Elijah offering sacrifices before Jehovah, apparently without any knowledge of such exclusive right of the descendants of Aaron. The great prophets from Samuel to Jeremiah show no such respect for priesthood, burnt offerings, and sacrifices as a knowledge of such a Mosaic appointment of Aaron's sons and the elaborate ritual of Levitical worship would naturally command. The probability is that this elaborate ritual of priesthood and offerings and multiplied ceremonies was of slow growth, and did not reach the completeness in which it now appears in the Priest Code of the Pentateuch until the time of Ezra and the second temple. But the story of the wandering Levite in Judg. xvii, 7-13, the eagerness of Micah to secure his priestly services, his subsequent capture by the Danites to be the priest of their tribe, and the fact that he is called "the son of Gershom, the son of Moses," and that "his sons were priests to the tribe of the Danites until the day of the captivity of the land" (xviii, 30), show the priestly standing of the Levites in those unsettled times. Moreover, the ministration of Eli, the priest, in a temple of Jehovah at Shiloh, and a going up "from year to year to worship and to sacrifice unto Jehovah of hosts in Shiloh," as recorded in 1 Sam. i, 3-9, point to a very ancient seat of Levitical worship at that place, where, according to Judg. xxi, 19, an annual "feast of Jehovah" was observed. The priestly prerogatives of the whole tribe of Levi are also clearly witnessed in Deut. xviii, 1-8. But our concern is not so much with the history of the Levitical priesthood as with its mediatorial significance. The officiating priest at the altar of sacrifice acted not for himself alone. He was mediator and representative of other worshipers before God. He was required to care for everything pertaining to the altar and the holy places (Num. xviii, 5, 7), to offer incense, light the lamps, attend to the showbread, and keep the fire continually burning on the altar of burnt offerings. The priests were also to be teachers of the law (Lev. x, 10, 11; Deut. xxxiii, 10). Their highest service, however, was to officiate in the offering of the various sacrifices described in the elaborate ritual of Lev. i—vii. In this they appear as the divinely ordained representatives of all Israel. The most solemn and significant service, developed in the later history of the Levitical priesthood, was that of the high priest on the day of atonement. Having washed his body and put on the hallowed garments, he proceeded to offer the burnt offering and the sin offering to make atonement for himself and for his house (Lev. xvi, 2-6). After this he took the censer full of burning coals, and burned incense so that the fragrant cloud arising therefrom covered the mercy seat above the ark; then he took the blood of the bullock which served as a sin offering for himself, and afterward the blood of the goat which served as the sin offering of the people, and, passing within the inner veil, sprinkled the blood of the bullock and goat upon the mercy seat, and thus "made atonement for himself, and for his household, and for all the assembly of Israel" (Lev. xvi, 12-17). In all this symbolical service the high priest appears as a representative of all Israel, a sanctified and sympathetic mediator between a sinful people and a holy God, and the mediation which he effects is supposed to accord with the holiness of God on the one hand, and the needs and necessities of the people on the other.

5. The Sacrificial Offerings. The office and work of the Levitical priesthood cannot be fairly set forth without at least a brief notice of the various offerings which were required by the laws and regulations of the Priest Code. These sacrificial offerings early acquired the threefold character of (1) self-surrender and self-dedication of the worshiper to God, (2) thanksgiving for his benefits and mercies, and (3) propitiation for sin. Cain and Abel are represented as bringing fruits of the ground and firstlings of the flock to present before Jehovah, and both fruits and firstlings are called a מנחה, *offering,* or gift (Gen. iv, 3-5). The burnt offerings of Noah after the flood (Gen. viii, 20-22) were of the nature of thanksgiving and dedicatory worship. The ancient records of the patriarchs show a noticeable connection of their sacrifices and their prayers. We are not able to determine how far the idea of sacrificial blood in the earliest times was conceived as an expiatory offering for sin, but it is evident that in every case the sacrifice offered was a formal expression of self-surrender to God. The animal sacrifice, in its pouring out of the warm lifeblood of the victim, was suggestive of a vicarious offering up of life in accordance with what was believed to be the good pleasure of God, and the accompanying acts of festivity and thanksgiving were expressive of the worshiper's trust in God and of his delight in the conscious acceptance of all his benefits.

(1) *Cereal Offerings.* The elaborate ritual of the Priest Code carefully distinguishes between bloody and bloodless offerings. The cereal offerings, or "meal offerings," consisted of corn in the ear, fine flour, and cakes baked or fried, and were accompanied with olive oil, frankincense, salt, and wine (Lev. ii). These were associated with libations, or drink offerings, of wine, and both together were a devout acknowledgment, as stated in 1 Chron. xxix, 11-14, that all things in the earth and heaven belong to Jehovah, and that all offerings which man can make to God are but a giving back to him some respectful portion of what he himself has bestowed.

(2) *Blood Offerings.* The offerings which involved the shedding of blood, according to the ritual of Lev. i—vii, were of four kinds: the burnt offering (עלה), the peace offering (זבח שלמים), the sin offering (חטאת), and the trespass offering (אשם). The first two were in large part, like the meal offering, expressive of self-dedication and thanksgiving. The "whole burnt offering" symbolized the offering up to God of all that the worshiper represented, himself body and soul, his family and household, his property of every sort. All these were regarded as God's gracious gifts to him, and were to be held in

readiness for any service of God to which they might be put. The peace offering was a public declaration of peaceful and friendly relationship between the worshiper and his God. The sacrificial feast which accompanied it was a joyful expression of fellowship with God, as if the happy participants were really eating and drinking in the presence of Jehovah.¹ But the sin offering and the trespass offering were preëminently designed to make atonement for the sins of the people. They presuppose a separation between the worshiper and God, and also a deep sense of guilt which must have, in order to remission, the shedding of the lifeblood of the vicarious victim. The law of the trespass offering (אָשָׁם), according to Lev. v, 14—vi, 7, and Num. v, 5-8, contemplated individual offenses which call for restitution. If the trespass were a criminal appropriation of another's goods, the guilty man was required to restore in full, and also to add a fifth of its value as a fine. When the offense was an act of carnal impurity with a bondmaid the priestly law contemplated the deed as an infringement of the rights of property which demanded open satisfaction (Lev. xix, 20-22). Probably also some similar thought of compensation for lost service, or of fine for censurable defect, entered into the reasons for the trespass offering required in the case of the Nazarite (Num. vi, 12) and of the leper (Lev. xiv, 11-18). The trespass offerings accordingly contemplated individual offenses involving the consciousness of personal guilt.

(3) *The Sin Offering.* But among all these offerings the most solemn and impressive appears to have been the חַטָּאת, *sin offering,* the detailed ritual of which is read in Lev. iv, 1—v, 13. A specific order of procedure and various sacrificial victims were ordained according to the rank and position of those for whom atonement was to be made. But whether the offender be the anointed priest, the whole congregation, the civil ruler, or one of the common people, in every case the atonement called for the shedding of blood. The only apparent exception is that of one so poor as not to be able to bring even "two turtledoves or two young pigeons" (v, 11-13). But the flour which in such case was allowed as a substitute, was not to be mixed with oil or frankincense, but to be burned upon the altar, and upon "the fire offerings of Jehovah" (אִשֵּׁי יהוה). Thus it was made to partake of the atoning efficacy of the animal sacrifices and reckoned as a real sin offering. The representative and propitiatory character of the sin offerings is seen

---

¹ Sacrifices on high places, like the one indicated in 1 Sam. ix, 12, 13, 23-25, were obviously of the nature of a public banquet at which the people and their God feasted and rejoiced together. 1 Sam. xx, 29, is evidence that families were wont to observe such sacrificial meals together. Comp. also xvi, 2-5, and Gen. xxxi, 54.

in the fact that they were required not only for individual offenses, and sins of ignorance, but also for the whole people. They were offered on the great national feast days, on the occasion of consecrating the priests, and at the dedication of the tabernacle. They appear in most solemn significance in the ritual of the day of atonement (Lev. xvi). Everything connected with the ceremonies of that day was of the most awe-inspiring character, and the service was ordained not for specific and individual sins, but rather to "make atonement for the holy sanctuary and the tent of meeting, and the altar, and the priests, and all the people of the assembly." After all the other expiatory rites of an individual character, and aside from those of the other annual feasts and of the new moons (Num. xxviii, 11-15), the ritual of the day of atonement on the tenth day of the seventh month assumes that there is yet some defilement or deficiency which ought to be provided for in most impressive form. And so on that day the high priest must take the censer full of burning coals from the altar, and sweet incense and the blood of the sin offering, and go within the veil and let the cloud of incense cover the mercy seat, and sprinkle the blood upon the mercy seat seven times.

6. The Goat for Azazel. The ceremonial of confessing all the iniquities of Israel over the head of the goat that was "sent away for Azazel into the wilderness," which formed also a notable part of the ritual of the day of atonement, deserves at least a passing notice. Whatever the origin of this part of the ceremonies, and whatever the real meaning of the word *Azazel*, formal confession of all their sins and putting them upon the head of the goat, which "bore upon him all their iniquities unto a solitary land," were a striking symbolical picture of the expulsion of sin and iniquity from the people of Israel. It was a public declaration that the sins of all the people were now sent away from them unto their own place, transferred to the abode of the evil spirits in the desert.[1] Thus both the people and their dwellings would be conceived as purged from the guilt and judgment of transgressions.

7. Symbolical Significance of the Blood. The classic passage in the Levitical law which defines the symbolical import of the expiatory offerings of blood is Lev. xvii, 11: "The life of the flesh is in the blood, and I have given (appointed) it to you upon the altar to make an atonement for your souls: for it is the blood that makes

---

[1] Compare the "passing through waterless places" (Matt. xii, 43), and the "casting into the outer darkness" (Matt. viii, 12), and "departing into the fire prepared for the devil and his angels" (Matt. xxv, 41), as a going forth to one's appropriate place.

atonement by reason of the soul (life)." It is not the mere blood, as a material substance, that possesses the efficacy here ascribed to it, but the blood yet warm with the life of the victim. When the worshiper brought his offering and placed his hands upon its head he openly confessed thereby his guilt and obligation, and must have conceived that the animal offered was in some sense a vicarious sacrifice for himself; and when the lifeblood was "poured out before Jehovah" the symbolic rite was itself a public declaration that the life of the victim without blemish or spot was substituted in the mercy of God for the life of the transgressor. Whether the blood were poured out at the foot of the altar, or sprinkled on the horns of the altar, or at the golden altar of incense, or on the mercy seat within the veil, it was in every case regarded as a divinely appointed offering to make atonement for the souls of men.[1]

8. The Consuming of the Flesh. In connection with these ideas of atonement, symbolized in the shedding of sacrificial blood, the disposition of the flesh of the animal victims was not without suggestions of purification. The burning of the fat upon the altar, as an offering made by fire unto Jehovah (Lev. iv, 26, 31, 35), signified a free offering up to God of the better part of the worshiper, and the burning of the flesh of the sin offering without the camp in the clean place where the ashes of the altar were carried (Lev. iv, 12, 21) suggested a complete removal of the sins of the flesh. For a thorough taking away of sin requires more than the atoning efficacy of the blood of expiation: there must be also a blotting out of all iniquity; and this was symbolized by devoting the flesh of the sin offerings, as if defiled by its contact with sin, to the consuming fire.

9. Significance of כפר and its Derivatives. The word כפר and its derivatives, which are usually translated by *atone* and *atonement,* deserve a passing notice in connection with the Levitical laws of expiation. The primary meaning seems to be indicated by a usage which involves the idea of *covering over,* or *hiding.* Thus in Gen. xxxii, 20, Jacob thinks he can *cover* the face of Esau with such a princely gift that his injured brother will not look upon the wrongs of the past.[2] Hence easily arose the meaning of covering over in the sense of appeasing, pacifying, propitiating,

---

[1] This was obviously the opinion, as we shall see farther on, of the author of the epistle to the Hebrews, who elaborates the idea in his ninth chapter, and concludes that "according to the law, I may almost say, all things are cleansed with blood, and apart from the shedding of blood there is no remission" (ix, 22).

[2] The word כסות is used in the same way in Gen. xx, 16, where Abimelech gives a thousand pieces of silver for a *covering* of the eyes of all who were with Sarah that they might not see the offense to which she had been exposed.

and in the sacrificial codes of the later priestly legislation the atonement offered was conceived as covering, concealing, and blotting out the sins of the guilty. The individuals thus covered or atoned for were regarded as delivered from exposure to the penal consequences of transgression. And this entire sacrificial arrangement appears in the biblical record not as an invention of men, nor as a service which recognized any merit in the person who brought the offering, but as a conspicuous condemnation of sin. It is Jehovah who has graciously provided this substitute of animal life for the life of the sinner, and has appointed the offering of blood upon the altar to make atonement for the guilty soul. It should also be noted that the Hebrew word commonly translated *mercy seat* is כפרת, the *cover,* or lid, of the ark of the covenant. The ark contained the two tables of the decalogue, God's testimony against sin, and this *capporeth,* or cover, was to be sprinkled with blood on the day of atonement (Lev. xvi, 11-17), and was thus made a significant symbol of "mercy covering wrath." [1]

10. Frequent Biblical Allusion to Sacrifices. Further details of priestly mediation and of sacrifices for sin, according to the Levitical ritual, need not detain us. But we shall find in other scriptures, and in the New Testament teaching, frequent allusion to the offerings of blood as an atonement for sin. How far these outward symbols of expiation entered into the eternal purpose of God, and were typical of holy mysteries which became manifest in the mediation of Jesus Christ, is a question not to be lost sight of as we pursue our inquiries. The Old Testament ritual of mediation and of service contains sundry object-lessons which were of the nature of a preparatory discipline, looking to the mediatorial ministry of the Son of God. And the same may be said of other religious systems which have served to cultivate the sense of spiritual need and to turn the yearnings of the human heart toward God. For all these methods of feeling after the Infinite Helper may be conceived as so many expedients through which the heart of unspeakable LOVE has been working to draw all men unto himself. They also evince the necessity which the guilty but penitent soul feels for some saving efficiency higher than himself in order to deliverance from the power of sin. Efficient rescue from depths of self-despair must needs come through some manner of suffering and sacrifice.

11. Human Sacrifices. The awful practice of offering human sacrifices is probably best explained as a giving up to God the best, the dearest, the most sacred treasure possible. Abraham's willing-

---

[1] For fuller showing of this symbolism, see Biblical Hermeneutics, p. 272, and Biblical Apocalyptics, p. 83.

ness thus to offer up his only son for a burnt offering obtained for him Jehovah's great blessing (Gen. xxii, 16, 17). Jephthah offered his daughter and only child as the noblest possible sacrifice (Judg. xi, 31, 39). The king of Moab in the extremity of battle as a last resort offered his eldest son as a burnt offering (2 Kings iii, 27). But the prophets of Jehovah condemned this practice (Mic. vi, 7; 2 Kings xvi, 3; xxi, 6; xxiii, 10); it was denounced as an "abomination to Jehovah" in Deut. xii, 31, and explicitly forbidden in the Levitical code (Lev. xviii, 21). The practice, however, shows to what extremes religious zeal will go in efforts to obtain and hold favorable relations with God. The devotion thus evinced may be most admirable, but its method of display is barbarous and abominable.

12. Priesthood and Sacrifice Express Deep Religious Convictions. One unavoidable conclusion, which forces itself upon us when we study those customs of priesthood and sacrifice which go back to primitive times, is that they are all the expressions of religious conviction, and evince the need, felt everywhere and at all times, of some kind of mediation between man and God. In earliest times the head of the family acted as priest and offered the sacrifice, as appears in the examples of Noah and Jacob and Job. Whether the Deity recognized were conceived as a household God, or the God of the tribe to which the worshiper belonged, or the one God over all, the worship in its essential elements would be the same. Hence we are to recognize the real depth and significance of the lowest forms of sacrificial worship, and to note that they all indicate desire and effort on the part of the worshipers to be on good terms with God. The offering seems in all cases to have been prompted by the query, "Wherewithal shall I come acceptably before my God?" The answer, of course, may take on various phases at different times and places. It may be in the form of fruits, libations of wine, whole burnt offerings, the blood of choice victims from flock and herd, and even a human sacrifice. The principle is the same in all. Along with such a variety of offerings would be associated divers conceptions of propitiation, atonement, expiation, and reconciliation, as also divers notions of priesthood. But in all ministrations of this kind the priest acts the part of a mediator between God and man. As it is well stated in Heb. v, 1, he is "taken from among men and appointed for men in things pertaining to God, that he may offer both gifts and sacrifices for sins, and bear gently with the ignorant and erring." And so, probably, the best explanation of priesthood and sacrifice, the wide world over, is that God himself thus put it into the heart of man to do his best to be on favorable terms with the Author of his being. Thus has the Father sought to draw men; but their forms of approaching him were often matters of their own devising.

13. Insufficiency of Animal Sacrifices. According to Heb. x, 1-4, all the Levitical offerings were insufficient to perfect the worshiper. The blood of animal sacrifices cannot take away sins. But those symbolical and typical ministrations of mediation were a "shadow of the good things to come." They serve to illustrate and in their measure reveal the greater and more perfect sacrifice of Christ, and the nature of his divine-human mediation. The earlier forms of worship, regarded as divine institutions, were graciously provided to assist man in his earnest feeling after God. The heavenly Father overlooked the misconceptions, the ignorance, and the errors; but in the fullness of time he brought in the clearer light to make known the mystery and the purpose of the ages. It is, accordingly, a great error to condemn, as some do, all the sacrificial offerings of the old time as inhuman, heathenish, and barbarous, arising out of superstitious fear of a vengeful Deity. No doubt demoralizing superstitions have too largely prevailed, but the degrading conceptions of placating an offended Deity spring from false views of God. The deities of the heathen world were often thought of as arbitrary, lustful, passionate beings, who deceived men by delusive dreams and subjected them to cruel plagues in order to gratify old feelings of revenge. Service offered to such a deity would naturally contemplate the removal of his wrath and spite. But we cannot regard such notions of God as having ethical content or value. The profound views of sin and guilt symbolized in the Levitical cult impart a nobler aspect to all offerings of blood. With the Hebrews atonement meant a divinely provided means of making God and man at one. The guilt-laden soul sought peace with the Holy One by means of the most sacred token of self-surrender he could bring. The real object was not to placate a revengeful Power, but to offer a reasonable, holy, and acceptable sacrifice before the Giver of all life, who had himself graciously instituted this means of reconciliation.

14. Ideas of Mediation in the Prophets. The prophets of the Old Testament present an ideal of mediatorial intercession and vicarious suffering which is far in advance of the Levitical ritual of sacrifice. They expose the emptiness of outward forms, and proclaim Jehovah as the God who yearns with infinite compassion after his erring people, and who would rather see in them a loving obedience than excessive observance of ritual. Isaiah proclaims Jehovah as having no delight in the oblations and burnt offerings of a people whose worship is only an outward heartless formality, while they fail to put away their evil doings (Isa. i, 10-17). Similarly Micah declares (vi, 6-8) that righteous action, loving affection, and walking humbly with God are a better means of approaching Jehovah than "thousands of rams, or ten thousands of rivers of oil." Vainly will one offer up his firstborn child for the sin of his soul. God looks rather for a deep struggle of the soul after purity and righteousness that results in spiritual transformation. The book of Hosea is remarkable for its doctrine of condemning judgment mixed with divine compassion. Israel is depicted as a faithless wife who has notoriously played the harlot in departing from Jehovah. Her guilt is set forth in the darkest colors, and the certainty of penal retribution is forcibly declared. Having sown the wind, she shall reap the whirlwind. Having plowed wickedness, she must needs reap iniquity. And yet through all this prophecy there breathes a spirit of divine affection for the sinful nation. Jehovah would fain receive back his faithless wife, notwithstanding all her running after other lovers. He cries out as if in bitter anguish: "O Ephraim, how shall I give thee up? O Israel, how shall I deliver thee over to judgment? My heart is turned upon me; my compassions are kindled together. I will not execute the fierceness of mine anger, I will not return to destroy Ephraim; for I am God and not man, the Holy One in the midst of thee" (xi, 8, 9). In a similar way Isaiah arraigns the "sinful nation, a people laden with iniquity, who have forsaken Jehovah and despised the Holy One of Israel" (i, 4), and he announces that because of their evil doings the judgments of fire and desolation have visited the land. But at the same time he pleads with them to put away the evil of their doings, and "though their sins be as scarlet, they shall be as white as snow; though they be red like crimson, they shall be as wool" (i, 18). Jeremiah recalls the piety of Israel's youth, the love of her espousal in the wilderness (ii, 2), but he cries out in astonishment over her backslidings, and her "playing the harlot with many lovers" (iii, 1). If one run to and fro through the streets of Jerusalem, he will seek in vain to find a man that doeth justly, that seeketh after truth (v, 1). And he speaks out the feeling of Jehovah himself when he cries: "Oh that my head were waters, and mine eyes a fountain of tears, that I might weep day and night for the slain of the daughter of my people! . . . For they proceed from evil to evil, and they know not me, saith Jehovah" (ix, 1, 3). The righteous judgment of God was signally executed on the sinful nation by Assyria, the rod of his anger (Isa. x, 5), and by the chastisements and woes of the Babylonian exile; but in all their woes the lovingkindness of

Jehovah continued toward them, and he brought his people back from the lands of their exile as he had in the older time brought them up out of the Egyptian bondage. His loving purpose of redemption never failed.

15. The Suffering Servant of Jehovah in Isaiah liii. The most remarkable prophetic portraiture of vicarious suffering is found in Isa. lii, 13—liii, 12. It is an old question of exegesis whether the servant of Jehovah in this passage is the same "Israel my servant, Jacob whom I have chosen, the seed of Abraham my friend," so frequently mentioned in preceding chapters (xli, 8, 9; xlii, 1; xliii, 10; xliv, 1, 2, 21; etc.), or some one individual of the nation, or the Messiah. Our use of the prophecy, however, need not wait for a final determination of that question; for the ideas of vicarious suffering presented in the language of the prophet are essentially the same in all these expositions, since the character described is that of "a man of sorrows," who leads Zion out of captivity, gives his soul as a trespass offering for sin, and makes intercession for the transgressors. Whatever, therefore, the possible explanations of the whole passage, the idea set before us is that of an individual.

(1) *The Preceding Context.* In the preceding context (lii, 1-12) the restoration of Zion and Jerusalem is portrayed in lively form. The captive daughter of Zion is called upon to shake herself from the dust and to go forth out of captivity, assured that her exodus from present oppression shall be more glorious than that from the Egyptian bondage. "For Jehovah hath comforted his people, he hath redeemed Jerusalem, hath made bare his holy arm in the eyes of all the nations, and all the ends of the earth have seen the salvation of our God." In departing from the present house of bondage they need not go out in such haste as in the ancient exodus, for Jehovah will go before and behind them like a pillar of cloud and of fire (ver. 12). Thereupon the prophet introduces his graphic picture of the servant who shall act wisely and become highly exalted.

(2) *The Contrasts.* In this graphic outline we cannot fail to observe several remarkable contrasts. The servant acts wisely and is exalted very high, yet is his form marred more than any man, and is also despised and rejected of men. He grows up as a tender plant, and as a root from the dry ground, but somehow he brings healing to a sick and sorrowing world. He is led as a lamb to the slaughter, yet he divides the spoil with the mighty. He is terribly stricken on account of the sins of the people, but he sees the fruits of the travail of his soul and is satisfied. He is even made a curse for others, being wounded and bruised for

their sins and bearing their iniquities, but by his knowledge he succeeds in making many righteous. It even pleases Jehovah to bruise him and put him to grief, but, as a result, "the pleasure of Jehovah shall prosper in his hand."

(3) *Mediatorial Soul-Passion.* Among the many facts of his humiliation and suffering is the notable statement of verse 6 that "Jehovah hath mediated in him (הפגיע בו) the iniquity of us all." The word which we here translate *mediated,* and which is commonly rendered *laid on,* or *made to light on,* is used in the same causative form (hiphil), but intransitively, in verse 12, where it means *maketh intercession.* It indicates in both places the mediatorial soul-passion and struggle of personal intercession, and what is remarkable is that in verse 6 Jehovah himself is the causative subject of the intercession, and in verse 12 the suffering servant of Jehovah, who pours out his soul unto death and bears the sin of many, is the one who intercedes for the transgressors. So it is Jehovah who causes the iniquity of others to strike (פגע) and work an agony of travail in the soul of his servant, and the servant's mediatorial intercession avails for the transgressors.

(4) *Triumph and Exaltation.* The final triumph and exaltation of this servant of Jehovah are as wonderful as his subjection to suffering. He becomes highly exalted, attracts the attention of many nations and kings, his days are lengthened, a great posterity is promised him, he brings righteousness to multitudes, his soul is satisfied with the result of its travail, and he is conceived at last as a great conqueror who divides the spoil among his mighty heroes. Though numbered with the transgressors, he is a revelation of the arm of Jehovah's power.

(5) *The Christian Interpretation.* Well might Christian interpreters have ever recognized in this prophetic picture of "a man of sorrows" a striking portraiture of Jesus Christ. For, whatever collective idea may here as in other parts of this book attach to the "servant of Jehovah," this description obviously contemplates a person who is distinguished from the whole house of Israel and who suffers for transgressions not his own. No less than seven times is it said in one form or another that he was smitten for the sake of others, and verse 9 declares that he himself was guilty of no violence or wrong. After the manner of the sin and trespass offerings of the Levitical ritual, his soul was made an offering for sin, poured out unto death, and he bare the sin of many.

16. Idea Given in Daniel ix, 24. The language of Dan. ix, 24, is worthy of attention as indicating the writer's idea of the termination of an old order, the end of certain forms of transgression and sin, and the introduction of a new order of everlasting righteousness. The passage is best translated in the form of Hebrew parallelisms:

Seventy heptades are decreed upon thy people and upon thy holy city,
To close up the transgression and to consummate sins,
And to expiate iniquity and to introduce eternal righteousness,
And to seal up vision and prophet, and to anoint a Holy of holies.

The expiation of iniquity here spoken of seems to be some propitiatory mediation of epochal significance, which is to be effected at the point of time to which the prophecy refers. The sealing up of vision and prophecy most naturally means the fulfilling and cessation of prophetic oracles by the opening of the Messianic age of universal knowledge (comp. Isa. xi, 9). The consecration of a new Holy of holies implies the institution of a "greater and more perfect tabernacle," with its new and living way of entrance for all the pure in heart (comp. Heb. ix, 11; x, 19). It is easy to see how these references to some new and superior methods of expiation were capable of a special Messianic application, and the song of Zacharias contains (Luke i, 68, 77) profound conceptions of "redemption for his people," "knowledge of salvation," and "remission of sins," which formed a part of Israel's Messianic hope as held among the most pious of the nation. And it was thus through sacrifices, and symbolic forms of worship, and soul-stirring oracles of prophets, and prayers of the psalmists, that God's purpose and the mystery of the ages were slowly working in the course of Israel's history and preparing the way for a clearer revelation.

17. Doctrine of the Penitential Psalms. The psalmists as well as the prophets magnify that inner spiritual conception of mediatorial self-offering which is better than all burnt offerings. The most acceptable "sacrifices of God are a broken spirit: a broken and a contrite heart, O God, thou wilt not despise" (Psa. li, 17). The deep inner struggles of the contrite heart partake of the nature of God's own yearnings to bring the truly penitent sinners into experiences of holy life and peace. The so-called "penitential psalms" are like so many cries out of the depths of profound sorrow for sin. They are full of confessions which acknowledge that rescue must come, if it come at all, from a lovingkindness of God which is able to blot out transgression and cleanse from all unrighteousness. Of all these penitential psalms the twenty-second is the most remarkable for the number and variety of its self-expressions of personal agony. Some expositors believe it to be a composition of David, describing a terrible struggle of soul through which he himself passed. Others have ascribed it to Hezekiah, and some to Jeremiah the prophet. Others discern in the pleading sufferer of this psalm a personification of Israel in exile, and not a few insist that the language can be legitimately explained only of the sufferings of Christ and the glorious results secured thereby. Whatever view one takes of its authorship and immediate occasion, the various sentiments of this impassioned lyric, like those of Isa. liii, are to be studied for their profound suggestions touching the personal agony that may be felt in mediatorial intercession. The exclamation at the beginning implies a terrible sense of abandonment by God: "My God, my God, why hast thou forsaken me?" This feeling of rejection is the more amazing and impressive in view of the suppliant's continual cry, and the trust and deliverance of his fathers, as stated in verses 1-5. He thinks of himself as a writhing worm rather than as a man, an object of reproach and contempt among the people. All who gaze upon him in his agony treat him with derision; they laugh him to scorn, wag their heads, and cry out with biting sarcasm:

> Roll it on Jehovah; let him deliver him;
> Let him rescue him, for he delighted in him.

In the midst of this great distress he finds no deliverer at hand, although God has been his trust from infancy. The following words show the extremity of his affliction:

> Many bulls have compassed me about,
> Strong ones of Bashan have surrounded me.
> They have opened their mouth upon me—
> As a lion tearing and roaring.
> Like waters am I poured out,
> And all my bones are sundered;
> My heart has become like wax,
> Melted in the midst of my bowels.
> My strength is dried up like a potsherd,
> And my tongue is cleaving to my jaws;
> And thou dost set me in the dust of death.
> For dogs have compassed me about;
> A crowd of evil-doers have encircled me.
> They have pierced my hands and my feet,
> I can number all my bones;
> They keep looking and gazing at me.
> They divide my garments among them,
> And upon my vesture they cast lots.

In this extremity of woe he directs his prayer again to Jehovah (vers. 19-21), and suddenly a marvelous answer comes. עניתני, *Thou hast answered me,* he cries;

> I will declare thy name to my brethren;
> In the midst of the assembly will I praise thee.

The remainder of the psalm (verses 23-31) is a triumphal declaration of the result of his sufferings and his prayers. He seems to struggle up out of depths of agony into heights of power, whence he calmly surveys "all the ends of the earth" returning to Jehovah and bowing down before him as their rightful ruler, whose righteousness is to be celebrated through all generations. This remarkable poem abounds with metaphors which run into hyperbole, but the extravagance of the figures serves to intensify to the uttermost the portraiture of personal affliction. The psalm is usually reckoned among the Messianic psalms, but it contains expressions which are inapplicable to Jesus Christ. This much, however, should be said, that the sufferer who gives utterance to these impassioned words is an innocent sufferer, and in all his agony he gives forth no vent of anger against those who revile him. No other Old Testament scripture suggests in equal space so many facts mentioned in connection with the crucifixion of the Son of man. Verse 1 was uttered by him on the cross (Matt. xxvii, 46; Mark xv, 34). The wagging of heads, the mockery and sarcasm, the thirst, the piercing of hands and feet, the parting of his raiment and casting lots for it, are all mentioned in the gospels in describing the last agony of Jesus. And the last word of the psalm, עשה, *he has done* it, or *it is accomplished*, reminds us of Jesus's last word, according to John xix, 30, τετέλεσται, *it is finished*. All these facts along with the representative character of the sufferer, who assumes that his triumph through unspeakable agony is destined to secure the redemption and reunion of "all the families of the nations," makes the twenty-second psalm a typical prophetic oracle. It sets before us an ideal Israelite, in whom is no guile, subjected to a passion of soul that makes him a representative partaker of the sufferings of Christ and of the glories destined to follow.

18. Connection with Israel's Messianic Hope. A study of the foregoing ideas of priestly and sacrificial mediation, as found in the Hebrew scriptures, will enable us also to see how this general concept of mediatorial intercession and salvation became naturally associated with Israel's Messianic hope. The Lord who sits at the right hand of Jehovah, according to Psa. cx, and is destined to subdue and judge among the nations, is declared by the oath of Jehovah to be "a priest forever after the order of Melchizedek." The epistle to the Hebrews (chaps. vi and vii) magnifies this saying as a most significant ideal of the priesthood of Jesus Christ, who is proclaimed (viii, 1, 2) as "a high priest who sat down on the right hand of the throne of the Majesty in the heavens, a minister of the sanctuary, and of the true tabernacle, which the Lord pitched, not man."

CHAPTER III

SAYINGS OF JESUS RELATIVE TO REDEMPTION

1. Comparatively Little on this Subject in the Gospels. It is preëminently desirable, in our study of the mediation of Christ, to know as accurately as possible the teachings of our Lord himself. It is the prevalent belief that the synoptic gospels furnish us with the most exact tradition of his words, and we shall first examine what they report touching the giving of his life for the salvation of man. But we shall also study in the same connection whatever the fourth gospel has to say upon the same subject. We should admonish ourselves, however, in advance, that the gospel records are not the class of biblical writings in which one would look for any extensive treatment of the doctrinal significance of Jesus's death. They are rather a record of the facts of his birth, life, works, death, and resurrection, and bear the style of memoirs. We do not find in them any formal or detailed instruction on the significance of these great facts. The disciples were strangely slow to understand what their Lord did say to them about his death and resurrection, but so far as we have any report of his teaching on these matters, whether in the synoptics or in the gospel of John, we study them as words of the highest value.

2. His Entire Life a Ransom for Many. Of all the reported sayings of Jesus, bearing on the doctrine of mediation, the most noteworthy is probably that which is recorded in Matt. xx, 28, and Mark x, 45: "The Son of man came not to be ministered unto, but to minister, and to give his life a ransom for many." The main question in this passage touches the precise meaning of the last three words, *a ransom for many* (λύτρον ἀντὶ πολλῶν). In defining the word λύτρον, *ransom,* in such a statement as is here made, we cannot fairly ignore the usage and connotation it holds in the Septuagint version of the Old Testament.[1] In Exod. xxi, 30, it means the price that may lawfully be put upon the life of one who is exposed to the penalty of death, and by the payment

---

[1] It is used alike for the translation of כפר, פדיון, and גאלה, all of which have in common the meaning of *ransom, redemption,* or *price of redemption.* The word ἀντίλυτρον in 1 Tim. ii, 6, seems to be substantially identical in meaning, and λύτρωσις (Luke i, 68; ii, 38; Heb. ix, 12) and ἀπολύτρωσις (Rom. iii, 24; Eph. i, 7, 14; Col. i, 14; Heb. ix, 15) also have the same general significance and connotation.

of which he is to be released from such penal exposure. In Exod. xxx, 12, the word is employed to designate the poll tax of half a shekel which "every man shall give as a ransom for his soul unto Jehovah." In Lev. xxv, 51, it stands for the price paid for the liberation of one who has been sold into bondage. The word is also used in connection with the redemption of land that had been sold (Lev. xxv, 24), and the redemption of the produce of the land which by the law of tithing belonged unto Jehovah (Lev. xxvii, 31). In all these examples and illustrations of the ransom the main idea is that of substituting one thing for another. Hence the preposition ἀντί, *for, in place of,* is naturally employed in Matt. xx, 28, as most consonant with the idea of a *ransom price.*[1] The Son of man gives his life as a ransom price for the liberation of many who are assumed to be held under some sort of bonds. In what this bondage consists nothing in the text or context tells; but the statement in Matt. xxvi, 28, that his blood "is shed for many unto remission of sins," and the use of the verb λυτρόω in Titus ii, 14, and 1 Pet. i, 18, in the sense of "ransoming from all iniquity," and "ransoming from a vain manner of life," are good evidence that the ransom contemplated by Jesus in the text under discussion is deliverance from the bondage of sin. The figure of "selling one's self to do evil" would probably have been familiar to readers of the Old Testament (comp. 1 Kings xxi, 20, 25; 2 Kings xvii, 17), and Paul develops this idea at length (Rom. vi, 16-23; vii, 14, 23). What Jesus himself taught about the impossibility of serving two masters and about repentance and remission of sins accords with the same idea. When, therefore, he declares that he "came to give his life a ransom for many" the most natural and obvious thought suggested is that of redemption from the bondage of sin. But the *process* or *mode* by which this redemption is accomplished is not here described; nor should we assume that the "giving of his life" in this text refers exclusively to his death on the cross. Jesus foretold his death and spoke of its necessity (comp. Luke ix, 22; xxiv, 7, 26, 46; John xii, 23-27); he recognized the closing period of his earthly life as a crucial hour; but when he says, "For this cause came I unto this hour," we are not justified in the inference that the events of his death on the cross were of more value in his work of mediation than many other events of his life. We must duly recognize all the great facts of his incarnation, and his resurrection and ascension, and the apostolic teaching that he ever lives to make intercession for us. The sacrifice of his life includes also every cup of agony

---

[1] The preposition περί is, however, used in connection with λύτρα in the Septuagint of Num. xxxv, 31.

which he drank (comp. Matt. xx, 22; xxvi, 42; John xviii, 11), and the baptism of overwhelming trials which he underwent (comp. Mark x, 38; Luke xii, 50). His severe temptations in the wilderness, his longsuffering with a "faithless and perverse generation" (Matt. xvii, 17), his upbraiding of Chorazin and Bethsaida, his weeping over Jerusalem, and his amazement and bloody sweat in Gethsemane were all of them together only a part of the mediatorial struggle involved in his giving his life a ransom for many. He recognized it as the high purpose of his mission "to seek and to save that which was lost" (Luke xix, 10). He "came not to call the righteous, but sinners" (Matt. ix, 13), and he would search far and labor long to gather in "the lost sheep of the house of Israel." In all these statements we read the struggle of an intensely sympathetic friend of the sinner, one who, like the ideally good shepherd, is ready to lay down his life for the sheep. He endured all manner of opposition of sinners, and "resisted unto blood, striving against sin" (Heb. xii, 3, 4). Such a giving of his life for the ransom of many from the bondage of sin need not and ought not to be complicated in thought by attempts to discover in the mediation of Christ something analogous to every idea which the figure of a ransom suggests. In what manner this heavenly Redeemer accomplishes his ministry of redemption is a legitimate inquiry, and will be considered in the pages which follow; but when Jesus says that his life was given to bring about the liberation of mankind from the power of sin it diverts attention from his main thought when one asks "to whom the ransom was paid," and how it could be an "equivalent satisfaction" of the debt which guilty man owed God.[1] Confusion of thought must needs attend the effort to press into dogmatic significance every suggestion and implication of a metaphor. In such a text as Deut. vii, 8—"Jehovah *redeeme*d you out of the house of bondage, from the hand of Pharaoh king of Egypt"—we do not suppose that a ransom price was paid to Pharaoh or to the Egyptians; nor do we once imagine

---

[1] It seems hardly necessary to make mention of the old patristic fiction of God giving the soul of Jesus as a ransom to Satan, who was thought of as holding humanity in captivity. Such an importance accorded to Satan formed part of a fanciful and absurd demonology now quite effectually exploded. The later Anselmic theory of substituting the infinite merit of Christ's sufferings as an equivalent satisfaction for the infinite demerit of sin moves in a realm of thought quite foreign to the Scriptures. It has a logical affinity with the later Romish doctrine of indulgences, and with ultra Antinomianism and its fictions of the imputation of man's guilt to Christ, and of Christ's personal righteousness to the elect. The originators and advocates of these theories failed to perceive that a ransom of such infinite merit, and such a complete satisfaction of justice, logically leave no reasonable ground for the doctrine of salvation by grace. Whatever grace may be alleged in such a monergistic scheme is by the hypothesis so essentially compulsory as to rob it of all the real qualities of mercy. But perhaps the worst feature of this monergistic scheme was its sovereign exclusion of the nonelect from any share in the imputed righteousness of Christ.

that Sheol and death receive a stipulation when we read Hos. xiii, 14: "From the hand of Sheol I will ransom them; from death I will redeem them." The great fact in this case is that Jesus Christ entered into all the experiences of human life. He was tempted in all points as we are; he confronted the scorn and malice and violence of a hostile world; and in all this struggle he sacrificed himself and gave up his own life to rescue men from sin. It seems, therefore, irrelevant and idle to inquire after some particular creditor to whom such a ransom must have been paid. When we think properly of a deliverer who of his own good will subjects himself to a fearful struggle, involving the sacrifice of his life to rescue others from the peril of death, we do not ask *to whom,* but rather *for whom,* that costly price of self-sacrifice was paid. Such ransoms are prompted by the purest emotion of love; one noble life is given instead of the many exposed to death, and the sufferings involved are even gladly borne for the sake of the rescued ones and for the glory that must result from such a work of redemption.

3. Words of Jesus at the Last Supper. Another important saying of our Lord bearing on the doctrine of his mediation is found in connection with the Last Supper, when he took the cup and gave it to the disciples, and said, according to Matt. xxvi, 28: "Drink of it all ye; for this is my blood of the covenant, which is shed for many ($περὶ πολλῶν$) unto remission of sins." The parallel text in Mark xiv, 24, reads: "This is my blood of the covenant, which is shed for many" ($ὑπὲρ πολλῶν$). The reading in Luke xxii, 20, is peculiar, is omitted from some ancient manuscripts, and has been thought by some critics to be an interpolation[1]: "This cup is the new covenant in my blood, that which is poured out for you" ($ὑπὲρ ὑμῶν$). Paul's statement in 1 Cor. xi, 25, corresponds closely to that of Luke: "This cup is the new covenant in my blood: this do, as oft as ye drink, in remembrance of me." These solemn words, together with what Jesus said in the same connection about eating the bread as a symbol of his body given and broken for them, have obvious allusion to some typical significance in the passover meal which our Lord and his disciples were eating togther. They clearly imply that in some sense he became for them a true paschal lamb and whatever else the paschal supper signified; and it agrees with this idea, that, according to Luke xxii, 16, 18, he himself

---

[1] Thus Westcott and Hort, after stating the difficulties of the critical problem, observe: "These difficulties, added to the suspicious coincidences with 1 Cor. xi, 24, 25, and the transcriptional evidence given above, leave no moral doubt that the words in question were absent from the original text of Luke, notwithstanding the purely Western ancestry of the documents which omit them."—Notes on Select Readings, p. 64.

partook of it neither by eating nor drinking. All the synoptists record Jesus's refusal to drink thenceforth from the fruit of the vine until he should drink it new (*καινόν*) in the kingdom of God. If, however, we suppose that he ate of the paschal lamb with them, but declined to eat of the bread and drink of the cup, we obtain nothing of essential value for determining the significance of our Lord's words on the occasion. He declared the bread to be his body and the cup his blood of the covenant which was shed for many, and the language can mean no less than that he himself was in some sense given as a sacrifice for many, whether he himself at that time ate of the paschal lamb or not. It is also well to note in passing that Paul conceived Christ as "our passover slain" (1 Cor. v, 7). Whatever the particular forms observed in the course of the paschal meal in the time of our Lord, there can be no doubt that the feast itself was celebrated as a memorial of Israel's deliverance from the bondage of Egypt (comp. Exod. xii, 14; xiii, 9). The story of that deliverance could not well be told apart from the memorable sprinkling of the blood of the first paschal lamb upon the side posts and lintel of the houses to defend the dwellers therein against the destructive plague. Thus the entire feast of the passover was on the one hand essentially a memorial of Israel's redemption unto Jehovah; on the other hand, the words *my blood of the covenant,* used by Jesus according to all the synoptists, can hardly be explained otherwise than as a conscious appropriation of the language of Exod. xxiv, 8, where the reference is to the blood of burnt offerings and peace offerings sacrificed unto Jehovah; but the emphatic statement that he would not drink of this symbol of the blood of the covenant until he should drink it *καινόν, new in kind,* with them in the heavenly kingdom, reminds us of the words of Jeremiah (xxxi, 31-34) about the new covenant between Israel and Jehovah,[1] and helps to point out the spiritual significance of all this language of Jesus at the paschal meal. It was a new kind of eating and drinking to which he would elevate their thoughts by means of this symbolic meal, a feasting together in the heavenly kingdom of his Father.[2] The eating of his body and drinking of his blood must mean a partaking of his spirit and of the eternal life which he imparts (comp. John vi, 53-58, 63). He surrenders himself, body and soul, to the death of the cross, for the redemption of many from a worse

---

[1] The use made of this passage from Jeremiah in Heb. viii, 6, ff., is worthy of careful study in connection with the words of Jesus. The plan of our treatise requires us to treat it in another connection.

[2] One might compare the figure of "reclining with Abraham and Isaac and Jacob in the kingdom of heaven" (Matt. viii, 11), and the blessedness of those "who are bidden to the marriage supper of the Lamb" (Rev. xix, 9).

than Egyptian bondage. For it is only as his spotless life is thus freely offered that he himself becomes the potent means and mediator of human salvation. The shedding of the blood of this paschal lamb has for its object, as Matthew (xxvi, 28) records it, "remission of sins." We cannot therefore with proper regard to the simplest suggestions of the language and its occasion divorce from the words of Jesus at the last supper the then current ideas of atonement through the sprinkling of blood. One may appropriately say, in the language of Isa. liii, 10, "It pleased Jehovah to bruise him and to make his soul an offering for sin." The institution of the new covenant of his gospel, like that of the old covenant of Mount Sinai, was accordingly ratified by the shedding of blood, and it was the blood of Jesus, the blood of the new covenant, shed for many because given for the life of the world. From all which it appears very evident that we cannot fairly or satisfactorily explain the teaching of Jesus touching his own divine mediation without admitting his obvious allusions to Old Testament ideas of atonement. In this fact we may also observe how the ritual of an inferior religious cult may prepare the way for something more spiritual and divine.

4. God's Great Love for the World. So far as the gospel of John sets forth the teaching of Jesus on the subject of his own divine mediation, it supplements and confirms the doctrine found in the synoptics. Perhaps the most noteworthy declaration in the New Testament touching the love of God as exhibited in the saving mediation of his Son is that which is written in John iii, 14-16: "As Moses lifted up the serpent in the wilderness, even so must the Son of man be lifted up: that whosoever believeth in him may have eternal life. For God so loved the world, that he gave his only begotten Son, that whosoever believeth on him should not perish, but have eternal life." It is an old question of exegesis whether all these are words of Jesus or an enlargement of his words made by the evangelist. The only trustworthy answer seems to be the general one that the teaching of Jesus had so thoroughly taken possession of the evangelist's thought and life as to find its true expression not in the exact terms employed by the Lord, but rather in the language and style of the disciple. Whether Jesus uttered these sentiments near the beginning or at the end of his ministry is a question of no essential importance to John. His aim is to present Jesus for all that he is worth to the believer (comp. xx, 31), and the words to Nicodemus in iii, 14-16, fairly interpreted, include the following truths: (1) The mediatorial offering of Christ has its origin in the love of God, which is a world-embracing love. (2) The offering involves the most affecting of all possible sacrifices, the giving of an only begotten Son[1] for the rescue and the eternal life of the perishing world of mankind. (3) The Son thus offered is in some sense a vicarious sacrifice for those who are liable to perish, but who, through faith in him, may have eternal life and be saved. (4) In the course of this divine procedure the Son of man is exalted before the eyes of men (comp. the προεγράφη, *openly portrayed,* of Gal. iii, 1) "even as Moses lifted up the serpent in the wilderness" (comp. Num. xxi, 9). (5) In order to accomplish this salvation of the world it was somehow necessary (δεῖ) that the Son of man should be thus lifted up (ὑψωθῆναι). This *being lifted up* refers most naturally to his being lifted up on the cross,[2] and the voluntary surrender of himself to the death of the cross is the mode, according to John's gospel, in which the love of God asserted itself and became effectual for the salvation of the world.

5. Giving of his Flesh and Blood for the Life of the World. This giving of the Son of man for the life of the world is further set forth in the remarkable words of John vi, 50, 51, and what is written in connection with them. The figure here is not that of a sacrificial victim offered on the cross, but of living bread out of heaven: "I am the living bread which came down out of heaven: if any man eat of this bread, he shall live forever: yea, and the bread which I will give is my flesh, for the life of the world." But the provision of such heavenly food necessarily involves the sacrifice of the life of the Son of man; for he goes on to say that, "Except ye eat the flesh of the Son of man and drink his blood, ye have not life in yourselves. He that eateth my flesh and drinketh my blood hath eternal life; and I will raise him up at the last day." This is no doubt mystical language and is to be spiritually interpreted (comp. ver. 63), but it has the most vital relation to the doctrine involved in the words of the Last Supper touching the eating of his body and the drinking of his blood. The gracious provision of God in giving his Son that the world through him might be saved becomes effectual in the individual believer only as he personally accepts the wonderful gift of the Father's love, and inwardly appropriates the living bread from heaven. So "he that believeth hath eternal life" (ver. 47).

---

[1] The offering of "the only begotten Son" may find some measure of its impressiveness in a conscious allusion to the offering of Isaac by Abraham in Gen. xxii, 2, 16.

[2] Compare John viii, 28; xii, 32–34. In the last-named passage the writer understands Jesus to "signify by what manner of death he should die"; but the words, *if I be lifted up from the earth* (ἐκ τῆς γῆς, *out of the earth*) are hardly compatible with the mere idea of being lifted up on the cross, and verse 33 has been suspected as an interpolation. But viii, 28, "When YE have lifted up the Son of man," indicates the crucifixion.

6. Dying for Others. The vicarious offering of his own life for the sake of others is also seen in John x, 11, 15, where Jesus declares himself the good shepherd who lays down his life for the sheep. The idea suggested in this illustration is not that of an expiatory offering for sin, but rather of an exposure to loss of life consequent upon faithful care of the flock. A similar thought is conveyed in the language of xv, 13: "Greater love hath no man than this, that a man lay down his life for his friends." A man may thus lay down his own life for the sake of his friends in one or another of many ways; and yet it is in keeping with the imagery of offering the blood of life upon the altar to speak of all such modes of giving up one's life for the sake of another as examples of vicarious sacrifice without which there could have been no salvation of the one that was rescued. This idea certainly pervades the gospel of John, and appears in the construction which the author puts upon the saying of Caiaphas, "That it was expedient that one man should die for the people, and that the whole nation perish not"; for he looked upon this utterance of the high priest as an inspired oracle, "That Jesus should die for the nation; and not for the nation only, but that he might also gather together into one the children of God that are scattered abroad" (xi, 50-52). The idea of sacrifice, even unto the laying down of life, appears also in the proverbial saying of xii, 24: "Except a grain of wheat fall into the earth and die, it abideth alone; but if it die, it beareth much fruit." This principle of sacrifice in order to reach some greater good is fundamental in the moral world, and the death of Jesus is its highest possible illustration.

7. Intercessory Prayer in Chapter xvii. But in no portion of the fourth gospel do we find a more impressive self-revelation of Jesus Christ as Mediator between God and man than in his high-priestly prayer in chapter xvii. With a sublime self-consciousness of oneness with the Father, and at the same time of oneness with the men who are given him out of the world, he stands as a great high priest who has already virtually passed into the heavenly places and "appears before the face of God for us" (comp. Heb. ix, 24). He is conscious of having come forth from the Father, of having glorified him on the earth, of having accomplished the ministry of his incarnation, and of having arrived at the crucial hour of leaving the world and being glorified with the glory which he had with the Father before the world was. He has manifested the Father's name and given his word to the disciples; and now, as he is about to leave them and go unto the Father, he prays for them that they may be kept and guarded from the evil of the world, and sanctified in the truth. As he had sanctified or consecrated himself in willing sacrifice, he prays that they also may be consecrated in a freewill offering of themselves in the truth. And finally he prays that they and those who should thereafter believe on him through their word "may all be one; even as thou, Father, art in me and I in thee, that they may be perfected into one; that the world may know that thou didst send me, and lovest them, even as thou lovest me." And so the one great Mediator pleads, desiring that those who are thus united in holy fellowship "be with me where I am, that they may behold my glory, which thou hast given me: for thou lovedst me before the foundation of the world." This remarkable intercession is equivalent to a declaration on the part of Jesus that he came forth from God as a divinely appointed Revealer of the Father's grace and glory, and as a Mediator divinely consecrated to effect the perfect union and fellowship of God and all them that are sanctified in the truth. He alone can say to the Father, "They are thine: and all things that are mine are thine, and thine are mine: and I am glorified in them." After the manner of Heb. ii, 13, and its context, we may here behold the sanctifier and the sanctified "all of one," and we see the author of their salvation, made perfect through suffering, leading many sons into glory, and saying, "Behold, I and the children whom God hath given me."

8. Words of Jesus on the Cross. At this place it seems most fitting to notice the sayings of our Saviour on the cross. Matthew and Mark inform us that "about the ninth hour Jesus cried with a loud voice: "My God, my God, why hast thou forsaken me?" Luke says nothing of this, but he reports three other sayings: (1) "Father, forgive them; for they know not what they do"; (2) "To-day shalt thou be with me in Paradise"; (3) "Father, into thy hands I commend my spirit." In John's gospel there is no mention of any of these sayings, but three others are recorded: (1) "Woman, behold thy son! Disciple, behold thy mother!" (2) "I thirst"; (3) "It is finished."[1] All reverent readers and expositors have felt the marvelous height and depth and breadth of these seven words. The cry of abandonment and agony is a citation of the first words of the twenty-second psalm. It expresses an awful sense of loneliness, and may be compared with the language of the mighty conqueror who speaks in Isa. lxiii, 3-6, and declares that he found no arm to help him in the terrible struggle with his foes. That conqueror was sprinkled with the lifeblood of his enemies whom he had trampled in his wrath; but the agony of Jesus on the cross, as well as in Gethsemane, was not a wrestling with

---

[1] These seven sayings appear in Matt. xxvii, 46; Mark xv, 34; Luke xxiii, 34, 43, 46; John xix, 26, 27, 28, 30.

flesh and blood, but rather with powers invisible. He had come to the last and supreme struggle of giving up his life as a ransom for the world of sinful men. If his soul was "exceeding sorrowful, greatly amazed, and sore troubled" in Gethsemane (Mark xiv, 33, 34), it is probable that there was even deeper anguish on the cross. But his God did not forsake him, and in his uttermost sense of vicarious suffering he revealed the Father also. For God was even thus in Christ, loving the world, yearning in unspeakable desire to save the world, "making intercession with groanings which cannot be uttered," and thus disclosing his holy passion to "reconcile the world unto himself." The prayer for the forgiveness of them that crucified him accords with the greatness of his dying love; the promise of paradise to the penitent soul that shared with him the ignominy of the cross enlarges our vision of the heavenly places prepared by the Christly Mediator for all them that believe on him; and his commending his own spirit at death into his heavenly Father's hands is an example which every one of his disciples may follow. The three sayings preserved in John's gospel show him to be very tenderly affectioned and human to the last, and the exclamation τετέλεσται, *it is finished,* expresses the calm, superhuman, godlike consciousness of one who is more than a conqueror.[1] Had we no other sayings of our Lord aside from these uttered on the cross, we should still possess the elements of a sevenfold gospel of the Son of God.

---

[1] Harnack observes the fact that those who looked upon the death of Jesus as a sacrifice "soon ceased to offer God any blood-sacrifice at all. Wherever the Christian message subsequently penetrated, the sacrificial altars were deserted and dealers in sacrificial beasts found no more purchasers. If there is one thing that is certain in the history of religion, it is that the death of Christ put an end to all blood-sacrifices." Das Wesen des Christentums, p. 99. Eng. trans., p. 169.

CHAPTER IV

DOCTRINE OF JOHN AND OF PETER

1. Doctrine of the First Epistle of John. The doctrine of the first epistle of John accords so closely with that of the fourth gospel that in now passing to a study of the apostolical epistles we may appropriately begin with this important document of the early Church. For though this epistle may be among the very latest products of the apostolic age its doctrine of the mediatorial work of Christ appears to be in substance identical with what we find in the very earliest examples of apostolic teaching. A remarkably close parallel to the great text in John iii, 16, is the comprehensive statement of 1 John iv, 9, 10, where, in immediate connection with the words "God is love," we read: "Herein was the love of God manifested in us, that God hath sent his only begotten Son into the world, that we might live through him. Herein is love, not that we loved God, but that he loved us, and sent his Son to be a propitiation for our sins." Verse 14 says that "the Father has sent the Son as Saviour of the world." Nothing is clearer in these statements than that the "propitiation for our sins" originates in the love of God. The work of Christ as "Saviour of the world" is not to appease a wrathful Deity, as was supposed in propitiatory sacrifices among the heathen, but rather a move on God's part to provide a covering of sins. This word ἱλασμός, translated *propitiation,* is employed in the Septuagint for the Hebrew כפרים, *coverings,* in the sense of atonement for sin and the consequent pardon and removal of the sin. So in this epistle of John the manifestation of Christ was for the purpose of *taking away sin* (iii, 5; comp. John i, 29), and thus *destroying the works of the devil* (iii, 8). This provision for the uttermost removal of sin centers in Jesus Christ, who "is the propitiation for our sins; and not for ours only, but also for the whole world" (ii, 2). He brings to the knowledge and within the reach of man the potent means by which sin is covered, blotted out, taken away; and such an effectual doing away with sin as the work of the devil is inseparably associated in John's thought with *purification from sin.* He who embraces the Christian's hope "purifieth himself even as God is pure" (iii, 3). A new and heavenly life is begotten through this divine propitiation, so that continuance in sin becomes utterly incompatible with the soul thus purified. For "whosoever is begotten of God doeth no sin, because his seed (that is, God's seed, the germ of heavenly life imparted ἄνωθεν, *from above,* John iii, 3) abideth in him: and he cannot sin because he is begotten of God" (iii, 9). The obstacle in the way of bringing the sinner into fellowship with God is the essential opposition of sin and holiness. This epistle emphasizes it as the contrast of light and darkness. "God is light, and in him is no darkness at all." If sinful man come into this light of God, and see and know and love the God of light, *he cannot go on walking in darkness.* He must become a child of the light. "If we walk in the light, as he is in the light, we have fellowship one with another, and the blood of Jesus his Son cleanseth us from all sin" (i, 5-7). The difficulty, accordingly, in the way of reconciliation between sinful man and God is not some imaginary exigency of divine government, but the fact of sin in man. This fact, however, is a breach of the divine order of life, and in that sense may be conceived as rebellion against God's rule. Righteousness and love alike require that this rebellion cease. No change is required in God. He is essentially unchangeable in love and truth and fidelity and righteousness. But "if we say that we have no sin, we deceive ourselves, and the truth is not in us. If we confess our sins, he is faithful and righteous (πιστός καὶ δίκαιος) to forgive us our sins, and to cleanse us from all unrighteousness" (i, 8, 9). Herein we discern the origin, the means, the process, and the result of Christ's "propitiation for our sins."

2. Old Testament Imagery of Blood Offerings. No faithful exposition of these texts can separate them from the imagery of Old Testament offerings of blood for the remission of sin. It is "the blood of Jesus Christ his Son" which is recognized as in some powerful way efficient for the purification of the sinner from all unrighteousness. The sinner has no means or resources within himself to effect a cleansing from all sin. His own penitence and confession of guilt have in them no cleansing power. There must come to his rescue some mediatorial ministry from a source higher than himself; the mediation must involve sacrifice of sufficient significance and worth to affect both God and man, and it should fulfill all those ideas of propitiation, expiation, removal of sin, reconciliation with God, atonement, and satisfaction which are symbolized in offering the blood of life upon an altar to make atonement for the souls of men (Lev. xvii, 11). Such mediatorial propitiation is manifested in the death of Jesus, and "hereby know we love, because he laid down his life for us" (1 John iii, 16). This laying down one's life for others is, as we have already read in John xv, 13, the greatest possible manifestation of love.

3. The living Paraclete. This manifestation of love in the person and ministry of the Son of God has an abiding value in the propitiation for our sins. For Jesus is conceived as now in actual living intercession with the Father, and thus his presence before God in the heavens is a perpetual ministry of reconciliation. "And if any man sin we have an Advocate (παράκλητον, *Comforter, Helper,* sympathetic and coöperative Intercessor) with the Father, Jesus Christ the righteous" (ii, 1). The concept of the holy and righteous Advocate ever living and making intercession for sinners (comp. Isa. liii, 12; Rom. viii, 34; Heb. vii, 25) helps us in the interpretation of all the scriptures which refer to his work of mediation and atonement. We are not to press to a literal significance every metaphorical suggestion of such terms as *expiation, intercession,* and *propitiation;* but we do recognize in them all, as employed by the New Testament writers, a true and profound conception of the saving work of Jesus Christ. He is the bleeding Sacrifice, the righteous Friend and Comforter, the interceding Advocate and Mediator between God and man, and by being all this and more he ever abides as a "propitiation for our sins." But all this ministry of atonement is of no avail for us except "we confess our sins" and "walk in the light" of God. It is noticeable that in this epistle Jesus Christ is set forth as Paraclete, while in the fourth gospel the Paraclete is the Holy Spirit, whom the Father sends in the name of the Son. The peculiar office and work of the Holy Spirit demands its own separate treatment, as showing the abiding and continuous operation of the heavenly ministrations of saving grace. Jesus Christ has finished the work given him to do in the flesh, but as the effective Paraclete he continues the same immanent Saviour of the world.

4. The Coming through Water and Blood. We cannot complete our study of Christ's mediation as found in this epistle without giving attention to the somewhat obscure passage in v, 6-8. The best accredited text may be thus literally translated: "This is he who came through (διά) water and blood, Jesus Christ; not in (ἐν) the water only, but in the water and in the blood. And the Spirit is that which is bearing witness, because the Spirit is the truth. Because three are they who bear witness, the Spirit, and the water, and the blood, and the three agree in one" (εἰς τὸ ἕν εἰσιν, *are directed toward the one thing;* that is, unite in one and the same testimony). There is no sufficient reason for supposing that the coming through water and blood refers to the "blood and water" which came out of Jesus' side when he was pierced by the spear of the soldier (John xix, 34); for that incidental fact, mentioned only in the fourth gospel, cannot be shown to have been any important feature of the Saviour's coming. The reference of the words to the sacraments of baptism and the Lord's Supper is also untenable; for the aorist tense of the verb *came* (ἐλθών) points to a definite historical fact in the past, and it is not true that he came or comes through the sacraments. The sacraments, moreover, are institutions for acknowledging covenant relations and for perpetuating the memory of Christ's death, and are not in any proper sense the accompaniment or means of his coming. And if the writer intended to refer to the two sacraments he should have employed terms more specific than the mere words *water* and *blood;* for while water may suggest baptism, the single word *blood* is not sufficient to indicate the Lord's Supper, in which the bread is as conspicuous as the wine. A satisfactory explanation of these words requires that we point out two conspicuous facts in the incarnate life of Jesus which may properly be designated by the phrases *through water and blood* and *in the water and in the blood.* And there are two signal events, one at the beginning and the other at the end of his public career, which most obviously answer to the expressions *water* and *blood* as here employed. Those events were his baptism in the water of the Jordan and his bloody death upon the cross. This exposition satisfies the requirements of the language, and is confirmed by the analogous statement of Heb. ix, 12, that Christ came near (παραγενόμενος) "through his own blood, and entered once for all into the holy place, having obtained eternal redemption." The water of his baptism and the blood of his cross mark two distinctive crises in the mediatorial ministry of Jesus, and a special emphasis is put upon the blood by the more definite formal repetition: "Not in the water only, but in the water and in the blood"; and the change in prepositions employed (ἐν after διά)[1] serves to indicate that the baptism and the cross were not only means through which, but also conditions in the bounds and elements of which, he came into the world to be a propitiation for our sins. This more definite statement not only presents an additional form of conceiving the two great events here referred to, but seems intended also to controvert the heresy of Cerinthus, who maintained, according to Irenæus,[2] that the Christly nature came upon Jesus at his baptism but withdrew from him before he suffered on the cross.

5. Testimony of the Spirit. The testimony of the Spirit as stated in verses 6-8 gives peculiar interest to this whole passage, and supplements the idea of the continuous heavenly ministry of Jesus Christ the righteous as our Advocate with the Father already

---
[1] Compare a similar use of the prepositions ἐν and διά in 2 Cor. vi, 4-8.
[2] Against Heresies, chap. xxvi, 1.

noticed (ii, 1). Along with these notable facts of the water and the blood we have also the abiding witness of the Spirit; and this fact is of the greatest possible value in the case, "because the Spirit is the truth," even as the Christ himself claims to be in John xiv, 6. Accordingly, no one of these great facts stands apart by itself, but all combine in threefold testimony to the saving ministry of Jesus; "for there are three who bear witness, the Spirit and the water and the blood, and the three agree in one." The Spirit is here assigned the precedence, and instead of the neuter the masculine form (τρεῖς) of the numeral is used, as if the writer's thought was mainly on the personal Paraclete, somehow identical with the Christ himself (ii, 1), whose living presence gives perpetual efficacy to the water and the blood. All this united testimony witnesses to the great central truth, stated in v, 11, but which is in fact the burden of the whole epistle: "God gave unto us eternal life, and this life is in his Son." His coming through water and blood was the manifestation of the mystery of the ages, to which the Spirit of truth is ever pointing.[1]

6. Doctrine of John's Apocalypse. The doctrine of John's Apocalypse is equally positive and unmistakable in presenting the saving work of Jesus Christ under the figures of atonement by means of the shedding of blood. In the salutation (i, 5) he is called the one "who loves us and loosed us from our sins by his blood," and in i, 18, he declares himself the Living One, who "was dead, and behold, I am alive for the ages of the ages." More than a score of times in this Apocalypse he is called "the Lamb." The Greek word employed is not ἀμνός (as in John i, 29, 36), but ἀρνίον, *little lamb*. A very suggestive passage is that in v, 1-6, where we read that, when no one could be found in heaven or on earth or under the earth able to open the sealed book, it was said that "the Lion who is of the tribe of Judah, the Root of David, would open the book; and when the seer looked to see the mighty Lion come forward, he beheld "a little lamb standing as though it had been slain." But though the diminutive form of the word for *lamb* may be suggestive of something small or feeble, the picture of this Lamb by the throne is otherwise portrayed so as to suggest the highest power and wisdom. He has seven horns and seven eyes, "which are the seven Spirits of God, sent forth into all the earth," and he was worshiped in the songs of heaven as the Lamb "who was slain and who purchased unto God with his blood men out of every

---

[1] So in substance Huther: "By means of the witness of the Spirit the whole redemptive life of Christ is permanently present, so that the baptism and death of Jesus, although belonging to the past, prove him constantly to be the Messiah who makes atonement for the world."—Meyer, Critical and Exegetical Handbook, in loco.

tribe and tongue and people and nation" (ver. 9). In vii, 14, the glorified multitudes of heaven are described as those who "washed their robes and made them white in the blood of the Lamb." In all these allusions, and others like them which appear in later portions of the book, there is unquestionable reference to sacrificial ideas of the blood of atonement.[1] In this particular the Apocalypse, the epistle, and the gospel of John are seen to be in thorough harmony, and their common doctrine of Jesus offering himself as a sacrificial lamb is witnessed also by the language put in the mouth of John the Baptist in John i, 29, 36: "Behold, the Lamb of God that taketh away the sin of the world." This form of expression obviously contemplates a sacrificial victim, and one without spot or blemish. His removing or *bearing away* ($αἴρων$) the sin of the world suggests the deepest and most far-reaching import of vicarious atonement, and accords with the doctrine of the new song in Rev. v, 9.

7. The Teaching of Peter. The early teaching of Peter, as recorded in the Acts of the apostles, makes prominent the provision for remission of sins in the name of Jesus Christ (Acts ii, 38; iii, 26; iv, 10-12; v, 31; x, 43). The emphasis placed on "the name of Jesus Christ," and on his work as Saviour from sin, can be satisfactorily explained only in the light of his mediatorial office and work as set forth in other scriptures. How else shall one interpret the strong words of Acts iv, 12, "In none other is there salvation: for there is not another name under heaven, that is given among men, wherein we must be saved"? If this teaching of Peter stood alone, unsupported and unexplained by other apostolic preaching, we might not cite these fragments of his sermons as conclusive proof that current ideas of the expiation of sin entered into his conception of the saving work of Christ. Nor are we to suppose that this apostle's doctrinal views of the death of Christ were fully developed at the time he spoke the words recorded in the Acts. We find upon further inquiry that he, as well as the other apostles, recognized from the first that Christ had made an atonement for sin. The preaching of Philip (Acts viii, 35), based upon Isa. liii, 7, 8, set forth Jesus in the figure of a sheep that is led to the slaughter, and would most naturally have explained that same scripture in the light of sacrificial offerings of blood to one who had come from Ethiopia to Jerusalem to worship.

8. Sprinkling of the Blood of Jesus. Passing to the first epistle

---

[1] It is an error, however, of some interpreters to find in the "garment sprinkled with blood" in xix, 13, an allusion to the blood of expiation or atonement. There we have the figure of a conquering hero, drawn from Isa. lxiii, 1-6, and the blood which stains his apparel is not his own blood, but that of his enemies whom he tramples down in the fierceness of his wrath.

of Peter, we observe in the salutation (i, 2) an allusion to the "sprinkling of the blood of Jesus Christ," and in verses 18 and 19 of the same chapter we read: "Ye were redeemed, not with corruptible things, with silver or gold, from your vain manner of life handed down from your fathers; but with precious blood of Christ, as of a lamb without blemish and without spot." No faithful exegesis of this scripture can fail to recognize the obvious allusion to such atonement as was wont to be made by the blood of sacrificial lambs. A comparison of the phrase *without blemish and without spot* with the requirements of sacrificial offerings in the law of Exod. xii, 5; Lev. xxii, 19-21; Deut. xvii, 1, puts this beyond all reasonable question. How could a Jew like Peter or any other of his time conceive redemption from sin by means of blood except in the light of that doctrine of vicarious blood of life enunciated in Lev. xvii, 11, and so familiar in the ritual of Jewish worship? The entire passage is one of the most explicit on record for showing the propitiatory character of the death of Jesus Christ.

9. Bearing our Sins in his Body. In 1 Pet. ii, 21-24, the mediatorial sufferings of Christ are further set forth in language which has obvious allusion to the Servant of Jehovah as described in Isa. liii, 4-9: "Christ suffered for you, leaving you an example, that ye should follow his steps: who did no sin, neither was guile found in his mouth: who, when he was reviled, reviled not again; when he suffered, threatened not; but committed himself to him that judgeth righteously: who his own self bare our sins in his body upon the tree, that we, having died unto sin, might live unto righteousness; by whose stripes ye were healed." The statement that he "carried our sins in his body up to the tree" ($\dot{a}\nu\acute{\eta}\nu\epsilon\gamma\kappa\epsilon\nu$ $\epsilon\pi\grave{\iota}$ $\tau\grave{o}$ $\xi\acute{\upsilon}\lambda o\nu$) conveys the idea that somehow our sins were crucified upon his cross. The thought is not that of bearing sins up to an altar and placing them thereon; for the cross was in no true sense an altar, nor can we think of sins as an offering upon an altar; but rather he carried the burden of our sins upon his soul up to the cross and nailed it with himself thereon. His soul was thus made an offering for sin (comp. Isa. liii, 10), and by his personal suffering and sacrifice we obtain remission of guilt and the power of living unto righteousness. But this vicarious suffering was no fictitious *quid pro quo,* no mechanical or commercial payment of a debt, no infinite equivalent for an inconceivable infinite demerit.[1] It was rather a mighty mediatorial struggle

---

[1] The theory that the sins of the world were imputed to Christ, or that the guilt of sin was thus imputed, and that he was *punished* for the same with an infliction of suffering and death equal in penal value to all the woe that must have come upon the guilty world, and that all this was necessary to satisfy the demands of justice in the nature of God, may now be treated as obsolete. The

even unto death, the death of the cross, whereby we, "having died unto sins," that is, having broken with sin and having become separate from its power by faith in the passion of our Lord, and by an intense sympathetic fellowship in his sufferings, "might live unto righteousness." And so again, to use Isaiah's words (liii, 5), "by his bruise ye were healed."[1] In this respect there is a vicarious element in the sufferings of Christ, and in his bearing our sins up to the cross, which is no example for us, and cannot be.

10. Partaking in Christ's Sufferings. But while some aspects of Christ's sufferings place him apart from other men, and render his the only name under heaven by which we may be saved, there is another point of view from which it appears that all who suffer for Christ's sake are partakers of his sufferings. We are told in 1 Pet. iii, 17, 18, that it is praiseworthy to suffer in the will of God for welldoing, "because Christ also suffered for sins once, the righteous for the unrighteous, that he might bring us to God." In iv, 1, we also read: "Forasmuch then as Christ suffered as to the flesh, arm yourselves with the same mind, for he that hath suffered in the flesh hath ceased from sin." The writer's thought is here turned to the more ordinary sufferings of our fleshly human nature in its struggle with temptations to sin. He who suffers in his struggle to overcome sin, and steadfastly refuses to yield to its power as Jesus did in the days of his flesh, "hath ceased from sin," that is, has utterly broken with it and ceased from its control. The brethren, therefore, who are exposed to fiery trial, are exhorted to rejoice in the thought that they are thus made "partakers of Christ's sufferings" (iv, 13). The writer of this epistle was himself "a witness of the sufferings of Christ" (v, 1), and he had confidence that he and all who followed the divine Master should also be partakers of the heavenly glory that was to be revealed; but Christ alone could be spoken of as "a lamb without blemish," whose precious blood makes expiation for the sins of men.

---

theory of full penal satisfaction made by Christ is logically at the basis of the Romish doctrine of indulgences and the later forms of Antinomianism. If Christ has truly paid all the penalty, divine justice can have no further claim on anyone for whom Christ died. A righteous God cannot exact his claims twice over. The theory of penal satisfaction, moreover, logically excludes grace. Where an obligation has been fully discharged, there is nothing left to pardon.

[1] *Healing* is to be taken here in the sense of cure and restoration from sin as a fearful disease. Comp. the figure in Isa. vi, 10; Jer. iii, 22; Hos. xiv, 5.

CHAPTER V

DOCTRINE OF THE PAULINE EPISTLES

1. Christ's Mediation the Substance of Paul's Gospel. In the Pauline epistles we find the mediatorial work of Christ set forth as the very substance of the gospel. The few allusions to the doctrine in Paul's preaching, as recorded in the Acts, accord also with the teaching of the epistles. Thus he proclaims, at Antioch of Pisidia, remission of sins and justification through the crucified and risen Jesus (xiii, 38, 39); at Athens he declares that "it was necessary for the Christ to suffer and to rise again from the dead" (xvii, 3); at Miletus he enjoins the elders of the church "to feed the church of the Lord which he purchased with his own blood" (xx, 28). In 1 Thess. i, 10, Jesus is mentioned as the one "who delivers[1] us from the wrath to come," and in v, 10, as our Lord "who died for us, that, whether we wake or sleep, we should live together with him." Such incidental allusions imply a well-defined doctrine of the saving work of Christ.

2. The Corinthian Epistles. The Corinthian epistles contain numerous allusions of a similar character, but do not attempt any elaborate treatment of the doctrine of the cross. In proclaiming at Corinth the mystery or the testimony[2] of God, Paul made "Jesus and him crucified" his great central theme (1 Cor. ii, 2). He held "the word of the cross" to be "the power of God to them that are saved" (i, 18), and that "Christ Jesus was made unto us wisdom from God, and righteousness, and sanctification, and redemption" (i, 30). The Christian believer is "bought with a price" no less or other than the death of the Lord Jesus (vi, 20; vii, 23; viii, 11; xv, 3), who "died for our sins according to the scriptures." It was therefore no new or exceptional idea for this apostle to recognize the bread and cup of the Lord's Supper as a symbol of the communion of the body and of the blood of Christ (x, 16; xi, 25-27), and for him to speak of Christ as our immolated paschal lamb (v, 7). In the light of all these statements it seems impossible to read 2 Cor. v, 14-19, without feeling that the writer is intending to give unmistakable expression to the vicarious nature

---

[1] Compare *the deliverer*, τὸν ῥυόμενον, of this text with the same word in Rom. xi, 26.
[2] There seems little to choose between the two alternative readings μυστήριον and μαρτύριον, both of which are well attested by ancient authorities.

of the death of Jesus: "The love of Christ constraineth us; because we thus judge, that one died for all, therefore the all died (οἱ πάντες ἀπέθανον); and he died for all, that they who live should no longer live unto themselves, but unto him who died for them and rose again." There is, no doubt, a certain mystical element, peculiar to Paul, in this manner of thinking and speaking (comp. Rom. vi, 5-11; Gal. ii, 20). All who partake of the saving grace of Christ are conceived as crucified and dying along with Christ. In this ideal but spiritually real sense *these all die,* because in fact and truth he died for the sake of all of them (ὑπὲρ πάντων). This entire ministry of saving mercy has its source in God (ἐκ τοῦ θεοῦ, ver. 18), "who reconciled us unto himself through Christ, and gave unto us the ministry of reconciliation."

3. God in Christ Reconciling the World. According to Paul, all men are, by the depraved tendencies of their nature and by their persistent habits of transgression, at enmity toward God; but from the bosom of God, as from a fountain of infinite love, spring the passion and the purpose of restoring the fallen, of redeeming the captives of sin, and of effecting a state of harmony and holy fellowship between himself and man. "The ministry of reconciliation" is the mediatorial work of Christ, who died for all, and its magnitude and scope are set forth in most impressive words: "God was in Christ reconciling the world unto himself, not reckoning unto them their trespasses." The object sought in this ministry of reconciliation is the whole world (κόσμον). Nothing less than this could satisfy the yearnings of infinite love, and no more profound or suggestive statement bearing on the doctrine of redemption can be made than finds expression in the words, "God was in Christ reconciling the world to himself." It may well seem strange that any exegete should argue, in the face of this statement, that we are to think of God as reconciled to the world rather than the world to God. But it has been maintained that, inasmuch as the Scriptures represent God as a righteous judge, indignant every day with the wickedness of the wicked (Psa. vii, 9-11), and as Paul himself speaks of "the wrath of God against all ungodliness and unrighteousness of men" (Rom. i, 18; comp. Eph. v, 6; Col. iii, 6), the reconciliation here spoken of must needs have reference mainly to the removal of God's wrath against the sinful world. It may be that the controversy is to some extent a vain wrangle over words, for there can be no question as to the attitude of the Holy One toward human sinfulness: he is "of purer eyes than to behold evil, and cannot look on miserable perverseness" (Hab. i, 13). But the question in 2 Cor. v, 18, 19, is not about the essential antagonism of the holiness of God and the sinfulness of the world, but about the object or aim of the reconciliation in Christ; and if the usage of the word καταλλάσσω, *reconcile,* in the New Testament is permitted to have its full weight in deciding the point at issue there ought to be no controversy. In the passage before us the word is employed three times in three successive verses (18-20), and in each case the reconciliation is unto God, not of God unto the world, or unto us. The noun καταλλαγή, *reconciliation,* occurring twice in this same passage, in the phrases *the ministry of reconciliation* and *the word of reconciliation,* is spoken of as something given and committed unto us, and in the absence of any other reference must be understood as in strict harmony with what the thrice repeated verb affirms—*the reconciliation unto God.* The use of these same words in Rom. v, 10, 11, is precisely the same: "Being enemies, we *were reconciled to God* through the death of his Son." The reconciliation thus received is affirmed in the most explicit terms to be a reconciliation *unto God* (τῷ θεῷ). The wrath of God against all unrighteousness of men is everywhere and always to be assumed or understood, but what is made conspicuous in Rom. v, 8-11, is not this wrath, but the adorable love of God which provides for the reconciliation of his enemies *unto himself.* The peace between God and the sinner effected by this reconciliation is conceived by Paul as a peace of the sinner *toward God* (πρὸς τὸν θεόν, Rom. v, 1) rather than a peace of God toward the reconciled and justified sinner. The incidental mention of the "reconciliation of the world" in Rom. xi, 15, is in perfect accord with the construction of the word given above, as is also the solemn charge of the apostle, in 1 Cor. vii, 11, that the wife who has improperly departed from her husband ought to be "reconciled to her husband." The wife is the erring party in the case supposed, and, like the sinner, is to be reconciled to the husband. And these are all the instances in the New Testament where the words καταλλάσσω and καταλλαγή occur. The intensified form ἀποκαταλλάσσω, which seems designed to add to the shorter word a suggestion of the completeness or thoroughness of the reconciliation, occurs only in Eph. ii, 16, and Col. i, 20, 21, and is in each of these texts employed to express the complete reconciliation *unto God* of those who stood in the relation of aliens and enemies to him. There would seem, therefore, to be no ground whatever, in the usage of this term, for the idea that it contemplates a reconciliation of God to man. Even the word διαλλάσσω, as employed in Matt. v, 24, shows that the reconciliation enjoined is *toward the injured brother.* The sinner in this case is the one who is about to offer his gift at the altar; he is to go at once and *be reconciled to the brother* who has good reason to complain against him.[1] The injured brother holds toward this offender a relation similar to that which God is supposed to hold toward the sinner in the texts previously cited, and here as there the reconciliation is explicitly spoken of as a reconciliation of the offender to the offended, not of the injured person to the transgressor. This latter may be understood as something necessarily involved in the transaction and sure to follow, but it is not the particular thing affirmed in any of these scriptures. All these scriptures, however, teach that the reconciliation of the sinner to God is effected through the mediation of Christ, and God and Christ are conceived as one in seeking to bring about this reconciliation. There is nothing in the entire passage of 2 Cor. v, 18-21, which speaks of God as an enemy to be reconciled toward man. There is no allusion to a wrath and hostility toward the sinner on the part of God, but, on the contrary, the whole process of reconciliation originated in him, is mediated through Christ, and proclaimed by the ministers of the word as ambassadors on behalf of Christ. It would seem, therefore, a perversion, not to say a caricature, of this scripture to read into it the idea of God standing afar off, filled with sovereign displeasure and hostility toward the world, and only to be appeased and reconciled to man by receiving some satisfactory compensation for offenses against his majesty. The apostle's representation is the most striking opposite of this. God is set forth as entreating and beseeching those who are estranged from him by their trespasses to become reconciled to himself: "As though God were entreating by us, we beseech you on behalf of Christ, be ye reconciled to God." When now we proceed to inquire into the nature of Christ's mediation in the reconciling of the world to God, we find that he embodies and illustrates by his humiliation and vicarious suffering on account of sin the spirit, the heart, the mind of God. In his saving ministry of reconciliation God is in Christ, not apart from him. Hence the remarkable words that follow in 2 Cor. v, 21: "Him who knew not sin he made sin on our behalf, that we might become the righteousness of God in him." That is, the perfectly sinless Christ, yearning with the emotion of God himself to rescue man from the power of sin, is appointed by God to the task of identifying himself with humanity so closely as to feel the burden and horror of all its sinfulness. The language is bold and striking, but no more so than Isa. liii, 10, where it is said that Jehovah was pleased to

---

[1] A very different course is prescribed in Matt. xviii, 15, for one who thinks that his brother has sinned against him. In such a situation he is to go after his faulty brother, show him his sin, and seek like God himself to gain him over to the Church.

bruise his servant and to make his soul a trespass offering (אשם; Septuagint, περὶ ἁμαρτίας). It is not improbable that the apostle had this very passage of Isaiah in his thought. The statement cannot mean that God in any literal or real sense made the sinless One an actual sinner. Many of the older interpreters maintain that the word *sin* is here to be understood in the sense of *sin offering,* and not a little may be said in favor of this explanation.[1] It is much to be preferred over that interpretation which holds that Christ was made to suffer the *punishment* of sin; for the conception of *punishing* the sinless for the sinful, and of imputing guilt to Christ and his personal righteousness to the credit of the guilty transgressor, is a scholastic fiction and abhorrent to the moral sense. But we may understand the apostle here as using the word *sin* in a bold, pregnant sense for a personal contact with sin, a subjection to suffering and death on account of sin, so real as to be mystically conceived as a terrible identification with the sins of the world. The divine purpose of his thus becoming sin for our sake was "that we might become the righteousness of God in him." Here too the word δικαιοσύνη, *righteousness,* is employed in the same bold way as the word *sin* in the previous sentence. The abstract is used for the concrete, and the strange brevity of each expression involves an obscurity in the thought which no exegesis has been able to clear away.

4. Epistle to the Galatians. We find a somewhat similar declaration in the epistle to the Galatians (iii, 13): "Christ redeemed us from the curse of the law, having become in our behalf a curse: for it is written, Cursed is every one that hangeth on a tree: that upon the Gentiles the blessing of Abraham might come in Jesus Christ; that we might receive the promise of the Spirit through faith." In this passage the word *curse,* κατάρα, is emphatic and bears a boldness of expression much like that of *sin* in 2 Cor. v, 21, and it is to be noticed that in both cases the words are used without the article, thus indicating some general character or quality of Christ's redeeming work, and the abstract is used for the concrete to intensify the rhetorical force of the statement. According to Deut. xxi, 22, 23, "a sin worthy of death" was to be punished by putting the criminal to death and hanging his dead body on a

---

[1] The fact that it is used in the Septuagint of Isa. liii, 10, for אשם, *trespass offering,* and regularly in the Priest Code for חטאת, *sin offering* (for example, Exod. xxix, 14, 36; Lev. iv, 3, 8, 20, 32, etc.; Num. vi, 11, 16; vii, 16, 22, etc.), furnishes a strong support for this view. In Ezek. xliii, 25; xlv, 17, 22, and other places it is used in the same sense and construed with ποιέω. The objection that the Septuagint usually has the phrase περὶ ἁμαρτίας is not insuperable. Codexes A and B have εἰς ἁμαρτίαν in Lev. iv, 32. Moreover, the explanation of *sin* in 2 Cor. v, 21, in the sense of *sin-bearer,* is virtually equivalent to what is represented by the sin offering.

tree; the body was not to be left all night upon the tree, but buried the same day; for, says the Hebrew text, "accursed of God is one that is hanged." Our apostle does not quote accurately either the Hebrew text or the Septuagint, but expresses the main thought in both. The publicly executed criminal was looked upon as an object of God's curse. In a similar manner in verse 10 he quotes another passage from Deut. xxvii, 26, to prove that "as many as are of the works of the law are under curse." That is, all who are conditioned in life by a law of works are under strictest obligation to *observe perfectly all* that the law prescribes and to *continue* in such perfect obedience. Otherwise they fall at once under the curse which the law of Deut. xxvii, 26, pronounces. But the apostle insists that as matter of fact no man is justified before God by way of such perfect continuance in keeping the whole law, and he cites in proof the words of Hab. ii, 4: "The one who is righteous shall live by faith." Here then is a way of salvation by faith, opened by the mediation of Christ, and availing to redeem the Jewish people from the curse which their law imposed on everyone who failed to perform all its requirements. The divine purpose of Christ's mediation, however, was not merely the redemption of the Jews from the curse of the law, but also that upon the Gentiles the gospel preached beforehand unto Abraham (ver. 8) might come with its fullness of blessing. Thus it is that both Jews and Gentiles "receive the promise of the Spirit through faith."

5. Becoming a Curse for Us. In order to accomplish this redemption from the curse of the law Christ "has become a curse for us" (ὑπὲρ ἡμῶν, *on our behalf; for our sake*). The reference to the curse of being hanged on a tree associates most naturally with the thought of Christ nailed upon the cross (comp. 1 Pet. ii, 24; Col. ii, 14). So in Gal. iii, 1, Christ is said to have been "openly set forth crucified." This public and shameful suffering of death had all the outer semblance of the curse of the law, and this open exhibition of Jesus as if he were an accursed criminal was a conspicuous part of his humiliation. It is, perhaps, a little less startling to say he "became a curse on our behalf" than to say that God "made him a sin on our behalf." But both statements are of the nature of metonymy, and cannot be literally understood. Both express the voluntary self-humiliation of Christ and his vicarious identification with man under the curse of sin. He entered into the depths of human suffering and felt most keenly the bitter exposure of sinful man to the curse of violated law, and being himself personally without sin and without any condemnation from law he was the more capable of becoming "greatly amazed and sore troubled" (**Mark xiv, 33**) over the desperate situation of sin-cursed humanity under the curse of holy law. In all this portraiture of the vicarious suffering of the Redeemer we should look, therefore, to see, not a victim of some extraneous demand of law, but rather a voluntary sympathetic friend of the sinner, the purest embodiment of love as well as of fidelity to truth and righteousness, in whom God's Spirit rules, and whose every action reveals the mind and feeling of God himself. Hence the peculiar force of the language employed further on in the epistle (iv, 4, 5): "God sent forth his Son, born of a woman, born under the law, that he might redeem them that were under the law, that we might receive the adoption of sons." This redemption from the curse of the law delivers one also from its dominion as a rule of life leading to salvation, so that the newly adopted sons of God are no longer in the position of bondservants, but of sons and heirs, in whose hearts the Spirit cries Abba, Father (vers. 6 and 7). Hence, too, the exultant confession of the apostle in vi, 14: "Far be it from me to glory, save in the cross of our Lord Jesus Christ, through whom the world hath been crucified unto me, and I unto the world." Being crucified with Christ he lives in Christ, as we have already heard him say in 2 Cor. v, 14, 15; and in this new and heavenly relationship there is no more curse of legal condemnation, but marvelous salvation from sin. Hence the mystical but characteristic Pauline confession of faith (Gal. ii, 19, 20): "Through law I died to law, that I might live to God. With Christ have I been crucified; and it is no longer I that live, but Christ liveth in me; and that which I now live in the flesh I live in faith, namely, that of the Son of God who loved me and gave himself up on my behalf." These words suggest how God is truly in Christ reconciling the world unto himself. The Lord Jesus Christ "gave himself for our sins, that he might deliver us out of this present evil world according to the will of our God and Father" (i, 4). Thus this epistle furnishes a most valuable contribution to the doctrine of the mediation of Christ.

6. Epistle to the Romans. Paul's epistle to the Romans is usually regarded as his masterpiece for the exposition of Christ's mediatorial work in the salvation of men. His great theme is the gospel considered as the "power of God unto salvation to every one that believeth" (i, 16). After a very full showing that all the world of mankind is under condemnation before God on account of a universal sinfulness he makes in iii, 21-26, one of the most formal and comprehensive statements in the New Testament touching the redemption from sin which is effected by the grace of God in Jesus Christ. The passage may be quite literally translated as follows: "But now apart from law a righteousness of God has been manifested, being witnessed by the law and the prophets; even the righteousness of God through faith of Jesus Christ[1] unto all them that believe; for there is no distinction; for all sinned and fall short of the glory of God; being justified freely by his grace through the redemption that is in Christ Jesus: whom God set forth as a mercy seat[2] through faith in his blood, for a showing of his righteousness because of the passing over of the sins done aforetime in the forbearance of God; for the showing of his righteousness in the present time, that he himself might be just and the justifier of him who is of the faith of Jesus."

7. Discussion of Romans iii, 21-26. There are numerous contrasted phrases and minute shades of thought suggested in this passage which it is scarcely the province of dogmatics to expound. Our aim must be to set forth as clearly as possible the apostle's conception of "the redemption that is in Christ Jesus," and the manner by which it becomes effective in showing forth the righteousness and grace of God and in securing the forgiveness and justification of the sinner. With this object in view we must study carefully the import of the more striking words and phrases of the text.

(1) *Not a New Teaching.* We observe first that Paul does not regard his teaching here as something new and original with himself, but as a truth which is "witnessed by the law and the prophets"; for he cites the Law, the Prophets, and the Psalms throughout the epistle to confirm his doctrine (comp. i, 17; iii, 10; iv, 3-8; ix, 25-33). We understand it, however, as Paul's exposition, the way in which this gospel of God was revealed in his conscious experience and thought (comp. Gal. i, 11-17). It accordingly bears the peculiarities of a gospel according to Paul.

(2) *Originates with God.* According to Paul's gospel the entire work of redemption in Christ originates with God, so that whatever Christ does God does; and "the redemption which is in Christ" is a manifestation[3] both of the righteousness and the free grace

---

[1] Genitive of the object: faith that takes hold on Jesus Christ. So too, in verse 26, "he who is of the faith of Jesus" is the one who has faith in Jesus, and believes unto salvation.

[2] ἱλαστήριον, *mercy seat.* Here used without the article, as is the word *Son* in Heb. i, 2 (ἐν υἱῷ), because the *nature, relative quality,* or *symbolic import* of the term is uppermost. This word occurs elsewhere in the New Testament only in Heb. ix, 5, where the writer is specifying the different articles of furniture in the holy places of the tabernacle.

[3] Two Greek words are employed in this passage to express the idea of *manifestation,* φανέρωσις and ἔνδειξις. The former seems to point to an outward sensible exhibition, which anyone so disposed may look upon, and so it differs from ἀποκάλυψις, *revelation,* which is a disclosure made subjectively to the individual soul. A manifestation, however, perceptible to all, may be the outcome of a series of revelations witnessed by prophets of God. The word ἔνδειξις, on the other hand, conveys the idea of a public *demonstration,* an evidential showing forth of some great fact or truth. Both ideas unite in the προέθετο of verse 25: *whom God set forth,* etc.

of God. Justice and love divine thus "meet and kiss each other" in this manifestation of God. Hence it follows that God may be shown to be righteous and to be at the same time a justifier of the man who has faith in Jesus Christ.

(3) *Passing over Former Sins.* This demonstrable proof of the righteousness of God explains also his forbearance in passing over the sins which had been committed in the times previous to the appearing of Christ. His righteousness and grace were never wanting, and were never separate from his eternal purpose in Christ (comp. Eph. iii, 11), but his forbearing mercy overlooked times and conditions of ignorance (comp. Acts xvii, 30). This, however, is not to be understood or construed as inconsistent with the fact that "the wrath of God is also revealed from heaven against all ungodliness and unrighteousness of men who restrain the truth in unrighteousness" (Rom. i, 18), but it is a vindication of his love and justice in all the ages of human history. What, therefore, finds an open demonstration in the manifestation of the historical Christ "in the present time" is essentially true for all times, and furnishes our only theodicy of the divine administration of the moral world.

(4) *Two Greek Words.* There are two Greek words in this passage which must necessarily have great significance in the apostle's doctrine of the mediation of Christ between God and man. They are ἀπολύτρωσις, in verse 24, and ἱλαστήριον, in verse 25. The first means *redemption* in the sense of deliverance from some condition of bondage, and does not differ in any essential or important manner from the main signification of the word λύτρον, *ransom,* which we have already considered in connection with the teaching of Jesus (p. 366).[1] Jesus offered his life "a ransom for many" (Mark x, 45), and that self-sacrifice provided for the redemption of the many. "The redemption that is in Christ Jesus" is the divine power in his person and work by the efficiency of which the sinner may be delivered from his sins. It is *through this redemption* that he "is justified freely by his grace." In all this more elaborate statement, however, we find thus far no essential thought which we have not already obtained from the simpler declaration of Mark x, 45, that Jesus "came to give his life a ransom for many."

But the word ἱλαστήριον seems designed to direct the reader to

---

[1] For the convenience of the reader disposed to examine all the passages in the New Testament where λυτρόω and its compounds occur we subjoin the following: The verb λυτρόω only in Luke xxiv, 21; Titus ii, 14; 1 Pet. i, 18; λύτρον only in Matt. xx, 28; Mark x, 45; λύτρωσις in Luke i, 68; ii, 38; Heb. ix, 12: λυτρωτής in Acts vii, 35; ἀντίλυτρον in 1 Tim. ii, 6; ἀπολύτρωσις in Luke xxi, 28; Rom. iii, 24; viii, 23; 1 Cor. i, 30; Eph. i, 7, 14; iv, 30; Col. i, 14; Heb. ix, 15; xi, 35. At the root of all these words is λύω, to *loosen,* or *set free.*

a more definite conception of "the redemption which is in Christ Jesus," and may be regarded as a concrete figurative illustration of ἡ ἀπολύτρωσις, *the redemption*. Here we meet with one of those niceties of biblical exegesis which is of sufficient importance to be studied with much patience and care. Four distinct interpretations have been put upon this word, which may be fairly represented by the Latin terms, *propitiator, propitiatorium sacrificium, propitiatio,* and *propitiatorium*.[1] The distinctive thought in each of these terms may be expressed by the corresponding Greek words, ἱλαστής, ἱλαστήριον θῦμα, ἱλασμός, and ἱλαστήριον, and in English by *propitiator, propitiatory sacrifice, propitiation,* and *propitiatory,* this last word in the concrete sense of place or instrument of propitiation. Of these different interpretations it is safe to say that the first named has too little in its favor to deserve extended notice. If the writer intended a personal reference to Christ as a *propitiator,* he should have used the word ἱλαστής, and not the neuter form, ἱλαστήριον. The second interpretation, which supplies the word θῦμα, *sacrifice,* or else maintains that, as a neuter substantive, ἱλαστήριον without any additional word like θῦμα understood here means *propitiatory sacrifice,* has been adopted by a goodly number of distinguished expositors.[2] The meaning, then, is that God has exhibited Jesus Christ conspicuously as a propitiatory offering for the sins of men. Against this interpretation there are several weighty objections: (1) The word does not appear to be elsewhere (unless very rarely) employed in this meaning.[3] If the writer wished to express the thought of sacrificial offering, he ought by all means to have added the word θῦμα, or some equivalent. (2) It is incongruous with New Testament thought and teaching to speak of God setting forth his Son Jesus Christ as a propitiatory sacrifice. As such an offering Christ rather *presented himself unto God* (Eph. v, 2; Heb. vii, 27; ix, 14, 26, 28; comp. John xvii, 19). (3) The phrase *in his own blood* would be superfluous and tautological if the preceding ἱλαστήριον meant an expiatory sacrifice.

The Authorized and Revised English Versions of the New Testament translate the word by the abstract term *propitiation,* thus following most copies of the Vulgate. This interpretation may

---

[1] The three forms *propitiator, propitiatio,* and *propitiatorium* are actually found in the different manuscripts of the Latin versions of the New Testament.

[2] So De Wette, Fritzsche, Meyer, Alford, Jowett, Hodge, Wordsworth, Conybeare and Howson.

[3] Dion Chrysostom (Orat. xi, 1) and Nonnus (Dionysiaca xiii) are cited by Meyer and others as sustaining the meaning of sacrificial offerings. Also 4 Maccabees xvii, 22, where, however, Swete (Septuagint, in loco) reads διὰ ... τοῦ ἱλαστηρίου θανάτου αὐτῶν, *through their propitiatory death*. Here the word is masculine and an adjective qualifying *death,* and hence not a parallel example.

construe ἱλαστήριον as a neuter noun in the sense of *means of propitiation,* or it may construe ἱλαστήριον as an adjective in the accusative masculine and as a predicate of ὅν, *whom.* Thus the margin of the Revised Version has it, *whom God set forth to be propitiatory.* Against the first construction lies the fact that the word is found nowhere else as a neuter in the abstract and general meaning of *propitiation.* No other example is adduced in which ἱλαστήριον appears as equivalent or synonymous with ἱλασμός. If the writer desired or intended to say *propitiation,* why did he not employ the unequivocal word which is so rendered in all versions of 1 John ii, 2, and iv, 10? Against the construction which makes it a masculine adjective qualifying ὅν, *whom,* and explains it as descriptive of a personal element in Christ, it may be urged (1) that the adjective is nowhere else applied to persons; (2) that in the examples adduced the object to which it is applied follows the adjective[1]; and (3) it is an uncouth and unexampled assertion to say that "God set forth Christ propitiatory," or "to be propitiatory." God has indeed sent forth and set forth his Son as a manifold revelation of himself in the Christ, but not as propitiatory to himself. So far as he is a sacrifice unto God he offered himself by the sacrifice of himself. Otherwise conceived, there is needless confusion of thought.

We prefer that interpretation of ἱλαστήριον in this text which accords the word the meaning which it bears everywhere else in the biblical Greek, and which has the support of the ancient Greek commentators and a large number of the ablest exegetes of modern times.[2] In the only other place where it occurs in the New Testament (Heb. ix, 5) it designates the "mercy seat," the lid or cover of the ark. This cover was the most central and sacred article of furniture in the Holy of holies in the tabernacle. According to Exod. xxv, 17-22, it was made of pure gold, and two cherubim were wrought into the same piece, one at each end, with their wings spread out over the mercy seat and their faces toward it and toward one another. This golden lid covered the two tables of "the testimony" which were placed within the ark, and there, "from above the mercy seat," Jehovah promised to meet and commune with Moses. Into this place the high priest entered alone, once in the year, and sprinkled the mercy seat with blood, "to make atonement (לְכַפֵּר, Sept., ἐξιλάσκεσθαι) for the children of Israel." The

---

[1] The examples often cited are ἱλαστήριον μνῆμα (Josephus, Antiquities xvi, 7, 1) and ἱλαστήριον θανάτου (4 Maccabees xvii, 22), already cited above.

[2] So Origen, Chrysostom, Theodoret, Cyril, Theophylact, Erasmus, Luther, Calvin, Grotius, Olshausen, Philippi, Tholuck, Umbreit, Liddon, Gifford (in Speaker's Commentary), Lange, Cremer (Biblico-Theological Lexicon), Ritschl (Rechtfertigung und Versöhnung, vol. ii, p. 169).

slab of gold thus fitted to cover the top of the ark was called in the Hebrew הכפרת, *the capporeth,* and this word is everywhere translated in the Septuagint by ἱλαστήριον. In Exod. xxv, 16 (17), where the word first appears, this Greek version reads: "Thou shalt make a propitiatory cover of pure gold" (ἱλαστήριον ἐπίθεμα χρυσίου καθαροῦ).[1] Elsewhere throughout the Septuagint כפרת is uniformly translated by ἱλαστήριον, without any further defining word. In view of these facts it is difficult to suppose that Paul would have employed a Greek word so familiar to all readers of the common version of the Old Testament in any other meaning than that which it bears in that version. The reasons, accordingly, for this meaning of the word in the passage under discussion are the following: (1) This is the only well-accredited meaning of the word in the biblical Greek. (2) The mercy seat was the most sacred and solemn symbol connected with the system of Levitical service in the tabernacle and in the temple. It was the secret place of the Most High, the throne of the presence chamber of Jehovah, the God of Israel. In that most holy place he would meet and commune with his people, through their anointed representative. (3) The symbolical significance of the mercy seat made it a very appropriate figure for the apostle to use by way of metaphor to illustrate "the redemption that is in Christ Jesus." It is worthy of special note that in Heb. ix, 7-12, immediately following the only other place in the New Testament where ἱλαστήριον occurs, the symbolism of the Holy of holies is spoken of as a figure (παραβολή) of the atoning ministry of Christ, who "through his own blood entered in once for all into the holy place, having obtained eternal redemption."[2] (4) This interpretation best explains the addition of the emphatic phrase *in his blood.* The mercy seat was a golden covering, over which were the faces and wings of the cherubim. It had no propitiatory significance until the priest sprinkled it with the blood of atonement. So, in the figure, it is only after Christ has entered the holy place through his own blood that God set him forth as a mercy seat and exhibited the saving mystery of eternal redemption "through faith in his blood." And so it was "that the way into the holy place was not made manifest while the first tabernacle was yet standing" (Heb. ix, 8). (5) The middle voice employed in the Greek verb προέθετο,

---

[1] It may be equally proper to construe the ἐπίθεμα in this exceptional text as in apposition with ἱλαστήριον, and so Gifford actually does: "Thou shalt make a propitiatory, a lid of pure gold." He also observes that this apposition of the two words "is the more natural, because on this first occurrence of כפרת the translators might wish to show that they had both meanings under their consideration."

[2] On the symbolism of the mercy seat, see further Biblical Hermeneutics, p. 272, and Biblical Apocalyptics, p. 83.

set forth for himself, also comports with this interpretation of ἱλαστήριον. It indicates God's own personal interest and participation in the redemption which is in Christ, and in the consequent "showing forth of his righteousness." God openly set forth in his own interest his Son Jesus Christ as the reality and fulfillment of all that was symbolized by the mercy seat.

Further confirmation of this interpretation will be seen, we think, as we pass under review the various objections that have been raised against it: (1) Some writers have declared that ἱλαστήριον is an incorrect translation of the Hebrew כפרת. To which it would be sufficient to reply, in view of the facts already adduced, that, whether it be a correct or an incorrect translation, it is the one word uniformly employed in the biblical Greek to represent the *capporeth,* and Paul would not have been likely to make use of it with another or an exceptional meaning. But the truth is that the verb כפר in its intensive form (piel), and the derivatives of the same, are almost invariably used in the sense of making an atonement for sin; *covering it over* as if putting it out of sight. And this is the obvious significance of the *capporeth* in the holy place. Sprinkled with the blood of atonement it was a perpetual symbol of the divine reconciliation secured thereby. It *covered* "the testimony" of the two tables of law deposited within the ark, and thus proclaimed how mercy covers wrath, and effects the reconciliation of the sinner unto God. And this idea was appropriately set forth by the Greek word ἱλαστήριον, a means and instrument divinely appointed to secure reconciliation between the sinner and his God, and hence it is appropriately translated into English by *mercy seat.* (2) It has been objected that there is an incongruity in the figure of the blood of a sacrifice and that of a mercy seat. But the incongruity, if any, is one of the objector's own making. The mercy seat as such was not without blood (Lev. xvi, 14; Heb. ix, 7), and the text under discussion affirms explicitly that Christ as a mercy seat effects the redemption by means of his own blood. We have already seen that ἱλαστήριον does not mean a sacrifice, or a propitiatory offering; but its significant symbolism is never apparent apart from the blood which the high priest sprinkled thereon in the day of atonement. (3) Others object that the idea of mercy seat would be inappropriate in view of the fact that Christ is here said to be set forth "for a showing (ἔνδειξις) of his *righteousness."* But this objection overlooks the fact that in Paul's thought the grace and the righteousness of God in Christ are never separate. No more emphatic statement appears in this whole passage than that we are *"justified* freely by his grace through the redemption that is in Christ Jesus." Moreover, both grace and righteousness are alike symbolized in the blood-sprinkled cover of "the ark of the covenant." (4) It is also objected that it would be violently abrupt to introduce such a figure here, without anything in the preceding context preparing the way for it. But this objection seems to forget that the word ἱλαστήριον occurs nowhere else in Paul's writings, and if its well-attested and uniform meaning elsewhere seem abrupt in this connection, how much more out of place would be an exceptional and questionable use of the word? We believe, on the contrary, that the emphatic mention in the preceding verse of the gracious "redemption that is in Christ Jesus" does prepare the way for this figure of atonement, and the repeated references to "the law," both before and after this verse, assume that the readers of this epistle were familiar with the means and methods of atonement provided in the law. (5) The last observation may also sufficiently dispose of the objection that such a reference to the *capporeth* would be out of place in an epistle addressed in part to Gentile readers. If this objection were valid, it must also apply to numerous other Old Testament references in the epistle. But Paul's contention throughout this epistle is first and mainly with the Jew, and he may as well have assumed that his first readers would be familiar with the mysteries of the holy place in the tabernacle, as does the author of Heb. ix, 7-14. (6) But it is urged that Christ is nowhere else in the New Testament presented under the figure of a mercy seat; to which it has been well replied that the same objection may be made to the figure of the brazen serpent (John iii, 14), the baptism unto Moses and the spiritual Rock (1 Cor. x, 2-4), Christ "made sin for us" (2 Cor. v, 21), and "a curse for us" (Gal. iii, 13). And it should also be observed that in the immediate context and argument following the only other mention of the mercy seat in the New Testament (Heb. ix, 5) we read quite an elaborate exposition of the "figure" (παραβολή) of Christ's mediation as seen in his entering in once for all into the holy place, through his own blood, and his thus obtaining eternal redemption (ver. 12; comp. x, 19, 20). (7) But the most weighty objection is generally felt to be the absence of the article before ἱλαστήριον. In the somewhat analogous illustration of 1 Cor. v, 7, the language of the apostle is τὸ πάσχα ἡμῶν ἐτύθη Χριστός, *Our passover* (that is, paschal lamb) *was sacrificed, even Christ*. Here the word *passover* is made definite both by the article and the pronoun, and it would seem to have been certainly proper, if not necessary, to qualify the word *mercy seat* in like manner, had the apostle used ἱλαστήριον in this specific sense.[1]

---

[1] And so Theodoret paraphrases it: "The Lord Christ is the true mercy seat" (τὸ ἀληθινὸν ἱλαστήριον).

The force of this argument is not to be denied, and it may be admitted that the more general term, *a propitiation,* would have suited the context. Nevertheless, as Schaff says in his additions to Lange's comments, this objection is by no means conclusive. For in expressing the main thought of 1 Cor. v, 7, Paul might truly have said, "Christ was sacrificed as a paschal lamb." This form would have emphasized *his character as a paschal lamb* rather than his being *our* paschal lamb. And so we believe that the absence of the article before ἱλαστήριον gives emphasis to the symbolical character and significance of the word. He was not manifested or set forth as *the mercy seat* of the sanctuary made with hands (comp. Heb. ix, 11), but as a mercy seat which embodied and represented all that was ever typified and symbolized in the well-known blood-sprinkled mercy seat of the tabernacle. Furthermore, the two clauses, *through faith* and *in his blood,* which follow and attach immediately to the word ἱλαστήριον, are of such a definitive character as to exclude the article before the word. God set forth Christ not as *the* mercy seat of the old tabernacle, but as *a mercy seat* in which the Christly redemption becomes eternally efficient *through faith in his blood.* These additional words, thus defining and enhancing the saving significance of Christ's priestly mediation, sufficiently account for the absence of the article. (8) Finally, it has been objected that προέθετο, *set forth,* would not be a suitable word to use in reference to the cover of the ark which was ever kept in the most holy place and hidden from the view of the people. But this objection is thoroughly refuted by the fact that Christ's mediation *makes known* the mystery of the ancient types and symbols. "The way unto the holy place was indeed not made manifest while the first tabernacle remained standing" (Heb. ix, 8); but the veil no longer hides that secret place; we may now enter "with boldness into the holy place by the blood of Jesus" (Heb. x, 19). The great thought in the *setting forth* of Christ as a mercy seat is that God has thus manifested the profound mystery of the most secret and sacred symbol connected with his ancient law and testimony. Every essential truth which is found in the words *propitiation, reconciliation,* and *atonement* is included in Christ's mediation conceived as the reality of what was symbolized by the mercy seat, and God's setting forth his Son in this light was the consummate revelation of his own glory, grace, and truth.

(5) *Realized through Faith.* This passage, furthermore, emphasizes the important truth that the righteousness of God manifested in Christ is a blessedness to be realized only "through faith in his blood." The Pauline phrase *righteousness of God* (comp.

Rom. i, 17; x, 3; 1 Cor. i, 30; 2 Cor. v, 21; Phil. iii, 9) is to be here understood as a righteousness which in some sense proceeds from God, and it is well-pleasing in his sight when it becomes the actual possession or state of him that believes in Jesus. It is "through the redemption that is in Christ," and "through faith in his blood" that a man may become "freely justified" by the grace of God. Like Abraham, one believes in God and in Christ, and it is reckoned unto him for righteousness (Rom. iv, 3). This doctrine of faith is something that may be verified in human experience. The gracious blessedness is mediated in Jesus Christ and appropriated by personal faith on the part of the believer. God's justice and grace are both magnified in the sacrifice of Jesus. While the first tabernacle stood the way into the Holy of holies was hidden from view (Heb. ix, 8), but the blood of Jesus has opened the way into the holy places not made with hands, and exposed to the eye of faith a mercy seat which assures the free and complete pardon of every sinner "who is of the faith of Jesus." In all this divine ministration God and Christ are one, and in the blood of the cross we have an exhibition of the way of salvation that was symbolized by the mercy seat.

(6) *Magnifies the Law.* It is to be noticed that this "righteousness of God," while attainable "apart from law," has in the highest possible manner honored the law. There can be no unrighteousness in the God who judges the world (iii, 5, 6), and his law is essentially holy and righteous and good (vii, 12). The symbolism of the mercy seat forever sets Christ forth as the "end[1] of the law unto righteousness to every one that believeth" (x, 4). The law is not dishonored, but rather enhanced, by the gracious provision of making faith in Christ the regulative principle which leads the believer unto righteousness. "Through the law cometh the knowledge of sin" (iii, 20; vii, 7), for in its inmost nature and essence "the law is spiritual" (vii, 14); that is, it is of the very nature of the Spirit of God. The law, in this deepest sense, is God himself revealing his essential holiness and righteousness to the hearts of men (comp. i, 15). But in the symbolism of the mercy seat the claims of this spiritual law, as represented in the "tables of testi-

---

[1] The word τέλος, *end*, is here to be understood in its ordinary meaning of *termination, conclusion.* Christ has ended the law as a condition and means leading unto righteousness. But, as Philippi has well said, "in a dogmatic point of view, the fact of Christ being the end of the law is no doubt based simply upon the fact that he is the *fulfillment* and *aim* of the law. For either the law itself would be without sanction, or its abolition by Christ without reason, if he had abrogated without fulfilling it. On the other hand, the law evinces its own as well as Christ's authority in the fact that it proposed as its object and aim to come to an end through fulfillment by Christ. It has come to an end, because now, in place of the requirement of works, the requirement of faith is established (vii, 1-6)."—Commentary on Romans, x, 4.

mony" within the ark and safely guarded there, are seen to be now *covered* and *ended* for him that believes in Jesus; for faith in the blood of Christ, instead of perfect obedience to the law, is reckoned unto him for righteousness.

(7) *Mysterious Necessities of the Moral World.* In this important passage in Romans we thus have in somewhat fuller form, and by means of symbolic illustration, the same truth that we have already studied in the profound statement of 2 Cor. v, 19, that "God was in Christ reconciling the world unto himself." We are not able to derive from either passage a particular theory of atonement. The sublime fact is declared; deep and far-reaching suggestions are put forward; but the holy mystery of God in Christ remains. The redemption in Christ is an exhibit of mysterious necessities of the moral world, and is mediated and becomes efficient unto salvation "through faith in his blood." Sin is shown to be "exceeding sinful" (vii, 13), and in the light of the holy, righteous, good, spiritual law every mouth is stopped and all the world is seen to be under the condemning judgment of God (iii, 19).

8. Continuous Reconciliation, Romans iv, 25. But according to Paul the redemption that is in Christ is effected and carried on to completion by the resurrection and heavenly life of Jesus as well as by his death on the cross. He says in iv, 25, that he "was delivered up for our trespasses, and was raised for our justification." In some places it is said that God delivered him up for us (viii, 32) and in others that Christ delivered himself up (Gal. ii, 20; Eph. v, 2; comp. 1 Tim. ii, 6; Titus ii, 14; Matt. xx, 28), but whichever way we state it, his being delivered up unto death was on account of human sinfulness, and his resurrection was equally necessary for the consummation of his mediatorial work. Hence the significance of what is written in v, 8-11: "God commendeth his own love toward us, in that, while we were yet sinners, Christ died for us. Much more then, being now justified in his blood, shall we be saved from the divine wrath through him. For if, while we were enemies, we were reconciled to God through the death of his Son, much more, being reconciled, shall we be continuously saved in his life; and not only so, but we also glory in God through our Lord Jesus Christ, through whom we have now received the reconciliation." The complete redemption is, accordingly, not only a remission of sins through the mediating death of Jesus, but a continuous and eternal salvation, in which the believer, being reconciled to God, lives the new life of righteousness by faith, and realizes that there is no enmity in his heart toward God, but a glorious state of reconciliation. To the same effect is that which is written in vi, 8-11: "If we died with Christ, we believe that we shall also live with him; knowing that Christ being raised from the dead dieth no more; death no more hath dominion over him. For the death that he died, he died unto sin once for all: but the life that he liveth, he liveth unto God. Even so reckon ye also yourselves to be dead unto sin, but alive unto God in Christ Jesus." This general trend of thought and argument is carried on to the close of chapter viii, where the apostle asks (ver. 32), as if in a rapture of emotion: "He that spared not his own Son, but delivered him up for us all, how shall he not also with him freely give us all things?" Again in xiv, 8, 9, he returns to this inspiring thought: "Whether we live or die, we are the Lord's. For to this end Christ died and lived, that he might be Lord of both the dead and the living."

9. The Great Antithesis of Romans v, 12-21. In the great antithesis set forth in v, 12-21, we should observe how the gracious mediation of Christ is made to offset all the consequences of Adam's transgression. "By the trespass of one the many died, but much more did the grace of God, and the gift in the grace of the one man Jesus Christ, abound unto the many" (ver. 15). In all these contrasts we note especially the difference in the *kind* of effects resulting from the acts of the two opposite representatives of humanity. Through the one, condemnation and death were imposed upon all men, but through the righteous act of Christ provision is made for the justification of all, so that "where sin abounded, grace did more exceedingly abound, in order that, as sin reigned in death, even so might grace reign through righteousness unto eternal life through Jesus Christ our Lord." In all these scriptures we may perceive the great thought of iv, 25, that Christ died for our sins, and was raised and ever lives for our justification and eternal life. And so the efficiency of Christ's redeeming work is perpetual. So long as sin and trespass and death continue in Adam's posterity, so long the Christly redeeming grace continuously avails to counteract the evil, and is not therefore to be conceived as a finished work. Because of Adam's trespass, sin abounds and death reigns; because of Christ's redemptive mediation, grace abounds more exceedingly and reigns through righteousness unto eternal life. The grace is greater than the sin.

10. The Doctrine in Ephesians and Colossians. So far as the Ephesian and Colossian epistles refer to the mediation of Christ they are in perfect accord with the other Pauline writings. In Eph. i, 6, 7, we read of "the glory of his grace, which he freely bestowed on us in the Beloved, in whom we have redemption in his blood, the forgiveness of our trespasses, according to the riches of his grace." According to ii, 13-16, the Gentiles who "once were far off are made nigh in the blood of Christ," and both Gentile and Jew are happily "reconciled in one body unto God through the cross, having slain the enmity thereby." With great confidence, therefore, the apostle speaks of the love of Christ, who "gave himself up in our behalf; an offering and a sacrifice to God for an odor of a sweet smell" (v, 2). Such an obvious allusion to Old Testament offerings (comp. Exod. xxix, 18; Lev. i, 9, 13, 17) shows beyond question that the writer had no hesitation in putting forward the sufferings and death of Christ as having something in common with the expiatory sacrifices of the Hebrew ritual. It was the offering up of a spotless life on behalf of the lives of many who were "dead through trespasses" that they might live and walk in light as beloved children of God. Further on (v, 25) it is said that "Christ loved the church and gave himself up on her behalf." Thus we observe that Christ's giving himself up as a sacrifice for the benefit of others is a very familiar Pauline thought (comp. Gal. i, 4; ii, 20; Rom. iv, 25). It is prominent in the great kenotic text (Phil. ii, 5-8) which emphasizes his humbling himself and becoming obedient even unto the death of the cross. It is equally explicit in the epistle to the Colossians, where we are told that it was the Father's good pleasure "through him to reconcile all things unto himself, having made peace through the blood of his cross" (i, 20). In him, the Son of the Father's love, "we have our redemption, the forgiveness of our sins" (i, 14). So far as Jew and Gentile were guilty of trespasses and felt the condemning power of the law upon their conscience, the death and resurrection of Christ effected complete deliverance. They are conceived as "buried with him in baptism," and "raised with him through faith in the working of God, who raised him from the dead, having forgiven us all our trespasses; having blotted out the bond written in ordinances that was against us, which was contrary to us: and he hath taken it out of the way, nailing it to the cross" (ii, 12-14). The condemning statute of the law hung like a bonded debt over us; but the Lord Jesus took it as he did the burden of all our sins, carried it in his own body upon the cross and nailed it there (comp. 1 Pet. ii, 24). Our faith lays hold with adoring wonder on this vicarious sufferer, so that we become crucified with him, but with him also live again.

11. In the Pastoral Epistles. The pastoral epistles have but few direct references to the doctrine of redemption in Christ, but these confirm the Pauline teaching. In 1 Tim. i, 15, we are admonished how "faithful is the saying, and worthy of all acceptation, that Jesus Christ came into the world to save sinners." In ii, 5, 6, we have the very comprehensive declaration, "There is one God, one mediator also between God and men, himself man,[1] Christ Jesus, who gave himself a ransom for all" (ἀντίλυτρον ὑπὲρ πάντων). The word here translated *ransom* occurs nowhere else in the New Testament, but seems to be intended for a more emphatic form of λύτρον, which is employed in Matt. xx, 28, and Mark x, 45. The meaning is substantially the same in all these texts. The Redeemer is a vicarious sufferer; he freely lays down his life in the place of and on behalf of many. The same truth is also affirmed in Titus ii, 14: "Christ gave himself for us, that he might redeem us (λυτρώσηται ἡμᾶς) from all iniquity, and purify unto himself a people for his own possession, zealous of good works." Thus we are assured that the grace of God brings salvation within reach of all men who deny themselves all ungodliness and live righteously (vers. 11 and 12). God and Christ work together in accomplishing this glorious salvation.

[1] Effective mediation between two parties, disparate as God and man, would seem to require the intervention of one who was at once partaker of the nature and secrets of both parties. And this was the peculiar qualification of Christ Jesus, who came into the world as the representative of "the King of the ages, the incorruptible, invisible, only God" (i, 17), and "came to save sinners" (i, 15). To accomplish this redemptive mediation he must needs be "manifest in the flesh" (iii, 16) in order to reveal the invisible God to men in the flesh, and to give himself a ransom for all. Hence the emphasis here put upon the humanity of the mediator. "The human nature of Christ," says Ellicott, "is specially mentioned as being the state in which his mediatorial office was visibly performed. The omission of the article (before *man*, in ii, 5) must be preserved in translation. In a different context Christ might clearly have been designated as *the man*, 'the representative man of humanity'; here, however, as the apostle only wishes to mark the nature in which Christ acted as mediator, but not any relation in which he stood to that nature, he designedly omits the article."—Commentary, in loco.

CHAPTER VI

DOCTRINE OF THE EPISTLE TO THE HEBREWS

1. Outline of the Epistle. Of all the New Testament writings the epistle to the Hebrews furnishes the most elaborate discussion of the mediatorial ministry of Christ. In that part of the epistle which we may regard as peculiarly doctrinal (i—x, 18) the Lord Jesus is set forth in several different relations, and an outline of the author's argument is in substance as follows: After an introductory paragraph (i, 1-4) in which the Son of God is extolled as heir of all things, maker of the ages, effulgence of God's glory, and very image of his being, upholding all things, effecting purification of sins, and enthroned with the Most High, the author proceeds to show (1) that as Son of God he is far above the angels (i, 5—ii, 18); (2) that he is worthy of more glory than Moses and Joshua (iii, 1—iv, 13); (3) that he is a great high priest, superior to Aaron and like Melchizedek (iv, 14—vii, 28); and (4) that he is minister of a more perfect tabernacle and mediator of a better covenant (viii, 1—x, 18). It will be seen upon the very face of this outline how largely the writer draws upon the Old Testament for imagery and illustration to enforce his argument. He seems never to forget that he is writing TO HEBREWS. Though Jesus is made for a little time lower than the angels, it is "that by the grace of God he should taste death for every one," and, "having made purification of sins," and "because of the suffering of death," should be "crowned with glory and honor." It was eminently fitting ($\xi\pi\rho\epsilon\pi\epsilon\nu$) that God, "for whom are all things, and through whom are all things, in bringing many sons unto glory, should make the author of their salvation perfect through sufferings" (ii, 9, 10).[1] This princely leader partook of the flesh and blood of the seed of Abraham that he might be truly identified in nature with the children he would save, and "that through death he might bring to naught him that had the power of death, that is, the devil, and might deliver all them who through fear of death were all their lifetime subject to bondage" (ii, 14, 15). He is not laying hold upon angels for the purpose of helping such beings as they are, but upon men of flesh and blood, beset with manifold temptations. It was, accordingly, a matter of obligation and necessity ($\ddot{\omega}\phi\epsilon\iota\lambda\epsilon\nu$,

---

[1] We have no English word that fully represents all that is suggested by $\dot{\alpha}\rho\chi\eta\gamma\acute{o}\varsigma$, here and in xii, 2, rendered *author*. It fairly means one who both *begins and leads on* in some great enterprise.

ver. 17) that he should "in all things be made like unto his brethren, that he might become a merciful and faithful high priest in things pertaining to God, to make propitiation (ἱλάσκεσθαι) for the sins of the people." Here for the first time in this epistle Jesus is called "high priest," and it deserves note that the word *propitiate,* profoundly suggestive in its metaphorical allusion to the mercy seat (ἱλαστήριον, comp. ix, 5; Rom. iii, 25), is employed to designate his priestly work. It is also worthy of note that Jesus is called priest and high priest only in this epistle to the Hebrews, and here the title of high priest is ascribed to him at least ten times.

2. Superior Priesthood of Jesus. Having introduced him (in ii, 17) as "a merciful and faithful high priest," and having further called him in iii, 1, "the Apostle and High Priest of our confession," he goes on to speak in chapters iii and iv of Christ's superiority to Moses and Joshua, and in iv, 14, returns to this subject of the high-priesthood of "Jesus the Son of God, who has passed through the heavens," and devotes the rest of the epistle mainly to a presentation of his heavenly ministry. Of this superior priest we are told that he is touched with the feeling of our infirmities, tempted in all points as we are, without sin, called and appointed of God, a man who prayed with strong cries and tears, who learned obedience by the things which he suffered, and, having been perfected through suffering, became to all who obey him the author of eternal salvation (iv, 15—v, 9). Psa. cx, 4, is cited and repeated several times (v, 6, 10; vi, 20; vii, 17), and the whole chapter vii is given to show that Christ is divinely styled "a priest for ever after the order of Melchizedek." The superior order or manner of Melchizedek is enhanced in chapter vii by a number of considerations, all well adapted to impress a devout Hebrew of the first Christian century. (1) First, it is pointed out that the ancient king of Salem, described only in Gen. xiv, 18-20, was both king and priest, and, being without recorded genealogy, and without record of his birth or his death, he remains a priest continually (vers. 1-3). (2) His superiority to Abraham and to the sons of Levi is next argued by means of a peculiar rabbinical argument (vers. 4-10). (3) Further, if the Levitical priesthood had been perfect, there could have been no reason for another priesthood after the order of Melchizedek rather than of Aaron (vers. 11-19). (4) Christ's priesthood, moreover, is confirmed by Jehovah's oath, giving it a majesty unknown to the Levitical priests (vers. 20-22). (5) It is also an unchangeable priesthood, for, ever living to make intercession, Christ can have no successor (vers. 23-25). (6) Finally, he is sinless, made higher than the heavens, and by the word of the oath perfected forever (vers. 26-28).

3. Symbolism of the Tabernacle. But the deeper mysteries of his priestly work are to be seen in the symbolism of the tabernacle and the mediatorial ministry of the new covenant in Christ. The Son of God is declared to be the minister of a more perfect tabernacle and the mediator of a better covenant, enacted upon better promises (viii, 1-6), and Jer. xxxi, 31-34, is cited as the word of the Lord in proof of this declaration. The old sanctuary and its holy places and vessels and ordinances of divine service were only "a copy and shadow of the heavenly things" (viii, 5; ix, 9, 23; x, 1), and were destined in the nature of things to grow old and vanish away (viii, 13), giving place to that which is essentially better and more spiritual. As every priest is appointed to offer gifts and sacrifices (viii, 3), so Christ entered once for all into the Holy of holies in the heavens (ix, 12, 24), as if sprinkling the heavenly mercy seat with his own blood. He has thus "been once offered to bear the sins of many" (ix, 28); "once at the end of the ages manifested to put away sin by his sacrifice" (ix, 26). This repeated mention of the offering of Christ through his atoning blood "once for all" (comp. vii, 27; ix, 12, 26, 28; x, 10; 1 Pet. iii, 18) has obvious allusion to the well-known law of the Jewish high priest going into the Holy of holies "once in the year" (ix, 7; Lev. xvi, 34), and sprinkling the mercy seat with "blood of goats and calves and bulls" (ix, 12, 13; x, 4; comp. Lev. xvi, 14, 15). The entrance of Christ "into heaven itself now to appear before the face of God for us" (ix, 24) has made that presence-chamber a "throne of grace," into which we too may boldly enter by the new and living way which he has dedicated for us in his blood (iv, 16; x, 19-21). Thus has he "obtained eternal redemption" (ix, 12; comp. Rom. iii, 24); "for if the blood of goats and bulls, and the ashes of a heifer sprinkling them that have been defiled, sanctify unto the cleanness of the flesh: how much more shall the blood of Christ, who through the eternal Spirit offered himself without blemish unto God, cleanse your conscience from dead works to serve the living God?" (ix, 13, 14.) All this language with its multiplicity of metaphorical allusion to the places and ordinances of the Levitical sanctuary, and especially to the divine service of the day of atonement, accords strikingly with our exposition of Rom. iii, 24, 25, and goes far to confirm it. Our high priest and minister of the true tabernacle "sat down on the right hand of the throne of the Majesty in the heavens" (viii, 1, 2); his throne is God's throne (i, 8); he is conceived as sprinkling that throne in the heavenly Holy of holies with his own blood, and abiding there forever as a heavenly mercy seat, "manifested to put away sin by the sacrifice of himself."

4. Mediator of the New Covenant, Hebrews ix, 15-18.

This manifoldness of metaphorical allusions all centering in the thought of a heavenly high priest, who enters the holy place offering his own blood and abiding thus continually, is also in accord with that interpretation of the difficult passage in ix, 15-18, which recognizes in "the mediator of the new covenant" one who in his own person and work is at once maker, mediator, and sacrificial offering.[1] This fact does not seem to be duly appreciated by those interpreters who insist that the word διαθήκη must in verses 16 and 17 mean a *testament, a will,* or *deed of bequest.* Outside of these two verses the word is used fifteen times in this epistle, always in the sense of *covenant.* Such is its meaning also in every other passage of the New Testament where it occurs, as also in the Septuagint, where it nearly always appears as the representative of the Hebrew ברית. It would seem, therefore, like a harsh and violent procedure in exegesis to import a new meaning of the word into these two verses, and such procedure can be justified only by most decisive reasons.

(1) *Reasons for "Testament" in Hebrews ix, 16, 17.* The following reasons for such a sudden change of meaning have been offered: (1) The language of verses 16 and 17, retaining the idea of a *covenant,* is exceedingly harsh and unmeaning; for (2) διαθέμενος in both these verses can only mean a maker of a will or testament, and not of a sacrificial offering; (3) it is not true that the death of a covenant maker is necessary to make a covenant valid; (4) the mention of "the eternal inheritance" in verse 15 suggests the idea of a will or testamentary document, and so justifies the change in meaning from *covenant* to *testament.* (5) Moreover, the statements of verses 16 and 17 are of the nature of a general well-known custom, and therefore most naturally

---

[1] It will be well for the reader to notice the following translations of Heb. ix, 16, 17. The Authorized Version reads: "For where a testament is, there must also of necessity be the death of the testator. For a testament is of force after men are dead: otherwise it is of no strength at all while the testator liveth." The Anglo-American Revision has: "For where a testament is, there must of necessity be the death of him that made it. For a testament is of force where there hath been death (margin, *over the dead*:) for doth it ever avail while he that made it liveth?" The American Standard Edition makes the last sentence affirmative instead of interrogative: "For it doth never avail while he that made it liveth." Macknight translates: "For where a covenant is made by sacrifice, there is a necessity that the death of the appointed sacrifices be produced. For a covenant is made firm over dead sacrifices, seeing it never hath force whilst the appointed sacrifice liveth." In a similar way "J. C.," in Adam Clarke's Commentary: "For where there is a covenant, it is necessary that the death of the appointed victim should be exhibited; because a covenant is confirmed over dead victims, since it is not at all valid while the appointed victim is alive." He further observes: "Διαθέμενος is not a substantive, but a participle, or a participial adjective, derived from the same root as διαθήκη and must have a substantive understood. I therefore render it the disposed or appointed victim, alluding to the manner of disposing or setting apart the pieces of the victim, when they were going to ratify a covenant."

explained as referring to the fact that the death of a testator is necessary to place his will and deed of bequest beyond question. These reasons, however, are not satisfactory or conclusive,[1] and whatever relief they may seem to afford in explaining some of the statements of verses 16 and 17, they leave other statements without a clear interpretation. Difficulties present themselves on any exposition, and our search should be for that view of the passage which best satisfies all the demands of the writer's argument.

(2) *Reasons for "Covenant."* Over against the reasons given for translating διαθήκη *testament* we may say (1) that the word appears to have that meaning nowhere else in biblical Greek; (2) that the context is very much against it: διαθήκη is the main word in the passage, and the "new covenant" and "first covenant" mentioned in verse 15 cannot be properly rendered *testament,* but unquestionably refer back to vii, 22; viii, 6-10; and the same thought of *covenant* is continued in verse 18, where the first covenant is again referred to as having been dedicated with blood.[2] (3) There is nothing, moreover, in the entire context to suggest the idea of a testamentary document, not even in the mention of "the eternal inheritance," for that is conceived as a matter of God's promise (ἐπαγγελία), not as an estate bequeathed through forms of legal attestation. But covenants and promises are correlative ideas.[3] (4) A mediator of a covenant and a testator of a deed of bequest are not correlative ideas; so that to use the word in such a different meaning would be to introduce without justification an idea foreign to the Hebrew mind and unlikely to be employed in addressing Hebrews. (5) It may also be urged that the death of a testator is not necessary to make his will valid in law; no more so, at any rate, than the death of a covenant-maker is necessary to confirm a covenant. If it be strange and harsh to say that "where a covenant is, there must be of necessity the death of him that made it" (ver. 16), is it not equally strange and very questionable as a matter of fact to say that a testament or will is valid only after the death of him that made it? In the case of the

---

[1] It should be observed that every one of them is either a bare assertion or virtually a begging of the question at issue. The third and fifth of the assertions may be as truly affirmed of the view which insists on the sense of *covenant*.

[2] The connection makes it most difficult to suppose that the key-word (διαθήκη), is used in different senses in the course of the verses, and especially that the characteristic of a particular kind of διαθήκη, essentially different from the *first covenant* of verses 15, 18, should be brought forward in verse 16. For it is impossible to maintain that the sacrifices with which the old covenant was inaugurated could be explained on the supposition that it was a *testament*. Nor does it appear that it could be called a *testament* in any sense.—Westcott, The Epistle to the Hebrews, p. 300. London, 1889.

[3] Compare the phrase *the covenants of the promise* in Eph. ii, 12, and compare Rom. ix, 4.

author, mediator, and finisher of our redemption from sin, such a statement about a testamentary deed has no relevancy, nor does it tend to illustrate any feature of the continuous mediatorial work of Christ, for he will never change his mind, or break his word. Any supposable word, testament, or declaration of the Christ must needs be as valid and sure before his death as after. (6) But the conspicuous fact of this new covenant is that the great mediator of it gave his own blood for the eternal redemption of those *who have been called* (οἱ κεκλημένοι), and the writer of this epistle makes this point most emphatic throughout the entire argument, and farther on he speaks of it as "the blood of the covenant," and "the blood of an eternal covenant" (x, 29; xiii, 20). (7) With this important fact in mind we should also observe that the *death*, which according to verse 15 "took place for the redemption of the transgressions that were under the first covenant," was the death of the mediator, Christ himself. (8) Accordingly, as stated above, the remarkable and unique feature of this new covenant is that its maker, mediator, and sacrificial victim, by whose blood the promise of the eternal inheritance is made forever fast and sure (βεβαία), are all one. This fact explains the boldness and apparent harshness of the language of verses 16 and 17, and it is in keeping with that style of thought which also conceives Christ as a throne of grace (iv, 16) and a mercy seat (Rom. iii, 25). (9) This interpretation, moreover, accords best with the word φέρεσθαι in verse 16. If one would speak of *proving, attesting,* or *announcing* a person's *death,* he could not appropriately use the word φέρεσθαι, which might, indeed, refer to the *bringing forward* of a legal document for probate, but not to prove the *testator's death*. But the one manifestation of the Christ at the end of the ages for the putting away of sin by the sacrifice of himself (ix, 26) is fittingly designated by φέρεσθαι, which points to the bringing of his *death* forward into prominence,[1] and is equivalent to the *open setting forth* of Jesus Christ crucified, as in Gal. iii, 1, and the *setting him forth* as a mercy seat through faith in his blood, as in Rom. iii, 25. In this case the *death* of Christ, referred to in verse 15, is conceived as brought forward and set in strong light as the seal of the new covenant. (10) The words ἐπὶ θυσίαις in verse 17, have peculiar force and significance in connection with the foregoing exposition, but are unsuitable for expressing the idea of the death of a testator.

---

[1] It is not said that he who makes the covenant must die, but that his death must be *brought forward,* presented, introduced upon the scene, set in evidence, so to speak. This sense of φέρεσθαι appears to be perfectly natural, and to be more simple than the sense commonly attributed to the word, either to be alleged as a fact, or to be pleaded in the course of an argument, or to be current as a matter of common notoriety.—Westcott, The Epistle to the Hebrews, p. 265.

The phrase is seen in its true significance in connection with ratifying a covenant in Psa. l, 5, where ἐπὶ νεκροῖς, is employed by the Septuagint translators for the Hebrew עלי זבח *over sacrifice:*

> Assemble unto me my pious ones,
> Those that ratify my covenant *over sacrifice.*[1]

To make or ratify a covenant it was necessary that a sacrificial victim or several victims be slain, and in the specific reference to the dedication of the first covenant which immediately follows in verses 18-22 Moses is mentioned as taking the blood of calves and goats and sprinkling it as the sign and seal of the covenant which God commanded (citing from Exod. xxiv, 8). Accordingly, the only suitable explanation of a covenant ἐπὶ νεκροῖς βεβαία would seem to be one *made strong over dead victims* slain for the purpose of ratifying the covenant. The death which "took place for the redemption of the transgressions" (ver. 15), and also for providing "the blood of an everlasting covenant" (xiii, 20), is the death of Jesus Christ the mediator of the new covenant. This death, which marked a crisis of the ages, is brought forward into prominence, and is to furnish the solution of the apparent incongruity of making the mediator and sacrificial victim of the covenant one and the same. As high priest Jesus entered the holy places "through his own blood" (ver. 12); as mediator and author and finisher of the new covenant he secures by his own death "the promise of the eternal inheritance" to all who have been called (ver. 15); and so we are assured that the new covenant as truly as the first covenant has been consecrated with blood (ver. 18), and it is as true under the one as under the other that "apart from the shedding of blood there is no remission" (ver. 22). This significant symbolism of sacrifice and blood is prominent throughout the entire context (vers. 13-22), and is not for a moment to be lost from view, or interrupted by a supposed irrelevant reference to the making and attesting of legal deeds of bequest. With such an understanding of the main thoughts in this passage it makes no essential difference whether we translate the last part of verse 17 affirmatively or interrogatively. The entire verse may

---

[1] The best illustration of the formalities of making or *cutting* a covenant (see the Hebrew Lexicons on the phrase כרת ברית) over sacrifice is read in Gen. xv, 8-18, where Abram divides the dead victims, and places the parts over against each other, and the flaming torch is seen to pass between the pieces. The same custom of cutting and dividing the victims, and of passing between the portions is referred to in Jer. xxxiv, 18, 19. It will be noticed that the phrase ἐπὶ νεκροῖς, *over dead ones*, in Heb. ix, 17 (A. V., "after men are dead"; R. V., "where there hath been death") when used in reference to the ratification of a covenant is virtually equivalent to ἐπὶ θυσίαις, *over sacrificial victims*, in Psa. l, 5. Compare also the phrases ἐπὶ βρώμασιν, πόμασιν, and βαπτισμοῖς, in Heb. ix, 10.

be rendered thus: "For a covenant over dead sacrificial victims is firm, since it never has any force while the maker of it lives." That is, a covenant is confirmed on the basis and with the accompaniment of sacrifice, so that in reality it is without force or validity unless the covenant maker signify the surrender of his own life by the blood of the slain victims which he offers in the course of the solemn transaction.[1]

5. This Not a Covenant between Equals. In studying these illustrations which rest upon the customs and the symbolism of covenants we must not overlook the fact that any covenant between God and man cannot be a covenant between equals. Such a covenant is, however, a most striking assurance of the gracious condescension of the Most High, and Jesus, as the mediator of the new covenant, represents in his redemptive work the interests of both God and man. These considerations serve to show also how, in the mind of the writer, covenant maker, mediator, and sacrificial offering all unite in the Son of God who is so remarkably described in the opening words of this epistle. This adorable mediator is heir of all things, maker of the ages, effulgence of the glory of God, upholder of all things, and purifier from all sin. Only such a transcendent Son of God can be at once maker, mediator, and sacrificial victim of an eternal covenant.

6. Alexandrian Cast of the Epistle. The foregoing study of Christ's priesthood and mediation as set forth in the epistle to the Hebrews has doubtless put beyond question our statement that no other book of the New Testament furnishes so elaborate a discussion of this subject. The entire treatment is unique, and the learned critic and exegete cannot fail to note the Alexandrian cast of thought and the extensive and peculiar use of the Old Testament writings. These are recognized as a sacred deposit of heavenly truth; but the Septuagint version, not the Hebrew text, is uniformly quoted, and passages where this version differs notably from the Hebrew are made the basis of special argument and illustration.[2] The tabernacle and its holy places are looked upon as

---

[1] Westcott has written so ably on this passage that we here add one more citation: "In ordinary covenants the death of the persons who made the covenant was represented of necessity in symbol only, and both parties were alike liable to change. . . . Here fresh considerations offer themselves which underlie the argument of the passage. The covenant to which the writer looks is not one between man and man, who meet as equal parties, but between man and God. The death of the covenant victim, therefore, assumes a new character. It figures not only the unchangeableness of death, but also the self-surrender of death. . . . Christ was himself the covenant victim. In this aspect he attested the inviolable force of the covenant which he established."—The Epistle to the Hebrews, p. 302.

[2] Most notably so in x, 5, where a citation of Psa. xl, 6, reads, according to the Septuagint, "a *body* didst thou prepare for me," but the Hebrew text of this passage reads, "*ears* thou hast dug for me," the word *dug* most naturally referring to the

figures of heavenly realities opened to us through the mediation of Jesus Christ, and Melchizedek is extolled as a type of our high priest who is now seated at the right hand of the throne of God. But with all these and other peculiarities, which scientific exegesis must duly note, the teaching of this epistle on the subject of Christ's mediation is in fundamental harmony with the other books of the New Testament. The writer treats the death, exaltation, and everlasting intercession of our Lord much after the manner of Paul. Neither of these writers seems to know much of Jesus Christ in the days of his flesh, but they both magnify his heavenly exaltation. Paul emphasizes the idea of righteousness, and the writer to the Hebrews that of holiness; but so closely do they agree in the main that the epistle to the Hebrews was long believed to be the work of Paul, and this opinion has not been without some advocates in quite recent times. On the offering of the body and blood of Christ the teaching of the epistle is also remarkably like that of the first epistle of Peter.

7. Substantial Agreement of All the New Testament Writers. We find, then, that on the sacrifice and mediation of Christ all the New Testament writers are in substantial agreement. After showing due respect to the various classes of writings, and to their obvious individual peculiarities of thought and diction, we are compelled to acknowledge that according to all the scriptures of the New Testament there is no salvation apart from Jesus Christ crucified, "nor is there any other name under heaven, that is given among men, wherein we must be saved." Peter and John and Paul and the author of Hebrews have their own ways of setting forth this truth, but none of them gets away from the doctrine which we trace in the words of Jesus at the Last Supper and at all those other times when he spoke of giving his life a ransom for many, or of laying it down in behalf of others.

---

hollow cavity of the ear. However the error of the Greek version arose, the author of the epistle makes the word *body* significant by regarding it as the organ of Christ's incarnation and the means of *doing the will* of God. This is seen further in verse 10, where "the body of Jesus Christ" has obvious reference to this citation from the psalm. God "takes away the first," that is, sacrifices and offerings, "that he may establish the second," that is, the will of God.

CHAPTER VII

SUMMARY OF THE BIBLICAL DOCTRINE

HAVING now examined with some care the import of the language of the biblical writers touching the mediation of Jesus Christ, we shall conclude this section with a brief statement of the principal truths which may be read in these scriptures and clearly proved thereby. Our statements in this epitome of doctrine are of the nature of so many expressions of conviction as to the real teaching of the various portions of Scripture which we have examined and endeavored to expound, and they should, accordingly, be read as the results of a faithful exegetical study of the word of truth rather than as the dogmas of a formulated creed.

1. A Continuous Process, Not a Finished Work. Our first observation is that the mediatorial ministry of Jesus Christ is a continuous process, not a finished work. We are not authorized by any biblical teaching to maintain that such terms as *atonement, propitiation, expiation,* and *redemption,* as applied to the saving ministry of our Lord, imply that he has completed or is near the completion of the work for which he came into the world. He truly died, and thus offered himself "once for all" (Rom. vi, 10; Heb. vii, 27; ix, 12, 26, 28; x, 10; 1 Pet. iii, 18); that fact is simple and definite matter of history; but that particular event was, relatively, only an incident in the vast work of Christ's mediation. It was only the passing of our great high priest into the heavenly Holy of holies "through his own blood," that he might appear in the presence of God for us, and there abide forever as our high priest and mediator. How could his being "delivered up for our trespasses" have availed had he not also been "raised for our justification"? (Rom. iv, 25.) According to Paul, "It is Christ Jesus that died, yea rather, that was raised from the dead, who is at the right hand of God, who also maketh intercession for us" (Rom. viii, 34). And according to this apostle it is also the Holy Spirit that "maketh intercession for the saints according to the will of God" (Rom. viii, 27), and in 2 Cor. iii, 17, he calls our Lord himself the Spirit who transforms us into the image of the glory of God. The eternal Spirit and Christ and God are one in all this ministry of reconciliation, and the Lord Christ has no more finished his work of mediation than has the Holy Father or the Holy Spirit finished yearning for mankind. The heavenly redemption is thus seen to be a process that must needs go on so long as there remains one sinner to be saved.

2. Largely Set Forth by Symbols and Metaphors. The nature of Christ's mediation is largely set forth by means of metaphors and symbols. This fact should admonish us that greatest care must be exercised in our interpretations of biblical texts bearing on this subject.[1] Human language is at best imperfect, and there are some figures of speech from which, perhaps, no two men would derive precisely the same idea. We need not wonder, therefore, that divers theories of atonement have sought support in what on close analysis appear to be only incidental features of an object referred to in a metaphor. We have seen that the New Testament writers speak often of the saving work of Christ in terms that plainly derive their significance from the sacrificial ceremonies of the Jewish people, and their language cannot be fairly interpreted without attention to Old Testament facts and teachings concerning the offering of blood upon the altar. Such words as *atonement, propitiation,* and *expiation*[2] are inseparable from sacrificial customs and the ideas such customs were adapted to inculcate. These customs and ideas are also part and parcel of the religious history of mankind. We have aimed to indicate in the foregoing pages the fundamental ideas which attach to the Old Testament ritual of sacrifices and offerings, and also to guard the reader against pressing incidental points of analogy and symbolism too far. Language and illustrations based upon popular customs should always be treated as popular, not as exact and scientific in its purpose. To apprehend aright the vicarious element in the self-offering of Christ, we must eliminate the pagan notion of

---

[1] Due regard must also be had for peculiar forms of expression which characterize particular writers. There are mystical sayings which are peculiarly Johannine, and for that very reason not to be understood as if they were of the nature of a dogmatic formula. There are also texts and paragraphs in Paul's writings which evince his rabbinical training, and also bold realistic statements which may by valid exegesis be resolved into mystical or ideal conceptions. It is a misleading procedure for anyone arguing in the interests of a disputed dogma to insist on a literal interpretation of such peculiar forms of speech.

[2] The word *atonement* occurs in the New Testament but once, in the common English version of Rom. v, 11, where the Revised Version substitutes *reconciliation.* In the Old Testament it is the common rendering of some form of the Hebrew כפר, the primary meaning of which is to *cover,* as we have elsewhere explained. Hence as an English word it can have no weight in determining the biblical conception. *Propitiation* is a Latin term, and appears in the New Testament only as a translation of ἱλαστήριον in Rom. iii, 25, which we have shown to mean a *mercy seat* (as in Heb. ix, 5), and of ἱλασμός in 1 John ii, 2, and iv, 10. The word in these two last-named texts has obvious reference to what Christ does for the forgiveness and removal of the sins of the world, but furnishes no explanation of the *method* of the propitiation. *Expiation* is not a biblical word, and so far as it suggests anything other than what Scripture teaches concerning atonement, propitiation, and reconciliation it has no place in a biblical theology.

placating a wrathful Deity, and look more deeply into the spiritual significance of "the blood of Christ, who through the eternal Spirit offered himself without blemish unto God."

3. Use of Current Forms of Speech. To make known a truth so far-reaching and profound, Christ and his apostles most fittingly appropriated figurative conceptions and forms of speech that were at once current and popular and sacredly associated with religious service. It is to be noted that our Lord chose the time of the passover for the laying down of his life in vicarious sacrifice, and that Paul speaks of the sacrifice of Christ as our passover (1 Cor. v, 7). Sacrificial worship, priestly intercession, and the lofty ideals of a covenant relation to God had furnished a large part of the providential preparation of the chosen people for the advent of the Christ. But the great prophets of Israel from Samuel onward had taught that sacrifices and burnt offerings were of no intrinsic value, and could not be acceptable before Jehovah unless expressive of a pure devotion of the heart of the worshiper and a faithful obedience to the word of God (comp. 1 Sam. xv, 22; Isa. i, 11-17; Hos. vi, 6; Mic. vi, 6-8; Amos v, 21-24; Jer. vi, 20; vii, 22, 23; Psa. xl, 6-8). Much more, then, may we suppose that our Lord and his apostles would penetrate beneath the forms of priestly service and of sacrifices (comp. Matt. xii, 5-8; 1 Cor. v, 7, 8; Rom. xii, 1, 2; Heb. ix, 9; x, 4), and fill their metaphorical allusions to them with the deepest spiritual significance. We should study in like manner to pass beyond the letter and to grasp the true spiritual import of such words as *atonement* and *propitiation* when applied to the sufferings of Christ. Our expositions, we trust, have shown that there is no need of loading the biblical writers with the pagan notions of placating a vengeful Deity, or of reconciling an offended God to the sinner. One may construct such a dogma, and many have so interpreted certain scattered texts of Scripture; but we think such a construction is unnecessary, and not justified in the light of the more authoritative statements of Christ and his apostles.

4. Necessity of Christ's Mediation. A certain divine necessity for the mediatorial sufferings of Christ is assumed in many scriptures (Matt. xvi, 21; xxvi, 54; Mark viii, 31; Luke ix, 22; xiii, 33; xvii, 25; xxii, 37; xxiv, 7, 26, 44, 46; John iii, 14; ix, 4; xii, 32-34; Acts iii, 18; iv, 12; xvii, 3; Heb. ix, 23); and aside from any such specific statement it would truly seem in the nature of things that such suffering and sacrifice must have been imperatively necessary or the only begotten Son of God would not thus have given up his life. Wherein, then, this necessity? Not, as we have read the Scriptures, in a demand of abstract justice to maintain God's honor and dignity as a Ruler of the moral world. God's righteousness, whether as Father, Ruler, or Judge, is sure to manifest itself in Love, so that even in the pardon of our sins and cleansing us from all unrighteousness he is ever "faithful and righteous" (1 John i, 9).

(1) *Necessity in Man.* The necessity for Christ's redeeming work is from our point of view most readily seen, first, in the sinfulness of man and his inability to release himself from its thraldom. The soul that sins must surely die (Gen. ii, 17; Ezek. xviii, 4, 20); "lust, when it hath conceived, beareth sin; and the sin, when it is full-grown, bringeth forth death" (James i, 15); "the wages of sin is death." When, therefore, we ask who shall deliver men from this fearful bondage of sin and of death our only answer is that such salvation is the free gift of God through Jesus Christ our Lord. It must come from above. There is no other way of life, no other name under heaven in whom we must be saved, if saved at all. Studying the whole manifestation of God in Christ, we are led, especially in John's gospel, to conceive him as light, life, love, righteousness, wisdom, power, and glory—a sevenfold revelation. Christ comes forth from the bosom of the Father, makes an end of the law for righteousness unto everyone that believeth, and brings life and immortality to light.

(2) *Necessity in Nature of God.* But there is also intimation in such scriptures as John iii, 16, that there exist mysterious necessities in the nature of God, as well as in the helplessness of perishing men, that required the giving of his only begotten Son to be the Saviour of the world. The creation of such a world as ours, with its myriad forms of life and its innumerable "offspring of God," capable of becoming children of God by heavenly birth and adoption, would seem to have involved obligations on the part of the Creator which no human mind can properly estimate. According to the profound conception of the fourth gospel, the Word that became flesh was with God in the entire process of creation, and no man has ever seen God or is capable of revealing him except "the only begotten Son, who is in the bosom of the Father." We may, accordingly, believe that, speaking after the manner of man, and not irreverently, the righteousness of love and the love of righteousness toward the dependent objects of his creation required on the part of God a redemptive manifestation of himself in the mediation of Jesus Christ. We thus conceive God as the eternal Father counting himself obligated by every conceivable bond of love and righteousness to exert himself to the uttermost to save from sin and its perdition every creature whom he permitted to come into being bearing the image and likeness of God. If, after

all such mighty provisions of love, the human offspring persist in sin and "sell himself to do evil," the Father has proven his own unspeakable affection, and has discharged his own obligation.

5. Such Suffering Not Penal. The sufferings of Christ, then, are not to be thought of as a penalty. No righteousness, human or divine, can inflict penalty on the righteous or on any being that is not convicted of sin. But, according to Paul (Rom. viii, 3), "God, sending his own Son in the likeness of sinful flesh and concerning sin (περὶ ἁμαρτίας)[1] condemned sin in the flesh." The entire manifestation of Christ as the holy, self-sacrificing Son of God has broken the power of sin in human nature, and thus put it forever under condemning judgment (comp. 1 John iii, 8; Heb. ii, 14). And if we inquire further why Christ must suffer in this public condemnation of sin, the true answer is, because God suffers and must needs have suffered concerning sin as soon as ever it appeared in the moral world. Whatever view we take of Christ's life, work, and suffering we must recognize in him some corresponding manifestation of his Father. And so when we behold Christ weeping and lamenting over Jerusalem, and crying, "O that thou hadst known the things that belong unto peace! How often would I have gathered thy children, but ye would not!" we behold the Father also. And in like manner in all his utterances of sorrow, of judgment, or of love, he is the divinely anointed Revealer of the thoughts and feelings of God.

6. Does Not Remove All Consequences of Sin. A fact not to be overlooked is that nothing which God in Christ has done or can do removes all consequences of sin. Sins that are past events, "the sins done beforetime," may be freely forgiven in the blessed forbearance of God, but they must forever remain as deeds of the past. They cannot possibly be undone, or cease to be facts in the history of the moral world. And the natural results or consequences of many sins work on through successive generations in spite of all the redeeming efficacy of the grace of God. These facts also serve to show that the great saving work of Christ is not to rescue man *from punishment* for wrongdoing, but rather to deliver him *from sin itself*. The sacrificial mediation of Christ is not a penalty for the sins of men, nor even a substitute for penalty; but it is rather to be apprehended as "a power of God unto salvation to every one that believeth."

---

[1] This phrase, being the usual rendering of the Hebrew for *sin offering* in the Septuagint (comp. Heb. x, 6, 8), may be explained in that sense here; or it may be explained as in substance equivalent to what this apostle expresses in somewhat stronger form in 2 Cor. v, 21. But it cannot be shown to mean that God visited *punishment* on Jesus Christ, as if by any sort of imputation he could be made a real substitute for the guilty and suffer the penalty due to them.

7. Not an Objective Process or Ground of God's Activity. The biblical conception of Christ's work is not that of an objective process going on outside of humanity. Such a notion seems possible only as we are taught to think of the atonement as "an objective ground" on which it is made possible for God to forgive sin. The logic of this conception implies that God's love and saving mercy could not be exercised *except as a result of Christ's offering his life as a ransom;* whereas, according to the Scripture, the entire mediation of Christ has its origin in the love of God. The sufferings of Christ are not the ground or cause of the exercise of God's saving grace; the love of God is the cause and source of the sufferings. So God is *in Christ,* not apart from Christ, reconciling the world unto himself. And the atonement, the propitiation, the reconciliation, is *in us, not apart from us.* Nor should we think of God as apart from his world, or outside of humanity, in any such way as to warrant our affirming objective grounds for his becoming reconciled to us.

8. Essentially Spiritual in its Operation. It is evident, therefore, that we are to think of Christ's work of mediation as something essentially spiritual. Sacrifices and offerings have no value except as figures of spiritual realities, or as illustrations of heavenly truths. In his coming to do the will of God, and so to manifest the nature and power of God, Christ taketh away such formal rites that he may establish the will of the heavenly Father (Heb. x, 9). And it is the will of God that all men should be saved from sin. His love for the world has given his only begotten Son to reveal a saving grace sufficient to embrace all humanity. But the grace and the mediation can become effective only as men in faith accept the heavenly provision and are born of the Spirit. Thus they "pass out of death into life," and "walk after the Spirit."

9. Effectual Through a Living Faith. Inasmuch, then, as Christ's mediation is a spiritual work, it becomes effectual in the heart and life of men only as they become united with Christ by a strong living faith. The Christ of God is a living Saviour, and in him we have our most blessed access to God. The personal experiences of life and light and peace and fellowship with God enable the Christian believer to apprehend the profound significance of such biblical concepts as a personal participation in the sufferings of Christ (comp. Rom. viii, 17; 2 Cor. i, 5, 7; Phil. iii, 10; 1 Pet. iv, 13), a being crucified with Christ (Gal. ii, 20; v, 24; vi, 14; Rom. vi, 6), dying and being buried with Christ (Rom. vi, 4, 8; 2 Cor. v, 14; Col. ii, 12; iii, 3), and also rising and reigning with him (Eph. ii, 2; Col. ii, 12, 13; 2 Tim. ii, 11, 12). As we are thus "partakers of the sufferings of Christ" (1 Pet. iv, 13), we may also "become partakers of the divine nature" (2 Pet. i, 4). And so the conviction of sin, the deep sense of guilt, the experience of repentance and conversion, the remission of sin, the new birth from above, and all the blessedness of the new spiritual life "hid with Christ in God" are brought about by means of the redemption in Christ, and are possible in no other name under heaven or among men. Like the new birth *from above,* all these gracious experiences of salvation are opened unto us by reason of the love and righteousness of God as revealed in the mediation of his Son Jesus Christ.

10. No Theory of Atonement in the Scriptures. We offer no theory or philosophy of atonement in Christ other than what may appear in these statements of the manifold Scripture teaching on the subject. The Scriptures certainly furnish us no theory of Christ's divine-human mediation, but we ought not therefore to condemn, as some do, all attempts to formulate such theories. For what is a theory of the atonement but an attempt to set forth a rational conception of the nature and necessity of Christ's redeeming work?[1] Regeneration and eternal life are impossible to man without the removal of his sinfulness and guilt, and the rational theorist inquires how this salvation is brought about in the manifestation of Christ. The result of our study has been to show that this divine redemptive mediation is so multifarious in its operation that no definitive theory can fairly express its depth and breadth and height. Whether we say with John iii, 16, "God so loved the world, that he gave his only begotten Son, that whosoever believeth on him should not perish, but have eternal life"; or with 2 Cor. v, 19, "God was in Christ reconciling the world unto himself"; or with 1 Pet. iii, 18, "Christ suffered for sins once, the righteous for the sake of the unrighteous, that he might bring us to God"; or with 1 John iv, 10, "God loved us and sent his Son as a propitiation for our sins"; or with Heb. ii, 10, "It became God in bringing many sons unto glory, to make the author of their salvation perfect through sufferings"—whether, I say, we appropriate any one of these or of a score of other biblical statements of similar character and import, we express at most only an incomplete idea of all that

---

[1] It would seem that each of the more notable theories of the atonement has had a sort of genetic relation to certain dominant ideas of the time when it originated. The patristic notion of a ransom paid to Satan for the release of mankind from his thrall could have been possible only at a time when crass doctrines of demonology were widely prevalent. The Anselmic theory of absolute satisfaction had a stronghold in mediæval ideas of absolute monarchy and the divine rights of kings. The "governmental theory" may be traced to Grotius and the prominence given in his day to international law. And the great humanitarian movements of the nineteenth century with their emphasis on altruism and moral reforms prepared the way for the "moral influence theory," and have supplied its chief arguments and illustrations.

belongs to Christ's mediation. The great work of redemption expressed in any one of these texts is generally found to be involved in one or more figures of speech which call for some measure of analysis and explanation. Hence appears the impossibility, also, of maintaining a doctrine of atonement in Christ on the basis of the language of divers texts of Scripture taken as so many authoritative utterances. A rational exegesis of each separate text and its immediate context often shows that men have read their doctrinal theories into biblical statements which furnish them no real support. While, therefore, a number and variety of observations may fairly summarize the teachings of Christ and his apostles on the subject, the doctrine of redemptive mediation in Jesus Christ is too broad and deep and mysterious to be satisfied with any single definition or theory.

11. Mystical Body of Christ. There is, however, an ideal of "the mystical body of Christ," given in the New Testament, which should receive distinctive attention in our study of the divine-human mediation of our Lord. The profound truth of the communion of saints in and through the Spirit of Christ finds, perhaps, its most remarkable expression in John xvii, 20-26, where Jesus prays that all those, whom the divinely appointed ministry of reconciliation shall gather together out of the world, may be PERFECTED INTO ONE ($\tau\epsilon\tau\epsilon\lambda\epsilon\iota\omega\mu\acute{\epsilon}\nu o\iota\ \epsilon\mathit{l}\varsigma\ \mathring{\epsilon}\nu$). They are all to be one, even as the Father is in the Son, and the Son is in the Father, that they may ultimately be with the glorified Christ in the heavenly light, and behold the glory and the love which were existent before the foundation of the world. There comes to us with these words an ideal of perfection in the love and fellowship of God which no comment of ours can place in clearer light. Paul's words about being raised up with Christ, and sitting "with him in the heavenlies" (Eph. ii, 6), seem like an echo of Jesus's intercessory prayer. "The heavenlies" of perfection in Christ and in God are not "heavenly places" merely, but heavenly fellowship of all saints, heavenly powers, heavenly wisdom and knowledge, and all heavenly glories of the life eternal.[1] The vital unity of the mystical body of Christ is also shown in the figure of the vine and its branches (John xv, 1-9). Jesus is himself the genuine living vine, his Father is the vinedresser, and his disciples are the branches which can have no fruit apart from the true vine. In strict accord with this ideal we are assured, in John vi, 53, that no one can possess the eternal life except he "eat the flesh of the Son of man and drink his blood." Thus only can the living Christ, "ascending up where he was

---

[1] See Biblical Hermeneutics, p. 276. New York, 1890.

before" (ver. 62), bestow the heavenly manna, and make good the word, "He that eateth my flesh and drinketh my blood abideth in me, and I in him." These words are offensive to the literalist and the man of a carnal mind, but to the man of spiritual intuition they are instinct with spirit and with life. In the first epistle of John (i, 3) we meet another statement of the same spiritual truth: "Our fellowship is with the Father, and with his Son Jesus Christ." Such fellowship is also called "abiding in the Son and in the Father," and constitutes the essence of "the life eternal" (ii, 24, 25).

12. The Communion of Saints. The same rich mystical thought appears in Paul's allusions to the communion of saints at the Lord's table: "The cup of blessing which we bless, is it not a communion (κοινωνία, *a joint participation*) of the blood of Christ? The bread which we break, is it not a communion of the body of Christ?" (1 Cor. x, 16.) So again in 1 Cor. xii, 12, 13, we read: "As the body is one and hath many members, and all the members of the body, being many, are one body; so also is Christ. For in one Spirit were we all baptized into one body." The saints of all ages and lands are to be thus conceived as constituting the mystical body of Christ, and they are "severally members thereof." They make up his "church, which is his body, the fulness of him that filleth all in all" (Eph. i, 23). This mystical body is not yet complete. Divers ministries of apostles and prophets and evangelists and pastors and teachers exist "for the perfecting of the saints, unto the building up of the body of Christ; till we all attain unto the unity of the faith, and of the knowledge of the Son of God, unto a full-grown man, unto the measure of the stature of the fulness of Christ" (Eph. iv, 12, 13). Here, surely, is an ideal of the great consummation contemplated in the mediation of Jesus Christ which inspires holiest thoughts. And when to all this we add the figure of the Church as the Spouse of Christ, who is at once her Saviour and her Lord, we but enhance our concept of the all-embracing love of God in Christ. The Lord Jesus is the Saviour of the mystical body, for he "loved the church, and gave himself up for her, that he might present the church to himself glorious, not having spot or wrinkle or any such thing" (Eph. v, 25-27). It is worthy of note that while in Pauline thought the Church of Christ was "purchased with his own blood" (Acts xx, 28), in the Apocalypse of John the great and glorious company of those who were, by the blood of the Lamb that was slain, "purchased for God out of every tribe, and tongue, and people, and nation" (v, 9), are shown in heavenly vision as "the Bride, the wife of the Lamb" (xxi, 9).

This picture is a consummation of our highest thought of "the redemption that is in Christ Jesus." By means of it we are elevated far above all special theories of the atonement. We "behold the Lamb of God, that taketh away the sin of the world." We behold the mystical body of Christ, all those who believe on him through the word of his apostles, sanctified and cleansed by the washing of water in the word, made one in the Father and in the Son, abiding in the heavenlies, and sharing in the glory of the risen and ascended Lord. The members of this mystical body are "a great multitude which no man can number, out of all peoples, arrayed in white robes, and palms in their hands, their robes washed and made white in the blood of the Lamb. *Therefore* are they before the throne of God, and he that sitteth on the throne shall spread his tabernacle over them, and the Lamb that is in the midst of the throne shall be their shepherd, and shall guide them unto fountains of waters of life: and God shall wipe away every tear from their eyes." And thus we behold the Author of our salvation made perfect through sufferings, bringing many sons into glory, and saying, as he presents them in the presence of that glory with exceeding joy, "Behold, I and the children whom God hath given me." Thus we behold God, in Christ, through the eternal Spirit, reconciling the world unto himself.

SECTION THIRD

THE KINGDOM AND COMING OF CHRIST

CHAPTER I

THE NATURE OF THE KINGDOM OF CHRIST

1. Heavenly Enthronement of Jesus Christ. Jesus, the great prophet and apostle of our confession, also our great high priest "after the order of Melchizedek," has, according to the epistle to the Hebrews, "passed through the heavens," has been "made higher than the heavens," and is enthroned at "the right hand of the Majesty in the heavens" (iv, 14; vii, 26; viii, 1). Such language has its necessary mystical and figurative element, but the essential thought is that our Lord Jesus Christ is our heavenly King as well as our heavenly Priest. According to Paul, who employs a similar style of speech, "he must reign till he hath put all his enemies under his feet" (Rom. viii, 34; 1 Cor. xv, 25). This heavenly enthronement of the Christ was a mighty inspiration to the first apostles and to the earliest converts of their preaching, and it finds conspicuous notice in the early part of the Acts of the apostles (i, 2, 9; ii, 33; iii, 21; v, 31; vii, 55). The Lord whom they had seen and heard had "gone up on high," and the holy heaven must receive him "until the times of the restoration of all things." According to the Revelation of John (xxi, 5) he that sitteth on the throne of God and of the Lamb is "making all things new." But along with this idea of his heavenly throne and dominion was also associated that of his coming again to judge the world, to raise the dead, to overthrow the powers of darkness, and to lead the sons of God into his everlasting glory.

2. Old Testament Doctrine of the Kingdom of God. The idea of the kingdom of God is presented in many ways in the Old Testament. That the Creator of the heavens and the earth must needs also be the everlasting Ruler of the same appears to be assumed without question. But what we have been accustomed to speak of as "second causes," and the operations of "natural law," found little or no place in Hebrew thought. The poets of Israel conceive God as immanent in all natural phenomena. Wind and storm, fire and earthquake, manifold lightnings, and rushing torrents of waters are but so many movements of the Almighty Ruler, who is never absent from his world (Psa. xviii, 7-15). "He covers himself with light as a garment; he stretches out the heavens as a curtain; he lays the beams of his chambers in the waters; he makes the clouds his chariot, and walks upon the wings of the wind" (Psa. civ, 2, 3). This mighty Ruler of the elements is no less the Ruler of men. "For the kingdom is Jehovah's, and he is the ruler over the nations" (Psa. xxii, 28). The prophets as well as the poets express the same great thought: "Jehovah shall be king over all the earth" (Zech. xiv, 9). "He sitteth upon the circle of the earth, and the inhabitants thereof are as grasshoppers; he stretcheth out the heavens as a curtain, and spreadeth them out to dwell in; he bringeth princes to nothing; he maketh the judges of the earth as vanity" (Isa. xl, 22, 23). Abraham cannot think that Jehovah, "the judge of all the earth," will fail to do what is right (Gen. xviii, 25), and Jeremiah speaks of him as judging righteously, and trying the reins and the heart (Jer. xi, 20). All these theistic concepts are profoundly truthful and sublime. Very frequently among the psalmists we also meet such lines as these:

> **Jehovah cometh to judge the earth;**
> **He shall judge the world with righteousness,**
> **And the peoples with equity.** Psa. xcviii, 9.

> **God reigneth over the nations;**
> **God sitteth upon his holy throne.** Psa. xlvii, 8.

In the book of Daniel these ideas of God's dominion are announced in a most positive manner and with noteworthy specifications. One of the most emphatic lessons taught by the prophet is that "the Most High ruleth in the kingdom of men, and giveth it to whomsoever he will. . . . He removeth kings and setteth up kings," and giveth the mightiest monarchs of the world to know "that the heavens do rule," and that God's kingdom "is an everlasting dominion" (ii, 21; iv, 17, 25, 26, 32, 34). Visions and prophecies of great kingdoms, like Babylon and Persia, rising and falling one after another, enhance these lessons of God's heavenly rule, and, in ii, 44, the prophet declares the specific purpose of the God of heaven to set up a kingdom that shall never be destroyed.

(1) *God Rules in Many and Divers Forms.* In studying the Old Testament ideals of the kingdom of God we are impressed with the fact that the dominion of the Most High is entirely compatible with divers forms of human administration. Ambitious leaders and princes may usurp authority, and think themselves able "to change times and seasons," but sooner or later they come to naught. The Most High is no less truly ruler among the nations though a

Babylonian Nebuchadnezzar, a Persian Cyrus, or a Grecian Alexander hold for a time the scepter of the world. These are all subordinate to the God of heaven, who puts each one of them aside in his own time.[1] And when their dominion finally gives place to that of "one like unto a son of man," and "the kingdom, and dominion, and the greatness of the kingdom under the whole heaven shall be given to the people of the saints of the Most High" (vii, 13, 14, 27), we are not to suppose that God will for a moment abdicate the throne of heaven, or cease to rule over the inhabitants of the earth. Neither the reign of the saints nor the reign of the Messiah is to exclude Jehovah, the righteous judge of the whole earth, from the government of the world. He abides the King eternal and invisible.

(2) *God as the Supreme Judge.* No truth of the Hebrew scriptures is more elaborately set forth than that God as supreme ruler of the world must needs also execute judgment. The manner in which this important doctrine is treated in the Scriptures deserves more attention than it has generally received from the confessional theologians. In narrative, in psalm, and in prophecy we find repeated allusions to the heavenly Ruler as the judge of men. As righteous judge of all the earth he visited destruction upon the cities of the plain (Gen. xviii, 25). As such he also enters into judgment with his people, and will purge away their blood-guiltiness with the burning blast of judgment (Isa. iii, 14; iv, 4). The psalms of Israel depict Jehovah sitting upon his throne and executing his judgments of righteousness (Psa. ix, 4, 7, 8; lxxv, 7; lxxxii, 8; xcviii, 9). The passage in Psa. l, 3-6, assumes an apocalyptic tone:

> Our God shall come, and let him not keep silence;
> A fire before him shall devour,
> And round about him it is very stormy.
> He calls to the heavens from above,
> And to the earth, that he may judge his people;
> Gather ye unto me my saints,
> Who make covenant with me over sacrifice.
> And the heavens declare his righteousness,
> For God is he that judges.

The spirit and form of poetry in which these sublime conceptions of judgment are wrought out do not detract from their value for doctrine but rather serve to enhance it. The psalmists and prophets of Israel discerned in plagues, and great calamities, and

---

[1] When Israel grew tired of judges and desired a king like all the nations, Samuel charged them with rejecting God as their king (1 Sam. viii, 7; x, 19). But such rejection of God, and the anointing of Saul as king, did not in the least remove Jehovah from being their real king and judge. And Samuel himself admonished all Israel to fear and obey Jehovah their God, lest his hand of power should be against them and consume both them and their king (1 Sam. xii, 14, 15, 25).

wars, and revolutions of kingdoms, the penal execution of judgment by him whose "throne is in the heavens and whose kingdom ruleth over all" (Psa. ciii, 19). According to Ezek. xxviii, 21-24, Jehovah executes his judgment against Sidon when he sends pestilence and blood in her streets; and he speaks in xiv, 21, of "the sword, and the famine, and the noisome beasts, and the pestilence" as his "four sore judgments upon Jerusalem," that is, his modes of executing judgment. In harmony with these conceptions of divine judgment we observe in other scriptures how the notable punishments of men and cities and peoples are put forward as so many examples of God's judgments in the earth. The deluge was a world-judgment on mankind because of excessive wickedness. Joseph's brethren felt in their trouble and confusion that they suffered a righteous judgment of God (Gen. xlii, 21, 28). The plagues of Egypt were so many judgments of Jehovah upon that idolatrous land and people (Exod. vi, 6; vii, 4; xii, 12; Num. xxxiii, 4). The disruption of the kingdoms of Israel and Judah and the bitter exile that followed were similar examples of the execution of divine judgment, and the whole series of prophetic oracles against the heathen nations, recorded in Isa. xiii—xxiii; Jer. xlvi—li; Ezek. xxv—xxxii, and Amos i—ii, inculcate the same doctrine that the Most High is both ruler and judge among the nations.

(3) *Apocalyptic Day of Jehovah.* The apocalyptic portions of the Old Testament portray Jehovah as the heavenly King who sits upon his throne of judgment, and assembles nations and kingdoms of men before him that he may execute upon them the decisions of his righteous will. Notable examples in illustration of this may be read in Zeph. iii, 8-20; Joel iii, 11-21; Ezek. xxxviii—xxxix; Isa. xxiv—xxvii, and xxxiv—xxxv. Such visitations of divine judgment are called "the day of Jehovah," "the great and notable day of Jehovah," and "the day of his anger." They are in each case a day of judgment, and this prophetic origin and usage of that phrase must not be ignored.[1] The poetic form and spirit in which these ideas of the day of judgment are set forth may be seen in the following passages:

> Alas for the day! for the day of Jehovah is near,
> And as a destruction from Shadday shall it come. Isa. xiii, 6.

> Blow ye a trumpet in Zion,
> And sound an alarm in my holy mountain;
> Let all the inhabitants of the land tremble;
> For the day of Jehovah cometh, for it is near;
> A day of darkness and of gloominess,
> A day of clouds and thick darkness. Joel ii, 1, 2.

---

[1] See Isa. ii, 12; xiii, 6, 13; Jer. xlvi, 10; Ezek. xiii, 5; xxx, 3; Joel i, 15; ii, 1; iii, 14; Amos v, 18, 20; Obad. 15; Zeph. i, 7, 18; Zech. xiv, 1; Mal. iv, 1, 5.

The reader should observe that this last-cited passage has reference to a great plague of locusts that had just spread desolation through the land, and the prophet makes use of the impressive imagery to depict the invasion of a still more hostile and destructive army from the north. That desolating invasion is conceived as a great and terrible day of Jehovah. Similar portrayals of the coming and the judgments of Jehovah are written in Isa. xiii, 9-19; xix, 1-4; xxxiv, 1-5; Mic. i, 1-5.[1] The unmistakable doctrine of all these scriptures is that the eternal God is Ruler and Judge of the world. The overthrow of mighty cities, like Nineveh and Babylon and Tyre, are so many signal examples of his "executing judgment in the earth," and the prophets call such a national catastrophe a "day of Jehovah."

(4) *Messianic Prophecies of the Kingdom.* The Messianic prophecies which speak of the coming of Christ as a king throw further light on the doctrine of the kingdom of God. One of the ancient promises to Israel was that they should be more than any other people the peculiar treasure of Jehovah, "a kingdom of priests and a holy nation " (Exod. xix, 5, 6). From the time of David onward the highest ideal of the Anointed One of Jehovah was that of a righteous and powerful king in Israel. Nathan gave David the prophetic assurance that his house and throne should be established forever (2 Sam. vii, 12-16), and this word of the prophet was of the nature of an eternal covenant of assured mercies (comp. 2 Sam. xxiii, 5; Isa. lv, 3). This idea finds expression in Psa. lxxxix, 4, 29, 36, 37. The name of David became the synonym of an ideal king and shepherd of the people (Hos. iii, 5; Jer. xxx, 9; Ezek. xxxiv, 23; xxxvii, 24). In Jer. xxiii, 5, 6, we read this specific oracle: "Behold, the days are coming, saith Jehovah, that I will raise up unto David a righteous Branch, and he shall reign as king and deal wisely, and execute judgment and righteousness in the earth. In his days shall Judah be saved and Israel dwell securely; and this is his name which he shall be called, Jehovah our righteousness" (comp. xxxiii, 15, 16). In Isa. ix, 6, 7, the Child of the wonderful name is to sit "upon the throne of David, and upon his kingdom, to order it and to establish it in judgment and in righteousness forever." The same Anointed One is represented in Isa. xi, 1-10, as a shoot out of the stump of Jesse, endued with spiritual gifts, girt about with righteousness, smiting the earth with the rod of his mouth, and filling it full of the knowledge of Jehovah as the waters cover the sea. Micah also foretells a ruler in Israel who is to come from Bethlehem of

---

[1] On these and other apocalyptic descriptions of "the day of Jehovah," see also Biblical Apocalyptics, pp. 90-180.

Judah, and be great unto the ends of the earth (v, 2-4). In the second psalm we read a dramatic representation of Jehovah establishing his Son as king upon his holy Mount Zion, and promising him the uttermost parts of the earth for a possession. The same Messianic ruler may also be recognized in the righteous king whose glorious reign is celebrated in Psa. lxxii, and whose name and glory are identified with those of Jehovah. The conquering hero of Psa. cx, to whom Jehovah says, "Sit thou at my right hand until I make thy enemies thy footstool," unites in himself the threefold office of king and priest and judge. In Dan. vii, 9-14, the Most High is represented as an ancient judge and ruler, seated upon his glorious throne in the heavens and surrounded with myriads of ministering angels. One like a son of man approaches him and receives at his hand the everlasting dominion of the world, and in verse 27 it is written that "the kingdom and the dominion, and the greatness of the kingdoms under the whole heaven, shall be given to the people of the saints of the Most High." Thus this "Son of man" and the saints of God live and reign together.

(5) *The Messiah an Associate with the Most High.* In all these and in other Messianic scriptures we observe that the Anointed of Jehovah is in some way an associate of the Most High. He bears the responsibility of executing judgment in the earth. But it is important to note that, in the loftiest elevation and glory of his reign, he possesses no wisdom or power apart from Jehovah. As we proceed, therefore, to a study of the New Testament doctrine of the kingdom of Christ and of God, let us keep in mind the following: (1) No prophecy of the reign of the Messianic King contemplates or suggests an abdication of the God of heaven from his throne or from his government of the world. However great and glorious the kingdom of the Messiah, it will be as true after his coming as before that "the kingdom belongs to Jehovah, and he is Ruler over the nations." (2) The transition from one period and dispensation to another involves no physical changes in the earth or heavens, or in the constitution of man upon the earth. But the advent of the Messiah was conceived as introducing a new era in the history of the people of God, and was destined to introduce new excellencies of religious life and worship. God, the eternal Ruler, however, abides forever the same, immanent in all the movements of the world. (3) The kingdom of the Messiah is not a dominion different from that of Jehovah, but it contemplates the introduction of new agencies and new enlightenment for the higher development of mankind. The outcome of the new dispensation is conceived as the creation of new heavens and a new earth (Isa. li, 16; lxv, 17; lxvi, 22). But Jehovah and his

Anointed will be united together in the dominion and they shall reign upon one throne.

3. Views of the Kingdom Current among the Jews. In passing on to a study of the kingdom of God as it is set forth in the New Testament we inquire, first of all, after the ideas of the Messiah and of his rule that were current among the Jewish people at the time when Jesus was born. We find in our gospels a very frequent use of the phrase *kingdom of God,* and *kingdom of heaven.* John the Baptist began his ministry by declaring, "The kingdom of heaven is at hand," and Jesus himself soon after followed with the same proclamation. No explanation of the phrase is given in connection with the records of its earliest publication by John or by Jesus. We naturally suppose that the words would be popularly understood as an announcement of the reign of the Messiah as foretold by the Hebrew prophets and expected by the Jewish people. But the Messianic ideal was not the same with all the people. Some enthusiasts were looking for a warlike chieftain, endowed with the gift of national leadership and able to throw off the Roman yoke and restore the political power of the Jewish nation to some such splendor as it held in the days of David and Solomon. Others seem to have entertained a more spiritual view, and like Simeon, and Anna, and Zacharias, connected with the hope of the redemption of Jerusalem thoughts of the confirmation of ancient covenants and promises, the remission of sins, unspeakable peace and consolation, and a life of holiness (comp. Luke i, 67-79; ii, 25-38). Between these two extremes there was a more prevalent belief that Israel was the elect people of Jehovah, destined to become a theocratic kingdom and to realize the glorious hopes portrayed in the writings of the prophets. From Matt. xi, 1-10, and its parallel in Luke vii, 19-28, we infer that John the Baptist shared largely in these current expectations of his time, and that he was disappointed in the failure of Jesus to fulfill what he regarded as the Messianic hope of Israel. Nevertheless, the various records of his own preaching accord with a high spiritual conception. He called upon the people to repent, and his baptism is called the "baptism of repentance for the remission of sins." He admonished his Jewish countrymen not to imagine that mere descent from Abraham would avail them before God, for every tree, whether sprung from Jewish or heathen soil, which does not bring forth good fruit must be cut down and cast into the fire. He advised the sharing of one's goods with those who are in need, and he spoke against extortion, violence, and insubordination. In all his references to the Messiah who was about to come he made it clear that he himself was only a forerunner, a voice in the wilderness to prepare his way. The coming One was to baptize with the Holy Spirit, purge the true from the false, gather the wheat into his garner and burn the chaff with unquenchable fire (Mark i, 2-8; Matt. iii, 7-12; Luke iii, 3-17).

4. The Doctrine of Jesus. For a true understanding of the nature of the kingdom of God and of Christ, we may seek our first and fullest information in the teachings of our Lord himself. In teaching the disciples how to pray Jesus gave the following as one of the leading petitions:

> Thy kingdom come,
> Thy will be done—
> As in heaven, so on earth.

The last clause may be understood as qualifying the coming of the kingdom as well as the doing of the will of "our Father in the heavens." It serves also the purpose of defining the preceding clause, and indicates, accordingly, that the coming of the kingdom is to result in the accomplishment of God's will upon earth as it is done in heaven. This doing the will of our heavenly Father must therefore be a fact of fundamental importance in guiding us to the true idea of the kingdom of heaven. It assumes in its very terms a moral and spiritual relationship and suggests the idea of a moral order. As the word *kingdom* implies an organized community of individuals having a common nature and life, the *will* of God also implies in those who do it a conformity to God in spiritual nature and action. The performance of all that the will of God requires in moral beings may vary in degrees of observance in heaven and in earth: we naturally predicate of heavenly things a measure of perfection above that of earthly things. But the members of the kingdom of God, whether in heaven or on earth, have this in common, that they all, according to knowledge and ability, do the will of the heavenly Father.

(1) *A Kingdom of Heaven.* The expression *kingdom of heaven* (ἡ βασιλεία τῶν οὐρανῶν, *the kingdom of the heavens*) is peculiar to the gospel of Matthew, being found elsewhere in the New Testament only in 2 Tim. iv, 18, where the phrase, *his heavenly kingdom*, is not identical but virtually equivalent. There is no good reason to doubt that our Lord made repeated use of the several expressions *kingdom of heaven, heavenly kingdom,* and *kingdom of God,* and we need not seek to find a significance in one of these phrases that is not really in the others. We simply note the fact that *the kingdom of the heavens* is peculiar to Matthew, the expression occurring therein about thirty times. The words suggest that the kingdom is of heavenly origin and nature. As the Christ

cometh from heaven to earth to reveal the will of God to men, so his kingdom is "of the heavens," and those who enter into it do the will of their Father who is "in the heavens." In Matt. vi, 14, 26, 32, occurs the phrase *your heavenly Father;* in xv, 13, and xviii, 35, *my heavenly Father;* in xxvi, 29, *my Father's kingdom.* The kingdom of God is heavenly just as God the Father is heavenly. In comparing the parallel texts of Matt. xxvi, 29, Mark xiv, 25, and Luke xxii, 30, we note what appears to be an interchangeable use of the expressions *my Father's kingdom, the kingdom of God,* and *my kingdom.* The term *kingdom of God* occurs four times in Matthew (xii, 28; xix, 24; xxi, 31, 43), and often in the other gospels, in the Acts, and in the Pauline epistles. We learn from these various terms that the kingdom of God and of Christ is a heavenly kingdom, in accord with the heavenly nature of God, and therefore "not of this world" (John xviii, 36).

(2) *Lessons of the Parables.* It is the main purpose of the parables of Jesus to make known to all truth-loving disciples "the mysteries of the kingdom of heaven" (Matt. xiii, 11). These mysteries are things unseen and eternal (comp. 2 Cor. iv, 18), but not unknowable. They pertain to spiritual life and experience, and must therefore be spiritually discerned, if known at all. This will at once appear when we inquire what the parables have to tell us about the kingdom of God. The parable of the sower and the seed, as Jesus himself explained it, shows us how "the word of the kingdom" (Matt. xiii, 19) is received by different classes of hearers, and what various results must follow according to the kind of soil upon which it falls. The word of the kingdom is the same as "preaching the gospel of the kingdom" (comp. iv, 23; xxiv, 14; Luke iv, 43), for "the seed is the word of God" (Luke viii, 11), the convincing truths of religion, which are scattered by the numberless ministries of Christ the great sower in the hearts of men. The hearts of men are like so many different kinds of soil conditioned by previous habits of life, and they are fruitful or unfruitful according to their various self-induced conditions. The kingdom of heaven, as illustrated in this first parable of Jesus, is thus seen to belong to things invisible, having to do with the spiritual possibilities of men. The parable of the good seed and the tares presents another aspect of the kingdom. Not only does the good seed of the gospel fall on different kinds of human soil, but after it is sown in good ground the enemy of all righteousness goes about sowing evil seed among the wheat, and producing growths which appear and remain to annoy and injure until the harvest time. The sons of the kingdom and the sons of the evil one are thus permitted to grow together until the consummation of their time,

but in the end all things that cause stumbling shall be gathered out of the kingdom, and the righteous shall shine forth as the sun (iii, 37-43). The other parables of this same chapter set forth other aspects of the kingdom. Its outward growth in the world is like a grain of mustard seed, among the smallest of seeds when planted, but greater than herbs and like a tree when it is grown. Its inward working in humanity is like that of leaven hidden in the meal which in due time leavens the whole mass. Sometimes the kingdom of heaven is found, as it were, by accident, like a treasure hid in the field; sometimes only after long and diligent searching, like a merchant who seeks far and near for goodly pearls; but in either case the obtaining of the treasure or the pearl is through the selling of all one has, for the heavenly kingdom is worth more than all other possessions. This kingdom is also like a net gathering out of the sea fish of every kind, but when filled and drawn to the beach there comes a separation: the good ones are preserved and the bad are cast away. In Mark iv, 26-29, it is said that "the kingdom of God is as if a man should cast seed upon the earth, and should sleep and rise night and day, and the seed should spring up and grow, he knoweth not how, . . . first the blade, then the ear, then the full grain in the ear." This parable, like those of the mustard seed and the leaven, conveys the idea of development after the law of an unseen and mysterious order of the world. But whether we understand it of the growth of the living word of truth in the individual heart, or of the more visible development of Christ's kingdom in human history, the parable clearly shows that this kingdom is a heavenly power in the world. It is no sudden phenomenon, no hasty growth. It matures and strengthens after the manner of a natural process, and thus follows the order of the God of heaven. The parable of the laborers in the vineyard (Matt. xx, 1-16) indicates how many may be distinguished as first or as last in the kingdom of heaven by the spirit they display. Of the three classes of laborers those last sent into the vineyard, although they served but one hour, receive equal reward with those who toiled from morning until even. The reason seems to be that the last, who were found standing in the marketplace at the eleventh hour only because no man had hired them, went into the vineyard without even the mention of wages or reward.[1] They did not, like Peter, ask, "What then shall we have?" (xix, 27) nor did they agree for a stipulated wage,

---

[1] The erroneous and misleading repetition of the words "whatsoever is right I will give you," found in the received text of verse 7, where they have no place in the true text, has been an effective obstacle to the correct interpretation of this parable. The spirit of the true laborer is the vital lesson; not the hours, nor the penny a day.

like those first hired; nor did they even hear the householder promise them, as he did those called at the third hour, "whatsoever is right I will give you." They represented rather that higher ideal of service for God which asks *What shall I do?* rather than *What shall I receive?* And so we are taught further on in the chapter that he who would be first among the followers of Jesus must be willing to act as a bondservant of them all. The parable of the servant, in Luke xvii, 7-10, furthermore admonishes us that after our best endeavors we may reckon ourselves unprofitable servants; and in the parable of the unmerciful servant (Matt. xviii, 21-35) we have our Lord's own comment on the petition, "Forgive us our debts, as we forgive our debtors." In the parable of the two debtors (Luke vii, 41-47) we are reminded of the wealth of love which is displayed where there is a lively sense of the forgiveness of many sins. We read in the picture of the Pharisee and the publican a condemnation of self-righteousness (Luke xviii, 9-14), but the duty of importunate prayer is encouraged by the parables of the friend at midnight (Luke xi, 5-13) and the unjust judge (Luke xviii, 1-8). We are shown in the parable of the rich man the fatal fallacy of laying up treasure for oneself and not being rich toward God (Luke xii, 15-21). Other lessons of like suggestiveness appear in the unrighteous steward who acted shrewdly in making friends by means of "the mammon of unrighteousness" (Luke xvi, 1-13), and in the story of the rich man and Lazarus, whose changed conditions after death exhibited the fearful mistake of failing to know one's responsibility to his fellow man (Luke xvi, 19-31). All these parables, it should be noticed, inculcate some very practical lesson and at the same time set forth important truths of the kingdom of Christ and show the spiritual nature of the kingdom. Another set of parables indicates some kind of a transfer of the kingdom of God from the Jews to the Gentiles. While furnishing a remarkable answer to the question, "Who is my neighbor?" the parable of the good Samaritan (Luke x, 29-37) suggests that even a heathen may illustrate the spirit which governs in the kingdom of Christ better than a narrow priest or Levite among the Jewish people. The parable of the two sons warned the Jewish priests and elders that the publicans and the harlots might go into the kingdom of God before them (Matt. xxi, 28-32). The parable of the wicked husbandmen (Matt. xxi, 33-34) employs the imagery of Isa. v, 1-7, and condemns the leaders of the Jews who had stoned the messengers of God and plotted against the life of Jesus; and the chief priests and Pharisees were told in terms of ominous import: "The kingdom of God shall be taken from you, and shall be given to a nation bringing forth the fruits thereof." This same lesson of the casting off of the Jewish people and the calling of the Gentiles into the kingdom is seen in the parable of the marriage of the king's son (Matt. xxii, 1-14), and also in that of the great supper (Luke xiv, 16-24). All these parables go to show that the kingdom of God of which they speak is the dispensation of divine grace which was inaugurated by Jesus Christ. The rejection of this spiritual kingdom was of the nature of a secession from the true inheritance of Abraham, Isaac, and Jacob. The rejection of the Christ was a rejection of the covenants and the promises, and "the sons of the kingdom" by natural descent must needs be given over to "weeping and gnashing of teeth," when they saw multitudes banqueting with the great patriarchs in the kingdom of heaven, and they themselves cast out (Matt. viii, 11, 12); Luke xiii, 28, 29). The parable of the pounds, in Luke xix, 11-27, was called forth by the supposition of some "that the kingdom of God was immediately to appear," and is not essentially different from that of the talents in Matt. xxv, 14-30. The lesson of each is the importance of making the greatest possible use of one's opportunities. In the twenty-fifth chapter of Matthew we have three vivid pictures which are the more suggestive by reason of their relation to each other. In the time of the end the kingdom will be like wise and foolish virgins who wait the coming of the bridegroom, but the foolish ones by careless and culpable lack of preparation fail to obtain admission to the marriage feast. Hence the admonition, "Watch, for ye know not the day nor the hour." The next parable shows that there is something more to do in this matter than to watch; great and useful service for the Lord should be done in his absence. Then the sublime picture of final judgment reveals the truth that our eternal destiny must be determined by the facts of our relationship to Christ and his brethren.

(3) *A Spiritual Kingdom.* So far, now, as the parables of Jesus explain the nature of the kingdom of God, they show upon their very face that the kingdom is essentially spiritual and to be spiritually discerned. It needs but a brief examination of the main lesson in each to perceive that the kingdom of heaven, which they all in some measure illustrate, is the dominion of Christ over the hearts of men. It is not an external visible establishment of this world, but it has its roots in the unseen and eternal, and enlarges its power according as the will of God is done on earth as in the heavens. All our experiences of regeneration and eternal life are vitally connected with the life of the kingdom of God.

(4) *The Greatest in the Kingdom.* But other teachings of Jesus, aside from his parables, are equally explicit touching the

spiritual nature of the kingdom of Christ. When the disciples asked, "Who is greatest in the kingdom of heaven?" he set a little child in the midst of them and said: "Except ye become as little children, ye shall in no wise enter into the kingdom of heaven. Whosoever therefore shall humble himself as this little child, the same is the greatest in the kingdom of heaven" (Matt. xviii, 1-4). On another occasion he said: "Suffer the little children to come unto me, and forbid them not: for of such[1] is the kingdom of God. . . . Whosoever shall not receive the kingdom of God as a little child, he shall in no wise enter therein" (Mark x, 13-15). In all these statements we learn what manner of spirit and disposition they must have who belong to the kingdom of God. True subjects of Christ's rule must put away ambition and jealous rivalry, and possess the simplicity and trust of a little child. Moreover, he who is to be called great in the kingdom of heaven is one who carefully performs and teaches the commandments of God, even the least of them (Matt. v, 19); for the surest evidence of love is a conscientious keeping of the commandments (John xiv, 15, 21; xv, 10). The happy subject of the heavenly kingdom is not the man who is self-righteous and self-satisfied, but the one who feels a real spiritual want within his soul, and hungers and thirsts after the living God. Such are pronounced blessed, and are called "poor in spirit," because of their own keen sense of insufficiency and need of help from above. "Theirs is the kingdom of heaven" (Matt. v, 3). For "the high and lofty One who inhabits eternity" chooses for his abode "the broken and humble spirit" (Isa. lvii, 15; Psa. xxxiv, 18; li, 17), and Jesus accordingly declared: "Except your righteousness exceed that of the scribes and Pharisees, ye shall in no wise enter into the kingdom of heaven" (Matt. v, 20). This kingdom belongs rather to those "that have been persecuted for righteousness' sake" (v, 10). The lovers of the truth and martyrs for its sake inherit the kingdom. "Not every one that saith unto me, Lord, Lord, shall enter into the kingdom of heaven; but he that doeth the will of my Father who is in heaven" (vii, 21). It is exceedingly difficult, nay, impossible, for one who is bound up with great riches of this world to enter this kingdom (Mark x, 23). Such an one, in order to be perfect and to deposit his treasure in heaven, must deny himself, give what he has to benefit the poor, and thereby show the depth of his love for God and man. And the faithful disciple of Christ, who is ready to leave everything else to follow his Lord with a loving

---

[1] Meyer says: "By *of such* we are not to understand literal *children,* for the Messianic kingdom cannot be said to belong to children as such, but to men of a childlike disposition and character."—Exegetical Handbook, in loco.

heart, "publishes abroad the kingdom of God" (Luke ix, 60). He becomes a living gospel and epistle of the kingdom, and by his service of love will come to know its heavenly mysteries more and more.

(5) *The Fundamental Law of Love.* It further appears that the fundamental law of the kingdom of God is that of love. The first and greatest commandment is, "Thou shalt love the Lord thy God with all thy heart"; and the second is, "Thou shalt love thy neighbor as thyself." These declarations of Jesus were no new revelation, but a selection from the ancient laws (comp. Deut. vi, 5; Lev. xix, 18) of those "two commandments," which embodied the spirit and substance of both tables of the decalogue, and on which the entire law and the prophets rested. And when the scribe acknowledged the wisdom of the great teacher's words, and said that such love "is much more than all whole burnt-offerings and sacrifices," Jesus responded: "Thou art not far from the kingdom of God" (Mark xii, 28-34).

(6) *Jesus's Teaching Different from John's Ideal.* We may learn further, from Matt. xi, 2-11, and Luke vii, 18-28, that the real nature of the kingdom of God and of the Messiah's work were quite different from the ideal which John the Baptist had conceived. While in prison John seems to have yielded to some doubts, and he sent to Jesus inquiring, "Art thou he that cometh, or are we to look for another?" Jesus referred him to his many miracles of mercy, and said, as a suggestive admonition: "Blessed is he whosoever shall not find occasion of stumbling in me." John the Baptist and all who shared his views were in danger of stumbling by reason of the manner in which Jesus went about his work. They were so far governed by current ideas of the Messiah who was to come that they failed to understand the spiritual significance of the ministry of Jesus. Although John had publicly proclaimed that the one who came after him would be mightier than himself, and would "baptize in the Holy Spirit and in fire," he did not perceive in what he heard about Jesus that which sufficiently fulfilled his expectations. It is noticeable that Jesus did not directly condemn the Messianic notions of his contemporaries; he aimed rather to correct them. By comparison, by contrast, by suggestion, he sought to turn men's thoughts to the spiritual nature of the kingdom of God. He extolled the real greatness of John the Baptist, declaring that "among them that are born of women there hath not arisen a greater," but he immediately added: "He that is an inferior ($\mu\iota\kappa\rho\acute{o}\tau\epsilon\rho\sigma$) in the kingdom of heaven is greater than he." Any little child in the kingdom, any of those common people who in the coming dispensation of the Spirit were to "taste

of the heavenly gift, and be made partakers of the Holy Spirit, and taste the good word of God, and the powers of the age to come" (Heb. vi, 4, 5), would be greater than the greatest of the pre-Messianic prophets. For these children of the coming kingdom would be more fully acquainted with the mysteries of its spiritual life. John's error, like that of many others, was in looking for outward, visible, worldly exhibitions of power rather than for vicarious sacrifices of love. This error begat the clamor and zeal which would fain have taken Jesus by force and made him king (John vi, 15). Hence the significance of Jesus's words in Matt. xi, 12: "From the days of John the Baptist until now the kingdom of heaven suffers violence, and violent ones are seizing on it." That is, from the time when John first announced that the kingdom of heaven was at hand many had been overzealous to behold some open and mighty display of Messianic power. Like the Israel of Samuel's day they wanted "a king like all the nations." The questions of John in prison betrayed an element of this mistaken zeal and impatience. The error naturally led to the presumption of seizing on the kingdom by some movement of violence, and it arose out of failure to understand the true nature of the kingdom of God.

(7) *Jesus's Teaching in John's Gospel.* In passing from the synoptic gospels to other New Testament writings, we find no different doctrine of the nature of the kingdom of heaven, but many additional lessons touching its spiritual character. In John's gospel we read the profound truth: "Except a man be born from above he cannot see the kingdom of God" (iii, 3, 5). The kingdom, then, is not a spectacle for worldly vision, but a matter of the inner life of man (comp. Luke xvii, 20, 21), and its powers and glories must accordingly belong to the things unseen and eternal. Accordingly, in viii, 23; xviii, 36, 37, Jesus says: "I am from above; I am not of this world. My kingdom is not of this world: if my kingdom were of this world, then would my servants fight, that I should not be delivered to the Jews." He further says, in answer to a question of Pilate: "I am a king: to this end have I been born, and to this end am I come into the world, that I should bear witness to the truth. Every one that is of the truth heareth my voice." These words explain themselves to a man of spiritual understanding. Christ's kingdom comes not forth out of (ἐκ) a world of matter or of physical sense, but is of heavenly origin. It makes no display of military forces for the purpose of establishing its empire in the world. It is especially remarkable in being a kingdom of truth. This may be a Johannine conception, for in the gospel and the first epistle of John

Jesus Christ is set forth as the embodiment and revelation of the truth of God (i, 17; viii, 32; xiv, 6; xvii, 17; 1 John iii, 18, 19; v, 20). Jesus Christ is the heavenly king who witnesses the truth, and whose subjects know, love, and obey the truth. They also love one another with an affection strong as life itself, and their devotion both to one another and to God is "not in word nor with the tongue, but in deed and in truth."[1]

5. Doctrine of Pauline Epistles. In the Pauline epistles we learn that the kingdom of God is the blessed spiritual inheritance of all who enjoy life in God through faith in Jesus Christ. It is a glorious possession into which one enters by faith. Its spiritual character is obvious from Rom. xiv, 17, where, in discussing certain questions of conscience about meats and drinks, he says: "The kingdom of God is not eating and drinking, but righteousness and peace and joy in the Holy Spirit." That is, it is not to be conceived as a dominion which concerns itself about subtle ceremonial questions of eating and drinking, but one which requires that its subjects shall know the blessedness of righteousness and peace and joy which is realized in living fellowship with the Holy Spirit of God. It is a kingdom that may be entered at any time by one who truly accepts the redemption of Christ. Paul also observes that "the kingdom of God is not in word but in power" (1 Cor. iv, 20); that is, not in the empty self-assertion of such as have little or nothing else than boastful words, but in the power of the Holy Spirit which had shown itself in the apostle's preaching among the Corinthians (ii, 4). The community of kindred spirits among whom the Holy Spirit works in such sanctifying power must needs be a kingdom of holy and heavenly character. It is impossible, therefore, for the unrighteous, and idolaters, and adulterers, and thieves, and revilers, and extortioners, and such like to inherit the kingdom of God (1 Cor. vi, 9, 10; Gal. v, 21; Eph. v, 5). It is common also for Paul to speak of this kingdom as an inheritance, and to contemplate it not only as a present possession but also as a future and eternal blessedness. The redeemed "shall reign in life through Jesus Christ" (Rom. v, 17), the eternal life of glory and honor and incorruption (comp. ii, 7). Being joint heirs with Christ they both suffer with him and are glorified with him. But while a real "inheritance in the kingdom of the Christ and of

---

[1] Harnack makes the following comprehensive statement: "The kingdom has a threefold significance. Firstly, it is something supernatural, a gift from above, not a product of natural, ordinary life; secondly, it is a purely religious good, the inner link with the living God; thirdly, it is the most important experience that a man can have, since it permeates and dominates his whole existence, because sin is forgiven and misery is banished."—Das Wesen des Christentums, p. 40. Eng. trans., p. 67.

God" (Eph. v, 5) includes every blessed hope and promise of eternal life, it cannot exclude the present possession realized in the spiritual fellowship of Christ and of God. For according to Col. i, 11-14, our heavenly Father makes us meet to be partakers of the inheritance; he has already by the operations of his redemptive grace "delivered us out of the power of darkness, and translated us into the kingdom of the Son of his love." Here Christian believers are spoken of as already "translated into the kingdom." They know the power of God in Christ that has delivered them from sin and spiritual darkness and introduced them into the heavenly light of spiritual life. Having believed, they are "sealed with the Holy Spirit of promise, which is an earnest of our inheritance unto the redemption of God's own possession" (Eph. i, 14). So the ultimate consummation of all future blessedness in Christ is but the glorious sequence of an inheritance already known as to its heavenly nature and in part bestowed.

6. Other New Testament Teaching. Other portions of the New Testament add somewhat to this doctrine of the kingdom of Christ by way of suggestion and illustration, but offer no different ideal. Mention is made in Heb. xii, 28, of "receiving a kingdom that cannot be shaken," and the argument of the context speaks of the removing of some things that were capable of being shaken in order "that those things which are not shaken may remain." In the two preceding verses the word of Hag. ii, 6, 7, is cited as finding fulfilment in the shaking and removal of that which is to give place to "a kingdom that cannot be shaken." The things that were then shaken were the old fabric of effete Judaism, with its burdensome ritual of feasts and fasts and sacrifices and burnt offerings. These had "become old and aged and nigh unto vanishing away" (viii, 13), but the main argument of this epistle is to show that they were at most only "a copy and shadow of the heavenly things" which are manifested through the mediation of Jesus Christ. They must needs be shaken and pass away in order that the immovable kingdom of heaven might be revealed and remain as an "eternal inheritance." Hence the great force and beauty of the language in Heb. xii, 18-24: "Ye are not come unto a mount that might be touched, . . . but ye are come unto mount Zion, and unto the city of the living God, the heavenly Jerusalem, and to innumerable hosts of angels, to the general assembly and church of the firstborn who are enrolled in heaven, and to God the judge of all, and to the spirits of just men made perfect, and to Jesus the mediator of a new covenant, and to the blood of sprinkling that speaketh better than Abel." In this most glorious fellowship we discern the "kingdom that cannot be shaken." Unto this heavenly inheritance the persons addressed had already come (προσεληλύθατε, *ye have come,* ver. 22). This important fact and teaching must not be overlooked. Like "the inheritance of the saints in light" and "the kingdom of the Son of his love" into which Paul conceived himself and his Colossian brethren to have been already transferred (Col. i, 13), so the immovable kingdom which supplants effete Judaism is "the heavenly Jerusalem," which affords personal communion and fellowship with God and Christ and all the holy ones. It is an inheritance which remains secure through ages of ages, and is held in common with "spirits of just men made perfect," but it is of such a spiritual nature as to be entered now by faith (comp. Heb. iv, 3). These two ideas of present and future inheritance do not exclude each other.

7. Contemplates Present and Future Blessedness. There are some texts in which the future glory and blessedness of the kingdom seem to be chiefly in the mind of the writer, and in which qualifying words are employed to indicate the thought which is uppermost. In 2 Tim. iv, 1, 18, and in 2 Pet. i, 11, both context and qualifying terms point our thoughts to a future deliverance and to the eternal heavenly kingdom. But when James (ii, 5) speaks of God's choosing "them that are poor as to the world to be rich in faith, and heirs of the kingdom which he promised to them that love him," one is reminded both of present riches of faith and of glories yet to come. In 1 Thess. ii, 12, the calling of men "into his own kingdom and glory," is to be understood as a process continually going on, and the being "counted worthy of the kingdom of God" (2 Thess. i, 5) is an expression which may contemplate both present and future possession of the kingdom. But the most specific allusions of this kind to a future inheritance in light do not in the least set aside the fact that the kingdom of heaven is of a spiritual nature and may be entered and possessed now through faith in Christ. Even "the holy city, new Jerusalem, comes down out of heaven from God," and is described as "the tabernacle of God with men" (Rev. xxi, 2, 3). And this dwelling of God with men is not essentially different from his coming with Christ and making his abode with the man who loves him and keeps his word (comp. John xiv, 23). All this and more may be understood and should be longed for when we pray, "Thy kingdom come, thy will be done, as in heaven, so on earth."

8. Concluding Summary. From the foregoing examination of scriptures bearing on the subject of the nature of the kingdom, we conclude, (1) that the kingdom of heaven so frequently mentioned in the teaching of Jesus, and illustrated by his parables, is not to be understood of a visible political organization. (2) The kingdom of Christ, or the Messianic kingdom, is no other than the kingdom of God and the kingdom of heaven. The exaltation of Christ to the right hand of the throne of God involves no essential change in the divine government of the world, but marks a new era in human history. (3) The method of Jesus in his self-manifestation did not accord with the current Messianic expectations of the Jewish people; but he did not formally controvert their expectations: he sought rather to give their thoughts a more heavenly and spiritual turn, and to inculcate the great fundamental truths which in time would be their own interpreter. (4) His teaching, however, logically involved the disruption of the religious system of effete Judaism, and the establishment of a new and higher religious cultus which embodied the truths of his gospel of salvation. (5) Membership in this heavenly kingdom is to be obtained through spiritual regeneration and a holy life, and it is open to all men of every nation who will accept its conditions of grace, and conform to its principles of righteousness and love. (6) In proportion as many individuals are brought into this kingdom and exhibit its heavenly virtues, the kingdom itself becomes more and more a manifested power of God in the world. Like the stone cut out of the mountain without hands (Dan. ii, 45), and like the mustard seed, it grows from small beginnings and is destined to bring the whole world into subjection to its truth. (7) The children of this kingdom are heirs of God and joint heirs with Christ, and accordingly participate in the kingdom, power, and glory which are perfected through the ages. They partake alike of Christ's afflictions and triumphs; they suffer with him and reign with him (Rom. viii, 17; 2 Tim. ii, 12). (8) This comprehensive view of the nature of the kingdom enables us to understand the noteworthy eschatological concept of Christ's dominion which we so constantly meet in the New Testament. From the point of view both of Christ and of his first apostles, the kingdom and the power and the glory of this new manifestation of the Father were essentially in the future. Throughout the entire period of Jesus' stay on earth the kingdom was not yet come, but only nigh at hand. And whenever and whatever the crucial hour of transition from the old covenant into the new, the coming of the kingdom and its development, as figured by the stone cut from the mountain without hands which became a great mountain and filled the whole earth, and by the parables of the mustard seed and the leaven, must needs fill the entire history of the Christian ages.

CHAPTER II

THE COMING OF THE KINGDOM OF CHRIST

1. Variety of Biblical Statements, Words, and Phrases. The essentially spiritual nature of the kingdom of Christ and of God appears more fully as we study the biblical statements of the time and manner of its coming. When we pray, "Thy kingdom come," we do not contemplate a sudden collapse of the physical heavens, nor an immediate revolution of human affairs. The coming of Christ and the progress of his kingdom in power and glory are sublime divine realities which appear in manifold ways and have gradual and continuous manifestation. There are many statements in the teachings of Jesus which declare the kingdom to have been near at hand while he himself was yet manifest in the flesh; but there are others which contemplate the coming of the Lord and his kingdom as an event of the future. The manner of his coming is also variously represented. Some scriptures speak of Christ coming in the clouds of heaven with great power and glory, while in another place we read that "the kingdom of God cometh not with observation." One naturally inquires whether these texts involve real contradictions and inconsistencies. There is also a number of words and phrases that must receive careful examination in connection with this subject, as for example, παρουσία *coming*, or *presence;* ἔρχομαι, to *come;* ἐπιφάνεια, *appearing;* παλινγενεσία, *regeneration;* ἀποκατάστασις, *restitution;* συντέλεια τοῦ αἰῶνος, *end,* or *consummation of the age.* These and some other like expressions will be duly noticed in connection with the discussion of the texts of scripture wherein they occur.

2. Coming in the Near Future. Those scriptures which speak of the coming as in the near future demand our first attention. Both John the Baptist and Jesus began their public ministry with the announcement that the kingdom of heaven was at hand (Matt. iii, 2; Mark i, 15). The disciples of Jesus were subsequently sent out to repeat the same important message (Matt. x, 7; Luke x, 9, 11), and were told, according to Matt. x, 23, that the Son of man should come before they completed their apostolic ministry in the cities of Israel. These several statements imply that the kingdom was not at the time fully come, but only near at hand; and yet the coming of Christ would take place before they should have gone through all the cities of Israel in fulfillment of their mission. In Luke xviii, 8, he observes: "When the Son of man cometh, shall he find faith on the earth?" This question follows the parable of the importunate widow and the unjust judge, as if to teach: If an unrighteous judge may be thus prevailed upon by persistent importunity, how much rather shall the righteous God hear and answer the prayers of those whom he loves? Howbeit, he adds, as if uttering an unpleasant reflection, when the Son of man comes he will not find on earth such persistent faith as he could wish.[1] Other declarations even more direct and unmistakable connect the coming of the Son of man in glory and for judgment with the coming of his kingdom, and affirm that some of those then living were not to taste of death until they had seen the coming and kingdom of Christ (Matt. xvi, 27, 28; Mark ix, 1; Luke ix, 27). Furthermore, when the Pharisees on one occasion asked him "when the kingdom of God cometh," he answered them that it "cometh not with observation." That is, the coming of the kingdom is not a public spectacle for men to look at and exclaim, Lo, there it is! For, he added, "the kingdom of God is among you."[2] All these scriptures show that the coming of the kingdom was not thought of as a far future event, and the statements of our Lord before the high priest imply that it is something that is to take place as a process, from that time and onward: "Henceforth ye shall see the Son of man sitting at the right hand of power, and coming on the clouds of heaven" (Matt. xxvi, 64; comp. Mark xiv, 62; Luke xxii, 69). To all these scriptures we add that most positive declaration of Matt. xxiv, 34 (and its parallels in Mark and Luke): "Verily I say unto you, This generation shall not pass away till all these things be accomplished." Whatever else, therefore, we learn concerning the time and manner of the coming of the kingdom of Christ, we cannot escape the conviction that it was proclaimed as an event of the near future by Jesus himself. Nothing in all his reported sayings is more emphatic and positive than that some of his contemporaries would live to see the coming of the Son of man in his kingdom and in the glory of his Father.

---

[1] It is to be observed that nothing in these passages requires us to suppose that apostolic ministries must cease, and all persecution and lack of faith disappear, at this coming of the Son of man.

[2] See Luke xvii, 20. Jesus evidently had in mind some aspect of his kingdom which these Pharisees did not comprehend. A kingdom may be represented and be in fact present in the person of its king, and so it truly was in the midst of them in the person and ministry of the Son of God and Saviour of men. These words of Jesus are thus best understood as one of his bold and impressive assertions. Similarly it is written in John i, 10, 11: "He was in the world, and the world was made through him, and the world knew him not. He came unto his own, and they that were his own received him not."

3. Jesus's Eschatological Discourse. Supposed difficulties of exegesis involved in these teachings concerning *the time* of the coming may disappear when we shall have more clearly apprehended *the manner* of the coming of the Son of man in his kingdom. The passages already cited will help us also in this further discussion. The important statements of Jesus in Luke xvii, 20-37, agree in all essential points with what the three synoptic gospels record as the great sermon of Jesus on the subject of his coming and of the end of the age, and Matthew actually incorporates them in his report of that remarkable discourse. This sermon on the Mount of Olives is in its main outline the same in all the synoptics, and appears to be as thoroughly attested as any of the teachings of Jesus. In fact, no discourse of Jesus of any similar length reported in our gospel is better authenticated than this one, and so far as concerns our present inquiry it matters not whether we confine ourselves to the report of one of these evangelists or take them all together. The incongruities which have perplexed interpreters are not materially relieved by eliminating sections or sayings peculiar to any one of these synoptic reports. Mark's gospel alone, which may be regarded as the most primitive of the three as we now possess them, contains all the supposed incongruities in these eschatological sayings of our Lord. Touching the relative nearness of the coming as well as the manner and the sign of it, all these gospel records are substantially at one in declaring things which must take place before the end of the age, the signs of its being close at hand, and an apocalyptic description of the event itself. They all agree, moreover, in reporting this discourse of Jesus as an answer to the twofold question of his disciples: "When shall these things be, and what shall be the sign of their coming to pass?" The question was prompted by the statement of Jesus that the buildings of the temple should be utterly overthrown.

4. The End of the Age. It is not our purpose in this volume to present a full analysis and discussion of the contents of this remarkable discourse of Jesus.[1] We shall first point out that "the end" (τὸ τέλος), and the "consummation of the age" (συντέλεια τοῦ αἰῶνος, peculiar to Matt. and Heb. ix, 26) are expressions which refer to the termination of a period of time then current, the close of a certain dispensation under which the speakers were living. There is really no room to doubt that in using these familiar phrases Jesus and his disciples appropriated the well-

---

[1] For such analysis and discussion the reader is referred to my Biblical Apocalyptics, pp. 213-252, where the different theories of interpretation, the parallel teaching of the synoptics, the occasion and scope of the discourse and an analysis of its contents, and a full exposition of the several parts, are treated in detail.

known Jewish designations of the age or period which preceded the coming of the Messiah and that age which was to follow his coming. It was common to speak of *this age* and *the age to come*,[1] and it can only be a source of error and of misunderstanding when these words are so translated as to convey to the popular mind the idea of the end of the physical world. The common version "end of the world" is naturally understood as the final collapse of the physical universe and the close of all human history. But the "end of the age" meant to Jewish hearers the end of the pre-Messianic age. The disciples of Jesus, according to Matt. xxiv, 3, evidently supposed that the ruin of the temple must needs also involve the end of the age preceding the time of the coming of Messiah; he would introduce some new order of things. So far now as the end of the pre-Messianic age was marked by some decisive crisis, we have no higher authority than this discourse of Jesus for determining the time and manner of that crisis. Does the answer of Jesus to this question of his disciples justify the opinion that the ruin of the Jewish temple did mark the end of the pre-Messianic age? We are persuaded that, if no dogmatic bias had come in to influence interpretation, and these and parallel scriptures had been permitted to explain themselves, there need have been no serious difficulty in perceiving that Jesus most positively affirms the end of the age and the triumphal coming of the Son of man as occurring in the near future, before that generation should pass away. For (1) it is all but universally conceded that a large part of what is here recorded as about to take place was actually and remarkably fulfilled in the events which preceded and accompanied the ruin of the temple. (2) It is also beyond question that Jesus explicitly said his coming *would immediately follow* the tribulation of those days; or according to Mark, would take place "in those days after that tribulation." (3) He further declared most emphatically: "This generation shall not pass away, until all these things be accomplished." We see no possible way of setting aside these facts except by reading into other statements

---

[1] The Hebrew phrases were עולם הזה, *this age*, and עולם הבא, *the coming age*. The uniform teaching of the New Testament is that the ministry of Christ and the apostles took place "in the end of the days," "the last days," "the end of the times"; that is, the last days or closing period of the pre-Messianic era. See Heb. i, 1; ix, 26; 1 Pet. i, 20; Acts ii, 17. In 1 Cor. x, 11, Paul speaks of himself and his contemporaries as those "upon whom the ends of the ages have come." Accordingly, the Messianic reign of our Lord Jesus, so far as any crucial turning point that marked the close of the one age and the beginning of the other may be pointed out, did not begin while Jesus was yet in the flesh. And after his enthronement at the right hand of God, the apostles did not regard the end of the pre-Messianic age as having yet fully come. They knew not the day, nor the hour, and they continued to speak of the parousia of the Lord as an event of the future.

of the discourse a meaning not necessary, and not justified by other teachings of the Scriptures.

5. Supposed Inconsistencies. Those other statements which have been supposed to be inconsistent with the time-limit are (1) the words of Matt. xxiv, 14: "This gospel of the kingdom shall be preached in the whole world for a testimony unto all the nations; and then shall the end come"; (2) the saying that *the day and hour* are not known to man, nor to the angels, nor even to the Son, but to the Father only; and (3) the language employed in Matt. xxiv, 29-31, and parallels in Mark and Luke, which is thought to be incompatible with the prophetic description of an event like the destruction of Jerusalem and its temple. But it can be easily shown that these suppositions are destitute of any sure ground in the Scriptures.

(1) *Matthew xxiv, 14.* Taking them in the order named we first observe that the preaching referred to in Matt. xxiv, 14, does not mean the conversion of all the nations of the habitable globe as we know it now, but is to be explained by the familiar usage of *world* and *nations* as seen in other New Testament statements. According to Acts ii, 5, "devout men from every nation under heaven were dwelling at Jerusalem" on the day of Pentecost, and the enumeration of Parthians, Medes, Elamites, etc., in verses 9-11, shows that the thought of the writer did not go beyond the limits of the Roman empire. We have already seen that Jesus advised his disciples that they would not complete their mission even in the cities of the land of Israel before the coming of the Son of man (Matt. x, 23). Paul declares in Col. i, 6, 23, that in his time the gospel was "bearing fruit and increasing in all the world," and that it "was preached in all creation under heaven."[1] It would seem, accordingly, that the most obvious meaning of Jesus, and in fact the only exposition of his words which fits the context, was that the promulgation of the gospel, so as to secure for it a firm and ineradicable hold on human life and thought, was necessary (δεῖ, Mark xiii, 10) before the old sanctuary and its cult be overthrown. In other words, the end of the then existing covenant with its ordinances, and ritual, and sanctuary (comp. Heb. ix, 1), should not come until the gospel of the new covenant had first been preached unto all the nations round about for a testimony that the kingdom of God was truly at hand, and that the Messianic King had appeared, born of the seed of David according to the flesh, but declared the Son of God with power by his resurrection and enthronement at the right hand of the Majesty on

---

[1] For other texts illustrating this usage of the terms *world* and *nations*, see Luke ii, 1; Acts xi, 28; xvii, 6; xxiv, 5; 2 Tim. iv, 17.

high. This explanation points out both the fact and the necessity of such a preaching of the gospel before the overthrow of the Jewish metropolis and its holy house of worship.

(2) *The Day and Hour Unknown.* In Matt. xxiv, 34-36, and Mark xiii, 30-32, it is written, in immediate connection with the statement that "this generation shall not pass away until all these things be accomplished," that "of that day or that hour no one knoweth, not even the angels in heaven, neither the Son, but the Father only." It is held by some that Jesus could not have spoken these two sayings in such immediate connection, and it is accordingly supposed that the apostolic tradition confused a number of things which he spoke in an entirely different connection. But this hypothesis involves a violent and very unsatisfactory piece of criticism, and it springs from the peculiar assumption that if Jesus knew an event as certain to come to pass within the time of a generation of thirty or forty years, he must also have known the day and the hour. All this seems to us quite arbitrary and untenable. It is perfectly natural and intelligible to affirm the certainty of a great event, foreseen to occur within the limit of half a century, and at the same time to disclaim any certain knowledge of the day or the hour of its occurrence. All the exhortations of Jesus to watch and pray in view of the uncertainty of the day and the hour accord with the presupposition that such unknown day and hour must of course come within the time limits of the generation of those whom he addressed, that is, before some of them should taste of death (comp. Matt. xvi, 28). The absurdity of a contrary opinion appears in the obvious stupidity of a solemn admonition which declared the great event as sure to come within the lifetime of some of them while the day or hour of its occurrence might be centuries after their generation should pass away!

(3) *Apocalyptic Language.* The allegation, made by literalistic expositors, that the language of Matt. xxiv, 29-31, is too majestic and world-significant to describe such an event as the fall of Jerusalem and the Jewish temple becomes utterly nugatory when we compare the words of Jesus with the language of other prophetic scriptures which describe events of far less moment to mankind. There is scarcely a word or phrase in this passage, and its parallels in Mark and Luke, which is not in substance appropriated from the apocalyptic portions of the Old Testament, where the reference is to the overthrow of such world-powers as Egypt, and Tyre, and Babylon.[1] On the day of Pentecost Peter quoted the words

---

[1] Compare Isa. xiii, 6-14; xix, 1; xxvii, 13; xxxiv, 1-5; Joel ii, 1-11; Mic. i, 3, 4; Dan. vii, 13, 14; Zech. ii, 6; xii, 11-14. The vivid portraiture of "the day of the Lord" in 2 Pet. iii, 10-13, consists of a free appropriation of such texts as

of Joel ii, 28-32, where we read of "wonders in the heavens and in the earth: blood, and fire, and pillars of smoke; the sun turned into darkness and the moon into blood, before the great and notable day of the Lord cometh"; and the apostle declared that this prophecy was fulfilled at that time (Acts ii, 14-21). But the ruin of the temple was the momentous crisis, which marked the fall of Judaism and the consequent outgoing and triumph of the kingdom of Jesus Christ, and we conceive it as the sign of the greatest event in the history of mankind, and therefore pre-eminently worthy to be described in sublime apocalyptic style, such as Jesus employed.

6. The Words παρουσία and ἔρχομαι. Matthew's gospel employs the word παρουσία, four times in this twenty-fourth chapter to designate the *coming* of the Son of man, but this term does not appear in the other gospels, although it is quite frequent in the apostolic epistles. The word strictly means *presence,* as opposed to *absence,* as one may observe in its usage in Phil. ii, 12: "Not as in my presence (παρουσία) only, but much more in my absence (ἀπουσία), work out your own salvation." When applied to Christ the word might be translated *presence,* and denote his personal spiritual fellowship with the believer who worships in his name (comp. Matt. xviii, 20; John xiv, 23); but as the personal presence of anyone implies some previous coming, παρουσία is very properly rendered in many passages by the word *coming,* and differs not essentially from what is also represented by the word ἔρχομαι. This latter word refers to the coming and kingdom of Christ in Matt. xvi, 27, 28; xxiv, 30; xxv, 31; John xiv, 3; Rev. i, 7; xxii, 7. And Luke xvii, 20, says that "the kingdom of God cometh not with observation." Nothing, therefore, in these words or in any statement of scripture bearing on the subject, necessarily teaches that the coming of Christ or of his kingdom is of the nature of a spectacle that is visible to fleshly eyes. We have already found that the nature of the kingdom of God is spiritual and to be spiritually discerned, and we accordingly believe that the coming of the Son of man in the clouds, in his kingdom, and in the glory of his Father, is not a matter of physical display in the world of

---

those just cited, and others like Isa. li, 6; lxv, 17; lxvi, 22; Ezek. xxxii, 7, 8. It is not at all improbable, nor to be wondered at, that some of the first apostles as well as those who came later misapprehended the real import of these apocalyptic words. The apostolic and post-apostolic interpreters of Hebrew prophecy, as well as the ancient seers themselves, "sought and searched diligently concerning what manner of time the Spirit did point unto" (1 Pet. i, 10, 11). The real question here is one of the interpretation of apocalyptic language, which we cannot here take space to discuss in detail, but which the reader may find elaborately treated in Biblical Apocalyptics, New York, 1898. See also Biblical Hermeneutics, pp. 338–389, New York, 1890.

sense, but perceptible only in such a deeper sense as "the invisible things of him since the creation of the world are clearly seen" (Rom. i, 20), and as faith "sees him who is invisible" (Heb. xi, 27).

7. Admonition of Luke xvii, 20-37. Jesus admonished his disciples that to some it was not given to know the mysteries of the kingdom of heaven (Matt. xiii, 11). The Pharisees eyed him with suspicion, and sought to ensnare him in his words. And so he spoke both to them and to his own disciples in mystic but suggestive forms of speech. His parables of the mustard seed, the seed growing secretly, and the leaven, showed that the kingdom of God comes according to an ordered progress, "first the blade, then the ear, then the full corn in the ear." It is worthy of note that in Luke xvii, 20-37, after he had admonished the Pharisees that the kingdom cometh not with observation, Jesus said to his disciples: "Days will come when ye shall desire to see one of the days of the Son of man, and shall not see." A study of verses 22, 24, 26, and 30 makes it plain that "one of the days of the Son of man" does not mean one of the days of his fleshly life, such as the disciples were then enjoying, but rather days of his future revelation from the heavens. The disciples were, like the Pharisees, slow to learn that the kingdom of God and the revelation of the Son of man were not matters of spectacular display. To the Pharisees Jesus suggested that the kingdom was already among them, and they knew it not. To the disciples he gave the timely admonition that days were coming on when they, too, would be zealously looking for one of the days of heavenly revelation of the Son of man, and would fail to see it for want of spiritual discernment. They, too, would be saying, Lo, here! and Lo, there! and so misunderstand its silent, pervasive, universal presence (παρουσία) which, like the sheet lightning, instantaneous from the far east to the remotest west, is yet quite intangible. Such a revelation is incompatible with local bodily presence.

8. Synoptic Testimony Quite Decisive. So far, now, as the synoptic gospels throw light upon the time and manner of the coming of Christ, we cannot escape the conviction that their testimony is decisive in connecting that great crisis of ages with the ruin of the Jewish sanctuary. Up to that point the new gospel of the kingdom had met its fiercest opposition from Judaism and its bitter zealots, but thereafter it went forth triumphantly among the Gentiles, being released from the entanglements of outward legalism which so seriously obstructed the ministry of Paul. Jesus announced that immediately after the tribulation of those days there would "appear the sign of the Son of man in heaven," and we are persuaded that both the *sign* of the Son of man and the *heaven* in which it appears must be understood in the same spiritual manner in which we understand all other mysteries of the kingdom of God. For Jesus declared to the Pharisees most emphatically that the kingdom comes not with observation. It is no public phenomenon to which men can point and say, Lo, it is here or there (Luke xvii, 21).[1] A spiritual kingdom can only be spiritually discerned. It may come in the same moment of time to persons and communities far apart in locality. "For as the lightning, when it lighteneth out of the one part under the heaven, shineth unto the other part under heaven, so shall the Son of man be in his day" (Luke xvii, 24). The salient point in this comparison is not the sudden glare of lightning which dazzles the eye, but the instantaneousness of its appearance in places as far apart as the east is from the west (comp. Matt. xxiv, 27). So where two or three meet in his name, one group in London and another in Calcutta, the Christ can come to each in the same moment of time. His coming is in every case a coming from heaven, and every manifestation of his saving grace is in some measure a coming of the kingdom of heaven.

9. Excludes Literalism. The foregoing exposition of the synoptic teaching on this subject will be of course unacceptable to the literalist. He must have spectacular phenomena, cosmic cataclysms, and a visible political organization exercising physical power over the nations of the earth. He can discern no coming of the kingdom in the silent progress of the gospel in the world. But such an interpreter of the scriptures is obliged to set aside in some unseemly way the most explicit statements of Jesus. He usually resorts to the vague hypothesis of a "double sense" in the words of prophecy. He is very like the Jewish scribes who looked here and there for something external and political in the world of sense, and fails to perceive the obvious aim of Jesus to correct such a misleading conception of the kingdom of God. He refuses to interpret the apocalyptic language of Jesus, appropriated

---

[1] Commenting on Luke xvii, 21, Alford says of the kingdom of God: "Its coming shall be so gradual that none during its waxing onward shall be able to point here or there for a proof of its coming."—Greek Testament, in loco. It is strange that so many expositors have failed to observe that, so far from confirming his contemporaries in their sensuous notions of the kingdom, Jesus aimed to lift them into a more spiritual way of thinking of it. It did, indeed, accord with Old Testament modes of prophetic announcement to picture the kingdom as coming "all at once" (as Beyschlag says, New Testament Theology, Vol. I, p. 52). The prophets, he observes, "had the complete picture of it before them in one great view, and they thought of its coming with observation, so that one on the watch might see it coming down from heaven by a great miracle of God." But Jesus taught the "progressiveness and development of the kingdom, in virtue of which it cannot fall ready made from heaven, but must develop itself in the earth, in the human race, and in the history of the world."

directly from Old Testament prophecies long ago fulfilled, after the manner of its usage in the Hebrew writers, and insists that symbolical portraitures of revolutions in human government and of appalling calamities of war and bloodshed connected with the ruin of cities and temples must needs be understood literally when spoken by the lips of our Lord. It is evident that the real issue with such an interpreter is over a principle of biblical hermeneutics, which must be determined by a calm appeal to the facts of usage in the great body of the prophetic scriptures.

10. Doctrine of John's Gospel. The synoptic teaching of the kingdom and coming of Christ is admirably supplemented by the doctrine of the fourth gospel. This was written some time after the fall of Jerusalem, and its peculiarly spiritual conception both of the ministry and the kingdom of Christ is worthy of special attention. The King and the kingdom are thought of as coming "from above." They are not of this world, and the heavenly King declares that his great purpose in coming into the world is to "bear witness unto the truth." His coming and his triumph are destined to effect the judgment of this world and to cast out the prince of darkness (xiii, 31).

(1) *John iii, 3-7, 31-36.* One of the most memorable lessons of this gospel is the necessity of being "born from above" in order to enter the kingdom of God (iii, 3-7). This teaching is not compatible with a physical and spectacular theory of the kingdom, but it supplements and confirms the lessons of Jesus in his parables. In John iii, 31-36, we have a correspondingly spiritual idea of the relation of the Father and the Son to them that enter the kingdom of God. It is the Son "who cometh from above" (ὁ ἐρχόμενος, *who is about to come*), who is truly also "above all," and into whose hand the Father has given all things. His coming from above (ἄνωθεν) is spoken of in the same verse as a coming from the heaven (ἐκ τοῦ οὐρανοῦ), and is conceived as a present and continuous manifestation,[1] so that, as an abiding truth, "he that believeth on the Son hath eternal life; but he that obeyeth not the Son shall not see life." To "see life" is evidently the same as "seeing the kingdom of God" (ver. 3). It accords with this spiritual doctrine of his kingdom that when Jesus perceived the disposition of the people "to come and take him by force to make him king," he went away and secluded him-

---

[1] In verse 13 we meet with the enigmatical saying of the descent of the Son of man out of heaven who is nevertheless in the heaven. These last words are wanting in some ancient copies, but it is difficult to explain how they came to be interpolated. It is far easier to account for their early omission than for their interpolation. They convey the thought of Christ's continuous existence in heaven even while incarnate among men.

self in the mountain (vi, 15). The popular ideal of the Messianic kingdom was not the one which he sought to inculcate, and his triumphal entry into Jerusalem, riding upon a young ass, was a symbolical act adapted to show forth the meekness and humility of this true king of Israel and the blessedness of his coming in the name of the Lord. But it was not until after Jesus was glorified that the disciples understood the significance of these things (xii, 13-16). His declarations before Pilate (xviii, 36, 37), which we have already cited to show the spiritual nature of his kingdom (comp. p. 437), are also to be recalled in this connection: "My kingdom is not of this world; my kingdom is not from hence." It cometh from above, and cometh as continuously and unostentatiously as truth itself.

(2) *John xiv, 3.* In this text Jesus tells his disciples that he is going away to prepare a place for them, and that he will come again and receive them unto himself. This coming again to receive his own disciples and friends ($\phi\iota\lambda\text{ους}$, xv, 14, 15) is most naturally understood as a process continually going on, as truly so as that which he affirms in verse 18: "I will not leave you as orphans: I am coming unto you." It would seem absurd to teach that the original disciples who heard these assurances, and all the devout and saintly friends of Jesus who have departed this life since these words were first spoken, are yet waiting for the coming of the Lord to receive them unto himself in the heavenly mansions.[1] Rather should we believe that Jesus's desire and prayer that they may be with him where he is and behold his glory (xvii, 24) is finding continual answer through the progress of the centuries. The fourteenth chapter of John's gospel is notable for a blending of the idea of spiritual life in Christ and the eternal life of fellowship and glory with Christ in a heavenly state. In verse 23 Jesus says: "If a man love me, he will keep my word: and my Father will love him, and we will come unto him, and make our abode with him." Here is a coming and abiding presence both of the Father and the Son. But in verse 19 he says: "Yet a little while, and the world beholdeth me no more; but ye behold me: because I live, ye shall live also. In that day ye shall know that I am in my Father, and ye in me, and I in you." Taken all together these various sayings teach that man may live a heavenly life on earth. The Father, the Son, and the Spirit abide with all such, and in his own time the Lord, who is himself the way and the truth and the life (ver. 6), will come and receive them unto himself in his Father's house of many mansions.

---

[1] The word $\mu\text{οναί}$, *mansions, abodes,* conveys the idea of dwelling places of a permanent character. Comp. "the eternal tabernacles" in Luke xvi, 9.

(3) *The Passage in John xxi, 22, 23,* is peculiar in its careful refraining from any attempt to explain what Jesus meant when he said to Peter in reference to the disciple whom he loved: "If I will that he tarry till I come, what is that to thee?" Some inferred from these words "that that disciple should not die." But it is written: "Jesus did not say unto him that he should not die; but, If I will that he tarry (μένειν, *remain*) till I come, what is that to thee?" This careful record ought to admonish us against hasty inferences from the reported words of Jesus touching his coming, as well as from the dogmatism which oracularly declares that his *coming again,* in John xiv, 3, cannot mean a coming of Christ to receive into heavenly life the spirit of a dying saint at the moment of its departure from this mortal state.[1] For anything that can be proven to the contrary, such a dying is perfectly compatible with remaining until the Lord come, and in spite of all that is said in opposition, this idea has somehow permeated the thought of Christendom, and has found strong and definite expression in the songs of the Church universal. How common to think and to say of any saint that passes from this mortal life, "The Lord has come and taken him away to himself in the heavens."

11. General Apostolic Allusions. Aside from the Apocalypse, there is comparatively but a small portion of the apostolic writings which treats directly of the time and manner of the coming of Christ and his kingdom. In James v, 7, 8; 2 Pet. i, 16; 1 John ii, 28, and 1 Thess. ii, 19; iii, 13; v, 23, we read examples of incidental allusion to the coming (*parousia*) of the Lord as of a common and well-known expectation of blessed hope. In these passages the word παρουσία, *presence,* does not necessarily mean a spectacular manifestation visible to fleshly eyes, but conveys the same idea of a spiritual coming and presence which we have already explained. Whensoever and wheresoever the kingdom of God comes with power, the coming and presence of the heavenly King must also be understood, and so far as seeing the kingdom of God and entering into the kingdom (John iii, 3, 5) contemplate being "set before the presence of his glory without blemish in exceeding

---

[1] Commentators like Meyer, who reject every interpretation of John xiv, 3, which leans towards "a merely spiritual import" of the words of Jesus, and who insist that the *coming* can here mean only the "parousia at the last day," seem to be unaware that their notion of a single spectacular coming, visible at one and the same hour to all men, is as unscriptural as it is unthinkable in the nature of things. The coming of which Jesus speaks is undoubtedly the same as his *parousia,* or presence; but whether he come to receive a Stephen up to his throne, or to execute his judgment upon his murderers, the parousia is not a spectacle such as the literalistic expositor assumes. The effects of such a judgment may be seen, but not the personal movements of the heavenly Judge. Such literal expositors have too one-sided a notion of Christ's parousia, and make too little of Christ's teaching in John xi, 26: "Whosoever liveth and believeth on me shall never die."

joy" (Jude 24), such reception into heavenly glory is an essential portion of the inheritance of the saints in light. Accordingly, any manifestation of the power and glory of Christ involves some certain aspect of his heavenly kingdom.

12. Import of the Word ἐπιφάνεια. At this point we may appropriately notice the import of the word ἐπιφάνεια, *manifestation,* or *appearing,* in its reference to God and to Christ. In 2 Tim. i, 10, "the appearing of our Saviour Christ Jesus" is his past historical manifestation in the flesh; but in chapter iv, 1, 8, of this same epistle the reference is less clear, although it is entirely compatible with the idea of a continual process, like that of the coming of his kingdom. The language in the first verse is: "I adjure thee in the sight of God and of Christ Jesus who shall judge the living and the dead, both by his appearing and his kingdom: preach the word." As the notion of the judgment of Christ ceases to be understood as a spectacular event, or as one that must needs be simultaneous with all the living and the dead of all ages, and as it adjusts itself to the doctrine of the kingdom of Christ as a process of spiritual conquest and dominion, it will become obvious that the appearing of Christ is not an event that occurs once for all, at a definite moment in the course of time. It occurs repeatedly and indeed continuously, as the children of the kingdom "fall asleep" and, like Stephen at his departure from mortal life, "see the heavens opened, and the Son of man standing on the right hand of God" (Acts vii, 56). In strictest harmony with this conception the apostle speaks, in 2 Tim. iv, 8, of his confident expectation of "the crown of righteousness, which the Lord, the righteous judge, shall give to me at that day: and not only to me, but also to all them that have loved his appearing." This appearing of Christ, according to 1 Tim. vi, 14, 15, the heavenly King "shall show forth *in its own times."* The day of its revelation is not one and the same point of time for every soul that has loved his appearing, but it has its various and innumerable times. So, too, God manifests his word in the gospel message *in its own times* (Titus i, 3), but the word comes not at the same time to all. In Titus ii, 13, we read of "the blessed hope and appearing of the great God and our Saviour Jesus Christ"; but nothing in this text or context obliges us to limit the realization of this "blessed hope and the appearing of the great God" to any one period of time for all the redeemed. Each must attain to that blessedness in his own time, and we are not to assume that the epiphany of the great God must be something visible to the eyes of men in the flesh. The writer contemplates rather the spiritual and eternal, and he speaks in verse 11 of the grace of God which "has appeared (ἐπεφάνη), bringing salvation to all men," and in iii, 4, of the like *appearance* of "the kindness of God our Saviour, and his love toward man." Nothing, therefore, in any one of these texts requires us to understand the *appearing* of Christ as a physical phenomenon yet to be revealed to mortal men, and to be perceived by all men at one moment of time. The only other passage which contains this word (ἐπιφάνεια) is 2 Thess. ii, 8, which we shall duly notice in connection with the doctrine of that epistle.

13. Import of ἀποκάλυψις and φανέρωσις. Two other words require a passing notice in this connection because of their occasional use in the same general meaning which we have pointed out in the word ἐπιφάνεια. In 1 Cor. i, 7, Paul speaks of "waiting for *the revelation* of our Lord Jesus Christ; who shall also confirm you unto the end, unreprovable in the day of our Lord Jesus Christ." Here the word *revelation* (ἀποκάλυψις) is obviously equivalent to *manifestation* or *appearing*, and may be understood, as we have explained the appearing of the Lord, of that heavenly revelation of himself which he makes in his own times. The *day* of Jesus Christ is the time at which he reveals himself and his heavenly glory (comp. John xvii, 24) to his redeemed saints, but as matter of fact this day of glorious revelation cannot be the same moment of time for all. For the New Testament doctrine of immortality and resurrection, as we have already seen, necessarily involves the fact that some saints are glorified with Christ before others are born. We cannot, therefore allow a literalistic exegesis to force the absurd conclusion that "the day of our Lord Jesus Christ" must be one and the same moment of his personal revelation to all generations of men. The same comments will apply to the word as it is employed in 1 Pet. i, 7, 13; iv, 13; 2 Thess. i, 7. The word φανερόω is also used to denote any kind of spiritual or heavenly manifestation. In Col. i, 26, the mystery of the ages is said to be "now manifested" to the saints of God; and in Col. iii, 4, it is written: "When Christ, our life, shall be manifested, then shall ye also with him be manifested in glory." There was a manifestation of Jesus Christ in the flesh, and there is to be a manifestation of the same Christ in glory; but this latter should not be thought of as occurring at one and the same time to all generations of mankind. In Heb. ix, 26, we are told that "now once at the consummation of the ages Christ has been manifested to put away sin"; but in verse 28 it is said that he "shall be seen (ὀφθήσεται) a second time, apart from sin, to them that wait for him, unto salvation." Similarly in 1 Peter: "Christ was manifested at the end of the times for your sake" (i, 20); and yet, "when the chief Shepherd shall be manifested (*i.e.*, whensoever to any one of you) ye shall receive the crown of glory that fadeth not away" (v, 4). Other statements of like character are made in 1 John i, 2; ii, 28; iii, 2. The noun φανέρωσις, *manifestation*, occurs only in 1 Cor. xii, 7, and 2 Cor. iv, 2. In the first passage mention is made of "the manifestation of the Spirit" through divers gifts, and in the second a commending of one's self to every man's conscience in the sight of God "by the manifestation of the truth." The one thing we here emphasize in all these scriptures is the obvious fact that the *appearing*, the *revelation*, and the *manifestation* of Christ are not to be understood as spectacular physical phenomena visible at one moment of time to all men. This fact being shown, there is left no solid ground for the exegesis of the literalist who insists that the coming of Christ and of his kingdom can be only a public event, once for all manifest to the whole world.

14. The Statement in Acts i, 11. In the first eleven verses of the Acts of the apostles we are told that Jesus showed himself as still living after his passion and death, and during forty days he spoke to his chosen apostles of "the things concerning the kingdom of God." To their question about the time of his "restoring the kingdom to Israel" he replied that it was not for them to know times and seasons which the heavenly Father kept within his own authority. He did not then say, as in Mark xiii, 32, that he did not know the time, but he turned their thoughts to something of more importance, the mighty coming upon them of the Holy Spirit not many days thereafter, and of their becoming his witnesses "in Jerusalem, and in all Judea and Samaria, and unto the uttermost part of the earth." All this was profoundly significant that his "restoring the kingdom" was to be a very much greater thing than their narrow Jewish concept of the kingdom contemplated. But "while they were looking, he was taken up, and a cloud received him out of their sight. And while they were looking stedfastly into heaven as he went, behold two men stood by them in white apparel; who also said, This Jesus, who was received up from you into heaven, shall so come in like manner as ye beheld him going into heaven." Peter was doubtless one of the witnesses of this event, and we recognize an allusion to it when he speaks, in Acts iii, 21, of the Lord Jesus, "whom the heaven must receive until the times of the restoration of all things." His coming again from heaven, whatever its *manner* (τρόπος), is doubtless the same "coming in his own glory" which he speaks of in Luke ix, 26, and parallel passages. Whatever essential fact or truth is expressed in his "coming on the clouds of heaven," whether written in Isa. xix, 1; Dan. vii, 13; Mark xiii, 26; Matt. xxvi, 64, or Rev. i, 7, the same is included in the statement of Acts i, 11. But the phrase ὃν τρόπον, translated *in like manner as,* does not warrant all that the literalistic interpreter is wont to read into it. Such a specific construction is seen to be misleading when applied to this phrase in Acts vii, 28; 2 Tim. iii, 8; Matt. xxiii, 37 (and the parallel in Luke xiii, 34)—the only other places where it occurs in the New Testament, and where, in each case, it is commonly translated simply *as,* or *even as.* It is not the specific manner in which Moses killed the Egyptian (Acts vii, 28), or in which Jannes withstood Moses (2 Tim. iii, 8), or in which a hen gathers her brood under her wings (Matt. xxiii, 37), but rather a general resemblance or likeness in the point of fact referred to. A proper translation of the phrase in all these texts would be simply *even as.* Jesus would often have gathered the children of Jerusalem under his protection, even as a mother bird protects her young. And so the psalmist would fain take refuge in the shadow of God's wings (Psa. lvii, 1). But neither the psalmist's metaphor nor the simile of Jesus would be helped by a literalistic interpretation which exhausts itself in looking into *the particular manner* in which the wings of God and of Christ cover those who trust in him.[1] The angels did not even say to those who saw Jesus ascend *that they should behold his return;* but they simply assured them that, as surely as Jesus had gone into heaven, even so he should again come from heaven. This coming from heaven is accordingly to be explained in the light of all parallel scriptures.

15. Doctrine of John's Apocalypse. This book of "the revelation of Jesus Christ" is most positive in its declarations that the great events of which it treats "must shortly come to pass" (i, 1, 3; xxii, 6, 7, 10), and there can be no reasonable denial or doubt of the fact that the main subject of the revelation is the kingdom and coming of the Christ. The language of xi, 1-3, 8, implies that the Jewish temple and courts, and the city where the Lord was crucified were yet standing, but nigh unto destruction when this book was written. The mystic riddles of xiii, 18, and xvii, 9-11, are best explained by the supposition that the book was written in the time of Nero, during whose reign the war was begun which ended in the overthrow of the Jewish temple and its local cult. The modern criticism, which essays to point out internal evidences of compilation in the book as we now have it, admits that the

---

[1] Is it, or is it not, true that the interpretation of Acts i, 11, which insists that the ὃν τρόπον must be the salient point of the passage, and can only mean a literal, visible coming in clouds just above the heads of those who "look for his coming and his kingdom," loses sight of the real kingdom and glory of Christ amid the clouds? It seems to put far more stress on the clouds than on the kingdom.

passages referred to must have been written in the time of Nero, and belonged to a smaller apocalypse which the compiler appropriated and wrought into his own larger work. Whatever theory of the date and composition one may prefer, it would seem that the exposition which best explains and harmonizes the contents of this remarkable prophecy is that which sees in the Babylonian harlot of chapter xvii another symbol of the corrupt and murderous city "which spiritually is called Sodom and Egypt" in xi, 8. The old Jerusalem became a harlot (comp. Isa. i, 21), and miserably fell; but that fall was followed by the coming down out of heaven from God of the New Jerusalem, the pure and glorious bride of Christ. We believe the New Testament Apocalypse of John to be a genuine product of earliest Christian doctrine, and a work remarkable for its symmetrical structure. The great theme is announced in true apocalyptic style in the language of i, 7: "Behold he cometh with clouds; and every eye shall see him, and they who pierced him, and all the tribes of the land shall mourn over him." This language is characteristic of apocalyptic writing and is in substance identical with that of Matt. xxiv, 30, and also with Zech. xii, 10, from which, in fact, it may well be supposed to have been appropriated. And the entire book appears upon analysis and exposition to be virtually an expansion of our Lord's discourse concerning the end of the age as reported in all the synoptic gospels.[1]

(1) *The First Part, i—xi.* The book is divisible into two nearly equal parts, which seem, like the double dreams of Joseph and of Pharaoh, to represent the same great events under different sets of symbols. The first part, which ends with chapter xi, portrays the terrible vengeance of the Lion of Judah and the Lamb of God upon his enemies, as if the author contemplated the ruin of Jerusalem and of those who pierced him and cried, "His blood be upon us and upon our children," in the light of the parable of the king "who sent forth his armies, and destroyed those murderers, and burned their city" (Matt. xxii, 7). This part contains three series of revelations, the seven churches, the seven seals, and the seven trumpets, and the final catastrophe is reached at the sounding of the last trumpet, which also signals the triumph of the heavenly king; for "there followed great voices in heaven, and they said, The kingdom of the world is become the kingdom (or possession) of our Lord and of his Christ: and he shall reign for ever and ever" (xi, 15). Thus the blood of Christian martyrs (comp. vi, 10) is avenged, the old temple disappears from view, and there opens "the new temple of God which is in heaven, and there was

---

[1] See all these points amply detailed and maintained in my Biblical Apocalyptics, in the sections on the Gospel Apocalypse, and the Apocalypse of John.

seen in his temple the ark of the covenant," which, according to Heb. ix, 8, could not be made manifest while the first tabernacle was yet standing.

(2) *The Second Part, xii—xxii.* The second part (xii—xxii) contains another series of apocalyptic visions which present other aspects of the same time of trouble, and other pictures of the coming and kingdom of Christ. There are the divers revelations of Antichrist and of the workings of the mystery of lawlessness. The dragon, the beast, and the false prophet appear, each in his own order. The seven last plagues are seen to correspond remarkably to the seven trumpets of doom. But most conspicuous of all is the detailed portrayal of Babylon the harlot, a symbol of the apostate Jewish Church, upon which Jesus charged the guilt of "all the righteous blood shed on the land" (comp. Matt. xxiii, 35-37). More lamentably than in Isaiah's time had the once faithful city become a harlot (Isa. i, 21; comp. Jer. ii, 20; iii, 1). But immediately after the fall of this great Babylon, the mother of harlots and of abominations, many glad voices in the heavens say: "Halleluiah; for the Lord our God, the Almighty reigneth"; the heavens open, and one, who bears the threefold title of "Faithful and True, the Word of God, and King of kings," goes forth leading the heavenly armies to the ultimate overthrow of beast, false prophet, and dragon. Thereupon the holy city, new[1] Jerusalem, is seen "coming down out of heaven from God, made ready as a bride adorned for her husband." The details given of the appearance of Jerusalem the Bride are in notable contrast with those of Babylon the harlot, and the crowning glory of the holy city is that "the throne of God and of the Lamb shall be therein: and his servants shall serve him . . . and they shall reign for ever and ever" (xxii, 3-5).

(3) *New Jerusalem a Symbol of the Kingdom of Heaven.* We understand this graphic picture of the heavenly Jerusalem to be an apocalyptic symbol of the kingdom of heaven. Its coming down from heaven to earth is the answer to the universal prayer, "Thy kingdom come: thy will be done, as in heaven, so on earth." The vision of John descries it in bold and glorious outline, filling the ages and covering the world with its blessedness. When "he that sitteth on the throne said, Behold, I make all things new" (xxi, 5), he expressed in a word the work which is to occupy the whole period of the Messianic reign. He who declares himself the beginning and the end portrays the true and faithful words of these prophecies as already come to pass (xxi, 6), even though they

---

[1] The use of καινή here suggests the idea of a *new kind* of Jerusalem. Comp. also verse 5.

contemplate a "reign unto the ages of the ages." Other scriptures explain to us that his reign begins with the regeneration of the individual heart, and thence works outward and onward to the renovation of all things. "If any man is in Christ, he is a new creation: the old things are passed away; behold they are become new" (2 Cor. v, 17). But when these separate new creations in Christ become multiplied by millions of millions, they prove that the kingdom of heaven is like the mustard seed and the leaven. Such divine growths go on night and day, one knows not how (comp. Mark iv, 27), but the kingdom and city which cometh down out of heaven is built upon the foundation of the apostles and the prophets, Christ himself being the chief corner stone, and the sublime structure groweth into a holy temple in the Lord (comp. Rev. xxi, 14, and Eph. ii, 20-22). Like the stone which became a great mountain and filled the world (Dan. ii, 35), the kingdom of heaven is destined to possess both earth and heaven, and to make all things new. A collation of all these scriptures and an analysis and comparison of their metaphors, symbols, and statements would seem sufficient to show with unmistakable certainty the spiritual manner of the coming and kingdom of Christ.

16. Biblical Doctrine of Antichrist. A full discussion of the doctrine of Christ's second coming must not ignore those scriptures which speak of the coming, the manifestation, and the destruction of the great enemy of God and man who is variously designated as the Devil, Satan, and Antichrist. The subject belongs to the peculiar concepts of angelology and apocalyptics, but takes cognizance of the facts of evil which force themselves upon the attention of mankind. These stern facts are made prominent in the theology of dualism which affirms two eternal principles or powers of light and darkness, good and evil. There can be no question that our Scriptures recognize the existence of a kingdom of darkness opposed to the kingdom of light, and the spiritual hosts of wickedness are conceived as organized and led on by a prince of demons, who is spoken of in Eph. ii, 2; vi, 12, as "the prince of the powers of the air, the spirit that now worketh in the sons of disobedience." This great enemy of truth and righteousness is destined to certain overthrow by the coming and manifestation of the Lord Jesus Christ. The concept has its elements of sublimity and opens into an inviting field of imaginative speculation. An extensive literature has grown up around the subject, and the Antichrist has been identified with Nero, the pope of Rome, Mohammed, and Martin Luther. A study of the biblical doctrine may well exclude the conflicting opinions of post-apostolic times and the whole mass of later speculations.

(1) *Old Testament Concepts.* We may trace elements of this doctrine in the use made of the names of mythological monsters by the Hebrew poets and prophets. Amos ix, 3, speaks of the serpent in the bottom of the sea, and in Isa. xxvii, 1, it is said that "Jehovah will punish leviathan, the swift serpent, the crooked serpent, and the monster (*tannin*) that is in the sea." Similar allusions are made in Isa. li, 9; Job iii, 8; xxvi, 12, and Psa. lxxxix, 10, to leviathan, Rahab, and the dragon or monster of the sea. In some of these scriptures the mythological names are applied to great world-powers, like Egypt and Babylon, which are conceived as terrible monsters arrayed in warlike opposition to God. What the Hebrew prophet thought or knew about the mythical monster whose name he appropriated for the special purpose, we cannot now tell. All we can say of the Old Testament use of such words is that they were employed to denote an ideal of monstrous opposition to God and his people. Similarly, but with less of the mythical aspect, Satan appears in Job i, 6; ii, 1, and Zech. iii, 1, as a great adversary and accuser, but it may also be noticed here that the great dragon of John's Apocalypse is identified with "the old serpent, the devil and Satan, the deceiver of the whole world" (Rev. xii, 9). It is not improbable that Jewish contact with Persian dualism and angelology during the Babylonian exile, and under the dominion of Cyrus and his successors, served to develop the idea of a kingdom of light persistently assailed by a kingdom of evil demons. What is said in Dan. x, 13, 20, about contending angelic princes of the different provinces is obviously in accord with the ideas of a highly developed angelology.

(2) *Antichrist in John's Apocalypse.* In this most Hebraic book of the New Testament we have not only a revelation of Jesus Christ, but also a most remarkable revelation of the nature and power of Antichrist. The name *Antichrist* is not employed by the apocalyptic writer, but the great enemy of God and his people is portrayed by means of a variety of expressive symbols. He first appears in chapter ix, 11, as king and angel of the abyss, from the smoking pit of which arose the tormenting locusts. His name is given in Hebrew and Greek in terms that mean Destroyer. Again, in xi, 7, he appears as "the beast which comes up out of the abyss," and destroys the two witnessing prophets of God. In xii, 3, 9, he is revealed as "a great red dragon, having seven heads and ten horns," and is called "the Devil and Satan, the deceiver of the whole world; he was cast down to the earth, and his angels were cast down with him." In xiii, 2, this dragon gives "his power and his throne and great authority" to the monstrous beast that came up out of the sea, breathing out great blasphemies against

God and making war with the saints. In xvi, 13, there is a vision of the dreadful trinity of dragon, beast, and false prophet, out of whose mouths proceed "three unclean spirits, as it were frogs; for they are spirits of demons, working signs; which go forth unto the kings of the whole world, to gather them together unto the war of the great day of God, the Almighty." In xvii, 1-8, he appears again as a scarlet-colored beast, carrying an abominable harlot, full of names of blasphemy, and possessing one after another of the kings that do his will. This is obviously the same old serpent and dragon that comes up out of the abyss and is destined "to go into destruction" (ἀπώλειαν). In the final picture of this enemy of God, which is given in xix, 19—xx, 10, we behold the beast, the false prophet, and the dragon utterly vanquished as they gather their armies together for a last desperate assault upon God and the camp of his saints; but the fire of God comes down out of heaven and devours them. It is evident that in all these prophetic visions we have a manifold apocalyptic portraiture of the great foe of God and Christ in his persistent warfare against truth and righteousness. It is the old conflict of light and darkness, of good and of evil, represented on the one side by "the throne of God and of the Lamb," and on the other by "the throne of the beast." The throne of the beast is the same as the throne and power and great authority of the dragon (xiii, 2). In the interpretation of such prophetic scriptures one naturally asks how far the biblical writer meant to be understood as describing events that were to occur in actual and literal accord with his statements. On this question expositors have long differed, and the literalist is still searching European history for some character that will answer to the beast out of the abyss. Is it not wiser and better to understand these various symbols as a graphic idealization of the age-long conflict between truth and error, righteousness and wickedness, as it is continuously going on in the world? These conflicts have historic crises, which signally emphasize the truth set forth in the ideal pictures of the prophet, and we may discern the spirit and actual working of Antichrist in every form of evil which hinders the progress of the kingdom of God among men.

17. The Pauline Doctrine of Antichrist. As in the Apocalypse so in Paul's writings the name *Antichrist* does not occur, but no portion of the New Testament is more directly involved in the subject than what is written in 2 Thess. ii, 1-12, concerning "the man of sin," "the son of perdition," "the lawless one," and "the mystery of lawlessness." These various titles, taken all together, make upon the reader a much stronger impression of the working of Satan than the mere word *Antichrist*. This lawless man of sin is one "who opposes and exalts himself against all that is called God, or that is an object of worship" (σέβασμα), and his coming is said to be "according to the working of Satan with all power and signs and lying wonders." That is to say, he works in accord with the well-known wiles of the devil, the great opposer of God and of Christ and of all that is good. But the Lord Jesus, we are assured, "shall slay him with the breath of his mouth, and bring him to naught by the manifestation of his coming."

(1) *Relation of Second Thessalonians ii, 1-12, to First Thessalonians iv, 13-18.* It has been alleged that the second epistle to the Thessalonians was written to correct some wrong impressions made by the first epistle touching the coming of the Lord from heaven. In the first epistle it is written: "The Lord himself shall descend from heaven with a shout, with the voice of the archangel, and with the trump of God." The resurrection, the reunion, and glorification of the saints are the main truths spoken of in connection with these words, and these truths we have already discussed (pp. 231-233). Here we only observe that, according to the apostle, the coming of the Lord from heaven was contemplated as an event of the near future. The words, "we that are alive, that are left unto the coming of the Lord" (1 Thess. iv, 15) are unnatural and insignificant when supposed to be applicable to people living centuries and millenniums afterward. The apostle's language is in perfect harmony with the declaration of Jesus that some of them that accompanied him in the days of his flesh should in no wise taste of death until they had seen the Son of man coming in the glory of the Father and with the angels (Matt. xvi, 28). The metaphorical and apocalyptic language of all these parallel scriptures is to be understood as the common biblical method of speaking of the heavenly things which are not seen by fleshly eyes, but are spiritual and to be spiritually discerned. The apostle's picture of the coming of the Lord from heaven agrees in substance and in imagery with what he writes about it in 2 Thess. i, 7-10, and in 1 Cor. xv, 51, 52. It would almost seem as if he had read and had in mind John's apocalypse of the seven trumpets in Rev. viii—xi. But what is most noteworthy is the fact that these words of Paul are in all essentials of description remarkably parallel with those of Jesus in Matt. xxiv, 29-31. Paul says nothing about the darkening of the sun, the falling of the stars, and the shaking of the heavens; but he does speak of a shout, the voice of the archangel, and the trumpet of God. He does not say that the Son of man comes with the clouds, but he does assure his fellow Christians that those who witness that coming shall be caught up in the clouds to meet the Lord in the heavens. Jesus also spoke of "sending forth his angels

with a great sound of a trumpet, and gathering together his elect from one end of heaven to the other." Both these descriptions of the coming of Christ are in striking harmony, and both employ the language of Hebrew apocalyptics to portray momentous realities of the kingdom and power of the Lord Jesus.

(2) *Meaning of Second Thessalonians ii,2.* The language of this verse does not justify the notion that Paul's first epistle to the Thessalonians had been misunderstood, and there is nothing in this second epistle to show that the coming of the Lord Jesus would not take place before that generation passed away. Nor are the apostasy and the revelation of the man of sin spoken of as events of a distant future. What the apostle urges upon the Thessalonians in this passage is that they be not suddenly and unreasonably disturbed by any person or persons assuming to speak to them in the spirit of prophecy, or by any word or epistle purporting to come from himself, or from Silvanus or Timothy, to the effect that "the day of the Lord is immediately present" (ἐνέστηκεν).[1] The apostle's language is in notable accord with what Jesus said to his disciples, admonishing them not to be led astray by false prophets nor troubled by rumors of wars, "for these things must needs come to pass; but the end is not yet" (Matt. xxiv, 6). The second epistle to the Thessalonians, therefore, is in strict harmony with the first epistle as to the time and manner of "the coming of our Lord Jesus Christ, and our gathering together unto him," and there is nothing in either epistle that naturally or necessarily carries the thought of the reader beyond the time of the generation then living.

(3) *Imagery of Paul's Picture of Antichrist.* A study of the various expressions found in 2 Thess. ii, 3-10, shows that the graphic picture of "the man of sin" is largely drawn from the language of Daniel, where Antiochus Epiphanes is described in highly wrought apocalyptic style. In Dan. vii, 8, 25, 26; viii, 9-12, 23-25; and xi, 21-45, we read of a "little horn" wherein "were eyes like the eyes of a man, and a mouth speaking great things," "wearing out the saints of the Most High, and thinking to change times and law," "waxing great even to the host of heaven, magnifying himself even to the Prince of the host and standing up against the Prince of princes," "profaning the sanctuary and setting up the abomination that maketh desolate," "exalting himself and magnifying himself above every god, and speaking marvellous things against the God of gods." Moreover, the phrase *man of sin*

---

[1] Comp. the use of ἐνεστώς in Rom. viii, 38; 1 Cor. iii, 22; vii, 26; Gal. i, 4; Heb. ix, 9. Lünemann renders: "As if the day of the Lord is already present"; Schmiedel: "immediately impending." According to Ellicott the verb denotes "the actual presence and commencement of the day of the Lord."

appears to have been derived from 1 Maccabees i, 10; ii, 62, where this same despicable persecutor of the Jews is called "a sinful root" and "a sinful man."[1] According to Daniel the terrible beast which bore the little horn "was slain and his body was destroyed and given to the burning flame," which issued as a fiery stream from the presence of the Ancient of days who sat upon the throne of fiery flame. When, therefore, Paul depicts "the man of sin, the son of perdition," as the one who "opposeth and exalteth himself against all that is called God or that is worshipped, so that he sitteth in the temple of God, setting himself forth as God," "whose coming is according to the working of Satan with all power and signs and lying wonders, and with all deceit of unrighteousness for them that perish"; and when he also declares that "the Lord Jesus shall slay[2] him with the breath of his mouth and bring him to naught by the manifestation of his coming," it is very obvious that the whole description is modeled after the language of Daniel. With anyone thus familiar with the Hebrew prophets the language also of Isa. xi, 4, naturally comes to mind, where it is said that the Messianic offspring of David, on whom the Spirit of Jehovah rests, "shall smite the earth with the rod of his mouth, and with the breath of his lips shall he slay the wicked." The phrase *son of perdition* is applied to Judas Iscariot in John xvii, 12, and may denote anyone who is destined to destruction.

(4) *Other Peculiar Words and Phrases.* According to this epistle the day of the Lord is to be preceded by a notable "falling away," in verse 3 called definitely ἡ ἀποστασία, the apostasy. It is difficult here to think of any other falling away than that which is spoken of in 1 Tim. iv, 1, 2, as having been expressly witnessed by the prophetic Spirit and generally known in the apostolic days, "that in later times some shall fall away (ἀποστήσονται) from the faith, giving heed to seducing spirits and doctrines of demons, through the hypocrisy of men that speak lies." In 2 Tim. iii, 1-9, we read a similar description of "the last days." These prophecies of great apostasy are clearly in accord with the utterances of Jesus who declared very explicitly that, before the end of that age, "many false Christs and many false prophets should arise and lead many

---

[1] The words of 1 Macc. ii, 62, are ἀνὴρ ἁμαρτωλός. The common text of 2 Thess. ii, 3, reads ὁ ἄνθρωπος τῆς ἁμαρτίας, *the man of sin;* but Tischendorf, Tregelles, Westcott and Hort, following codices ℵ and B, read ἀνομίας in place of ἁμαρτίας, thus making it *the man of lawlessness.*

[2] This reading, ἀνελεῖ, *slay,* seems on the whole to be best supported, and agrees with the text of the Septuagint in Isa. xi, 4. But the other reading, ἀναλώσει, *shall consume,* is also well attested. The Aramaic of Dan. vii, 11, has the equivalent of both these words in saying that "the beast was *slain* and his body given to the *burning of fire.*"

astray, and because iniquity should be multiplied, the love of the many should wax cold" (Matt. xxiv, 5, 11, 12). As a matter of fact and of record such apostasy and all the forms of wickedness here specified did show themselves during the later days of that age whose decisive end was marked by the overthrow of Jerusalem and its Jewish cult and temple. But this great "falling away" seems to be closely connected in Paul's thought with what he calls, in verse 7, "the mystery of lawlessness," and which he says "is already in operation" (ἤδη ἐνεργεῖται). It is a mystery which is characterized by utter disrespect for law. Evidences of its operation in Thessalonica may be read in the record of Paul's treatment there (Acts xvii, 1-9). Jewish jealousy and fanaticism roused up the rabble and set the whole city in an uproar, thus exhibiting the spirit and the methods of the lawlessness (τῆς ἀνομίας). This spirit of lawlessness, especially among the Jews, met the apostle in all the world in which he traveled. It followed him from Thessalonica to Beræa, and drove him from that place. It opposed him with blasphemous raillery at Corinth (Acts xviii, 6), and finally secured his imprisonment at Jerusalem, and Cæsarea, and Rome. It is conceived as a "mystery," more deep and subtle than anything we call apostasy. Its nature was that of an evil leaven working in the hearts of men who make and speak lies. As "the mystery of godliness" (1 Tim. iii, 16) is revealed in the Christ of God, so the "mystery of lawlessness" is revealed in the Antichrist. But there is another word in this passage, so indefinite and uncertain, that no one is now able to explain it with any measure of assurance. The revelation of Antichrist and the day of the Lord are delayed by what is called in verse 6 τὸ κατέχον, and in verse 7 ὁ κατέχων. What is "that which restrains," and who is "he who restrains?" The true answer seems to have been part of a secret which the apostle imparted to the Thessalonians when he was yet with them, but of which we now have and can have no certain knowledge. It is an old and widespread opinion that τὸ κατέχον refers to the Roman empire, the instrument and representative of "the higher powers" (comp. Rom. iii, 1) ordained of God to maintain law and order among men; ὁ κατέχων would then refer to the emperor, who embodied in himself the civil power, and was God's minister to restrain outbreaks of lawlessness. Theodore of Mopsuestia and Theodoret explained "that which restrains" as the limiting decree involved in the statement of Matt. xxiv, 14, according to which the end could not come until the gospel had first been preached in all the world. It has also been argued that "the restrainer" was the Jewish state itself, whose continued existence opposed a strong check to the persecution of the Christians, and so enabled the gospel to obtain a sure foundation in the world.[1] In view of these different opinions and of the indefiniteness of the apostle's allusion, it seems presumptuous and futile to determine the exact meaning of the statement; but whoever the restrainer may have been, he was sooner or later to "be taken out of the way," and no revelation of Antichrist has followed the removal of the Roman empire or of any of its emperors which may not also be seen in "the working of Satan with all power and signs and lying wonders" which occurred before the overthrow of Jerusalem and the Jewish state.

(5) *Essential Content and Import of the Pauline Doctrine.* In attempting to state the essential meaning of a scripture like that of 2 Thess. ii, 1-12, we may distinguish between the writer's concept and construction of a current belief of his time and the deeper essential truth of the doctrine thus expressed. The leading thought running through this graphic picture of the man of sin was not original with Paul, and we have shown how largely the description is derived from the prophecies of Daniel. While thus appropriating much from common sources it is to be supposed that he would add some things of his own. But it is quite impossible for anyone now to know just how far Paul accepted without modification various current opinions of Jewish eschatology and demonology. His picture of Antichrist is that of a monster of impiety and lawlessness, but in the times of peril and great expectation in which his ministry fell, he may not always have analyzed and weighed the full import of his apocalyptic language. It may be that when he wrote these earlier epistles his thoughts found expression in terms with which he had been familiar in the Jewish synagogues and rabbinical schools, but which he gradually discarded. The picture of Antichrist here given is peculiar to this one epistle, and must be accepted as an individual construction of popular belief in the great enemy of God and his people. It is in its own way a part and parcel of the current Jewish demonology, and, if we accept it as a genuine composition of Paul, we should interpret it in the light of his other epistles and of the whole New Testament teaching on the same subject. We need not suppose Paul to have been ignorant of what Jesus said about the coming of false Christs and false prophets (Mark xiii, 22), and of Satan

---

[1] So B. B. Warfield, in The Expositor, 3rd Series, Vol. IV. London, 1886. Bengel observes: "The ancients thought that Claudius himself was the restrainer; so they supposed that Nero, Claudius' successor, was the man of sin."—Gnomon, in loco. Grotius, Le Clerc, Wetstein, Whitby, and others maintained a similar view, but they differed among themselves as to which emperor was the man of sin. J. S. Russell argues forcibly that Nero was the man of sin here described. See his The Parousia, pp. 179–189. London, 1887.

fallen as lightning from heaven (Luke x, 18). But the New Testament prophets and apostles, like those of more ancient time, did not always fully comprehend the time and manner of the things which the Spirit within them pointed out (1 Pet. i, 11). One notable thought common to all the biblical conceptions of Antichrist and of the end of the age is that "evil men and impostors shall wax worse and worse, deceiving and being deceived" (2 Tim. iii, 13), until the Lord God himself crush Satan under the feet of his saints (Rom. xvi, 20). And this seems to be the law of destiny for all impious men and systems whose existence hinders the progress of truth and righteousness. Even a heathen proverb says that "whom the gods would destroy they first make mad." So it was most conspicuously with that generation of the Jewish people from whom Paul experienced his fiercest opposition. They waxed worse and worse, furnished occasion for many false Christs and deceivers, and multiplied transgressions so that Josephus wrote of them that "no age ever bred a generation more fruitful in wickedness from the beginning of the world."[1] It would seem, therefore, that "the lawless one" described by Paul was a graphic impersonation of all the antichristian forces of his time coming to a head, reaching a climax of "all power and signs and lying wonders," and perishing before the manifestation of the Lord Jesus.

In speaking of such a crucial epoch as that of the signal fall of Judaism and the triumph of the new covenant of God in Christ, all the biblical writers make use of apocalyptic modes of thought and expression. We need not suppose that they knew the times, or the manner, or the details of those mighty events of which they spoke by the word of the Lord. But we have lived to see that the "revelation of the Lord Jesus from heaven" is a manifestation as continuous and enduring as his throne in the heavens, and that it has its seasons and epoch-making crises "which the Father hath set within his own authority" (Acts i, 7). The apostle uttered a fundamental and abiding truth when, in 2 Thess. i, 7, 8, he spoke of "the revelation of the Lord Jesus from heaven with the angels of his power in flaming fire, rendering vengeance to them that know not God, and to them that obey not the gospel of the Lord Jesus, who shall suffer punishment, even eternal destruction from the face of the Lord and from the glory of his might, when he shall come to be glorified in his saints." This is the same coming in power and in glory of which Jesus himself

---

[1] Wars of the Jews, book V, chap. x, 5. In chap. xiii, 6, of the same book he speaks of that last period of Jewish nationality as having "brought forth a generation of men much more atheistical than were those that suffered such punishments (as Sodom); for by their madness all the people came to be destroyed."

spoke in Matt. xvi, 27, 28. Such a coming of the Lord must needs slay the man of sin and bring his Satanic power to naught. But it was probably not given to Paul to comprehend the continuous comings and judgments of the Lord Jesus which were to fill millenniums of human history with revelations of his heavenly power. He seems not to have elaborated the world-historic import of his own statement in 1 Cor. xv, 25, that the Christ "must reign till he put all his enemies under his feet," but he could write in all confidence to his Christian brethren in Rome: "The God of peace shall bruise Satan under your feet shortly" (Rom. xvi, 20). In this confidence he was not mistaken or ever put to shame, for his prophetic eye saw the decisive beginning of what would require ages to consummate. The end of the old order and service, which for a thousand years had centered in the Jewish temple, was near at hand when the apostle wrote, and it marked the crisis of the ages; and a writer accustomed to thinking and speaking in terms of Jewish apocalyptics would naturally portray the coming both of Christ and of Antichrist in the language of current popular beliefs. The idea of a spectacular coming of Antichrist rests on the same literalistic exegesis as that of a spectacular coming of Christ in the visible physical heavens. A deeper insight into "the mystery of lawlessness" is obtained by giving more attention to what is in fact the real and essential nature of Satanic opposition to God. In other epistles Paul speaks of Satan as "the prince of the powers of the air, of the spirit that now worketh in the sons of disobedience" (Eph. ii, 2). He speaks of "the wiles of the devil," and admonishes us that "our wrestling is not against flesh and blood, but against the principalities, against the powers, against the world rulers of this darkness, against the spiritual hosts of wickedness in the heavenly places" (Eph. vi, 11, 12). Here is the concept of a prince of the demons, the great leader and inspirer of all that is antichristian. His hosts of wickedness operate in the invisible realms of the air; and are not to be opposed by weapons of the flesh (2 Cor. x, 4); for in his workings "with all deceit of unrighteousness" we are told that "even Satan fashioneth himself into an angel of light" (2 Cor. xi, 14). How he worked in the sons of disobedience and with signs and lying wonders is seen in the example of Elymas the sorcerer whom Paul addressed as "full of all guile and all villainy, thou son of the devil, thou enemy of all righteousness" (Acts xiii, 10). All such works of darkness, at all times and by whomsoever performed, are manifestly "according to the working of Satan, and with all deceit of unrighteousness for them that perish."

In Paul's doctrine of Antichrist we accordingly recognize a

graphic concept of the workings of Satan as they were to reveal themselves in the last days of the age and generation to which the apostle belonged. He conceived all the evils of those last days as summed up and impersonated in the great prince of the demons, and his description of the man of sin and son of perdition is his peculiar construction of the current Jewish demonology in its relation to the Antichrist.[1] But his language is appropriated mainly from Daniel, and his portraiture of "the lawless one" is to be understood and interpreted of the operations of Satan himself. The fundamental truth to be recognized in it all is the fact that the coming of Christ and the ultimate triumph of his kingdom are destined "to destroy the works of the devil."

18. The Antichrist of the Johannine Epistles. In the first and second epistles of John we meet what may be regarded as a later construction of the doctrine of Antichrist and a more general and spiritual conception of the operations of the evil one. The writer is an elder who feels that he is living in "the last hour," and that "the darkness is passing away, and the true light is already shining." He assumes it to be commonly understood that, when Antichrist comes, such fact is evidence of its being the last hour, and he affirms that "even now there have arisen many antichrists" (1 John ii, 18). He declares further on (ver. 22) that "he is the antichrist who denies the Father and the Son," and in iv, 3, he writes: "Every spirit that confesseth not[2] Jesus is not of God: and this is the spirit of antichrist, whereof ye have heard that it cometh; and now it is in the world already." In denying that Jesus is the Christ he makes himself emphatically the liar (ὁ ψεύστης), for he thereby openly falsifies the Messiahship of the

---

[1] How far the apostle Paul was familiar with the current literature of his time bearing on the doctrine of Antichrist is not apparent. One of the earliest post-apostolic descriptions of Antichrist, and one quite in harmony with Paul's picture of "the lawless one," may be read in the Teaching of the Twelve Apostles, chap. xvi. The following passage from the Sibylline oracles, book iii, lines 63–70, is worthy of note:

> From the Sebastenes Beliar shall come
> Hereafter, and shall make the hills stand high,
> And he shall also make the sea stand still,
> And the great fiery sun, and the bright moon;
> And he shall raise the dead, and many signs
> Perform for men; but nothing shall in him
> Be brought unto perfection but deceit,
> And many mortals shall he lead astray,
> Faithful and chosen Hebrews, and some others,
> Lawless men, such as never heed God's word.

The Sebastenes are perhaps most naturally understood as the people of Sebaste, or Samaria. A Jewish writer at the time of Christ might readily have conceived Beliar-Antichrist as a product of the hated and despised Samaritans. Others have understood the Sebastenes to be the race of Augustus Cæsar.

[2] A very remarkable ancient reading substitutes ὁ λύει, *who destroys*, or *does away with*, in place of ὁ μὴ ὁμολογεῖ, *who does not confess*. It is represented in the Latin version by *solvit*, and appears also in a number of the early patristic citations. See Westcott, Epistles of John, pp. 163–166.

Lord Jesus and the divinity of his person. In this statement the writer seems to be raising a note of warning against the Gnostic heresy which was then beginning to trouble the Church and to pervert the true doctrine of the relations of "the Father and the Son." In 2 John, 7, we find the language even more explicit: "Many deceivers are gone forth into the world, even they that confess not that Jesus Christ cometh in the flesh. This is the deceiver (ὁ πλάνος), and the Antichrist." That is, in the spirit and operations of the many deceivers who are abroad in the world, denying the truth of "God the Father, and of Jesus Christ, the Son of the Father" (vers. 3 and 9), we must recognize the arch-deceiver and the Antichrist. These antichrists are apostates from the Christian body, for "they went out from us, but they were not of us" (1 John ii, 19). Their apostasy made it manifest that they possessed not the Spirit of the Lord Jesus nor the love of God the Father. In all essentials, however, this general concept of the Antichrist is in thorough harmony with that of Paul in 2 Thess. ii, 1-12. According to both these views the revelation of Antichrist is preceded and accompanied by a great apostasy, and the spirit of Antichrist is the spirit of presumptuous opposition to Jesus Christ and to "all that is called God, or that is worshipped." All false teaching and deceptive prophesying is of the evil one, and every malicious and blasphemous enemy of the gospel of Jesus is an embodiment of the Antichrist. To the same effect we read in 2 Pet. ii, 1: "Among you also there shall be false teachers, who shall privily bring in destructive heresies, denying even the Master that bought them, bringing upon themselves swift destruction." This agrees also with what we have already cited from 1 Tim. iv, 1, 2, and Matt. xxiv, 5, 11, and with what is written in 2 Pet. iii, 3, and Jude 18. Wheresoever such a spirit of opposition to the truth of God prevails, there is the Antichrist.

19. General Conclusion. In all the scriptures bearing on this doctrine of Antichrist one may recognize a portraiture of Satan, the great enemy and opposer of God. He manifests his working and his spirit in manifold ways, and we are so advised of his wiles, and power, and signs, and lying wonders as not to be taken unawares in his crafty deceptions. According to our Lord's teaching in John viii, 14, "the devil was a murderer from the beginning, and standeth not in the truth, because there is no truth in him. When he speaketh a lie, he speaketh of his own; for he is a liar, and the father thereof." Here we have, in the style of the fourth gospel, a noteworthy statement of the whole New Testament doctrine of Antichrist. The various portraitures of the great adversary by the different biblical writers are to be studied as so many individual modes of conception peculiar to men of different mental characteristics, while amid sundry diversities of expression there is a common substance of doctrine. All these writers contemplate a great antagonist of God and his people. The conflict deepens in intensity at certain extraordinary crises of the ages; but, in the ultimate struggle, all antichristian evils must perish before the irresistible power of God. Most of these teachings are cast in apocalyptic form, and we may distinguish between the form and the essential truth within the form. When we have the picture of Michael and his angels at war with the dragon and his angels we observe at once the mythical character of the imagery, and two courses of inquiry open before us: one is to trace the origin of the imagery and compare its analogies in the various religious cults and literatures of the nations; another, and the one we are concerned with, is to seek the essential truth that is hidden under the pictorial forms of thought. Whether there be an actual host of personal spirits of wickedness, led on by a mighty prince of the demons; or whether these terms are to be explained as figurative but necessary modes of speech by means of which we express ideas of the terrible power of physical and moral evil in the world of men, may be left an open question. There can be no reasonable doubt that the biblical writers conceived and spoke of the devil and his angels as real beings, working in the sons of disobedience, and often possessing them and rushing them to their own destruction. Much of that which is written touching the Antichrist implies such a realistic view on the part of the writers. Each interpreter of the scripture must determine for himself this question of the invisible "principalities and powers." But of this much we may speak with the greatest assurance, and affirm as an unquestionable fact of the moral world that the good and the evil are mighty realities with men. Whatever their strongholds among invisible spirits in high positions or in low, they may well be conceived and spoken of as essentially antagonistic kingdoms, and as the kingdom and coming of Christ have been shown to be most glorious facts of revelation and experience, so, too, the oppositions of the kingdom of Satan are continuously showing their power "with all deceit of unrighteousness," and in manifold delusions of error. This is the great conflict of the ages, but, to use biblical terms of thought, the woman's seed shall bruise the old serpent's head, the God of peace shall bruise Satan under the feet of his saints, and in his own times the Lord Jesus shall slay and consume the lawless son of perdition, and bring him to naught by the manifestation of his presence.

CHAPTER III

CONTINUOUS DEVELOPMENT OF THE KINGDOM OF CHRIST

1. Christ to Overcome the World. Both the nature and the coming of the kingdom of Christ have further illustration in a study of those scriptures which relate to his spiritual conquest of the world. We are told in 1 Cor. xv, 25, that Christ "must reign till he hath put all his enemies under his feet," but this is simply a Pauline way of expressing the psalmist's ideal of the Messiah, who obtains from Jehovah the nations and the uttermost parts of the earth for his possession (Psa. ii, 8), and sits enthroned at his right hand until his enemies are made his footstool (cx, 1). From another point of view the workers and witnesses for Christ share in these Messianic triumphs. Paul spoke of himself and his Christian brethren as "God's fellow-workers" (1 Cor. iii, 9; comp. 2 Cor. vi, 1; Mark xvi, 20). According to 1 John v, 4, 5, the victory that overcomes the world is to be recognized as inherent in the faith that Jesus is the Son of God; for it is affirmed of every one who has this faith that "God abideth in him and he in God" (iv, 15). He suffers with Christ, and shares with him in the kingdom and the power and the glory. If any of these witnesses lay down their lives for the truth, they are caught up unto God and unto his throne. In such self-sacrifice, according to the apocalyptic mode of thought, "the salvation, and the power, and the kingdom of our God, and the authority of his Christ" are advanced and enhanced when his martyrs love not their lives even unto death, but overcome the evil one by reason of the blood of the Lamb and the word of their testimony (Rev. xii, 10, 11). Manifold, therefore, must be the aspects of the kingdom of Christ in connection with the innumerable agencies of its continuous spread and triumph in the world.

2. Old Testament Messianic Ideals. In order to obtain a full biblical conception of the heavenly kingdom we must revert again to the Old Testament Messianic hopes, and the suggestions they furnish touching the development and duration of the kingdom of the saints of the Most High. For every ideal of growth, prosperity, overthrow of hostile powers, diffusion of truth and peace and righteousness which is traceable in the various Messianic prophecies, may be brought forward to show what is contemplated in the coming of the kingdom of the Christ. Oracles already cited for other purposes must be again adduced to show that the kingdom foretold is no temporary display of power, but a dominion extending through a long period of growth and expansion.

(1) *Ancient Promises.* The ancient Abrahamic promises assure the patriarch that his seed shall become a great and mighty nation and be made a blessing to all the families of the earth (Gen. xii, 3; xviii, 18; xxii, 18). David is also assured that his house and throne and kingdom shall be established forever (2 Sam. vii, 16), and the Messianic psalms take up the thought and repeat it with poetic embellishment:

> Once have I sworn by my holiness;
> I will not lie unto David;
> His seed shall endure forever,
> And his throne as the sun before me.
> It shall be established forever as the moon,
> And as the faithful witness in the sky. Psa. lxxxix, 35-37.

(2) *Psalms cx and lxxii.* In Psa. cx the Messianic King sits at the right hand of Jehovah, judges among the nations, and overthrows all the hostile kings. The rod of his power moves forth out of Zion, and his people rally around him like young warriors, numerous as the dewdrops of the morning. He is also a priest like Melchizedek as well as king and conqueror. A similar ideal is also found in Psa. lxxii. The king executes the judgments of God, rules the people in righteousness, shows kindness to the poor, and breaks the cruel oppressor in pieces:

> He shall come down like rain upon the mown grass;
> As showers that water the earth.
> In his days shall the righteous flourish
> And abundance of peace, till the moon be no more.
> He shall have dominion also from sea to sea,
> And from the river unto the ends of the earth.

(3) *Isaiah ii, 2-4.* So far as these poetic ideals of the kingdom of the Messiah serve to indicate the extent and duration of that dominion, they point to a gradual growth that ultimately fills the habitable world. The same distinguishing feature appears in the triumphs of the Messianic time as portrayed in the prophets. The remarkable oracle of uncertain date, which is found in Isa. ii, 2-4, and Mic. iv, 1-4, may be shown to be a very truthful outline of the origin and progress of Christianity. Jerusalem was the conspicuous starting point of this new law and word of Jehovah. The gospel of the kingdom went forth out of Zion as a new revelation of the righteousness of God, but its spirit and power exalted Zion

into the higher conception of "the city of the living God, the heavenly Jerusalem" (comp. Heb. xii, 22). A going up to this mountain of Jehovah involves no pilgrimage to earthly heights like Zion and Gerizim, as the ignorant Samaritan might vainly imagine (John iv, 20-24), but simply a worshiping of the Father in spirit and in truth. No literal interpretation can be put upon the language which says that the temple mountain shall be elevated above all other hills, and that all the nations shall flow as a stream to that particular place, and that the peoples shall literally beat their swords into plowshares. But when we discern in this figure of supernatural elevation a symbol of "the general assembly and church of the firstborn who are enrolled in heaven, and Jesus the mediator of a new covenant" (Heb. xii, 23, 24), we recognize the whole passage as an ideal of the glorious Messianic era, when nations shall learn war no more, and every man shall dwell at peace with his neighbor. But all this implies a long period for its accomplishment, as is also the case with those other oracles of like significance written in Isa. lvi, 6-8; lx, 18-22; lxvi, 18; Zech. viii, 20-23.

(4) *Isaiah ix, 1-7, and xi, 1-10.* We derive the same necessary inference from the prophecy of the Messianic Child in Isa. ix, 1-7, who bears the wonderful name of manifold significance.[1] The dominion of this heir of David breaks the yoke and rod of the oppressor, puts an end to bloody wars, introduces peace and righteousness, and continues forever. The Christian expositor sees at once that all these ideals are notably fulfilled in the New Testament kingdom of Christ, when understood of the rule of Jesus in the hearts of men; and in the assurance that he must reign until all things are put in subjection under him. The same teaching is also apparent in the prophecy of Isa. xi, 1-10, which outlines the work and ultimate triumph of the Messianic Son of David. He is represented as a shoot from the stock of Jesse, endued with the wise and holy Spirit of Jehovah, a righteous and holy judge, who effects a universal peace as ideal as that of Eden. This peace is to be accompanied by a universal knowledge of Jehovah, filling the earth as the waters cover the sea, and all the nations shall seek his glorious rest. So, too, in Zech. ix, 9, 10, the king of Zion is portrayed as one who "shall speak peace unto the nations, and

---

[1] The critical reader may well study the series of symbolical names in Isa. vii, 2, 14; viii, 3; ix, 6: "*Shear-jashub, Immanuel, Maher-shalal-hash-baz*, and *Pele-yoets-el-gibbor-abi-ad-sar-shalom*. This last, a compound of four double names, is usually translated "Wonderful-Counsellor, Mighty-God, Father of eternity, Prince of Peace." But, except for its length, there appears no more reason for translating it than *Maher-shalal-hash-baz*. The whole section is a kind of Apocalypse of symbolic names. See Biblical Hermeneutics, pp. 331-334.

his dominion shall be from sea to sea, and from the river to the ends of the earth."[1] These are only a few out of many examples of the Old Testament Messianic hope, and they all point out an ideal of progress and conquest which in the nature of things requires long ages for complete accomplishment.

(5) *Daniel ii, 44, and vii, 13.* A few things in the book of Daniel, bearing on this point, demand our special attention. The kingdom which the God of heaven is to set up (ii, 44) is a power which shall break in pieces and consume the kingdoms of the world. It is like a stone cut out of the mountain by some unseen supernatural force, and it was seen to smite the colossal image and to become a great mountain and fill the whole earth (ver. 35). The same kingdom is represented in vii, 13, 14, 27, as a triumphing and everlasting dominion, to which all peoples and nations and languages shall be in subjection.

It would seem beyond controversy that all these Messianic prophecies contemplate a kingdom which in the nature of things must gradually acquire its universal dominion over all peoples. Its conquests are not the miraculous triumphs of an hour, a day, or a year of human reckoning: they imply a long period of development and progress. In the prophetic pictures of overwhelming disaster and ruin of the world-powers we are briefly shown in bold outline what must take ages of ages to fulfill. Reading these lively oracles in the light of the teaching of Jesus, we perceive that this Messianic kingdom is a supernatural power that works silently in the progress of human history. It aims first of all to subdue the hearts of men and bring men into subjection to the spirit of Christ. Thence it works outwardly upon society, operating as a holy leaven upon the entire mass of humanity till the whole is leavened by the potent elements of its great mystery of godliness. We are compelled, therefore, by all these facts, to conclude that the period of the kingdom of Christ began with his enthronement at the right hand of God, and with that consequent crisis of dispensations which was marked by the ruin of the Jewish temple and its cult. Then the word of the Lord went forth from Jerusalem as never before, proclaiming its heavenly ideals of a kingdom of righteousness, and peace, and joy in the Holy Spirit. Its future stretches onward indefinitely, and can be known to us only in the broad outline

---

[1] The suggestions of Zech. vi, 12, 13, are worthy of note: "The man whose name is Branch (comp. iii, 8, and Jer. xxiii, 5; xxxiii, 15; Isa. iv, 2) shall grow up and build the temple of Jehovah, and shall bear the glory, and shall sit and rule upon his throne, and he shall be a priest upon his throne, and the counsel of peace shall be between them both." Thus priest and king are conceived as united in one person, and no conflict between the two could then arise. And the ruling upon his throne and at the same time building the temple show that his period of dominion is to be of long duration and of manifold development.

suggested in the prophecies of its filling the earth and bringing all things in subjection to Christ.

3. Christ as Ruler and Judge. Other aspects both of the past and the future of this kingdom are to be seen when we consider the work of Christ as ruler and judge of mankind. In Rom. xiv, 10, Paul tells us that "we shall all stand before the judgment-seat of God"; but in 2 Cor. v, 10, he says: "We must all be made manifest before the judgment-seat of Christ; that each one may receive the things done in the body, according to what he hath done, whether it be good or bad." In his view, therefore, the judgment seat or tribunal (βῆμα) of God and Christ are the same. In John v, 22, we are told that the Father judgeth no man, but hath committed all judgment unto his Son, and this agrees with the statement in Acts xvii, 31: "He hath appointed a day in which he will judge the world in righteousness by the man whom he hath ordained (ὥρισεν, *set apart by decree*, Psa. ii, 7); whereof he hath given assurance to all men, in that he hath raised him from the dead." We have already had occasion to point out that, according to the Old Testament, the execution of judgment is a conspicuous prerogative of the supreme Ruler of the world. We have also pointed out the poetic and apocalyptic forms in which his days of judgment are described (see pp. 426, 427), and the Messianic passages in which the Anointed of Jehovah is conceived as an associate judge with the Most High and engaged with him in executing judgments in the earth. God is therefore not to be thought of as abdicating his throne when the Messiah sat down at his right hand; nor are we to think of "the day of Jehovah," or the day of judgment, as one definite moment, hour, or day, fixed at the end of all human history. We miss the true scriptural doctrine of *judgment* (משפט, κρίσις) when we limit it to such a single point of time. The day of judgment is always the day on which the penal execution occurs. This is true alike of nations, communities, and individuals. There is no ground for the supposition that the methods of executing judgment during the reign of Christ are at all different from those of Jehovah as described by the prophets. The very phrase *judgment-seat of Christ* is essentially a metaphor.[1] So far, therefore, as the present and future government of the world is under the control of the supreme Judge, God the Almighty and his Christ are one. Jehovah has enthroned his anointed Son upon his holy hill of Zion, and all men must honor the Son even as they honor the Father (John v, 23).

---

[1] See Biblical Apocalyptics, p. 80.

4. Days of Judgment. This execution of judgment, like the mediation of the Son of man, is accordingly to be understood as a continual process. But there are exceptional days of judgment. As in the older scriptures we read of "the day of Jezreel" (Hos. i, 11), and "the day of Midian" (Isa. ix, 4), and "the day of Jerusalem" (Psa. cxxxvii, 7), so we understand that the great and terrible day of the Lord came upon Jerusalem, which killed the prophets and stoned them that were sent unto her, at that bitter hour when her holy house was left unto her desolate (Matt. xxiii, 37, 38). That crisis may be recognized as the first signal act of judgment under the reign of the Lord Christ, and it marked, as we have seen, the decisive end of the pre-Messianic age.

5. The Judgment in Matthew xxv, 31-46. The continuous administration of the Son of man as judge of all men and nations is pictured in strong parabolic outline in Matt. xxv, 31-46. The whole chapter is peculiar to Matthew and profoundly suggestive touching matters of final judgment. The parable of the virgins, in verses 1-13, emphasizes the importance of constant watchfulness. The parable of the talents advances to the thought that the coming of the Lord may be long delayed, and that every good and faithful servant should be working for the interests of his master in his absence as well as in his presence. But the third lesson, which combines the symbolic form of apocalypse and the simplicity of parable, enhances the solemnity of the judgment and of Christ's rendering to every man according to his works. He will separate the righteous from the wicked. He discerns the thoughts of the heart, and knows the springs, and motives, and principles of all human action. No man can conceal anything from his penetrating glance. He will expose every refuge of lies, so that no sinner can escape conviction before his tribunal. And this process of divine judgment is ever going on and must continue so long as the heavenly Ruler and Judge sits upon his throne.

6. Times and Modes of Judgment Not Specifically Revealed. It appears also, that the judgment of Christ takes cognizance of individuals, and renders to every man "according to what he hath done, whether it be good or bad" (2 Cor. v, 10). But when and how this judgment is to be executed in each particular case no one may presume to say. The times and seasons and modes of retribution and reward are not for us to know. It would be foolish and futile to say in advance just when, where, and how "he who sows unto his own flesh shall of the flesh reap corruption." But many things come to judgment in ways that may be recognized by men at once. We are told in 1 Tim. v, 24, 25, that "some men's sins are openly manifest, going before into judgment; but some also they follow after. In like manner also the good works are openly manifest; and those which are otherwise cannot be hidden." That is, some men's sins are so open to the eyes of their contemporaries that a righteous judgment of condemnation is immediately passed upon them, and so they really go into judgment before any formal or final sentence is pronounced upon the sinner himself. His sins precede him into the judgment. They plainly show beforehand what the ultimate judgment upon their author must be. But with other men the case is quite different. Their sins become evident only upon competent trial and conviction, and so come to light afterwards. This is true of the good works of men as well as of the evil. Some are made conspicuous beforehand, while others are not brought into the light until the day disclose them (comp. 1 Cor. iii, 13). But we should note in all this work of judgment that the day and the hour of final disclosure are not the same with every man. It is not said that we must all appear at one and the same moment before the judgment seat of Christ. But this is the essential doctrine: "There is nothing hid save that it should be manifested; neither was it made secret, but that it should come into manifestation" (Mark iv, 22). Just when, where, and how this final manifestation and judgment will take place with each individual is not for us to know.

7. Eternal Issues of the Judgment. The epistle to the Hebrews (vi, 2) places the doctrine of "eternal judgment" among the first principles of Christian truth, and the final issues of the judgment depicted in Matt. xxv, 31-46, assign the wicked to eternal punishment and the righteous to eternal life. We must accordingly include in the biblical doctrine of eternal judgment the final issues both of retribution for sin and of recompense for righteousness, and these results of "the things done in the body" appear in the state of existence in which each one will find himself after he has put off the body of mortal flesh. And so it is written: "As it is appointed unto men once to die, and after this judgment; so also the Christ, having been once offered to bear the sins of many, shall appear a second time, apart from sin, to them that wait for him unto salvation" (Heb. ix, 27, 28). This second appearing of Christ, apart from sin, to them that wait for him unto salvation, as well as the judgment here spoken of, is something to come to each man after death. The great unseen hereafter presents to the wilful sinner "a certain fearful expectation of judgment, and a fierceness of fire which shall devour the adversaries" (Heb. x, 27); but for all who live and die in the true faith of God there is the promise of a heavenly country, a blessed fatherland ($\pi\alpha\tau\rho\iota\varsigma$), an abiding city, which has the foundations, whose builder and maker is God (Heb. xi, 10, 16; xiii, 14). This homeland and heavenly city is no other than the Father's house of many abiding places, of which Jesus spoke assuringly to his disciples (John xiv, 2). Nor need we doubt that "the city which has the foundations" is the holy Jerusalem apocalyptically portrayed in Rev. xxi, 10-27. Into the fellowships of this heavenly Jerusalem the pure in heart now come (Heb. xii, 22), but, as elsewhere shown, they never die, but exchange mortality for life, eternal in the heavens.

8. Judgment of God and of Christ One. And thus we perceive that the judgment seat of God and the judgment seat of Christ are the same, and that the future of the kingdom of Christ must needs be a process of divine judgment and rule, in no essential element different from the dominion of the Most High as depicted in the Old Testament. If it be said that this doctrine makes Christ's kingdom the same as God's "general government of the world," it is well to answer that God knows no general government of the world which is essentially different from his particular government. The great distinguishing fact in the kingdom of Christ is that it is a new dispensation of the Father Almighty, in which new truths and new responsibilities are brought to bear on human life. God rules and judges as really after having committed all judgment unto the Son as he did before. He is never absent from the throne of the universe, and from the beginning God is in Christ reconciling the world unto himself. The distinguishing feature of this dispensation of the mystery of the ages (comp. Eph. iii, 8, 9; Col. i, 26; Rom. xvi, 25) is the fuller and more specific revelation of heavenly things which it opened to the world. God overlooked the former times of ignorance, but now requires repentance everywhere, "inasmuch as he hath appointed a day in which he will judge the world in righteousness by the man he hath ordained; whereof he hath given assurance unto all men in that he hath raised him from the dead" (Acts xvii, 30, 31). Such a revelation of God in Christ opens a new era in the history of mankind, and imposes its heavier obligations. "A man who set at naught the law of Moses died, without compassion, on the word of two or three witnesses: of how much sorer punishment shall he be judged worthy who has trodden under foot the Son of God?" (Heb. x, 28, 29; comp. xii, 25; Matt. x, 15; xi, 20-24; xii, 41, 42).

9. A New Power in the World. We are, accordingly, to understand that the kingdom of Christ is a new heavenly power introduced into the governing forces of this world. It is not of the world, but it aims to subjugate the world to the truth. The Lord Jesus Christ is exalted to the right hand of the throne of God as the supreme judge and ruler of the world, and as prophet, priest, and king he must needs exercise his power in accordance with the nature of his kingdom. It has pleased the Almighty Father that all the fullness necessary to his world-wide mission should dwell in the Son of his love (Col. i, 19), and according to John's gospel (v, 19-27) the Father has given the Son power to make alive whom he will, and authority to execute judgment because he is Son of man; and so all men should honor the Son even as they honor the Father. We must, therefore, keep constantly in mind that in all his work of revelation, mediation, salvation, and dominion the Christ of God represents no separate or independent power. Rather, as he himself affirms (John x, 30), "I and my Father are one."

10. Its Period One of Untold Ages and Generations. It is thus in a broad and truly scriptural way of thinking that we conceive the continuous development and advance of the kingdom of Christ in the world. Its period of development is one of untold ages and generations. Through all the passing centuries, and probably for many millenniums of human history yet to come, this King of glory sits upon his throne, directing and overruling all. He has come to execute judgment many times since he ascended to the glory of the Father. And he has appeared in glorious revelations of heavenly life to millions of his saints at the hour of their departure from this world. Thus in a very true and holy sense were they caught away to a meeting of the Lord in the air. Such a departing to be with Christ is not to be deemed incompatible with the Lord's coming to receive them unto himself. And this glorious process is continually going on, and has been since the time when Stephen saw the heavens opened, and beheld the glory of God, and the Son of man standing at the right hand of God.[1] We should not suppose that the exit from the world of the Lazarus who was carried by the angels into Abraham's bosom (Luke xvi, 22) was essentially different from that of every other child of God who departs this mortal life in the faith of Jesus. It is equally proper for us to think of angels coming in like manner and gathering to the heavenly home all those who are counted worthy to obtain that world; and in no case are we to suppose that such ministering spirits are sent forth without the Lord. He who was with the disciples always, even to the consummation of the age (Matt. xxviii, 20), and who is present wherever two or three are gathered together in his name (Matt. xviii, 20), is competent to be in like manner with every angel that ministers to such as shall

---

[1] Comp. Biblical Apocalyptics, p. 481.

inherit salvation. In every event of the departure from this life of those whose names are written in heaven, "the Lord Jesus is revealed from heaven with the angels of his power to be glorified in his saints, and to be marvelled at in all them that believed in that day" (2 Thess. i, 7-10). Thus is he continually coming to verify the promise of John xiv, 3, and to receive unto himself and glorify the devout Stephens and Pauls who long for that heavenly manifestation as their most blessed hope. Blessed is that disciple who is thus ready to depart and to be with Christ; for he can say in fervor of spirit: "Henceforth there is laid up for me the crown of righteousness which the righteous judge shall give me at that day" (2 Tim. iv, 8). *That day* is the day or time of his departure (ver. 6). For why should we commit this scripture to the notion that even now, after nearly two thousand years, Paul is still waiting and longing for the crown of righteousness!

11. Regeneration and Restitution of All Things. This incalculable period of Christ's dominion over the world is requisite for the regeneration and restitution of all things. In Acts iii, 21, we read of the "times of restoration of all things, of which God spoke by the mouth of his holy prophets from of old." This word *restoration* (ἀποκατάστασις, *restitution, reconstruction*) seems to point to the rectifying of all that has gone wrong in the world, and the ultimate abolishing of all rule and authority and power that oppose the progress of the kingdom of God. In Matt. xix, 28, we read of "the regeneration, when the Son of man shall sit on the throne of his glory." The word *regeneration* (ἡ παλιγγενεσία) fitly points out the spiritual character of Christ's rule in the world, and suggests the unseen forces which he employs in executing the saving work of the gospel of his kingdom. The period of this regeneration is coëxtensive with the Messianic era, and must continue as long as the Son of man sits upon the throne of his glory; but "the times of restoration of all things" suggests rather the idea of a finished work, when the Lord shall have put all his enemies under his feet (comp. 1 Cor. xv, 25). The times are those of an indefinite future when Israel's highest hopes are to be realized. The restoration of the kingdom to Israel, referred to in Acts i, 6, entered into the Messianic hope of the disciples. The expectation that in some way Elijah must first come and restore all things is witnessed in Matt. xvii, 11, and Mark ix, 12. This expectation appears to have been based upon the prophecy of Mal. iv, 6, and it should be noted that our Lord assured his disciples that Elijah had already come, and that they understood him to refer to John the Baptist (Matt. xvii, 12, 13). We find no detailed exposition of what the biblical writers understood by these allusions to a "restoration of all things," but, in general, we may well believe that they included all that was ever contemplated by the Old Testament prophets as destined to result from the coming of the Messiah in the world. His kingdom would sooner or later put an end to the evils introduced by sin, and restore the world to a state of universal peace and happiness somewhat like that blissful ideal which the traditions of Eden and Paradise suggested. Some such ideal may be inferred from what Paul writes about "the earnest expectation of the creation waiting for the revealing of the sons of God," and his hope that "the creation itself shall be delivered from the bondage of corruption into the liberty of the glory of the children of God" (Rom. viii, 19-21). Both "the regeneration" and "the restoration of all things" imply some such glorious future, but its times and seasons of accomplishment are not made known to us. Such regeneration and restoration of the world are not the work of a day or a year. But the ages of ages belong to Him at whose right hand the Son of man is seated, and in his own times and ways the Christ of God shall receive "the nations for an inheritance and the uttermost parts of the earth for a possession."[1]

12. Paul's Statement in First Corinthians xv, 24-28. It remains to add here the statements of Paul in 1 Cor. xv, 24-28, that there will come an end of the redemptive ministry of the Son of God, "when he shall deliver up the kingdom to the God and Father; when he shall have abolished all rule and all authority and power. . . . And then shall the Son himself be subjected to him that did subject all things unto him, that God may be all in all." This terminus ($\tau\grave{o}$ $\tau\acute{\epsilon}\lambda o\varsigma$) seems to imply the ultimate completion of the entire work of Christ's mediation, including the resurrection and the putting of all things in subjection, even the abolition of death. But that final issue is far away in the future times eternal, and it is not now manifest to us what its full significance shall be.

---

[1] Comp. Biblical Apocalyptics, p. 481.

CHAPTER IV

THE MISSION AND MINISTRY OF THE SPIRIT OF CHRIST

1. Vital Relation of the Kingdom of Christ and the Ministry of His Spirit. The biblical doctrine of the Holy Spirit furnishes additional light upon the mediation, the kingdom, and the coming of Christ. According to John's gospel the departure of Jesus from the world was expedient both for the highest good of the disciples and for the coming of the kingdom of God. The Lord Jesus must needs go away from the gaze of fleshly eyes in order that he might come again in the more heavenly glory of a living spiritual presence, and abide permanently with his disciples and with all those who should believe on him through his word. Herein we may see how the fourth gospel supplements the synoptics in a more spiritual disclosure of the kingdom of the truth and of the presence of the King invisible. The withdrawal of Jesus from the sight of men and his spiritual coming again in ways unseen by mortal eyes are to be understood as an essential part of the manner in which the Son of man was to be glorified. And so the doctrine of the Holy Spirit is essential to a complete presentation of the New Testament teaching concerning the parousia, the coming and dominion of the Christ of God.

2. The Spirit Operative Before End of Age. The true doctrine of the Holy Spirit will serve to obviate difficulties which some have felt in determining the exact date of the beginning of the gospel-dispensation. We have seen that so far as any traditional sayings of Jesus set a time limit to the pre-Messianic age and the coming of the Son of man in his power and glory, the end of that age was to be reached before the generation then living should pass away, and it was specifically connected with the overthrow of the Jewish temple. That significant event marked a crisis of the ages, a decisive turning point between the old and the new; but, as a matter of fact, the spirit of the new age became very powerful in the world sometime before that fearful day of judgment on the Jewish nation. It is also a fact that the spirit of the old age lingered as a shadow over many hearts long after that decisive event. There was no such clash between the dispensations of Sinai and Zion that the whole wide world must needs pause and say, Lo, there! Before the crisis it was richly given to the disciples of our Lord to be made partakers of the Holy Spirit, to taste of the heavenly gift of saving grace and "the powers of the age to come" (Heb. vi, 4, 5). The coming and kingdom of Christ may have epochal times and seasons, but it is so spiritual and heavenly in its real nature that it may also transcend limitations of time and place. By duly observing different points of view and the manner of expression peculiar to different writers, we shall come to see that such a statement as John vii, 39, "The Spirit was not yet," does not mean that the Holy Spirit was not in the world and active in human hearts before the glorification of Christ. It was the Holy Spirit that spoke through the prophets and psalmists of Israel, and according to Gen. i, 2, the Spirit of God was distinctly active in the very beginning of the creation of the world.

3. Meaning of the Word "Spirit." The Scriptures furnish us no definition of the word *spirit*. The Hebrew רוּחַ and the Greek πνεῦμα have the same meaning, usage, and connotation as the Latin *spiritus* which has become familiarly Anglicized, and is employed in the same variety of significations, namely, *breath, wind, courage, disposition, temper,* vital principle which animates all sentient life, and especially, in the highest sense, that rational element, or entity in man in which we find the constituent powers of feeling, thinking, and volition. These powers we have already seen to be essential elements of human personality. We have also seen that the words *spirit* and *soul,* when referring to man, are often used interchangeably (pp. 52, 53), but the word *soul* is used in the Old Testament rarely (*e.g.,* Judg. x, 16; Jer. xiv, 19; xv, 1; li, 14; Amos vi, 8), and never in the New in reference to God. In a general way we may understand the word *spirit* to mean the same when applied to God as when applied to man. In man it is that center and substance of his higher nature which is distinguished from his bodily form. We think and speak of God, however, as altogether spirit. "God is Spirit" (John iv, 24). Spirit constitutes, so to speak, the characteristic element and totality of his nature.

4. Threefold Elements of Personality. But in the unity of this divine spiritual nature as in that of man we may naturally look for the same trinal constituents of personality, Will, Feeling, and Intelligence. We have been told again and again that man exists as the image and glory of God (comp. Gen. i, 26; 1 Cor. xi, 7), and we may therefore appropriately inquire whether at least some essential elements of this image of God be not the trinal spiritual unity of personal thought, desire, and will. The trinitarian formula, in 2 Cor. xiii, 14, of "the grace of the Lord Jesus Christ, and the love of God, and the communion of the Holy Spirit," recognizes a distinction of the Holy Spirit from God and from Christ. The same distinction is expressed in "the name of the Father and of the Son and of the Holy Spirit" in Matt. xxviii, 19. A like trinitarian distinction appears in the impressive salutation of Rev. i, 4, 5: "Grace and peace (1) from him who is and who was and who is to come; and (2) from the seven Spirits before his throne; and (3) from Jesus Christ." And while each of these hallowed names is again and again mentioned in the New Testament as the source, power, and means of all heavenly help, it is also noticeable that at times the Father is spoken of as distinctively the source *from whom* (ἐξ οὗ), and the Son as the one *through* (διά) whom, and the Holy Spirit as the one *in* (ἐν) whom or by whose efficient agency all things are.[1] We have seen that "God was in Christ reconciling the world unto himself," and "in him dwelleth all the fulness of the Godhead bodily." Conceived as the Logos or Word of God, he is the wisdom of God, the thought, reason, intelligence of the divine Personality, and in his manifestation through incarnation he reveals at once the glory of heavenly wisdom, love, and power. But as all the fullness of Deity found bodily expression *through him,* and yet he was distinctively the Logos, so in the Father dwelleth all the fullness of the Godhead potentially and actively, and all things are accordingly *from him;* while in the Holy Spirit dwelleth all the fullness of the Godhead efficiently. All the fullness of the Deity becomes operative and personally present in the world and in the heart of man by the power of the Holy Spirit. In him we live and move and have our being. It is therefore natural and proper that God and the Holy Spirit of God should be often spoken of in the Scriptures as one. If in the deepest and truest sense God is a Spirit, the Spirit of God and God himself must needs be one. Whatever mysterious distinctions, therefore, exist in the personal nature of the Godhead, we recognize the Holy Spirit as essentially identical with God. We are not to think of this eternal Spirit as merely an influence, an energy, or an impersonal emanation flowing out from God, but rather as God himself, the personal, creative, sustaining, ever-present Spirit. The Spirit of God is described in Gen. i, 2, as "brooding upon the face of the waters," and thus acting as the all-pervading Generatrix of the swarms of living creatures which come forth (comp. ver. 20) from the waters by the Word of God. The Hebrew poets conceive the heavens as made and garnished by

---

[1] Comp. 1 Cor. viii, 6; xi, 12; xii, 3; Rom. vi, 23; xv, 16; xvi, 27; 1 Thess. i, 5. "In every work effected by Father, Son, and Holy Ghost in common, the power *to bring forth* proceeds from the Father; the power *to arrange* from the Son; the power *to perfect* from the Holy Spirit."—Kuyper: The Work of the Holy Spirit, p. 19. New York, 1900.

the Spirit as truly as by the Word of God (Psa. xxxiii, 6; civ, 30; Job xxvi, 13; xxxiii, 4). When the psalmist says, "Whither shall I go from thy Spirit, or whither shall I flee from thy presence?" (cxxxix, 7) he thinks of the Spirit of God as identical with his personal presence. The prophets also conceive the Spirit of Jehovah to be the same as Jehovah himself (Isa. xl, 13; xlviii, 16; lxi, 1; lxiii, 10; Ezek. xi, 5; Zech. iv, 6; vii, 12).

5. Epithets Applied to the Spirit of God. The epithets which are applied to the Spirit of God in the Old Testament are those which involve the essential qualities of the divine nature. Three passages make use of the expressive term *thy* (or *his*) *Holy Spirit* (Psa. li, 11; Isa. lxiii, 10, 11), and we cannot suppose that this Holy Spirit is any other than "the Holy One of Israel." In Isa. xi, 2, where "the Spirit of Jehovah," which is to rest upon the Messianic Branch out of the roots of Jesse, is foretold, that Spirit is defined as "a spirit of wisdom and understanding, a spirit of counsel and might, a spirit of knowledge and reverence of Jehovah." Here the Spirit of God is contemplated as a communicated gift, but the qualities specified are essential attributes of the Holy One himself. This same Holy Spirit was imparted to the prophets and psalmists in order to qualify them to utter the messages of God (Mic. iii, 8; Isa. li, 1; Ezek. ii, 2; iii, 24; xi, 5; xxxvii, 1; 2 Sam. xxiii, 2; Neh. ix, 20, 30; comp. 1 Pet. i, 11; 2 Pet. i, 21), and such inspiration was effected by the personal presence and inworking of God himself. The same is true of Moses's remarkable prayer in Num. xi, 29: "Would God that all Jehovah's people were prophets, that Jehovah would put his Spirit upon them!" In all these and similar scriptures there is no essential distinction to be made between God and his Spirit. He is himself in every case the Spirit.

6. The Spirit Capable of Grief. The idea of grieving his Holy Spirit, expressed in Isa. lxiii, 10, suggests that so far as we may attempt distinguishing the Holy Spirit from God himself the Spirit represents the affectional or emotional nature of God, the feeling as distinct from intellect and will. It is this element of the human personality that is specifically the subject of passion; and the admonition, "Grieve not the Holy Spirit of God" (Eph. iv, 30), has the same significance in the Old Testament as in the New. Grieving or in any way disturbing the spirit of a man (or the heart of a man) is affecting the emotional nature of the man himself. So the rebellious people of God "grieved, tempted, and provoked the Holy One of Israel" (Psa. lxxviii, 40, 41). This divine emotion is expressed in such sayings as "it repented Jehovah that he had made man on the earth, and it grieved him at his heart"

(Gen. vi, 6; comp. Exod. xxxii, 14; Judg. ii, 18; 1 Sam. xv, 11; Jer. xxvi, 19, etc.). These anthropopathic forms of speech, which have given offence to superficial readers, show that in the personality of God as of man the capacity for emotion is an essential element. And so in the broadest and deepest sense it may be affirmed that as no man knoweth the things of a man save the spirit of the man which is in him, even so none knoweth the things of God save the Spirit of God (1 Cor. ii, 11). And in all these ways we recognize in the Old Testament as in the New that the Spirit of God and God himself are essentially one.

7. Advance in the New Testament Doctrine. But we find in the New Testament a more specific doctrine of the work of the Holy Spirit than is anywhere apparent in the Hebrew scriptures. The phrases *God's Spirit, the Spirit of God,* and *the Holy Spirit of God* are no doubt to be understood in the New Testament in the same way as "the Spirit of God" in the Old, and the classic text in John iv, 24, "God is a Spirit," confirms what we have already sufficiently shown, that God and his Spirit are one and the same divine Being. Those New Testament texts also, which refer to the personal inspiration of the Old Testament writers (*e.g.,* Mark xii, 36; Acts i, 16; xxviii, 25; Heb. iii, 7; x, 15), recognize the Holy Spirit as in some sense the author of those scriptures, and hence every sacred scripture is appropriately said to be "God-breathed" ($\theta\epsilon\acute{o}\pi\nu\epsilon\nu\sigma\tau o\varsigma$). But we shall see, as we proceed, that the same divine inbreathing of the Spirit of God is through the mediation of Jesus and along with his heavenly glorification imparted as a blessed gift to every member of the body of Christ. "To each one is given the manifestation of the Spirit to profit withal" (1 Cor. xii, 6, 7).

8. Christ and the Holy Spirit. We notice first those passages which speak of the Holy Spirit in connection with the life and work of Jesus. According to Matt. i, 20, the child Jesus was begotten of the Holy Spirit in the womb of the virgin Mary. This great mystery is thus explained to Mary in Luke i, 35: "The Holy Spirit shall come upon thee, and the power of the Most High shall overshadow thee: wherefore also the holy thing which is begotten shall be called the Son of God." In these words, which readily fall into the form of Hebrew parallelisms, "the Holy Spirit" in the first clause is equivalent to "the power of the Most High" in the second, and that which is begotten is "God's Son." The Holy Spirit, the power of the Most High, and God himself are essentially one. All the four gospels mention the descent of the Spirit of God upon Jesus at the time of his baptism, and all declare that the Spirit descended in the form of a dove. Immediately afterward he was impelled or "led up by the Spirit into the wilderness to be tempted of the devil" (Matt. iv, 1; comp. Mark i, 12; Luke iv, 1). According to Luke (iv, 14) he returned after the temptation "in the power of the Spirit into Galilee," and in Matt. xii, 28, he assumes to cast out demons by the Spirit of God. In Peter's discourse before Cornelius (Acts x, 38) he speaks of "Jesus of Nazareth, how God anointed him with the Holy Spirit and with power: who went about doing good, and healing all that were oppressed of the devil, for God was with him." In Heb. ix, 14, it is said that he "through the eternal Spirit offered himself without spot unto God," and Peter declares that "being by the right hand of God exalted, and having received of the Father the promise of the Holy Spirit, he poured forth" the Holy Spirit upon the disciples on the day of Pentecost (Acts ii, 33). In connection with this outpouring of the Spirit, as an effect of Christ's ascension to the Father, we may also cite Paul's idea of his ascending on high, leading captivity captive, and bestowing gifts on men, giving some to be apostles, and some prophets, and some pastors and teachers (Eph. iv, 7-11). From his birth until his ascension into the heavens Jesus was vitally connected with the Holy Spirit of God. He was conceived by the Spirit, baptized and anointed by the Spirit, filled with the Spirit, wrought miracles by the Spirit, offered himself through the Spirit, and after his ascension received and shed forth the Spirit of God upon his worshipers.

9. The Johannine Teaching. But aside from this relation of the Holy Spirit to the personal manifestation of Christ in his incarnation, we should devote special attention to the doctrine of the Spirit as it appears in the gospel of John. Here we find the dispensational aspects of the Spirit's ministry more definitely set forth, and here we meet the title of Paraclete, or Comforter, and most important revelations touching the nature of his work. At the close of Luke's gospel and at the beginning of the Acts of the apostles we read the command of Jesus for the disciples to tarry in Jerusalem until "clothed with power from on high" (Luke xxiv, 49). This power from above is called "the promise of the Father," and is the same as baptism in the Holy Spirit (Acts i, 4, 5, 8). But in the fourth gospel Jesus says to his disciples: "It is expedient for you that I go away; for if I go not away, the Comforter (ὁ παράκλητος) will not come unto you; but if I go, I will send him unto you" (John xvi, 7). In another place (xv, 26) he says: "When the Comforter is come, whom I will send unto you from the Father, even the Spirit of truth that proceedeth from the Father, he shall bear witness of me." In 1 John ii, 1, Jesus is himself called "a Comforter (or Advocate) with the

Father," and this fact adds force to the words of Jesus in John xiv, 16-20: "I will pray the Father, and he shall give you another Comforter, that he may be with you forever, even the Spirit of truth: whom the world cannot receive; for it beholdeth him not, neither knoweth him: ye know him; for he abideth with you and shall be in you. I will not leave you desolate (like orphans): I will come unto you. Yet a little while, and the world beholdeth me no more; but ye behold me: because I live, ye shall live also. In that day ye shall know that I am in my Father, and ye in me, and I in you." There can be no reasonable misapprehension of the main import of these words. The continued visible presence of Jesus Christ in the flesh was not for the highest good of the disciples. It was for their advantage, and for the consummation of the highest purposes of divine Love, that Jesus disappear from the gaze of the world. The spiritual and eternal things of God are not seen (comp. 2 Cor. iv, 18). The Holy Spirit of God, the Spirit of truth, is not a being whom the world can behold. Jesus must therefore go away into the holy heavens unto the Father (xiv, 12, 28; xvi, 28; xvii, 11), in order that the Spirit of truth, the Paraclete, the Comforter, the Helper, the Advocate, may come to the disciples and to all those who should afterward believe on Christ through their word.

10. Procession and Personality. Two things first of all deserve attention in these declarations of Jesus concerning the Paraclete. (1) "He proceedeth from (ἐκπορεύεται, *goeth forth from*) the Father" (xv, 26). He is given, or sent by the Father at the prayer and in the name of Jesus (xiv, 16, 26), and yet Jesus also says: "I will send him" (xv, 26; xvi, 7). Thus going forth from the Father and being sent by the Son, this Spirit of truth may be properly called both "the Spirit of God" and "the Spirit of Christ" (comp. Rom. viii, 9; Gal. iv, 6; Phil. i, 19; Acts xvi, 7; 1 Pet. i, 11). In 2 Cor. iii, 17, 18, the Lord Christ is himself called the Spirit. So in the mystic and mysterious relations of the Godhead the Father, the Son, and the Holy Spirit are conceived as essentially one God. The Son, however, is conceived as begotten of the Father, and the Spirit proceedeth from the Father, and Son and Spirit are alike sent by God, and the Spirit is sent both by the Father and the Son. (2) Another thing to notice in these scriptures is the direct personality attributed to each of these divine names. Not only have we the masculine ὁ παράκλητος, but the masculine demonstrative ἐκεῖνος is repeatedly employed when this Holy Spirit of truth is referred to. Personal acts are thus ascribed to him: "he shall teach"; "he shall bring to remembrance"; "he shall bear witness"; "he shall guide unto all the truth." These and other like references, to be noticed more fully in another connection, cannot be fairly explained by the figure of personification, for they essentially involve personal acts of God himself.[1]

11. The Power of the Spirit After the Glorification of Jesus. The glorification of Jesus, according to John's gospel, was accomplished when he went away from the world and ascended unto the Father. In the great intercession recorded in John xvii, Jesus prays for the heavenly glorification: "Father, glorify me with thine own self with the glory which I had with thee before the world was." Many other scriptures witness also that he attained the throne of his glory when he ascended on high and poured forth the gifts of the Spirit (Acts ii, 33; Rom. i, 4; Eph. iv, 8). In the light of all these facts we can the better understand the statement of John vii, 39: "The Spirit was not yet; because Jesus was not yet glorified." That is, the Holy Spirit was not yet given as the gospel Comforter and guide. Before Jesus could send the Comforter for his greater ministrations of causing the "rivers of living water" to flow within the souls of Christian believers (vii, 38), he must first lay down his life, and take it again, and ascend unto the Father. The Spirit, accordingly, has his own times and seasons of special manifestation, and in the order of ages and dispensations there was to be a definite fullness of times for an epoch-marking gift of the Holy Spirit of God. That day of the coming of the Spirit as "the promise of the Father" was witnessed at the Pentecost, when the disciples "were all filled with the Holy Spirit, and began to speak with other tongues, as the Spirit gave them utterance" (Acts ii, 1, 4). Why Jesus should remain forty days on earth after his resurrection, why ten days should pass after the ascension before "the promise of the Father," and why a whole generation should pass away after the Pentecost and before the end of the pre-Messianic age, are all questions relating to "times and seasons which the Father hath set within his own authority" (Acts i, 7; comp. Mark xiii, 32). But in the wisdom of God they all have their reason and their purpose. We have elsewhere (pp. 222-224) suggested reasons why Jesus should for the space of forty days after his resurrection show himself alive by many proofs; it was fitting that the disciples should for ten days after the ascension

---

[1] The Spirit here spoken of is a personal existence. Personal epithets are applied to him, and the actions ascribed to him are personal actions. He is to be the substitute of the most marked and influential personality with whom the disciples had ever been brought in contact. He is to supply his vacated place. He is to be to the disciples as friendly and staunch an ally and a more constantly present and efficient teacher than Christ himself.—Marcus Dods, in the Expositor's Bible, Gospel of John, in loco.

continue steadfastly in prayer and expectation of the baptism of the Holy Spirit; it was also necessary that the gospel of the kingdom of Christ should be preached unto all the nations by the Holy Spirit sent forth from heaven (Matt. xxiv, 14; Mark xiii, 10; 1 Pet. i, 12) before the end of that pre-Messianic age should come. But the baptism of the Holy Spirit was essential to the successful preaching of the new gospel of the kingdom, and was therefore shed forth soon after the ascension of Jesus to the right hand of God. During this apostolic period as well as afterward it was all-important that the teachers and builders of the Church should be "made partakers of the Holy Spirit, and taste the powers of the age to come" (Heb. vi, 4). And all this came to pass in order that "the age to come," the Messianic era, might be preëminently the era of the dispensation of the Spirit. The Holy Spirit is now the abiding presence of God Most High; the living executive of the Father and the Son. His mission and ministry are "for the perfecting of the saints," and the "building them together into a holy temple in the Lord, for a habitation of God in the Spirit," "till we all attain unto the unity of the faith, and of the knowledge of the Son of God, unto a fullgrown man, unto the measure of the stature of the fulness of Christ" (Eph. i, 19-22; iv, 12, 13). And so it is the mission of the Spirit to carry forward the work of the kingdom of Christ and of God unto ultimate completion.[1]

12. The Pentecostal Gifts of Power. The marvelous outpouring of the Holy Spirit on the day of Pentecost must accordingly be recognized as having epochal significance both for the coming and for the completion of the kingdom of heaven. This was the first signal fulfillment of the words of John the Baptist, that there was to come after him One far mightier than himself who should baptize in the Holy Spirit (Matt. iii, 11; Mark i, 8; Luke iii, 16; John i, 33). That last and greatest prophet of Old Testament revelation foresaw that he was standing on the verge of a new

---

[1] In line with these thoughts Luthardt observes: "Jesus Christ rules the **ages.** He has become the ruling power of the world and its history; and that not merely in the sense of general intellectual power, for we do not mean merely that the spirit of Christianity as combined with the intellectual life of mankind rules the world. It would then be no power of inward renovation and moral regeneration. Neither have we to deal with the influence left behind by the person of Christ; an influence which, propagated from generation to generation by that vital power which proceeded from him, is thus communicated to every individual who comes within the radius of its agency. Christ is not merely a past greatness, but a present living power. When he took leave of his disciples it was with the words, 'Lo, I am with you always, even to the end of the world.' He is gone to God that he may be near to us. He has cast aside the limitations of space that he may be everywhere present. He departed from the circle of his disciples that he might be with his Church at all times and in all places. . . . His departure from earth marked the commencement of a higher kind of presence, a higher order of agency. He rules the ages; and he will rule hearts."—*Saving Truths of Christianity*, pp. 174–176. Edinburgh, 1880.

era, and preparing the way of One who should fulfill all the promises made to the older prophets and to the fathers of the Jewish race. In order now to appreciate the real greatness of this event on the day of Pentecost we should duly observe the following facts:

(1) *Foretold by Jesus.* This baptism of the Holy Spirit was, according to Acts i, 5, distinctly foretold by Jesus: "John indeed baptized with water; but ye shall be baptized in the Holy Spirit not many days hence." Similarly, in Luke xxiv, 49: "Tarry ye in the city until ye be clothed with power from on high." Both the manner and the matter of these words show how indispensable in the thought of Jesus was this outpouring of the Spirit as a qualification for the subsequent ministry of the apostles. At one of his appearances after the resurrection Jesus "breathed on the disciples, and said unto them, Receive ye the Holy Spirit: whose soever sins ye forgive, they are forgiven unto them; whose soever ye retain, they are retained" (John xx, 22, 23). This act of the risen Lord, however, seems to have been prophetic of their future ministry rather than an actual enduement of power then and there bestowed upon those disciples.

(2) *Expected and Prayed For.* The steadfast and prayerful waiting in the upper chamber in Jerusalem is also a noticeable fact. Luke says (xxiv, 52) that the disciples "returned to Jerusalem with great joy, and were continually in the temple blessing God." Thus they sacredly obeyed the injunction of their Lord, and waited for the promise with pious and confident expectation.

(3) *The Promise Fulfilled.* The promise was fulfilled with accompanying supernatural manifestations of power. The record of it in Acts ii, 1-13, is brief but very direct and positive. The great fact was that "they were all filled with the Holy Spirit and began to speak with other tongues," and a similar remarkable outpouring of the Spirit occurred on several subsequent occasions (comp. Acts iv, 31; viii, 17; ix, 17; x, 44-47; xi, 15, 16; xix, 6).

(4) *Peter's Interpretation.* Peter's interpretation of the great event showed that it was a fulfillment of Joel's prophecy of what was to occur "in the last days," namely, a pouring out of God's Spirit upon all flesh so that all should prophesy.[1] In the closing days of the pre-Messianic age the notable prayer of Moses (Num. xi, 29) was thus to be answered, and other signs and wonders in heaven and on earth were also to take place before the great and notable day of the Lord should come. Peter's discourse also (in Acts ii, 33) helps us to understand why this pouring forth

---

[1] See the exposition of Joel's words in Biblical Apocalyptics, pp. 174, 175.

of the Holy Spirit is called "the promise of the Father" (Acts i, 4; Luke xxiv, 49), for not only had Joel prophesied of these things, but in Isa. xxxii, 15, and xliv, 3, we read of the promise of the pouring out of the Spirit from on high upon the seed of Jacob (comp. also Ezek. xxxvi, 27; Zech. xii, 10). It was a promise given by God through many ancient prophets, and, according to John xiv, 26, and xv, 26, the Spirit himself "proceedeth from the Father." Peter also in this same discourse exhorted his convicted hearers to repent and be baptized and receive the same "gift of the Holy Spirit," inasmuch as the promise was to them and to their children and to all whom God should call. And so also Paul teaches that Gentiles as well as Jews may "receive the promise of the Spirit through faith" (Gal. iii, 14). He also speaks of being "sealed with the Holy Spirit of promise, which is an earnest of our inheritance, unto the redemption of God's own possession, unto the praise of his glory" (Eph. i, 13, 14). This "promise of the Father" was thus conceived as in a very marked way the culmination of all the Old Testament promises to the fathers and in the prophets.

(5) *Immediate Results.* The immediate results of the outpouring of the Spirit at Pentecost were seen in the mighty quickening of the disciples, their speaking with tongues, their preaching and prophesying (of which Peter's sermon is an example), the conviction of multitudes who heard their word, and the consequent addition of thousands to their numbers, the boldness of their ministry, and the unflagging zeal with which, in the face of persecution and death, they all with one accord persisted in publishing abroad the new gospel of salvation.

(6) *Typical Significance.* The typical significance of the great events of that day of Pentecost is profound and far-reaching. Being in a preëminent way the culmination of the promises of God given through the prophets, this pouring out of the Spirit signified that then and thenceforward, to the end of that age and onward through the coming Messianic age, God himself would come into closer personal relations with men than before. What had been the peculiar privilege and glory of illuminated prophets was thenceforth through the mediation of Christ to be the heavenly Father's free gift to all who would receive it. Sons and daughters, young men and old men, servants and handmaidens should all be made partakers of the Holy Spirit and of the visions and dreams and oracles of life which it is the province of God's Spirit to bestow. The rushing, mighty wind, the firelike tongues distributing themselves, and the multitudes hearing, every man in his own language, were symbolically significant of the power and purpose of the

new gospel in the world. If the confusion of tongues at Babel scattered men abroad, the gift of Pentecostal tongues was prophetic of the new word of life that was destined to translate itself into all the tongues of men, and bring all the scattered nations into spiritual concord.

(7) *Three Fundamental Truths.* As a result and summary of all these observations of the work of the Spirit three fundamental truths may be affirmed: (1) God is essentially the Spirit. The Spirit of God is no other than the Holy One himself, but the specific operations of the Spirit, so far as they are impliedly distinctive and special in character, may be regarded as the more immediate manifestations of the active sympathy of our heavenly Father in his personal coöperation with the children who delight to do his will. (2) This affectionate ministry of the Spirit could not be perfectly accomplished without the manifestation of Jesus Christ among men, and his subsequent glorification at the right hand of God. After this glorification the Spirit, the Comforter, was sent forth to consummate the ministry of Jesus and to be the efficient executive of the Father and the Son in the regeneration of the world. (3) The signal event of the outpouring of the Spirit at Pentecost was the fulfillment of Jesus's promise of the Comforter. That event indicated the near approach of a new era, "the age to come," of which the prophets and Christ himself had spoken. From that time onward men were to learn that heavenly excellence and eternal life must be realized through faith in the Unseen. It was the breaking of the dawn of the Messianic age, the dispensation of the Spirit.

13. Ministrations of the Spirit. The gifts and operations of the Spirit of God, as indicated in the Scriptures and witnessed in the heart of man, are manifold. The Spirit worketh from above and has its essential mysteries. We may feel the presence and become familiar with the effects of this "power from on high," but human eye has never seen nor can it see the things of the Spirit of God. We hear the sound of the wind as it blows hither and thither, but we cannot behold it or know whence it comes or whither it goes. And so we must think and speak of the works of the Spirit as of things unseen but very powerful. Paul speaks of diversities of gifts and of ministrations, workings, and manifestations of the Spirit (1 Cor. xii, 1-11), and in the mystic symbolism of the Apocalypse we read of "the seven Spirits which are before the throne" (Rev. i, 4), and of "the seven Spirits of God, sent forth into all the earth" (v, 6). These we take to be an apocalyptic manner of designating the one eternal Spirit of universal presence and power. The mystical significance of the number seven, used thus in connection with the Holy Spirit, is recognized in the ancient Christian hymn:

> Thou the anointing Spirit art,
> Who dost thy sevenfold gifts impart.

It is not important that we assign the manifold workings of the Spirit to just seven modes of gracious activity. These may be more or fewer, as various experiences show, but we mention seven distinctive works of the Spirit, which fairly represent the fullness of his heavenly ministration.

(1) *Conviction of Sin, Righteousness, and Judgment.* According to what we read in John xvi, 8, it is one leading purpose of the Comforter to "convict the world in respect of sin, and of righteousness, and of judgment." The word here rendered *convict* (ἐλέγχω) carries with it the idea of exposing things in their true light. It involves the process and the result of a searching test which is sure to bring condemnation, reproof, and shame to the evildoer. "All things when they are *reproved* (ἐλεγχόμενα) are made manifest by the light" (Eph. v, 13). And so it is said in John iii, 20, that the evildoer hates the light and refuses to come to the light lest his works should be reproved (ἐλεγχθῇ, *exposed to severe censure* and the shame of open conviction). But according to Jesus the conviction effected by the Spirit of truth has regard to sin, righteousness, and judgment in a manner which he goes on to indicate in verses 9-11: "Of sin, because they believe not on me; of righteousness, because I go to the Father, and ye behold me no more; of judgment, because the prince of this world hath been judged." The meaning of these words is not apparent at first sight, for it involves a depth and scope of religious conception peculiar to the most profound sayings of the fourth gospel. The Lord Jesus is speaking from his own elevated point of view, and seems to contemplate the whole period and work of the Spirit's operations in one comprehensive glance. As the devil once "showed him all the kingdoms of the world in a moment of time" (Luke iv, 5), so now the eternal Spirit opens in one moment the vision of all the ages to his eye. The language implies a crucial hour like that of chapter xii, 31, 32: "Now is the judgment of this world: now shall the prince of this world be cast out. And I, if I be lifted up from the earth, will draw all men unto myself." The words should therefore be interpreted as a momentary æonic conception of the world (κόσμος). There are three things concerning which the Spirit works conviction, namely, sin, righteousness, and judgment. (1) The world is convicted περὶ ἁμαρτίας, "*concerning sin,* because they believe not

on me." As in the judgment picture of Matt. xxv, 31-46, all sin and all righteousness of the persons judged were determined by the relations and activities of those persons toward the Son of man, who there appears upon his judgment throne, so here all sin is viewed as a failure or a refusal to believe on Christ. Being the Light of the world, he becomes the supreme test of all human hearts in their relation to truth, for "this is the condemning judgment, that the light is come into the world" (iii, 19). And therefore Jesus says: "If I had not come and spoken unto them, they had not had sin: but now they have no excuse for their sin" (xv, 22; comp. Acts xvii, 30, 31). Christ is the supreme revelation of God, and the most fearful and fatal form of sin is a persistent and blasphemous rejection of the truth when it comes with the clearest conviction of the Spirit to one's heart. And so all sin is shown, in its real nature, by persistent refusal of the manifested truth of God. We need not say that all sin consists in unbelief of Christ, but rather that he is the typical sinner whose attitude toward Christ as "the way, and the truth, and the life" (xiv, 6) is that of persistent unbelief. It is in the light of this sort of conviction concerning sin that John writes: "Who is the liar but he who denies that Jesus is the Christ? This is the antichrist—he who denies the Father and the Son" (1 John ii, 22). The Spirit of truth that proceeds from the Father, and witnesses of Christ, is the living agent who convinces the sinful heart of its personal guilt by disclosing what sin is. It is by the direct working of this Spirit that the word of God becomes "living, and active, and sharper than any two-edged sword, and piercing even to the dividing of soul and spirit, of both joints and marrow, and quick to discern the thoughts and intents of the heart" (Heb. iv, 12). (2) But the convincing power of the Spirit deals also with *righteousness,* the direct contrast and opposite of sin. And as sin has its seat and manifestation in the heart of the unbelieving world, so, on the other hand, righteousness has found its supreme exhibition in Him who could calmly say before his enemies, "Who among you convicteth me of sin?" (viii, 46.) The spotless righteousness of Christ is the most conspicuous possible antithesis of the sin of the world, and his going unto the Father so that his disciples behold him no more in the flesh has exalted, completed, and glorified this ideal of righteousness into absolute perfection. He was and shall forever be "the righteous one" (Acts iii, 14; vii, 52; xxii, 14; 1 Pet. iii, 18; 1 John ii, 1; James v, 6). He is the only being who could pray: "O righteous Father, the world knew thee not, but I knew thee; and these knew that thou didst send me; and I make known unto them thy name, and will make it known" (John xvii, 25, 26). It was expedient for him to go unto the Father, and being thus glorified, to send forth the living Spirit of truth, convince the world concerning righteousness, and make this perfect ideal of righteousness forever monumental. It was also expedient for him to go away from the gaze of his disciples in order that they henceforth might live by faith, not by sight, and that the righteousness of faith might become the blessed possession of every believer (comp. Rom. iii, 21, 22). (3) Furthermore, the Spirit is to convict the world *"concerning judgment,* because the prince of this world has been judged." Twice before in this gospel has "the prince of this world" been mentioned (xii, 31; xiv, 30), and he is no doubt to be identified with the devil, of whom it is said, in viii, 44, that "he was a murderer from the beginning, and stands not in the truth, because there is no truth in him." He is the arch-antichrist, and hath nothing in common with the Son of God (comp. xiv, 30). The Prince of light stands in essential opposition to the prince of darkness, and according to 1 John iii, 8, "The Son of God was manifested that he might destroy the works of the devil." Therefore the eternal Spirit of truth, who witnesses of Christ and reveals the things of God, must needs pass condemning judgment on the enemy of all righteousness. This judgment of the prince of this world, as expressed here and in xii, 31, covers the whole period of the dispensation of the Spirit, and yet seems like the vision of a moment, as when Jesus "beheld Satan fallen as lightning from heaven" (Luke x, 18). It is in truth a process extending through all the centuries required for drawing all men unto Christ.[1] It is a judgment that exposes the wiles of the devil, exhibits him as the bitter enemy of all truth, and declares what his penal sentence has been and must ever be. Hence the force of the perfect in the verb κέκριται, *has been judged;* is already adjudged to condemnation. And such judgment of the prince of this world is also the condemnation which the Spirit of truth must needs pronounce against all workers of iniquity who, like Satan, oppose and exalt themselves against God. And so, in the parable of eternal judgment in Matt. xxv, 31-46, the Son of man, sitting on the throne of his glory, executes this judgment of the Spirit when he says to those on his left hand, "Depart from me, ye cursed, into the eternal fire, which is prepared for the devil and his angels." Thus, in every case, the work of conviction concerning sin, righteousness, and judgment, brings out

---

[1] That which was to be effected by his Spirit in the Church during the whole course of ages down to the end of the world, he concentrates, as it were, into a single point of space, and a single moment of time; even as our eye, with the help of distance, concentrates a world into a star.—Hare, The Mission of the Comforter, p. 38. London, 1876.

into unmistakable certainty the real nature of both the evil and the good.

(2) *Regeneration.* That mighty work of the Holy Spirit of God whereby one is "delivered out of the power of darkness and translated into the kingdom of the Son of his love" (Col. i, 13; comp. 1 Pet. ii, 9) is spoken of in John iii, 5-8, as being "born of the Spirit." Whosoever is thus begotten of God is conceived as a "new creation" (2 Cor. v, 17; Gal. vi, 15), "created in Christ Jesus for good works" (Eph. ii, 10), "the new man, who after God hath been created in righteousness and holiness of truth" (Eph. iv, 24). This mighty change is also conceived as being raised from the dead so as to "walk in newness of life" (Rom. vi, 4); and even the quickening of our mortal bodies into the resurrection life is through the power of the indwelling Spirit (Rom. viii, 11). The new birth, conceived as a new creation and a resurrection from a state of death, is thus enhanced in our thought as essentially a supernatural work wrought within us, which is effected by the specific agency of the Spirit of God. And so it is written, "According to his mercy he saved us, through the washing of regeneration and renewing of the Holy Spirit" (Titus iii, 5).

(3) *Sanctification.* Regeneration, strictly speaking, only introduces one into newness of spiritual life. "The law of the Spirit of life in Christ Jesus" makes and keeps one free from the law of sin and of death (Rom. viii, 2). He that is dead unto sin cannot live any longer therein (Rom. vi, 2). "Whosoever doeth not righteousness is not of God," and "hereby we know that we abide in him, and he in us, because he hath given us of his Spirit" (1 John iii, 10; iv, 13). All growth in the Christian life, and all deepening and perfecting of Christian graces, come through the continual supply and ministration of the Spirit (Phil. i, 19; Gal. iii, 5). So we read of the "sanctification of the Spirit" (1 Pet. i, 2; 2 Thess. ii, 13; comp. Rom. xv, 16). All the saints of God "are sanctified in Christ Jesus" (1 Cor. i, 2), but the sanctification, like the washing of regeneration, and justification in the name of Christ, is effected and realized "in the Spirit of our God" (1 Cor. vi, 11). The Holy Spirit operates directly in the human spirit by means of every instrument of truth, and Jesus prayed that the disciples might be sanctified in the truth (John xvii, 17). We noticed above that the Spirit's work of conviction was wrought through the word of divine revelation, which discerns the thoughts and intents of the heart (Heb. iv, 12); sanctification of the heart is effected by the same mighty instrument of truth. "The Spirit of truth" must needs appropriate and employ the truth in the entire sanctification of one's spirit and soul and body (1 Thess. v,

23). He who truly walks in newness of life lives by the Spirit and walks by the Spirit (Gal. v, 25). The purified soul that is blessed with the vision of God is "transformed into the same image from glory to glory by the Lord, the Spirit" (2 Cor. iii, 18). Here the Lord Jesus Christ is himself called the Spirit (ver. 17), and those who are transformed into his image[1] are also spoken of as "epistles of Christ, written with the Spirit of the living God" (ver. 3). The abiding presence of the Spirit is a personal fellowship or communion (2 Cor. xiii, 14; Phil. ii, 1) which promotes sanctification of the human spirit, and the love of God is shed abroad in the heart by the Holy Spirit (Rom. v, 5). "Joy in the Holy Spirit" (Rom. xiv, 17) is a phrase worthy of notice in the same connection, for fellowship, love, and joy point to high and blessed attainments of the sanctified. "The earnest of the Spirit" (2 Cor. i, 22; v, 5), which is given the believer as both a foretaste and a pledge of his inheritance in God's own possession (Eph. i, 14), is an expression which richly enhances the holy fellowship of God, and being "sealed with the Holy Spirit of promise" (Eph. i, 13; iv, 30) adds to the thought of foretaste and pledge the idea of God's fixing thereon the special stamp of his personal assurance. The privilege of being "filled with the Spirit" (Eph. v, 18; Acts ix, 17; xi, 24) is also a good assurance that the pentecostal baptism of the Spirit (comp. Acts ii, 4) is available unto all who will receive it. By these manifold attainments of holy life in the Spirit one "comes to know the love of Christ which passeth knowledge," and apprehends how he "may be filled unto all the fulness of God" (Eph. iii, 19).

(4) *Witness and Communion.* Another specific work of the Holy Spirit is to impart directly to each child of God the assuring testimony that he is born from above. The classic text is Rom. viii, 16: "The Spirit himself beareth witness with our spirit, that we are children of God." This divine assurance is also necessarily involved in the establishing and anointing, referred to in 2 Cor. i, 21, 22, as a work of God, "who also sealed us and gave us the earnest of the Spirit in our hearts." Paul speaks in Rom. ix, 1, of his own conscience bearing witness with him in the Spirit. John says (1 John v, 7) that "it is the Spirit that beareth witness, because the Spirit is the truth." Hereby we know that he abideth in us, by the Spirit that he gave us" (1 John iii, 24). This witness of the Spirit is the assuring conviction of the new birth and

---

[1] Mahan observes: "The Spirit sanctifies by presenting Christ to the mind in such a manner that we are transformed into his image. The common error of Christians, in respect to this subject, seems to be this: looking away from Christ to the Holy Spirit for sanctification, instead of looking for the Spirit to render Christ their sanctification."—Christian Perfection, p. 172.

of the spiritual life which is wrought in the heart by the direct agency of the Holy Spirit of God. The abiding presence or "communion" (κοινωνία, *fellowship*, 2 Cor. xiii, 14; Phil. ii, 1) of the Holy Spirit" must needs be of essentially the same nature, an assuring continual conviction that our new life in the Spirit "is hid with Christ in God" (Col. iii, 3). Our filial relation to God is thus impressed upon us as a blessed conviction, and so long as that conviction remains we cry, Abba, Father, thereby witnessing on our part that we are children of God.

(5) *Revealing the Truth.* Along with this assuring witness of the Spirit we should also notice the direct agency of the same Spirit in communicating light and knowledge and wisdom to the soul. He is called emphatically "the Spirit of truth," and comes to "guide into all the truth," to take of the things of Christ and declare them to the heart and conscience of the believer (John xvi, 13-15). In this passage the Spirit is spoken of as *hearing* the things he makes known, just as in xv, 15, Jesus says, "All things that I heard from my Father I have made known unto you." The Son and the Spirit hear of God the things they reveal: they are alike partakers of those divine secrets which it has pleased the heavenly Father to reveal unto men. But the Spirit declares the things of Christ and so continues his ministry of heavenly revelation. It is this Spirit of truth who enables us "to know the mysteries of the kingdom of heaven" (comp. Matt. xiii, 11, and xi, 25). Thus the Holy Spirit bears witness of Christ (John xv, 26). All this accords most closely with what is written in 1 Cor. ii, 9-14: "Things which eye saw not, and ear heard not, and which entered not into the heart of man, whatsoever things God prepared for them that love him, these things God revealed unto us through the Spirit." These are called "the things of the Spirit of God," which the natural man cannot receive or know. This communicating of truth by the Spirit is called in 1 John ii, 20, 27, "an anointing from the Holy One." "The anointing which ye received of him abideth in you, and ye need not that anyone teach you; but his anointing teacheth you concerning all things, and is true." This Spirit also reveals the future and "declares the things that are to come" (John xvi, 13), and also brings to mind the sayings of Jesus (xiv, 26). These operations of the Spirit show that he is the great Illuminator, who flashes light upon the human understanding, so that in his light we see light (Psa. xxxvi, 9). So the psalmists and prophets were in some sense organs of the Spirit (comp. Heb. iii, 7; Matt. xxii, 43; 2 Sam. xxiii, 2), when they uttered the oracles of God. "Men spake from God, being moved by the Holy Spirit" (2 Pet. i, 21; comp. 1 Pet.

i, 11). The Holy Scriptures were thus God-breathed (2 Tim. iii, 16), and hence their profitableness for teaching and instruction in righteousness. For thus one becomes "filled with the knowledge of God's will in all spiritual wisdom and understanding" (Col. i, 9; comp. Eph. i, 17, 18). The sons of God are led by the Spirit of God (Rom. viii, 14; Gal. v, 18). And we should not overlook the fact that the Messianic Branch to come forth from the stock of Jesse was to be gifted with the spirit of wisdom and understanding, the spirit of counsel, and the spirit of knowledge (Isa. xi, 2). It is also profoundly suggestive in the symbolism of Rev. v, 5, 6, that the Root of David appears as a Lamb "having seven eyes, which are the seven Spirits of God, sent forth into all the earth." He thus represents "the wisdom of God."

(6) *Imparting Gifts of Power.* The Spirit of Jehovah which was to rest upon the Branch of Jesse, according to the prophecy of Isa. xi, 2, was to be also a "spirit of power," and Jesus bade the disciples tarry in Jerusalem "until clothed with power from on high" (Luke xxiv, 49). "Ye shall receive power," he said (Acts i, 8), "when the Holy Spirit is come upon you." The great outpouring of the Spirit which came upon the disciples at Pentecost was the first signal fulfillment of that "promise of the Father"; but the same blessed gift is an abiding power in the Church of God. Jesus went to the Father and was seen no more; but the Spirit was sent as his invisible Executive to abide permanently. "He abideth ($\mu\acute{\epsilon}\nu\epsilon\iota$) with you and shall be in you" (John xiv, 17). Paul speaks of "the power of the Holy Spirit" (Rom. xv, 13, 19), and of "being made powerful in all power according to the might of his glory" (Col. i, 11), and "being strengthened with power through his Spirit in the inward man" (Eph. iii, 16). After his temptation Jesus "returned in the power of the Spirit into Galilee" (Luke iv, 14), and every disciple who has since that time triumphed over evil has done so in the power of the same Holy Spirit. "It is the Spirit that giveth life" (John vi, 63; 2 Cor. iii, 6), and "the last Adam, the man from heaven, is a life-giving Spirit" (1 Cor. xv, 45); and so the power of God which effects the resurrection of the dead (comp. Matt. xxii, 29; 1 Cor. vi, 14) is exerted and becomes effective through the Spirit (Rom. viii, 11, 23). As the first awakening of the soul of man from the death of sin and his regeneration into newness of life is accomplished by the power of the Holy Spirit, so the uttermost consummation of his redemption is to be realized by means of the mighty working of the same Spirit. And all this is "according to the working ($\dot{\epsilon}\nu\acute{\epsilon}\rho\gamma\epsilon\iota\alpha$) whereby the Lord Jesus Christ is able to subject all things unto himself" (Phil. iii, 21). Thus we see

that the phrase *the power of the Holy Spirit* (Rom. xv, 13, 19) is essentially equivalent to the power of God. The apostle speaks of preaching the gospel "in demonstration of the Spirit and of power" (1 Cor. ii, 4; comp. 1 Thess. i, 5; 2 Cor. vi, 6, 7), and all human efficiency in the ministries of the gospel and the propagation of the truth of God in the world must needs be through the power of the Holy Spirit, which is the only real "power from on high." Among the Spirit's gifts of power we also note those extraordinary charisms of the early Church which are referred to in Heb. ii, 4: "God bearing witness both by signs and wonders, and by manifold powers and distributions of the Holy Spirit, according to his will." These remarkable manifestations are thus described in 1 Cor. xii, 4-11: "Now there are diversities of gifts, but the same Spirit. . . . To each one is given the manifestation of the Spirit to profit withal. For to one is given through the Spirit the word of wisdom; and to another the word of knowledge, according to the same Spirit: to another faith, in the same Spirit; and to another gifts of healings, in the one Spirit; and to another workings of powers (δυνάμεων, *of miracles*); and to another prophecy; and to another discernings of spirits: to another kinds of tongues: but all these worketh the one and the same Spirit, dividing to each one severally even as he will."[1] These manifold gifts of power have been distributed into great diversities of ministrations, manifesting themselves at certain times and places more notably than at others. But altogether they give assurance of the mighty energy with which the Holy Spirit ever worketh to consummate the age-long triumphs of the kingdom of God and of Christ.

(7) *The Comforter.* Finally, if in the foregoing outline we have omitted any distinctive form or quality of the manifold operations of the Spirit, all that remains to be noticed may be comprehended under the word *Paraclete* (παράκλητος), which our English versions of the New Testament have commonly translated *Comforter*. The word is found only in the writings of John (xiv, 16, 26; xv, 26; xvi, 7; 1 John ii, 1), and we have already observed that, in the one passage in the first epistle where it occurs, it is explicitly applied to Jesus Christ as our "Advocate with the Father." And when Jesus says, in John xiv, 16, that the Father "will give you another Paraclete" he clearly implies that the title is also truly descriptive of himself. It is generally admitted that

---

[1] Whedon classifies these divers charisms "into gifts of *mind*, of *voice*, and of *action;* thought, word, and deed. Under mind are gifts of wisdom, knowledge, faith, discerning of spirits, and interpretation; under gifts of voice or utterance, prophecy and tongues; under gifts of action, healing and working of miracles."—*Commentary* on the New Testament, in loco.

Comforter is not an adequate translation of παράκλητος; the primary meaning of the Greek word is that of *advocate,* as commonly rendered in 1 John ii, 1. It designates one who pleads the cause of another, and acts as his legal counselor and friend. The Paraclete is a helper, an official friend at court, an advocate, who not only keeps himself in closest touch with those who desire his assistance, but is also very ready to plead their cause in time of need. And so "the Spirit helpeth our infirmity," and "maketh intercession for the saints according to God" (Rom. viii, 26, 27). Such a divine helper in our times of need is a great Comforter, and hence the propriety of this title to represent the Spirit of truth as an abiding Helper. There is unspeakable comfort in the promise that "he may be with you for ever"; "he abideth with you, and shall be in you" (John xiv, 17). Moreover, the Greek words παρακλέω and παράκλησις are not infrequently used in the sense of bringing comfort and consolation. "The God and Father of our Lord Jesus Christ, the Father of mercies," is called "the God of all comfort, who comforteth us in all our affliction, that we may be able to comfort them that are in any affliction, through the comfort wherewith we ourselves are comforted of God" (2 Cor. i, 3, 4). In Acts ix, 31, we read of "the comfort of the Holy Spirit," in which the church throughout Judea, Galilee and Samaria was greatly edified and enlarged.

Such, according to the Scriptures, are the sevenfold manifestations of the Spirit, and these divers ministrations of the personal "Power from on high" are the source of all life and growth in the kingdom of God. Through the continuous and unfailing work of the Holy Spirit of truth the kingdom of heaven is coming, and the will of God is done on earth as in heaven. And in all these ways our Lord continues his saving mediation, and "God is in Christ reconciling the world unto himself."

14. The Greater Works of the Spirit. The many and marvelous ministrations of the Holy Spirit accomplish the highest fulfilling of the Law and the Prophets, and place the little child of the kingdom of Christ far in advance of the greatest prophets of the older time (Matt. xi, 11). Not only was it expedient for Jesus to go away to the Father that the Comforter might come, but his departure was to open the way for his disciples and apostles to perform greater works than even those which he himself had wrought. Hence the emphatic statement of John xiv, 12: "Verily, verily, I say unto you, he that believeth on me, the works that I do shall he do also; and greater works than these shall he do; because I go unto the Father." This is a most remarkable declaration, and it points to a truth of the kingdom of Christ which men are prone to ignore. Here we find our Lord exalting the works of the Spirit above all that is fleshly, material, and spectacular.

(1) *Greater than Physical Signs and Wonders.* The "greater works" to which Jesus referred were certainly not miracles in the realm of physical nature; for as matter of fact no greater signs and wonders of the miraculous kind than those wrought by our Lord have ever been performed by any of his followers. The apostles did indeed show forth many "mighty works" similar to those of the great Master. Peter healed a lame man at the temple (Acts iii, 7); at Lydda he healed Æneas who was palsied and had kept his bed for eight years; and at Joppa he raised up Dorcas from the sleep of death (ix, 34, 41). Many other miracles of this kind were wrought by other apostles (Acts v, 15, 16; viii, 7; xix, 12). But it cannot be shown that any one of the disciples or that all of them together ever performed miracles of this sort greater than those of Jesus. Nor can it be shown that all the reported miracles of the apostolic age were either greater in kind or in number than those that were wrought by Jesus during his earthly ministry.

(2) *Jesus's Estimate of Miracles.* The masses of men have been strangely slow to perceive that Jesus himself set a relatively low estimate upon the outward signs and wonders which accompanied his ministry. It taxed his patience and disturbed his soul to note the lack of faith and of prayer which sought for strength in outward signs. "O faithless generation," he cried, "how long shall I be with you? how long shall I bear with you?" (Mark ix, 19.) It is as with a sigh of pity that he says: "Except ye see signs and wonders, ye will in no wise believe" (John iv, 48). It is said in Mark viii, 12, that "he sighed deeply in his spirit" when the Pharisees came to question him and to seek of him a sign from heaven. According to Matt. xii, 39, he said to them: "An evil and adulterous generation seeketh after a sign." When the multitude asked in a similar manner for a sign, and referred to the manna in the wilderness, Jesus pointed them to deeper mysteries of the bread out of heaven, and declared himself to be the bread of eternal life (John vi, 30-35). With gracious tenderness of condescension he showed his hands and side to Thomas, but at the same time added the words of profound significance: "Blessed are they that have not seen and yet have believed" (John xx, 29). When the seventy returned and exulted that the demons were subject unto them in his name, he bade them the rather rejoice that their names were written in heaven (Luke x, 20). And so at many times and in many ways our Lord intimated that his working of miracles was a compassionate condescension to the morbid

weakness of human nature and the conditions of his time.¹ But he clearly taught that the mission of the Comforter would introduce greater things and nobler examples of power from on high.

(3) *Lesson from Elijah.* The comparative worthlessness of external signs and wonders as a power to change the spiritual life is strikingly shown in the story of Elijah the prophet. He challenged all Israel and the prophets of Baal to meet him on mount Carmel, and to test by prayer and sacrifice whether Jehovah or Baal were the true God. The details of Elijah's marvelous triumph are written in 1 Kings xviii, and depicted with dramatic impressiveness. The prophets of Baal, four hundred and fifty in number, prepared their victim and called on the name of their god from morning until noon, but without any sign of answer. Then Elijah mocked them with words of stinging irony, "and they cried aloud, and cut themselves after their manner with knives and lances, till the blood gushed out upon them." But long after midday "there was neither voice, nor any to answer, nor any that regarded." Then Elijah prepared his altar, and made a trench about it, and piled on the wood and placed his victim thereon, and then, to make the miracle the more astounding, he poured four buckets of water over the whole place, and poured them on a second and a third time, until the water filled the trench about the altar. And when Elijah prayed, behold, "the fire of Jehovah fell, and consumed the burnt offering, and the wood, and the stones, and the dust, and licked up the water that was in the trench." So overwhelming was the immediate impression that "all the people fell on their faces, and they said, Jehovah, he is the God! Jehovah, he is the God!" It would be difficult to portray a triumph in the way of miracle more decisive than this. Generations of devout readers have admired the demonstration of the transcendent greatness of Jehovah and his prophet. But how few have had the discernment to see that all this display of miracle effected no change in the faith of the people. The worship of Baal went on in the kingdom of Israel without any sign of abatement. There is no evidence that a single thorough and permanent conversion was secured by all that sublime exhibition on mount Carmel. Jezebel was enraged at the slaughter of the prophets of Baal, and threat-

---

¹ Edersheim observes: "So far from being a mere worker of miracles, as we would have expected if the history of his miracles had been of legendary origin, there is nothing more marked than the pain, we had almost said the humiliation, which their necessity seems to have carried to his heart. . . . In truth, when, through the rift in his outward history, we catch a glimpse of Christ's inner being, these miracles, so far as not the outcome of the mystic union of the divine and the human in his person, but as part of his mission, form part of his humiliation."—The Life and Times of Jesus the Messiah, Vol. I, p. 489. London and New York, 1883.

ened the life of Elijah; and that great prophet, who seemed so omnipotent on Carmel, fled before the word of the idolatrous queen, and hid himself in a cave in mount Horeb. There "a word of Jehovah came to him" (xix, 9), a revelation adapted to rebuke his self-conceit and to correct his error. "What doest thou here, Elijah?" inquired a heavenly voice. "And he said, I have been very jealous for Jehovah, the God of hosts; for the children of Israel have forsaken thy covenant, thrown down thine altars, and slain thy prophets with the sword; and I, even I only, am left; and they seek my life." Then followed Jehovah's apocalypse of the still small voice, mightier than wind and earthquake and fire. Truth in the heart, faith, hope, love, are greater gifts than power over fire and earthquake and storm. Such physical forces may "break in pieces the rocks before Jehovah," but have no power to change one human heart. In the light of this suggestive revelation, we can the better appreciate the proverb,

He that is slow to anger is better than the mighty;
And he that ruleth his spirit than he that taketh a city. Prov. xvi, 32.

(4) *Paul's Estimate of External Wonders.* The language of Paul is no less suggestive and significant when he says: "Though I speak with the tongues of men and of angels, and have not love, I am become sounding brass, or a clanging cymbal. . . . And if I have all faith, so as to remove mountains, but have not love, I am nothing" (1 Cor. xiii, 1, 2). Elsewhere he also writes: "The things which are seen are temporal; but the things which are not seen are eternal" (2 Cor. iv, 18). The eternal things are no less real because unseen, and as the eternal is greater than that which is temporal, so the spiritual things which are not seen are greater than the things which are material. The obvious teaching of all these scriptures is to magnify the things of the spirit above all signs and wonders of the world of sense, and we must not look in the realm of physical nature for the "greater works" which Jesus declared his followers should perform as a consequence of his going unto the Father (John xiv, 12). These greater mighty works include all the spiritual operations of the kingdom of Christ until he shall have given up that kingdom to the Father, having abolished all adverse rule and authority and power (1 Cor. xv, 24). He that converts one sinner from the error of his way shall save a soul from death and shall cover a multitude of sins (James v, 20), and one such work is unspeakably greater than the miraculous healing of a palsied arm. Such miracles of salvation are wrought through the power of the Holy Spirit. Thus those who were dead through their trespasses and sins are made alive (Eph. ii, 1; Col.

ii, 13; comp. Eph. v, 14). This quickening and raising up into spiritual life is the continuous work of the Spirit of truth and of power, who convicts the world of sin and of righteousness and of judgment.

15. Shows the Real Nature of the Kingdom of God. A proper apprehension of the essential superiority of spiritual things enables us the more clearly to discern the real nature of the kingdom of God, and the continuous mission and ministry of the Holy Spirit. We worship the holy Father, the holy Christ, and the holy Spirit; but it is the more frequent usage of the Scriptures to call the Spirit holy, and so we commonly employ the title, *the Holy Spirit*. The Father, the Son, and the Spirit are mysteriously one, but their metaphysical interrelations in the Godhead are not matters of direct biblical revelation. We honor the Son even as we honor the Father, and we recognize in the continuous ministry of the Holy Spirit the fullness of the Godhead working in all, through all, and over all, for the perfection of the kingdom of Christ and of God.

16. Personal Presence of the Living God. From all that we have now presented touching the mission and ministry of the Holy Spirit it must be apparent that herein we become personally acquainted with the living God. All the longing of pious mysticism, and the affinity for pantheistic union with the Eternal Existence which have shown themselves in millions of the religious peoples of the earth may find deepest satisfaction in this doctrine of the Spirit. The human soul cries out for a God that is personally present, and not afar off; an abiding Comforter, whom the world cannot receive nor cast out. The Spirit of truth reveals himself with all this blessed assurance to them that worship in spirit and in truth. Herein we recognize the blessed reality which was from the beginning but has been sadly overlooked at times—the reality of the vital, everlasting IMMANENCE of God.

PART THIRD

OUR FATHER IN HEAVEN

SECTION FIRST

THE UNIVERSAL REVELATION

CHAPTER I

THE MYSTERY OF THE INVISIBLE

1. Witnessed Among All Nations. The most mysterious of all facts within us and beyond us is the presence of an unseen Power whom we call God. In the discussion of this mystery we enter, as it were, the Holy of holies in our exposition of biblical doctrine. At no point of our foregoing study have we been able to escape the pressing fact of the immanence of God; for no rational treatment of the common experiences of religion is possible without constant recognition of the invisible but all-pervasive Being who is the ultimate ground of the universe and of all that it contains. But at this point we must pause to make note of those lower forms of religious thought and practice which show, as an apostle teaches, that "a living God, who made the heaven and the earth and the sea, and all that in them is, . . . left not himself without witness" among any of the nations of men in any generation of the past (Acts xiv, 15-17). It is now quite generally conceded that there are, and probably have been, no tribes of men so degraded as to be destitute of religious conceptions.[1] Somehow the most primitive savages conceive the idea that every moving thing in nature is endowed with life. The sun and moon and stars possess an invisible force or energy by which they move regularly through the heaven. The winds and the waters are instinct with life, possessed, it may be, each with its own self-conscious spirit; the

---

[1] See above, pp. 60-63, in our discussion of the religious element in man, and comp. E. B. Tylor, Primitive Culture, Vol. I, pp. 416–423. Third American ed. New York, 1889.

flowering plant, the waving leaf, nay, even the very sticks and stones that are stirred before the eye, have been conceived as having an invisible life and power within themselves. The superstitions of fetishism, the practices of divination, the belief in ghosts and goblins, and the manifold conceptions of another world, invisible to mortals on the earth, witness in almost countless forms the universal fact that man possesses a sort of instinctive, intuitive, and necessary sense of dependence upon some Higher Power whom he cannot find out to perfection. Nor should we overlook the fact that the concepts of animism, fetishism, and magic survive in numerous religious rites of our own time, and in the midst of prevailing enlightenment and scientific culture. How many among us can rid ourselves of the superstition of haunted houses, and haunted wells, and haunted caves? What reverence is felt by thousands for the crucifix, or the mere sign of the cross made with the hand, or for the uplifted host, or for sacred relics, amulets, rings, lucky coins, talismans, charms, incantations of wizards, or the touch of "holy water"? These all, wherever found, bear witness to man's universal belief in the existence of a Power or of powers invisible.

2. The Divers Interpretations. It was but natural that there should arise among men divers interpretations of this universal consciousness of the influence of Powers unseen. The various religious cults and the poetic creations of mythology are but so many different attempts to explain the nature and operations of the Eternal Energy which is the real basis of all phenomena. It is to be expected that these divers attempts at explaining the Invisible should be fraught with more or less error, but the all-commanding and impressive fact remains in spite of every failure to resolve its mystery. It may be that the phenomena of sleep and dreams, of swoons and ecstasy, of life and death, developed the notions of ghosts and of good and evil angels. These all suggest a preternatural, if not a supernatural world of beings. But inferences from these phenomena do not explain the higher concepts of God and the facts of religion. The most noteworthy nature-myths, which purport to explain the regular recurrence of night and day, sunset and dawn, winter and summer, are obviously based upon those manifestations of the forces of nature which evince the existence of an unseen law and order of the world. The myth itself is the poetic or imaginative creation of a story out of an idea. It arises from a natural impulse of the mind to account for some striking fact or some existing custom. A solar myth is a story about some doings of the sun conceived in a realistic way, as if the sun were a real person endowed with life and thought.

Such myths spring from an instinct in primitive peoples to see some sort of personal intelligence and will in all the more noticeable objects and processes of nature. There is, or is supposed to be, a real "Soul of the world," the *Anima Mundi*, which lives and moves through all things; and thence it is easy to imagine, further, that there are also many distinctive souls in possession of the various phenomena of sun, moon, stars, winds, clouds, and waters. Of course there are many myths which have no vital connection with religion, and some men will argue that the belief in God as the Creator of the world is itself a myth. All we need here say to facts of this kind is that in all mythologies and in all forms of religion rational and irrational elements have been strangely mixed, and the divers interpretations of the mysterious Energy that works unseen through all the world and through all ages bear unmistakable witness to the fact of God, the mysterious Power, whom no man hath seen or can see.

3. Philosophical Theories. It was also but natural that the sages and the philosophers of the most enlightened peoples should exercise their wisdom upon the mysterious problems of the world. Cosmic philosophy ancient and modern is an effort of the cultivated human mind to penetrate into the mystery of things and to tell us how they came to be what they are and how they all hold together. The ancient Ionic philosopher Thales, who is said to have traveled far in quest of knowledge, and to have studied with the priests of Memphis, maintained that all nature is endowed with life, everything is full of gods, and water is the primordial element of the universe. Anaximander put forth the doctrine of "the Infinite," a sort of illimitable original substance or first principle, out of which all things arise and into which they return again. According to Heraclitus the origin of all things and the principle of perpetual motion are to be found in fire, a clear light fluid or dry vapor, out of which all the visible forms of nature and the souls of men are evolved, and each particular soul, accordingly, partakes of the quality of the natal environments and the soil from which it springs forth. According to Plato, spiritual entities are the only real things in existence, and the material world is in perpetual change, flowing into forms of being and then flowing out. He argued that the great Soul of the world must have existed before the world itself, and so likewise must all human souls have existed before the bodies they inhabit here. Still more subtle, speculative, and dreamy are the cosmic theories of Brahmanic literature, especially as found in the philosophic and theosophic treatises known as the Upanishads. Modern theories of evolution were anticipated in part by the ancient thinkers of India and of Greece; but of one and of all these theories we may say that they fail to explain the riddle of the universe. They are at most and best only so many attempts at an explanation of the great mystery of being. The invisible secret is recognized as the most real of things existing, but the explanations are defective and unsatisfactory. One may search through the entire history of modern philosophy, from Descartes to Hegel, and observe that the one mysterious fact, around which as a center all inquiries and all theories move, is the invisible Reality of things.

4. Current Theistic Arguments. We are, furthermore, obliged to affirm substantially the same judgment concerning the current standard arguments of rational theism. So far as they go, they appear to be valid and helpful to faith in the Unseen, but they leave us without any clear knowledge or conviction as to the real nature of God. The so-called "cosmological argument" is a familiar syllogism: (1) All things existing must have a sufficient first cause; (2) no such cause is found in the things which do appear; (3) therefore the first cause must be the self-existent and eternal Being whom we call God. The "teleological argument" is a worthy associate of the foregoing, and is virtually a counterpart and corollary of it. We are shown that the great world of which we form a part exhibits manifold adaptations of means to ends, adaptations so obvious as to imply an intelligent Designer, without whose power and wisdom many things could not have been made as they are made. The "anthropological argument," or, as some call it, "the moral argument," is only an application of the two preceding modes of reasoning to facts which are conspicuous in the moral and spiritual constitution of man. The "ontological argument" is less intelligible; it moves in a line of *a priori* assumptions, and has been so variously constructed and modified as to beget with some a doubt of its having any real value as an argument. But admitting that all these arguments are irrefutable as proofs of the existence of God, and that they open the way for legitimate inferences touching his power and wisdom, they still leave us without satisfactory knowledge of his personal character. We think that in various forms of the creation we behold unmistakable proofs of benevolent design; yet are we confronted with other facts which seem rather like the contrivances of horrible malevolence. What means the fearful struggle for life, which has been going on in the animal world for incalculable ages? Sharp claws, crushing jaws, and poisonous fangs are not always indicative of beneficent design. We are often told that the world of animal life is on the whole a very happy world. Earth, air, and waters "teem with delighted existence," and "shoals of the fry of fish are so happy that they know not what to do with themselves."[1] But while this is true for a time, we should not close our eyes to the fact that there are also shoals of larger swimmers that never seem more happy than when in the act of gulping down the smaller fry. And these larger fish become in turn the prey of others greater than themselves. The great shark and the powerful lion exhibit no signs of more exquisite delight than when they crunch the yielding bones and devour the quivering flesh of their helpless victims. What evidences of divine goodness shall we find in this class of facts, or what sort of beneficent design planned millenniums of such torture and death? Some of these difficulties may be obviated by a wider induction of facts, but after all that our reason can formulate into arguments like those of theism, the heart is not satisfied. We yearn to know more about the moral and personal qualities of the Great Designer.

5. Words of Zophar and Elihu. And so the all-pervading mystery remains, but it is a certain fact from which we cannot get away. It ever confronts us in our thoughtful hours; we cannot lawfully thrust it from our immediate cognition; all men in all times have felt the presence and the power of some invisible Person or Energy that holds the world together. We may call it Fate, or Force, or God; but whatever its proper name, it seems to possess the qualities of wisdom and will. The poetic language of Zophar and Elihu, in the book of Job, expresses very forcibly our consciousness of limitation and lack of knowledge in the presence of this mystery:

> Eloah's secret, canst thou find it out?
> Or Shadday's perfect way canst thou explore?
> Higher than heaven's height, what canst thou do?
> Deeper than Sheol's depths, what canst thou know?
> Its measurement is longer than the earth,
> And broader than the sea. Job xi, 7-9.

> Lo, God is great, we know him not;
> Unsearchable the number of his years.
> For he it is who draws the water drops;
> Whence they distil to rain in place of mist;
> Even that with which the heavens flow down,
> And drop on man abundantly.
> Is there who understands the floatings of the cloud,
> The thunderings of his canopy?
> Behold upon it spreadeth he the light,
> Whilst darkening the sea's profoundest depths.[2]
> Job. xxxvi, 26-30.

---

[1] Paley, Natural Theology, chapter xxvi.
[2] Translation by Tayler Lewis in the American ed. of Lange's Commentary.

CHAPTER II

BIBLICAL RECOGNITION OF THE GODS AND CULTS OF THE NATIONS

1. **Gods of the Nations.** Allusions to the various gods of the nations with whom Israel came in contact are frequent and abundant in the Scriptures. We are told that the ancestors of Abraham, who dwelt in old time beyond the Euphrates, served other gods (Josh. xxiv, 2). In Egypt the Hebrews came into close touch with an ancient and elaborated religious cult, with its temples, and sacred scribes, and magicians and sorcerers (Gen. xli, 8; Exod. vii, 11), and upon the exodus of the chosen people from that land of bondage Jehovah "executed judgments against all the gods of Egypt" (Exod. xii, 12; Num. xxxiii, 4). During their journeys and in the land of Canaan Israel "chose new gods" (Judg. v, 8; Deut. xxxii, 17), and ran away after the gods of the nations that were round about them, and all through their history, down to the time of the Babylonian exile, they persisted more or less openly in the idolatrous practices of the nations with whom they had intercourse. They found no nation or people without a god and a religious cult.

2. **Traces of Heathen Myths.** Even the myths of the nations are recognized in such names and monsters as "leviathan the swift serpent, the crooked serpent, and the monster (תנין) that is in the sea" (Isa. xxvii, 1). Rahab is mentioned in a similar way in Isa. li, 9; Psa. lxxxix, 10; Job xxvi, 12. For while these words are employed by the poets and prophets to designate hostile powers like Egypt and Babylon, they go back linguistically and historically to ancient nature-myths. Compare the allusions to Leviathan in Job iii, 8; xli, 1; Psa. lxxiv, 14; and to Behemoth in Job xl, 15, and to the serpent at the bottom of the sea, in Amos ix, 3. Helal-ben-Shahar (or Lucifer), in Isa. xiv, 12, has also the appearance of a mythological name, and Lilith (night-monster) in Isa. xxxiv, 14, has similar suggestions of ultimate derivation from the realm of nature-myths. It has long been seen that the Hebrew word *Tehom,* translated the *deep* in Gen. i, 2, has its connection with the raging *Tiamat* of the Babylonian story of creation. Other allusions of like character appear in the poetic metaphors found in the Psalms and the Prophets,[1] and comparative research shows

---
[1] See Gunkel: Schöpfung und Chaos, pp. 82–87. Göttingen, 1895.

that there are numerous myths and symbols which travel from race to race, and from one religious cult to another, and whose power of life is not extinguished with the century, the people, or the religion in which they had their origin.

3. Names of the Gods. The names of the various deities of the nations found in the Scriptures give a more specific witness to the actual religious thought and worship of the ancient peoples with whom the Israelites came in contact. The most common Hebrew word for God is *Elohim* (אלהים), and we find it applied both to the gods of the nations and to the God of Israel. Dagon, Chemosh, and Baal as well as Jehovah are called Elohim (comp. 1 Sam. v, 7; Judg. xi, 24; 1 Kings xviii, 24), and even magistrates and rulers bear the same title (Exod. xxi, 6; Psa. lxxxii, 1, 6). The word seems to have a natural linguistic connection with *El* (אל), which is also used to designate the gods of the nations as well as Israel's God. Both these words express primarily the idea of power. Israel's God is spoken of as "a great and terrible El" (Deut. vii, 21), and "the great, the mighty and the terrible El" (Neh. ix, 32). The plural form of Elohim has been accounted for in different ways: some are of opinion that the plural indicates a polytheistic origin and usage of the name; others explain it as the plural of majesty, and others as a designed recognition of the manifold powers inherent in the divine nature. So Elohim is conceived as the pluripotent Being, who combines in himself and represents all the powers on high. The word is often used with the article, *the Elohim,* to designate the only true God (comp. Deut. vii, 9; 1 Kings viii, 60; xviii, 39; Isa. xlv, 18). The same is true of El (האל). The name *Baal* is frequently mentioned in connection with the idolatrous cults of Canaan, and may be regarded as an appellative rather than a proper name. It means owner, lord, master, and when applied to the deity it designates him as the possessor and lord of the particular province or district of country where the worship is performed. Thus we read of Baal-Peor, Baal-Hermon, and Baal-Zephon. The fertility of the land and the blessings of rain and corn and wine and oil are the beneficent gifts of the god of that particular land. The name in some places seems to have been associated with sun-worship, and we have also the compounds Baal-gad, "lord of fortune," "Baal-zebub, "lord of flies," that is, the deity who delivers from the pest of flies. The plural of this word, *Baalim,* would thus refer to the numerous local Baals, which seem to have had their individual names (Hos. ii, 17), had their altars on high places (Jer. xix, 5), and were probably worshiped under different forms in different localities. The name *Ashtaroth* appears in several texts in connection with

Baal (comp. Judg. ii, 13; 1 Sam. vii, 4; xii, 10), but the form *Ashtoreth* appears in 1 Kings xi, 5, 33, as the name of "the goddess of the Sidonians." The name is found in other forms, as Astarte, Ashtart, and is doubtless to be in some way associated or identified with the Assyrian goddess Ishtar, the queen of the gods and "the queen of heaven" referred to in Jer. vii, 18; xliv, 17. By the Phœnicians and the Greeks this same goddess seems to have been identified with Aphrodite, and was probably connected with the rites of Tammuz referred to in Ezek. viii, 14. The cult of this goddess Ashtoreth was of a pernicious tendency, encouraged unchastity, and is called in 2 Kings xxiii, 13, "the abomination of the Sidonians." Chemosh was the name of the national deity of the Moabites, and in Num. xxi, 29, and Jer. xlviii, 46, the Moabites are called "the people of Chemosh," as if they were sons and daughters of the god. We learn from 2 Kings iii, 26, 27, that this deity was worshiped by human sacrifices. Hence, in 2 Kings xxiii, 13, Chemosh is called "the abomination of Moab." In the same verse mention is made of "Milcom, the abomination of the children of Ammon." Ammonites and Moabites occupied contiguous territory, and their religious cults were probably quite similar. The names *Molech, Moloch,* and *Milcom* are but different forms of the same word which means a king, and designates the deity as the great ruler of the land and people where he is worshiped. Human sacrifices were common among the Ammonites as well as among the Moabites. The argument of Jephthah, in Judg. xi, 24, implies that Chemosh was also recognized as the god of the Ammonites. Dagon is mentioned in Judg. xvi, 23, and 1 Sam. v, 2-7, as the name of the god of the Philistines. The Hebrew etymology would suggest that the images of this deity had, at least in part, the form of a fish, but this is questioned and denied by recent lexical authorities. Passing beyond the borders of Canaan we meet the name of Rimmon, a Syrian deity, in whose temple Naaman and his king were wont to worship (2 Kings v, 18). The name is probably the same as that of Ramman, the Assyrian god of the wind, the thunderstorm, and the lightning. It is noteworthy that when Naaman, "knowing that there is no God in all the earth but in Israel," asked pardon for bowing with his royal master when he thereafter accompanied him into the house of Rimmon, the prophet Elisha bade him "go in peace," and did not forbid him to carry home with him "two mules' burden of earth" that he might, even in Syria, worship on the holy soil of Israel's God. In 2 Kings xvii, 30, mention is made of Succoth-benoth (probably identical with Sakkuth in the Hebrew text of Amos v, 26), Nergal, Ashima, Nibhaz, Tartak, Adrammelech, and Anammelech, names of so many gods of the nations whom the king of Assyria transported from the eastern provinces of his empire and settled in the cities of Samaria. Some of these names are probably corrupt, and little or nothing is known now of the cults which they represented. The same is to be said of the Assyrian god Nisroch, in whose temple Sennacherib was worshiping when slain (2 Kings xix, 37). In Isa. xlvi, 1, Jer. l, 2; li, 44, we meet the names of the Babylonian deities Bel, Nebo, and Merodach. Bel is probably the same as Baal, meaning lord, and when connected with the name Merodach may be regarded as an appellative, Lord Merodach. The Babylonian inscriptions speak of him as "the great Lord," "the King of the heavens and the earth." The form of the name found on the monuments is Marduk. Nebo, or Nabu, had a temple near Babylon, and was worshiped as the god of wisdom and learning.

It is not important here to enlarge upon these names. From extra-biblical sources we may learn the names and attributes of many other deities which were worshiped by the nations with whom Israel had more or less intercourse. The vast pantheon of Babylonian, Assyrian, Persian, Egyptian, Greek, and Roman cults has been brought to our knowledge by learned specialists, who have given their lives to the study of the monuments of the life and thought of these ancient nations. No evidence is found to show that any of the tribes and peoples of antiquity were without gods and religious practices. In every case the names of the deities worshiped commanded the reverence of the worshiper, and it is worthy of our attention that, in spite of the prohibition of Exod. xxiii, 13—"Make no mention of the name of other gods"—so many of the names of foreign gods are recorded in the sacred books of Israel. These records show in how many ways the chosen people were brought in realistic touch with the religious life of other nations; and the names of the deities mentioned, and also corresponding names of all the gods of other peoples not known to the Israelites, point in every case to a religious cult through which innumerable human hearts were feeling after the mystery of the Invisible.

CHAPTER III

ORIGIN OF THE CONCEPT OF GOD

1. Involved in the Origin of Religion. Inquiry after the origin of the idea of God is virtually the same as asking after the origin of religion. In our study of the natural constitution of man we have noticed the religious element which appears in all races and generations of men, and we observed that it always and everywhere involved a sense of necessary dependence on some unseen higher Power. The notion of that higher Power may be very vague and imperfect, but in civilized man and in the savage alike it persistently asserts itself. It includes in many cases a belief in the existence of spiritual beings who have power over man's life and destiny, and whose favor is to be sought by some form of service or of sacrifice. It appears that wherever human life has existed upon the earth religion has been manifest as an essential element of that life. It is, accordingly, as proper and as pertinent to inquire after the origin of human life on earth as after the origin of religion and the concept of God.

2. Inadequate Theories. Accordingly, one's views of the origin of religion and of the concept of God are likely to be governed largely, if not wholly, by his views of the origin of man. Religion itself inheres in man's spiritual nature and includes his consciousness of relationship to the unseen Power on whom he is dependent; it would therefore seem that the origin of religion and its concept of God must have been the first human recognition of such mystic and divine relationship. But who shall presume to say when, where, and how that consciousness and concept of the superhuman Mystery first dawned on the soul of man? The various theories of the origin and earliest forms of religion fail to account for all the facts which enter into the concept of God. We possess an immense literature on the ideas and culture of prehistoric man, and on the facts of animism, fetishism, totemism, ancestor worship, and the mythologies and folk-lore of peoples ancient and modern, but the vast collection of these facts contains no certain testimony touching primitive man's conception of a supernatural Power. All religion is essentially animistic. It is the feeling of a finite soul after the great Oversoul. Whether we suppose the earliest form of religion were fetishism, or animism, or ancestor worship, we have at most only the facts and forms of an existing cult, not any certain knowledge of the origin of that cult. The hypothesis that primitive man elaborated his concept of Deity by a process of observation and inference as he pondered things visible and invisible, the phenomena of sleep, and dreams, and swoons, and ecstasy, and death, and thence came to believe in ghosts and to worship them out of a sense of fear that they might injure him if not propitiated—all this is but a fine-spun series of suppositions utterly incapable of demonstration. It is not difficult to ascertain with much accuracy what were and are the thoughts and practices of sundry very primitive tribes of men; but when we inquire what were the first ideas of God and what the first forms of religious worship among the first one hundred or one thousand human beings that appeared on earth, we obtain no satisfactory answer in any naturalistic theory that has been proposed.

3. A Question of Psychology Rather than of History. We shall not obtain much light upon this question by turning our whole attention to the supposed conditions of primitive man. He is too far away from us, and his thoughts and practices too indistinct for us to trace with scientific certainty. We shall do far better to study man as he now is. All evidence goes to show that religion is as old and primitive as human life, and as universal as the human race. The original concept of God in man is therefore a question of psychology rather than of history. It matters little for this question whether one or another known form of religion first appeared in human life, for back of any and of all forms of religious expression must have been some sense or concept of the invisible Mystery. Why should there be any such concept in man more than in the fish of the sea or the fowl of the air? We can find our only worthy answer in the facts of human personality. We can conceive no satisfactory definition of religion that does not recognize in man a feeling of relationship to the invisible Power whom we call God, and such feeling is inseparable from certain conceptions of the Deity and certain voluntary acts which the feeling and the concept inspire.

4. The Concept a Revelation. Is it or is it not a fact that our first concept of a higher Power is of the nature of a revelation coming directly from that Power? We may call it a discovery, a perception, or an intuition, but it is inseparable from the influence upon us of the mystic Reality. The dawn breaks in upon us and we recognize the light that expels the darkness; the infantile mind may, for its convenience, construct out of the phenomena the myths of Ushas, Eos, and Aurora, but we know that our thoughts and mythic tales did not originate the dawn. The light first revealed itself to man and was never a creation of his thoughts, but his explanations of it have been many and various. So, too, the infant soon recognizes the mother's tender touch and care, but who can describe the dawning consciousness of a child's perception of parental nursing, or tell what dreams and fancies inchoate first flashed upon the infant soul? In like manner may we affirm that the first concept of God, whenever or wherever apprehended, is never a product of human reason but always a revelation coming from above. The initial stages of the experience may be a feeling after God, just as the infant clings instinctively to its mother's breast; but it is also true that no such feeling after God occurs without God's previous feeling after the human soul, and making manifest his presence and superior power. We accordingly maintain that among all the tribes and nations of men, from the beginning until now, God has made himself known. He is the Light which has imparted and ever imparts spiritual light and life to everyone who comes into this world. Men have misconceived and misinterpreted this heavenly Light, but it keeps continuously shining, and it is impossible that man, who exists in the image of God, should fail to reflect that image in the dawning and growing consciousness of his own personal emotions, ideas, and acts of volition.[1]

5. Revelation Gradual and in Parts. But some man will ask why it is that God should reveal himself so feebly and so variously among the nations. Our inability to answer the question does not alter the fact that all knowledge of God and all progress in every department of human knowledge has come gradually, in many different portions and in divers ways. Shall we not also ask why the omniscient Creator of heaven and earth and man produces anything by way of birth and growth? Why especially should man be born a helpless infant and require the slow and patient nourishment and the long and tedious discipline of years? Why should he not come to maturity in an hour and be gifted from the

---

[1] The following passage from Professor C. B. Upton's Lectures on the Bases of Religious Belief may be appropriately cited here: "If it be true, as we have seen reason to conclude it is, that the individual man, though in respect to God a finite and dependent being, has yet, immanent in his consciousness, the presence and activity of the universal ground of his own being, and that it is the presence of this universal principle within him which alone enables him to have dynamic and cognitive relations with the other finite existences in the cosmos, it follows from this very fact that man, as a thinking, a moral and a spiritual being, is conscious of wholly transcending his own finitude, and can discriminate between the action of this universal or higher self, as we term it, and that of his own finite self, that there is a certain self-revelation of the Eternal and Infinite One to the finite soul, and therefore an indestructible basis for religious ideas and religious beliefs as distinguished from what is called scientific knowledge."—The Hibbert Lectures for 1893, p. 16. London, 1894.

first with a perfect knowledge of his origin, his manifold relations, and his ultimate possibilities? We do not presume to answer such questions. We point out the facts as they present themselves to us and affirm that God's ways must be sought therein. The individual man, the family, the clan, the tribe, the race, and the nation all reach their highest and best through gradual stages of advance, not by sudden or instantaneous coming into perfection. Why should we be slow to believe that our Father in heaven has been disclosing parts of his ways, here a little and there a little, to every family and race of man? We need not think it strange that he has at sundry times revealed his eternal power and goodness even through shadowy mythical forms of heathen superstition. Who knows but those vague, childlike images of nature-myths and current folk-lore were the only language the babes could understand? And who can tell what concepts of wisdom, power, and love were awakened by the naïve traditions of gods and spirits immanent in clouds and waters and trees? Some of the most degrading forms of polytheism are found in connection with the idea of one God over all. We are of opinion that to a greater extent than has been generally allowed there may be traced in all the known religions of mankind evidences of a belief in one supreme Power, the God and Father of us all, working in sundry ways to make himself known to his human offspring. The wisdom which is from above has cried aloud in the high places and along the pathways of the sons of men much after the manner of the Hebrew prophet: "If I be a father where is my honor?" And the men who have heard this heavenly voice have shown "the work of divine law written in their hearts, their conscience bearing witness therewith, and their thoughts one with another accusing or else excusing them" (Rom. ii, 15). Too generally, however, it must be confessed, as Paul wrote it long ago, that these offspring of the scattered tribes of men have "not approved of having the God in their knowledge," and so, though "knowing God, they glorified him not as God, neither gave thanks, but they became vain in their reasonings, and their foolish heart was darkened" (Rom. i, 21, 28). Hence it would seem that, so far from evolving the concept of God out of a process of reason, human reason has too often perverted the self-revelation of God in the hearts and consciences of men. And so it has ever been that the light that is in us may become darkness, but he that diligently follows the light will not fail to find God.

6. Childhood of the World. We accept as a fact the universal revelation of God in the heart of man, but we do not overlook the other fact that the revelation has always been in relative accordance with the environment and intelligence of men reared under conditions of animal life on earth. Some men in every generation have risen above their fellows, and have been, according to the measure of their gifts and wisdom, lights in the world. But the masses of mankind, in all ages and among all the peoples, have been (to use Paul's figure) until now in a state of infancy and childhood, imperfect in understanding, minors untaught and unskilled, babes (νήπιοι, Gal. iv, 1, 3). Millions of Christians are yet, religiously, in a state of pupilage, and need, like the millions of other cults, to be under wise and sympathetic tutors. The progress of the world in enlightenment has been, from the outlook of any one generation, tediously slow. Men naturally become restless and discouraged. But God's eternal purpose moves steadily onward to its distant goal, and "one day is with him as a thousand years, and a thousand years as one day." The eight, ten, or twenty thousand years of human life on earth are probably, in proportion to its entire extent and destiny, only as so many hours would be in one man's life of three score years and ten. Our previous study of the kingdom and coming of Christ warrants the blessed thought that through all the ages thus far our Father in the heavens has so loved the world as to impart some measure of his kindly light to every man. But we see only parts of his ways, and even these we do not always understand or interpret aright. The gifted apostle to the Gentiles wrote: "We know in part and we prophesy in part." We cannot tell why God should take so long to unfold the mystery of the ages, but with the apostle we cheerfully and hopefully accept the self-evident truth that "when that which is perfect is come, that which is in part shall be done away."

SECTION SECOND
THE HEBREW REVELATION

CHAPTER I

THE CALL AND COVENANT OF ABRAHAM

1. The Migration and the Promise. According to the biblical tradition the series of divine revelations imparted to the Hebrew people began with the call of Abraham. His migration from the far East and his journey throughout all the land of Canaan brought him from first to last in constant touch with divers people who served other gods. When he pitched his tent near Shechem he found that the Canaanite was already in the land. He traveled on into the South country, and went down into Egypt, and found everywhere tribes and nations that were given to the worship of various deities. We now know, from other than biblical sources, that, at the supposed date of Abraham's migration, the Babylonians in the East and the Egyptians in the Southwest were already possessed of a highly developed religious cult and priesthood, and the same was probably true, in some measure, of all the intervening nations. It is noteworthy and significant that, at such a time and under such conditions of that vast Orient, the great ancestor of the Hebrew people should be called of God to go out from his country and kindred, and journey from the Euphrates to the Nile, and receive the promise that his posterity should be a great nation and a blessing to all the families of the earth (Gen. xii, 1-3). He surely was no type or representative of what is now commonly spoken of as "primitive man," for he moved during his entire career amid civilizations that were already aged.

2. Meeting with Melchizedek. According to Gen. xiv, 18-20, Abraham met in the land of Canaan a remarkable king and priest to whom he reverently gave a tenth of the spoils he had taken, and from whom he received a blessing in the name of his God El 'Elyon. Thus he acknowledged Melchizedek superior to himself, for "without any dispute the less is blessed of the better" (Heb. vii, 7). Melchizedek was priest of El 'Elyon, a name which is commonly and appropriately rendered "God Most High." The name means, strictly, "the Power which is above" (אל עליון), that is, the Supreme Power, or the Being who rules on high.[1] So Abraham stands not alone in that ancient time as the friend of God, but rather as an inferior to the great king and priest of Salem.

3. Defective Ethical Standards. We should also notice here the ethical shortcomings of Abraham. His duplicity was rebuked by Pharaoh (Gen. xii, 18), his bigamy and polygamy are mentioned in the records of his life, and the service of the three hundred and eighteen trained men who were "born in his house" (Gen. xiv, 14) implies a body guard of servants who were virtually slaves of his family. The traditions of Isaac and of Jacob make mention of like matters in their personal and family life, and the banishment of Hagar and her child into the wilderness was an exhibition of cruelty which our Christian sense condemns. But these defective morals were not estimated in those ancient times and among the Oriental peoples as we judge them in the light of a developed Christian conscience. And in Palestine and adjacent lands, even to this day, may be found many a nomadic sheik, whose tents, and flocks, and slaves, and wives, and concubines, and habits of duplicity are remarkably like those of Abraham, Isaac, and Jacob.

4. Nomadic Life Favorable to Religious Thought. Notwithstanding the defective moral sense implied in the records of the ancient patriarchs, the nomadic life was, on the whole, favorable to reflection and the cultivation of high religious sentiment. When Abraham walked forth abroad and looked toward heaven and the innumerable stars (comp. Gen. xv, 5), he received revelations from on high and had communion with God. Not the ancient patriarchs only, but also Moses, and David, and Amos in later times knew the solemn blessedness and the stern discipline of the shepherd life. Exposed to extremes of heat and cold, to lack of food, and to attack by wild beasts and robbers, the heroic virtues were developed in their souls; and, on the other hand, repose by restful waters, wandering in the green pastures, climbing among the hills, and watching the sky, and clouds, and changing seasons, naturally inspired ideals of what is beautiful and good. Through all these visions, and struggles, and meditations came various revelations of the mystery of God.

5. The Covenant of Promise. To all this must be added the divine covenant with Abraham, and the repeated promise that his posterity should be multiplied as the stars of heaven. The various passages in Genesis which relate to this subject may be combined

---

[1] It may be an interesting inquiry of comparative theology to ascertain how closely the idea and import of the name *El'Elyon* correspond to the Chinese conception of *Shangti*.

into a kind of sevenfold apocalypse.¹ But the more formal account of the covenant and its seal of circumcision is written in the priestly narrative of Gen. xvii, in which the heavenly covenant-maker announces himself as *El Shadday*, that is "God Almighty."² The great pledge and promise of this covenant is thus recorded (ver. 7): "I will establish my covenant between me and thee and thy seed after thee throughout their generations for an everlasting covenant, to be a God unto thee and to thy seed after thee." The sign and seal of this covenant was circumcision, a bloody rite, suggestive of the consecration of the source of paternal virility to the God of the covenant. Like other forms of bodily mutilation this rite became a sort of tribal mark and bond of indissoluble fellowship between the men of a community set apart for a particular purpose. It seems to be in essential accord with the rite of blood-covenanting still common in the East and going back to times immemorial.³ While this practice was observed by the ancient Egyptians, the Colchians, the Syrians, the Arabians, and other peoples, it seems to have been elevated in the thought of the Hebrews to the high distinction of representing a sacred bond of friendship with God. In the later time Abraham was commonly spoken of as "the friend of God" (Isa. xli, 8; 2 Chron. xx, 7; James ii, 23). A covenant was generally understood to be a compact between equals, but it was a revelation of surpassing friendship and heavenly favor for God the Almighty to condescend to enter into a sort of blood-relationship with a man. Accordingly, the idea of a plighted agreement and abiding friendship between God and the descendants of Abraham runs through the entire biblical literature. It was as if God had promised and had bound himself by a solemn oath (comp. Gen. xxii, 16; Heb. vi, 13) to multiply the offspring of his friend Abraham, give them the land of the Canaanite, and make them eventually a blessing to all the nations.⁴

6. Anthropomorphic Conceptions. Quite related in thought to this idea of God entering into covenant with man is the anthropo-

---

¹ See my Biblical Apocalyptics, pp. 71-74.
² Comp. this name as found also in Gen. xxviii, 3; xxxv, 11; xliii, 14; xlix, 25, and Exod. vi, 3.
³ See the numerous forms and the accompanying comments on them in H. C. Trumbull's The Blood Covenant; A Primitive Rite and its Bearings on Scripture. New York, 1885.
⁴ The figure of a covenant between God and Noah, and God and Abraham, and God and Israel has its very natural and interesting significance, and the doctrine of Christ as "the Mediator of the new covenant" of God with the new Israel is a familiar New Testament idea. But these biblical conceptions furnish no sufficient warrant for the complicated notions of "a covenant between the Father and the Son" as a basis of human redemption. The doctrine of "the covenant of works" and "the covenant of grace" belongs to the postulates of the so-called "Federal Theology," and is a portion of the speculative and scholastic methods of thinking prevalent in the sixteenth and seventeenth centuries. Such speculation has no legitimate place in modern biblical dogmatics.

morphism so frequently occurring in portions of the Hebrew scriptures. In no chapter of Genesis is this peculiar manner of describing the Deity so striking as that which narrates the visit and conversation of Jehovah with Abraham, at his tent by the oaks of Mamre (xviii). He appeared unto the patriarch and feasted with him, and when about to depart he spoke as follows: "Because the cry of Sodom and Gomorrah is great, and because their sin is very grievous, I will go down now and see whether they have done altogether according to the cry of it, which is come unto me; and if not, I will know." The narrative goes on to relate Abraham's intercession for Sodom, which secured the promise of "the Judge of all the earth" to spare the wicked city if only ten righteous persons could be found therein. Other parts of Genesis exhibit the same peculiar human way of representing God. In ii, 7, Jehovah is conceived as fashioning man's body out of the dust of the ground and breathing life into his nostrils. In vi, 6, he beheld the great wickedness of man and was sorry that he made him; "it grieved him at his heart." In xi, 5, it is written: "Jehovah came down to see the city and the tower which the children of men builded." In xxxii, 24, we read that "there wrestled a man" all night with Jacob, and at the breaking of the day he revealed himself as God. Similar anthropomorphisms appear in other scriptures, and they are apt to strike the reader at first as so many naïve and almost crass conceptions of the Deity. But we must not overlook the fact that such a manner of conceiving and speaking of God is not confined to the earliest periods of religious history. The later Hebrew writers who maintained a lofty monotheistic idea of God, and even the gifted authors of most popular Christian hymns make use of the same vivid portraitures of the Most High as sharing the human form and moved with human affection. Anthropomorphism may have its explanation partly in the nature of poetic composition and partly in the necessities of human speech. The oldest narratives of the Old Testament exhibit a considerable element of poetry, and an ancient war song, a national ballad, or even a prose composition based upon an earlier poetic celebration of a great event, may employ concepts of the Deity which the author and first readers did not understand literally. In Exod. xv, 3, 6, 8, Jehovah is called "a man of war"; "his right hand dashes in pieces the enemy," and the "blast of his nostrils piles up the waters"; but such imagery may be found in the poetry of all cultivated nations. In 1 Kings viii, 23-30, we observe that Solomon's prayer of dedication recognizes no God like Jehovah; "the heaven and the heaven of heavens cannot contain him"; but this only true God "keeps covenant and loving-kindness with his servants," hearkens to their cry, and keeps his eyes open night and day toward the temple in Jerusalem. It is also true that an individual author, or a school of religious writers, may be characterized by peculiar ways of describing the activity of the Creator and Ruler of the world. The more noteworthy anthropomorphisms of Genesis are all found in those narratives which the modern critical analysis of the book ascribes to that ancient Judæan prophetic writer who is commonly designated by the symbol J, and who thought and spoke of the worship of Jehovah as dating from earliest times. The priestly writer of Exod. vi, 2-8, informs us, however, that the God of Abraham, Isaac, and Jacob was not known to them by the name of Jehovah, but as El Shadday.

7. Other Patriarchal Revelations. The revelation of God seen in the call and covenant of Abraham was continued and confirmed in Isaac and in Jacob: "I will establish the oath which I sware unto Abraham thy father" (Gen. xxvi, 3); "I am the God of Abraham thy father, and the God of Isaac" (xxviii, 13). Thus over and over again the endearing pledge of divine favor is renewed. Jacob's dream at Bethel brings to him a new and fuller revelation of the God of his fathers, and prompts him to record a vow of allegiance to him. The ladder reaching from earth to heaven, with God's angels going up and down, opens the concept of a supernatural world. The covenant between Jacob and Laban in the mountain of Gilead has its pillar of witness, and its solemn appeal to "the God of Abraham, and the God of Nahor and the Fear of Isaac" (xxxi, 53). The struggle at Peniel marks a crisis in the religious life of Jacob, gives him the new name of Israel and the gracious blessing of "having seen God face to face" (xxxii, 30). The chastened sequel of that patriarch's life, the loss of Joseph, and the going down into Egypt, involve numerous additional communications from the God of Abraham and of Isaac, and the final scene, when, having pronounced his prophetic blessing on his sons, "he gathered up his feet into the bed, and expired, and was gathered unto his people," was certainly a most remarkable euthanasia.

8. The Biblical Narratives Give Truthful Pictures. The pictures of patriarchal religion portrayed in the book of Genesis do not conceal the fact that ethnic idolatry found some recognition and toleration in the household. Rachel concealed and carried with her into Canaan the teraphim of her father Laban (Gen. xxxi, 20, 34). These teraphim seem to have been small images of supposed guardian deities of the household, like the Penates among the ancient Latins, and were probably "the foreign gods" which Jacob required his household to put away at Shechem (xxxv, 2). The divining cup of Joseph (xliv, 5, 15) may also indicate more or less infection received almost unawares from contact with the magicians of Egypt. Moreover, the readiness of Abraham to obey the divine voice which bade him go and offer his only son for a burnt offering implies the patriarch's familiarity with the practice of human sacrifices. Altogether, we may say that the outlines of ancient nomadic life in and about Canaan, as portrayed in the Hebrew traditions of Abraham, Isaac, and Jacob, are faithful and true. The oral transmission of such stories was, of course, likely to embellish them in many ways. Each narrator would naturally set forth his own ideal, and we accordingly find in the biblical records of the most ancient time distinguishable narratives of different cast and structure. Our theology makes no contention with that critical analysis which finds evidences of three different writings (known as J, E, and P) in the book of Genesis, but maintains, rather, that this analysis enables us the more clearly to trace changes and development in the Hebrew conception of God. The oldest Judæan, or Jehovistic narrative (J) is graphic and poetical and abounds in anthropomorphism. The somewhat later Elohistic record (E) is probably the product of an Ephraimite of the northern kingdom of Israel who held a more spiritual conception of God. The priestly narrative (P) is written in a more formal and prosaic style and from the standpoint of a highly developed monotheism. But taken as a whole these narratives supply us with a fascinating idea of the divine element in the call of Abraham and the religious development of the patriarchal shepherds. Those ancient worthies walked and talked with God, and with them began a new departure and an exceptionally lofty series of divine revelations destined to be a blessing to all the nations.

CHAPTER II

THE DIVINE LEGATION OF MOSES

1. The Hebrew Exodus. In the divine call and mission of Moses we discern a new and epoch-making advance in the Hebrew revelation. The exodus from the land of Egypt, of which he was the great leader under God, was the traditional Independence Day of the Hebrew people and nation. For centuries they had been in bondage and their deliverance was attended with such marvels that their national poets and prophets of all after time ceased not to celebrate it as a momentous interposition of Jehovah, their God, and a sublime display of his power and glory. The following passage from Isa. lxiii, 12-14, is characteristic of the prophetic way of viewing the great event and expressive of the national belief. Jehovah is extolled as the affectionate friend and savior of the people, and their real father and redeemer,

Who caused his glorious arm to go at the right hand of Moses;
Who divided the waters before them, to make himself an everlasting
    name;
Who led them through the depths, as a horse in the wilderness, so that
    they stumbled not;
As the cattle that go down into the valley, the Spirit of Jehovah caused
    them to rest;
So didst thou lead thy people, to make thyself a glorious name.

2. The New Name Jehovah. According to Exod. vi, 2, 3, a most noteworthy element of the divine revelation through Moses was the announcement of the name Jehovah: "I am Jehovah; and I appeared unto Abraham, unto Isaac and unto Jacob as El Shadday, but by my name Jehovah I did not reveal myself (לא נודעתי) to them." This is the unmistakable revelation of a new name unknown to the ancient patriarchs of the nation, and this fact is confirmed by the (Elohistic Ephraimite) writer of Exod. iii, 13-15, where God says to Moses: "I am who I am (אהיה אשר אהיה);[1] say unto the children of Israel I AM (אהיה) hath sent me unto you. . . . Jehovah (יהוה), the God of your fathers, the God of Abraham, the God of Isaac, and the God of Jacob, hath sent me unto you; this is my name for ever, and this is my memorial unto all generations." It is evident from this passage

---
[1] Others render: *I will be who I will be.*

that, in the mind of the writer, I AM and JEHOVAH were one and the same, and this memorial name is one which contains both suggestion and assurance that the God of the patriarchs will be with his people Israel forever.[1] The correct pronunciation and the significance of the name יהוה have been matters of dispute. It is said that a rigid but erroneous interpretation of Lev. xxiv, 11, 16 ("blaspheme the Name"),[2] begat among the Jewish people a superstitious fear of pronouncing this divine name. The Massoretes attached to it the vowels of the word אדני (LORD), and hence the current pronunciation *Jehovah*. But the name is most naturally explained as the imperfect of the verb הוה, *to be,* or *become,* and as implying continuous existence. It should accordingly be written *Yahweh*,[3] and be understood as the *One who is and will forever be.* Yahweh is the everlasting God who wills to make himself known in his own ways and times. He is the same Almighty God, *El Shadday,* who revealed himself to Abraham, Isaac, and Jacob, and purposes also to manifest his personal intelligence and activity throughout all generations. He revealed himself to Moses as to no other before his time (comp. Num. xii, 8; Exod. xxxiii, 11; Deut. xxxiv, 10), and by his name Jehovah he established in new form his ancient covenant with Abraham and his seed.[4] And so the gifted poet sings, in Deut. xxxii, 9-12:

> Jehovah's portion is his people;
> Jacob is the lot of his inheritance.
> He found him in a desert land,
> And in the waste howling wilderness;

---

[1] This explanation of the sacred name holds as an opinion of remote antiquity, whether the words of Exod. iii, 14, be the language of E, or an explanatory insertion made by a later hand. The explanation has certainly a very natural correlation with the statements of Exod. vi, 3, and *Ehyeh* and *Yahweh* are from the root הוה, or היה.

[2] In Lev. xxiv, 11, the Septuagint translates נקב, *blaspheme,* by ἐπονομάζω, and in verse 16 by ὀνομάζω, indicating that even at the time of this Greek version it was deemed fatal to *name* the name יהוה.

[3] The pronunciation *Yahweh* is favored by the contracted poetic form יה, *Yah,* and also by the Greek transliteration 'Ιαβέ. Some believe that *Yahweh* is the hiphil, or causative form of the verb, thus indicating *one who causes things to be,* the Creator.

[4] The frequent use of the name *Jehovah* in the accounts of the patriarchs, as, for example, in Gen. xii, 8; xv, 7; xxi, 33; xxviii, 13, seems to be in conflict with the statement of Exod. vi, 3. The harmonistic explanation that the name was well known to the patriarchs but not understood by them is quite unsatisfactory. Much more simple and natural is the explanation furnished by the critical analysis of the documents out of which the book of Genesis was compiled. The priestly annalist (P) of Exod. vi, 2–8, does not employ this name in his previous narratives, but the Jehovistic writer (J) observed no such distinction in the names of the God of Abraham. The assertion sometimes made, that the introduction of a new name for Israel's God at that eventful epoch would have been equivalent to the setting up of a new God, is neither self-evident nor demonstrable. The significance of a proper name, and particularly when a new name is given, should be obvious at the time it is first employed, and the new name *Yahweh* was notably relevant to the time when the God of Israel was to be magnified above all the deities of the nations by the mission and ministry of Moses.

> He compassed him about, he cared for him,
> He kept him as the apple of his eye.
> As an eagle that stirreth up her nest,
> That fluttereth over her young,
> He spread abroad his wings and took them,
> He bare them on his pinions.
> Jehovah alone did lead him,
> And there was no foreign god with him.

3. The Sinaitic Legislation. Moses, Mount Sinai, and the giving of the law to Israel are inseparably associated in the traditions of the Hebrew people. The substance of the Sinaitic legislation appears in most remarkable form in the decalogue, the "ten words," which were uttered by Jehovah himself amid the most sublime accompaniments of thunder, lightning, sound of a trumpet, quaking and smoking mountain. They were also delivered unto Moses in the mount in the form of two tables of stone graven with the finger of God. They were the divine basis of the covenant between Jehovah and Israel at Sinai, and were called "the two tables of the testimony." The two tables were in substance as follows:

FIRST TABLE

1. Thou shalt have no other gods before me.
2. Thou shalt not make for thyself any graven image.
3. Thou shalt not take the name of Jehovah thy God in vain.
4. Observe the sabbath day to sanctify it.
5. Honor thy father and thy mother.

SECOND TABLE

6. Thou shalt not commit murder.
7. Thou shalt not commit adultery.
8. Thou shalt not steal.
9. Thou shalt not bear false witness against thy neighbor.
10. Thou shalt not covet thy neighbor's house.

These tables of the fundamental law and testimony of God are supplemented in Exod. xxi—xxiii by numerous "judgments" which Moses was to set before the people. They are mainly of a simple and primitive character and notably adapted to the needs of an agricultural and nomadic populace. The statutes relating to domestic slavery receive prominent attention, and divers laws appear in modified forms and with noticeable repetitions and additions in the different sections of the Pentateuch. As the nation developed in strength, met new emergencies or faced new conditions, the relevant laws were codified anew and adjusted to the demands of the times. All subsequent legislation of this kind would naturally and properly be called Mosaic.

4. Comparative Legislation of the Nations. We find no civilized people or nation without laws, and we must not forget the profound observation of Paul that the Gentile nations are not without the law of God written in their hearts. Although without such laws and oracles of God as were the advantage and glory of the Hebrew people, they nevertheless possessed revelations from heaven of the wrath of God "against all ungodliness and unrighteousness of men." We have recently recovered the code of Hammurabi, believed to be the Amraphel of Gen. xiv, 1, the contemporary of Abraham. The laws are written on a huge stone about eight feet high, and are cast in the form of judgments conspicuously after the manner of the Sinaitic legislation of Exod. xxi—xxiii. Many of the laws are in substance identical with those of the Mosaic code, and Hammurabi himself is represented on the stone tablet as receiving them from Shamash, the God of the sun and the source of light. We have also the sacred laws or "Institutes of Manu," whose origin eludes us amid the mists of Hindu antiquity and legend; but they claim, nevertheless, to have been first given by the Creator of mankind to the ten great sages whom he made at the beginning and trained in sacred things. We are familiar also with the legends of Minos, the king and lawgiver of Crete, the son of Zeus, who received from "the Father of gods and men" the laws which he delivered to his people. He was wont to resort to a cave in Crete in which he obtained his laws by dictation from the deity and afterward reported them in different portions and at different times. His name also connects in Grecian story with Lycurgus, the Spartan lawgiver, who made a journey to Crete to confer with Minos, and who also extended his researches into Egypt and other countries. When he went to Delphi, to consult the oracle of Apollo, he was declared to be the beloved of the gods, even more of a god than a man, and it was promised him that his laws should be the best in the world. Similar legends are told of Solon, the famous Athenian lawgiver, whose statutes and ordinances were cast in metric form, like those of Manu, and were inspired by Apollo and the Muses. There, too, was Numa Pompilius, the second king of Rome, born, according to tradition, the day that Rome was founded. He was wont to wander in the sacred groves, had frequent interviews with the goddess Egeria, and received from her the revelations which enabled him to become the founder both of the religion and the legislation of his people.

There are those, perhaps, who fear that such comparisons tend to disparage Moses and his divine legation. We believe, on the contrary, that a faithful study of all that can be known of these men and nations and their laws will magnify and enhance the Hebrew legislation. Vainly will we seek to honor Moses by denying that God himself has also spoken to other prophets and other peoples. Moses himself would in spirit rebuke such narrow jealousy, and say rather: "Would to God that Jehovah would put his Spirit upon all the peoples and make them all prophets!" It is both interesting and noteworthy that Moses, who was learned in all the wisdom of the Egyptians, stands forth in the biblical records as the great lawgiver of Israel, and that Hammurabi, the contemporary of Abraham, and so living more than five hundred years before Moses, proclaimed the same laws in great part as the gift of the God of light. The great ethical commandments, like those of the decalogue, did not originate with Moses or with Hammurabi; they were spoken from heaven to men and written in human hearts before the times of Abraham. Abraham was called out of the land of Hammurabi, and his migration extended into Egypt where the future Hebrew lawgiver was born. There is no evidence that the different codes of these lawgivers were dependent on each other. The Hebrews did not copy their laws from the stones of Babylon, nor from the sacred scribes of Egypt. Law, in its deeper, fuller, higher meaning, is essentially a revelation of God to man. Moses, Confucius, Hammurabi, Manu, Minos, Lycurgus, Solon, and Numa represent so many different aspects of divine legation, and show the essential relations of law and religion. "One only is the lawgiver and judge, even he who is able to save and to destroy. Every good gift and every perfect gift is from above, coming down from the Father of lights" (James i, 17; iv, 12). Law and religion alike, but each in its own way, disclose the spiritual relationship between God and man.[1] And so the Sinaitic legislation of Moses, and its various modifications and codification in the subsequent history of Israel, form an important portion of the Hebrew revelation.

---

[1] In perfect accord with this deep truth, and beautiful in its expression, is that classic passage of Richard Hooker: "Of Law, there can be no less acknowledged than that her seat is the bosom of God, her voice the harmony of the world. All things in heaven and earth do her homage, the very least as feeling her care, and the greatest as not exempted from her power; both angels and men, and creatures of what condition soever, though each in different sort and manner, yet all, with uniform consent, admiring her as the mother of their peace and joy."
—Ecclesiastical Polity, at end of First Book, Section 16.

CHAPTER III

CANAANITISH CONFLICTS AND MESSAGES OF THE PROPHETS

1. Israel's Apostasy from Jehovah. Nothing seems to come to perfection of itself, and that which seems to us most excellent is found to be the result of long and serious struggles. Seasons of great moral and religious awakening have quite generally been followed by long periods of decline. The history of Israel is no exception, but rather a monumental exhibition of this fact, and, withal, an admonition of corresponding weight. All the traditions of the Hebrew people and all their sacred records witness a uniform report of their tendency to forsake the commandments of Jehovah. Even while Moses was yet with them they murmured and rebelled, and when they encamped in the plains of Moab they "joined themselves unto Baal-peor" (Num. xxv, 3, 5; Hos. ix, 10; Psa. cvi, 28). In their conquest and settlement of the land of Canaan they did not succeed in utterly driving out the idolatrous inhabitants who were there before them, but made alliances with some of them, and for a long time lived on friendly terms with neighboring states and princes. According to Josh. xxiv, 14-28, the people entered into a solemn covenant before Joshua and before God to put away the strange gods and serve Jehovah only, their God who brought them out of Egypt and drove out the Amorites and other peoples before them; but the book of Judges tells us over and over how these children of Israel persistently ran into evil, "forgat Jehovah their God, and served the Baalim and the Asheroth," and were again and again delivered by Jehovah into the hand of various heathen oppressors. Thus they became leavened with the superstitions and idolatry of the nations that were round about them. Ephod and teraphim and molten images were connected with the priestly service of a descendant of Moses in the house of Micah in Ephraim and in the tribe of Dan (Judg. xvii, 5, 12; xviii, 18, 30). David's wife, Michal, had one of these images in her house (1 Sam. xix, 13), and we can hardly suppose that Josiah succeeded in thoroughly eradicating all such idolatry from the land (comp. 2 Kings xxiii, 24). The use of the ephod as a means of ascertaining the mind of God is repeatedly mentioned in the history of David (1 Sam. xxiii, 9; xxx, 7), and seems in no essential principle to be different from the methods of divination practiced by the king of Babylon (comp. Ezek. xxi, 21). The prevailing worship on high places, and that of the golden calves at Bethel and at Dan, witness the strong trend of the popular worship to idolatrous customs. The traditions of Samuel and of Elijah confirm these facts, and we find that, in spite of all laws to the contrary and of all the efforts of the great prophets to correct this evil, such idolatrous modes of worship and defective conceptions of God were maintained in Israel and in Judah until they were carried away into exile.

2. The Concept of Monolatry. The language of the biblical record favors the belief that the concept of God, prevalent with the ancient Hebrew patriarchs and with the Israelites long after the exodus from Egypt, was that of monolatry rather than of absolute monotheism. Whether the gods of other nations had a real existence was at that time no concern of the children of Israel; it was sufficient for them to know that Jehovah was greater than all the gods (Exod. xviii, 11). The first commandment of the decalogue neither assumes nor affirms the nonexistence of other gods, but simply forbids the worship of any other by the people of Jehovah. The language of Jephthah, in Judg. xi, 23, 24, recognizes Chemosh as the god of the Ammonites in the same manner that it recognizes Jehovah as the God of Israel. Even David seems to have supposed that to be exiled from the land of Israel was to be driven out of the inheritance of Jehovah into the service of other gods (1 Sam. xxvi, 19). Such a concept of a national or a local deity was widespread among the ancients, and it finds expression in the language of the Samaritan colonists in 2 Kings xvii, 26. Absolute monotheism, moreover, was scarcely consistent with the Deuteronomic legislation which aimed to localize the worship of Jehovah at one central sanctuary (Deut. xii, 5-7). Such legislation had a certain value and was a means of breaking down other local sanctuaries and the idolatry connected with them, but it inculcated monolatry rather than monotheism. It was not adapted to elevate the masses of common worshipers above the idea that each nation and country must have its own Deity. It begat the custom of pilgrimages to the holy place and, so far, prevented the higher conception of God which Jesus opened to the woman of Samaria when he declared God to be a Spirit who reveals himself everywhere to the true worshiper. It should be seen, however, that the symbolism of profane, and holy and most holy places serves the purpose of a suggestive object-lesson of approach unto God, and may be very helpful to the popular mind that is not prepared to receive the doctrine of the omnipresent Spirit. The graduated sanctity of holy places in the Levitical tabernacle and in the temple had an educating value, and the sacred structure with its furniture and services was a figure for the time of spiritual mysteries which could be clearly discerned only after the manifestation of the Christ (Heb. ix, 8-10).

3. **Jehovah a Terrible God.** The concept of monolatry and the national struggle for life against the gods and peoples of Canaan combined to beget the idea that Jehovah was a most fearful Deity. The Sinaitic theophany, as described in Exod. xix, 10-20, and xx, 18-21, inspired and was intended to inspire an awful sense of Jehovah's power and majesty. Gideon saw Jehovah's angel face to face, and was smitten with overwhelming fear (Judg. vi, 22, 23). Manoah feared that he must die because he had seen God (Judg. xiii, 22). Fearful also were the judgments which befell the men of Beth-shemesh and Uzzah because of their presumption in meddling with the ark of Jehovah (1 Sam. vi, 19; 2 Sam. vi, 6-8). Such excessive fear of God led to strained and erroneous notions of his justice. It sanctioned the law of retaliation (Exod. xxi, 24; Deut. xix, 21) and many other statutes of a revengeful and barbarous character. It was in full accord with the archaic jurisprudence which destroyed the sons and daughters and all the possessions of a family because of the sin of the father, as in the case of Achan (Josh. vii, 24-26). In this same spirit Samuel "hewed Agag in pieces before Jehovah in Gilgal" (1 Sam. xv, 33), the seven sons of Saul were "delivered over and hung up unto Jehovah in Gibeah of Saul" (2 Sam. xxi, 6), and Elijah called down fire from heaven to consume his enemies (2 Kings i, 10). Jehovah himself was thought of as "a man of war," dashing his enemies in pieces and consuming them as stubble (Exod. xv, 3, 7). As a reason for prohibiting the worship of graven images he declares: "I Jehovah thy God am a jealous God, visiting the iniquity of the fathers upon the children, upon the third and fourth generation of them that hate me." And this concept of the wrath, fury, jealousy, and anger of Jehovah is traceable throughout the Old Testament. It speaks out fearfully in the vindictive psalms. Both the earlier and the later prophets express the same sentiment in many an oracle. So far as any of these scriptures convey the thought of Jehovah's essential hostility to all manner of evil they contain a fundamental truth important in every stage of divine revelation. The language employed is also largely figurative. The jealousy of God is to be understood as a metaphorical allusion to the true marriage relation. Jehovah is thought of as a faithful husband moved with a deep sense of wrong when his chosen people, who are plighted to him in the bonds of a sacred covenant, become unfaithful and act the part of a harlot (comp. Hos. ii, 2, 5; Isa. i, 21; l, 1; Jer. ii, 2; iii, 1, 8; Ezek. xvi, 8). Against such atrocious wrong the outraged love of God becomes a consum-

ing fire and burns in fury as against the crime of highest treason (comp. Deut. iv, 24; xxxii, 19-23).

4. Jehovah of Hosts. The phrase *Jehovah of hosts* occurs so frequently in the Old Testament as to deserve a brief examination. It comports with the poetical concept of Jehovah as a man of war, the captain and leader of innumerable armies. The word צבא (plural *sebhaoth, hosts*) is used in Exod. vii, 4; xii, 41, and frequently elsewhere in referring to the armies of Israel, and nothing was more familiar in the traditions of the nation than that Jehovah led the hosts of Israel out of the land of Egypt, and "went before them by day in a pillar of cloud, to lead them the way, and by night in a pillar of fire, to give them light" (Exod. xii, 51; xiii, 21). But the word is used also in referring to the sun, moon, and stars as "the host of heaven" (Deut. iv, 19; 2 Kings xvii, 16; Jer. viii, 2) and as objects of worship, since the vast array and splendor of the heavenly luminaries have from earliest times elicited the adoration of many peoples. The word is used also of the angels of heaven, conceived as a mighty host standing in Jehovah's presence and ever ready to execute his orders (1 Kings xxii, 19; Psa. ciii, 21). In course of time the phrase came to indicate in common usage the Most High God, who rules the earth and the heavens and all that is therein (Isa. xl, 22-26). His dominion is alike over the hosts of the earth and of all the heavens.

5. Human Sacrifices. In view of the defective conceptions of God in the earlier stages of religious thought and life, and also in view of the terror and vengefulness of Jehovah as apprehended by the Israelites, we need not wonder that many pious souls were led to think that a human sacrifice must needs be the greatest possible offering one could make to God. Abraham's apparent readiness to offer up his only son Isaac; Jephthah's offering of his daughter in sacrifice, and Saul's purposed sacrifice of his son Jonathan (1 Sam. xiv, 45), imply that such offerings to God were not looked upon as an abomination at the time. The offering of children to Moloch at a later period (2 Kings xvi, 3; xxiii, 10) shows how strong a hold this practice had upon multitudes in Israel. Such a spectacle as the king of Moab sacrificing his eldest son for a burnt offering upon the wall of the besieged city (2 Kings iii, 27) was adapted to make a profound impression, and may have commended itself to many Israelites in spite of all laws to the contrary. See above, pp. 357, 358.

6. Ideas of God Enlarged with National Growth. But while contact with other nations exposed the Hebrew people to many corruptions of belief and morals, it also served at times to furnish occasion and motive for enlarging their ideas of God and the world.

From the time of the exodus until their final dispersion the tribes of Israel were brought in touch with the other peoples, and their political and commercial relations together with their various experiences of exile compelled them to come face to face with the religious customs of such civil powers as Egypt, Phœnicia, Syria, Assyria, Babylon, Persia, and Greece, not to speak of their home contact with powerful tribes on their immediate border. Enlarged ideas of the world prepared the way for more exalted ideas of God, and monolatry would gradually be displaced or supplemented by the grander concept of monotheism. It was sufficient for the nomadic Hebrew, and the Israelite domiciled in his land of promise, to know that Jehovah was greater than all the gods of the heathen, and to worship no other god besides. But when, under David and Solomon, the tribes of Israel became a united nation and a kingdom that ruled over all the kingdoms from the border of Egypt to the river Euphrates (1 Kings iv, 21), possessing a navy of ships that traversed the seas afar (1 Kings ix, 26; x, 22), it became apparent that there could be no God in heaven or on earth like Jehovah, the God of Israel, whom even the heaven of heavens could not contain (1 Kings viii, 23, 27). Solomon, however, with this lofty concept of Jehovah, fell into lamentable coalition with the religious cults of his foreign wives, and thus entailed irreparable harm upon his kingdom and nation. Nevertheless, from his time onward great prophets arose in Israel and inculcated the monotheism which in the darkest times of the nation's exile proclaimed: "I am Jehovah, and there is none else; besides me there is no God" (Isa. xlv, 5).

7. Significance of the Temple. The temple built by Solomon served in a very powerful way to inculcate the doctrine as well as the worship of Jehovah. Whatever the exact facts as to the tabernacle at Shiloh (Josh. xviii, 1; Judg. xxi, 19, 1 Sam. i, 3) and its history previous to the time of David, there is no question as to its general plan of graduated holy places and its theocratic significance for the Hebrew people. These were the same in temple and tabernacle. As a matter of fact, the temple of Solomon may have had its pattern modeled after the plans of older structures in Egypt and in Syro-Phœnicia, for the king of Israel procured Sidonian architects and builders from Hiram, king of Tyre. In Solomon's prayer of dedication the thought of God, whom the heavens cannot contain, dwelling on earth, keeping his covenant of lovingkindness with his faithful servants, and hearkening to their supplications, is expressed as a marvelous revelation (1 Kings viii, 23, 27, 29). Three things of prime importance were emphasized by means of the temple worship: (1) the holiness of Jehovah; (2)

his condescending grace in dwelling with his people, and (3) the conditions on which his people may approach him and secure his favor. The concept of monolatry was not without ethical content, and the God whose worship was united with the moral code of the decalogue must have been regarded as unapproachable in majesty, "glorious in holiness and fearful in praises" (Exod. xv, 11). The most secret and unapproachable places in Egyptian and Syro-Phœnician temples were adapted to inspire feelings of awe in the worshiper. But the idea of the ethical separateness and sanctity of Jehovah was a revelation peculiar to Israel. It is noteworthy that the song unto Jehovah, in Exod. xv, 1-18, celebrates the sanctuary, the holy habitation of Jehovah in the mountain of his inheritance, as well as the overthrow of Pharaoh and his host in the Red Sea. And no conceivable object-lesson could better express and impress the absolute holiness of the God of Israel than the symbolism of the Holy of holies in his sanctuary. Within that secret place Jehovah was conceived as "enthroned above the cherubim" (Psa. lxxx, 1), and when the consecrated priest stood at the golden altar of incense, with his face to the veil which hid the holiest place from view, having the golden candlestick on his left hand and the showbread on his right, he represented the pure worshiper in his nearest approach unto the Holy One of Israel. This conception appears in the vision of Isaiah, when he saw Jehovah on his throne, attended by the seraphim and heard them saying one to another, "Holy, holy, holy, is Jehovah of hosts; the whole earth is full of his glory" (vi, 3). The same symbolism also enhances the idea of a covenant of grace, reaffirmed again and again since the call of Abraham: "O Jehovah, the God of Israel, there is no God like thee in heaven above nor on earth beneath; who keepest covenant and lovingkindness with thy servants that walk before thee with all their heart" (1 Kings viii, 23). Such a holy covenant requires also becoming obedience on the part of all the people. They must "be perfect with Jehovah, to walk in his statutes and to keep his commandments" (ver. 61).

8. Concept of a Theocratic Kingdom. The idea of a theocratic government of the chosen people would be a very natural outgrowth of the idea of a covenant between God and a tribe or nation. In Exod. xix, 4-6, Jehovah thus speaks through Moses to the house of Jacob: "If ye will obey my voice, and keep my covenant, then shall ye be mine own possession from among all the people: and ye shall be unto me a kingdom of priests, and a holy nation." Whatever the exact time of its origin this concept of Jehovah as King of Israel is very ancient, and it grew with the nation's growth. When the elders of the people urged Samuel to appoint over them a king to judge them after the manner of the other nations, their request was construed as equivalent to a rejection of Jehovah that he should not be king over them (1 Sam. viii, 7; x, 19). Up to that time there had been no established ruler of the people, no executive officer having permanent position and authority in the state. God raised up the great leaders who from time to time were recognized by the nation as lawgivers, judges, and shepherds of the people. Moses, Joshua, and the successive judges like Barak and Gideon, were each called out to meet emergencies, as the times demanded. To seek justice before such a leader was "to inquire of God" (Exod. xviii, 15), and the decision rendered was "the judgment of God" (Deut. i, 17). And so the idea of Jehovah as Israel's immanent Ruler took strong hold of the nation, and found expression in the great prophets, as in Isa. xxxiii, 22: "Jehovah is our judge, Jehovah is our lawgiver, Jehovah is our king; he will save us." Whatever was the civil and religious organization of the tribes at any period of their history, the various princes, elders, officers, judges, and priests were but so many subordinate ministers of Jehovah. And this theocratic idea was by no means displaced by the establishment of the monarchy in Israel. Jehovah was the great King, whom all kings and judges of the earth should serve with fear and trembling (Psa. ii, 10, 11). But Israel was Jehovah's peculiar treasure among the nations, a chosen people, destined to serve a lofty purpose in the world. Hence this people was shown peculiar favors:

> When Elyon gave the nations their inheritance,
> When he separated the children of men,
> He set the bounds of the peoples
> According to the number of the children of Israel.
> For Jehovah's portion is his people;
> Jacob is the lot of his inheritance. Deut. xxxii, 8, 9.

It was in perfect accord with this Hebrew particularism that the earlier monolatry should expand into the higher prophetic monotheism.

9. Apocalyptic Visions of Jehovah. The thought of Jehovah as the great King of Israel naturally led to the apocalyptic portraitures of his heavenly throne and his hosts of ministering angels. For when it was common to speak of God as "King of all the earth, reigning over the nations, sitting upon his holy throne" (comp. Psa. xlvii, 7, 8), it was easy to feel the power of such a vision as that of Micaiah, in 1 Kings xxii, 19: "I saw Jehovah sitting on his throne, and all the host of heaven standing by him on his right hand and on his left." A similar picture is seen in "the sons of God coming to present themselves before Jehovah," in Job 1, 6; ii, 1. Traces of the same imagery may be found in Gen. i, 26; iii, 22, where God speaks as in the presence of a heavenly assembly, and the plural form of utterance, "let us make," etc., is best explained, as in Isa. vi, 8, by supposing it addressed to the angelic ministers of his royal court. In the first chapter of Ezekiel this visional picture is drawn out in great detail, and "the likeness of the glory of Jehovah" is enhanced by the opening of the heavens, the four cherubic living creatures, radiant with the brightness of burning coals of fire and flashes of lightning, moving the wheels of a chariot that seemed instinct with life and bearing above it the likeness of a throne, and "a likeness as the appearance of a man upon it above." Quite similar is the vision, in Dan. vii, 9, 10, of the "Ancient of days," sitting enthroned amid a heavenly host; "his raiment was white as snow, and the hair of his head like pure wool; his throne was fiery flames, and the wheels burning fire. A fiery stream came forth from before him, and thousands of thousands ministered unto him." Such portraitures served to set forth the glory of the heavenly King of Israel, and to cultivate the most exalted conceptions of his majesty and power; and yet, with all their grandeur and impressiveness, they contain elements of anthropomorphism.

10. The Biblical Angelology. This apocalyptic concept of the God of Israel, enthroned above the hosts of heaven and earth, with thousands of thousands ministering unto him, furnishes the logical basis of the biblical angelology. Even the Sinaitic theophany was spoken of by the poets as a shining forth and a coming of Jehovah "from the ten thousands of his holy ones" (Deut. xxxiii, 2). As gods and goddesses form the machinery of the epic poets in their descriptions of heaven, earth, and hell, so innumerable angels of varying rank and power figure in the apocalyptic scriptures. In Jacob's dream at Bethel there appeared "angels of God ascending and descending" upon a ladder that reached from earth to heaven (Gen. xxviii, 12). In the book of Daniel they are not only "ten thousand times ten thousand" in number, but have distinctive ranks and provinces. In Job i, 6; ii, 1; xxxviii, 7, "the sons of God" are commonly understood to be a title for the angels of God. In Zech. i, 8-11, we read the apocalyptic vision of the angel of Jehovah standing among the myrtle trees, accompanied by others who appeared as so many riders upon horses of different colors, and in vi, 1-8, of the same book is a similar vision of four chariots, drawn by horses of varying color, and "going forth from standing before the Lord of all the earth." They are called the four winds or messengers of heaven (comp. Psa. civ, 3, 4). These visional chariots are also to be compared with the elaborate vision of the four cherubim and the mighty wheels of Jehovah's chariot in Ezek. i, 4-28. All these are apocalyptic scriptures and symbolic of God's immanence in the whole domain of creature life. He is the divine Ruler of this world, and he is conceived as employing innumerable messengers and ministers of his will. He is the regal Commander of all the heavenly hosts, and no part of his dominion is to be supposed to be left without the immediate oversight of one or more such ministering spirits. How much of all this is imagery and how much is reality we may not presume to say. It may all be interpreted as a highly embellished doctrine of animism, the animism of the Hebrew faith. It is immeasurably above that form of animism which is found in primitive cults of nature worship, and has its entire setting in the doctrine of a personal Deity,

> Who covers himself with light as with a garment;
> Who stretches out the heavens like a curtain;
> Who sends forth springs into the valleys;
> Who waters the mountains from his chambers;
> Who causes the grass to grow for the cattle;
> Who touches the mountains and they smoke.

These and other like statements of Psalm civ present the true biblical animism, all nature instinct with the life of God; and whenever the concept employs the interposition of angels, the fundamental fact in every case is that God himself, the Infinite Spirit, is immanently present and active. Herein we find the sure basis of our doctrine of universal Providence, so minute in its oversight and care that never a bird, a beast, or an insect is without the sympathetic attention of the omnipresent Spirit of the world. The doctrine of angels is, accordingly, a phase of the biblical doctrine of God. The glory of the "holy angels" is, in part, the glory of the everlasting Father, and the whole concept of their heavenly ministries in the interests of men has close affinity with the Jewish ideas of the *Shechinah,* the manifested presence and glory of Jehovah among his people. Thus Jehovah went before them at the exodus "in a pillar of cloud," and in Exod. xiv, 19, this pillar seems to be identified with "the angel of God." On the whole, it is to be observed: (1) The angel of Jehovah and Jehovah himself are mysteriously identified in Gen. xvi, 11, 13; Exod. xxiii, 20-23; xxxii, 34; xxxiii, 14; Isa. lxiii, 9. The angel of Jehovah who called to Moses out of the burning bush spoke as being himself the God of Abraham, Isaac, and Jacob (Exod iii, 2-6). So the angel of Jehovah is the personal manifestation of Jehovah himself. (2) In a similar way the angels of the seven churches and "the angel of the waters" (Rev. xvi, 5), in the Apocalypse of John, are in some sense identified with the churches and with the waters. The idea arises out of visional and symbolical modes of thought. (3) The wide and varied use of the word *angel* in the sense of agent or messenger of God accords with the idea that any ministrant angel is really God himself working in the particular way described. Thus priests and prophets are Jehovah's angels (Mal. ii, 7; iii, 1); pestilences and winds also fulfill his word (2 Sam. xxiv, 17; Psa. civ, 4), and thus act as his agents and messengers. The angels of God are invisible and innumerable powers of God immediately present and active in every part of his universe. (4) But this poetic and apocalyptic concept of God's angels is by no means exclusive of the actual existence and ministry of countless personal spirits, who lovingly and intelligently coöperate with the Most High in his dominion of the world. As we conceive the illimitable universe alive with God in every part, we can as easily associate with this idea the thought of ten thousand times ten thousand holy angels whom he elects and constitutes to share his glory. This idea has found a place in all the religions of mankind, but notably in Mazdaism, from which it is not improbable that the Jewish people borrowed somewhat during the time of Babylonian exile and under the Persian domination, with which latter they were on most friendly terms. As a people's doctrine of immortality and the future life rises in dignity, coherency, and beauty in proportion to the excellence of their doctrine of God, so the doctrine of angels and principalities in the heavens of God is found to correspond with the prevailing concept of the glory of God. That millions of spiritual beings should be going up and down this earth in ministries of wisdom and love is a thought so far from detracting from the power of God that it rather enhances in us the concept of his heavenly majesty. The highest revelation of God in Christ is depicted as an appearing in the glory of his Father with the holy angels.

11. The Prophetic Monotheism. The Hebrew revelation of God, as traceable in the Old Testament, appears in its highest and fullest excellence in the writings of the great prophets and poets. The lofty monotheistic conception seems to have taken full possession of Amos, whose rapt soul hears the voice of Jehovah in the thunder that roars out of Zion and withers the top of mount Carmel (i, 2). Jehovah is no local deity, concerned for one land and people only, for he sends his penal judgments on Damascus, and Gaza, and Tyre, and Edom, and Ammon, and Moab, as well as on Judah and Israel. He led the Philistines from Caphtor and the Syrians from Kir as truly as he led Israel out of Egypt (ix, 7). No one can escape his searching gaze, though he hide in the top of Carmel or in the bottom of the sea, in the depths of Sheol or in the heights of heaven (ix, 1-3). He controls the rain, sends abroad the wasting pestilence, forms the mountains, creates the wind, and declares unto man his inmost thought (iv, 7, 9, 13). No evil may befall a city but Jehovah has something to do with it (iii, 6). His hand spreads out the constellations of heaven, and "turneth the shadow of death into the morning" (v, 8). But he is a moral Ruler, who hates the evil, and loves the good, and establishes justice and is very gracious and merciful (v, 14, 15); he will not accept feasts and burnt offerings in place of righteousness (v, 21-24), and "the day of Jehovah" will come as a woeful darkness upon all transgressors (v, 18-20). In the prophecy of Hosea we find the same lofty monotheism. The God of Israel rules over the whole creation, and makes Egypt and Assyria serve his purposes. He has power over death and Sheol (xiii, 14). Besides him there is no savior (xiii, 4). He abhors and punishes all manner of sin, and "has a controversy" with the land whose inhabitants do any sort of evil (iv, 1-5). He "desires goodness and not sacrifice, and the knowledge of God more than burnt-offerings" (vi, 6). But that which is specially prominent in Hosea is the doctrine of God's tender compassion for Israel in their backsliding: "How shall I give thee up, Ephraim? how shall I cast thee off, Israel? My heart is turned within me, my compassions are kindled together" (xi, 8; comp. xiv, 4-7; 18-20). Micah is not behind his contemporaries in magnifying the universal power and dominion of Jehovah, and he, too, in exceptionally strong terms, declares the relative worthlessness of ritual offerings as a substitute for doing justice, lovingkindness, and walking humbly with God (vi, 7, 8). Who is a God like unto Jehovah, who pardons iniquity, delights in loving-kindness, and performs the truth and the lovingkindness which he swore unto Abraham and Jacob from the days of old? (vii, 18-20.) Isaiah even surpasses his contemporary prophets in extolling the glory and power of Jehovah. His vision of "the King, Jehovah of hosts," "sitting upon a throne, high and lifted up" (vi, 1-5) imparts peculiar impressiveness to his descriptions of the supernatural power by which the Assyrian is used as a sharp razor and as a rod to execute the purposes of God (vii, 20; x, 5, 33). Egypt, and Elam, and Shinar, and Hamath, and the islands of the sea are under Jehovah's oversight and power as truly as are Judah and Ephraim (xi, 11-16). This great prophet also proclaims the worthlessness of burnt offerings, and incense, and solemn meetings, when the worshipers are spiritually unclean and do not "seek justice, judge the fatherless, and plead for the widow (i, 10-17). In the book of Jeremiah the same high doctrine appears again and again. "Jehovah is the true God; he is the living God and an everlasting King; at his wrath the earth trembles and the nations are not able to abide his indignation" (x, 10). He is ruler of the sun and moon and stars, and the waves of the sea (xxxi, 35); nothing is too hard for him (xxxii, 17, 27). He fills heaven and earth (xxiii, 24), and executes judgments upon all the nations of the earth (chaps. xl—li). In like manner six chapters of Ezekiel (xxv—xxx) declare Jehovah's absolute dominion over all nations and kingdoms. The same doctrine appears also in the words of Nahum, Habakkuk, and Zephaniah. But more impressive than any other prophet in portraying the absolute dominion of God in the world is the great author of Isa. xl—lxvi. In many forms of rhythmic oracle he speaks of Jehovah as "the Holy One of Israel," as the almighty Being "who hath measured the waters in the hollow of his hand, and meted out heaven with the span, and comprehended the dust of the earth in a measure, and weighed the mountains in scales and the hills in a balance. . . . He sitteth above the circle of the earth and the inhabitants thereof are as grasshoppers; he stretcheth out the heavens as a curtain, and bringeth princes to nothing, and maketh the judges of the earth as vanity" (xl, 12, 22, 23). There is no other God besides him, and he forms the light and the darkness (xlv, 5-7). His thoughts and his ways are immeasurably above those of men (lv, 8, 9). But though heaven is his throne and earth his footstool (lxvi, 1), his special delight is to attend to "him that is poor and of a contrite spirit." His loving-kindness, great goodness, and mercies toward Israel were so deep that "in all their affliction he was afflicted" (lxiii, 7-9). He loves justice and hates robbery, and he anoints his prophet to "preach good tidings unto the meek, to bind up the broken-hearted, to proclaim liberty to the captives, to comfort all that mourn" (lxi, 1-3). Such oracles of God reach no higher strain than in the writings of this great poet-prophet of the Babylonian exile.

12. Theology of the Psalter. The Hebrew Psalter contains many conceptions of the power, wisdom, and love of God which are well worthy of a place beside the noblest monotheistic teachings of the Prophets. The five books of the collection, as they now stand in the Hebrew canon, contain psalms of various dates and authorship. It is impossible for us to determine the origin or the age of many of these sacred lyrics, but as touching the creation and dominion of the world, they all present one common idea of God. He is the Author of all things, and the visible universe is an open book from which we may learn of God's wisdom and power. The heavens declare his glory and the firmament shows the work of his hands (xix, 1).

> By the word of Jehovah were the heavens made,
> And all the host of them by the breath of his mouth.
> He gathereth the waters of the sea together as a heap;
> He layeth up the deeps in storehouses.
> For he spake, and it was done;
> He commanded, and it stood fast. Psa. xxxiii, 6-9.

His omnipresence is magnificently celebrated in Psa. cxxxix, 7-10. He is also described as laying the foundations of the earth, stretching out the lofty heavens, sending forth springs into the valleys, caring for the birds and the beasts, and making the grass grow for the cattle. Whether these thoughts be expressed in a song of praise or formulated into a creed, their doctrine is that of a personal Power and Intelligence who brought all things into existence, and on whom all things depend. Other psalms proclaim his tender mercies, his holiness, righteousness and truth. There is probably no hymn or spiritual song that has comforted more human souls than the twenty-third psalm, in which Jehovah is extolled as a tender shepherd and a royal host. Beautiful also is the beginning of Psa. lxxxix: "I will sing of the lovingkindness of Jehovah for ever; with my mouth will I make known thy faithfulness to all generations." This gracious Lord is the dwelling place of his people in all generations, and with him a thousand years are but as one day (xc, 1, 4). He gives his angels charge over the faithful soul that abides in his secret fellowship (xci, 1, 3, 11). He reigns also in heavenly splendor and majesty, discloses his righteousness before the nations, while at the same time his loving-kindness toward them that fear him is great as the heavens are high above the earth (xciii, 1; xcviii, 2; ciii, 11).

13. Hebrew Ideal of Creation. The post-exile Judaism added little or nothing to the high monotheistic teachings of the Prophets, for the later psalms do no more than repeat in substance the older concepts of the God of Israel. At this point, however, we may well adduce the ideal of creation as depicted in the first chapter of Genesis. This magnificent composition is now quite generally believed to be the work of a great Jewish theist of the exile period, who was inspired to write the sacred traditions of his people from the priestly point of view. Whatever interpretation of this creation-narrative one may hold, there is no mistaking the author's sublime conception of the divine origin of the world. God who in the beginning made the heavens and the earth must himself have been without beginning. He is the source of light and of all life, and by the word of his power he brings the things which now appear out of that which is not seen (comp. Heb. xi, 3). All the growths of nature and all kinds of animal life spring forth at his command, and the advance in the order and ranks of creaturehood from lower to higher, from vegetable up to man, reveal the Creator as a being of infinite power and intelligence who sees the end from the beginning. The entire description is as charmingly simple as it is impressively sublime. Its doctrinal content is in substantial agreement with the Prophets and the Psalms. Even the New Testament repeats without any noticeable addition these Old Testament ideas of creation by the immediate agency of God.[1]

14. The Messianic Hope of Israel. One of the most noteworthy portions of the Hebrew revelation of God's wisdom and love is the Messianic hope which appears variously set forth in the Law, the Prophets, and the Psalms. This Messianic hope appears like a prophetic gospel running through all the sacred literature of the chosen people. The various oracles point to a future birth of an anointed Person and a new era destined to bring the highest good to men. According to Gen. ix, 27, God is somehow to enlarge Japheth and dwell in the tents of Shem. A future seed of Abraham is to be made a blessing to all the families of the earth (Gen. xii, 3; xxii, 18). The seed of the woman is to bruise the head of the serpent (Gen. iii, 15). God will raise up a prophet like unto Moses out of the midst of Israel (Deut. xviii, 15, 18). David is not permitted to build a temple for Jehovah, but he is told that one of his sons shall build the house, "and I will establish the throne of his kingdom for ever. I will be his father and he shall be my son" (2 Sam. vii, 13, 14). This thought is taken up and celebrated in the Messianic psalms (*e.g.*, ii; cx). Amos declares that Jehovah will raise up the fallen booth of David (ix, 11). Other prophets repeat the hopeful promise in a variety of ways. Zephaniah and Jeremiah, in the face of appalling calamities, when Judah is about to be carried into Babylonian exile, express the unwavering confidence that the mighty God of Jacob will redeem his people from exile and establish David's throne forever (Zeph. iii, 8-20; Jer. iii, 14-18; xxiii, 5-8; xxxii, 36-42; xxxiii, 14-26). Ezekiel assures the captive people of a restoration that shall be like a resurrection from the dead, and indicates that the temple,

---

[1] See the exposition of these creation records in Biblical Apocalyptics, pp. 38–49. But no exposition of the biblical records furnishes us with any certain information of the *method* of God's creation. All things that appear might have been brought forth by a process of evolution continuing through ages of ages, for all that the Scriptures teach to the contrary. Nor is there anything in these ancient records to assure us that God created the material world "out of nothing." Some such thought may be implied in 2 Macc. vii, 28, but the language of Heb. xi, 3, is more guarded: "That which is seen has not been made out of things which do appear." This is not equivalent to saying that the visible creation was produced out of nothing. God is of himself the cause and source of all things, and all things are dependent upon him. Comp. Bowne, Philosophy of Theism, pp. 170, 178, 179.

and city, and land of Israel shall become the dwelling place of Jehovah. The great prophecy of the exile (Isa. xl—lxvi) abounds with words of comfort for the people of Jehovah. "Israel shall be saved in Jehovah with an everlasting salvation" (xlv, 17), and Jehovah will even create new heavens and a new earth, in which the seed and name of Israel shall remain forever (lxv, 17; lvi, 22). The post-exilic prophets continue this Messianic hope, and Zechariah speaks of "the man whose name is Branch," who shall grow up and build the temple of Jehovah, and be a priest upon his throne (iii, 8; vi, 12, 13). This hope continued to strengthen in the nation's heart, and was never more expectant than at the time of the birth of Jesus Christ.

15. A Purposed Goal in Human History. This magnificent series of prophetic oracles, taken as a whole, contains a most remarkable revelation of the character of God. They show that he who created the heavens and the earth, and placed man over all other orders of living things, yearns over his offspring with the affection of a father. Though his children disobey, and provoke him to anger, and grieve his heart, the everlasting Ruler purposes in his infinite wisdom to destroy the operations of evil and to introduce eternal righteousness (comp. Dan. ix, 24). He is both a loving Father and a righteous Judge. He chooses Israel as a firstborn son, a child, however, subjected to chastisement, and exile, and many sorrows, in order that he and all others who learn to obey the truth may become partakers of a glorious inheritance. He reveals himself to them in many ways, and confirms his covenant with the fathers in spite of all their unfaithfulness. In the darkest days of oppression he cheers them with the prophetic word: "Arise, shine; for thy light is come, and the glory of Jehovah is risen upon thee. . . . Nations shall come to thy light, and kings to the brightness of thy rising. . . . Thy sun shall no more go down, neither shall thy moon withdraw itself; for Jehovah shall be thine everlasting light, and the days of thy mourning shall be ended" (Isa. lx, 1, 3, 20, 21). Thus in all this series of divine revelations we may see how times and nations and individuals are made to contribute to the consummation of a goal of humanity, so that God and man shall at last meet and dwell together in glorious felicity. These oracles of prophecy point us to an all-comprehending Mind, who sees the end from the beginning, and who has a blessed purpose running through the ages. Just when and where and how the purposes of his grace shall reach fulfillment, the prophets themselves are not gifted to make known, but they are assured that God rules over the dominion of men, and their psalmists cry:

> Blessed is the nation whose God is Jehovah;
> The people whom he hath chosen for his own inheritance.
> Jehovah looketh from heaven;
> He beholdeth all the children of men.
> Let thy lovingkindess, O Jehovah, be upon us,
> According as we have hoped in thee. Psa. xxxiii, 12, 13, 22.

This prophetic concept of a goal of human history, toward which the wisdom and love of God made a chosen people contribute in an exceptional way, enables us to understand the real character of the divine election of Israel. One great thought was impressed upon the nation, from first to last: "Jehovah thy God hath chosen thee to be a people for his own possession above all the peoples that are upon the face of the earth" (Deut. vii, 6). Here is the solemn announcement of a personal act of choice. Why he thus chose and favored one people above all others is no more difficult to answer than why he ever chooses one child of a family, or one individual out of the thousands of a nation, to stand out separately and conspicuously above the others. But exceptional favors impose corresponding obligations, and in the revelation of the one true God of heaven and earth Israel led the way, and has fulfilled the promise made to Abraham and the purpose of God as declared by the prophets.

16. Concept of God as Father. The highest and most endearing concept of God, whether found in the Old Testament or in the New, or among the nations anywhere, is that of Father. The prophet Hosea (xi, 1) represents Jehovah as saying: "When Israel was a child, then I loved him, and I called my son out of Egypt." Similarly, we read in Jeremiah, "I am a father to Israel, and Ephraim is my firstborn" (xxxi, 9; comp. iii, 4, 19), and in Exod. iv, 22, Moses is commanded to tell Pharaoh that Israel is the firstborn son of Jehovah. In Mal. i, 6, Jehovah pleads with Israel and says: "If I be a father, where is mine honor?" He promised through the word of Nathan to be a father to the son of David (2 Sam. vii, 14), and the author of Psa. lxxxix, 26, 27, seems to allude to this when he makes Jehovah say concerning some royal son of David,

> He shall cry unto me, Thou art my father,
> My God and the rock of my salvation.
> I also will make him my first born,
> The highest of the kings of the earth.

In Psa. lxviii, 5, God is proclaimed as "a father of the fatherless, and a judge of the widows," and in Psa. ciii, 13, it is written, "As a father pitieth his children, so Jehovah pitieth them that fear him." With all these statements one may also associate the words of Isa. lxvi, 13: "As one whom his mother comforteth, so will I comfort you." In Isa. lxiii, 16, the Israelites in exile, feeling that their ancient fathers Abraham and Jacob no longer acknowledge them as true and worthy descendants, are represented as crying out unto Jehovah and saying: "Thou, O Jehovah, art our father, our redeemer from everlasting is thy name." But in the next chapter (lxiv, 8) the relation of father is spoken of as equivalent to that of creator: "O Jehovah, thou art our father; we are the clay, and thou our potter; and we all are the work of thy hand." In most of these passages the Fatherhood of God is conceived as a national relationship rather than a personal one, and the idea is nowhere fully developed in the Hebrew scriptures. But wherever the personal relation is suggested, it is that of God's gracious tenderness and sympathy toward them that keep his law.

17. Summary of Old Testament Doctrine. The doctrine of God derived from the Hebrew scriptures as a whole is worthy of our highest admiration. In no nation or tribe of men before the time of Jesus Christ can we find anything comparable to it as a revelation of the unseen mystery of the world of being. If the Deity be at times conceived after the manner of a man, it is also made emphatic that man himself bears the image and likeness of God. If passions of jealousy and wrath are ascribed to him, it is because he can have no fellowship with the wicked who disobey his law. As far back as the oldest Hebrew records give us any light upon the subject, the God of Abraham and the God who made the world was conceived as a mighty Personality. He is no personification of the forces of nature, and is never identified with the world or with any of its visible forms of life. But he is worshiped as the almighty Power who is back of all phenomena. He is conceived as marching forth out of the fields of Edom, and making earth and heaven tremble at his presence (Judg. v, 4, 5). He leads the armies of Israel and causes the stars in their courses and the floods of the ancient rivers to fight against Sisera. His interpositions in behalf of his servants David and Elisha are heard like "the sound of marching in the tops of the mulberry-trees" (2 Sam. v, 24), and like the "noise of chariots, and of horses, and of a great host" (2 Kings vii, 6). He rides upon the whirlwind, utters his voice in the thunder, sets bounds to the seas, sends forth springs in the valleys, and makes the grass grow upon the mountains. There is no spot in all the world where he is not. Heaven is his throne; earth his footstool. And all these concepts of Deity are in perfect accord with the purest theism, and find a place in Christian hymnology as well as in Hebrew psalmody. For this "high and lofty One who inhabiteth eternity" dwells not only "in the high and holy place," but also "with him that is of a contrite and humble spirit" (Isa. lvii, 15).

(1) *Essential Qualities of Nature.* Speaking more particularly of the essential qualities of the nature of God, as revealed in the Hebrew scriptures, we should specify his unity. The distinguishing watch cry of Israel was, "Jehovah is one," and the monotheistic teaching declared that besides him there is and can be no God. He is essentially omnipresent, eternal, immutable, the everliving One. He is essentially spiritual in his nature, for "the Spirit of God," and "the Spirit of Jehovah" are terms expressive of this truth.

(2) *Personality of God.* The unity and spirituality of the divine nature necessarily involve the fact of personality. Any being who knows and delights in what is good, ordains laws for his subjects and punishes transgression must needs be a personal agent. The God of Israel expressed himself as a self-revealing personality in the utterance of the memorial name, I AM WHO I AM. The greatest thing cognizable in human thought is personality, and in the sublime picture of creation drawn by the Hebrew theist at the beginning of his narrative, the final and highest act in the order of the creation was the making of man in the image of God We recognize this divine image in the personality of intelligence, sensibility, and will. Man, thus made in God's image, may discern the elements of the divine Personality in his own spiritual nature.[1] All the categories of human thought assert themselves in the personal consciousness of intellections, emotions, and acts of volition. And all our ideas of time and space, of cause and effect, of law and freedom, are without possible explanation, and, indeed, impossible of statement, except as they are distinctively known in the personal consciousness of each individual of the race.

(3) *Divine Attributes in Personality.* In accord with the foregoing analysis of personality the attributes of God may all be comprehended under the trine division of omnipotence, omniscience, and omnisentience, or, in simpler terms, power, wisdom, and love.[2] In the human being these three are manifest in acts of

---

[1] "Personality," says Mansel, "comprises all that we know of that which exists; relation to personality comprises all we know of that which seems to exist. And when from the little world of man's consciousness we would lift up our eyes to the inexhaustible universe beyond, and ask to whom all this is related, the highest existence is still the highest personality; and the Source of all being reveals himself by his name, I AM."—Limits of Religious Thought. Bampton Lecture III, p. 105. Boston, 1859.

[2] Miley discriminates, we think very properly, between essence and attribute in God. Such essential qualities of the divine nature as unity, eternity, and spirituality are not strictly attributes, but designations of essential being. Attributes inhere in personality, and, thus conceived, are capable of the most simple classification. See Miley, Systematic Theology, Vol. I, pp. 160–164. New York, 1892.

the will and in states or operations of the intellect and the feelings, and the same is true in God, the highest personality. The great distinction between the divine and human personality is that in God these attributes exist in absolute perfection.

OMNIPOTENCE. Our study of such names of God as El, Elohim, and El Shadday led to the belief that the earliest conceptions of the Supreme Being regarded him mainly as one possessed of unlimited power. Those scriptures which imply a current monolatry rather than monotheism extol the God of Abraham and of Israel as the Mighty One who can send floods of waters to destroy mankind, and rain fire and brimstone to overthrow the wicked cities of the plain of Sodom. The marvels of the exodus made known Jehovah's absolute control over all the elements of nature. And so annalist and poet and prophet alike declare that there is nothing in heaven or earth too difficult for him to accomplish (comp. Jer. xxxii, 17, 27; Dan. iv, 35). He can "measure the waters in the hollow of his hand, mete out heaven with a span, comprehend the dust of the earth in a measure, and weigh the mountains in scales" (Isa. xl, 12). As in the memorial name he announced himself as I AM THAT I AM, so from beginning to end of the Hebrew revelation he virtually declares I WILL DO WHAT I WILL. "He doeth according to his will in the army of heaven, and among the inhabitants of the earth, and none can stay his hand, or say unto him, What doest thou?"

OMNISCIENCE. Wherever occasion offers, the Scriptures affirm or assume that the Creator and Ruler of the world is infinitely wise. By his wisdom he created the heavens and the earth. In the bold imagery of Prov. viii, 22, 23, Wisdom is personified as abiding with Jehovah "from eternity, from the beginning, before the earth was." Within this rich envelope of poetic thought we perceive the Hebrew doctrine of wisdom as an eternal attribute of the Creator. In some deep sense wisdom and God are one. He knows and is able to declare the end from the beginning, for he is the first and the last (Isa. xliv, 6; xlvi, 10). He knows the innermost thoughts of man (Psa. xciv, 11). Such omniscience must needs comprehend foreknowledge of the goal of all human history, and whatsoever enters into his eternal purpose of the ages and generations.

OMNISENTIENCE. We adopt this term for want of a better and because of its obvious conformity to the very common words *omnipotence* and *omniscience*. It serves to describe the God of Israel as an infinitely sentient Being, capable of emotion, affection, and the uttermost sensitiveness to all that is right and wrong, pure and impure. This attribute comprehends all the moral qualities, such as goodness, faithfulness, righteousness, and holiness, in divine perfection, for these may be properly thought of as expressions of the moral sense of God. It has been too much the habit of theologians to overlook the biblical revelations of divine emotion. It has even been deemed a disparagement of the heavenly nature of God to suppose him capable of any kind of suffering. To be a perfect and blessed Deity he must needs be without passions. And yet all relevant facts show that the most refined and exalted spiritual natures are most susceptible of intelligent emotion. Beings least capable of tender feeling are found among the lowest orders of animal life. The notion that various emotions in God must imply a limiting of his divine perfection has no basis in the Scriptures. Rather may it be affirmed that incapability of the various emotions of pleasure and of pain would be a reprehensible limitation of the God of the Hebrew revelation. He is represented as yearning in wonderful pity and compassion over the objects of his care, and also as angry and deeply grieved over the sins of men. "His soul was grieved for the misery of Israel" (Judg. x, 16). "How shall I give thee up, O Ephraim? how shall I cast thee off, O Israel? My heart is turned upon me, my compassions are kindled together" (Hos. xi, 8). Whatever element of anthropopathism, or of poetic license, be recognized in such representations of God, there is no mistaking the main thought. In all the affliction of his people he was afflicted, and in his love and in his pity he redeemed them (Isa. lxiii, 9). They often rebelled against him, and "grieved his Holy Spirit," but he did not cast them off. His loving favors were adapted to cheer those who trusted him "as one whom his mother comforteth" (Isa. lxvi, 13; comp. xlix, 15). He was the loving Shepherd of Israel, and carried the lambs in his bosom (Isa. xl, 11). The queen of Sheba said that "Jehovah was in love with Israel for ever" (1 Kings x, 9), and, according to Psa. ciii, 13, "as a father pitieth his children, so Jehovah pitieth them that fear him." Emotions of tenderest affection are thus attributed to Jehovah. But the passion of hostility toward that which is evil is as pure as the passion of love for that which is good. Hence in numerous other texts of Scripture the righteousness, truth, fidelity, loving-kindness, and tender mercies of Jehovah are extolled together. In Deut. vii, 9, the faithfulness of Israel's God is thus declared: "Know that Jehovah thy God, he is God; the faithful God, who keepeth covenant and mercy with them that love him and keep his covenant to a thousand generations." The idea of faithfulness is naturally associated with goodness and mercy. It is noteworthy how frequently the words *lovingkindness* (חסד) and *tender mercies* (רחמים) occur together in the Hebrew Psalter. The righteousness and holiness of Jehovah are also intimately associated. Righteousness and judgment are the foundation of his throne, for "Jehovah of hosts is exalted in judgment, and the holy God is sanctified in righteousness" (Psa. lxxxix, 14; Isa. v, 16). He is extolled by psalmists and prophets as "the Holy One of Israel." So pronounced are the references to his holiness that some writers would rank the title קדוש, *holy,* among the names of God.¹ Others treat it as a synonym of the majesty and glory of the divine nature, designed to sum up all the other perfections of God, while others explain it as denoting Jehovah's peculiar relations to Israel.² Some truth attaches to all these views of קדוש and yet it remains obvious that the *holiness* of Jehovah is that quality of his emotional nature which separates him personally from everything that can defile. He can have no fellowship with the impure. This truth was made prominent in the Levitical legislation. The graduated sanctity of the holy places in the tabernacle, the consecration of priests and altar, the numerous and minute distinctions between things clean and unclean, the entire body of statutes embraced in Lev. xvii—xxvi, and now commonly called the "Law of Holiness," and, above all else, the symbolism and solemnity of the Holy of holies, in which only the high priest was permitted to enter, once in the year, wearing a miter with a golden plate inscribed "Holiness to Jehovah"—these provisions served as an object-lesson to teach the immaculate separateness and moral purity of the God of Israel. All these moral perfections, as well as all affections of loving tenderness, are comprehended in the divine attribute of omnisentience.

---

[1] Piepenbring, Theology of the Old Testament, p. 106.
[2] Schultz, Old Testament Theology, Vol. II, pp. 131, 168, 169. W. R. Smith, Prophets of Israel, pp. 224–229.

SECTION THIRD

THE REVELATION IN JESUS CHRIST

CHAPTER I

THE THREEFOLD MANIFESTATION

1. Love, Wisdom, and Power in the Person, Mediation, and Kingdom of Christ. Our Lord Jesus Christ, to the study of whose person, mediation, and kingdom we have devoted the chief portion of this volume, has made known to us the most perfect revelation of God yet vouchsafed to mankind. That threefold manifestation exhibits in each of its wonderful phases the love, the wisdom, and the power of our heavenly Father, and we have seen that the blessed Son of his love is the very incarnation of the invisible God, the image of his substance, who in the days of his flesh declared that "no man knows the Father but the Son, and he to whomsoever the Son willeth to reveal him." Our previous study of this Christ has prepared us to see and now to point out the fact that, whether we contemplate him in his person, his mediation, or his kingdom, he is a revelation of the Father who sent him. His adorable personality and his heavenly kingdom, as truly as his ministry of reconciliation, disclose the eternal will, wisdom, and love of the invisible Being, who has not left himself without witness among any of the nations, but who spoke of old time to the Hebrew fathers and prophets in an exceptional way, and made that peculiar people a chosen possession "above all the peoples upon the earth."

2. Complemental to Old Testament Revelation. The New Testament revelation of God is, accordingly, a fulfillment or a complement of truths given of old in the Law and the Prophets. We find in the gospels and epistles a recognition of the same essential attributes of God which are extolled in the Hebrew scriptures. The majesty and glory of Jehovah are there set forth in a manner so marvelous that it would seem impossible to conceive anything more awful and impressive. The unity, omnipotence, omnipresence, righteousness, and holiness of the God of Israel find such a fullness of statement in the Prophets and the Psalms as to leave little if anything additional to be expected in the New Testament. But the Old Testament revelation is at its best incomplete and one-sided. The almighty God of Israel is portrayed as high and lifted up, dwelling in the thick darkness, true and righteous altogether, but his holiness is conceived in such solemn and awful separateness from man as to repel rather than attract the common soul. The severity of his judgments is so terrific that his lovingkindness is thrown into shadow. His choice of a peculiar people for his own special possession has been construed too often into a relative hatred of other nations, and the vindictive psalms witness the extremes to which this feeling of vengeance toward enemies gave way among the pious Israelites. The book of Esther is a monument of this vindictive spirit, and there is little in the Hebrew scriptures to correct or counteract it. While the Abrahamic promise contemplated the blessing of all the families of the earth, and the prophets at times caught the ideal of nations coming to the light of Israel, the national partialism and the historical separateness of the people were so strong as to make the broader view of no effect. The coming of Christ was to fulfill all that was excellent in the older revelation, supplement defects, correct the one-sidedness of exclusive partialism, and introduce the universalism of the gospel of a spiritual kingdom of heaven that was destined to make all things new.

3. Christ the Power of God. In the manifestation of Christ we behold a new revelation of the power of God. The prevalent idea of God's power in the Old Testament and among the nations is that of physical force. The Almighty is he who sends out his lightnings, hurls the destructive thunderbolt, makes the mountains tremble, and controls the proud waves of the sea. The New Testament does not ignore that supreme power; it rather magnifies our concept of omnipotence; but the manifestations of the power of God in Christ are more conspicuously powers of the Spirit. It is written that, after his temptations, "Jesus returned in the power of the Spirit into Galilee" (Luke iv, 14), and from his person went forth a kind of "authority and power" that healed all manner of diseases, cast out unclean spirits, and wrought many other "mighty works" which filled the hearts of multitudes with gladness. This divine power was not only a wisdom and subtle force that could analyze all kinds of sickness and impart the healing touch, but also an authority to forgive the sins of men. As he that rules his own spirit is mightier than the hero who takes a city (Prov. xvi, 32), so the heavenly power that works a revolution in one's inner life is immeasurably greater than any physical force. The still small voice of the unseen Spirit of Christ is mightier than the strong wind and earthquake and fire, and it reveals a power that never operates apart from infinite wisdom and love; for it is a spiritual energy that thrills the soul, convicts of sin, regenerates the moral life, and proves itself to be "the power of God unto salvation to every one that believeth." Hence the consciousness of superhuman, spiritual authority over life and death, which, in accordance with the Father's love, declared: "I lay down my life that I may take it again. No one taketh it away from me, but I lay it down of myself. I have power to lay it down, and I have power to take it again" (John x, 18). In accordance with such authority Christ also further revealed the infinite resources of the power of the Spirit in the whole work of his divine mediation; for we have seen that in all his mission and ministry of redemption "God was in Christ reconciling the world unto himself." And his enthronement at the right hand of God is but another concept of the heavenly power. All authority has been given unto him in heaven and on earth, and it is no other than the authority and power of God, which irresistibly, silently, steadily puts all things in subjection under his feet, "all rule, and authority, and power, and dominion, and every name that is named, not only in this world, but also in that which is to come" (Eph. i, 21). In all this Christ Jesus our Lord is a manifestation of the power of our heavenly Father, and so we honor the Son as we honor the Father, and worship and say, "Thine is the kingdom, and the power, and the glory."

4. Christ the Wisdom of God. But in Christ we behold the wisdom as well as the power of God. The Old Testament extolled the wisdom of Jehovah, and in Proverbs (viii, 22-31) we have the personification of this eternal attribute conceived as rejoicing always before the Creator of the world, and present as a master workman when God established the heavens and the earth. The New Testament makes Christ the embodiment of this heavenly wisdom. The apostle speaks of a "full assurance of understanding" by means of which one may "know the mystery of God, even Christ, in whom are hidden all the treasures of wisdom and knowledge" (Col. ii, 3). This fullness of wisdom in Christ is seen in "his understanding and his answers" which amazed the rabbinical teachers in the temple while as yet he was but twelve years old. While he was thus growing, waxing strong, and advancing in wisdom and stature, he was filled in the developing capacities of his manhood with "all the fulness of the Godhead bodily." The biblical records clearly show his human limitations, and he himself declared most emphatically, even when he was near the end of his earthly career, that he was limited in his knowledge as the angels in heaven (Mark xiii, 32); but there was no defect in the quality of the wisdom with which he was divinely filled. There is great significance in the phrase πληρούμενον σοφίᾳ, *becoming full of wisdom,* in Luke ii, 40. His perfect human nature in its normal growth from infancy to manhood was continuously filled with wisdom, love, and power to his utmost capacity; but the human limitations of his incarnation remained until he was received up into heaven. This limitation, however, was not of a nature to admit of any error in thought, word, or deed. We make an absolute distinction between defective knowledge that expresses itself in terms of ignorance and in false opinions, and fullness of wisdom and knowledge that declines to utter a word that is not true and righteous altogether. The teachings of Jesus are a marvelous treasury of divine wisdom and knowledge. No other man ever thus spoke. His mission was to "bear witness unto the truth," and in his heavenly wisdom to found and administer a kingdom "not of this world" (John xviii, 36, 37). His mediation and his kingdom are alike a manifestation of the "great mystery of godliness." The redemption of the world through Christ is to be conceived as "God's wisdom in a mystery, even that hidden wisdom which God foreordained before the ages unto our glory" (1 Cor. ii, 7). In his entire ministry of personal teaching, of self-sacrificing mediation, and of ruling until he shall have subdued the last enemy, he appears as revealer of "the depth of the riches both of the wisdom and knowledge of God."

5. Christ the Love of God. In all the depths of the riches of heavenly revelations in Christ nothing so tenderly affects the heart of man as his manifestation of the love of the Father. At his baptism in the Jordan a voice from heaven proclaimed, "Thou art my beloved Son; in thee I am well pleased." The entire message of the gospel centers in the blessed thought that God so loved the world that he gave his only begotten Son to save the world. The apostolic exhortation is: "Be ye imitators of God, as beloved children, and walk in love even as Christ loved you." All this is in deepest harmony with Christ's own prayer: "Holy Father, keep them in thy name whom thou hast given me, that they may be one, even as we are: I in them and thou in me, that they may be perfected into one; that the world may know that thou didst send me, and lovedst them even as thou lovedst me." Alike then in his person, his mediation, and his heavenly kingdom, Christ is the supreme manifestation of the love of the Father, so that he may well say, "He that hath seen me hath seen the Father." The beloved disciple reiterates the blessed truth that "God is love." All the ideals of tender affection, and even of passionate emotion, which we found in the Old Testament doctrine of omnisentience, appear in actual human manifestation in Jesus Christ. Whether he takes little children into his arms and blesses them, or tenderly heals the sick and opens the eyes of the blind, or groans in the spirit and weeps at the grave of Lazarus, or cries over Jerusalem, "How oft would I have gathered thy children together even as a hen gathereth her chickens under her wings, and ye would not!" or forgives the sins of the erring, and says even to the adulteress, "I do not condemn thee; go and sin no more," or instructs his disciples to forgive offenders unto seventy times seven; whether in his last hour he commends his mother to the care of a beloved disciple, or prays for the forgiveness of them that crucified him, and lays down his own life in behalf of his friends and his foes—in all these acts of love we behold not Jesus only, but the Father also. The God and Father of our Lord Jesus Christ is imaged in the incarnate Christ himself, and every divine attribute which we have comprehended under omnisentience is manifested in the same adorable personality. He is the faithful and true witness and example of the righteousness and the holiness as well as the love of the Father. God did not lay aside any divine attribute, nor empty himself of any essential quality of his nature in order to manifest himself in the likeness of men, but, as we have shown in our study of the person of Christ, it pleased the Father that in the Son of his love should dwell "all the fulness of the Godhead bodily." The incarnation was not a kenotic but a pleromic revelation of God.

CHAPTER II

CHRIST'S OWN TESTIMONY AND TEACHING

1. Jesus's Testimony in Matthew xi, 25-27. There is no saying of Jesus preserved to us in the gospels that bears more directly on the subject before us than the one written in Matt. xi, 25-27: "I thank thee, O Father, Lord of heaven and earth, that thou didst hide these things from the wise and understanding, and didst reveal them unto babes: yea, Father, for so it was well pleasing in thy sight. All things have been delivered unto me of my Father, and no one knoweth the Son, save the Father; neither doth any know the Father, save the Son, and he to whomsoever the Son willeth to reveal him" (comp. Luke x, 21, 22). It is quite arbitrary and unjustifiable to question this text, as some critics have done, solely on account of its remarkable harmony with the doctrine and style of the fourth gospel. Its sentiment is in thorough harmony with the general spirit and teaching of our Lord, and the three things which demand our careful attention are the following: (1) The filial relationship of Jesus to God, and the consciousness that he is personally the medium of a very special and superior revelation of his Father; (2) this superior revelation is intelligible to babes in understanding, that is, people of simple and receptive hearts like guileless children, as against those who pride themselves in their own wisdom and knowledge; (3) the Father himself enjoys a real pleasure in thus revealing himself to such as are, like Jesus, "meek and lowly in heart." These three noble truths find ample support in other teachings of our Lord recorded in the synoptic gospels, as we proceed to show.

(1) *Fuller Revelation of the Father.* The consciousness that he came to reveal the Father in a more complete manner than had been made known in the Law and the Prophets, is apparent in the teaching of Jesus in the Sermon on the Mount. Both the substance of his teaching and the authority with which he spoke astonished the multitudes that heard him (Matt. vii, 28, 29). I came not to destroy the law or the prophets, he says, but to fulfill. I declare unto you a deeper sense in the old commandments than the world has yet recognized. The law against murder is violated by every one who is angry with his brother. The law against adultery is broken even by the lustful look and thought. He is guilty of

swearing profanely who allows his speech to go beyond the simple, straightforward yea and nay. The law of personal retaliation and hatred of enemies is to be superseded by the new commandment, "Love your enemies and pray for them that persecute you; that ye may be sons of your Father who is in heaven: for he maketh his sun to rise on the evil and the good, and sendeth rain on the just and the unjust" (v, 44, 45). In the matter of prayer he puts stress on one's personal approach to the Father. The psalmist uttered one of the most affecting conceptions of Jehovah to be found in the Old Testament when he said, "As a father pitieth his children, so Jehovah pitieth them that fear him" (ciii, 13). But the utterance is general, and is based on the conception of reverential awe rather than of love in the heart of the child. Jesus speaks of "thy Father," and inculcates personal confidence and affection in one's approach unto God: "When thou prayest, enter into thine inner chamber, and having shut thy door, pray to thy Father who is in secret, and thy Father who seeth in secret shall recompense thee" (vi, 6). He assures us that our heavenly Father knows our needs before we ask him. Be not anxious, he says, about food and drink and clothes. Your heavenly Father feeds the birds, and clothes the lilies, and are ye not of much more value in his sight than they? And so, in addressing God in prayer, he teaches us to say, "Our Father; give us our daily bread; forgive us our debts; bring us not into temptation." Elsewhere he says: "Not one sparrow shall fall on the ground without your Father; but the very hairs of your head are all numbered" (x, 29, 30). With what personal confidence, then, ought we to pray unto our Father who is in the heavens! We are, accordingly, admonished to be perfect children, inasmuch as we have such a perfect heavenly Father (v, 48), and to let our light shine before men, that they, too, may see, and know, and glorify our Father who is in the heavens (v, 16). Other teachings of Jesus in the synoptic gospels involve this same impressive doctrine of our heavenly Father. He assures those who are persecuted and brought to bear witness for him before governors and kings that it shall be given them in that hour what they shall say by the Spirit of their Father (Matt. x, 20). This is in noteworthy harmony with the doctrine of the Comforter in John's gospel. "Call no man your father on the earth," he says (xxiii, 9), "for one is your Father, the heavenly." This means that the filial relation to God should be realized in a manner so enhancing to our thought that no merely human title, not even that of father, should for a moment lead us to forget our blessed relationship to our heavenly Father. His frequent use of the expression *my Father* has also its suggestions. "Whosoever shall do the will of my Father who is in the heavens, he is my brother, and sister, and mother" (xii, 50). Here, surely, Jesus reveals his Father in a most personal and affectionate way. Every pure human relationship is thus sanctified with those whose lives are "hid with Christ in God," and all the blessed possibilities of regeneration and eternal life take on an overwhelming heavenly aspect by the suggestions of such spiritual relationship to "the God and Father of our Lord Jesus Christ." Add to this the solemn words of Matt. x, 32, 33: "Every one who shall confess me before men, him will I confess before my Father who is in the heavens. But whosoever shall deny me before men, him will I also deny before my Father who is in the heavens." Also those of Matt. xv, 13: "Every plant which my heavenly Father planted not, shall be rooted up." In all such statements Jesus not only assumes a unique relation to God as his heavenly Father, but also implies the provision for a personal filial relation to God of all that love him. He also reveals the Father in various aspects of his heavenly tenderness in such other sayings as, "If two of you shall agree on earth as touching anything that they shall ask, it shall be done for them of my Father who is in the heavens" (Matt. xviii, 19). "It is not the will of my Father who is in the heavens, that one of these little ones should perish" (ver. 14). "Verily I say unto you, that in heaven their angels do always behold the face of my Father who is in the heavens" (ver. 10). "The righteous shall shine forth as the sun in the kingdom of their Father" (xiii, 43). "I appoint unto you a kingdom, even as my Father appointed unto me, that ye may eat and drink at my table in my kingdom; and ye shall sit on thrones, judging the twelve tribes of Israel" (Luke xxii, 29, 30; comp. Matt. xix, 28). It is impossible to study these sayings of our Lord and fail to see that in a variety of profoundly suggestive ways he is making the Father known to them that are willing to know him. His language has at times the style of metaphor and proverb, but the essential thought is never difficult to grasp, and in every instance we catch some new and impressive glimpse of the love of our Father who is in the heavens.

(2) *Simplicity of Christ's Gospel of the Father.* Furthermore, this manner of revealing the Father has its peculiar adaptation to those who possess childlike simplicity and willingness to learn the truth. Things that concern our deepest needs, things of a very practical character but of far-reaching importance, are often hidden, by reason of barriers of their own construction, from those who are wise in their own conceit. The simplicity of the gospel of Christ is one of its highest claims upon our confidence, and the

beatitudes, pronounced in Matt. v, 3-8, upon the poor in spirit, the sorrowful, the gentle, the merciful, and the pure in heart surpass in beauty and tenderness even such exceptionally comforting words of the Old Testament as, "Jehovah is nigh unto them that are of a broken heart, and saveth such as are of a contrite spirit" (Psa. xxxiv, 18); or those of Isa. lvii, 15: "I dwell in the high and holy place, with him also that is of a contrite and humble spirit." The simple adaptation of Christ's teaching to touch the heart of humanity everywhere is its crowning excellence. Herein he surpasses psalmists and prophets that were before him. While it is written, in Dan. vii, 27, that "the kingdom and the dominion, and the greatness of the kingdoms under the whole heaven, shall be given to the people of the saints of the Most High," Jesus says, "Fear not, little flock, for it is your Father's good pleasure to give you the kingdom" (Luke xii, 32). In explaining the purpose of his parables he said to the disciples: "Unto you it is given to know the mysteries of the kingdom of heaven, but to them (who vainly pride themselves in ability to see and hear) it is not given. . . . Blessed are your eyes, for they see; and your ears, for they hear. For verily I say unto you, that many prophets and righteous men desired to see the things which ye see, and saw them not; and to hear the things which ye hear, and heard them not" (Matt. xiii, 11-17; comp. Luke x, 21-24). All this and much more of a similar kind illustrates the simple, direct, and touching manner in which Jesus made known the Spirit of his Father and our Father who is in heaven.

(3) *The Father's Delight in His Children.* But these same teachings also reveal the delight of our heavenly Father in communicating his grace to those who are of a receptive heart. Such revelation is a positive pleasure ($εὐδοκία$, *a delightful satisfaction*) unto him. He is as well pleased to impart the riches of his kingdom to his children as he is well pleased in his beloved Son (Matt. iii, 17; xvii, 5). As the Father loves his anointed Son, and delights to honor him, he reveals in this conspicuous fact that he has exquisite joy in all his obedient children. The great commandment which Christ extols as comprehensive of the whole Law and the Prophets would be without force if we did not assume that the Father himself loves us with an affection that passeth understanding. How wonderfully and genuinely must he love us to expect that we love him with all the heart and soul and mind and strength! He surely expects reciprocal affection, and in the entire ministry of his Son Jesus Christ he has given us assurance of his unspeakable pleasure in manifesting his holy love for man, and in receiving from man the simple, childlike response of a love unfeigned.

2. Great Advance on the Old Testament View. In this more personal revelation of the love of our heavenly Father, Jesus made a noteworthy advance beyond the general teaching of the Old Testament. He spoke with an authority greater than that of Moses and the prophets, and in proportionate clearness brought God nearer to the human heart. For while the Law and the Prophets and the Psalms extol the loving-kindness and long-suffering of the God of Israel, and in a few instances ascribe to him the title of Father, the power, majesty, righteousness, and holiness of God receive by far the more elaborate treatment. In that older time the nation and the family were put so far above the individual that personal interests were comparatively lost from sight. Hence when Jehovah says in Jer. xxxi, 9, "I am a father to Israel, and Ephraim is my first-born," it is the nation, the people as a collective body, not the individual Israelite, that is thought of as "the dear son, the darling child" (ver. 20). So, too, in Hos. xi, 1, "when Israel was a child, then I loved him and called my son out of Egypt," it is not an individual but all the tribes of Israel that the prophet has in mind. The same appears in Exod. iv, 22: "Thus saith Jehovah, Israel is my son, my first-born." Also in Isa. lxiii, 16; lxiv, 8, "Thou, O Jehovah, art our Father," is the cry of Jehovah's servant Israel, who calls himself "thy holy people, the tribes of thine inheritance." While such a collective idea of Jehovah's first born son was the prevailing thought, the true personal relation of each individual to God as his heavenly Father could not be fully made known. This highest and holiest personal relationship was first brought to light in Jesus, who at twelve years of age spoke confidently of "my Father" (Luke ii, 49), and whom at the Jordan the voice out of heaven proclaimed as "my beloved Son, in whom I am well pleased." What the prophet Hosea (xi, 1) said of Israel as a people, the evangelist sees fulfilled personally in Jesus (Matt. ii, 15). The magnificent language, which in Isa. xlii, 1-4, is addressed by Jehovah to Jacob his servant and Israel whom he has chosen, is in Matt. xii, 18-21, applied directly to Jesus Christ. And, similarly, in all the teaching of our Lord relative to his Father and our Father who is in heaven, he puts forward the more personal revelation of the Father to the individual heart of everyone "to whom the Son willeth to reveal him."

3. The Only One Good. It is further to be remarked that in his revelation of the Father Jesus declares him as the one God who is the impersonation of all goodness. To the man who addressed him as "good Master," he said: "Why callest thou me good? None is good save one, the God" (εἶς, ὁ θεός; Mark x, 18). This declaration should not be construed into a denial of Christ's goodness, but is designed rather to put forward the highest conception of personal goodness and center it in God. Somewhat after the manner of Eliphaz (in Job iv, 18; xv, 15), who would enhance the thought of God's holiness by suggesting that his holy ones and even the heavens themselves are comparatively unclean, Jesus affirms that God alone is absolutely good. This characteristic quality of the divine nature must needs comprehend all those moral attributes which we have classified under omnisentience, namely, faithfulness, goodness, loving-kindness, emotionality, righteousness, and holiness; and hence we learn that the God and Father of our Lord Jesus Christ possesses all these qualities in absolute perfection. The Pharisee, whose notions of righteousness and goodness were altogether conventional, and who was wont to "tithe mint, and rue, and every herb, and pass over the justice and the love of God" (Luke xi, 42), was hardly susceptible to such a revelation of divine goodness as these words of Jesus contain. This declaration concerning goodness might perhaps be paraphrased so as to conform to what our Lord said about his knowledge of the day and hour (Mark xiii, 32): "No one is absolutely good, not even the angels in heaven, neither the Son, but the Father."

4. Doctrine of Jesus in the Fourth Gospel. The peculiarities of the fourth gospel are such as to justify our study of its doctrine of God in connection with the same doctrine found in the first epistle of John. In both gospel and epistle we find the teaching of Jesus touching his heavenly Father set forth in language and style peculiar to the Johannine writings, but the doctrine is in all essentials in complete harmony with that of the synoptic gospels. The doctrine of the Logos, in whose incarnation was beheld "a glory as of an only begotten from a Father full of grace and truth," has its commanding significance for the true revelation of God. There are also other statements of a general character, which here call for only a passing notice. The Father is "the only true God" (xvii, 3; comp. vii, 28; viii, 26); he is the "holy Father," and the "righteous Father" (xvii, 11, 25), also "the living Father," who has life in himself, and has given to the Son to have life in himself (vi, 57; v, 26). In the first epistle (i, 9; ii, 29; iii, 7; v, 20) we meet with the same general statements, and from all such teaching we derive the concept of a blessed Father, full of grace and truth, existing through eternity but manifesting himself in time as holy and righteous altogether, and that supreme manifestation is in and through his Son.

(1) *God is Spirit*. The most specific declaration of the essential nature of God to be found in John's gospel is in iv, 24, where Jesus says to the woman of Samaria, "God is Spirit." The Greek

word πνεῦμα, *Spirit,* is here without the article and occupies the emphatic position in the sentence, thus notably describing the nature rather than the personality of God. The Samaritan woman seems to have held the old notion of her ancestors (comp. 2 Kings xvii, 26, 27) that each country has its local deity, and that within that region one place of worship would be more acceptable than another. Over against this notion Jesus set forth the sublime spiritual and monotheistic concept of God, the one universal Father, whose presence may be known in any place. Nay, instead of presuming to find God in this mountain or in that, the Father himself is the one who seeks the true worshipers. The real concern of one who would know the Father must be, not a question of time, and place, and outward forms of reverence, but the spirit and truth in which he opens his inmost soul to the reception of that which is good. Spiritual truth may be spiritually discerned in any place, and every spot where God thus makes himself known to his true worshiper is holy ground. The essential attributes of a spirit are not and cannot be seen by fleshly eyes, but they may be felt and known in personal consciousness. Spirit answers to spirit, and God's wisdom, love, and power are spiritual verities to be truly apprehended by spiritual intuition. Only the spiritual man can truly discern, examine, and receive the things of the Spirit of God.

(2) *God is the Life and the Light.* We have noticed that, in John vi, 57, Jesus calls God "the living Father." In another place (v, 26) he says: "As the Father hath life in himself, even so gave he to the Son also to have life in himself." Accordingly, the prologue of this gospel declares that "in him was life, and the life was the light of men" (i, 4). The coming of Christ is that men "may have life, and may have it abundantly" (x, 10). Life and light are thus closely associated in the mind of this evangelist, and the main thought is that of spiritual life and its heavenly illumination. God is the one eternal source of life and light, and these he imparts to man through the incarnation of the Word through whom all things were made. Hence by necessary implication the Father is the source of all life and all light in the universe. All possibilities of life, vegetable, animal, and spiritual, exist primordially in him. Life and light associate naturally together, and since "the life was the light of men," Jesus says with great force, "I am the light of the world: he that followeth me shall not walk in darkness, but shall have the light of life" (viii, 12). In this connection the language of 1 John i, 5, may well be cited: "God is light, and in him is no darkness at all." He became incarnate that he might appear and witness "the true light which lighteth every man" (i, 9; ix, 5; xii, 46).

(3) *God is Love.* The love of the Father finds highest expression in the person and work of his "only begotten Son." The language of John i, 18, is very remarkable. It is "the only begotten Son, who is in the bosom of the Father," who alone can fully reveal him. This statement is in substance the same as that of Jesus himself in Matt. xi, 27, but in this fourth gospel we note the phrases *only begotten Son,* and *the bosom of the Father.* These are terms of holiest affection, and the concept of the eternal Word, in the beginning with God, existing in the glory of the Father, and beloved of the Father before the world was (comp. xvii, 5, 24), yet becoming flesh and manifesting himself as a man among men, is unique and marvelous among all the self-revelations of God. While this Son of the Father makes known the truth and holiness and righteousness of God, and magnifies all moral excellencies to the highest conceivable perfection, his manifestation of the love of God has noteworthy preëminence. The classic text, which embodies the whole gospel in one sentence, is John iii, 16: "God so loved the world that he gave his only begotten Son, that whosoever believeth on him should not perish, but have eternal life." This is the love divine which, when duly felt, prompts our loving God with all the heart and soul. "As the Father hath loved me, I also have loved you: abide ye in my love" (xv, 9). The same idea of God's love is emphasized in the first epistle of John. We are to love one another because "love is of God, and every one that loveth is begotten of God, and knoweth God." Thus every true child of God is to know the love of the Father, and all such are to love one another also, as dear children, in whom God delights to abide and perfect his own heavenly love. "God is love; and he that abideth in love abideth in God, and God abideth in him" (iv, 7-16). "Behold what manner of love the Father hath bestowed on us, that we should be called children of God" (iii, 1). All these sayings are but echoes of the teaching of Jesus in the gospel according to John. God is the tender, affectionate, all-compassionate Father. As truly as he is a Spirit so also God is love, and we think of his omnisentience as preëminently the delicate sensitiveness of an infinite loving-kindness toward his whole creation. The groaning and travailing world of life suffers no emotion that is not also felt in the bosom of the Father. How unfathomable the love that so grasps the world as to feel every joy and every pang of insect, bird, beast, and child of man that ever lived and moved upon the face of the earth, in the depths of the sea, or in the heavens above!

(4) *Johannine Concept of the Fatherhood.* The name of the Father is employed in referring to God about one hundred and twenty times in the gospel, and twelve times in the first epistle of

John. The expression is generally "the Father," and frequently "my Father," but, with the sole exception of xx, 17, "your Father" does not appear as in the synoptic gospels. To the unbelieving Jews who claimed God for their Father he said: "If God were your Father, ye would love me, for I came forth and am come from God. . . . Ye are of your father the devil" (viii, 42-44). So in the parable of the tares those who offend and work iniquity are called "sons of the evil one" (Matt. xiii, 38). There is nothing in the nature of fatherhood nor in the yearnings of love to coerce filial obedience in any human heart. And so while all men are offspring of God, and the whole world of life has its origin in the eternal Spirit, men have rebelled against God, rejected his truth, alienated themselves from his fellowship, and "sold themselves to do evil." But on the other hand, to as many as receive this Son of God, "gave he the right to become children of God" (i, 12). This "right to become children of God" is a Johannine phrase, and the idea is not very different from Paul's doctrine of adoption ($\upsilon\iota o\vartheta\varepsilon\sigma\iota\alpha$). It is the gracious bestowal of a peculiar power or authority ($\dot{\varepsilon}\xi o\upsilon\sigma\iota\alpha$) for personal fellowship with God and with Christ. To those who enjoy such filial right the fatherhood of God becomes in Christ a blessed and glorious vision. "He that hath seen me hath seen the Father" (xiv, 9). The everlasting Father lives, loves, and shows his wisdom and power in the person of his Son, whom he has sent to be the Saviour of the world. There are many mansions in the Father's house prepared for and awaiting those that love him (xiv, 2), and it is the only begotten Son who prepares them, and comes and receives his own, and takes them away to behold his heavenly glory. The Father is thus manifested and glorified in the Son. Hence the force and suggestiveness of the words, "I am in the Father and the Father in me." At the same time the dependence of the Son upon the Father is declared in most positive terms: "The Son can do nothing of himself, but what he seeth the Father doing; for what things soever he doeth, these the Son also doeth in like manner. For the Father loveth the Son, and showeth him all things that himself doeth" (v, 19, 20; comp. viii, 28; xii, 49). It is in accordance with this self-testimony that he can both say, "I and the Father are one" (x, 30), and "the Father is greater than I" (xiv, 28). The Father as the infinite source of all love, wisdom, and power holds the essential relationship of fatherhood, but in the outworking of his purpose of redemption he acts in dynamic unity of fellowship with the only begotten Son, and the real basis of such fellowship is a spiritual unity of nature and of life.

CHAPTER III

APOSTOLIC CONCEPTS OF THE FATHER

1. In the Epistle of John. It is a revelation in itself to study and discover the concept of "our Father who is in heaven" as it appears in the teachings of the first apostles of our Lord. We have already observed that the doctrine of the first epistle of John is in substance identical with that of the fourth gospel. There are, however, a few passages in the epistle which deserve additional notice as illustrating the writer's conception of the Father. His controlling thought may be supposed to have had its origin in that profound supplication of Jesus that Christian believers everywhere "may all be one, even as thou, Father, art in me, and I in thee, that they also may be in us, that the world may believe that thou didst send me" (John xvii, 21). For at the beginning of his epistle he observes: "Our fellowship is with the Father, and with his Son Jesus Christ" (i, 3). Hence the whole company of believers are as "little children," who "have an Advocate with the Father," and "know the Father," and know also that "all that is in the world, the lust of the flesh and the lust of the eyes and the vainglory of life, is not of the Father, but is of the world" (ii, 1, 13, 16). What manner of love such sonship and such knowledge of God display! (iii, 1.) Hence the great lesson that "every one that loveth is begotten of God and knoweth God, and he that loveth not knoweth not God; for God is love" (iv, 7, 8). Such knowledge of God and loving fellowship with his Son Jesus Christ bring the purified believer as a little child into the very bosom of the Father.

2. In the Other Catholic Epistles we meet only incidental references to God as "the Father" (James i, 27; iii, 9; 1 Pet. i, 2, 3, 17; 2 Pet. i, 17; Jude 1; 2 John, 3, 4, 9). The expression *Father of lights,* in James i, 17, is peculiar, and points to God as the creator of the heavenly luminaries, sun, moon, and stars, as told in Gen. i, 14-16. In Heb. xii, 9, God is called "the Father of spirits," that is, of such spirits as angels and the "spirits of just men made perfect" (comp. ver. 23 and i, 7, 14). But these few references attest a prevalent apostolic concept of God as the blessed Father of our Lord Jesus Christ and of all who enter into the life and fellowship of Jesus.

3. In the Pauline Epistles we find the same vivid conception of God as the Father of Jesus Christ and of all them that believe in him. In his address to the men of Athens Paul proclaims "the God that made the world and all things therein," and who also "made of one every nation of men, and determined the bounds of their habitation." He accordingly teaches that men are "the offspring of God," and that "in him we live and move and have our being" (Acts xvii, 24-29). Here is a broad and profound concept of God as the universal Father, the maker and upholder of the visible universe, without whom nothing lives and acts. It is a lofty theism, an all-embracing monotheism, and mankind at large is thought of as begotten (γένος) of him as an eternal Father.

(1) *Various Striking Phrases.* At the beginning of every epistle this apostle makes mention of "God our Father." The same phrase occurs many times in other parts of the epistles, and varies with such forms as "God the Father," "our God and Father," "God and Father of our Lord Jesus Christ." In Rom. viii, 15, and Gal. iv, 6, we meet the intensified expression, *Abba, Father.* The Aramaic word *Abba* had often fallen from Jesus's lips in prayer (comp. Mark xiv, 36), and it came to have a charming significance in the worship of the first Christian congregations. The tenderness and assurance implied in these phrases may be further noticed in such exquisite conceptions as "the Father of mercies and God of all comfort, who comforteth us in all our affliction" (2 Cor. i, 3); "the God of patience and of comfort" (Rom. xv, 5); "God our Father who loved us and gave us eternal comfort and good hope through grace" (2 Thess. ii, 16); "God rich in mercy, for his great love wherewith he loved us" (Eph. ii, 4); "God commendeth his own love toward us, in that, while we were yet sinners, Christ died for us" (Rom. v, 8). In Phil. i, 8, the apostle calls God to witness his deep longing after the saints "in the tender mercies of Jesus Christ." Christ's divine love and personality have so taken possession of his heart that his affection for the Philippians is truly Christ's affection working in him. What he feels is what Christ feels, and God himself is witness to it all and shares the same tender feeling. In Phil. ii, 1, mention is made of the "consolation of love, fellowship of the Spirit, and tendermercies[1] and compassions," and at the close of the epistle (iv, 19) the writer says: "My God shall supply every need of yours according to his riches in glory in Christ Jesus." As recognizing the common source of all Christian comfort we notice also in the salu-

---

[1] In Luke i, 78, we have the word here rendered *tendermercies* connected with another of similar import, and the compound expression is employed as designating an attribute of God: σπλάγχνα ἐλέους, *bowels*, or *heart of mercy* of our God.

tation at the beginning of the pastoral epistles the invocation of "grace, mercy and peace from God the Father and Christ Jesus our Lord."

(2) *Monotheistic Attributes.* The God and Father of our Lord Jesus Christ is conceived in the Pauline epistles as possessed of every quality and attribute ascribed to him in the highest prophetic monotheism. He is "the King eternal, incorruptible, invisible, the only God." He is "the blessed and only Potentate, the King of kings, and Lord of lords; who only hath immortality, dwelling in light unapproachable; whom no man hath seen or can see: to whom belong honor and power eternal" (1 Tim. i, 17; vi, 15, 16). How adorable "the mystery of God" and "the mystery of Christ," in whom are hidden "all the treasures of wisdom and knowledge"! (Col. ii, 2, 3.) "O the depth of the riches both of the wisdom and knowledge of God! how unsearchable are his judgments and his ways past finding out!" (Rom. xi, 33.)

(3) *Sympathy with the Groaning Creation.* The profound concept of "the whole creation groaning and travailing in pain along with us," as expressed in Rom. viii, 22, implies that God is not only immanently present and active in his entire creation but that he is also intensely and unspeakably sympathetic with all its suffering. It is the eternal Spirit of God who himself "maketh intercession for us with groanings which cannot be uttered." There is no throb of pain in all the universe which finds not responsive pulsation in the bosom of the Father. Whatever elements of mystic and poetic thought may be traceable in this passage, the apostle's teaching suggests that the whole suffering world, through all its millenniums of struggle for life and the accompanying pains of death, has somehow shared in corresponding emotions and intercessions of the Spirit of God. As the magnificent objects of the visible creation evidence "his everlasting power and divinity" (Rom. i, 20), so the long travail of all the tribes of flesh and blood upon the earth shows signs of the unutterable groanings and sympathy of the Spirit himself. Not a sparrow falls on the ground without the Father, and "not one of them is forgotten in the sight of God" (Luke xii, 6). His tender mercies cannot ignore but they rather embrace the pains of all sentient life, and out of all its anguish and struggle he purposes to effect a glorious deliverance of this whole suffering creation. For Paul's conception of the power, wisdom, grace, mercy, and peace of God the Father, as revealed in Jesus Christ, is large enough to include such a redemptive deliverance "from the bondage of corruption." All this belongs to the mystery of God in Christ, the mystery of the ages.

CHAPTER IV

THE EVERLASTING FATHERHOOD

1. Monistic, Immanent, Transcendent. It is only after a thorough study of the revelation of God in Jesus Christ that we can look back over the bygone generations of mankind and observe how our heavenly Father has been ever present and active in all the world of being. The biblical doctrine of God involves the profoundest monism and also the facts of divine immanence and transcendence. The eternal Spirit is the one principle and ground of all that exists, both visible and invisible. All the infinite and infinitesimal variations of phenomena are the products of his living energy, and without him was nothing ever made or unmade. His abiding immanence is but a necessary correlative of this primary concept of monism. There is and can be no place or entity from which he is absent, and so the Scripture speaks of him as in all and through all, from everlasting to everlasting. And this is the true pantheism, the only rational concept of omnipresence; and the divine immanence of God our Father is made the more affecting to our thought and feeling by reason of his attributes of omnisentience. Being an eternal personality of wisdom, power, and love, he must needs also be transcendent in the sense that he ever exercises conscious dominion over all that is. He is not separate from his world, or above and outside the things that exist, but he is consciously in all, through all, and over all, to make all things work together for good in the accomplishment of his eternal purposes of love and of wisdom. All, therefore, that we conceive and speak of as "the laws and order of the universe" are but the methods by which our heavenly Father worketh hitherto, and will work forever.

2. God Conceived as Generator and Generatrix. Our concept of the creations of God should not ignore the fact that the heavens, the earth, and the sea, and all that in them is, are products of divine generation. According to Gen. ii, 4, "These are the generations (תולדות, *begettings*) of the heavens and of the earth." God, the eternal Spirit, is the Generator and the Generatrix of every seed, and herb, and tree, of every living creature that moves upon the face of the earth, of every winged bird, and of whatsoever passeth through the paths of the sea, as well as of man to whom he has assigned a rank and dominion over them all.¹ Every argument and conclusion of a rational theism point to God as the great First Cause and intelligent Designer of all that has been made; the revelation of God in Christ adds to this the blessed thought that the Creator of the world and of all its living tribes of flesh and blood is an everlasting Father. The times and methods of his creative work are beyond our ken. We conceive them under our necessary limitations of thought, but there is no word or name that represents God's causal relations to the world more suggestively and more fittingly than that of Father. He has begotten out of his own illimitable resources of power, wisdom, and love "all things that are in the heavens above, in the earth beneath, and in the waters that are under the earth."

3. Providential Oversight and Rule. The doctrine of divine Providence cannot be separated from that of creation, and the idea of God as the eternal Father fills the doctrine with a personal significance. It implies that there is no natural government of God that is not moral in its end and aim. The divine order is, first the natural, then the spiritual. The one prepares the way for the other, and it is God's way. And so the natural is for the spiritual rather than the spiritual for the natural, just as the sabbath was made for man, not man for the sabbath. There is for man an inestimable moral value in the very conditions of his existence in a material body and a material world.² His subjection to physical wants, his limitations in time and space, and the natural ties of kinship and obligation are part and parcel of a providential discipline adapted to cultivate the ethical nature. The doctrine of God's superintending providence is logically inseparable from the biblical concept of his immanence and his omniscentience. The æsthetic sentiment expressed when God beheld and pronounced all his creations "very good" (Gen. i, 31) evinces the moral sense as

---

¹ In the grand biblical picture of creation God is represented as dividing the light from the darkness, and " the Spirit of God was *brooding upon* (מרחפת) the face of the waters." In obedience to God's life-imparting Word (אמר) the waters swarmed with swarms of living things (Gen. i, 2, 20). Many expositors have noticed the suggestiveness of the feminine participle מרחפת, *brooding*, and some have seen in it an allusion to the mythical conception of the world-egg which figures in some ancient cosmogonies. Dillmann (on Genesis, in loco) admits such a reference, but he remarks that "here the sensuous and gross representation is transfigured into a tender, thoughtful figure; as the bird over her nest, so the all-penetrating Spirit of God moves over the primeval waters, producing therein, or communicating to them, vital powers, and so rendering creation possible." Whatever its recognition in the myths of the world, the concept of the Creator as both Generator and Generatrix is worthy of all acceptation, and has its noteworthy biblical setting. The creations of God are the generations of his eternal Spirit of life. In him is the fountain of life, not only of the life of men, but of every living creature in the earth and the heavens.

² See J. T. Crane's article on "The Moral Value of a Material World," in the Methodist Quarterly Review for April, 1858, pp. 228–241.

well as the intelligent judgment of the great "Master Workman." His minute personal care extends to every sparrow and to the cattle on a thousand hills; how much more must he care for man who exists in his own image! For the most ignorant and degraded savage is of more value than all birds and cattle, and no nation or tribe of men has been left without the witness of his fatherly concern. Moreover each individual receives as minute attention as if there were no other in the world. "All the earth is mine" has been our Father's declaration from of old (Exod. xix, 5), and the great purpose of the call of Abraham and of the divine election of Israel was to secure innumerable blessings for all the families of the earth. For each and for all of these alike the everlasting Father cares with unspeakable tenderness, and makes all things work together for their good. He is at once the abiding and faithful Sustainer, Preserver, and Ruler. Our heavenly Father is in love with all his world, not willing that anything should perish.

4. Suffers with the Groaning Creation. The idea of our heavenly Father as the continuous Generator of all that lives and moves involves the further thought of his abiding sympathy with the suffering world. The Pauline hint of "the whole creation groaning and travailing in pain together until now" comports with this idea, and gives to the providence of God a still more profound significance. When we contemplate the ages of ages of physical struggle and death which preceded the appearance of man upon earth and keep in mind that never one living thing suffered and died without our Father, we obtain a most thrilling concept of the omnisentience of God. How appalling to our thought the millions of millions of living creatures that have gone down in the struggle for existence! And the groaning and travail and dying still go on. Our inference is that he who is the personal Generator and Generatrix of all forms of sentient life suffers along with them, and not a pang of insect, reptile, fish or bird or beast ever fails to move the emotions of his love. And not these only, "but ourselves also, who have the first-fruits of the Spirit, we ourselves groan within ourselves, waiting for the redemption of our body." In this same connection we are assured that "the Spirit helpeth our infirmities, and maketh intercession for us with groanings which cannot be uttered" (Rom. viii, 23, 26). Whatever else this means, it shows the whole suffering world of God's creation to be groaning as with travail pains, and the eternal Spirit himself to be in sympathetic emotions of unspeakable affection. There seems to be no such thing as "dead matter," for its most inert forms appear to be in such subserviency to the eternal Force that thrills all things that we may not think of them as dead. There is no force in the universe but the conscious energy and activity of the eternal Spirit, the loving, sympathetic Spirit of our heavenly Father. Oh, what a passionately loving Soul is this, the Soul of the world! It is in and through this all-embracing Spirit that we live and move and have our being. This paternal sentiency must needs have embraced all the tribes and families of mankind, the prehistoric races from the first man onward. However obscured and sunken in depravity, no human being could ever have escaped the affectionate notice and yearning of the Father, for "God so loved the world" as to give his only begotten Son for its redemption.

5. The Cry, "How Long, O Lord?" The suffering creation may well cry out, as the ages pass, "How long, how long, O Lord?" It is quite natural for us, with our limited knowledge, to think God "slack concerning his promise," as men in all times have had their notions of slackness in the management of this world (comp. 2 Pet. iii, 9). We may well wonder why the struggle of life should go on through such immense periods of time, and yet reach no end apparently worth such incalculable pains and toil. Why should our heavenly Father, who has all power and wisdom, tolerate such apparent waste of energy? Why permit the long, long times of ignorance, and vice, and wars, and oppressions, and crimes? Perhaps we ask such questions in our ignorance, and look too little upon other aspects of the facts. Why birth and growth at all? Why not have fruit without seed, and without blade, stem, bud, or blossom? Why should anyone be born blind, or live for fifty years an invalid and helpless? We do not find that God makes any organism perfect at the start. There may be, each in its order, a perfect seed, a perfect bud, a perfect full-grown fruit. But the higher we rise in the order of life the more sensitive to pain becomes the being capable of suffering. Why should the Christ of God be born a helpless babe, and slowly grow into youth and afterward become a man of sorrows and give his life a ransom for many? Alas, the questions of theodicy are many, and it is not given unto any of us to answer them.[1] We can at most only see in part, but if we look with care, we shall see enough to establish us in faith and hope and love. God's method in all the world of life is evolutionary. Organisms grow and pass by processes of

---

[1] Men wonder and question how God can be truly the Father of all men, and yet permit anyone to "suffer punishment, even eternal destruction from the face of the Lord and the glory of his might" (1 Thess. i, 9). We answer that this is not a question of God's might, or will, or love. Our Father willeth not the ruin of any angel, or spirit, or man. If any perish eternally, it must be in spite of the utmost exertions of God's love and wisdom and power. See our discussion of penal consequences of sin (pp. 122–135).

development from simple to complex forms of being. But when our thought turns to the unknown extent of all cosmic suffering we find ourselves incompetent to judge of the times and seasons which the eternal Father "has set within his own authority" (Acts i, 7). With him "a thousand years are but as yesterday when it is past, and as a watch in the night" (Psa. xc, 4), and the days of the years of our suffering are not worthy to be compared with the ages of struggle through which the Father sees it needful to subject the whole creation to frailty and to travail. But since he is a Father, acting in the perfection of wisdom and of love, his long and varied chastening must aim to bring many sons into glory, fit them for the highest liberty of sons of God, and make them partakers of his holiness. We may be assured he wastes no time in the consummation of his holy purposes, but he provides that when that which is perfect is come it shall not possess the frailty and immaturity of childish things. It shall be an imperishable growth of God's own planting and development.

6. No Waste of Material or Energy. Not only is there no waste of time with our everlasting Father; there is also no waste of material or of force in the evolution of his universe. From our limited point of view there are no doubt many seeming wastes in the earth and in the heavens. The immensity of the universe transcends all our calculations. Astronomers have estimated the distance of the sun from us to be somewhat over ninety millions of miles; the earth, then, must in her annual circuit move around a space of more than one hundred and eighty millions of miles in diameter, and yet this immense circle forms comparatively but an inconsiderable measure of that vaster circle of the heavens in which the fixed stars appear to us as so many little points of light. Even the utmost bounds of our entire solar system would include a space of relatively small extent if viewed from any one of those distant points of light. But the stars which we call fixed are found to be in immeasurably rapid motion, and many of them are suns a thousand times larger than our own, and rushing through depths of space with a force and a swiftness that utterly amaze us and baffle all human computation. What an incalculable waste of power is this, and what good purpose can it serve?[1] Or shall we

---

[1] Scientists have computed "that the sun emits as much heat each second as would result from the burning of 11,600,000,000,000,000 tons of coal, and of this enormous amount of energy the portion utilized (that is, in our solar system) corresponds only to that due to the consumption of about 50,000,000 of tons. Remembering that what is true of the sun is true of his fellow suns, the stars, that all the thousands of stars we see, all the millions revealed by the telescope, as well as many myriad times as many more that lie beyond the range of our most powerful telescopes, are suns similarly pouring heat and light into space, how enormous, according to our conceptions, is the waste of energy!" But what man

rather say that the everlasting God who made and upholds these suns and systems knows perfectly what he is doing and what he intends to do forever? It is not only in the immensities that we find what seem like wastes of energy. Wherefore the myriad flowers that "blush unseen, and waste their sweetness on the desert air"? What countless seeds fall into the earth and never bring forth fruit unto perfection! What shall we think of the enormous loss of life in all the vegetable and animal world? Some will think we do not answer wisely, and many may say that our answer is a worthless fancy; but we hesitate not, in view of the revelation of our Father which the Lord Jesus has made known, to affirm that the infinitely wise and beneficent Power that numbers the hairs of our heads and watches with care every sparrow that falls to the ground, must needs care for every atom of his universe. With him there are no wastes, as we count wastes. No life of insect, shrub, or flower, no living soul in any animal (least of all in man) goes out of being. Every atom of matter, every energy or force, however great or small, and every living soul of fish, or fowl, or beast, or man, must needs be utilized. It is not ours to know or tell how these things are, but, once possessed with the concept of the everlasting Father of the universe, we argue *a priori* that all things work for good, and not a fragment of the whole is lost. Whatever endless suffering and possibilities of self-depravity are inherent in beings made in the image of God, they cannot change his eternal purpose to make the whole creation move on toward the goal for which he is working hitherto and forever. In the working out of that blessed purpose nothing in time or space is wasted. And in view of this illimitable operation and abiding presence of God in all the universe of being, it is, perhaps, suggestive that in the language of the Lord's Prayer, as given in Matt. vi, 9, our Father is the one who is "in the heavens" (ἐν τοῖς οὐρανοῖς). This plural form suggests that our heavenly Father is in all the heavens. He fills the illimitable universe, and nothing in earth or in the uttermost heavens beyond us can for a moment be apart from him. Such is the Father

---

is competent to speak of all the possibilities and purposes of such stupendous manifestations of energy? We believe there is no Energy, but that of the living Father, immanent in all his works. The same devout scientist, from whom we have just quoted, beautifully adds: "Our faith in the wisdom of God need not be shaken unless we assume that our science teaches us the whole of that which is. But inasmuch as science itself has taught us over and over again how little we really know, how little we can know, I think that we may very well believe in this instance that the seeming mystery arises from the imperfection of our knowledge. If we could see the whole plan of the Creator instead of the minutest portion, if we could scan the whole of space instead of the merest corner, if all time were before us instead of a span, we might pronounce judgment."—R. A. Proctor, Our Place Among Infinities, pp. 43, 44. New York, 1876.

who has given us his most blessed revelation of himself in the incarnation of Jesus Christ.[1]

7. Defective Concept of Monarchy and Absolutism. This larger concept of our heavenly Father should offset and clarify such other concepts of him as are based upon the imagery of conventional terms, like king, ruler, governor, potentate, lord, and master (δεσπότης). These all have their place and propriety in the biblical writings, but when any one of them is exalted into such prominence as to magnify the idea of an absolute monarchy and a monergistic sovereignty over man and his eternal destiny, the true doctrine of God is perverted, and the concept of the everlasting Fatherhood is lost from view. No small portion of Christian theology took shape at a time when absolute monarchy and the divine right of kings were acknowledged widely in human government. The Anselmic doctrine of atonement has its roots in the notions of absolute sovereignty prevalent in mediæval times. Many rulers even seemed to act upon the principle that "might makes right." It may be easily seen how such a habit of thinking should develop a one-sided doctrine of the everlasting Father. His sovereignty is ever to be acknowledged and adored, but it is no arbitrary dominion. His lordship and power are those of a loving Father rather than those which most men associate with a powerful king. The kingdom of Christ and of God, as we have seen, is a kingdom of truth, having for its fundamental law the commandment of love. It is like seed growing secretly, by night and by day, and putting forth "first the blade, then the ear, then the full grain in the ear" (Mark iv, 28). The great Sovereign of this kingdom is a nourishing Father, who welcomes with joy every returning prodigal son. He goes far and suffers long to seek and to save that which was lost. In the light of such revelations of the God and Father of our Lord Jesus Christ such deistic terms as *the Absolute* and *the Unknowable* become irrelevant. They express at best only a vague philosophical concept which can have no real value to one in whose heart has been

---

[1] The idea of incarnation is repugnant to some. Herbert Spencer slurs the notion that the Cause to which we can put no limits in space and time, and of which our entire system is a relatively infinitesimal product, took the disguise of a man for the purpose of covenanting with a shepherd chief in Syria. But he seems to be awed by the vision of the astronomer, who sees in the sun a mass so vast that even into one of his spots our earth might be plunged without touching its edges. To which a Scotch minister replies that "no conception of God is less imposing than that which represents him as a kind of millionaire in worlds, so materialized by the immensity of his possessions as to have lost the sense of the incalculably greater worth of the spiritual interests of even the smallest part of them." That which the universal heart of man cries out after is not a God of vast bulk, absolute and unknowable, but a heavenly Father, who is abundant in loving-kindness and truth.

given the "illumination of the knowledge of the glory of God in the face of Jesus Christ" (2 Cor. iv, 6).

8. The Idea of Divine Maternity. We cannot overlook the fact that in some religious cults and from ancient times the idea of divine maternity has been associated with the concept of God. In the polytheistic cults we meet with the names of male and female deities. The greatest gods of the pagan peoples have had their female consorts, and the worship of such deities has naturally resulted in practices of most revolting sensuality. But these facts should not prevent our observing the biblical intimations of the qualities of maternal affection in our heavenly Father. The divine unity and fatherhood are not compromised by any new or enlarged conception of the love of God which truly magnifies him in our hearts. The Old Testament has not a few suggestions of motherly qualities in God. The feminine participle employed in Gen. i, 2, conveys the thought that the Spirit of God was brooding like a mother bird over the face of the waters. Further on in the same chapter, where it is said that "God created man in his own image," it is immediately added, "male and female created he them," as if it required both male and female in the creature to represent fully the image of man's Maker. Accordingly, as we have already seen (p. 572), the Creator may well be thought of as both Generator and Generatrix. All "the generations of the heavens and the earth" (Gen. ii, 4) are his offspring. In Isa. xlix, 15, it is written: "Can a woman forget her nursing child? Yea, they may forget, yet will not I forget thee." In the same chapter the prophet speaks of "nursing fathers" as well as "nursing mothers," and in lxvi, 13, he represents Jehovah as dandling and caressing his people like little children, and saying to them: "As one whom his mother comforteth, so will I comfort you." And such tenderness of motherlike affection became incarnate in the Lord Jesus. When he took little children in his arms and blessed them, and also when he said that his heavenly Father numbers the hairs of our heads, he leads us to think of a loving, fondling mother rather than of a mighty Ruler of worlds. Even the Mariolatry of the Church of Rome has its relevant suggestions here, and a scientific student of religion may do well to inquire whether this form of madonna worship was not the product of a deep yearning in the human heart for some tender maternal element in God. It is noteworthy that this Romish practice arose about the fourth century of our era, when many a yearning heart might well have turned away in disgust from the cold, metaphysical concepts of God and of Christ, which were forced upon the Church in the storms of the trinitarian controversies, and sought elsewhere for something more human and divine. A wholesome reaction from one-sided and superstitious notions on this subject must be sought in a recognition of the real maternal qualities inherent in the essential nature of our Father in heaven. Paternal and maternal love abide eternally in the bosom of our God. "The highest human is divine," and has been manifested in the person and mediation of Jesus Christ, whom a beloved disciple could speak of as "what we have heard, what we have seen with our eyes, and our hands have handled, concerning the Word of life."

This union of paternal and maternal qualities in our concept of God well fits the truth that GOD IS LOVE. In the divine personality as in the human there abideth wisdom, power, and love, these three; and the greatest of these is love. For Love is the most active energy in creation, in redemption, and in providence. With a fatherly and motherly tenderness, in all creation, God is active hitherto and evermore so as to make all things work together for good to them that love him. All manner of love implies some sort of reciprocal affection. It is no mere poetic license that speaks of "mother earth." The seed that falls into the ground, the blade that springs up, and the ear and the full grain in the ear respond at every stage of growth to the maternal nursing of earth and light and air. We find the qualities of male and female in the forms of vegetable life. The glad springtime is redolent with what seem to be emotions of mingling joy and struggle in grass, and blossom, and bird, and the cattle on a thousand hills. And though the whole creation groans and travails, what is it but the striving after an object of desire?—"the liberty of the glory of children of God." But first comes the natural, then the animal (which, alas! too often shows its beastly aberrations), and then the spiritual and the heavenly, in which the male and female natures become exalted into the perfection of deathless angels of God. For they become one in the glory of the Father and the Son and the Eternal Spirit, who loved before the foundation of the world.

9. The Everlasting Trinity of Wisdom, Power, and Love. The revelation of God in Christ makes manifest the everlasting Trinity of Wisdom, Power, and Love.[1] These correspond with intellection, volition, and sensibility in our self-conscious personality, and these three are so essentially one that we cannot conceive any one of them existing or acting apart from and independently of the others. One or another may become prominent on occasion, and

---

[1] This trinal concept of the divine personality is admirably stated in W. N. Clarke's lectures entitled, Can I believe in God the Father? In the chapter on "Divine Personality" he elaborates the propositions that God is a great Thinker, a great Willer and a great Lover.

for the time seem to leave the others out of sight or in abeyance, but a thorough analysis of the facts of personality shows the essential unity of these faculties of the living soul of man. We conceive the personality of God to be like that of man, and herein we recognize the image and glory of God in which man exists and was originally made (Gen. i, 27; 1 Cor. xi, 7). That this trinal personality of God is something immeasurably more than that of man should be assumed, since omniscience, omnipotence, and omnisentience must needs transcend all human knowledge. It is to be observed also that in the trinity of Father, Son, and Holy Spirit each of these essentials of personality is manifest. The Holy Spirit is the Spirit of wisdom and of power by whose divine ministrations the love of God is shed abroad in the hearts of men. Jesus Christ, the Son of God, is the manifested wisdom of God and the power of God, and his mission of divine mediation is the supreme demonstration of the love of God; and the love of the Father, the wisdom and the knowledge of God and his everlasting power and divinity are everywhere extolled in the biblical revelation. Besides all this, it may, perhaps, be truthfully affirmed that in some deeper sense the everlasting Father is preëminently the Almighty; the eternal Word or Son of the Father is the revealer of all heavenly wisdom; and the eternal Spirit fills our fullest and richest concept of the all-pervading omnisentience of God. According to the Johannine teaching, the Son is the only begotten of the Father (John i, 14, 18; iii, 16); the Spirit proceeds from the Father (xv, 27); the Son and the Spirit are sent by the Father (iii, 34; xiv, 26); and the Spirit is sent both by the Father and the Son (xiv, 26; xv, 26). The holy and heavenly Personality that exists and acts in these mysterious interrelations is "the only God" (ὁ μόνος θεός, v, 44; xvii, 3), but he exists and acts as Father, Word, and Spirit, an adorable UNITY. Men may never be able to resolve the difficulties of the Trinity as they have been magnified by the polemics of centuries; but if we turn our thought to the trinal unity of every normal human personality, and keep in mind that man exists in the image and glory of God, we shall be able the better to worship the Father, the Son, and the Holy Spirit, and at the same time behold and believe that the Spirit and the Son of his love are truly one with the Father, essential and inseparable in the divine personality, and evermore revealing the nature of the everlasting Father.

10. The Everlasting Goal. It remains for us only to observe that in the everlasting power, wisdom, and love of God the entire universe moves onward toward a goal of perfection and glory worthy of the Father, the Son, and the Holy Spirit. Our limited vision can set no bounds to God's future operations. As he has been working hitherto, so doubtless he will keep on working through the ages of ages. Every stage of progress and accomplishment serves only to open into illimitable possibilities beyond. The apostle Paul looked forward to an END, when Christ shall have abolished all adverse powers, and shall have brought all things into subjection to himself, and "shall deliver up the kingdom to the Father" (1 Cor. xv, 24-28). But whatever glorious revelations and triumphs that grand event may show, they will not and cannot exhaust the resources of eternal Wisdom and Love. In these mysteries of the ages we may safely argue *a priori* on the basis of the nature and power of the God whom Jesus Christ reveals. All things are possible to his Father and our Father, his God and our God. In the order of his wisdom there seems to be no stage or state of being which is not of the nature of an intermediate state between what went before and what is sure to follow it in glory. "From glory to glory" is the motto of his continuous transformation of the sons of God. We need have no manner of doubt that in his own times the whole travailing creation shall be delivered from its pains and bondage and corruption and become transfigured into higher forms of life and power. The Omnisentience of eternal Wisdom and Power will not refrain from his sympathetic intercession and groaning so long as any living creature is waiting and yearning for the glorious liberty of the children of God. For as a father pitieth his children, and as a mother comforteth, so shall our Father who is in the heavens comfort and glorify his own.

SELECT BIBLIOGRAPHY

(When there are satisfactory English translations of the foreign works named in this list the original titles are not given.)

ADENEY, WALTER F.—The Theology of the New Testament. New York, 1894.
A brief, readable, and useful compendium.

ALEXANDER, W. LINDSAY.—A System of Biblical Theology. 2 vols. Edinburgh, 1888.
Consists of theological lectures, abridged, arranged, and edited from the author's manuscripts by James Ross. Is comprehensive, and combines some features of both biblical and systematic theology.

ALGER, WILLIAM R.—Critical History of the Doctrine of a Future Life. Boston, 1860. Many later editions.
A classical treatise, indispensable to the student of the doctrine.

ARMINIUS, JAMES.—The Works of. Translated from the Latin by James Nichols. 3 vols. Third volume by W. R. Bagnall. Auburn and Buffalo, 1853.
Valuable as original disputations in defense of the main points of doctrine at issue between the Arminian and the Calvinian theology.

BANKS, JOHN S.—A Manual of Christian Doctrine. Edited with Introduction and Additions by J. J. Tigert. Nashville, 1897.
A convenient handbook, condensed and comprehensive.

BAUER, GEORG LORENZ.—Theologie des alten Testaments, oder Abriss der religiösen Begriffe der alten Hebräer, von den ältesten Zeiten bis auf den Anfang der christlichen Epoche. Leipzig, 1796.
Biblische Theologie des neuen Testaments. 4 vols. Leipzig, 1800–1802.
Valuable for studying the early attempts to distinguish Old and New Testament theology, and for noting the various types of doctrine in the different biblical writers.

BAUMGARTEN-CRUSIUS, L. F. O.—Grundzüge der biblischen Theologie. Jena, 1828.
Interesting mainly as one of the earlier efforts to construct a biblical rather than a confessional theology.

BAUR, FERDINAND CHRISTIAN.—Vorlesungen über die neutestamentliche Theologie. Leipzig, 1864. New edition with Introduction by Otto Pfleiderer. Gotha, 1892.
These lectures were first edited by F. F. Baur, son of the author. They give the distinguished professor's views on the teaching of Christ and of the apostles more fully than any one of his other works.

BECK, J. T.—Outlines of Biblical Psychology. Translated from the German. Edinburgh, 1877.
......Vorlesungen über christliche Glaubenslehre. 2 vols. Edited by Lindenmeyer. Gütersloh, 1886–1887.
Productions of a devout and painstaking study of the Scriptures. The second volume of the *Vorlesungen* gives under four main sections a valuable outline of biblical dogmatics.

BECKWITH, CLARENCE AUGUSTINE.—Realities of Christian Theology. An Interpretation of Christian Experience. Boston and New York, 1906.
Interprets the central truths of the Christian faith in condensed and comprehensive form, in accord with true scientific method, and with constant reference to the facts of personal experience.

BEET, JOSEPH AGAR.—A Manual of Theology. London and New York, 1906.
Consists of sixty-six chapters, arranged under eleven parts and notably exegetical. The result of many years of faithful study; combines to some extent apologetics and exposition, and treats with noteworthy clearness the main doctrines of the gospel. Somewhat original and noteworthy in its eschatology.

BERNARD, THOMAS D.—The Progress of Doctrine in the New Testament. New York, 1867. New ed., 1900.

> The Bampton Lectures for 1864, and worthy of note as an early English attempt at biblical theology.

BEYSCHLAG, WILLIBALD.—New Testament Theology, or Historical Account of the Teaching of Jesus and of Primitive Christianity according to the New Testament Sources. English Translation by Neil Buchanan. 2 vols. Edinburgh, 1894.

> The most able and commanding work on New Testament theology that is now accessible to English readers. No student in this department can afford to do without it.

BIEDERMANN, ALOIS EMANUEL.—Christliche Dogmatik. 2 vols. Second ed. Berlin, 1884–1885. Vol. II edited by J. Rehmke.

> A rationalistic and somewhat pantheistic exposition of the doctrines of Christianity in accord with the Hegelian philosophy. The first 169 pages of the second volume contain a very interesting outline of biblical dogmatics under the title of *Die Schriftlehre*.

BOVON, J.—Théologie du Nouveau Testament. 2 vols. Lausanne, 1893–1894.

> In this learned and valuable treatise the New Testament is recognized as the historical foundation and beginning of the author's proposed Study of the Work of Redemption. The first volume discusses the life and teaching of Jesus, and the second presents the apostolic teaching under five sections: (1) Jewish Christianity; (2) Paulinism, to which the epistle to the Hebrews belongs as "Paulinism of the second degree"; (3) the catholic epistles; (4) the Apocalypse, and (5) the Johannine Theology.

BRETSCHNEIDER, KARL GOTTLIEB.—Handbuch der Dogmatik der evangelischen Kirche. 2 vols. Leipzig, 1838.

> A comprehensive treatise, clear in statement, coldly critical, somewhat rationalistic, but maintaining the positions of supernaturalism.

BROWN, WILLIAM ADAMS.—Christian Theology in Outline. New York, 1906.

> A strong, clear, compact, and comprehensive restatement of the main truths of Christian doctrine in the light of modern philosophical and scientific thought.

BRUCE, ALEXANDER BALMAIN.—The Kingdom of God; or, Christ's Teaching according to the Synoptic Gospels. Edinburgh, 1890.
...... St. Paul's Conception of Christianity. New York, 1894.
...... The Epistle to the Hebrews. The First Apology for Christianity. Edinburgh and New York, 1899.

> These, like all the works of Professor Bruce, are of permanent value, and deserve repeated study.

BUELL, SAMUEL.—A Treatise on Dogmatic Theology. 2 vols. New York, 1890.

> Consists of lectures given in the General Theological Seminary of the Protestant Episcopal Church, and gives much space to sacramentarian dogmas.

BUESCHING, A. F.—Dissertatio exhibens epitomen theologiæ e solis literis sanctis concinnatæ. Göttingen, 1756.

> Deserving notice chiefly as one of the very earliest efforts to construct a biblical rather than a dogmatic and scholastic theology.

BURWASH, NATHANIEL.—Manual of Christian Theology on the Inductive Method. 2 vols. London, 1890.

> A convenient, readable, comprehensive treatise.

CAIRD, JOHN.—The Fundamental Ideas of Christianity. 2 vols. Glasgow, 1899.

> The Gifford Lectures of 1892-3 and 1895-6. The author treats the chief topics of Christian faith with such masterly skill that no well read theologian can afford to ignore these volumes.

CALVIN, JOHN.—Institutes of the Christian Religion. Translated from the original Latin, and collated with the author's last edition in French, by John Allen. Presbyterian Board of Publication, Philadelphia.

> This monumental masterpiece of the dogmatics of the Protestant Reformation has appeared in more editions and translations than are easily told. The first edition (Basel, 1536) was a book of only six chapters, written before the author was twenty-seven years old; the latest during his lifetime, in Latin (1559), when he had reached the age of fifty. The work is arranged in four parts, or books, corresponding to four parts of the Apostles' Creed, Father, Son, Spirit, and Church.

CHARLES, R. H.—A Critical History of the Doctrine of a Future Life, in Israel, in Judaism, and in Christianity. London, 1899.

Exceedingly valuable and indispensable to the student of the later Jewish literature on the subject of the future life.

CLARKE, WILLIAM N.—An Outline of Christian Theology. Cambridge, 1894.

A volume of the greatest intrinsic value. Probably the most readable, intelligible, and popular statement of Christian doctrine produced in modern times.

COELLN, DANIEL GEORG CONRAD VON.—Biblische Theologie, mit einer Nachricht über des Verfassers Leben und Wirken, herausgegeben von David Schulz. 2 vols. Leipzig, 1836.

Exhibits extensive learning, but follows the method of De Wette and adopts his headings for the main divisions. The Old Testament theology is given under the two heads of Hebraism and Judaism, and that of the New Testament under (1) The Teaching of Jesus, and (2) The Teaching of the Apostles.

CONE, ORELLO.—The Gospel and its Earliest Interpreters. New York, 1893.

A suggestive work, well worthy of attention.

CRAMER, L. D.—Vorlesungen über die biblische Theologie des neuen Testaments. Edited by Næbe. Leipzig, 1830.

CREMER, AUGUST H.—Biblisch-theologisches Wörterbuch der neutestamentlichen Gräcität. Gotha, 1866. Many later editions. English translation by William Urwick. Edinburgh, 1872. Several later editions.

An invaluable work, indispensable to the scientific student of New Testament theology.

CURTIS, OLIN ALFRED.—The Christian Faith, Personally given in a System of Doctrine. New York, 1905.

A unique, original, and very readable presentation of the main truths of the Christian religion, adapted to stimulate thought and encourage religious inquiry.

DAHLE, LARS NIELSEN.—Life after Death and the Future of the Kingdom of God. Translated from the Norse by John Beveridge. Edinburgh, 1896.

An interesting specimen of dogmatic literalism in biblical exegesis, and especially elaborate in its treatment of the intermediate state and "the great events of the time of the end."

DENIO, FRANCIS B.—The Supreme Leader: A Study of the Nature and Work of the Holy Spirit. Boston, 1900.

A very excellent and helpful monograph.

DENNEY, JAMES.—Studies in Theology. New York, 1895.
......The Death of Christ. Its Place and Interpretation in the New Testament. New York, 1902.
......The Atonement and the Modern Mind. New York, 1903.

These volumes are suggestive, learned, conservative in sentiment and often strong in argument where not altogether convincing.

DE WETTE, WILHELM MARTIN LEBERECHT.—Biblische Dogmatik des alten und neuen Testaments; oder kritische Darstellung der Religionslehre des Hebraismus, des Judentums and Urchristentums. Berlin, 1813. Third improved ed., 1831.

Like all the productions of this author, a masterpiece of lucid, concise, and comprehensive presentation of the subjects which it handles. The first and larger part of the volume sets forth the religion of the Old Testament under the heads of Hebraism and Judaism. The apocryphal books, Philo and Josephus, are drawn upon as sources of information, as well as the canonical books. The New Testament part treats the teaching of Jesus and that of the apostles under two distinct divisions.

DICKSON, WILLIAM P.—St. Paul's Use of the Terms Flesh and Spirit. Baird Lecture for 1883. Glasgow, 1883.

A critical, scholarly, and exceedingly valuable contribution to the study of biblical psychology and of Pauline theology.

DILLMANN, AUGUST.—Handbuch der alttestamentlichen Theologie. Herausgegeben von R. Kittel. Leipzig, 1895.

Accurate in its statements, thorough in exegesis, and always helpful.

BIBLICAL DOGMATICS

DORNER, ISAAC AUGUST.—A System of Christian Doctrine. Translated from the German by Alfred Cave and J. S. Banks. 4 vols. Edinburgh, 1880–1882.

One of the most important and comprehensive contributions to the modern literature of Christian doctrine, and in full sympathy with the evangelical Protestant spirit. Following in the steps of Schleiermacher, the author made this ripe product of his study a worthy companion of his earlier great classic on the History of the Development of the Doctrine of the Person of Christ.

DRUMMOND, ROBERT J.—The Relation of the Apostolic Teaching to the Teaching of Christ. Edinburgh, 1900.

The Kerr Lectures for 1900. Somewhat discursive, but contains much of real worth.

DU BOSE, WILLIAM PORCHER.—The Soteriology of the New Testament, New York, 1892.

...... The Gospel in the Gospels. New York, 1906.

These excellent monographs discuss with marked ability and thoroughness the saving ministry of Jesus Christ, his Person and his Humanity. They belong to the highest order of theological exposition.

DUFF, ARCHIBALD.—Old Testament Theology; or, The History of Hebrew Religion from the Year 800 B. C. London, 1891.

This volume deals mainly with the books of Amos, Micah, and portions of Isaiah, and furnishes much valuable material for the study of Old Testament theology.

DUHM, BERNHARD.—Die Theologie der Propheten, als Grundlage für die innere Entwicklungsgeschichte der israelitischen Religion. Bonn, 1875.

A valuable help in tracing the historical development of biblical doctrines in the prophets of the different periods of Assyrian, Babylonian, and Persian supremacy.

EBRARD, J. H. A.—Christliche Dogmatik. 2 vols. Königsberg, 1851.

An interesting and useful presentation of the substance of Christian doctrine as held by the Reformed Churches of Germany, France, and Switzerland.

EWALD, HEINRICH.—Old and New Testament Theology. English translation by T. Goadby. Edinburgh, 1888.

Ewald's German work consists of four volumes and covers a wide field. This translation is confined mainly to the second and third volumes, and treats of God and the universe, the nature of faith in Christ, the Christian Trinity, and immortality.

FAIRBAIRN, A. M.—The Place of Christ in Modern Theology. New York, 1893.

Not a formal treatise on systematic theology, but, according to the author, "an attempt at formulating the fundamental or material conception of such a system." It is one of the ablest contributions of modern times to the exposition of fundamental Christian truth.

FOSTER, RANDOLPH S.—Studies in Theology. 6 vols. New York, 1889–1899.

The plan of this opus magnum contemplated eleven volumes, of which six were published before the author's death. These volumes contain much of real value, but are needlessly diffuse and enlarged by extensive quotations from other writers.

FOSTER, ROBERT VERRELL.—Systematic Theology. Nashville, 1898.

A bulky volume, dealing with biblical theology, cosmology, anthropology, Christology, soteriology, ecclesiology, and eschatology.

FRANK, F. H. R.—System der christlichen Wahrheit. 2 vols. Second ed. Erlangen, 1885–1886.

Belongs to the Lutheran school of dogmatics, constructs the system of Christian truth on the basis of the totality of realities ascertained in personal experience (a subject previously discussed in his System der christlichen Gewissheit), makes all Christian truth center in the thought of God's becoming man in Jesus Christ, and expounds it under the three main heads of the Principle, the Execution, and the Aim of God's redeeming work.

FULLIQUET, GEORGES.—La Pensée religieuse dans le Nouveau Testament. Étude de Théologie Biblique. Paris, 1894.

A popular and interesting exposition of New Testament doctrine, with special emphasis on the relation of doctrines to spiritual life and experience.

GOULD, EZRA P.—The Biblical Theology of the New Testament. New York, 1900.

An admirable treatise in small compass, and quite comprehensive in its plan and method.

GUNKEL, HERMAN.—Die Wirkungen des heiligen Geistes nach der populären Anschauung der apostolischen Zeit, und der Lehre des Apostels Paulus. Eine biblisch-theologische Studie. Göttingen, 1899.
   An excellent specimen of thorough historical criticism in biblical theology.

HASE, KARL AUGUST.—Evangelische protestantische Dogmatik. Leipzig, 1826. Sixth ed., 1870.
   A condensed and very interesting treatise, which arranges all the doctrines under the two heads of Ontology and Christology.

HAUPT, ERICH.—Die eschatologischen Aussagen Jesu in den synoptischen Evangelien. Berlin, 1895.

HITZIG, FERDINAND.—Vorlesungen über biblische Theologie und messianische Weissagungen des alten Testaments. Herausgegeben von Kneucker. Karlsruhe, 1880.
   Apparently lacking in unity of aim and in comprehensiveness, but, like all this author's works, incisive, suggestive, and critical.

HOFMANN, JOHANN CHR. KARL VON.—Der Schriftbeweis. Ein theologischer Versuch. 2 vols. Nördlingen, 1852–1856. 2d ed., 1857–1860. (2d vol. in two large parts.)
...... Biblische Theologie des neuen Testaments. Nach Manuskripten und Vorlesungen bearbeitet von W. Volck. Nördlingen, 1886.
   The older work is a mine of valuable exegetical discussions of biblical doctrine, and has exerted wide influence on subsequent writers. The later work, edited by Volck, is an excellent compendium of New Testament theology.

HODGE, CHARLES.—Systematic Theology. 3 vols. New York, 1871–1873.
   A work of great learning and wide scope, maintaining the older Calvinian system of doctrine as against Arminian interpretations. It is a monumental contribution to its school of thought, and worthy of the careful study of the specialist in confessional dogmatics.

HOLSTEN, KARL JOHANN.—Zum Evangelium des Paulus und des Petrus. Rostock, 1867.
...... Das Evangelium des Paulus dargestellt. Berlin, 1880.
...... Paulinische Theologie dargestellt. Berlin, 1898.
   Valuable as the successive contributions of one who was a leader in the formulation of Pauline theology.

HOLTZMANN, HEINRICH JULIUS.—Lehrbuch der neutestamentlichen Theologie. 2 vols. Leipzig, 1897.
   Somewhat radical in its critical treatment of the documentary sources of New Testament theology, but easily to be ranked among the most thorough, scientific, comprehensive, and masterly works on the subject extant.

HUDSON, THOMSON JAY.—A Scientific Demonstration of the Future Life. Chicago, 1896.
   A work that may be very profitably studied without admitting that its argument amounts to a demonstration.

IMMER, A.—Theologie des neuen Testaments. Bern, 1877.
   This learned and comprehensive treatise discusses (1) the Religion of Jesus; (2) the Jewish Christianity of the primitive apostles; (3) Paulinism; (4) the post-Pauline Jewish Christianity; (5) the mediating course between Paulinism and Jewish Christianity; and (6) the Johannine Gospel and First Epistle.

KAFTAN, JULIUS.—Dogmatik. Freiburg, 1897.
   The author is a prominent representative of the Ritschlian theology, and here presents in a noteworthy manner the main dogmas of the Christian faith as seen from his somewhat modified point of view.

KAYSER, AUGUST.—Die Theologie des alten Testaments, in ihrer geschichtlichen Entwicklung dargestellt. Nach des Verfassers Tode herausgegeben mit einem Vorwort von Ed. Reuss. Strassburg, 1886.

KENNEDY, H. A. A.—St. Paul's Conception of the Last Things. New York, 1904.
   These "Cunningham Lectures for 1904" are a very valuable contribution to the literature of the Pauline eschatology.

KNAPP, GEORGE CHRISTIAN.—Lectures on Christian Theology, translated by Leonard Woods. 2 vols. Andover, 1831–1832. 8th American ed. 1 vol. New York, 1859.

An elaborate work of real value. It is cast in the form of a systematic theology, but is, in fact, a very full treatise on biblical dogmatics. In its English translation it has had an extensive circulation.

KROP, FREDERIC.—La Pensée de Jésus sur le Royaume de Dieu d'après les Évangiles synoptiques avec un appendice sur la question du "Fils de l'homme." Paris, 1897.

KUYPER, ABRAHAM.—The Work of the Holy Spirit. Translated from the Dutch with Explanatory Notes by Henri De Vries. Introduction by B. B. Warfield. New York, 1900.

Probably the most elaborate work on the subject extant, rigidly Calvinistic, and pointing out in great detail the relations and work of the Spirit in the creation and redemption of the world.

LADD, GEORGE T.—The Doctrine of Sacred Scripture. A critical, historical, and dogmatic Inquiry into the origin and nature of the Old and New Testaments. 2 vols. New York, 1883.

An exceedingly valuable work, but too diffusely written to serve the most helpful purpose. It treats many of the most important topics of biblical doctrine, and is a storehouse of information.

LAIDLAW, JOHN.—The Bible Doctrine of Man; or, The Anthropology and Psychology of Scripture. Edinburgh, 1879. New ed., 1895.

Belongs strictly to works on biblical dogmatics, and is well worthy of thoughtful study.

LANGE, JOHN PETER.—Christliche Dogmatik. 3 vols. Heidelberg, 1849–1852.

A ponderous and comprehensive work, suggestive and interesting in many places, but sometimes fanciful.

LIDDON, H. P.—The Divinity of our Lord and Saviour Jesus Christ. London, 1867.

Bampton Lectures of 1866, which have been published in many editions and have had an immense circulation. Their real value as a contribution to fundamental Christian doctrine is generally conceded.

LIPSIUS, RICHARD A.—Lehrbuch der evangelisch-protestantischen Dogmatik. Third ed. Braunschweig, 1893.

This edition contains some noticeable changes from the two previous editions of 1876 and 1878, and was published after the author's death under editorial care of Otto Baumgarten. The work is a comprehensive presentation of Christian dogmatics in the light of the coöperating life and experience of the individual and the Christian community.

LOBSTEIN, P.—An Introduction to Protestant Dogmatics. Translated from the French by Arthur Maxson Smith. Chicago, 1902.

Admirable as an introduction to the scientific statement of the task and the methods of the modern theologian.

LUTHARDT, CHRISTOPH ERNST.—Apologetic Lectures on the Fundamental Truths of Christianity. Translated from the German by Sophia Taylor. Edinburgh, 1865.
...... The Saving Truths of Christianity. Edinburgh, 1868.
...... The Moral Truths of Christianity. Edinburgh, 1873.

Though assuming an apologetic purpose and claim, these volumes are a substantial contribution to the exposition of Christian truth, and they belong to the department of Christian dogmatics.

LUTZ, J. L. S.—Biblische Dogmatik. Nach dessen Tode herausgegeben von Rudolf Rütschi, mit einem Vorwort von Schneckenburger. Pforzheim, 1847.

A comprehensive and valuable contribution for its time.

MACPHERSON, JOHN.—Christian Dogmatics. Edinburgh, 1898.

A compact but comprehensive and learned treatise, representing a moderate Calvinism.

MARHEINEKE, PHILIPP.—System der christlichen Dogmatik. Edited by Mitthies and Vatke. Berlin, 1847.
> Follows the trinitarian method of grouping all biblical and Christian doctrine under the headings God, God the Son, and God the Spirit, and views the several doctrines from the standpoint of the Hegelian philosophy.

MARTENSEN, H.—Christian Dogmatics. A Compendium of the Doctrines of Christianity. Translated from the German by William Urwick. Edinburgh, 1866.
> Presents briefly and with distinguished ability the chief doctrines of Christianity, and, like Marheineke, groups them all under the three divisions of the Father, the Son and the Spirit.

MÉNÉGOZ, EUGÉNE.—Le Péché et la Redemption d'après Saint Paul. Paris, 1882.
......La Prédestination dans la Théologie Paulinienne. Paris, 1884.
......La Théologie de l'Épitre aux Hébreux. Paris, 1894.
> These are all treatises of sterling value.

MILLIGAN, GEORGE.—The Theology of the Epistle to the Hebrews, with a critical Introduction. Edinburgh, 1899.
> A volume to be cordially commended to students.

MILEY, JOHN.—Systematic Theology. 2 vols. New York, 1892–1894.
> One of the most able and thorough presentations of the Arminian theology extant, and ranks as an authority in American Methodism.

MUELLER, JULIUS.—The Christian Doctrine of Sin. Translated from the German of the Fifth Edition by William Urwick. 2 vols. Edinburgh, 1868.
> Holds the rank of a theological classic on the important subject which it treats quite exhaustively.

NEANDER, JOHANN AUGUST W.—History of the Planting and Training of the Christian Church by the Apostles. Translated by J. E. Ryland. Revised by E. G. Robinson. New York, 1865.
> An old standard work, having permanent value for the student of New Testament theology.

NITZSCH, CARL IMMANUEL.—System of Christian Doctrine. Translated from the fifth German edition by Robert Montgomery and John Hennen. Edinburgh, 1849.
> A very interesting and suggestive manual.

NITZSCH, FRIEDRICH AUGUST BERTHOLD.—Lehrbuch der evangelischen Dogmatik. In two parts. Freiburg, 1889–1892.
> A comprehensive and scientific statement of current evangelical doctrines, and of the principles needful to the study of the same.

NOACH, LUDWIG.—Die biblische Theologie. Einleitung in's alte und neue Testament, und Darstellung des Lehrgehaltes der biblischen Bücher nach ihrer Entstehung und ihrem geschichtlichen Verhältniss. Halle, 1853.
> Treats the Old and New Testaments in two parts, but bestows much more attention upon the literature than upon the doctrinal contents.

OEHLER, G. F.—Theology of the Old Testament. A revision of the translation in Clark's Foreign Theological Library, with additions of the second German edition, an Introduction and Notes by George E. Day. New York, 1883.
> A comprehensive and standard work, arranged under the three heads of Mosaism, Prophetism, and Old Testament Wisdom.

ORR, JAMES.—The Christian View of God and the World as Centering in the Incarnation. Being the Kerr Lectures for 1890–1891.
> These lectures cover a wide range of fundamental Christian truths, and combine a scientific with a thoroughly evangelical treatment of the several doctrines.

PFLEIDERER, OTTO.—Der Paulinismus. Leipzig, 1873. 2d ed., 1890.
...... Paulinism: a Contribution to the History of Primitive Theology. Translated by Edward Peters. 2 vols. London, 1877.
...... The Influence of the Apostle Paul on the Development of Christianity. Translated by J. F. Smith. New York, 1885.

All these works are indispensable to the critical study of New Testament theology, but the author's views are often radical, and have not met with general favor.

PIEPENBRING, CH.—Theology of the Old Testament. Translated from the French by H. G. Mitchell. New York, 1893.

Exhibits the development of religious thought among the Hebrew people.

POPE, WILLIAM BURT.—A Compendium of Christian Theology. 3 vols. London, 1875–1876. New York, 1880.
...... A Higher Catechism of Theology. London, 1883.

These volumes rank among the fullest and ablest expositions of the English Wesleyan Arminian theology.

RAYMOND, MINER.—Systematic Theology. 3 vols. Cincinnati, 1877–1879.

A very clear and readable presentation of Arminian theology. It deals also with Apologetics, Ethics and Ecclesiology.

RIDGELEY, THOMAS.—A Body of Divinity, wherein the Doctrines of the Christian Religion are explained and defended. 2 vols. London, 1831–1833. New ed. revised by John W. Wilson. New York, 1855.

A profusely elaborate series of lectures on the Westminster Confession, following its order of questions and answers.

RIEHM, EDWARD KARL AUGUST.—Der Lehrbegriff des Hebräerbriefes dargestellt und mit verwandten Lehrbegriffen verglichen. Basel. In two parts, 1858–1859. New and improved ed. in one vol., 1867.

An elaborate and masterly exposition of the doctrines of the epistle to the Hebrews, along with comparison with corresponding ideas in the other biblical writers.

RITSCHL, ALBRECHT.—Die christliche Lehre von der Rechtfertigung und Versöhnung. 3 vols. Bonn, 1870–1874.

The second volume of this famous work (2d ed., 1882) treats the "biblical material of the doctrine," and is an important contribution to biblical theology. The influence of Ritschl on the modern theological thought of Germany has been powerful and far-reaching, and is now felt in much of the English world. The translation of the third volume (New York, 1900) has placed the author's own statement of his system within the reach of English readers.

ROTHE, R.—Dogmatik. 2 vols. Heidelberg, 1870.

Edited from the author's manuscripts by D. Schenkel. An important contribution to Christian doctrine, somewhat after the ideas and spirit of Schleiermacher. His previous work on theological ethics had treated the chief doctrines of Christianity as the essential basis of sound morals.

SABATIER, A.—The Apostle Paul. A Sketch of the Development of his Doctrine. Translated by A. M. Hellier. Edited, with an additional Essay on the Pastoral Epistles, by George G. Findlay. 3d ed. New York, 1896.

An important contribution to the Pauline theology.

SALMOND, STEWART D. F.—The Christian Doctrine of Immortality. Edinburgh, 1895.

A full and helpful discussion of the doctrine of man's future life.

SCHENKEL, DANIEL. Die christliche Dogmatik vom Standpunkte des Gewissens. 2 vols. Wiesbaden, 1858–1859.

Expounds German liberalism in doctrine, and emphasizes conscience as the organ of religious truth.

SCHLEIERMACHER, F. D. E.—Der christliche Glaube nach den Grundsätzen der evangelischen Kirche im Zusammenhange dargestellt. 2 vols. Berlin, 1821–1822. Reutlingen, 1828. Berlin, 1884.

One of the most important contributions to religious dogma that has ever appeared. In connection with his earlier *Reden über die Religion*, this ripe product of the distinguished author opened an era in the scientific treatment of theology.

SCHLOTTMANN, KONSTANTIN.—Compendium der biblischen Theologie des alten und neuen Testaments. Herausgegeben von Ernst Kühn. Leipzig, 1889. 2d ed., 1895.

    A very convenient and comprehensive manual, covering both the Old and the New Testaments.

SCHMID, CHRISTIAN FRIEDRICH.—Biblical Theology of the New Testament. Translated by G. H. Venables. Edinburgh, 1871.

    One of the earlier and best-known books on the subject, and still worthy of consultation.

SCHMIDT, WILHELM.—Die Lehre des Apostels Paulus. Gütersloh, 1898.

    Critical, and deserving the attention of students in Pauline theology.

SCHNEDERMANN, GEORG.—Jesu Verkündigung und Lehre vom Reiche Gottes in ihrer geschichtlichen Bedeutung. Erste Hälfte: Die Verkündigung Jesu vom Kommen des Königsreiches Gottes. Leipzig, 1893.

SCHULTZ, HERMANN.—Old Testament Theology. The Religion of Revelation in its pre-Christian Stage and Development. Translated from the fourth German edition by J. A. Paterson. 2 vols. Edinburgh, 1892.

    The learned and accomplished author modified his critical views of Old Testament literature and doctrine after his first German edition of this work was issued (1869), and his more matured opinions appear in this translation (made from the 4th German ed.). It holds a commanding place among works on Old Testament theology.

SEEBERG, ALFRED.—Der Tod Christi in seiner Bedeutung für die Erlösung. Eine biblisch-theologische Untersuchung. Leipzig, 1895.

    A remarkably comprehensive discussion of the saving significance of the death of Christ, and an important contribution to biblical theology; but not altogether satisfactory. It maintains the essential harmony of all the New Testament writers in their views of Christ's death. The author begins with the epistle to the Hebrews, and then examines, in order, the teaching of John, of Paul, of Peter, the speeches recorded in the Acts, and, last of all, the synoptic gospels.

SHEDD, WILLIAM G. T.—Dogmatic Theology. 2 vols. New York, 1888. Vol. iii. Supplement, 1894.

    An elaborate work, learned and comprehensive, aiming to state and defend the Augustinian and older Calvinian theology.

SHELDON, HENRY C.—System of Christian Doctrine. Cincinnati, 1903.

    A very complete and able exposition of the doctrines of the Christian faith, comprehensive and scientific in thought and statement, and worthy of special commendation to students and ministers.

SMEATON, GEORGE.—The Doctrine of the Holy Spirit. Edinburgh, 1889.

    An able and comprehensive discussion of the doctrine after the manner of biblical dogmatics.

SMITH, HENRY B.—System of Christian Theology. Edited by William S. Kerr. New York, 1884.

    A unique and very able treatise, which aims to make all Christian theology center in the person and ministry of Christ.

SOMERVILLE, DAVID.—St. Paul's Conception of Christ; or, The Doctrine of the Second Adam. Edinburgh, 1897.

    A book that cannot well be overlooked in the study of Paul's Christology.

STADE, B.—Biblische Theologie des alten Testaments. Erster Band: Die Religion Israels und die Entstehung des Judentums. Tübingen, 1905.

    A masterly treatise, thoroughly scientific, critically historical, the product of ripe scholarship and patient study.

STEARNS, LEWIS FRENCH.—Present Day Theology. New York, 1893.

    A series of twenty-seven essays on as many different Christian doctrines, all of which are treated with ability and sober thought.

STEUDEL, JOH. CHRISTIAN FRIEDRICH.—Vorlesungen über die Theologie des alten Testaments. Nach dessen Tode herausgegeben von G. F. Oehler. Berlin, 1840.

> One of the older books that deserves study. It adopts the method of biblical dogmatics in three parts: (1) the Doctrine of Man; (2) the Doctrine of God, and (3) the Doctrine of the Relation between God and Man.

STEVENS, GEORGE B.—The Theology of the New Testament. New York, 1899.
...... The Pauline Theology: a Study of the Origin and Correlation of the doctrinal teaching of the Apostle Paul. New York, 1892.
...... The Johannine Theology: a Study of the doctrinal contents of the Gospel and Epistles of the Apostle John. New York, 1894.
...... The Christian Doctrine of Salvation, New York, 1905.

> These volumes constitute the most important and valuable contribution which American scholarship has thus far made to biblical theology. They all deserve cordial recommendation to students of New Testament doctrine.

STRONG, A. H.—Systematic Theology. New York, 1886.

> One of the most valuable and comprehensive works on systematic theology that has appeared during the last generation.

SUMMERS, THOMAS O.—Systematic Theology: A Complete Body of Wesleyan Arminian Divinity. Revised and edited by J. J. Tigert, Nashville, 1888.

> Consists of lectures on the Twenty Five Articles of Religion, and holds the rank of an authoritative exposition of Arminian theology in Southern Methodism.

TITIUS, ARTHUR.—Jesu Lehre vom Reiche Gottes. Freiburg, 1895.

> A very thorough and systematic statement of the doctrine of the kingdom of God, and worthy of special commendation.

TURRETIN, FRANCIS.—Institutio Theologiæ Elencticæ. 3 vols. Geneva, 1688. New ed., Edinburgh, 1847–1848.

> A systematic and elaborate work, following the catechetical method of questions and answers in the order of the prevalent confessions of the time, and maintaining the most rigid orthodoxy of the Calvinian theology.

TWESTEN, AUGUST D. C.—Vorlesungen über die Dogmatik der evangelische lutherischen Kirche. 2 vols. Hamburg, 1826, 1837.

> An unfinished work, but interesting as a modification of the Lutheran theology under the broadening influence of the teaching of Schleiermacher.

VAN OOSTERZEE, J. J.—The Theology of the New Testament. A Handbook for Bible Students. Translated from the Dutch by M. J. Evans. New York, 1871.
...... Christian Dogmatics.—A Text Book for Academical Instruction and Private Study. Translated from the Dutch by J. J. Watson and M. J. Evans. 2 vols. New York, 1874.

> The first named is a condensed, convenient, and useful manual; the later and larger work is a mature and elaborate exposition of Christian truth worthy of attention and study.

VATKE, WILHELM.—Die biblische Theologie wissenschaftlich dargestellt. Die Religion des alten Testamentes, nach den kanonischen Büchern entwickelt. Erster Theil. Berlin, 1835.

> The first part is devoted to a presentation of the religion of the Old Testament, and the work was never completed by a further setting forth of the theology of the other canonical books. This work is noted as one of the first attempts to construct the historical development of the Old Testament theology after the manner now generally adopted by the more advanced biblical criticism.

VOLZ, PAUL.—Jüdische Eschatologie. Von Daniel bis Akiba. Tübingen und Leipzig, 1903.

> An invaluable help for tracing the history of the later Jewish eschatological opinions from B. C. 300 to A. D. 200.

WATSON, RICHARD.—Theological Institutes, or a View of the Evidences, Doctrines, Morals, and Institutions of Christianity. 3 vols. 1823–1824. New ed., with a copious Index and an Analysis by J. McClintock. 2 vols. New York, 1850.

The monumental contribution of the earlier Wesleyan Methodism to systematic theology. The work is unequal in its parts, obsolete now in some of its discussions, and abounds in extensive quotations from others. But it ranks with the ablest productions of its time.

WEBER, FERDINAND.—Jüdische Theologie auf Grund des Talmud und verwandter Schriften gemeinfasslich dargestellt. Leipzig, 1880. 2d revised edition, by F. Delitzsch and G. Schnedermann. 1897.

Invaluable as a guide to theological opinions as set forth in the literature of the later Judaism.

WEINEL, HEINRICH.—Die Wirkungen des Geistes und der Geister im nachapostolischen Zeitalter bis auf Irenæus. Freiburg, 1899.

A work of the greatest value for the study of the operations of the Spirit and an important contribution to biblical dogmatics.

WEISS, BERNHARD.—Biblical Theology of the New Testament. Translated from the third German edition by David Eaton. 2 vols. Edinburgh, 1882.

A work of exceeding value and a thesaurus of material for working out the problems of New Testament doctrine. It ranks among the foremost of its class.

WEISS, JOHANNES.—Die Predigt Jesu vom Reiche Gottes. Göttingen, 1892. 2d ed., 1900.
......Die Idee des Reiches Gottes in der Theologie. Giessen, 1901.

The last named was read at a theological conference at Giessen, and is a supplement to the preceding. They both maintain the eschatological conception of the kingdom of God.

WENDT, HANS HINRICH.—The Teaching of Jesus. Translated by John Wilson. New York, 1892.

This English translation gives only the second part of the German original, but it contains the author's exposition of the teaching of Jesus. The first part is a critical discussion of the gospel as sources of doctrine. A second edition of the German work (Göttingen 1901) has condensed the two volumes of the first edition into one of 640 pages. No other work on the teaching of our Lord holds a higher place among New Testament scholars.

WITTICHEN, CARL.—Beiträge zur biblischen Theologie:
......1. Die Idee Gottes als des Vaters: ein Beitrag zur biblischen Theologie, hauptsächlich der synoptischen Reden Jesu. Göttingen, 1865.
......2. Die Idee des Menschen: zweiter Beitrag zur biblischen Theologie hauptsächlich der synoptischen Reden Jesu. Göttingen, 1868.
......3. Die Idee des Reiches Gottes: dritter Beitrag zur biblischen Theologie, inbesondere der synoptischen Reden Jesu. Göttingen, 1872.

These three small volumes present all together an admirable outline and discussion of the biblical doctrine of the Father, of Man, and of the Kingdom of God. While dealing mainly with the teaching of Jesus, they also pay becoming attention to the other biblical writings, especially the Old Testament and the Apocrypha.

WOOD, IRVING F.—The Spirit of God in Biblical Literature. A Study in the History of Religion. With an Introduction by Frank C. Porter. New York, 1904.

Biblical, historical, critical, comprehensive. One of the most satisfactory books on the biblical doctrine of the Holy Spirit that has been written.

ZACHARIÄ, GOTTHILF TRAUGOTT.—Biblische Theologie, oder Untersuchung des Grundes der vornehmsten biblischen Lehren. 4 vols. Göttingen, 1771–1775.

Interesting as one of the elaborate treatises of its time, and one of the early attempts at biblical theology, but of little intrinsic value for a modern student.

INDEX OF SCRIPTURE TEXTS

This index includes only those texts on which some comment is made

Genesis.

I, 2.	154, 485, 486, 514, 573n, 579.	
" 3.	154.	
" 11.	64.	
" 24.	64.	
" 26-28.	76.	
" 26.	79.	
" 27.	59, 79.	
" 28.	64, 73.	
" 31.	76, 178, 573.	
II, 7.	65, 71, 526.	
" 17.	118.	
" 18.	59.	
" 24.	59.	
" 25.	76.	
III, 3.	118.	
" 5.	309.	
" 15.	185.	
" 16-19.	113.	
" 17-18.	119.	
" 24.	185.	
IV, 1-5.	62.	
" 10.	47.	
V, 1-3.	79.	
" 3.	64, 65.	
VI, 6.	488.	
VIII, 20-23.	353.	
IX, 4.	47.	
" 9-17.	185.	
XI, 1-9.	67.	
" 5.	526.	
XIII, 1-3.	7.	
XIV, 1.	30.	
XVII, 7.	525.	
XVIII, 23-32.	188.	
" 25.	424.	
XXV, 8.	199, 253.	
" 17.	199.	
XXVIII, 13.	527.	
XXXI, 20.	527.	
" 34.	527.	
" 53.	527.	
XXXII, 24-30.	188.	
" 24.	526.	
" 30.	527.	
XXXV, 29.	199.	

Genesis.

XL, 5.	528.	
" 15.	528.	
XLIX, 29.	199, 253.	
" 33.	199, 253.	

Exodus.

III, 2-6.	330, 542.	
" 6.	226, 227, 353.	
" 7.	304.	
" 8.	304.	
" 13-15.	529.	
IV, 22.	159, 164.	
VI, 2.	529.	
" 3.	529.	
XIV, 19.	330.	
XV, 1-18.	539.	
" 3.	526.	
" 6.	526.	
" 8.	526.	
XVIII, 15.	540.	
XIX, 5.	159.	
XXI, 4-21.	104.	
" 23-25.	104.	
" 24-25.	105.	
XXIII, 13.	517.	
XXV, 17-22.	394.	
XXXII, 34.	330.	
XXXIII, 2.	330.	
" 12-16.	188.	
" 14.	330.	
XXXIV, 7.	106.	
XL, 34-38.	326.	

Leviticus.

IV, 13.	90.	
" 26.	356.	
" 31.	356.	
" 35.	356.	
XVI, 2-6.	252.	
" 11-17.	252, 357.	
XVII, 11.	47, 355.	
" 14.	47.	
XIX, 17.	59, 436.	
" 18.	436.	
XXIV, 11.	530.	
" 16.	530.	
XXVI, 14-21.	123.	

Numbers.

XI, 11-15.	138, 351.	
XIV, 22.	102.	
" 23.	102.	
XVI, 22.	66.	

Deuteronomy.

I, 17.	540.	
VI, 5.	52, 436.	
VII, 6.	549.	
" 8.	368.	
X, 16.	150.	
XII, 23.	47.	
XIII, 13.	104.	
XXI, 22.	388.	
" 23.	388.	
XXIV, 1.	104.	
XXVII, 26.	389.	
XXVIII, 15-45.	123.	
XXX, 6.	150.	
" 19.	57.	
XXXII, 8.	540.	
" 9-12.	530.	
" 9.	540.	
" 39.	213.	

Joshua.

VII, 24.	104.	

Judges.

I, 6.	104.	
X, 16.	553.	
XI, 23.	535.	
" 24.	535.	
XVII, 7-13.	352.	
XIX, 22.	104.	
XX, 6.	104.	
" 16.	86.	

1 Samuel.

I, 3-9.	352.	
II, 6.	213.	
VIII, 7.	425n, 540.	
X, 9.	150.	
" 19.	425n, 540.	
XV, 22.	109.	
" 33.	104.	
XXIV, 5.	55.	
XXVI, 19.	535.	

595

INDEX OF SCRIPTURE TEXTS

2 Samuel.
VII, 14.	266.
XII, 13.	138.
" 16–18.	189.
" 23.	253.
XXIII, 2.	20.
XXIV, 10.	55.

1 Kings.
VIII, 23–30.	526.
" 23	538.
XVIII, 20–40.	506.
XIX, 9	507.
XXII, 19.	540.

2 Kings.
I, 10.	105.
" 12.	105.
III, 27.	537.
V, 18.	516.
XVII, 26.	535.
" 30.	516.

Job.
I, 5.	350.
" 12.	111.
II, 6.	111.
III, 8.	461.
XI, 7–9.	513.
" 7.	171.
" 8.	201.
XIV, 10–12.	215.
XVII, 13–16.	202.
XIX, 25–27.	201.
XXI, 24.	49.
XXVI, 5.	202.
" 6.	202.
" 12.	461, 514.
XXXVII, 6.	55.
XXXI, 33.	113.
XXXVI, 26–30.	513.
XXXVIII, 4.	111.
XLII, 7–17.	111.

Psalms.
I, 3.	164.
V, 10.	105.
VIII,	72.
" 4.	268.
IX, 16.	107.
" 17.	107.
XVI, 8–10.	203.
" 10.	200.
" 11.	200.
XVII, 15.	212.
XVIII, 4.	122n.
" 5.	122n.
" 7–15.	424.
XIX, 7–11.	32.
XXII	363–365.
" 28.	424.

Psalms.
XXVII, 1.	201.
" 4.	178.
XXIX, 2.	178.
XXXIII, 6–9.	70.
XXXVII, 20.	134.
XXXVIII, 1–4.	138.
XL, 8.	283.
XLIII, 1.	107.
XLIV, 22.	128.
XLV, 6.	324.
XLVII, 8.	424.
XLIX, 15.	200.
L, 3–6.	425.
" 5.	410.
LI, 1–3.	138.
" 4.	108, 138.
" 5.	84, 138.
" 10.	150.
LVII, 1.	457.
LVIII, 3.	84.
LIX, 23.	105.
" 28.	123.
LXXII.	474.
LXXIII, 18.	123.
" 23–26.	199.
LXXVIII, 40.	487.
" 41.	487.
LXXXII, 7.	113.
LXXXIV, 11.	175.
LXXXIX, 10.	461, 514.
" 35–37.	474.
XC, 17.	178.
XCII, 12.	165.
XCVI, 9.	178.
XCVIII, 9.	424.
CIII, 13.	533.
CIV, 2.	424.
" 3.	424.
CIX, 6–13.	105.
CX.	365, 428, 474.
" 3.	178.
CVI, 3.	128.
CXIX.	32.
" 71.	177.
" 73.	66.
CXXXVII, 7.	478.
" 8.	105.
" 9.	105.
CXXXIX, 7.	487.
" 14.	155.
" 15.	155.

Proverbs.
I, 20–23.	109.
" 24–31.	94.
III, 17.	178.
IV, 18.	193, 256.
V, 5.	122n.
" 12.	110.

Proverbs.
V. 13.	110.
" 22.	110.
" 23.	110.
VI, 12–19.	110.
VII, 27.	110.
VIII, 22–31.	110, 312, 329, 557.
" 22.	552.
" 23.	552.
X, 2.	122n.
XI, 4.	122n.
XII, 1.	110.
" 28.	122n.
XIII, 5.	110.
XIV, 34.	110.
XVI, 32.	507.
XX, 27.	48.
XXIII, 7.	169.

Ecclesiastes.
II, 1–11.	112.
" 12–23.	112.
III, 10.	112.
" 11.	198.
" 21.	198.
XI, 5.	155.
XII. 5.	198.
" 7.	65, 198.

Isaiah.
I 4.	360.
" 10–17.	109.
	360.
" 18.	360.
" 19.	57.
" 20.	57.
" 21–23.	106.
II, 2–4.	474.
VI, 1.	19.
" 10.	94.
IX, 1–7.	475.
" 4.	478.
" 6.	427.
" 7.	427.
XI, 1–10.	427, 475.
" 2.	487.
" 4.	465.
XIII, 6.	426.
" 9–19.	427.
XIV, 9–11.	202.
" 11–19.	124.
" 12.	514.
" 15.	253.
" 16.	253.
XIX, 1–4.	427.
XXV, 8.	213.
XXVI, 12–21.	214, 215.

INDEX OF SCRIPTURE TEXTS

Isaiah.

XXVI,	19.	214.
XXVII,	1.	461, 514.
XXX,	33.	123.
XXXI,	9.	123.
XXXIII,	12.	123.
"	14.	123.
"	22.	540.
XXXIV,	1-5.	427.
"	14.	514.
XL,	22.	424.
"	23.	424.
XLII,	1-4.	564.
"	1.	266.
"	5.	66.
XLIX,	15.	579.
LI,	9.	461, 514.
LII,	13—LIII, 12.	361, 362.
LIII,	5.	383.
"	7.	381.
"	8.	381.
"	10.	387.
LVII,	20.	86.
LXIII,	3-6.	374.
"	10.	487.
"	12-14.	529.
"	16.	564.
LXIV,	8.	564.
LXVI,	13.	579.
"	24.	124.

Jeremiah.

I,	9.	19.
IV,	4.	150.
VII,	12-16.	94.
IX,	1.	360.
"	3.	360.
XII,	4.	119.
XVII,	9.	84.
XXIII,	5.	427.
"	6.	427.
XXX,	2.	19.
XXXI,	9.	564.
"	20.	564.
"	29.	31, 109.
"	30.	109.

Ezekiel.

XI,	19.	150.
XIV,	21.	119, 426.
XVIII,	2.	31.
"	3.	109.
"	4.	66, 109.
"	20.	109.
XXII,	4.	90.
XXVIII,	21-24.	426.
XXXVI,	25.	152, 153.
"	26.	150.
XXXVII,	1-14.	216.

Daniel.

II,	28.	48, 49n.
"	35.	460.
"	44.	476.
IV,	5.	48.
VII,	9-14.	428.
"	9.	541.
"	10.	541.
"	13.	268, 271, 476.
"	15.	46, 48.
"	18.	258.
"	27.	206.
IX,	7.	55.
"	8.	55.
"	24.	362, 363.
X,	13.	461.
"	20.	461.
XII,	2.	124, 130, 217. 218, 227, 248.
"	3.	217, 218.

Hosea.

I,	2.	106.
"	11.	478.
IV,	12.	106.
VI,	1-3.	214.
"	6.	108.
"	7.	113.
IX,	1.	106.
XI,	1.	564.
"	8.	360, 553.
"	9.	360.
XIII,	14.	213.
XIV,	5.	165.
"	6.	165.

Joel.

II,	1.	426.
"	2.	426.
"	28-32.	448.

Amos.

V,	12.	108.
"	21-24.	108.
IX,	3.	461.

Micah.

I,	1-5.	427.
IV,	1-4.	474.
V,	2-4.	428.
VI,	6-8.	108, 360.

Habakkuk.

II,	4.	389.

Haggai.

II,	6.	439.
"	7.	439.

Zechariah.

VI,	12.	476n.
"	13.	476n.
IX,	9.	475.
"	10.	475.
XII,	1.	66.
XIV,	9.	424.

Malachi.

IV, 6.		482.

Matthew.

I,	1.	22n.
II,	15.	564.
III,	2.	442.
"	6.	146.
IV,	1-11.	99.
"	3.	266.
"	6.	266.
V,	3.	435.
"	9.	159.
"	12.	209.
"	17.	3, 15, 265.
"	18.	171.
"	20.	169.
"	21.	90, 169.
"	22.	90, 169.
"	24.	386.
"	28.	58.
"	44.	105.
"	45.	159.
VI,	9.	577.
"	10.	430.
"	13.	182n.
"	20.	209, 255.
"	23.	89.
VII,	12.	59.
"	29.	280.
VIII,	11.	370n.
"	36.	284.
IX,	13.	368.
"	14-17.	16.
"	22.	146.
"	29.	146.
X,	7.	442.
"	15.	90.
"	23.	442.
"	28.	52, 126, 133, 134.
"	29.	67.
"	30.	280.
"	32.	562.
"	33.	562.
XI,	1-10.	425.
"	2-5.	275.
"	2-11.	436.
"	11.	16.
"	12.	437.
"	25-27.	560.
"	27.	265, 267.
"	28.	265, 267.

INDEX OF SCRIPTURE TEXTS

Matthew.

XII,	6.	265.
"	8.	265.
"	18–21.	564.
"	31.	92, 131, 132.
"	32.	92, 131, 132.
"	39.	277, 505.
"	41.	265.
"	42.	265.
"	50.	562.
XIII,	10–16.	34.
"	19.	431.
"	38.	159, 468.
"	43.	159, 210, 562.
"	52.	5.
XIV,	26.	222.
XV,	13.	562.
"	28.	145.
XVI,	13–20.	272.
"	17.	286.
"	28.	463.
XVII,	2.	223.
"	9.	210.
"	11.	482.
XVIII,	1–4.	435.
"	10.	562.
"	14.	562.
"	15.	387.
"	19.	562.
"	21–35.	433.
XIX,	21.	171.
"	28.	258, 482.
"	29.	194, 210.
XX,	1–16.	432.
XXI,	28–32.	433.
"	33.	433.
"	34.	433.
XXII,	1–14.	434.
"	23–33.	225, 226.
"	37.	52.
"	39.	59.
XXIII,	9.	569.
"	23.	169.
"	37.	57, 457.
XXIV,	1.	180n.
"	3.	445.
"	5.	466.
"	11.	466.
"	12.	466.
"	14.	446, 466, 492.
"	29–31.	447, 463.
"	34–36.	447.
"	34.	443.
"	36.	247.
XXV,	1–13.	478—

Matthew.

XXV,	14–30.	434.
"	31–46.	126, 231, 478, 479, 497, 498.
"	41.	130.
"	46.	131.
XXVI,	24.	127.
"	28.	369, 371.
"	64.	443.
"	66.	90.
XXVII,	46.	374.
XXVIII,	3.	224.
"	19.	182, 182n, 486.

Mark.

I,	10.	342.
"	11.	342.
"	15.	142, 445, 442.
"	41.	284.
II,	10.	284.
"	27.	181.
III,	4.	284.
"	5.	89.
"	28–30.	92.
"	29.	90, 94, 123.
IV,	22.	256, 479.
"	26–29.	432.
VI,	3.	261.
VIII,	12.	505.
"	38.	126.
IX,	3.	224.
"	10.	225.
"	12.	482.
"	19.	505.
"	23.	146.
"	43.	129.
X,	2–12.	59.
"	13–15.	435.
"	18.	564.
"	23.	435.
"	29.	194.
"	30.	194.
"	45.	366–369.
XII,	18–27.	225, 226.
"	28–34.	436.
"	36.	488.
XIII,	10.	446, 492.
"	11.	20.
"	30–32.	447.
"	32.	267.
XIV,	22–24.	265.
"	24.	369.
"	33.	375.
"	34.	375.
"	64.	90.
XV,	34.	374.
XVI,	12.	308.
"	16.	145, 182.

Luke.

I,	32.	259.
"	35.	266, 273, 488.
"	51.	50.
"	67–79.	429.
"	78.	570n.
II,	1.	74.
"	24.	262.
"	25.	272.
"	25–38.	429.
"	38.	272.
"	40.	558.
"	49.	280.
"	52.	271.
IV,	1–13.	99.
"	13.	275.
"	14.	275, 556.
"	39.	284.
VI,	31.	59.
"	44.	101, 170.
VII,	18–23.	275.
"	19–28.	429, 436.
"	41–47.	433.
VIII,	11.	431.
"	31.	129.
IX,	29.	224.
"	30.	210.
"	43.	278.
"	54.	105.
X,	18.	287.
"	19.	287.
"	20.	505.
"	21.	560.
"	22.	560.
"	27.	52.
"	29–37.	433.
"	54.	286.
XI,	5–13.	433.
XII,	10.	92.
"	15–21.	433.
"	47.	90.
"	48.	90.
XIII,	1–5.	119.
"	16.	276.
XIV,	14.	225.
"	16–24.	434.
XVI,	1–13.	433.
"	9.	254.
"	19–31.	433.
"	22.	481.
"	23.	127, 129, 133, 203, 253.
"	24.	127, 129, 133.
XVII,	7–10.	433.
"	20–37.	444, 449.
"	20.	443.
"	21.	450.
"	24.	450.

INDEX OF SCRIPTURE TEXTS 599

Luke.		
XVIII,	1–8.	433.
"	8.	443.
"	9–14.	433.
"	12.	169.
XIX,	10.	368.
"	11–27.	434.
XX,	27–38.	225, 226.
"	35.	248, 254.
"	36.	254.
XXII,	19.	265.
"	20.	265, 369.
"	29.	562.
"	30.	562.
XXIII,	34.	374.
"	42.	229n, 254.
"	43.	133, 229n, 254, 374.
"	46.	282, 374.
XXIV,	4.	224.
"	31.	223n.
"	39.	223, 278.
"	49.	493.
"	51.	221.
"	52.	493.

John.		
I,	1.	326, 332, 337.
"	4.	192, 322, 567.
"	9.	2.
"	12.	155, 568.
"	13.	155.
"	14.	267, 326.
"	18.	267, 268, 281, 327n, 567.
"	49.	267.
III,	3–8.	151, 451.
"	5–8.	449.
"	5.	151, 154.
"	8.	155, 162.
"	13.	334, 451n.
"	14–16.	371.
"	16.	267, 416, 419, 567.
"	18.	267.
"	20.	496.
"	30–36.	451.
"	36.	145, 191, 204.
IV,	1.	182.
"	2.	182.
"	14.	194.
"	22.	7.
"	24.	82, 485, 488, 555.
"	36.	194.
"	48.	277, 337, 505.

John.		
V,	19–27.	481.
"	19.	277, 281.
"	21.	225.
"	22.	477.
"	24.	140, 156, 191, 228.
"	25.	228.
"	26.	566.
"	29.	130.
"	30.	277, 281, 283.
"	36.	277.
"	40.	141.
VI,	30–35.	505.
"	35.	265.
"	38.	211, 283.
"	39.	211, 283.
"	40.	225, 284.
"	44.	141.
"	48.	265.
"	50.	372.
"	51.	284, 372.
"	53.	265, 420.
"	54.	191.
"	57.	566.
"	62.	283, 334.
VII,	39.	485, 491.
"	46.	281.
VIII,	12.	256, 284, 566.
"	21–24.	127.
"	23.	283, 437.
"	28.	372n.
"	32.	192.
"	36.	163.
"	42–44.	568.
"	42.	283.
"	44.	498.
"	46.	283.
"	58.	283, 334.
IX,	1–3.	120.
"	3.	112.
"	5.	283.
X,	10.	566.
"	11.	373.
"	15.	373.
"	18.	221, 557.
"	30.	568.
"	38.	267.
XI,	3–5.	338.
"	25.	210, 229, 265, 285.
"	26.	210, 229, 265, 285.
"	33.	229.
"	50–52.	373.
XII,	13–16.	452.
"	24.	119, 372.
"	31.	498.
"	32–34.	372n.

John.		
XII,	32.	250, 265.
"	45.	283.
"	46.	284.
XIII,	3.	210.
XIV,	1–3.	210.
"	2.	568.
"	3.	452, 453.
"	6.	265.
"	9.	283, 568.
"	10.	267, 283.
"	11.	267.
"	12.	504, 507.
"	16–20.	490.
"	20.	191.
"	23.	452.
"	26.	20.
"	28.	282, 568.
"	31.	282.
XV,	1–9.	420.
"	13.	373.
"	18.	452.
"	19.	452.
"	22.	497.
"	26.	490.
XVI,	8.	496.
"	9–11.	496.
"	13–15.	501.
"	28.	210.
XVII,	3.	191.
"	5.	283, 334.
"	12.	127.
"	17.	33, 168.
"	18.	283.
"	20–26.	420.
"	24.	211n, 283, 334, 337, 452.
"	26.	64.
XVIII,	36.	437, 452.
"	37.	437, 452.
XIX	11.	91.
"	26.	338, 374.
"	27.	338, 374.
"	28.	374.
"	30.	374.
"	34.	378.
XX,	19.	223.
"	22.	493.
"	23.	493.
"	26.	223.
"	27.	222.
"	29.	505.
"	31.	146.
XXI,	22.	453.
"	23.	453.

Acts.		
I,	1–11.	222.
"	3.	222, 223.
"	5.	493.

INDEX OF SCRIPTURE TEXTS

Acts.

I,	6.	482.
"	11.	456.
"	16.	488.
II,	1–13.	493.
"	5.	446.
"	14–21.	448.
"	14–40.	289, 290.
"	27.	203.
"	31.	203.
"	33.	491, 493.
"	38.	381.
III,	13–15.	290.
"	19.	141, 147.
"	21.	290, 456, 482.
"	26.	381.
IV,	10–12.	381.
"	12.	290, 381.
"	25.	400.
V,	31.	141, 381.
VII,	28.	457.
"	38.	33.
"	51.	58.
"	56–60.	254.
"	56.	454.
"	59.	133.
VIII,	4.	33.
"	35.	381.
IX,	3–9.	234.
"	17.	234.
X,	36.	149.
"	40.	222, 223.
"	41.	222, 223.
"	42.	290.
"	43.	381.
XI,	18.	140, 141.
"	28.	74.
XIII,	10.	469.
XIV,	15–17.	509.
XV,	28.	35.
"	29.	35.
XVII,	1–9.	466.
"	16.	62.
"	22–25.	62.
"	24–29.	82, 156, 570.
"	30.	480.
"	31.	477, 480.
XVIII,	24.	330.
XX,	28.	320.
XXII,	11.	224.
XXIV,	15.	231.
XXVI,	13.	224, 234.
XXVIII,	25.	488.

Romans.

I,	3.	300.
"	4.	300, 491.
I,	7.	181.
"	17.	148.
"	18–20.	27.
"	18–32.	85.
"	18.	136.
"	20.	311.
"	21.	521.
"	25.	88.
"	28.	521.
II,	3–11.	128.
"	4.	141.
"	9.	58, 122, 131.
"	14.	27, 56, 521.
"	15.	27, 56, 521.
III,	2.	7.
"	9.	85.
"	10–18.	85.
"	19.	90.
"	21–26.	391–400.
"	21.	143, 148.
"	22.	143, 148.
"	23.	85.
IV.		143, 144.
"	5.	148.
"	6.	148.
"	11.	148.
V,	1.	148, 149, 386.
"	8–11.	386, 400.
"	11.	149, 386.
"	12–19.	64, 85, 117, 121.
"	12–21.	401.
"	17.	257.
VI,	1.	144.
"	4.	156, 499.
"	5–14.	244.
"	7.	139.
"	8–11.	400.
"	12.	120.
"	13.	115.
"	14.	115.
"	17.	162.
"	18.	162.
"	19.	162.
"	21.	121.
"	23.	120, 160, 193.
VII,	5–11.	385.
"	5.	114.
"	6.	16.
"	7–24.	117.
"	9–14.	120.
"	14–24.	115, 116.
"	14.	114.
"	18.	114.
"	22.	115.
"	23.	115.
"	24.	114.
"	25.	114.
VIII,	1–11.	162, 166.

Romans.

VIII	2.	116, 193.
"	3.	315, 417.
"	3–5.	114.
"	6–8.	114.
"	6.	120.
"	11.	244, 499.
"	13.	114.
"	14–16.	158.
"	15.	570.
"	16.	51, 160, 500.
"	17.	159, 205.
"	18.	208.
"	19–22.	119, 483, 574.
"	21.	163.
"	22.	571.
"	23.	49, 159, 574.
"	25.	49.
"	26.	504, 574.
"	27.	504.
"	32.	401.
"	36.	128.
"	38.	208.
"	39.	208.
IX,	4.	159.
"	5.	300, 319.
X,	4.	399.
"	6–10.	148.
"	9.	146.
"	10.	146.
XI,	15.	386.
XII,	4–8.	181.
XIV,	8.	401.
"	10.	477.
"	17.	438, 500.
"	18.	178n.
XV,	4.	21, 185.

1 Corinthians.

I,	7.	455.
"	14.	21.
"	16.	21.
"	17.	183.
II,	6.	173.
"	10–14.	82, 501.
"	11.	51, 161, 488.
"	13.	21n.
"	14.	52.
"	15.	52.
III,	1.	114.
"	3.	114.
"	9.	179.
IV,	20.	438.
V,	4.	306.
"	7.	184, 370, 397.
VI,	19.	66.
VII,	11.	386.
"	25.	21.
"	34.	52.

INDEX OF SCRIPTURE TEXTS

1 Corinthians.

VII,	40.	21.
IX,	24–26.	172.
"	27.	114.
X,	4.	117, 315, 316.
"	16.	184, 421.
XI,	7.	309.
"	27.	90.
XII,	4–7.	180.
"	4–11.	503.
"	6.	488.
"	7.	488.
"	12.	421.
"	13.	182, 421.
XIII,	1.	507.
"	2.	507.
"	4–8.	175.
"	10.	173, 256.
"	12.	252, 256.
XIV,	15.	49.
"	19.	49.
"	20.	48, 173.
XV,	1–11.	233.
"	8.	224.
"	12–19.	234.
"	20–26.	248.
"	20–28.	234.
"	22.	121, 250.
"	23.	249.
"	24–28.	135, 483, 581.
"	25.	473.
"	29–34.	235.
"	31.	128.
"	35–49.	235–240.
"	36.	119.
"	36–38.	242, 246.
"	44.	53.
"	45–49.	316.
"	50–58.	240, 241.
"	51.	232.
"	52.	232.

2 Corinthians.

I,	12.	161.
"	22.	500.
III,	6–11.	16, 165.
"	15–18.	34.
"	17.	162, 192, 299, 490.
IV,	4–6.	299.
"	4.	88.
"	6.	155, 192, 257.
"	16–V, 10.	241–244.
"	17.	120, 177.
"	18.	507.
V,	1–8.	208, 249.
"	1.	46.
"	5.	500.
"	6.	208.

2 Corinthians.

V,	10.	126, 477.
"	14.	121.
"	14–19.	384, 385, 386.
"	17.	154, 164.
"	18–21.	149, 387.
"	19.	147, 419, 385.
VI,	10.	317.
"	21.	387, 388.
VII,	1.	168.
"	10.	122n, 140.
VIII,	2.	176.
"	9.	317.
XI,	14.	469.
XII,	8.	189.
XIII,	14.	297, 485, 501.

Galatians.

I,	4.	390.
"	6.	102.
"	7.	102.
"	14.	117.
II,	19.	299, 390.
"	20.	121, 156, 184, 299, 385, 390.
III,	1.	102, 389.
"	13.	388, 389.
"	27.	182.
IV,	4.	273, 315, 390.
"	5.	390.
"	6.	570.
"	10.	163.
"	22–26.	117, 162.
V,	1.	162.
",	6.	174n.
"	13.	162.
"	17.	116.
"	19.	87, 114.
"	20.	87, 114.
"	22.	173.
"	23.	173.
VI,	8.	114.
"	10.	180.
"	14.	390.
"	15.	153, 164.

Ephesians.

I,	1.	168.
"	9–11.	349.
"	10.	302.
"	13.	153, 195, 439, 494, 500.
"	14.	195, 439, 500.
"	18–23.	303.
"	20.	245.
"	21.	557.
"	23.	305.
II,	1–3.	116, 121, 158.
"	5.	121.
"	6.	192, 245, 420.
"	8.	142.

Ephesians.

II,	10.	154.
"	14–18.	149.
"	16.	386.
"	19–22.	179.
III,	8–11.	303, 349.
"	8.	317.
"	10–12.	142.
"	12.	161.
"	14–19.	174.
"	16–19.	116, 303.
"	19.	305.
"	21.	258.
IV,	5.	183.
"	8.	491.
"	9.	303n, 304, 305.
"	10.	304, 305.
"	11.	304, 305.
"	11–16.	180.
"	12.	421.
"	13.	305, 421.
"	15.	164.
"	18.	89.
"	24.	80, 164, 168.
"	30.	94, 487.
V,	1.	159, 175.
"	2.	175, 402.
"	5.	319.
"	8.	159, 192.
"	8–11.	173.
"	10.	178n.
"	19.	181.
"	20.	181.
"	25–27.	168.
"	26.	152, 153.
VI,	11.	469.
"	12.	469.
"	17.	153.

Philippians.

I,	8.	570.
"	9–11.	174.
"	21–24.	133, 208, 243.
"	25.	174.
II,	1.	501, 570.
"	2–8.	174.
"	5–11.	307–310.
"	12.	488.
"	15.	159.
III,	9.	148.
"	10.	244, 248.
"	11.	244, 248.
"	13–15.	172.
"	20.	192.
"	21.	244, 245.
"	22.	244, 245.
IV,	7.	49.
"	8.	172, 174, 178.
"	9.	172, 174, 178.
"	19.	570.

INDEX OF SCRIPTURE TEXTS

Colossians.

I,	6.	74, 446.
"	9–13.	257.
"	10.	164.
"	11–14.	439.
"	12.	195.
"	13–18.	312–314.
"	15.	309.
"	20.	386.
"	21.	386.
"	22.	311.
"	23.	74, 446.
"	26.	349, 455.
"	28.	309.
II,	2.	161, 311.
"	3.	311, 557.
"	5–7.	175.
"	9.	311.
"	10.	311.
"	11–12.	183.
"	11.	114.
"	12–14.	402.
"	14–15.	312n.
"	18.	114.
"	19.	164.
III,	1–4.	245.
"	1.	192, 311.
"	3.	80, 81, 156, 191.
"	4.	455.
"	5.	87, 88, 114.
"	9.	80, 81, 154.
"	10.	80, 81, 154.
"	14.	173, 174.
IV,	12.	173.

1 Thessalonians.

I,	10.	384.
II,	12.	440.
"	19.	453.
III,	13.	168, 453.
IV,	3–7.	168.
"	13–18.	231–233, 463.
"	14.	208.
"	15.	463.
"	17.	208.
V,	10.	208.
"	17.	189.
"	19.	94.
"	23.	51, 52, 168, 453.
"	25.	189.

2 Thessalonians.

I,	3.	164.
"	5.	440.
"	7–10.	482.
"	7.	468.
"	8.	468.
"	9.	126, 131.

2 Thessalonians.

II,	1–12.	462, 463, 467.
"	2.	464.
"	3–10.	464, 465.
"	3.	88, 465.
"	4.	88.
"	6.	466.
"	7.	466.
"	11.	94.
"	12.	94.
"	13.	168.

1 Timothy.

I,	11.	301.
"	15.	301.
"	17.	82.
II,	5.	301, 346, 403.
"	6.	403.
III,	13.	161.
"	16.	288, 302, 318.
IV,	1.	465.
"	2.	465.
V,	24.	478.
"	25.	478.
VI	14.	454.
"	15.	454.
"	16.	82.

2 Timothy.

I,	10.	209, 454.
II,	10.	209.
"	12.	257.
"	18.	219.
"	25.	140, 141.
III,	1–9.	465.
"	8.	117, 457.
"	13.	468.
"	16.	21, 185, 502.
"	17.	185, 502.
IV,	1.	440, 454.
"	6–8.	209, 245.
"	8.	454, 482.
"	18.	430, 440.

Titus.

I,	3.	454.
II,	13.	318, 454.
III,	5.	152.

Hebrews.

I,	1–4.	322.
"	3.	323.
"	6.	321, 321n.
"	8.	322, 324, 325.
"	10.	325.
II,	1.	102.
"	7.	323.
"	9.	323, 404.

Hebrews.

II,	10–17.	269.
"	10.	404, 419.
"	13.	374.
"	14.	404.
"	15.	404.
"	17.	405.
III,	1.	102, 322.
"	3.	322.
"	7.	488.
IV,	9.	254.
"	12.	33, 49, 52.
"	14.	405.
"	16.	161.
V,	1.	358.
"	12.	33.
VI,	1.	164.
"	2.	479.
"	4–8.	93, 485.
"	11.	161.
VII.		405.
"	3.	322.
"	10.	67, 86.
"	18.	17.
"	19.	17.
VIII,	1–6.	406.
"	2.	322.
"	6.	17.
"	7.	17.
"	8.	17.
"	13.	17, 439.
IX,	7–12.	395.
"	12.	379.
"	15–18.	406–411.
"	24.	406.
"	26.	444.
"	27.	479.
"	28.	479.
X,	1.	17.
"	1–4.	359.
"	5.	322, 411n.
"	6.	322.
"	7–9.	283.
"	15.	488.
"	19.	161.
"	19–25.	190.
"	22.	161.
"	26.	93, 103.
"	27.	93, 103.
"	28.	131.
"	29.	131.
"	39.	145.
XI,	1.	145.
"	3.	145, 322, 347n.
"	4.	145.
"	6.	145.
"	10.	480.
"	13–16.	255.
"	16.	480.
"	33–38.	176.

INDEX OF SCRIPTURE TEXTS

Hebrews.

XII,	2.	322.
"	4–11.	176.
"	9.	66, 569.
"	18–24.	439.
"	22–23.	207.
"	28.	439.
XIII,	8.	323.
"	14.	480.
"	18.	56.
"	20.	322.
"	21.	325.

James.

I,	2–4.	176.
"	4.	171, 172.
"	12.	176.
"	15.	120.
"	17.	533, 569.
"	18.	163, 170.
"	20.	170.
"	25.	163, 170.
II,	1.	292.
"	5.	293, 440.
"	10.	170.
"	21–23.	144.
III,	2.	172.
IV,	12.	533.
V,	7.	453.
"	8.	293, 453.
"	20.	120.

1 Peter.

I,	2.	168, 171, 382.
"	3.	291.
"	6.	176.
"	7.	176, 291.
"	8.	291.
"	9.	291.
"	13.	291.
"	18.	382.
"	19.	291, 382.
"	20.	291.
"	22.	171.
II,	1.	164.
"	2.	164.
"	4.	291.
"	9.	171.
"	11.	168.
"	16.	163.
"	19.	56.
"	21–24.	382.
"	22.	291.
"	25.	291.
III,	4.	177.
"	10–13.	447n.
"	15.	291.
"	17.	383.
"	18–20.	132.
"	18.	383, 419.

1 Peter.

III,	21.	182.
"	22.	291.
IV,	1.	383.
"	6.	133.
"	11.	33.
"	12.	176.
"	13.	176, 291, 383.
"	17.	133.
"	18.	133.
V,	1.	383.
"	4.	291.
"	10.	291.

2 Peter.

I,	1.	292.
"	4.	156.
"	8.	292.
"	11.	292.
"	16.	292, 453.
"	17.	292.
"	21.	501.
II,	1.	471.
"	4.	129.
"	20.	103, 292.
"	21.	103, 292.
III,	4.	167.
"	6.	167n.
"	8.	325.
"	16.	8, 25.
"	18.	164, 292.

1 John.

I,	1.	323, 338.
"	3.	421, 569.
"	5–7.	377.
"	5.	192, 256, 323, 566.
"	7.	192, 256.
"	8–10.	167.
"	9.	146, 323, 377.
"	11.	440.
II,	1.	167, 378, 489, 504, 569.
"	2.	376.
"	11.	88.
"	16.	99.
"	18.	470.
"	19.	471.
"	20–27.	20.
"	20.	501.
"	22.	497.
"	24.	421.
"	25.	421.
"	27.	501.
"	28.	161, 453.
"	29.	156.
III,	1–3.	160.
"	1.	567.
"	4.	87.

1 John.

III,	5.	376.
"	6.	167.
"	8.	376.
"	9.	156, 166, 377.
"	10.	166.
"	14.	140, 156, 161.
"	16.	377.
"	19.	161, 323.
"	21.	161.
"	22.	178n.
IV,	2.	256.
"	3.	470.
"	7–16.	567.
"	7.	156, 469.
"	8.	469.
"	9.	267, 376.
"	10.	376, 419.
"	14.	376.
"	16–19.	174.
"	17.	161.
V,	1.	156.
"	4.	146n, 156, 473.
"	5.	473.
"	6–8.	378, 379.
"	11.	156.
"	12.	156, 191.
"	14.	161.
"	17.	88.
"	18.	156.
"	19.	276.

2 John.

7.		338, 471.

3 John.

7.		338.

Jude.

1.		292.
4.		292.
17.		292.
21.		292.
25.		292.

Revelation.

I,	4.	486, 495.
"	5.	486.
"	6.	205, 325.
"	7.	458.
"	12–16.	295.
II,	7.	205.
"	17.	205.
III,	5.	205.
"	12.	205.
"	21.	205, 230, 257.
IV,	5.	295.
V,	1–6.	380.
"	5.	502.
"	6.	295, 495, 502.

Revelation.			Revelation.			Revelation.		
V,	9.	206.	XIII,	2.	461.	XX,	6.	257.
"	10.	205.	"	11.	457.	"	14.	130.
"	13.	296.	XIV,	10.	129.	XXI,	2.	153n, 440.
VI,	9–11.	206, 230.	"	11.	129.	"	5.	206.
VII,	9–17.	177, 206, 255.	XVI,	13.	462.	"	6.	459.
X,	1.	296.	XVII,	1–8.	462.	"	7.	206, 296, 459.
XI,	1–3.	457.	"	9–11.	457.	"	8.	127, 130.
"	1.	294.	"	10.	294.	"	25–27.	255.
"	2.	294.	XVIII,	18.	294.	XXII,	1–5.	206.
"	3–12.	230.	XIX,	3.	381n.	"	1.	295.
"	8.	457.	"	9.	370n.	"	5.	206, 256, 257, 258.
XII,	3–9.	461, 462.	"	11.	296.			
			XX,	4–15.	230.			

GENERAL INDEX

The letter n placed after a page-number indicates that the reference is in the footnote.

Abbott, Ezra, 319n, 320n.
Accadian Psalms, 63n.
Adoption, 158.
Alexander, W. L., 41.
Alford, 154n, 162n, 325n, 450n.
Angelology, 460, 541.
Angelophany, 329.
Animism, 542.
Annihilation, 133.
Anselmic Theory, 419n, 578.
Anthropomorphism, 525, 526.
Antichrist, 460–472.
Apostasy, 101.
Assurance, 160, 161.
Ascension of Jesus, 222, 224, 278.
Attributes of God, 551.
Augustine, 219n.
Authority of Scripture, 28.
Avatara, 331.
Avesta, 9, 29, 63n, 212, 218.

Bacon, 261n.
Baldensperger, 285n.
Baptism, 151, 152, 182, 183.
Baruch, cited, 113, 218n.
Beautiful, The, in Religion, 177.
Beck, 47n.
Beet, 81, 180n.
Bengel, 155n, 322n, 325n.
Beyschlag, 239n, 272n, 315n, 335n, 450n.
Bhagavat Gita, 347n.
Bigamy, 58.
Blasphemy of the Spirit, 92, 96.
Bleek, 325n.
Blood of Life, 47.
Blood Covenant, 525.
Blood Offerings, 353, 354, 377.
Blood, Symbolism of, 355, 356.
Body, The, 46.
Bowne, 547n.
Box, G. H., 261n.
Brahm, 331, 347.
Briggs, 261n.
Buddha, 348.
Bull, Bishop, 77n.
Burwash, 41.

Caird, E., 61.
Caird, J., 60n, 115n.
Calixtus, 38.
Calvin, 37.
Canon, Limits of, 9, 10.
Canon, Hebrew, 13.
Canon, New Testament, 14.
Capital Punishment, 118.
Carpzov, 8.
Cereal Offerings, 353.
Cerinthus, 379.
Charles, R. H., 2n, 125n, 239n, 271n.
Cheyne, 124n, 215n.
Church, The, 179, 180.
Childhood Piety, 137.
Chinese Classics, 9, 29.
Circumcision, 525.
Clarke, Adam, 212, 407n.
Clarke, W. N., 41, 62n, 580n.
Communion of Saints, 421.
Comforter, The, 378, 489, 490, 503.
Concept of God, 518.
Confession, 146.
Conscience, 55, 56.
Conversion, 140, 141.
Conversion of Paul, 297.
Conviction of Sin, 137, 496.
Cooke, R. J., 261n.
Crane, J. T., 573n.
Creation, 70, 73, 546.
Creationism, 65.
Curtis, O. A., 42.

Day of Jehovah, 426.
Day of Judgment, 478.
Death, Physical, 118.
Death, Spiritual, 120.
Death, The Second, 130.
Decalogue, 15, 531.
Degrees of Penalty, 130.
Degrees of Sin, 90.
Deities, Names of, 62.
Delitzsch, 51n, 124n, 325n, 331n.
Demonology, 274, 461, 462, 467, 469.
Denney, 78n.
Depravity of Race, 84.
Dillmann, 573n.

Dispersion of Men, 67.
Dods, 491n.
Dorner, 58n, 328n.
Drummond, H., 73, 74n, 155n.
Dwight, 314n, 319n.

Ecclesiasticus, cited, 113, 328.
Edersheim, 506n.
Egyptian Ritual, 63n.
Elijah, Lesson from, 506.
Ellicott, 152n, 310n, 403n, 464n.
End of the Age, 445.
Enoch, Book of, cited, 125, 129n, 219n, 269, 270.
Enthronement of Jesus, 423.
Esdras, Second, cited, 113, 125, 218.
Eternal Judgment, 479.
Eternal Life, 191-196.
Eternal Punishment, 131.
Eusebius, 10, 14, 275n.
Evolution, 71.
Expiation, 414n.

Fairbairn, A. M., 326n.
Fairbairn, P., 217n.
Faith Defined, 142.
Fatherhood of God, 157, 549.
Federal Theology, 525n.
Fiske, John, 73n.
Freedom in Christ, 162, 163.
Freedom of Will, See Will.
Future Punishment, 128.

Gardner, 261n.
Gehenna, 125, 126, 129, 130.
Generator, 572.
Generatrix, 486, 572.
Gfroerer, 328n.
Gifford, 395n.
Gloag, 322n.
Goal in History, 548.
Goal, The Everlasting, 581.
Godet, 248n.
Godhead of Christ, 344.
Godliness, Practical, 187.
Gods, Names of, 62, 515.
Golden Rule, 59.
Gore, 261n.
Gregory of Nyssa, 37.
Griesbach, 133n.
Growth, Spiritual, 164, 165, 175, 177.
Guilt, 89, 90.
Guilt-Offering, 90.
Gunkel, 514n.

Hades, 125, 126, 127, 129, 203.
Hahn, 39.
Hammurabi, 532.
Hardening the Heart, 91.
Hare, 498n.

Harnach, 264n, 375n, 438n.
Harris, J. R., 133n.
Hase, 39.
Head, The, 48.
Heard, 51n.
Heart, The, 47, 48.
Heavenly Recognition, 252-255.
Helvetic Creed, 8, 23.
Hoben, 261n.
Hodge, 40.
Holiness, 167, 168, 554.
Hooker, 533n.
Hopkins, S., 88n.
Hort, 222n, 318n, 320n, 334n, 369n.
Hottinger, 10n.
Human Sacrifice, 357, 358, 537.
Huther, 56n, 380n.
Huxley, 68n.

Ignorance, Errors of, 90.
Image of God in Man, 78-82.
Immortality, 197.
Imprecatory Psalms, 104, 105.
Imputation, 382n.
Incarnation, 331, 346, 347.
Inerrancy, Dogma of, 18, 23.
Infallibility, Dogma of, 24.
Immanence of God, 508.
Inspiration, 8, 18-23.
Intermediate State, 243n, 258.
Illingworth, 63n.
Irenæus, 379.

Jehovah, new Name, 529, 530.
Jehovah of Hosts, 537.
Jerusalem, The New, 206.
Jewish Traditions, 7, 8.
John of Damascus, 37.
Josephus, 10, 125, 219n, 468n.
Jubilees, Book of, cited, 113.
Judgments of God, 426, 477, 480.
Judith, Book of, cited, 125, 218.
Justification, 148.
Justin Martyr, 18.

Kojiki, The, 9, 29.
Koran, The, 9, 29.
Kuyper, 486n.

Lange, 39.
Lawgiving among Nations, 532.
Le Conte, 71n.
Levitical Priesthood, 351.
Lewis, T., 513n.
Leydecker, 38.
Liberty in Christ, 162.
Life in Blood, 47.
Lightfoot, J. B., 143n, 307n.
Logos in John, 326.
Logos in Philo, 327.

Lord's Supper, 184.
Love, 174, 436.
Lünemann, 325n, 464n.
Luthardt, 492n.
Lycurgus, 432.

Maccabees, First, cited, 465.
Maccabees, Second, cited, 547.
Maccabees, Fourth, cited, 391n.
Macpherson, 41.
Macloskie, 70n.
Macknight, 407n.
Mahan, 500n.
Manu, 532.
Mansel, 551n.
Marheineke, 38.
Martensen, 38.
Maternity in God, 579.
McFadyen, 35.
Mediation, 346, 350.
Melanchthon, 37.
Mercy-seat, Christ a, 393–399.
Merrill, 148n, 161n.
Messianic Hope, 365, 473–476, 547.
Meyer, 160n, 174n, 236n, 299n, 303n, 310n, 316n.
Miley, 551n.
Millennial Reign, 481.
Mind, The, 49, 50.
Ministry of Word, 185, 186.
Ministrations of Spirit, 495.
Minos, 532.
Miracles of Christ, 275–277.
Mohammedanism, 2.
Monogamy, 58.
Monolatry, 535.
Monotheism, 543.
Moral Sense, 55.
Moses, Divine Legation of, 529.
Mueller, J., 101n.
Mystery of Ages, 348.
Mystery of God, 345.
Mystery of Spiritual Life, 155.
Mystical Body of Christ, 420, 421.
Myths, Allusions to, 510, 511, 514.

Names of God, 515.
Necessity of Mediation, 415, 416.
New Birth, 150.
New Creation, 153.
New Testament superior to Old, 15–17.
Nitzsch, F. A. B., 39.
Nitzsch, K. I., 39.
Numa, 532.

Oehler, 52n.
Omnipotence, 552.
Omniscience, 552.
Omnisentience, 552, 553.

Origen, 37.
Origin of Man, 69.
Origin of Sin, 95–99.

Paley, 513n.
Papias, 14.
Parables, Lessons of, 431.
Paraclete, 378, 380, 490, 503.
Parousia, 448, 453.
Pauline Rabbinism, 116.
Paul's Conversion, 297.
Penal Blindness, 94.
Penitential Psalms, 94, 108, 138, 363.
Pentecost, 492, 494.
Perfection, 171, 172.
Personality, 56, 57, 82, 97, 485, 551.
Philippi, 399n.
Philo, 327, 328.
Plato, 254n.
Polygamy, 58.
Prayer, 188, 189.
Pre-Adamites, 64n.
Preëxistence, 282, 314, 334, 342.
Priesthood, 351, 358.
Primitive Man, 77.
Proctor, 576n.
Propitiation, 376, 378, 394, 414n, 415.
Providence, 573.

Quarry, 134n.
Quenstedt, 8.

Ramsay, 261n.
Ransom, 366.
Raymond, 40.
Realities, Primary, 45.
Reconciliation, 148, 149.
Regeneration, 150, 499.
Reigning with Christ, 257.
Religion Universal, 1, 60, 61, 63.
Religion, The Christian, 3.
Religion, Philosophy of, 2.
Remission of Sin, 147.
Repentance, 140, 141.
Restitution of All Things, 482.
Resurrection, 212.
Resurrection, Jewish Opinions, 218.
Retribution, 122.
Revelation, Universal, 509.
Revelation, Gradual, 520.
Rhees, 261n.
Righteousness, 169, 170.
Ritschl, 85n, 159n, 163n, 313n.
Russell, 467n.

Sabbath-Rest, 255.
Sacraments, 181.
Salmond, 128n, 134n.
Sanctification, 167, 168, 499.
Sanday, 261n.

Schleiermacher, 38.
Schmiedel, 261n, 464n.
Schoettgen, 154n, 315n.
Schultz, 554n.
Second Death, 130.
Self-Consciousness of Jesus, 280.
Shades, The, 202.
Shedd, 40.
Sheldon, 41.
Sheol, 125, 126, 129, 201, 203.
Sibylline Oracles, cited, 219n, 470n.
Sinfulness, 83.
Sinlessness of Jesus, 265.
Sin Offering, 354, 355.
Smith, H. B., 41.
Smith, W. R., 354n.
Smyth, N., 58n, 98n.
Social Relations, 59.
Socrates, 254n.
Solon, 532.
Son of God, 266.
Son of Man, 268.
Sons of God, 159.
South, 77n.
Spencer, H., 578n.
Spirit, 51, 53.
Spirit, The Holy, 484.
Strong, A. H., 40.
Stuart, 325n.
Sufficiency of Scriptures, 24, 27, 35.

Tabernacle, Symbolism of, 406.
Talmud, cited, 11.
Targum, 142n, 315n, 330n.
Tartarus, 129.
Tennant, 114n, 117n.
Terminology, Theological, 42.
Tertullian, 219n.
Testament XII Patriarchs, 218n.
Thackeray, 117n.
Theistic Arguments, 512.
Theocracy, 539.

Theodicy, 134, 135.
Theodoret, 397n.
Theophany, 329.
Tholuck, 325n.
Thomas, J., 261n.
Tobit, cited, 11, 213n.
Traditions, Jewish, 7, 18.
Trial, Discipline of, 176.
Trichotomy, 51, 52.
Trinity, 485, 486, 580.
Tripitaka, 9, 29.
Trumbull, H. C., 525n.
Turretin, 37.
Tyler, C. N., 178n.
Tylor, E. B., 509n.

Unity of Race, 64.
Upton, 520n.
Usener, 261n.

Vedas, 9, 29, 63n.
Virgin Birth, 260, 261n, 273.
Virtues, Christian, 173.

Warfield, 261n, 467n.
Weber, 77n, 114n.
Weiss, 48n, 151n.
Westcott, 324n, 325n, 408n, 409n, 411n.
Wesley, 22n, 160n.
Whedon, 58n, 100n, 503n.
Whitby, 239n.
Will, Freedom of, 56, 57, 98, 99, 100.
Wisdom, Book of, cited, 81, 213, 218, 322, 328.
Wisdom Personified, 328.
Witness of the Spirit, 160, 500.
Word of God, The, 32, 33.
Word, Ministry of, 185, 186.

Young, 264n.

Zenos, 261n.

www.ingramcontent.com/pod-product-compliance
Lightning Source LLC
Chambersburg PA
CBHW052040290426
44111CB00011B/1571